SAP PRESS e-books

Print or e-book, Kindle or iPad, workplace or airplane: Choose where and how to read your SAP PRESS books! You can now get all our titles as e-books, too:

▸ By download and online access
▸ For all popular devices
▸ And, of course, DRM-free

Convinced? Then go to **www.sap-press.com** and get your e-book today.

Implementing SAP HANA®

SAP PRESS is a joint initiative of SAP and Galileo Press. The know-how offered by SAP specialists combined with the expertise of the Galileo Press publishing house offers the reader expert books in the field. SAP PRESS features first-hand information and expert advice, and provides useful skills for professional decision-making.

SAP PRESS offers a variety of books on technical and business-related topics for the SAP user. For further information, please visit our website: *www.sap-press.com*.

Merz, Hügens, Blum
SAP BW on SAP HANA
2015, approx. 450 pp., hardcover
ISBN 978-1-4932-1003-9

Schneider, Westenberger, Gahm
ABAP Development for SAP HANA
2014, 609 pp., hardcover
ISBN 978-1-59229-859-4

James Hanck et al.
SAP Data Services: The Comprehensive Guide
2015, approx. 625 pp., hardcover
ISBN 978-1-4932-1167-8

Christian Ah-Soon, Peter Snowdon
Getting Started with SAP Lumira
2015, 540 pp., hardcover
ISBN 978-1-4932-1033-6

Jonathan Haun, Chris Hickman, Don Loden, Roy Wells

Implementing SAP HANA®

Galileo Press

Bonn • Boston

Galileo Press is named after the Italian physicist, mathematician, and philosopher Galileo Galilei (1564 – 1642). He is known as one of the founders of modern science and an advocate of our contemporary, heliocentric worldview. His words *Eppur si muove* (And yet it moves) have become legendary. The Galileo Press logo depicts Jupiter orbited by the four Galilean moons, which were discovered by Galileo in 1610.

Editor Kelly Grace Weaver
Copyeditor Miranda Martin
Cover Design Graham Geary
Photo Credit Shutterstock.com/72997021/© Shkanov Alexey
Layout Design Vera Brauner
Production Kelly O'Callaghan
Typesetting III-satz, Husby (Germany)
Printed and bound in the United States of America, on paper from sustainable sources

ISBN 978-1-4932-1176-0
© 2015 by Galileo Press Inc., Boston (MA)
2nd edition 2015

Library of Congress Cataloging-in-Publication Data
Loden, Don.
Implementing SAP HANA / Jonathan Haun, Chris Hickman, Don Loden, Roy Wells. -- 2nd edition.
pages cm
Revision of: Implementing SAP HANA / Don Loden, Jonathan Haun, Chris Hickman, and Roy Wells.
Includes index.
ISBN 978-1-4932-1176-0 (print : alk. paper) -- ISBN 1-4932-1176-5 (print : alk. paper) -- ISBN 978-1-4932-1177-7 (ebook) -- ISBN 978-1-4932-1178-4 (print and ebook : alk. paper) 1. Database management. 2. Business enterprises--Data processing. 3. SAP HANA (Electronic resource) I. Haun, Jonathan. II. Hickman, Chris. III. Wells, Roy. IV. Title.
QA76.9.D3L638 2014
005.74--dc23
2014039989

Contents at a Glance

Dear Reader,

Normally, I like to give authors a break between their first and second editions: two years, three years, maybe even four. But for this book, like for all things SAP HANA, speed was the name of the game. Thanks to new releases of SAP BusinessObjects BI, SAP Data Services, and—of course—SAP HANA itself, these authors didn't get much breathing room from this editor. Fortunately, they handled it the same way it seems they handle all things: with aplomb.

So, dear reader, I'm pleased to present you with the second edition of this best-selling book, updated and improved based on both technology changes and the feedback of readers like you. I trust you'll find it chock-full of exactly the information you're looking for.

Whether you're new to this edition or are coming back for seconds, we hope you'll share your opinion with us. What did you think about *Implementing SAP HANA*? As your comments and suggestions are the most useful tools to help us make our books the best they can be, we encourage you to visit our website at *www.sap-press.com* and share your feedback.

Thank you for purchasing a book from SAP PRESS!

Kelly Grace Weaver
Editor, SAP PRESS

Galileo Press
Boston, MA

kelly.weaver@galileo-press.com
www.sap-press.com

Contents

PART III   Multidimensional Modeling in SAP HANA

10 Multidimensional Modeling in Practice 479

11 Securing Data in SAP HANA 535

PART IV Integrating SAP HANA with SAP Business Intelligence Tools

Contents

Acknowledgments

We would like to dedicate this book to our families and loved ones for their support and understanding during the endless hours and many weekends that were committed to the completion of this project. To Lauren Loden, Parks Loden, Gray Loden, Samantha Haun, Addison Haun, Mason Haun, Curry Bordelon, Adam Bordelon, and Jennifer Wells: Without your thoughtfulness and support, this book would not have been possible.

We would also like to thank our customers for trusting us with their SAP HANA initiatives. Without these experiences from the field, this book would not be possible.

We would also like to recognize Decision First Technologies and show our appreciation to co-owners Scott Golden and Taylor Courtnay. Without their support and the use of their SAP HANA environments in the Decision First Technologies SAP HANA Center of Excellence, most of the content of this book could not have been created.

Special thanks to Hillary Bliss for her knowledge of and esteemed expertise with the SAP Predictive Analysis product and her track record on the subject. Her guidance and input on predictive analysis, statistics, and modeling made the level of depth possible and offered far more valuable content for the reader.

Finally, our sincere and utmost thanks go to everyone at Galileo Press, especially to Kelly G. Weaver and Emily Nicholls, for their patience, dedication, and guidance in helping us through this process and seeing this dream become reality.

Preface

As a powerful, new technology with a lot of hype, SAP HANA is often misunderstood. Many believe that they can simply place their data into SAP HANA, and all of their business intelligence (BI) problems will disappear. However, the technology alone is not a magic bullet; there is indeed a methodology behind a BI implementation of SAP HANA, and other software tools are needed to complement such a solution and fully leverage its substantial benefits.

Purpose

This book was written with the goal of educating readers about implementing an SAP HANA solution. Specifically, we focus on delivering BI solutions using SAP HANA as a data warehouse platform. We begin with an overview of SAP HANA and all of the ways organizations can implement BI solutions using SAP HANA. We then walk you through a specific solution that harnesses the power of SAP Data Services and SAP BusinessObjects BI to complete an end-to-end BI solution.

Who Should Read This Book

This book will help an organization's project teams and technology consultants, as well as anyone looking for a one-stop guide to implementing SAP HANA from a BI perspective. Note that this book is not intended to teach basic BI concepts, and we try to always focus on specific SAP HANA implementation knowledge. We also address specific functionality not often discussed in standard SAP documentation or training materials. The book goes well beyond the typical SAP HANA sales cycle conversation.

Before reading this book, we recommend the following prerequisites:

- General knowledge of data warehousing concepts
- Familiarity with BI tools and constructs

▶ Foundational knowledge of traditional database provisioning, multidimensional modeling, and reporting technologies

This book strives to offer a uniquely real-world perspective to follow the academic sections of each chapter. Each chapter is structured to offer background and theory around the technology. The theory is then followed with a case study—the story of the fictitious AdventureWorks Cycle Company—to show a real-world example of the topics covered in the book. You can download the data used for the AdventureWorks Cycle Company case study from this book's website at *http://www.sap-press.com/3703*. Our goal is to provide you with a unique perspective of how these solutions have worked in the field based on real customer engagements.

Structure of This Book

The book is structured into four parts. The first part offers an introduction to the tools covered in this book (SAP HANA, SAP Data Services, and SAP BusinessObjects BI), explains how to set up a secure system environment, and gives the technical details on how data is stored in SAP HANA. The second part of the book is all about getting data into SAP HANA, from preprovisioning steps to the actual loading process. The third part of the book covers the unique multidimensional modeling capabilities built into SAP HANA, as well as how to secure these multidimensional models (or *information views*, as they're known in SAP HANA) via analytic privileges. Finally, the fourth and final part of the book explains how to integrate SAP HANA with SAP's business intelligence tools. We cover universe design for SAP HANA, the use of predictive analysis within SAP HANA, and how the various reporting and visualization tools found in the SAP BusinessObjects BI suite consume SAP HANA data.

These parts are explained in more detail next.

Part I: Introduction

Chapter 1: SAP HANA, SAP BusinessObjects BI, and SAP Data Services

An implementation of SAP HANA isn't just an implementation of SAP HANA—it also requires other products, such as SAP BusinessObjects BI and SAP Data Services. By explaining how these three products work together in a successful SAP HANA BI implementation, we'll lay the foundation for the entire book.

Chapter 2: Securing the SAP HANA Environment

Before we can interact with SAP HANA, we need to understand how to connect to it and secure it. This chapter takes a deep dive into the core components of the SAP HANA security model. It discusses key items such as provisioning users, provisioning roles, and configuring privileges.

Chapter 3: Data Storage in SAP HANA

This chapter takes a deep dive into data storage in SAP HANA and answers several key questions: How is data stored? What type of data models perform best on SAP HANA? Why? The goal is to give an understanding of how data is stored in memory in order to provision data most effectively.

Part II: Getting Data into SAP HANA

Chapter 4: Preprovisioning Data with SAP Data Services

Before provisioning or data loading can occur, you must first perform source system analysis to see what aspects of the data need repair. Learn how to provide high-quality data as a base for SAP HANA using SAP Data Services.

Chapter 5: Provisioning Data with SAP Data Services

This chapter explains the design and build of the data loading process for SAP HANA. For standalone SAP HANA, you must load your data, and this can be done via SAP Data Services or replication, which we outline here.

Chapter 6: Loading Data with SAP Data Services

In this chapter, we provide an in-depth overview of the various options for batch-loading data into SAP HANA tables. We also discuss SAP Data Services' ability to process and load data in real-time.

Part III: Multidimensional Modeling in SAP HANA

Chapter 7: Introduction to Multidimensional Modeling

One of the many features of SAP HANA is its ability to natively expose data as a multidimensional model. In this chapter we will give you a basic understanding of multidimensional modeling. We will also share how multidimensional modeling benefits both business users and IT departments.

Chapter 8: Tools and Components of Multidimensional Modeling

Before you can build multidimensional models within SAP HANA, you need to understand SAP HANA Studio and how SAP HANA schemas and packages act as a core component of the multidimensional model.

Chapter 9: Creating SAP HANA Information Views

SAP HANA's multidimensional models are called *information views*. Developers can create three different types of information views within SAP HANA. This chapter will bolster your understanding of the three types: attribute views, analytic views, and calculation views.

Chapter 10: Multidimensional Modeling in Practice

As you develop information views, you need to understand how physical data is processed by SAP HANA, specifically with respect to normalized and denormalized data. You also need to understand the difference between traditional data modeling and multidimensional modeling as it relates to performance. After explaining these key concepts, we will then walk you through two case studies designed to provide detailed, step-by-step instructions for creating information views.

Chapter 11: Securing Data in SAP HANA

Now that we have data stored in SAP HANA and have set up information views to expose data for consumption, we need to think about how to secure that data. This chapters walks you through the process of securing data by creating analytic privileges and assigning them to users and roles.

Part IV: Integrating SAP HANA with SAP Business Intelligence Tools

Chapter 12: Building Universes for SAP HANA

This chapter provides an in-depth look at the semantic layer built into SAP BusinessObjects BI. You'll gain a basic understanding of the SAP BusinessObjects BI universe and how it is used to provide access to data within SAP HANA. We conclude the chapter with two case studies that walk you through the processes of developing universes on SAP HANA tables and analytic views.

Chapter 13: Predictive Analytics with SAP HANA

This chapter discusses the various tools and methodologies for integrating predictive analytics within the SAP HANA platform and SAP BusinessObjects BI tools. Many organizations need to tap into insights within their operational data, and SAP has developed several tools that integrate with SAP HANA to run predictive algorithms on very large data sets.

Chapter 14: Professionally Authored Dashboards with SAP HANA

This chapter focuses on both SAP BusinessObjects Dashboards and SAP BusinessObjects Design Studio (the intended successor to SAP BusinessObjects Dashboards). It discusses the two SAP products available to generate dashboards and outlines the process for connecting dashboards to SAP HANA. The chapter concludes with a case study for developing an SAP BusinessObjects Design Studio dashboard on top of SAP HANA.

Chapter 15: Data Exploration and Self-Service Analytics with SAP HANA

This chapter covers the major activities of connecting SAP BusinessObjects Explorer and SAP Lumira to SAP HANA. The chapter concludes with a case study for developing an SAP Lumira visualization for sales data on top of SAP HANA.

Chapter 16: SAP BusinessObjects Web Intelligence with SAP HANA

This chapter provides an in-depth overview of how SAP BusinessObjects Web Intelligence can interact with data from SAP HANA, as well as features of SAP BusinessObjects Web Intelligence that are specifically relevant when run on top of SAP HANA. The chapter concludes with a case study showcasing some SAP BusinessObjects Web Intelligence features that are especially relevant with SAP HANA.

Chapter 17: SAP Crystal Reports with SAP HANA

This chapter provides an in-depth overview of how SAP Crystal Reports for Enterprise can interact with data within SAP HANA. We conclude with a case study on how an accounting department can leverage financial data with SAP HANA using SAP Crystal Reports.

PART I
Introduction

An implementation of SAP HANA isn't just an implementation of SAP HANA—it also requires other products such as SAP BusinessObjects BI and SAP Data Services. By explaining how these three products work together in a successful SAP HANA implementation, we'll lay the foundation for the entire book.

1 SAP HANA, SAP BusinessObjects BI, and SAP Data Services

SAP HANA is an exciting technology from SAP. When conversations about SAP HANA are initiated, mystique often surrounds the discussion. This mystique is often related to the multiple ways that SAP HANA can be implemented within an organization, as well as its hardware and software features. To help clarify any misconceptions, this book will introduce you to a specific SAP HANA business intelligence (BI) solution that can be implemented by any organization, regardless of its data sources or requirements: an implementation of SAP HANA that uses SAP Data Services and SAP BusinessObjects BI.

However, before we venture too deep into this particular solution, we first aim to fortify your general knowledge of SAP HANA in the first part of this chapter. We'll start by describing SAP HANA itself by exploring both its software and hardware aspects (Section 1.1) and then guiding you through the various ways that SAP HANA can be used as a BI appliance (Section 1.2). For a glimpse of other use cases, we'll also discuss how SAP HANA can be used with SAP Business Suite applications (Section 1.3)—in particular, how SAP Business Suite on SAP HANA might change the traditional concepts of a BI solution.

The second half of this chapter discusses the aspects of an implementation of SAP HANA using both SAP Data Services and SAP BusinessObjects BI. Our hope is that you'll gain insight into how these three components make up the core solution that is discussed within this book. We'll start by helping you understand why SAP BusinessObjects BI and SAP Data Services are needed in an SAP HANA implementation (Section 1.4). After that, we'll guide you through the traditional enterprise information management (EIM) process to introduce you to SAP Data Services and the ways it can benefit an SAP HANA implementation (Section 1.5). We'll then walk through a traditional landscape running SAP BusinessObjects BI to help you understand how it exposes the power of SAP HANA to an organization's users (Section 1.6). Finally, in Section 1.7, we'll discuss the overall solution architecture to show how each component functions within the overall solution architecture.

What Are SAP BusinessObjects BI and SAP Data Services?

SAP BusinessObjects BI represents the core platform and tool sets that are used to analyze, secure, and visualize data. It comprises a server platform that can be configured to secure, distribute, and manage BI content within an organization. It also supports multiple reporting and visualization tools that are capable of facilitating multiple BI requirements.

SAP Data Services represents the core platform and tool sets that are used to extract, transform, and load data. It also contains several data quality tools to help organizations manage their data quality. SAP Data Services is data source agnostic, meaning that it can connect to both SAP and non-SAP data sources. It can also target both SAP and non-SAP data sources during the load process.

1.1 What Is SAP HANA?

In short, there's no single statement that can fully describe what SAP HANA is. Some consider SAP HANA just another database, while others consider it an analytics appliance. The truth is that SAP HANA is more than just a database or an analytics appliance. SAP HANA is the next-generation data appliance. It can facilitate many solutions throughout an organization. This includes both solutions in which SAP HANA is used to manage data for an application and instances where it's used to process BI queries.

However, even these descriptions do not fully describe SAP HANA. To understand SAP HANA better and to answer this question, we must first examine both the software layers and hardware layers of SAP HANA.

1.1.1 Software Layers and Features

At the software layer, some components of SAP HANA act as a database, while others facilitate multidimensional models. In fact, there are also parts that act as an application server, a geospatial engine, a predictive analytics engine, and even an online transaction processes engine. Let's not forget that SAP HANA can also act as an unstructured data processor and full-text search engine.

> **Multidimensional Models: Definition**
>
> Multidimensional models provide metadata-rich access to SAP HANA database tables using constructs that convert raw data elements into user friendly or easy to understand objects. They also shield the user from the traditional complexities of Structured Query Language (SQL) while facilitating a single version of the truth. In subsequent chapters we will provide more details on the SAP HANA multidimensional modeling capabilities.

At a high level, Figure 1.1 depicts the software features and layers of the SAP HANA appliance that allow it to facilitate more than just standard relational data queries. The SAP HANA in-memory database layer contains multiple query processing engines, such as the calculation engine, OLAP engine, row engine, and join engine. This layer also contains the row store tables, columnar store tables, and Smart Data Access logical database tables. There are also engines designed to specifically manage text processing and text search. The SAP HANA software appliance layer, which includes the SAP HANA in-memory database layer, also includes the *Extended Application Services* (XS Engine) to enable SAP HANA as a development platform. There are also embedded features, such as the *Predictive Analytics Library* (PAL), *Business Function Libraries* (BFL), *planning engines*, *rules engines*, and *geospatial engines*. Because SAP HANA is a robust data platform, it also requires dedicated management services to ensure that everything is running properly. In total, these layers build upon each other to form the SAP HANA appliance.

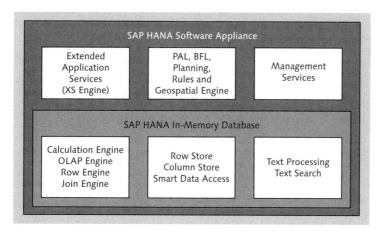

Figure 1.1 A High-Level Overview of the SAP HANA Software Appliance Layers

SAP HANA incorporates columnar tables to aid in the processing of analytic queries. Columnar tables use a special type of storage mechanism that results in two advantages.

The first advantage centers on their ability to facilitate analytic queries. These queries typically incorporate the use of grouping, ranking, sorting, and aggregating. Columnar tables are perfect candidates to facilitate these queries because the process of storing data in a columnar store effectively creates indexes that describe the location of each unique value in the column. In addition, a columnar store provides a better mechanism for querying large quantities of data because data is quickly pinpointed in each column without the need to scan every row in the table. In general, this reduces the amount of CPU time that is required to pinpoint data in a table and increases the response time of queries.

The second advantage of a columnar table is that it effectively compresses the data stored in each column of the table. Identical values in each column are replaced with smaller surrogates that require less storage than the original values. If we account for this process on each column, the total storage for the entire table can be reduced as much as 20 times. But in reality, there is no set number for describing the amount of compression that a table will experience; the amount of compression that a table yields depends largely on how many times values are repeated in a column and the type of data that exists in the column. In general terms, SAP agrees that you'll experience anywhere from three to seven times compression. However, there can be a plus or minus factor at both ends of this expectation.

> **SAP HANA Sizing**
>
> Compression contributes a great deal to making SAP HANA a reality. In general, the sizing requirements for SAP HANA can be obtained using the equation $(SD \times 2) / CF$. SD represents the uncompressed size of the source data. CF represents the compression factor expected within SAP HANA.
>
> Pay close attention to the equation, though. Notice that the SD is multiplied by a factor of two before it's divided by the CF. Within the SAP engines, we need about 50% of the available RAM to manage the computation of data. This leaves the remaining 50% for data storage, code, and other items.
>
> There is also a difference in the sizing requirements for SAP Business Warehouse (BW) on SAP HANA compared to a native SAP HANA solution. This is mostly due to the abundance of row-store tables that are needed in an SAP BW on SAP HANA implementation. However, there are other factors to consider, as well.

The CF, or compression factor, can vary depending on the structure of the data. Columns that have more repeated values will compress better than columns with a majority of unique values.

SAP has provided several documents and tools to help you determine the correct size for an SAP HANA appliance. Please refer to the following links for additional information:

▸ SAP HANA Sizing Note 15149: *https://service.sap.com/sap/support/notes/1514966*

▸ Quick Sizer tool for SAP HANA: *http://service.sap.com/sap/bc/ bsp/spn/quicksizer/main.do?sap-language=en&bsp-language=en*

▸ Quick Sizer for Beginners Guide: *http://service.sap.com/~sapidb/ 011000358700000523272005*

▸ Links to sizing: *http://help.sap.com/hana_platform#section9*

Within the SAP HANA software layers are unique query processing engines that are well optimized to retrieve columnar or row data stored in-memory using parallel processing:

▸ The *OLAP engine* processes basic analytic queries. These queries are often defined by an underlying physical or logical data model in which the tables, when joined, produce a logical star schema. In data modeling terms, you can identify a star schema when one or more conformed dimensions are joined to one or more facts. This engine is massively parallel and best used to process BI queries.

▸ The *calculation engine* processes complex queries or choreographs basic logical data modeling. It is often required to produce highly tailored, business-centric views of data.

▸ The *join engine* processes standard SQL queries. The join engine is best described as the engine to process the standard SELECT, FROM, and WHERE SQL statements that have become an industry standard.

▸ The *row engine* processes complex SQL query logic, row-store tables, or logic that is recursive in nature.

Each engine is well optimized because it is accessing data that is stored in RAM. However, each engine also has a unique ability to process different types of queries. As a result, their capabilities and performance will vary.

Starting with SAP HANA SPS 6, a *Smart Data Access* feature was added to the platform to provide real-time data federation from a variety of supported data sources. With Smart Data Access, tables from a remote RDMS can be presented within SAP HANA as logical tables. These logical tables can then be incorporated into SAP HANA calculation views, stored procedures, SQL statements, and custom-built applications. Please note that, as of this writing, virtual tables cannot be utilized in SAP HANA analytic views and attribute views as of SAP HANA.

Because the tables are logical, they do not have a storage footprint within SAP HANA. However, at execution time, SAP HANA accesses the remote RDMS and retrieves the data. Under some circumstances, Smart Data Access attempts to optimize the retrieval of data using a variety of pushdown operations. Depending on how the virtual table is utilized, the SAP HANA Smart Data Access engine optimizes the retrieval query by passing filters, group-by statements, aggregations, semi-joins, standard joins, and other functions to the source RDMS. In turn, these pushdown operations should reduce the size and quantity of the data that is transferred from the source to SAP HANA in real time. We can then assume that the performance of these virtual tables used in a query will increase as the amount of data transferred is decreased.

1.1.2 Hardware Layers and Features

The hardware components of SAP HANA are also fundamentally important in understanding what SAP HANA is. With SAP HANA, data is stored in *dynamic random-access memory* (DRAM) and within the *central processing unit* (CPU) cache. This allows the software to deliver exceptional performance because data is stored close to the CPU. Traditional databases store and access data on disk drives that are architecturally farther away from the CPU and slower in accessing data for a variety of technical reasons.

Each server is also configured with 20 or more CPU cores and two or more CPU sockets so that the software can process multiple requests concurrently. For example, when data is stored in a column store, the software can reduce the processing of each column of data into one or more parallel requests. Because there are multiple CPU cores available, each request can be processed by one or more CPU cores in parallel. The net result is more data being processed at the same time for an individual query.

As we mentioned earlier, compression is an important component of the SAP HANA appliance and is significant in today's implementations. Despite all of the hardware advancements over the past 20 years, an individual server is still limited to somewhere between eight and 12 terabytes (TB) of *random access memory* (RAM) depending on the vendor and CPU chipset. Even though modern servers can accommodate 8–12 TB of RAM, most of these servers are not certified to operate SAP HANA for analytic purposes. For example, the current generation of certified servers, based on the Ivy Bridge v2 CPU, have a maximum of eight CPU sockets and 2 TB of RAM when utilized for analytics.

To overcome the single-server RAM limitations, SAP HANA also supports the ability to scale out. This allows SAP HANA to manage data in memory, on multiple servers, while acting as a single unit. Most SAP HANA hardware vendors certified their multi-node appliances with a maximum of 16 nodes. In most cases, each server node has between 512 GB and 1 TB of RAM. IBM currently has a certified appliance cluster that scales to 56 TB of total RAM. With compression, the top systems are able to accommodate anywhere from 56 TB to 196 TB of data, given a compression of 7.

Because of these memory limitations, compression is an extremely important benefit of the SAP HANA appliance; without it, most large enterprises would not be able to implement SAP HANA because their data needs would exceed the limitations of the hardware.

Even though there are current limitations on hardware, we can expect the amount of RAM supported on an SAP HANA server to increase significantly over the next few years. There are rumors that some hardware vendors are working on technologies that would allow a single logical server node to incorporate 16 TB or more of RAM in the near future. If this rumor is true, SAP HANA servers will likely one day accommodate over a petabyte of RAM.

Because DRAM is volatile or erased when the server loses power, it's important that the data in DRAM be backed up to a nonvolatile storage layer both automatically and periodically. The SAP HANA appliance manages these periodic snapshots of memory to disk automatically. It incorporates a fast storage layer to manage database logging. Within the first generation of single-node servers, this logging layer was managed on solid state disk (SSD) arrays or NAND flash cards like those developed by the company Fusion-io. However, the requirement for NAND flash drives seems to have dissipated due to recent changes in the SAP HANA software. Many of the second-generation SAP HANA servers, based on the Ivy Bridge v2 CPU, no longer incorporate high-speed NAND flash storage. With that said, all certified SAP HANA appliances incorporate RAID-level disk arrays to manage nonvolatile storage. These arrays offer a persistence storage partition, which is used to house the logging files, logging snapshots, and snapshots of the row or columnar tables.

SAP HANA is *ACID compliant*—a term that describes a database that has *atomicity*, *consistency*, *isolation*, and *durability*. ACID compliance guarantees that each database transaction is reliable, even if the server loses power.

Although SAP HANA does rely on traditional disk-based storage, data is stored and accessed in DRAM first. With that said, data is also simultaneously preserved in persistent nonvolatile disks to provide ACID compliance, data recovery, and data integrity.

Figure 1.2 depicts an overview of the hardware features and layers of a single-node SAP HANA appliance. Data is stored in-memory and close to the CPU for faster processing. The SAP HANA software also makes precise use of the CPU cache to bring frequently accessed data even closer to the CPU. The storage layer is used in conjunction with DRAM to provide ACID compliance and data integrity.

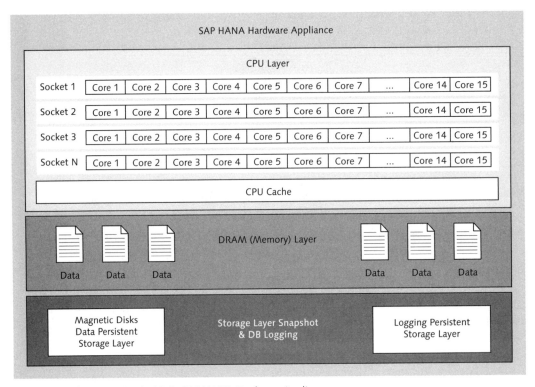

Figure 1.2 Single-Node SAP HANA Hardware Appliance

As we mentioned above, SAP HANA can run on a single server, or it can be scaled out to run on multiple servers that act as a single instance. It acts as a single appliance when scaled over multiple nodes, giving users a single point of access. When distributed on multiple nodes, the core software engines are active on each node and used to manage the distributed data in-memory.

In the multi-node or scale-out SAP HANA appliance, all nodes share a single logical persistent storage layer. This ensures that the in-memory data on each node is written to the same shared persistent storage when it performs its regular in-memory data snapshots and backups. Figure 1.3 depicts the SAP HANA appliance running as a single instance distributed over multiple nodes. Note that SAP HANA is ACID-compliant even when it's scaled to multiple nodes.

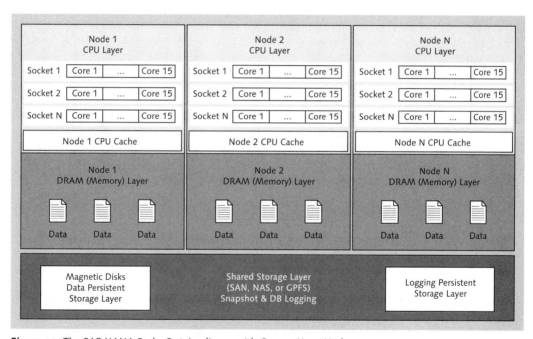

Figure 1.3 The SAP HANA Scale-Out Appliance with One or More Nodes

SAP HANA scale-out configurations are also the foundation for providing disaster recovery (DR) and high availability (HA) options. When an HA SAP HANA implementation is required, typically, one or more active nodes are clustered with one or more passive nodes. In these instances, a single physical or logical persistent storage array is shared among all of the nodes. If any single node fails, you can activate a passive node to carry the workload of the failed node by reloading the data from the shared persistent store tier back into memory. This is possible because each node is capable of accessing the same shared storage layer. When we study the certified SAP HANA configurations, we find that one of the following storage mechanisms is utilized: local disk arrays, *Storage Area Network* (SAN) arrays, *Network Attached Storage* (NAS) arrays, or the IBM *General Parallel File System* (GPFS). Which devices or methodology is used depends on the selected vendor's solution. When an SAP HANA DR implementation is required, this same storage layer is often replicated to an offsite location. In the event that the main site is lost, passive SAP HANA nodes can be activated on the DR site and reloaded to the replicated persistent storage data.

SAP HANA Hardware Selection

A variety of server hardware vendors provide prebuilt certified systems to run SAP HANA. Each hardware vendor is required to undergo a strenuous certification process to ensure that its hardware platform meets or exceeds the standards set by SAP. Because the SAP HANA software was developed to take advantage of the Intel Nehalem EX, Intel Westmere EX, and Ivy Bridge v2 E7 processors, it can't be installed on just any off-the-shelf x86 server. For a complete listing of certified servers by vendor, refer to the SAP HANA Product Availability Matrix (PAM) at *http://www.saphana.com/docs/DOC-4611*. For a complete list of the second-generation SAP HANA servers based on the Ivy Bridge v2 CPU, please review the document located at *http://scn.sap.com/docs/DOC-52522*.

The available persistent storage technologies vary from vendor to vendor, and the selection is even more diverse when we study the different configurations that vendors choose in the scale-out SAP HANA scenarios. It is important that we study the different available options as they relate to the various SAP HANA HA, DR, and backup solutions.

In addition to the certified SAP HANA systems, customers can design their own certified systems using the *Tailored Datacenter Integration* (TDI) program. This program allows customers to use their own internal network infrastructure and storage infrastructure to build a fully supported SAP HANA system. With that said, customers can utilize only servers or nodes that are listed on the SAP HANA PAM. For more information, please review the following document: *http://www.saphana.com/docs/DOC-4380*.

Starting with SAP HANA SPS7, customers can also implement a production instance of SAP HANA on VMWare ESX 5.x, but there are a few stipulations. Non-production use of SAP HANA has been certified on VMWare since SAP HANA SPS5. Please review the following document for more details: *http://www.saphana.com/docs/DOC-4192*.

At its heart, SAP HANA is built from the ground up to manage, store, and process data in-memory while leveraging multiple CPU cores and the CPU cache. It's a fusion of both software and hardware that was designed to take advantage of today's server hardware capabilities. If SAP were to attempt to deliver technology such as SAP HANA just 20 years ago, it would have found the task to be both technically difficult and cost prohibitive. The cost of DRAM per megabyte has decreased more than 250 times during the past 20 years. During the same time period, the speed and capacity of networks, CPUs, motherboards, and disk drives have increased substantially. SAP recognized this trend and designed SAP HANA to be the true next-generation data appliance.

Traditional database vendors are in a position that limits their ability to quickly adapt to modern hardware because they still need to support legacy technologies designed when hardware was significantly more limited than today's. Most database vendors are also restricted by the costs and risks associated with redesigning their database software to take advantage of today's hardware. This isn't to say that other database vendors won't *try* to make the transition, but rather, an indication that it will be difficult for them to make the transition without requiring their customers to make renewed investments in their legacy database technologies.

The net result of this fusion between hardware and software is a platform that can process queries 1,000 times faster than the traditional magnetic disk–based database. Speed alone doesn't justify SAP HANA, nor does it create an instant value proposition. There are other components of the SAP HANA platform that also add value. Some of those components are built directly into the SAP HANA appliance, while others work closely with SAP HANA to deliver solutions and value for an organization. SAP has made a considered effort to incorporate other technologies into the SAP HANA appliance landscape. An SAP HANA instance contains a development platform and web application server that allows organizations to not only move the data closer to the CPU, but also move application code closer to the CPU and data. In addition, SAP has incorporated predictive analytics, geospatial analysis, multidimensional models, and row-store tables in the SAP HANA platform. When you consider all of the capabilities internal to the SAP appliance, you'll find that it's more than just a database.

In addition to the components built directly into SAP HANA, there are other technologies that SAP HANA incorporates to deliver an end-to-end BI solution. As we continue throughout this chapter, we'll discuss the different solutions that are built upon the SAP HANA appliance foundation and how they are used to deliver a complete BI SAP HANA solution. Although there are multiple ways to implement SAP HANA, the core of this book is based on a solution that incorporates the use of two specific tools: SAP Data Services, which can work with data from any source, and SAP BusinessObjects BI, which is the recommended BI solution to run on top of SAP HANA.

1.2 Business Intelligence Solutions with SAP HANA

Although the purpose of this book is to explain a native implementation of SAP HANA for analytics using SAP BusinessObjects BI, organizations interested in a business intelligence solution running on top of SAP HANA can also choose to implement SAP BW on SAP HANA. We'll briefly introduce you to the differences between these options in this section. Each solution that is discussed in Section 1.2.1 and Section 1.2.2 has its own unique set of benefits, components, and use cases. With this knowledge, you should gain a better understanding of SAP HANA and the different ways it can be implemented before we spend the rest of the book on the discussion of implementing a native solution using SAP Data Services and SAP BusinessObjects BI.

1.2.1 SAP BW on SAP HANA

SAP BW is a BI solution that was designed by SAP to facilitate reporting, analytics, data security, master data management, and general data warehouse principles. It's predominantly for use with data generated in the SAP Business Suite applications, but solutions are available that provide support for third-party data, as well. SAP BW comprises a software layer and an underlying *relational database management system* (RDBMS).

Historically, SAP BW performed many of its functions in the software layer while agnostically using the underlying RDBMS to store the data. This decision was largely based on the need for SAP BW to support multiple vendor RDBMSs. As the use of SAP BW became more prominent and the volumes of data it stored began to increase, the application layer component of SAP BW became a hindrance to its scalability. SAP's initial attempt to solve this problem was found in a solution called the *SAP BW Accelerator* (BWA). While this solution solved many of the scalability and performance issues associated with querying SAP BW, it was largely focused on fixing the response times of queries. Architecturally, it didn't solve all of the fundamental issues associated with SAP BW. For example, the SAP BW application layer was still predominantly used for extracting, transforming, and loading (ETL) data. For many organizations, the inefficacies of the ETL processes in the SAP BW application layer were not solved with BWA.

In response to the need to better respond to customers' requirements, SAP developed SAP HANA. Initially, SAP HANA was used alongside SAP BW much like BWA. Data was moved from SAP BW InfoProviders into SAP HANA for faster query response times. Much like the BWA solution, using SAP HANA in this capacity didn't solve the fundamental issues associated with the SAP BW ETL processes.

In November 2011, SAP officially released SAP BW on SAP HANA. While SAP HANA and BWA were already usable solutions for SAP BW, the release of SAP BW on SAP HANA fundamentally changed the way SAP BW interacted with the underlying RDBMS. With its release, SAP began the process of integrating the software layer of SAP BW with the underlying RDBMS of SAP HANA.

Here, SAP HANA serves as the underlying RMDS of SAP BW. Given the powerful features of SAP HANA, this marriage was destined to resolve many of the historical performance and scalability issues associated with SAP BW running on legacy RDBMS. SAP BW on SAP HANA simultaneously solves the issues associated with both the SAP BW ETL processes and the SAP BW querying processes.

In addition to the overall performance gains, SAP BW on SAP HANA incorporates many changes to the application layer. Many of the traditional software features of SAP BW are now pushed to SAP HANA for processing. As a result, many traditional SAP BW functions are accelerated throughout the complete SAP BW development lifecycle. This is truly the first step in leveraging SAP HANA and SAP BW as the preferred data warehouse for SAP Business Suite applications. Figure 1.4 illustrates a high-level depiction of the architecture for SAP BW on SAP HANA.

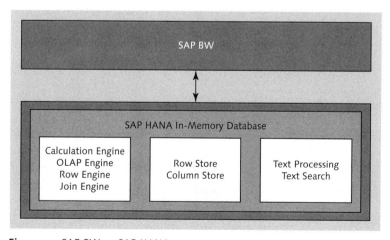

Figure 1.4 SAP BW on SAP HANA

For organizations that currently run SAP BW with a third-party RDBMS, SAP BW on SAP HANA will be an easy transition. Because SAP BW is still the primary software interface, very few changes have been made to the current development tools and processes. That is, while it contains several SAP HANA–specific optimizations, all development and administrative tasks continue to be performed using the SAP GUI or the existing BI tool sets associated with SAP BW.

To implement SAP BW on SAP HANA, your organization needs to create a new SAP BW on SAP HANA environment and then migrate its existing SAP BW environment to the new landscape—that is, you can't simply do an in-place upgrade of your existing architecture to support SAP HANA. Based on firsthand experience, the process is very straightforward.

Let's examine some of the reasons that an organization would implement SAP BW on SAP HANA:

▶ **Minimal changes**
The most compelling reason to implement SAP BW on SAP HANA is that there are very few changes required for an organization to adopt this SAP HANA solution. Of course, this is assuming the company is currently running SAP BW. The SAP BW application layer continues to be the primary point of contact with this solution. Unlike solutions that replicate SAP BW or SAP Business Suite data to SAP HANA, SAP BW on SAP HANA results in a minimal learning curve in its adoption. Developers don't need to use the SAP HANA development tools or models to adopt this solution. In addition, this solution leverages all of the historical development investments associated with the legacy SAP BW environment.

▶ **Faster load times**
Due to enhanced integration between the SAP BW application layer and the overall power of the SAP HANA appliance, organizations can expect a significant boost in load times and the overall ETL process.

▶ **Faster query response times**
Due to the enhanced integration between the SAP BW application and the overall power of the SAP HANA appliance, organizations can expect a significant boost in BI query response times. Based on firsthand experience, SAP BW on SAP HANA can result in a query response time that is 70 to 100 times faster for BI queries in SAP Business Explorer (BEx) and SAP BusinessObjects BI.

▶ **Integration with SAP Business Suite applications**
Because SAP BW is delivered with pre-built content and direct integration with SAP Business Suite applications, SAP BW on SAP HANA also has these same benefits. Again, this solution merely changes the underlying RDBMS that operates SAP BW. All remaining SAP BW on SAP HANA enhancements are minimal and easy to adopt.

▶ **Reduced storage footprint**
With SAP BW on SAP HANA, there are several optional application-layer enhancements that allow developers to reduce the overall storage footprint of SAP BW by moving legacy operations from the application layer to the SAP HANA platform. In addition, some InfoCubes can be replaced with direct reporting on SAP BW on SAP HANA in-memory optimized DataStore Objects (DSOs).

▶ **Reduced reliance on the application layer**
With SAP BW on SAP HANA, there are several operational steps that can be pushed directly to the SAP HANA engines for processing. This reduces the number of round trips between the application layer and RDBMS layers that were associated with traditional SAP BW systems. The end result is faster development cycles and load times.

▶ **Near-line storage**
SAP BW offers the ability to directly integrate an independent storage tier into the SAP BW landscape. While SAP HANA offers in-memory data processing, it's not always the most cost-effective medium to store legacy or infrequently accessed data. Near-line storage offers organizations an option to store select data in a storage system that incorporates the benefits of the SAP (Sybase) IQ columnar store database. Near-line storage uses cost-effective disks to store the data.

▶ **Expected future enhancements**
While there are no guarantees about what future enhancements will look like for SAP BW on SAP HANA, there have been several rumors that future versions will further remove the dependencies on the SAP BW application layer and move more processing to the SAP HANA appliance. In addition, many of the persistent steps associated with legacy SAP BW processes will likely be removed. If the rumors turn out to be true, the SAP BW application layer will eventually serve as a logical modeling tool, and data will need to be stored only once within an SAP HANA table.

1.2.2 Native Implementation of SAP HANA for Analytics

Business intelligence solutions that use SAP HANA natively are fundamentally different from SAP BW on SAP HANA. A native implementation of SAP HANA represents solutions that provision and access data within SAP HANA directly. After the data is provisioned within SAP HANA, the multidimensional modeling views can be created to express the data in a business-centric, multidimensional model. SAP BusinessObjects BI can then be used to access the data using its powerful reports, dashboards, and visualization tools.

SAP HANA native solutions require an organization to use the tools and processes within SAP HANA, such as its multidimensional models, columnar tables, and other supported SAP provisioning tools to facilitate analytics and reporting. An organization's resource will also need to become knowledgeable in the methods for provisioning, modeling, and managing data that will be stored directly in SAP HANA.

Although many organizations implement SAP Business Suite applications to run their businesses, not everyone does. Many of the legacy SAP BusinessObjects BI customers fall into this category. Many organizations support both SAP Business Suite applications and third-party applications within their organizations, while other organizations use systems that have no association with SAP. To that end, SAP BW isn't always the most appropriate choice when you're implementing SAP HANA. Fortunately, SAP HANA native solutions offer several viable alternatives that can accommodate multiple types of data sources. Later in this section, we'll discuss different SAP HANA native provisioning solutions, but before we discuss these solutions, let's compare and contrast a native implementation of SAP HANA to SAP BW on SAP HANA. This comparison will give you further insight into the distinctions.

Solutions running with SAP HANA natively offer organizations the opportunity to directly leverage SAP HANA without any additional software layer to impede data access. Granted, independent software tools are used to provision and interact with SAP HANA natively. However, this isn't exactly the same methodology that SAP BW uses. With SAP BW on SAP HANA, query and reporting tools access the SAP BW software layer and then broker requests to SAP HANA. Figure 1.5 depicts, at a high level, the overall process flow of using SAP BusinessObjects BI to access SAP BW on SAP HANA. As you can see, SAP BW brokers requests to SAP HANA.

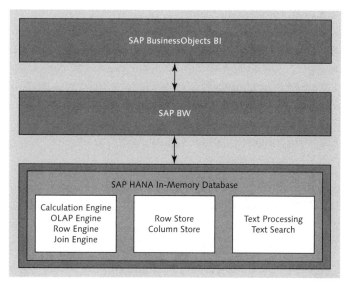

Figure 1.5 Query and Analysis Tools Accessing SAP HANA via SAP BW when Running SAP BW on SAP HANA

With SAP HANA as a native solution, query and reporting tools interact directly with the SAP HANA engines instead of through SAP BW. Our firsthand experience has been that accessing data directly within SAP HANA currently offers a slightly faster experience than accessing data through the SAP BW layer. Figure 1.6 depicts, at a high level, the way that that SAP BusinessObjects BI interacts directly with a native implementation of SAP HANA.

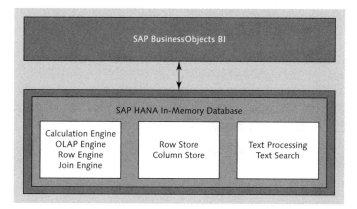

Figure 1.6 Query and Analysis Tools Accessing SAP HANA Directly in a Native Implementation of SAP HANA

Figure 1.5 and Figure 1.6 depict the current state of the two integrations. As we have already observed, with each release, SAP has enhanced SAP BW to better leverage the SAP HANA platform natively. Starting with SAP BW 7.4 SP5, organizations can fully import SAP BW metadata and security into SAP HANA and represent it as a secure native SAP HANA information view. The process automatically creates a calculation view or analytic view that can be accessed natively by SAP BusinessObjects BI. With each new release, we can expect more and more traditional SAP BW features to be converted to native SAP HANA functions.

Now that we've compared SAP BW on SAP HANA to a native implementation of SAP HANA, it's time to better understand the reasons that organizations would choose to implement SAP HANA native solutions. As it pertains to the core subject of this book, we'll be discussing a solution that uses SAP Data Services and SAP BusinessObjects BI to manage an SAP HANA native solution.

We can cite five specific reasons that an organization would choose to implement SAP HANA natively. Individually, they might not provide a compelling justification. However, if you find that your needs match more than one of the reasons listed, you'll likely find a native implementation of SAP HANA to be an appropriate solution.

▸ **Third-party data**
  In the context of this book, third-party data refers to data that is generated and stored using applications that have no association with SAP Business Suite. While SAP dominates the overall market share with its SAP Business Suite applications, Forbes has reported that it still accounts for only about 25% of the overall ERP market share. In this regard, there are more overall applications generating data than those developed by SAP.

  It's our opinion that SAP BW isn't the appropriate solution to manage mass amounts of third-party data. This is especially true when organizations predominantly use non-SAP systems to run their businesses. This isn't to say that it can't manage third-party data, but rather to express the opinion that there are better solutions available within the SAP portfolio.

  If an organization wants to leverage SAP HANA, the amount of third-party data the company chooses to load into SAP HANA has a direct bearing on which solution the company should choose. SAP HANA native solutions support tools that are well equipped to manage data from third-party sources. At the same time, SAP BW is better equipped to manage data from SAP systems. Third-party data alone should not be the deciding factor, but it does play an important role in making the right decision.

▶ **Custom solutions**
When organizations require a custom information management or BI solution, they will find that both a native implementation of SAP HANA and its accompanying tools offer a great deal of flexibility.

The SAP HANA platform has several embedded scripting languages, a development platform, a web application server, and support for industry standard connectivity. This makes SAP HANA an ideal development platform for custom solutions. SAP HANA also supports several data source–agnostic extraction and loading tools that further enhance the flexibility of a custom solution.

▶ **Native performance**
Because SAP HANA native solutions directly leverage the SAP HANA engines and platform, the performance of such solutions will be unimpeded by additional software layers.

▶ **Real-time replication**
When an organization needs a platform that supports both real-time data replication and real-time analytical modeling, a native implementation of SAP HANA will prove to be the best solution.

▶ **Complex transformations**
When the source data requires complex transformation, data cleansing, and complex data merging, a native implementation of SAP HANA that uses SAP Data Services will provide the most flexibility and capability.

To further understand a native implementation of SAP HANA, we need to first examine all of the methods that are used to provision the data it will manage. Before we can create meaningful reports and analytics, we must first decide how best to extract data and load it into SAP HANA. SAP currently supports several main provisioning solutions for a native SAP HANA implementation: SAP Landscape Transformation (SLT), Direct Extract Connector (DXC), SAP Event Stream Processor, SAP Replication Server, SAP Data Services, and SAP HANA Studio. Let's take a closer look at each of these.

SAP Landscape Transformation

SAP Landscape Transformation (SLT) is one way that an organization can choose to implement SAP HANA. The key technology behind SLT is its ability to perform real-time source system trigger–based replication of data from both an SAP Business Suite application or from a third-party source. The mechanism that SLT uses for replication is commonly referred to as *trigger-based replication*.

SLT can also process data in batch mode, but it's more appropriately used to provision data within SAP HANA in real-time mode. Organizations will benefit from SLT when they need to create analytics using data that has near zero latency. With the goal of SLT centered on the concept of real time, there is little room for complex transformations of the data within the SLT engines. This is where SAP HANA plays an important role in an overall SLT solution. As you'll discover in later chapters, SAP HANA has the capability to transform basic, raw data into multidimensional or analytic models in real time, as well.

Figure 1.7 depicts the SLT provisioning processes at a high level. Logging tables and database triggers are created within the source system. As data is inserted, updated, or deleted within the source, triggers are executed to populate the logging table with the details of these operations. The SLT server monitors the source logs and replicates the source system changes to a mirrored table in the SAP HANA appliance. SLT can make a few changes to the data as it's transferred, but the changes are limited to basic filtering and a few linear functions. The end result is a mirror or near-mirror copy of the source system's data and tables. After the data lies in SAP HANA, multidimensional models can be created to further transform and calculate the data.

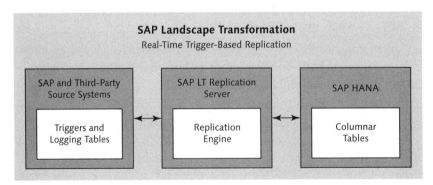

Figure 1.7 Replicating Data from an SAP System or Third-Party Database into SAP HANA in Real Time

SLT supports replication from many popular third-party RDBMs, such as Microsoft SQL Server, Oracle Enterprise Edition, IBM DB2, and SAP MaxDB. This is in addition to its support of the SAP Business Suite applications. This makes SLT an ideal solution for organizations that need to deliver real-time analytics.

Because an implementation of SAP HANA has many possible solutions, let's take a look at the main reasons an organizations would choose to implement SAP HANA with SLT:

▶ **Real-time access to data**

Many organizations have a legitimate need to provide data to decision makers in real time. The use cases are vast and vary from one industry to the next. While the organization as a whole might not need all of its data in real time, an organization might have one or more processes that can be successful only when data is provided in an actionable and real-time way. In these cases, SLT will prove to be a successful tool that complements the capabilities of SAP HANA.

▶ **Use of SAP HANA Live**

SAP HANA Live represents a set of prebuilt code that can be downloaded from the SAP Service Marketplace. The downloadable code contains content and applications that can be imported into SAP HANA and SAP BusinessObjects BI. It consists of various prebuilt SAP HANA virtual data models, SAP BusinessObjects BI reports, and metadata. The code is prebuilt by SAP to accommodate basic reporting and analytic needs from a variety of standard SAP Business Content. SAP BusinessObjects BI is then used to analyze and visualize the data. It can also be customized to meet the specific needs of the organization. For many organizations, these packages will help streamline their implementation of SAP HANA and SLT. In general, it will reduce the time and resources required to implement such a solution. SAP HANA Live can also be implemented with *SAP Business Suite on SAP HANA*. In this case, SLT is not a hard requirement. Organizations can also implement SAP HANA Live directly within their SAP HANA instance that is running SAP Business Suite on SAP HANA.

▶ **Reduced complexity**

For some organizations, SLT will simplify overall BI processes by eliminating many of the traditional barriers associated with a rigid ETL process. Data is moved from the source to SAP HANA using an incremental and automatic process. The SAP HANA platform is then leveraged to convert the raw data into a logical, multidimensional model. This can prove to be a very simple and agile process for many organizations.

▶ **Increased flexibility**

Because the data isn't persisted beyond the initial SLT provisioning step, organizations will find that an SLT and SAP HANA solution are very flexible. SAP HANA's multidimensional models are logical, meaning that they don't move the data into subsequent tables. Traditional ETL processes sometimes require that data be moved from one table to the next as it undergoes its transformation process. This often requires a very long and complex development lifecycle that can impact an organization's ability to react to changing requirements and business rules. SLT and SAP HANA remove these barriers because only code and logical changes are required. There is also little need to physically move data within the SAP HANA platform, which also increases flexibility.

In addition to these benefits, we recommend that you consider a few other items before deciding on SLT. This isn't to say that SLT is an inappropriate means of managing data, but rather to expose common issues that can make SLT difficult to implement. Consider the following:

▶ **Data quality**

One of the most compelling reasons to be cautious about SLT is based on the quality and governance of the source data. Data is effectively replicated from the source as is. Within an SLT and SAP HANA solution, there are very few effective mechanisms to clean and manage bad data. The old adage of, "garbage in, garbage out," is a very real concern with an SLT-based solution. To be effective, the source data must be tightly governed independently of SLT.

▶ **Complex transformations**

Depending on the state of the source system data, there is a chance that SLT and SAP HANA will be unable to properly transform complex data into meaningful analytics. In subsequent chapters, we'll discuss these concepts in more detail. However, at this stage, we must anticipate that there will be some limitations associated with the processing of data using a combination of SLT and SAP HANA.

▶ **Multiple sources**

SLT and SAP HANA have a limited ability to work with data that originates from multiple sources. Take, for example, an organization that has four subsidiaries. If each subsidiary has its own product master table, it will be difficult to merge, conform, and de-duplicate this data in real time.

▶ **Diversity of data sources**

Given these points, take a moment to fully grasp all of the data sources that an organization can have. Using SLT alone to provision SAP HANA isn't a replacement for a data warehouse. On the achievable side, SLT and SAP HANA do an excellent job of replicating and presenting a focused subset of an organization's data to end users because SLT supports a limited list of data sources. On the cautious side, SLT and SAP HANA will likely fail in acting as a substitute for a traditional central store of the organization's data or a data warehouse. Organizations will find that ETL tools such as SAP Data Services are much better at obtaining and managing data from a variety of sources.

As with all technology, not all rules are black and white. Organizations could choose to replicate data into SAP HANA in real time and then leverage SAP HANA's scripting code to address many of these concerns. There's more to an SAP HANA appliance than its capability to deliver data through its multidimensional modeling views. SAP HANA supports a higher level of programming through its SQLScript, stored procedures, and other coding languages. When you combine these capabilities with the hardware and software capabilities of SAP HANA, there are few technical barriers within the SAP HANA platform. Organizations could also look at hybrid solutions that leverage all of the provisioning methods supported by SAP HANA. For example, transactional tables could be replicated into SAP HANA using SLT in real time. At the same time, descriptive tables could be managed using traditional ETL-based tools that better manage complex transformations. The SAP HANA multidimensional models could then be used to conform these tables into a comprehensive logic model.

SLT is an excellent means of replicating a focused set of data from a supported SAP and non-SAP source in real time. SAP HANA provides logical modeling tools that can convert raw data into multidimensional models in real time, as well.

Direct Extract Connect

Direct Extract Connect (DXC) is another solution that can to be leveraged to move data from an SAP Business Suite application directly to SAP HANA. Because it interacts directly with the SAP HANA appliance, it too is considered an SAP HANA native solution. DXC uses the same *SAP Business Content DataSource Extractors* that are found in SAP BW to move data into SAP HANA. DXC extracts the data from the SAP source in batch mode on a scheduled and reoccurring basis. DXC has limited transformation capabilities, but it's ranked in the same class as many ETL tools.

Figure 1.8 depicts the DXC extraction processes at a high level. Starting with SAP NetWeaver 7.0, SAP BW is embedded in the standard application stack. While this stack isn't used to run all of the features of SAP BW, a limited set of its components can be leveraged to provision data directly into SAP HANA. In essence, DXC uses the same extraction process that is found in a standalone SAP BW stack. However, DXC redirects the extracted data directly into the SAP HANA system. DXC creates an in-memory DSO (IMDSO) within the SAP HANA system. The IMDSO consists of a series of SAP HANA columnar tables. Note that the embedded SAP BW modules can't be used to model the extracted data. Within the SAP HANA appliance, multidimensional models should be created based on these columnar tables to serve as the primary modeling tools.

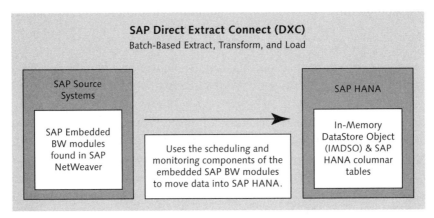

Figure 1.8 Moving Data from an SAP Application to SAP HANA Using DXC Extractors

Because the DXC modules run directly within the SAP source system, the overall architecture of the DXC solution is simplified. There is no need to maintain and run an intermediary server to broker the movement of data. This is an ideal solution for organizations or hosting companies that need a simplified architecture capable of moving data from an SAP source to an SAP HANA target.

For many tables in the SAP source system, DXC offers a very simple mechanism to extract only changed data—the *delta load process* or *change data capture process*. In fact, this is the same technology that is used by SAP BW to extract data from the SAP source. Organizations will also find this to be an added benefit of the DXC solution.

The DXC extraction process is very different from those used in the SLT solution because the data is moved on a scheduled basis in batch. However, after the data is provisioned within SAP HANA, DXC also relies on the multidimensional models or other SAP HANA code to transform the data. DXC transfers the data from the SAP source to a special web dispatcher service or XML processor that is embedded in the SAP web application server or XS Engine. It's also important to understand that not all data sources found in SAP sources can be managed with DXC.

Be mindful that DXC can fall victim to many of the same limitations described within the SLT section of this chapter. However, the extractors used by the DXC process contain code that facilitates some of the most common transformations. We should also reiterate that the DXC only supports SAP applications as a data source.

Additional References

For more information on the SAP DXC setup, implementation, and other limitations, refer to the ETL-based *Data Acquisition by SAP HANA Direct Extractor Connection* guide found within the SAP Service Marketplace. You can also refer to SAP Note 1665602 to obtain additional details by going to *https://service.sap.com/sap/support/notes/1665602*.

SAP Event Stream Processor

SAP Event Stream Processor (ESP) is also a viable real-time solution for provisioning data within SAP HANA. The ESP engine is capable of processing large volumes of data from a variety of sources using *complex event processing* (CEP). As opposed to capturing and storing all source data, ESP allows organizations to pick and choose what information is significant using user-defined functions and business rules. It can be utilized to stream data, in real-time, from a variety of sources. It supports industry-standard message busses, such as Java Message Services (JMS), TIBCO, and IBM Web-Sphere Message Queuing. It supports streams obtained from RDMS using industry-standard ODBC and JDBC connectivity. It can read input events from files or sockets. If the ESP standard adapters do not provide access to the desired data source, custom adapters can be developed to support the desired data source. Once the data is obtained and processed, it can be stored or provisioned in SAP HANA columnar tables. Like SLT and DXC, we can then develop SAP HANA multidimensional models that can be consumed by SAP BusinessObjects BI tools.

Beyond the traditional BI application of these replicated data streams, organizations could also leverage SAP HANA's predictive libraries and application development platform to create highly customized applications, dashboards, alert engines, rules engines, and enterprise performance management applications.

These possibilities are all achievable because SAP HANA is more than just a database—it is also a development platform. By adding components like ESP to the solution, we can truly expand its capabilities beyond the traditional RDMS.

SAP Replication Server

SAP Replication Server supports real-time replication of data from a variety of non-SAP sources. SAP Replication Server is similar to SLT; however, it uses a replication agent to monitor the source database's transaction logs. This is commonly referred to as *log-based replication*. Log-based replication is less invasive or disruptive on the source system. As an example, SLT requires the creation of database triggers, functions, and logging tables on the source system. This often adds overhead to the source system or RDMS. The SAP replication agent monitors the source RDMS logging mechanism. When changes to the transaction logs are detected, they are sent to the SAP Replication Server. The target replication server will then commit the transaction to a desired SAP HANA instance. Because the data is stored or provisioned in SAP HANA columnar tables, we can then develop SAP HANA multidimensional models that can be consumed by SAP BusinessObjects BI tools.

SAP Replication Server should be considered when non-SAP sources are needed in an SAP HANA real-time solution. SLT is also capable of replicating non-SAP data, but the SAP Replication Server option is less invasive. Based on personal experience, most third-part DBAs are unlikely to allow the creation of triggers and logging tables on their source RDMS. SAP Replication Server uses log-based replication, which is asynchronous to the source RDMS system. It does not create tables or triggers on the source RDMS. It simply uses the SAP Replication Agent to monitor the standard transaction logs of the source RDMS. The net result is that little or no overhead is added to the source RDMS.

SAP Data Services (ETL)

Now, let's turn our attention to the solution that we'll discuss throughout the core of this book: SAP Data Services.

The core technology behind SAP Data Services is based on a product originally named ActaWorks. In 2002, the organization Business Objects acquired Acta Technologies and enhanced the product that is now commonly referred to as *Data Integrator*. When SAP acquired Business Objects, the product was renamed SAP Data Services.

Although the name has changed, the core technology behind SAP Data Services has not. SAP Data Services is a data source–agnostic ETL tool. Its primary purpose is based on an organization's need to manage, centralize, and govern data that exists in one or more data sources. It's capable of extracting data from almost every commonly used data source. After the data is extracted, it's then cleansed, transformed, and merged into the desired data model. Its final feat is then to load the data into one or more databases or formats. Figure 1.9 shows the generic ETL process as managed by SAP Data Services.

SAP Data Services and other ETL tools have traditionally been used to manage several common data processes within an organization and integrate data between source systems.

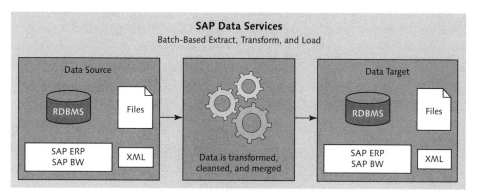

Figure 1.9 The Generic ETL Process of SAP Data Services

Take, for example, a large enterprise that has acquired another organization. Let's assume that both organizations managed their business by collecting data using software applications. After the two entities are legally combined, there will be a need to migrate one organization's customer data into the other organization's existing applications. Because SAP Data Services is capable of extracting, transforming, and loading the data, it will serve as an ideal tool to manage this process.

SAP Data Services can also be used to create a comprehensive central store of data or a data warehouse. For that data to be useful, it must be conformed into a clean, denormalized, and relational series of data tables. SAP Data Services can also be used to create data marts or datastores that are well optimized for multidimensional analysis. Finally, SAP Data Services provides several data quality tools to help organizations track, manage, clean, and identify problems within their data.

> **The Data Warehouse versus the Data Mart**
>
> A *data warehouse* describes a system of database tables and their relationships that encompasses all relevant information within an organization. All information is organized by business constructs or terms, rather than the source fields or tables. The information, obtained from multiple sources, is conformed into business concepts and relationships.
>
> A *data mart* describes a similar system of database tables and their relationships. However, it's generally focused on a subset of data. It's typically well optimized for multidimensional analysis. Its source can be the data warehouse or staged data from various sources. In short, a data mart is often a better source for reporting and analytics.

Because SAP Data Services is the ideal tool to manage an ETL process, it too can serve as an important tool in an SAP HANA native solution. SAP Data Services is maintained by SAP, so its integration with SAP HANA and other SAP applications is very sound. However, its legacy capabilities also mean that it integrates well with third-party applications and data sources. This makes SAP Data Services an ideal tool to manage both SAP and third-party data that needs to be moved into a native implementation of SAP HANA.

From a technology standpoint, SAP Data Services uses a massively parallel processing engine that makes excellent use of RAM and multiple CPU cores when processing data. These technology features result in a tool that is capable of not only managing data, but also managing data while achieving outstanding throughput. It supports x86 64-bit servers running the Windows, AIX, Linux, or Solaris operating systems. Because it supports these commonly used operating systems, most organizations will find it easy to implement within their unique environments.

From a software standpoint, SAP Data Services uses an intuitive graphical user interface (GUI) to manage and develop the ETL processes. This interface is also very mindful of an organization's need to leverage metadata; several UI features allow data managers to quickly identify the relationships between data processing elements. There are even tools that give data managers a comprehensive view of the data lineage and impact analysis. This is all possible because SAP Data Services makes excellent use of the source, transformation, and target metadata. In subsequent chapters, we'll discuss this interface in more detail, but for now, it's important to understand its basic capabilities.

In the context of this book, we'll thoroughly discuss a solution that uses SAP Data Services to provision data within SAP HANA, and we'll continue our discussion of

SAP Data Services in Part II of the book. SAP Data Services can load data into either SAP HANA columnar or row tables. Figure 1.10 depicts the process flow of this solution. Data is retrieved from one or more types of sources. It's then transformed into a data model that best suits the analytic and performance requirements of the organization. The model is then loaded into an SAP HANA columnar table.

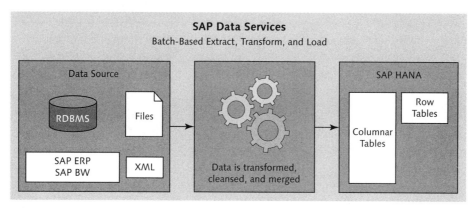

Figure 1.10 The Process Flow of Moving Data from an Agnostic Data Source to SAP HANA Using SAP Data Services

After the data is physically stored in SAP HANA, Part III of the book will walk you through the processes of designing a logical multidimensional model within SAP HANA. These models will act as views that can serve as the basis for end-user consumption of the data. Finally, you can then connect the SAP BusinessObjects BI platform using either the SAP HANA base columnar tables or SAP HANA information views to deliver stunning reports and visualizations. This is the subject of Part IV of the book.

SAP HANA Studio

The final option for provisioning data within a native implementation of SAP HANA involves the use of SAP HANA Studio, which is the development and administration tool for SAP HANA. It can be run from the SAP HANA server or on a separate computer.

With SAP HANA Studio, there are options that allow you to import flat files into an SAP HANA table in supported formats (*.csv*, *.xls*, and *.xlsx*). When you import the flat file, the UI allows you to either create a new target table based on the source flat file metadata or use an existing table that has the required data types and columns.

This feature is intended for quick proof-of-concept projects that need the data to be loaded only on a limited basis. The process is entirely manual, and subsequent imports will always append to the existing data set. It offers no transformation, delta load, or direct-from-database import options. Figure 1.11 depicts the workflow of the file import process. An administrator collects the needed files. Using the SAP HANA Studio application, the administrator launches the file import wizard and imports the file data directly into either a columnar or row-store table.

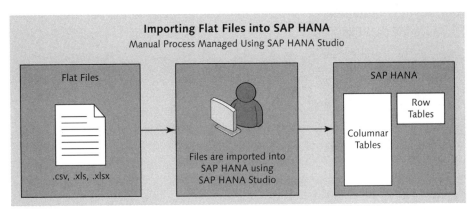

Figure 1.11 Importing Flat Files into SAP HANA Using SAP HANA Studio

Additional Resources

For more information about the process and steps required to import flat files into SAP HANA, we recommend that you watch the video located on the main SAP HANA website at *http://www.saphana.com/docs/DOC-2191*.

Summary

There are multiple ways to provision data within SAP HANA. Each option has a unique and appropriate use case. One or more of the described methods can be used together to provide a hybrid SAP HANA native solution. SAP Data Services is the ideal provisioning method when you're designing a data mart or data warehouse hosted in an SAP HANA native solution. SLT is the ideal solution for replicating SAP data that requires real-time analysis. DXC is a viable solution that can quickly and easily move SAP application data into SAP HANA on a recurring basis. SAP offer two additional real-time replication technologies from the Sybase acquisition, each with its own benefits and use cases. When data needs to be quickly imported into SAP HANA for temporary analysis, SAP HANA Studio can be used to import flat files.

1.3   SAP Business Suite on SAP HANA

Although the focus of this book is on using SAP HANA as a BI appliance, it's important that we also discuss the evolution of SAP HANA as the engine for SAP Business Suite applications. With SAP Business Suite on SAP HANA, we have found that there are a few viable options to implement a BI solution.

Tens of thousands of organizations use SAP Business Suite applications to run and operate their businesses. In terms of BI, these applications are the machines that produce the data that inevitably supports the analysis of data. Traditionally, these applications used a standard RDBMS to store and process the data inputs that were generated by an organization's operations. In 2013, SAP announced its support for SAP HANA as the engine to replace the standard RDBMS. This solution is commonly referred to as *SAP Business Suite on SAP HANA*.

With the power of SAP HANA, several lines of business processes can now be enhanced, in the form of both processing speed and the scripting capabilities of SAP HANA. Business processes that require the analysis of mass amounts of data can now be managed in seconds. Complex procedural processing can also be enhanced in the same manner. Statistical calculations can be performed within SAP HANA without the need to marshal data into third-party applications.

While SAP Business Suite on SAP HANA is a relatively new technology, many organizations are already reaping the benefits of it in terms of performance and BI capabilities. For many organizations, the prospect of implementing SAP BW or a data warehouse or extracting data using ABAP code is not a cost-effective or ideal solution. SAP Business Suite on SAP HANA offers a viable alternative because of two factors. First, SAP HANA Live can be implemented within SAP Business Suite on SAP HANA. Its prebuilt SAP HANA calculation views and SAP BusinessObjects BI reports will offer instant BI benefits to an organization. Second, using the SAP HANA Live views as a basis, custom calculation views can be developed to further expand the operational reporting capabilities of SAP Business Suite on SAP HANA. SAP BusinessObjects BI can then connect directly to the SAP HANA instance that is operating the SAP Business Suite platform.

As depicted in Figure 1.12, SAP Business Suite on SAP HANA uses SAP HANA as its RDMS. SAP HANA Live and custom information views can be developed to provide real-time operational access to the data. Custom reports, dashboards, and analytics can then be defined within SAP BusinessObjects BI. This is all achieved on a single platform.

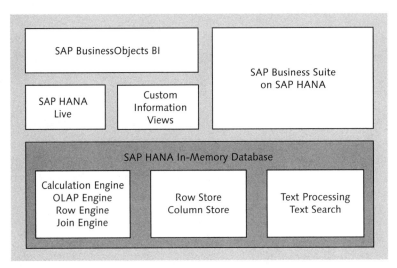

Figure 1.12 SAP Business Suite on SAP HANA and SAP HANA Live

As an alternative to running SAP Business Suite directly on SAP HANA, organizations can also implement a sidecar implementation of this same solution. The *SAP Business Suite on SAP HANA sidecar* implementation uses SLT to replicate the data from the SAP system to SAP HANA without the need to change the RDMS that operates the SAP Business Suite platform. For many organizations, this option is more practical because fewer changes to the SAP Business Suite platform are required. There is no need to migrate the data or set up a new SAP Business Suite environment. In many cases, there is also no need to upgrade the SAP Business Suite Application. Data can simply be replicated, in real-time, from the existing SAP Business Suite platform to SAP HANA. SAP HANA Live virtual data models and custom information views can then be developed within SAP HANA to provide real-time access to the data using SAP BusinessObjects BI or SAP Lumira Server.

Regardless of how an organization chooses to implement SAP Business Suite on SAP HANA, it will find that an effective, agile BI solution can be quickly implemented using SAP HANA Live. This same solution can also be quickly extended through custom virtual data models, which are technically called SAP HANA information views.

For those who have been involved in the BI field for the past few decades, this idea is a reversal of well-established BI best practices. However, the power and speed of SAP HANA, plus all of its built-in features, make this solution a possibility for many originations. With that said, our experience has shown that it does not always replace the need for SAP BW, a data warehouse, or data mart for all organizations. Most organizations must consider their need to analyze and confirm both non-SAP data and SAP data into a single point of access. They must also consider the volume of data that needs to be analyzed and conformed. In reality, implementing reporting and analytics directly upon SAP Business Suite on SAP HANA can succumb to the same limitations described within the "SAP Landscape Transformation" section in Section 1.2.2.

Additional Reference

For more information about SAP Business Suite on SAP HANA, we recommend that you visit *http://www.saphana.com/community/learn/solutions/sap-business-suite-on-hana*.

Now that we've discussed the current BI solutions available for use with SAP HANA, it's time that we focus on the core solution of this book. As we've discussed, there are several ways to leverage SAP HANA as a BI appliance. You can choose to run SAP NetWeaver BW on SAP HANA, SAP Business Suite on SAP HANA, or one of the six native SAP HANA provisioning methods that are currently available. It's hard to say that any one solution is the right choice for an organization—the diversity of available solutions is a product of the diversity that exists around an organization's requirements—but we'll now turn our focus to implementing SAP HANA using SAP Data Services and SAP BusinessObjects BI.

To better understand this solution, we'll first provide you with a view of a traditional BI implementation with SAP BusinessObjects BI and SAP Data Services. There are two aspects to a traditional SAP BusinessObjects BI implementation:

- **An organization's requirement to manage its data**
  Traditionally speaking, this process involved the creation of a data warehouse or data mart. If we assume that data can be useful only when it's organized and correct, we must then allow it to be managed, conformed, and cleaned. This is where SAP Data Services plays a key role.

- **An organization's requirement to provide access to its data**
  Decision makers need tools that allow them to visualize and analyze their data. This is where SAP BusinessObjects BI plays a key role. The SAP BusinessObjects

BI platform is home to multiple features and tools, all of which were designed with the idea of presenting data to data consumers.

1.4   Traditional EIM with SAP Data Services

Let's begin our traditional data loading conversation with a high-level overview of the data management process. In many ways, getting data into SAP HANA is more than simply moving data into SAP HANA tables—you need to develop a strategy and a series of rules that help you manage the process on a recurring basis. When you're designing a data warehouse or data mart, these strategies and rules are critical to the success of the implementation.

There are multiple aspects to an implementation of a data warehouse or data mart. In all, we refer to this solution and its tool sets, processes, and methodologies as *enterprise information management* (EIM). You use the tools to help manage the process, but there are other aspects of an EIM implementation that must be implemented outside the control of software. At a high level, there are five main aspects to the EIM process: the alignment of IT resources with the business, establishment of processes to manage the data, analysis of the data sources, development of a data model, and loading or provisioning of the data. As you'll see, there are aspects of the EIM processes that aren't simply managed with tools such as SAP Data Services.

1.4.1   Align IT with the Business

The most important step of an EIM implementation—and, unfortunately, the one that is most often overlooked—is the alignment of IT and the business community. In some ways, this step gets skipped because IT tends to lead these projects and this step isn't a strictly technical process. In reality, this step involves strong management, teamwork, and leadership.

The goal of the alignment is twofold. First, IT needs to fully understand the data analysis requirements of the business community. This helps IT to identify the source of the information and any gaps that exist in obtaining the data. It also helps IT understand the needs of the business when architecting the technical aspects of the EIM solution. Second, the business needs to take ownership of the data. This helps the business understand that IT can't solve all data issues with IT resources alone. Sometimes, the data simply needs to be entered into the frontend systems better. This is where leadership and management on the business side play a key role.

SAP HANA is capable of many technical wonders, but it relies on traditional tools and processes to obtain data. When implementing SAP HANA with SAP BusinessObjects BI and SAP Data Services, aligning the business community with IT is critical.

1.4.2 Establish Processes to Manage the Data

Once the IT and business resources are aligned, both a technical and procedural process should be established to manage the collection and distribution of data. Data should be treated as if it were a corporate asset—an asset that requires routine maintenance, care, and constant tracking. This is an area where a data governance discipline or program is often needed. At a high level, data governance involves the management and distribution of source system data, data quality, data transformation, data conformity, business process management, change management, and communication between data stewards and data custodians through an organization. ETL tools play a key role in the distribution and conformity of data, but a well-managed business process is just as important. With any SAP HANA BI implementation, we need to remember that data management is just as important as the need for fast access to the data.

1.4.3 Source System Analysis

After IT and the business are aligned, it's time for the two sides to fully analyze both the source data and the processes that help form the source data. IT resources generally profile the data or collect statistics about source data. SAP Data Services contains tools to help automate this process and collect the data. IT resources then identify the relationships between the data sources to help identify gaps in the data. Based on the results of the data profiling, the business owners then analyze their business processes to help IT understand the gaps. In some cases, these gaps must be solved with a change in the business process. In other cases, IT resources can fill the gaps using the technology at their disposal.

In the context of an SAP HANA implementation, SAP Data Services provides several tools that help with source system analysis. Other add-ons to SAP Data Services, such as SAP Information Steward, can also be used to help with this step.

Without proper source system analysis, it will be hard for an implementation of SAP HANA to be successful. Understanding the state of the data and where it exists is very important. Without this step, the benefits native to SAP HANA will be overshadowed by the lack of coherent data.

1.4.4 Develop a Data Model

Before you can load data into SAP HANA, you have to develop a data model. In a data mart or data warehouse, the data model describes the relationships between the various data elements in the form of database tables and technical diagrams. A data model comprises both *dimensions* and *facts*. Dimensions are tables that are used to describe or characterize a transaction. Fact tables are used to store transactions. A typical fact table contains keys that link back to one or more dimensions. Dimensions are often conformed to link to one or more fact tables. A proper data model is based on the need to conform the various dimensions to one or more fact tables. However, as we'll demonstrate in subsequent chapters, the traditional data model approach might need to be updated because of the ways that SAP HANA stores data.

1.4.5 Load the Data

With sound business community support and an understanding of the source data, IT resources are now ready to move data into SAP HANA. Using SAP Data Services, data is obtained from the various sources, staged into SAP HANA or another RDBMS, and then transformed into the prescribed data model within SAP HANA.

In subsequent chapters, we'll dive deeper into this phase of the SAP HANA implementation by exposing the capabilities of SAP Data Services. At this point, it's important that you understand that the full life cycle of an EIM process is composed of more than just provisioning data.

1.5 Traditional Business Intelligence with SAP BusinessObjects BI

In the traditional BI landscape, SAP BusinessObjects BI is the quintessential platform for managing the presentation and analysis of data stored in SAP HANA. On its own, SAP HANA can't properly present data to the business community—it needs the SAP BusinessObjects BI platform to form a proper BI solution. In other words, you need SAP BusinessObjects BI to properly implement SAP HANA.

In the SAP landscape, SAP BusinessObjects BI has become the de facto standard reporting and analytics tool for all SAP systems and applications. Based on its legacy support for third-party data sources, it's also capable of working with most enterprise data sources found within an organization.

The SAP BusinessObjects BI platform and SAP's other business intelligence offerings include multiple reporting tools such as SAP Crystal Reports, SAP Business-Objects Web Intelligence, SAP BusinessObjects Analysis (edition for Microsoft Office and edition for OLAP), SAP Predictive Analysis, and SAP InfiniteInsight (formerly KXEN). SAP offers dashboard tools such as SAP BusinessObjects Dashboards and SAP BusinessObjects Design Studio. It also offers a new breed of BI self-service tools, such as SAP BusinessObjects Explorer and SAP Lumira, and multiple mobile-enabled versions of these tools.

We use the term *platform* to describe SAP BusinessObjects BI because it's more than just a single application or service. It's composed of multiple layers and processes that can be scaled to meet the needs of any size organization. It's capable of pushing BI content to the users, as well as providing them with mechanisms to interact directly with the data. It contains multiple features that are essential to all BI implementations, such as the capability to properly secure the data, serve up analytical content, distribute the content, and integrate the content with existing systems.

Before we venture further into the book, let's establish a few high-level concepts surrounding the SAP BusinessObjects BI solution. These concepts are important because they highlight the fact that SAP BusinessObjects BI is more than a single tool. These concepts also introduce you to many of the topics that will be discussed through this book and how they facilitate a proper implantation of SAP HANA.

SAP BusinessObjects BI is a portfolio of applications and solutions. Within this portfolio, there are four main concepts and solutions: the semantic layer, ad hoc reporting, self-service BI, and IT-delivered content.

1.5.1   The Semantic Layer (Universe)

The semantic layer within the SAP BusinessObjects BI platform is a metadata rich data access layer. It's most commonly referred to as a *universe*. A semantic layer is a logic layer that sits between the data source and the data consumer. It's designed to provide an intuitive, central, and secure point of access to a supported data source. This layer shields the report developer from the common complexities of querying data by presenting data in business terms as opposed to crude technical terms. In many ways, it's similar to the InfoCubes that are found in SAP BW. However, the universe, or semantic layer, is a logical layer, which means that no data is physically stored in the universe.

When implementing SAP HANA, you'll discover that the universe is often needed to provide access to the data that is stored within SAP HANA. You'll also discover that some tools can bypass the universe and interact directly with SAP HANA. In Chapter 12, we'll discuss the universe in more detail. In addition, we'll provide you with instructions for connecting the universe to SAP HANA.

1.5.2   Ad Hoc Reporting

The term *ad hoc reporting* has been somewhat redefined in recent years. In the legacy Business Objects landscape, ad hoc reporting referred to tools that empowered users to create their own reports and analyze data. Before the existence of ad hoc reporting tools, the report design process was largely managed by IT developers. This was due in part to the complexity of such reporting tools. SAP BusinessObjects Web Intelligence, for example, has the goal of empowering non-technical users to interact with data. In recent years, new self-service BI tools like SAP Lumira have evolved in the SAP BI portfolio to further simplify the data analysis process for non-technical users, although SAP BusinessObjects Web Intelligence continues to be a powerful ad hoc reporting tool for many technical and non-technical report developers. We'll talk more about SAP BusinessObjects Web Intelligence in Chapter 16.

In the context of an SAP HANA implementation, most organizations will find ad hoc reporting tools to be a valuable solution. In many ways, ad hoc reporting tools possess more power and features than many of the more recent self-service alternatives. For this reason, SAP BusinessObjects Web Intelligence will likely be a critical part of your SAP HANA implementation.

1.5.3   Self-Service BI

Self-service BI, or self-service analytics, is a relatively new term used to describe tools within the SAP BusinessObjects BI platform. They are derived from the fundamental ideas of ad hoc reporting tools, but they focus more on the delivery of information to the business community.

In the traditional ad hoc reporting landscape, data needs to be consolidated, standardized, and secured before it can be consumed, which requires significant time and resources to implement (see Section 1.4 and Section 1.5 of this chapter). In the meantime, the business community is forced to wait for the solution to be developed. For many in the business community, this isn't acceptable. However, at the same time, we can't disregard the reasons that a proper EIM and BI process are needed. In some ways, we're then left with a paradoxical situation with few alternatives.

Self-service BI tools are designed with the goal of allowing users to consume data and analytics quickly, without barriers. Tools such as SAP Lumira are built on a foundation that allows the average user to quickly merge, transform, and then share data within the SAP HANA or SAP BusinessObjects BI platform. Other tools, such as SAP BusinessObjects Explorer, are built on a foundation that allows the user to effortlessly search and explore open-ended data sets without the need to leverage an IT resource. Both tools can also be used in tandem to empower the user community because they define BI content without a reliance on IT developers, and both tools also have a stunning visualization layer that can produce analytics in the form of charts and graphs.

Developing a self-service BI solution can be a challenge for most organizations. While it's essential for users to gain access to their data quickly, it's also essential that they produce accurate, consistent, and secure results. Based on our experience, we find that self-service BI plays an important role in allowing users to form a hypothesis and then test their theory. In a BI solution, such tools can provide a very cost-effective alternative to the established EIM and BI process. This is especially true when the business users need only a one-time answer to a BI-related question. If the user community finds that their solution provides value, that solution can then be implemented under the guise of the standard EIM and BI process. With these goals in mind, organizations will find a proper avenue to implement self-service BI tools.

In the context of SAP HANA, the self-service BI tools within the SAP BusinessObjects BI platform are capable of directly leveraging its power and performance. SAP Lumira can query and write data directly from and to SAP HANA. SAP BusinessObjects Explorer can bypass its native engines and use the SAP HANA platform engines to explore millions and even billions of detailed records. Based on the need for self-service BI, this combination can prove to be a powerful solution. We'll discuss these self-service BI tools in more detail in Chapter 15.

1.5.4 IT-Developed Content

While ad hoc reporting and self-service BI tools are essential to an SAP HANA implementation and solution, you'll find that business communities' requirements often exceed the capabilities of such tools. This is where tools such as SAP Crystal Reports, SAP BusinessObjects Dashboards, and SAP BusinessObjects Design Studio play an important role. IT-developed content refers to content that can be developed only by an experienced and skilled professional resource. When pixel-perfect reports need to be developed, SAP Crystal Reports will prove to be the ideal tool. When highly formatted and interactive dashboards are required, SAP BusinessObjects Dashboards and SAP BusinessObjects Design Studio will prove to be the ideal solution. Although SAP BusinessObjects Web Intelligence was mentioned in the ad hoc reporting section, it too can serve as an ideal tool for IT resources when an organization's requirements exceed the capabilities of the average business user.

When implementing SAP HANA with SAP BusinessObjects BI, you must understand that a skilled technical resource will often be required to develop content to the business communities' specifications. In the ideal world, an IT resource would only need to set up the environment and then push content development entirely to the business community. However, you'll often find that some BI needs can be developed only by IT. In subsequent chapters, we'll discuss IT-developed content under the concept of professionally authored dashboards (Chapter 14) and SAP Crystal Reports (Chapter 17).

1.6 Solution Architectural Overview

Before we dive into the details of an SAP HANA implementation with SAP BusinessObjects BI and SAP Data Services, we should discuss the product versions and basic architecture that will be covered within this book and give you an overview of each product's core architecture to help you better understand the solution.

1.6.1 SAP Data Services

SAP Data Services is responsible for managing the ETL aspects of a native implementation of SAP HANA. SAP Data Services comprises four main layers. There is the web application server layer and the tools it hosts. There is the SAP Data Services *job server* and the *information platform services* layer. SAP Data Services also uses several RDBMS repositories to manage the platform and developed code. Finally, there are several management and development desktop tools. Figure 1.13 depicts these layers at a high level. We'll now discuss each layer in more detail.

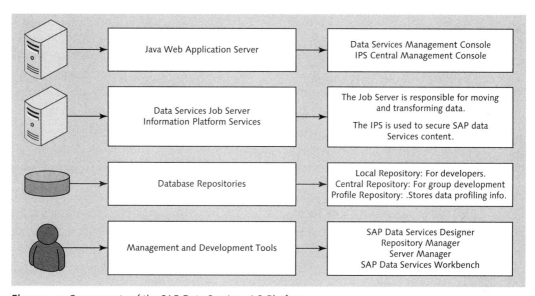

Figure 1.13 Components of the SAP Data Services 4.2 Platform

The Java Web Application Server

The default installation of SAP Data Services includes Apache Tomcat to serve as the SAP web application server for Java. The main web applications that are managed at this layer include the SAP Data Services *Management Console* and *Central Management Console*. Both tools are used, in one form or another, to manage application access, security, or ETL jobs. The Java web application server can be installed with the services found in other layers of the platform, or it can be deployed on a dedicated server. These tools can also be deployed to an existing SAP BusinessObjects BI Java application server or to a number of supported third-party Java application servers.

The Job Server and Information Platform Services

The job server is used to process the ETL code. Specifically, it's responsible for the read, transformation, and write processes that are orchestrated within the ETL code. The job server process runs under the main operating system process named `al_jobservice`. Multiple child processes, with the name of `al_engine`, will be generated by this process, depending on the level of parallel execution defined in the ETL code. This is important to understand when you deploy your SAP Data Services architecture because you need to make sure to include a sufficient number of CPUs and RAM on the job server host to accommodate the parallel processing. It's also possible to cluster the job servers across multiple hosts to facilitate the appropriate level of scalability.

The *information platform services* (IPS) package is a scaled-down version of the SAP BusinessObjects BI platform. It doesn't have to be explicitly deployed in the SAP Data Services architecture because it's possible to use an existing SAP BusinessObjects BI platform to serve as its replacement. However, in our experience, most organizations choose to separate their SAP Data Services platform from their existing SAP BusinessObjects BI platform by using the IPS. The IPS contains many of the core services found in the SAP BusinessObjects BI platform. This includes the SAP BusinessObjects BI *Central Management Service* (CMS) and the *File Repository Services* (FRS). As a result, a dedicated CMS database and audit schema are needed to facilitate the requirements of the IPS. There are other core services available, as well. The IPS can be deployed either on the same host with the job server or to a dedicated host.

The Database Repositories

Several database repositories are required to facilitate the use of SAP Data Services. There are three main types of repositories. One or more *local repositories* are required to facilitate individual developers and job execution. A *profile repository* is needed to host the static results of data profiling requests. The *central repository* will serve as the main software versioning and team development repository within the platform. ETL code can be versioned, checked in, and checked out using this repository. It's ideal for environments where multiple developers are responsible for managing the code.

Your SAP Data Services environment will require one or more database schemas to host each repository. When you're using the IPS, a CMS and audit repository will also be required. All repositories are typically hosted on a dedicated RDBMS to provide peak performance and scalability. However, the default installation of SAP Data Services and IPS will provide you with an option to install a local RDBMS.

The Management and Development Tools

Several management and developer desktop tools are included in the SAP Data Services platform. Four main tools will be used:

▶ **Data Services Designer**
The *Data Services Designer* and its GUI are used by developers to create the ETL code. It can also be used to manage data profiling requests, metadata, job execution, and the central repository. In subsequent chapters, we'll discuss this tool in more detail.

▶ **Data Services Server Manager**
The *Data Services Server Manager* is executed using either a command line interface (CLI) or a GUI, depending on the selected operating system. It's responsible for the configuration of the job server. This includes the ability to associate a repository with a job server, the ability to configure clustering, the ability to configure email server integration, and many of the job server–related tasks. For more information on the role of this tool, please consult the SAP Data Services documentation.

▶ **Data Services Repository Manager**
The *Data Services Repository Manager* is responsible for the creation of a local repository, central repository, or profiler repository. It, too, is either a CLI tool or GUI tool, depending on the operating system. Before a repository can be used by any layer of the SAP Data Service platform, it must be set up using the Data Services Repository Manager.

▶ **Data Services Workbench**
The *Data Services Workbench* is a new tool that will eventually replace the SAP Data Services Designer client. In its current state, it can be used to quickly batch replicate data into SAP HANA or other RDBMS targets.

Understanding the key components and layers of the SAP Data Services platform is important when implementing SAP HANA and SAP Data Services. In subsequent chapters, we'll provide you with additional information that will further enhance your understanding of the SAP Data Services platform.

1.6.2 SAP BusinessObjects BI

Because the SAP BusinessObjects BI platform is used to manage and facilitate end-user functions such as reporting, visualization, and analysis in a native implementation of SAP HANA, we want to give you an overview of the SAP BusinessObjects BI platform as it pertains to the overall solution.

The SAP BusinessObjects BI architecture comprises four main layers: the Java web application server layer, server architecture layer, database repositories layer, and management and development tools layer. The server architecture layer is further divided into three main sub-layers. Figure 1.14 depicts the four main platform layers found in the SAP BusinessObjects BI architecture.

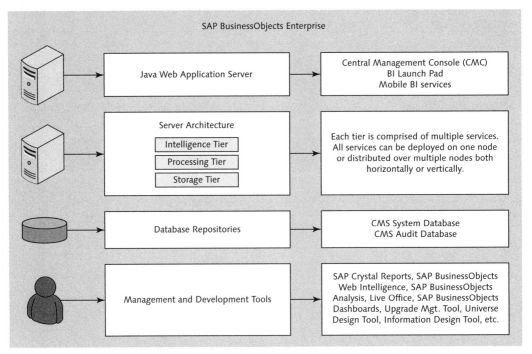

Figure 1.14 Components of the SAP BusinessObjects BI Platform

The Java Web Application Server

The default installation of SAP BusinessObjects BI includes Apache Tomcat to serve as the Java web application server. However, SAP provides support for several additional mainstream Java applications servers. The main web applications that are managed at this layer include the *SAP BusinessObjects BI Launch Pad* and the *SAP BusinessObjects BI Central Management Console* (CMC). This layer hosts the web services servlet, RESTful APIs, and a few other management functions, as well. It can be installed with the remaining layers of the platform, but most often, it's hosted on a dedicated host. This layer can also be clustered using a supported IP load balancer or proxy server.

In the SAP BusinessObjects BI architecture, the SAP BusinessObjects BI Launch Pad is the main point of contact for most BI consumers. Depending on the number of expected users, it can manage several concurrent sessions. Therefore, it's an important layer in the overall SAP BusinessObjects BI platform.

The Server Architecture Layer

The server architecture layer is composed of three main sub-layers: the intelligence tier that represents the core services used to manage the platform (including the CMS, lifecycle management service, platform search service, monitoring service, SAP BusinessObjects Explorer master services, and other administrative services); the processing tier layer that represents the services used to process, schedule, and render reports and visualizations (including the adaptive job services, adaptive processing services, SAP Crystal Reports services, SAP BusinessObjects Web Intelligence services, and SAP BusinessObjects Explorer services); and the storage tier that represents the services used to store and cache content and data (including FRS, the cache for the various processing services, and the SAP BusinessObjects Explorer data).

By default, these services are installed to a single host or node. However, it's recommended that they be distributed both horizontally and vertically to achieve proper performance. You must also ensure that your storage tier services have sufficient storage to manage all of the content and data within the platform. In some cases, components of the storage tier will need to be shared between hosts. This is especially true when deploying a clustered SAP BusinessObjects BI environment.

> **Additional References**
>
> For additional information about the installation and sizing of SAP BusinessObjects BI, look for the *SAP BusinessObjects BI Sizing Companion Guide* and the *Business Intelligence Platform Installation Guide* that is appropriate for your operating system. There is also an SAP PRESS book that covers this and other administration topics: *SAP BusinessObjects BI System Administration* (Myers, Vallo, 2015).

The Database Repositories

SAP BusinessObjects BI uses two key database repositories to manage the platform. The first repository is the central management server repository, which stores content metadata, security information, system information, and other platform-specific data. The second repository is used to store the audit history. This information can be used to track user activities and configuration changes within the system.

The default installation of SAP BusinessObjects BI includes a local database server that will manage these repositories. However, it's generally advised that these repositories run on a supported database server that is independent of your SAP BusinessObjects BI deployment.

The Management and Development Tool

Multiple management and development client tools are available within the SAP BusinessObjects platform that runs on the desktop, as opposed to within the Java Application Server. Therefore, it's important that we identify the main tools discussed in this book and provide a brief description of their use. There are several other client and management tools in the platform:

▸ **Universe Designer**
  The Universe Designer is the legacy developer tool used to create an SAP BusinessObjects BI universe. It creates universe files that end in the UNV extension.

▸ **Information Design Tool (IDT)**
  The IDT was introduced with SAP BusinessObjects BI 4.0. It's used to create universe files that end in the UNX extension.

▶ **Web Intelligence Desktop**

Web Intelligence Desktop is a full client desktop version of SAP BusinessObjects Web Intelligence. The SAP BusinessObjects Web Intelligence client can also be run in the client browser using the Java web application server layer.

▶ **SAP Crystal Reports 2013**

SAP Crystal Reports 2013 is the legacy Crystal Reports developer tool. It's used to create SAP Crystal Reports.

▶ **SAP Crystal Reports for Enterprise**

SAP Crystal Reports for Enterprise was a offering starting with SAP BusinessObjects BI 4.0. It's used to create SAP Crystal Reports. We expect it to be the eventual replacement for SAP Crystal Reports 2013.

▶ **SAP BusinessObjects Dashboards**

SAP BusinessObjects Dashboards is a full client desktop application that is used to develop dashboards.

▶ **SAP Lumira**

SAP Lumira is a full client desktop application used to develop self-service analytics.

▶ **SAP BusinessObjects Design Studio**

SAP BusinessObjects Design Studio is a full client application that is used to design dashboards. It's best suited to connect directly to SAP HANA or SAP BW when OLAP-style navigation is required. Ultimately, it is our understanding that it will replace SAP BusinessObjects Dashboards.

▶ **QaaWS Designer**

Query as a Web Service (QaaWS) Designer is used to create web service–based connections within the SAP BusinessObjects BI platform.

1.6.3   SAP HANA

At a high level, Figure 1.15 depicts the basic architecture of SAP HANA. The SAP HANA system is composed of several core services, such as the *name server, preprocessor server, compile server, script server, index server,* and *XS Engine.* Each service provides one or more of the many features available within the SAP HANA platform. SAP HANA Studio is the core desktop application that is used by SAP HANA administrators and developers.

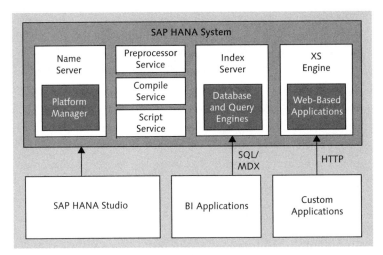

Figure 1.15 Basic SAP HANA Architecture

To better understand the functions of each SAP HANA server, let's review what each server is responsible for managing in the platform.

The Index Server

The core service of the platform is the *index server*. The index server is responsible for all database, data storage, and data processing tasks. When data is stored in-memory, it resides within the index server process. This includes data stored in row- or columnar store tables. When SQL or MDX queries are executed by a BI application, the index server processes the query and returns the results. It is responsible for queries executed in the OLAP engine, calculation engine, join engine, or row engine. When it comes to analytics, it is the most important service in the platform.

The XS Engine

The *XS Engine* acts as a web application server and is used to manage and process application code deployed to the SAP HANA platform. Applications such as *SAP Lumira Server* reside in the XS Engine. Developers can also design custom applications, using JavaScript and HTML5 code, and host them in the XS Engine.

The Name Server

The *name server* is responsible for managing the topology of the SAP HANA architecture. With SAP HANA scale out, the name server keeps track of which services are active and where data tables reside in the cluster.

The Preprocessor Server

The *preprocessor server* helps the index server process text-based searches. This includes features such as sentiment analysis, text analysis, full-text search, and fuzzy search of both structured and unstructured text.

The Compile Server

The *compile server* is responsible for helping the index server compile L language–based procedures. Presumably, it was removed from the index server in SAP HANA SPS 6 to prevent compiling tasks from crashing the index server. However, the exact reasons it was isolated from the index server have never been officially published by SAP.

The Script Server

The *script server* is responsible for helping SAP HANA process operations that require the *Application Function Libraries* (AFL). This includes the BFL and PAL libraries. Developers or applications using SAP HANA for predictive modeling will utilize this service.

When you implement the SAP HANA solution that is discussed within this book, it's important to understand the different types of human resources that are required for its implementation and administration. Figure 1.16 depicts the areas where different resource types will be required. To properly manage the ETL process with SAP Data Services, an experienced ETL developer is required. This resource should also have specific SAP Data Services experience. To properly manage the SAP HANA components, an experienced SAP HANA modeler and SAP HANA database administrator are required. Finally, an experienced SAP BusinessObjects BI developer and administrator should also be selected.

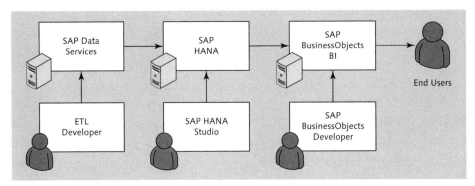

Figure 1.16 An Overview of the SAP HANA Solution Discussed within This Book

1.7 Summary

SAP HANA is more than just a database—it's a next-generation data management platform. It can be characterized and implemented in many ways. As a result, organizations that have heavily invested in SAP applications will find multiple ways to leverage SAP HANA in their BI landscapes. At the same time, organizations with little or no investment in SAP applications will also find that there are multiple ways to implement SAP HANA.

As you've discovered in this chapter, an implementation of SAP HANA requires more than just SAP HANA. You need to identify the best means to provision SAP HANA or load data into SAP HANA. Although there are multiple ways to provision SAP HANA, this book explores how to leverage SAP Data Services to provision data within SAP HANA.

In subsequent chapters, we'll also discuss the different components and parts within SAP HANA. These components are used to manage the data and produce multidimensional models of the data. We'll also discuss the different ways SAP BusinessObjects BI is then used to access the data stored in SAP HANA. In the end, you should have a thorough understanding of what it takes to implement SAP HANA with SAP Data Service and SAP BusinessObjects BI.

Deploying a comprehensive security model with SAP HANA is a key step in delivering an end-to-end solution that satisfies end users' needs to the fullest.

2   Securing the SAP HANA Environment

When you start a new SAP HANA project, you are likely to be starting from a blank slate with a new SAP HANA system. This system won't be ready for developer or end-user access until you lay down a base set of structures and security to enable your team to use the system.

Although all systems have to deal with authentication, authorization, and user provisioning, SAP HANA deviates from typical database platforms in the amount of security configuration that is done inside the database. This stems directly from the main benefit of the SAP HANA platform: collapsing the complex application infrastructure and pushing more work down close to where the data resides, in the database.

In analytic systems based on other database management platforms, much of the security configurations we discuss here would be handled by application server layers sitting on top of the database. The database in those scenarios is often a dumb repository of data. Those upper-tier applications mediate the end users' access to the data, and it is only DBAs and developers who have direct access to the data. Often, even developer access to the database is tightly controlled and limited.

In contrast, SAP HANA is a complete application development platform and database rolled together. This is what makes security in an SAP HANA system different. Because the business logic and interaction of users with the data are being performed directly in SAP HANA, the system needs to know who is doing what. This means almost every user who interacts with data from an SAP HANA platform will have a database user with access to at least some database resources. This doesn't mean that they can login and write arbitrary SQL, but they will have query access to various sections of the database via one tool or another.

Another difference between SAP HANA and other database platforms is the focus on application development in the database; much of the work developers would normally do in an application layer sitting on top of the database is instead done directly in the database using SAP HANA's development tool SAP HANA Studio. This means you need to define a security model to ensure that developers have the correct amount of access to the system.

This level of access to the sacred database can often give traditional DBAs a heart attack. Easing them through this paradigm shift can be one of the significant human factors of the SAP HANA implementation. In the end, the simplified application structure offered by the SAP HANA platform, centralizing data and logic in one place, will lead to a superior overall solution, but it may take some convincing to get your DBAs over that hump.

Don't Let Human Factors Derail Your Project

A common oversight is proper preparation of the team members who will have an impact on your SAP HANA implementation. Make sure key personnel are on board with the strategic changes that SAP HANA can bring to your IT operations.

In this chapter, we will provide the tools and guidelines for configuring a new system and setting up a proper authentication and authorization model. We'll discuss the basic platform setup steps necessary to start development of a security model (Section 2.1). From there, we will introduce the core security concepts of authorization, user provisioning, and authentication (Section 2.2, Section 2.3, and Section 2.4) and how they are applied to SAP HANA-specific scenarios. Finally, we'll wrap up this chapter with a case study that brings together all the pieces of a new system setup (Section 2.5).

2.1 Configuring the SAP HANA Environment for Development

Before you can let developers load data into SAP HANA or construct analytic content, you need to configure the base structures and security for the system. To do that, you need to become familiar with some core SAP HANA concepts that are somewhat unusual compared to other database platforms. These new concepts stem from the paradigm shift of SAP HANA as an application platform. In this section, we will introduce you to the SAP HANA repository, where all development artifacts reside in SAP HANA. We will then review the setup of the SAP HANA

Studio tool to access the repository. Finally, we will talk about the setup of packages, development projects, and database schemas.

2.1.1 Introduction to the SAP HANA Repository

As we've mentioned, a major difference between SAP HANA and other databases is that SAP HANA is an application development platform in addition to a database. Because of this, SAP HANA borrows concepts from more traditional application development environments that are unusual in the context of a database platform. One of these is the way SAP HANA manages much of its development content.

In a typical database, objects are created in schemas typically using SQL CREATE statements. Once an object is created, the database retains the runtime version of it in the schema but makes no attempt to retain the script used to create the object. It's up to the developer to keep and manage all the creation scripts. Although SAP HANA can create objects in schemas using this traditional approach, it also offers an alternative that allows the developer to store the creation scripts for objects in a well-defined source code repository, simply known as the *SAP HANA repository*.

SAP HANA also offers a well-defined mechanism for executing object creation scripts from the repository. This process is known as *activation*. We will be discussing some of the security implications of repository content and activation throughout this chapter. For now, simply be aware that the repository exists and that it is where most of the development content, including security definitions, will be stored.

Another key aspect of the repository and activation is the ownership of the runtime objects that are created by the activation of object definitions. There is a special system user account known as *_SYS_REPO*. This user is the owner of all activated repository objects. _SYS_REPO cannot be deleted, nor can you log on to the system as _SYS_REPO. We will discuss the implications of _SYS_REPO's ownership of objects in detail in Section 2.2.

Content stored in the repository is organized into logical structures that are known as *packages*. Packages are essentially like folders in a file system. They group content into a nested hierarchy. Packages are one of the crucial objects that will be secured when we discuss authorization in Section 2.2. They also serve as a definition of a namespace for objects so that all objects created in the repository are uniquely identified by their full package path and name. We'll discuss recommendations for organizing content in packages and setting up the initial package structures in Section 2.3.

Now that we have introduced you to some of the base concepts that we will be using to construct an initial security model for your SAP HANA system, we'll proceed to introduce the tool used to create objects in the repository: SAP HANA Studio.

2.1.2 Configuring SAP HANA Studio

SAP HANA Studio is the primary user interface for both system administrators and developers for interacting with SAP HANA. SAP HANA Studio has various modes of operation that focus on certain sets of tasks, like system administration or development. These task-focused user interface modes are known as *perspectives*. We'll primarily be using the SAP HANA DEVELOPMENT perspective in this chapter.

This perspective is relatively new and started coming to prominence over other perspectives in SAP HANA SPS 6. With each new SAP HANA service pack, more of the development efforts are moved into this perspective. Security objects fall into the category of content this is primarily worked on using this new perspective.

The SAP HANA DEVELOPMENT perspective allows us to access the repository like a traditional source code management system and uses the features of SAP HANA Studio to check code in and out and to work on it locally. One of the benefits of the SAP HANA DEVELOPMENT perspective is that every developer ends up with a copy of his or her repository objects in his or her local system repository, which serves as an extra form of backup.

Before we can start working in SAP HANA Studio, we need to log on to the SAP HANA database via SAP HANA Studio. When you first gain access to your SAP HANA system, the only user that will be able to log on is the SYSTEM account, which has full access to all aspects of the system in its initial state. The initial setup actions we'll cover in this section have to be done using the SYSTEM user until we establish the base security model and begin provisioning developer users and roles. This account is critical and should be used with care during the initial environment setup. Once the base security structures are established, you should stop using the SYSTEM account for further development efforts.

In the next few sections, we'll review the SAP HANA Studio environment and specifically the SAP HANA DEVELOPMENT perspective, add a connection to SAP HANA

Studio so we can log on to the system and perform work, and configure SAP HANA Studio for access to the SAP HANA repository for code check in and check out.

Now, let's open SAP HANA Studio and learn how to access the DEVELOPMENT perspective.

Accessing the SAP HANA Studio Development Perspective

When you launch SAP HANA Studio for the first time in a new environment, you are presented with a WELCOME screen. This screen has links that take you to one of the core perspectives. You can access the ADMINISTRATION CONSOLE perspective to perform DBA-type tasks. You can open the MODELER perspective to work on multidimensional modeling objects (although you can now do all the work of the MODELER perspective in the DEVELOPMENT perspective). You can manage installed patches with the LIFE CYCLE MANAGEMENT perspective. The perspective we are looking for is DEVELOPMENT. In Figure 2.1, you can see an example of SAP HANA Studio opened to the WELCOME screen.

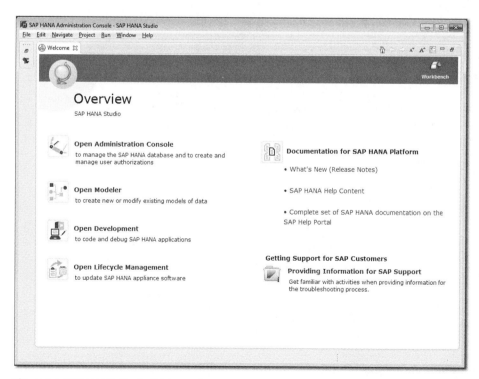

Figure 2.1 SAP HANA Studio Welcome Screen

Let's open the DEVELOPMENT perspective by clicking the OPEN DEVELOPMENT link and familiarize ourselves with the screens and their functions. When you arrive at the DEVELOPMENT perspective, you see several different tabbed sections spread around the screen. On the left of the screen, you should see a main navigation set of tabs, which includes the PROJECT EXPLORER, REPOSITORIES, and SYSTEMS tabs. We'll explain each of these as we go.

> **Note**
>
> At the bottom of the screen, you should see some extraneous screens, which we aren't going to go into. These include PROBLEMS, PROPERTIES, HISTORY, and CHANGE MANAGER.

In the upper-right of the screen, you find the perspective selection portion of the UI. From there, you can switch to different open perspectives, like the ADMINISTRATION CONSOLE, or open a new perspective entirely from the OPEN PERSPECTIVE button. Take a look at Figure 2.2 for an overview of the SAP HANA Studio opened to the DEVELOPMENT perspective.

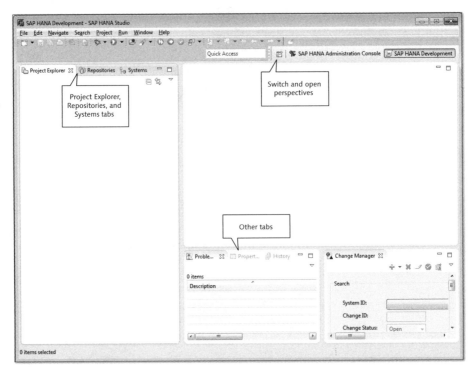

Figure 2.2 SAP HANA Studio Development Perspective

The tabs and screens in an SAP HANA Studio perspective are known as *views*. Views can be moved around the screen and docked wherever you like; they can also be minimized to one edge of the screen or closed completely to be recalled later, when needed. You can recall a closed view from WINDOW menu WINDOW • SHOW VIEW.

To give yourself more room to work and to learn how to interact with views in SAP HANA Studio, close or minimize the CHANGE MANAGER and other tabs at the bottom of the screen. From here on out, we will be focused on the SYSTEMS, REPO-SITORIES, and PROJECT EXPLORER views.

Now that you are familiar with the DEVELOPMENT perspective environment, we will log on to the system and begin exploring it in more detail.

Adding a Connection

To log on to an SAP HANA system from SAP HANA Studio, you must define a systems connection. This is done in the SYSTEMS view. Switch to that tab now, and follow these steps to add a system connection to connect to your environment as the SYSTEM user:

1. Right-click in the SYSTEMS view and select ADD SYSTEM. From there, you are presented with the system configuration wizard. See Figure 2.3 for an example of this screen.

Figure 2.3 Adding a System to SAP HANA Studio

2. You need the host name and instance number of your SAP HANA server, which you should have from your SAP HANA installer. Optionally, you can organize systems into folders. When you have filled in this page, click NEXT.

3. On the next page, select the account to log on as. As we've mentioned earlier, the only account that can log on at this point is the SYSTEM account. In Section 2.3, we'll talk about enabling operating system user authentication instead of requiring a user name and password on this screen. See Figure 2.4 for an example of the CONNECTION PROPERTIES screen.

Figure 2.4 Setting Connection Properties

4. Once you have filled in this screen, you can click FINISH to create your new connection.

   You now have a connection defined in your systems view. From this connection, you can view the various pieces of the SAP HANA environment. This includes the following sub-sections:

   ▸ BACKUP: Provides access to backup configuration and triggering of backups

   ▸ CATALOG: Provides access to all the schemas defined in the system, including system schemas

- ▶ CONTENT: The systems representation of the SAP HANA repository

- ▶ PROVISIONING: Where you can configure Smart Data Access

- ▶ SECURITY: Provides access to users, roles, and security policies

We will be focusing on the catalog, content, and security sections in this chapter.

Take a look at Figure 2.5 for an example connection configured in the DEVELOPMENT perspective.

Figure 2.5 System Connection in the Development Perspective

Now that you have a connection configured, we can proceed to connect SAP HANA Studio to the SAP HANA repository in order to enable check-in/check-out of repository content. This is required before we can build any of our initial security objects.

Configuring the Repositories View

The repositories view in the DEVELOPMENT perspective connects your local development environment to the source code repository managed by SAP HANA. From this view, you can check developed content in and out. This content resides on your local development system while you are working on it. This is similar to how most source code repository systems function. The first thing to do is establish a repository connection in the repositories view. Follow the steps below:

1. Start by switching to the REPOSITORIES view, which will initially be empty.

2. Start the repository connection process by right-clicking in the view and choosing CREATE REPOSITORY WORKSPACE.

3. This opens the CREATE NEW REPOSITORY WORKSPACE dialog, which you can see an example of in Figure 2.6.

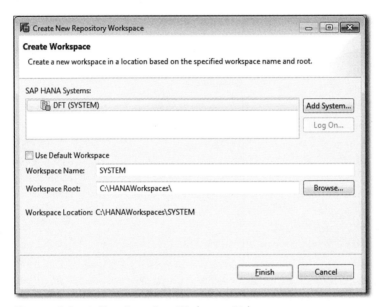

Figure 2.6 Create New Repository Workspace Dialog

4. From this screen, you select the system connection we established earlier. This is the SAP HANA system from which we will retrieve repository content. You also select where on your local system the repository working directory will be located.

5. After making your selections, click FINISH to create your repository workspace.

You now have a repository workspace defined where you can browse the content of the SAP HANA repository and check in/check out local copies of development objects. Take a look at Figure 2.7 for an example of a newly created repository workspace.

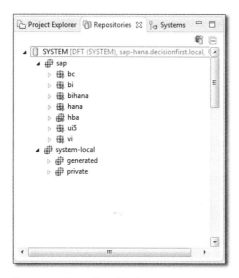

Figure 2.7 Repository Workspace

With your development environment configured, you are now ready to set up your own packages for developing content and creating your first development project.

2.1.3 Setting Up Packages and Development Projects

One of the very first things you need to do when setting up a new SAP HANA implementation is lay out the naming conventions and name spaces you will use for SAP HANA–developed content. If you leave this until later, you will quickly find that excited developers eager to play with their new SAP HANA toy have cluttered the root package name space with a plethora of experimental packages. Coming back later and cleaning this up, figuring out what needs to be kept and what needs to be disposed of, is a serious inconvenience and will lead to slower overall development.

To avoid this scenario, take time at the start of your project to arrange the root-level structures in SAP HANA and develop rigorous naming conventions. As the adage says, "Sometimes you have to go slow to go fast." In the end, spending this time up front will lead to a better, more successful implementation.

In this section, we will cover the default package structures that SAP HANA provides out of the box, and then we will review best practices for setting up your own package structure and naming conventions. Finally, we will introduce the PROJECT EXPLORER view in SAP HANA Studio and show you how to create your development projects to access your package structure.

Default Packages

Before you plan the layout of your package structures, you need to better understand the structures that come in the default layout of a delivered SAP HANA system. Look back to Figure 2.7 for an example of the root package structures you will see in a new SAP HANA system.

There are two top-level packages in a new SAP HANA system: `sap` and `system-local`. Both of these packages are structural packages. This means that no content can be directly created in them, only subpackages can. They have a slightly different icon from other packages to help indicate this.

The `sap` package is the root package for all SAP-delivered content. The subpackages you find in here depend on which products/content from SAP you have deployed. Common things you are likely to find in this package are the SAPUI5 libraries for SAP HANA XS application development, SAP HANA administration web applications like the SAP HANA Life Cycle Management application, and, if you opted to install it, demo content showing the capabilities of the SAP HANA XS application platform. You should not alter any of the content in this package, but most developers should have read access to this package because it can be educational to see how SAP has configured its own content.

The `system-local` package has two default subpackages: `generated` and `private`. These are also structural packages. The name `system-local` is intended to indicate the purpose of these packages. They should contain content that is local to just this SAP HANA instance, and they are not intended for transport to other SAP HANA systems.

The `generated` subpackage is intended for any programmatically generated information views or other content. In general, this is something that would likely be used only by SAP-provided applications.

The `private` subpackage is intended for content that is not meant for end-user consumption. This is your developers' playground and experimental sandbox, where they can try out features and techniques without polluting the content intended for transport to QA and Production.

It is possible that you will find additional packages outside of these listed here in your environment, depending on what additional products have been installed in your environment. For example, the SAP BusinessObjects Design Studio 1.3+ add-on for the SAP HANA platform creates two top-level packages outside the `sap` root package. Other SAP or third-party products may do the same.

Custom Packages

The fact that SAP, and possibly third parties, might add additional top-level packages to a system during the installation of an SAP HANA add-on should indicate that, if you let developers create any packages they desire at the root of the package hierarchy, it could conceivably lead to a name collision at some later date when you install a new add-on. Therefore, you need to carefully organize any custom packages you create.

To avoid this scenario, we recommend creating a structural root package with a name that comes from your company's public domain name. This is a similar naming strategy to Java and other programming languages, which typically have software package names like `com.somecompany.xxx`. The "com." prefix is probably overkill, so simply creating a root package like `mycompanyname` is sufficient. This custom package and system-local.private are the only locations where you should create custom content.

Within your company's custom package, you can further subdivide developed content using different subject areas. These sub-packages are your content packages. One key set of content that needs to be kept separate from other areas are security objects. In Section 2.2, we will review package security in detail, but for now, know that you need to keep all security objects in their own subpackage, and only a small audience will be given access to this package. You can name this package anything you want, but something that indicates its central importance is appropriate. For example, we use the name `core` for this package.

How you arrange the remaining packages under your company package will depend on the complexity of your development environment. In many cases, just one other subpackage is sufficient to house all custom content that is planned for deployment. In other cases, you may want to have multiple subpackages that break down content by developer sub-teams or subject areas.

Combining all of these ideas together, you can come up with a fairly standard top-level package structure that will work for a wide variety of scenarios. In Figure 2.8, we show a complete structure following the recommendations we just reviewed. This scenario assumes a single developer team collaborating on all public-facing content.

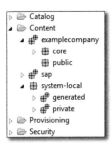

Figure 2.8 Example Package Structure

Now that we have reviewed what a typical package structure looks like, we will learn how to create one, and a development project to go along with it.

Creating Development Projects and Packages

To create our initial package structure following the guidelines we just discussed, we need to set up two things. First, we define the structural package that forms the root of our company content. Second, we create a development project in the PROJECT EXPLORER view for our security content. You can then create as many additional projects as you see fit to divide up your development artifacts by subject area.

Creating Structural Packages

Structural packages can be created only from the SYSTEMS view in the SAP HANA DEVELOPMENT perspective. We want to make sure our root package is a structural package because we don't want developers ever creating objects at the root of the corporate content name space. Follow these next steps to create your root package:

1. Open the SYSTEMS view in the SAP HANA DEVELOPMENT perspective.

2. Open the content section of the connection you created earlier. If this is the first package you are creating, the only other top-level items should be sap and system-local.

3. Right-click the content folder and choose NEW • PACKAGE….

4. This opens the NEW PACKAGE screen (Figure 2.9).

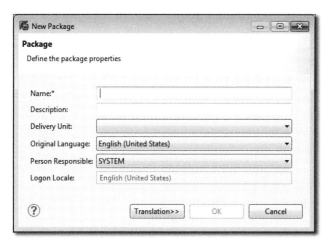

Figure 2.9 New Package Screen

5. You need to give your package a name. Based on our recommendations, enter your company's domain name here. Other properties are optional and not important for our current efforts, so simply click OK.

6. Currently, you can convert an existing package to structural only by editing the package after it is created. So, select the package you just created in the content section, right-click, and choose EDIT. You are presented with the EDIT PACKAGE DETAILS screen (Figure 2.10).

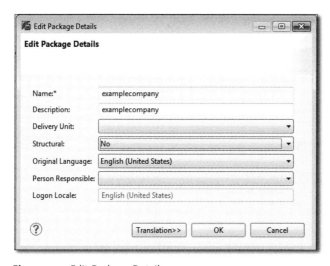

Figure 2.10 Edit Package Details

7. From this screen, you can select Yes from the Structural dropdown, and then click OK.

You now have your company's root structural package created, and you are ready to start setting up development projects to manage sub-packages. Most importantly, we need to create a subpackage to house all future security content that we will be creating in the rest of this chapter.

Creating a Development Project
Although we can continue to create packages from the Systems view, it is better if we combine our content packages with development projects in the Project Explorer. Follow the next set of instructions to create your first development project, where we will house all of our future security objects:

1. Switch to the Project Explorer view to set up a project to store your work in.

2. Create the project by right-clicking in the Project Explorer view and choosing New Project.

3. This opens the SAP HANA Studio New Project screen. See Figure 2.11 for an example.

Figure 2.11 New Project Screen

4. Select SAP HANA • Application Development • XS Project as the project type, and then click Next. This takes you to the New XS Project screen. Figure 2.12 shows an example of this screen.

Figure 2.12 New XS Project Screen

5. Give your project a name. The project name should be the same as your desired SAP HANA package name and should include the parent package name you created earlier. For example, EXAMPLECOMPANY.CORE would be an appropriate project name. Note the period (.) as the separator between name components. This is key to this having the desired outcome of creating sub-packages.

6. Leave the SHARE PROJECT checkbox clicked, and select NEXT.

7. The SHARE PROJECT screen is displayed (Figure 2.13).

8. From this screen, you select the repository you created earlier, which is where the project will be shared. Unfortunately, the default for the repository package will not be correct. You can correct this by unchecking the ADD PROJECT FOLDER AS SUBPACKAGE checkbox.

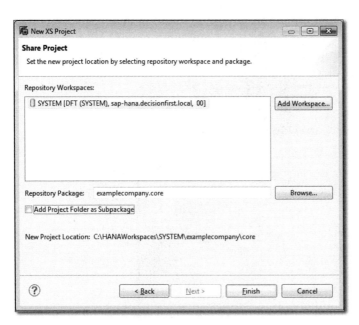

Figure 2.13 Share Project Screen

9. Click FINISH, and you will see your new project in the PROJECT EXPLORER. See Figure 2.14 for an example of the PROJECT EXPLORER with a new project created.

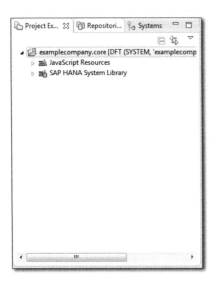

Figure 2.14 New Project in Project Explorer

Any objects you create in this new project and then activate are synchronized to the SAP HANA package you set up during creation.

One of the types of objects you can create in a project is a schema to hold data. In the next section, we'll talk in detail about schemas and how to create them.

2.1.4 Setting up Schemas in SAP HANA

Before we can load any data or create any analytic content in an SAP HANA system, we need a schema to store that data. A schema can be created in SAP HANA using traditional SQL CREATE statements or by simply creating a dedicated user to own the schema. This process should be familiar to any DBA for most databases in existence. It is quite common to have a dedicated user in the database whose sole purpose is to own the data.

However, SAP HANA also offers another mechanism for creating and managing schemas: They can be created as repository objects in a development project and activated using the repository activation mechanism. This method is particular to SAP HANA and has some advantages over the more traditional approach.

Next we will review the properties of schemas in SAP HANA. We will then discuss both approaches for creating schemas.

Properties of SAP HANA Schemas

Schemas in SAP HANA are no different from other database systems. They hold tables, views, procedures, and other typical database objects. Much like other databases, schemas in SAP HANA are owned by a particular user. That is, if a particular user issues the CREATE SCHEMA command, they own the created schema. Additionally, all users automatically get a private schema created for them when the user is created, and that user is the owner of their private schema.

Unlike other databases, SAP HANA does not allow the SYSTEM account or any other account to take control of, or grant themselves access to, a schema that they are not the owner of. Only the original schema owner can allow others to access a schema. This fact has implications for the setup of schemas that will hold data for analytic purposes: we will likely need to grant multiple users access to a schema.

> **Schemas and Information Views**
>
> Access to schemas is especially important when you're using SAP HANA's information views, a subject we will cover in depth in Part III of the book. Information views are repository objects that also go through the activation process we described earlier for object creation. Recall that all activated repository objects are owned by the system account _SYS_REPO. For _SYS_REPO to activate information views, it needs access to the schema holding the data that is to be displayed in those views, and only the schema's owner can grant that access to _SYS_REPO.

This leads us to the process of creating schemas in SAP HANA and managing the access to those schemas.

Creating Schemas with Users

Creating a schema with the traditional approach is simply a matter of creating a user and giving the user the name of the schema that you want to create. In Section 2.3, we'll cover user creation in detail. However, recall that creating the schema this way will not allow any other user, including the key system accounts like _SYS_REPO, to access the schema. We will cover the specific process of granting access to database objects like schemas in detail in Section 2.2, but for now, you need to know that as soon as you create a user that will own data in their schema, you need to immediately log on as that user and grant the _SYS_REPO and SYSTEM account access to the schema. The amount of access you grant to _SYS_REPO and SYSTEM can vary depending on how much access you ever want to pass on to other users, but at a minimum, you should grant those users SELECT and EXECUTE permissions.

The above method for managing schemas is exactly what you will see when working with SAP applications deployed on top of SAP HANA. This includes SAP BW on SAP HANA and SAP Business Suite on SAP HANA. The installation process for the SAP NetWeaver stack will create a dedicated user that will own the SAP NetWeaver schema. If you want to set up analytics or do development on top of data in an SAP NetWeaver schema, you will have to grant _SYS_REPO access to the schema. Luckily for SAP NetWeaver–specific solutions, a set of predefined database roles are generated for you, which makes it easier than logging in and manually granting the required access.

Creating Schemas as Repository Objects

Because we are focusing on using SAP HANA with SAP Data Services to build data warehousing solutions in this book, we won't have a predefined schema or roles generated for us by the application install. Instead, we need to define our own schemas and set up security for them. When you're creating your own schemas outside of an application install on top of SAP HANA, there are some distinct advantages to creating schemas as repository objects.

Remember that any object activated from the repository is owned by _SYS_REPO. This means that, if we create a schema as a repository object, the owner—and, therefore, the user with full access to the schema—will already be _SYS_REPO. This means there is no need to worry about setting up access to the schema for system accounts because it is handled in the simple act of activating and creating the schema.

Additionally, repository objects participate in SAP HANA's life cycle management process and can be transported between landscapes like Dev, Test, and Production. This can simplify the whole security process by ensuring that all objects that need to be created and managed are part of the repository life cycle. If we use the traditional approach of users that own schemas, we have to ensure that we create the correct users and grant all the correct access in each landscape tier manually. Using the repository handles this for us.

The process of creating a schema in the repository is quite straightforward now that we have already configured our core SAP HANA development project. Follow these steps to create your first schema:

1. Switch to the PROJECT EXPLORER view in the SAP HANA DEVELOPMENT perspective.

2. Right-click the project you created earlier and select NEW • OTHER from the pop-up menu.

3. This opens the NEW OBJECT screen.

4. Navigate to the SAP HANA • DATABASE DEVELOPMENT folder, select the schema object type, and click NEXT. See Figure 2.15 for an example of this screen.

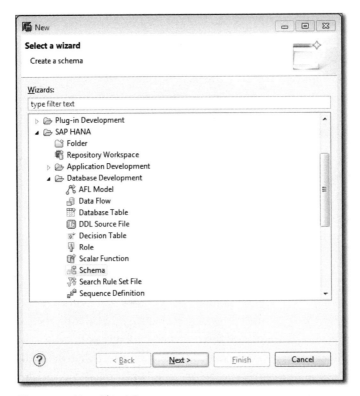

Figure 2.15 New Object Screen

5. After clicking NEXT, you are presented with the NEW SCHEMA screen. You will select the project to create the schema in and give your schema a file name. The file name must match the name of the schema you would like to create.

6. From the TEMPLATE dropdown, select BASIC, and click FINISH to create the schema definition. See Figure 2.16 for an example of this screen.

7. After you click FINISH, your new schema definition opens automatically in an editor window. You will notice that the definition is a simple text file with a single line of code defining the schema and a comment at the top. See Figure 2.17 for an example of the schema opened in the editor.

Figure 2.16 New Schema Window

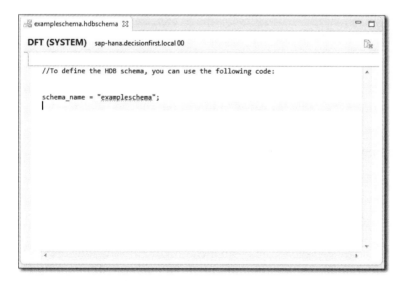

Figure 2.17 Schema Definition Editor

8. To complete the creation of your schema and deploy it back to the server, you need to activate the definition. You can do this from the editor by pressing `Ctrl`+`F3` on the keyboard. Or you can click the ACTIVATE SAP HANA DEVELOPMENT OBJECT button on the toolbar, a green circle with white arrow.

You now have all the necessary components to begin full development of an SAP HANA security model, including the development project, system access, and base package and schema structures.

2.2   SAP HANA Authorizations

In this section, we will examine the authorization process and learn about the different types of authorization checks the SAP HANA system can perform. We will also review the specific definitions of each type of privilege that can be granted.

Once a user is authenticated to an information platform like SAP HANA, the system is able to determine what actions the user is allowed to perform based on a set of rules set up by the systems administrators. The application of these rules makes up the process we call *authorization*. When authorization is configured correctly, users are only able to perform actions and access data that they have been explicitly granted access to.

Authorizations typically fall into two broad categories: functional authorizations and data authorizations. Functional authorizations allow a user to perform specific actions on specific objects. An example of a functional authorization in a system like SAP HANA is a rule allowing a user to DELETE data from a specific table. Data authorizations, on the other hand, operate at a more granular level than functional authorizations. They are specific to individual rows of data in a table and are dependent on the values of key columns in the controlled tables.

Data authorizations are a common scenario in almost all business areas. A common example of the need for data authorization shows up in sales data reporting. Typically, a sales organization is grouped around some sort of hierarchical structure, like a region. Managers of each region should be able to review only the sales transaction data that falls in their managed region. This can be achieved in SAP HANA with data authorizations managed by analytic privileges.

In SAP HANA, data authorizations can be applied only to information views, i.e., attribute, analytic, and calculation views, a subject we will introduce in detail in

Chapter 9. You cannot limit data access in base tables beyond the level of the table itself. Because information views are read only, you can use data security to limit only read access, not data manipulation. Finally, SAP HANA does not provide a security mechanism that controls access to specific columns of data at this time. For example, you can't use a data authorization to limit access to a column containing Social Security numbers. Instead, you would have to keep sensitive columns in separate models that only authorized personnel could view.

The process of applying authorizations to a user is fairly straightforward. An example of an authorization check for a user in SAP HANA that is trying to query an information model might look like the following:

1. Is the user allowed to log on via JDBC/ODBC to the SAP HANA platform?
2. Is the user allowed to execute a `SELECT` statement on the runtime version of the information view stored in the _SYS_BIC schema?
3. Does the model enforce data-level security?
4. Does the user have authorization to access some or all of the model's data based on the data-level security rules?
5. Return the authorized data to the user.

Each of these checks gets applied by the system as it prepares to do the work requested by the user. If at any step, the system determines that the current user is not authorized to perform the given action, an error message is returned to the invoking process detailing the missing privilege.

In the rest of this section, we will be focusing on the introduction of authorization types, known as privileges. After introducing the types of privileges, we will examine more closely how privileges are granted and the life cycle of a granted privilege. We will not go into the details of data authorizations in this chapter; instead, we will return to that topic in Chapter 11, after we have introduced you to the concepts of information views in more detail.

2.2.1   Types of SAP HANA Privileges

The rules controlling authorization for users in SAP HANA are managed by the granting of privileges to a user. Privileges define the specific features or functions the user is being authorized to access. Privileges come in several different flavors for different aspects of the SAP HANA system. In Table 2.1, we'll list each type and its definition, and in the following sections, we'll drill into each kind in detail.

Privilege Type	Definition
System Privilege	Enables broad, system-wide functions for the authorized user
Object Privilege	Enables a set of rights on a specific database object
Package Privilege	Enables access to and management of content in the SAP HANA repository
Application Privilege	Enables access to a custom SAP HANA XS application feature
Privileges on Users	Enables debugging procedures in another user's session
Analytic Privilege	Enables access to specific data in information models

Table 2.1 SAP HANA Authorization Privilege Types and Definitions

Now, let's go into more detail about each of the privileges listed in Table 2.1.

System Privileges

System privileges are the least granular type of privilege that can be assigned to a user. The majority of the system privileges that exist will only ever be given to system administrators. The granting of a system privilege enables the specific functionality across the board for the target user. Thus, there is no need to define a particular target object when granting the rights.

Examples of system privileges include user and role administration, which allow the target user to administer the security of the SAP HANA platform. Other examples include privileges that enable the administration of the auditing or backup sub-systems. The granting of a system privilege should be considered carefully before proceeding.

Additional Resources

A complete list of system privileges is available in the SAP HANA Security Guide, Section 9.2.1, at *http://help.sap.com/hana/SAP_HANA_Security_Guide_en.pdf*.

Object Privileges

Object privileges are where you control traditional database SQL access to specific tables, schemas, procedures, etc. Unlike a system privilege, an object privilege must be granted in the context of a specific target object. This makes object privileges considerably more granular than system privileges, and you will find that they are granted to a much wider audience than most system privileges.

Examples of object privileges include the granting of SELECT, INSERT, UPDATE, or DELETE rights on tables or schemas, as well as the EXECUTE right on individual procedures or a schema. Broader object privileges that control creation and destruction of catalog objects include the CREATE ANY and DROP rights.

Additional Resources

A complete list of object privileges is available in the SAP HANA Security Guide, Section 9.3.1. *http://help.sap.com/hana/SAP_HANA_Security_Guide_en.pdf*

Package Privileges

A package privilege allows a user to access information in the SAP HANA repository. As we introduced in Section 2.1, the repository is where all information models and application objects are stored during development. Thus, package privileges are mostly of interest for controlling developer access. Package privileges are similar to object privileges in that they are granted in the context of a specific package. Package privilege management is one of the areas where SAP HANA is quite different from a traditional database, and this stems from the fact that it is a complete application development platform.

To understand package privileges, we first need to further understand that there are different types of packages. So far, all the packages you have been introduced to are either default packages for a new system or packages you created in development. However, packages are a core aspect of SAP HANA life cycle management. Packages that have been transported from one landscape to another are distinguished from local packages so that security on them can be managed separately. This helps prevent developers from making changes to objects in downstream landscapes. Therefore, SAP HANA categorizes packages into the two following types:

▸ **Native packages**
Native packages are those created by a developer in the SAP HANA system. In your development environment, this will be almost all packages not provided by SAP.

▸ **Imported packages**
Imported packages are any packages imported into the SAP HANA system via delivery units. This will include packages provided by SAP or third-party vendors, as well as any packages you promote out of development environments to QA and Production.

Examples of package privileges include the ability to see and traverse the folders of the repository, which is controlled by the REPO.READ privilege. The ability to modify the state of an object in the repository depends on the package type. Users can be granted access to edit and activate one or both of these package types with the privileges shown in Table 2.2.

Package Privilege	Description
REPO.READ	The ability to see a package and its child contents
REPO.EDIT_NATIVE_OBJECTS	The ability to make changes to an object in a native package
REPO.ACTIVATE_NATIVE_OBJECTS	The ability to activate an object in a native package, altering the runtime version that will be consumed by end users
REPO.MAINTAIN_NATIVE_PACKAGES	The ability to create, update, or delete a native package or subpackage
REPO.EDIT_IMPORTED_OBJECTS	The ability to make changes to an object in an imported package
REPO.ACTIVATE_IMPORTED_OBJECTS	The ability to activate an object in an imported package, altering the runtime version that will be consumed by end users
REPO.MAINTAIN_IMPORTED_PACKAGES	The ability to create, update, or delete an imported package or subpackage

Table 2.2 List of Package Privileges and Descriptions

Note: Limit Access to Imported Packages

It is a best practice to limit access to altering imported content. Otherwise, developers could make changes in a production system. Typically, the versions of the package privileges related to imported objects are given only to system administrators or developers in emergency firefighter scenarios.

Application Privileges

Application privileges are used to control access to custom application content developed using the SAP HANA XS application server. There are no application privileges defined by the system itself. Instead, developers can define an application privilege as a repository object during development, and then that privilege can be granted to users. Only custom application logic that checks the application privilege will be controlled by the presence or absence of the privilege. This allows the SAP HANA security model to extend into custom solutions.

Examples of application privileges primarily come from some of the out-of-the-box XS applications that SAP delivers with the SAP HANA platform, such as the web-based integrated development environment (IDE) that allows developers to edit and view repository content without opening SAP HANA Studio. The role `sap.hana.xs.ide.roles::TraceViewer` grants the custom application privilege `sap.hana.xs.ide::LandingPage`, which allows the user to access the main UI of the web-based IDE, as well as `sap.hana.xs.ide::Traces`, which grants access to the trace viewing portion of the IDE.

Privileges on Users

These privileges are very specific and narrow in purpose. They allow one user to grant another user the ability to attach a debugger to a procedure executing in their session. Obviously, this is only really pertinent in development and debugging scenarios of custom procedure development.

Analytic Privileges

Analytic privileges are the mechanism used in SAP HANA to control data authorization. Like application privileges, they are created by developers, and once they are activated, they can be granted to other users. Unlike application privileges, there is one predefined system analytic privilege called _SYS_BI_CP_ALL, which grants access to all data in all information models.

Analytic privileges come in two basic forms. The most common is the structured analytic privilege, which is created as a repository object, just like information views, and has a graphical user interface (GUI) for its definition. The second type of analytic privilege is the SQL-based analytic privilege. This privilege is created as a catalog object in a schema using SQL `CREATE` statements. It uses a more flexible expression language for defining the rules for access to data, but it has some complexities for deployment due to the fact that it is not a repository object.

We will be reviewing analytic privileges in detail in Chapter 11.

> **Note**
>
> As catalog objects, SQL-based analytic privileges cannot be transported between systems, and they are owned by the user who creates them, not by _SYS_REPO.

2.2.2 Granting of Privileges and the Life Cycle of a Grant

Now that we are familiar with the various types of privileges that can be used in an authorization scheme, we will examine how those privileges are assigned to a user to enable a specific scenario and review the life cycle of a granted privilege and the implications of that life cycle on our security models.

Granting Privileges

There are two ways to grant privileges to a user. You can grant the privilege directly to an individual user or, instead, grant the privileges to a role that acts as a stand-in for the user. If you have many privileges to grant to enable a scenario and there are many users who should have the same privileges, you will quickly find ourselves in a maintenance nightmare in which you spend all of your time granting and revoking privileges to users.

This is where *roles* come in to make this process much more manageable. A role is just a collection of granted privileges. Instead of manually granting many privileges to many users, you can simply assign one single role to a user, and they will receive all the privileges defined for the role. If you later need to remove a privilege, you simply make one change to the role instead of changing all the affected users directly.

Roles have an added benefit for managing privileges. One role can extend another role, granting all the privileges of the original role plus any additional privileges the role grants on its own. This allows you to build up an authorization scenario in layers, without requiring you to repeat the definition of granted rights at each layer. Thus, if a privilege needs to be granted to everyone from a base layer and to all the higher layers as well, you can simply add one granted privilege to a base role, and the inherited roles will pick up the granted privilege.

We will review the methods of role creation in detail in Section 2.3.

> **Best Practices for Managing Authorizations**
>
> Because of the complexity of managing the assignment of the many required authorizations for even a simple task, it's always a best practice to assign privileges to roles instead of attempting to assign them to individual users.

Life Cycle of a Granted Privilege

All privileges must be granted by some other user. In order for one user to grant a privilege to another user or role, the granting user must already have the privilege in question with the added property of WITH GRANT OPTION, which allows the user to pass the privilege on to other users. A user can never grant a privilege to themselves.

When an SAP HANA system is initially installed and configured, the only user that can log in is the SYSTEM user. The SYSTEM user has all privileges WITH GRANT for the initial system state. Thus, when setting up an initial security model, all security would have to flow outward from the SYSTEM user in a chain of grants.

Limits of SYSTEM User Privilege

The one exception to the privileges of the SYSTEM user is access to user schemas. When a user is created, they get a personal schema created as well. When the user is first created, only that user has access to the personal schema. The SYSTEM user cannot access the data stored in tables in that schema. The SYSTEM user can, of course, destroy the schema by removing the user in question from the system.

The life cycle of a granted privilege is tied closely to the chain of authorization that stems from the original grantor, i.e., SYSTEM. If the chain is broken at any point, all downstream grants that flow from that chain are revoked.

Let's look at an example scenario:

1. SYSTEM creates a user T1 and grants T1 USER ADMIN WITH GRANT.

2. T1 creates a user T2 and grants T2 USER ADMIN WITH GRANT.

3. T2 creates a user T3 and grants T3 USER ADMIN WITH GRANT.

4. SYSTEM deletes T1, breaking the chain of authority.

5. T2 and T3 no longer have the privilege USER ADMIN.

The above scenario applies to grants of privileges to roles, as well as users. Thus, if one user creates a role and grants privileges to it and the granting user is ever deleted, that role loses those privileges.

This chain of authorization creates a management complexity that must be considered. If a security administrator grants a privilege but you later terminate that administrator and remove his account, then all the work they ever did is removed, possibly breaking your entire security model and locking users out of the system.

In early versions of SAP HANA, the solution to this was to perform security operations using a dedicated service account that would never be deleted. This has its own downsides in that it limits audit ability. Anyone with access to the service account can change the security of the system, and it could have been anyone with access to the account that made the change. You would have to drop down to network logs to see where the login came from to get an idea of who was actually driving at the time a change was made. The other alternative was to never delete a user that was part of a security chain. Instead, simply disable their account.

Neither of those scenarios is very appealing from a security point of view. Thus, in the latest editions of SAP HANA, a new solution was introduced based on the SAP HANA repository. In this solution, you create role objects using the repository activation mechanism. Doing this ensures that all grants stem from the dedicated _SYS_REPO user, which can never be deleted. Additionally, all object activations are auditable, so you can have a dedicated service account perform the grants, maintaining the chain of authorization, while at the same time giving you an auditable system.

You should now have a clear picture of the types of privileges that can be granted to users and roles and the importance of carefully managing how and by whom those privileges are granted.

2.3   User and Role Provisioning

In this section, we will review the specific processes used to create and manage roles and users. We will start with role creation. As we've indicated, there are two ways to create roles: a traditional database approach that has issues with chains of authority and a new mechanism using repository object activation that alleviates these issues. We'll follow up role creation by looking at some important considerations for package design when you're using repository roles. We'll then wrap the role creation portions of this section with a detailed review of common role scenarios and the rights that need to be granted.

We'll follow that by looking at user provisioning in SAP HANA. It's important to have a well-thought-out plan for how to manage user creation. Otherwise, you will quickly find yourself in another maintenance nightmare of having to manually provision and make changes to users as the system grows. In this section, we'll also look at granting roles to users.

2.3.1 Creating Roles (the Traditional Approach)

To create a role in the traditional database approach, you will need the system privilege ROLE ADMIN. You will also require any additional privileges that you wish to grant to the role with the WITH GRANT option. By default, in a new system, only the SYSTEM user would be authorized to do this. In Figure 2.18, we show an example of the role creation/editing user interface. As you can see, there are tabs that correspond to each of the privilege types we covered previously. Under each tab, you can grant or revoke the required privileges.

When you use this interface, you are really just executing SQL CREATE ROLE and GRANT statements in the background, and you could achieve all the same outcomes by executing these statements directly in script.

Figure 2.18 New Role Window

To access this screen and create a new role, follow these steps:

1. Switch to the Systems view of the SAP HANA Development perspective.

2. Open the connection you created earlier, and expand the Security folder.

3. Right-click the Roles folder and choose New Role.

4. The Role Creation/Editing window appears. See Figure 2.18 above.

5. Give the role a name.

6. You can inherit all the privileges of other existing roles by granting roles on the Granted Roles tab.

7. Each of the other tabs allows granting or revoking of the specific privilege type listed on the tab. There is a green plus sign (+) icon used to add a new privilege of the appropriate type, and an X icon for removing already-granted privileges.

8. Clicking the + icon opens a privilege selection dialog, allowing you to pick from either the set of privileges of that type or select a target object for object and package privileges. See Figure 2.19 for an example of selecting a system privilege from the privilege selection screen.

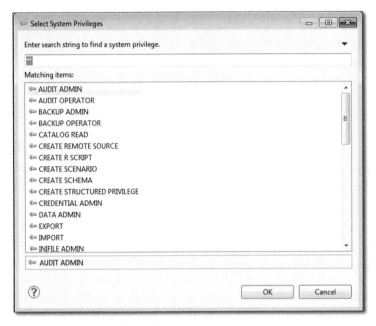

Figure 2.19 System Privilege Selection Screen

9. Once all necessary privileges are granted, click the DEPLOY ([F8]) button in the upper-right of the screen.

Your new role is created, and you can turn around and grant it to users.

2.3.2 Creating Roles as Repository Objects

As we've discussed, creating roles as repository objects helps resolve the complexity of managing the chain of authority. To better understand how roles created as repository objects helps this situation, let's review repository activation in a bit more detail.

The first thing to remember about objects created in the repository is that they are always created and owned by the dedicated _SYS_REPO user. When you activate an object in the repository, what you are really doing is requesting that _SYS_REPO do some work on your behalf. This is the key element in simplifying the chain of authorization we discussed previously. If you create roles as repository objects, it is _SYS_REPO who actually creates the role and grants privileges to it. Since the _SYS_REPO user can never be deleted, you don't have to worry about the chain of authorization being broken.

If _SYS_REPO is doing all the role creation and privilege granting, then _SYS_REPO must have the necessary privileges with the WITH GRANT option. Luckily, _SYS_REPO has nearly every privilege in the system you might want to grant, including all system privileges. However, _SYS_REPO has the same limitations that the SYSTEM user has. That is, data in private schemas belonging to created users isn't initially accessible to _SYS_REPO unless that user first grants _SYS_REPO access to the schema with the WITH GRANT option. This is why we emphasized the importance of ensuring that owners of schemas always grant _SYS_REPO access to the schema and why it's much more beneficial to create the schema as a repository object itself, ensuring that the _SYS_REPO already has full access to the schema in the first place.

An additional benefit to creating roles in the repository is that you don't necessarily need the system privilege ROLE ADMIN because you are simply editing a repository object and activating it. It's _SYS_REPO that has the ROLE ADMIN privilege. This can help ensure that developers and administrators create roles only as repository objects.

The process of creating a role as a repository object follows a similar path to our earlier creation of a schema as a repository object. We'll create the role as an object in our development project from the PROJECT EXPLORER view. Like the schema object we created, the role definition will simply be a text file using a specialized syntax. Unfortunately, there is currently no graphical interface for editing the role definition files. However, the text editor for role files is aware of the role definition syntax and provides hints and text completion as you type.

Follow these steps to create your first role:

1. From the PROJECT EXPLORER view of the SAP HANA DEVELOPMENT perspective, right-click a PROJECT and choose NEW and then choose OTHER from the slide-out menu.

2. Select the SAP HANA • DATABASE DEVELOPMENT • ROLE option from the list of wizards. You can see an example of this selection in Figure 2.20.

Figure 2.20 New Object

3. Clicking Next opens the New Role screen. Here, you can give the role a name. See Figure 2.21 for an example.

Figure 2.21 New Role Screen

4. Click FINISH on this screen, and an empty role definition file is displayed, which is essentially an empty text file with a cryptic heading at the top.

As you can see, the role editing language doesn't give you much to go on when you are starting out. However, the displayed text editor is aware of the semantics of the role domain specific language and can provide context-sensitive help as you type, guiding you to valid values. You can access the help by pressing `Ctrl`+`Space`. Figure 2.22 shows an example of accessing the help.

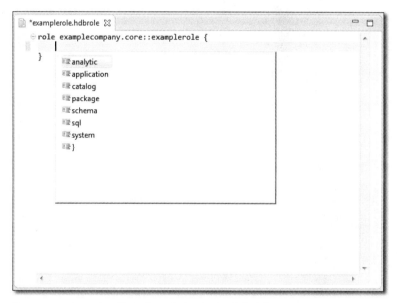

Figure 2.22 Accessing Code Completion in the Role Editor

To grant privileges to a role, we issue statements inside the role definition listing each privilege to be granted. The general form of the statements follows a pattern:

- Privilege type identifier
- Followed possibly by a named object on which the privilege is being granted
- Followed by a colon (:)
- Followed by one or more specific named privileges of the type being granted
- Terminated by a semi-colon (;)

Some examples are the best way to clarify this, so look at Figure 2.23 to see several different privileges granted to an example role.

Figure 2.23 Example Role with Privileges

Some key takeaways from this example are listed below:

▸ We've commented the privilege grant statements with lines that start with two forward slashes (//).

▸ Some grant statements are prefixed with the keyword catalog. This signifies granting access to an object that exists outside the management of the repository, i.e., an object not necessarily owned by _SYS_REPO. For most objects delivered with the system in its default state, _SYS_REPO has access to grant these rights, but new catalog content created by users has to be explicitly granted to _SYS_REPO before it can be granted to others via a repository role. Also note that catalog object names are surrounded with double quotes ("").

▸ In contrast, the granting of the analytic privilege exampleprivilege and the schema exampleschema is not prefixed with the catalog keyword. However, we must use the fully qualified name of the object in the repository starting with its topmost packages all the way down to the object name, and the object type file extension is also required. Note the separation of the last package from the start of the object name with a colon (:).

▶ We've extended two existing roles, which grant all the rights contained in those roles to our new role.

The first role extended is another repository role. Strangely, in contrast to other repository objects, we do not include the file extension when granting repository roles, and we use two colons instead of a single one as a separator between package and role name.

The second role is a pre-existing catalog role delivered with the systems default state.

▶ Finally, note the fully qualified name of the role itself. Quite often, when you create the role, if it is in a nested subpackage, the wizard does not include all the parent packages for you. You won't be able to activate the role until you correct this.

To activate a role file created in a project, you can click the activate button in the tool bar (white arrow in a green circle), or simply press Ctrl+F3. If there is any mistake in your syntax, an error message is displayed when you attempt to activate the file.

Additional Resources

For complete reference to the role creation domain specific language, see the SAP HANA Developer Guide, Section 11.3, at *http://help.sap.com/hana/SAP_HANA_Developer_Guide_en.pdf*.

2.3.3 Preventing Rights Escalation Scenarios

There are some important restrictions that must be set up to prevent users with repository edit access from elevating their own rights in the system when using repository roles. Because a repository role is a repository object by definition, it can be altered by any user who has REPO.EDIT_NATIVE_OBJECT and REPO.ACTIVATE_NATIVE_OBJECT privileges on the package containing the role. If a developer has been granted a repository role and is given these privileges on the package containing that role, they can alter the role and activate the new privileges, which immediately take effect, giving themselves the new privilege.

To prevent this from happening, it's important to separate packages containing roles from other development objects and grant the edit and activation rights only on packages containing roles to the team of system administrators or security team entrusted with full rights to the system.

This is the reason we defined a separate `core` package at the start of this chapter when establishing our base package structure. Only the system administrators should be given edit and activate rights on this package. All other developers should be given those rights only on other content packages that contain the analytic content they are charged with creating. Placing our data schema definition in the `core` package also keeps regular developers from altering the schema containing the systems data.

2.3.4 Common Role Scenarios and Their Privileges

In any organization, beyond the smallest and simplest of scenarios, there will need to be a division of labor for the proper management of a platform like SAP HANA. In general, this division of labor falls into four broad categories: system administrators, security administrators, content developers, and end users. In some larger organizations, these categories may be further subdivided, and in smaller organizations, individual users might handle multiple roles, i.e., the common combination of system administration and security. In addition to these common functional roles it is important to consider data access concerns and what roles are needed for ETL processes.

In this section, we will examine the out-of-the-box roles that are distributed with a new SAP HANA environment. These roles are not recommended for production usage but can be informative about which privileges are useful in various use cases. We will then review the four functional role categories we discussed and lay out specific recommendations for sample roles to fill these categories. Finally, we will look at what a data access role looks like for an ETL service account.

SAP HANA Standard Roles

As we mentioned above, we do not recommend using the SAP-provided roles for most scenarios. Generally, this is because these roles grant too broad of an access for real-world scenarios. Instead, you will want to build more limited roles that constrain users. These roles are useful to better understand what privileges are required to perform certain types of actions, and you can look to them for some guidance.

However, some of the provided roles are useful or required to be used for certain scenarios. For example, almost all users are automatically granted the PUBLIC role, and there is no downside to that usage. Similarly, the SAP_INTERNAL_HANA_

SUPPORT role is required for times when SAP support staff wants to connect to your SAP HANA environment during a support call. There is no need to change this role.

CONTENT_ADMIN

This role has all the privileges necessary for an SAP HANA modeler to manage and produce information views within SAP HANA Studio. It also allows these privileges to be granted to other users and a user to import and export content within the SAP HANA package repository.

This role has very broad privileges and should never be granted to an actual user. It is best when used as a template to help an administrator understand the various rights and privileges required by an SAP HANA modeler.

MODELING

The modeling role allows a user to create information views within SAP HANA Studio. By default, it has full analytic privilege (_SYS_BI_CP_ALL) access and root package access. Users with this level of access have full data (row level) access to all information models and packages within SAP HANA Studio. They also have full edit access to all repository content. The role is not capable of assigning any of its privileges to other users. Like the CONTENT_ADMIN role, it's only really useful as an example of types of privileges.

RESTRICTED_USER_JDBC_ACCESS/RESTRICTED_USER_ODBC_ACCESS

These roles are pertinent only when used in conjunction with restricted users, a feature we will talk more about in Section 2.3.5. These roles grant the absolute minimum rights necessary to log on via JDBC/ODBC and no other rights. They are most likely to be used in scenarios with custom applications built with the SAP HANA XS Engine for very limited user accounts.

MONITORING

This role contains the privileges necessary to query tables that contain SAP HANA system state data; this includes the CATALOG_READ system privilege and SELECT access to _SYS_STATISTICS. This is a role that could be useful to grant read-only access to system state information.

PUBLIC

This role is the default role assigned to all non-restricted users within SAP HANA. It is not possible to remove this role from a standard user. It contains a variety of

SELECT and EXECUTE object privileges on tables, views, and procedures found in the SYS schema. Access to these objects is what allows a user to perform the most basic operations of logging in and using the system. Without access to these objects, a user has extremely limited capabilities. The PUBLIC role is not and cannot be assigned to restricted users.

SAP_INTERNAL_HANA_SUPPORT

This role is intended for use by SAP Support personnel when they are investigating root causes for issues in your SAP HANA environment during a service call. The role grants the following privileges, which cannot be changed:

▶ CATALOG_READ

▶ TRACE_ADMIN

▶ SELECT/EXECUTE on _SYS_STATISTICS schema

▶ EXECUTE on MANAGEMENT_CONSOLE_PROC stored procedure in the SYS schema

These limited rights allow the support admin to read and configure system log files and view statistics about the SAP HANA server but do not allow them access to any corporate data or models. Therefore, this role is safe for use in production environments.

Custom Functional Roles

Now that you are familiar with some of the default roles available in your SAP HANA system, it's time to begin building a set of useful corporate roles that you can base your SAP HANA security model around. As we introduced at the beginning of this section, these roles typically handle four broad functional categories: end users, developers, security administrators, and system administrators. You can think of these as a hierarchy of access, with subsequent levels generally having more access than the previous level.

Before we drill into individual role types, there are some things to consider about the management of all roles in the system. A common issue with security design is that users and developers who have access to lower-tier environments like development and QA are typically given broader access than they might have in production environments. However, we want to design and test our security model in lower-tier environments and then promote it to the higher tier like any other development product, without being required to alter it in the upper tier.

We can achieve this with SAP HANA roles, but it requires a little organization. The first step is to clearly identify the roles that are granting production-level access and differentiate them from the ones granting development-level access. By having different roles, we can assign the appropriate role to users in each environment but still be able to design and test our production roles in development.

Since development environment roles typically grant additional access, we can leverage the role inheritance features to avoid repeating the definitions of privileges in more than one role. We can create the production version of a role first and then extend it with additional privileges for development environments.

End-User Roles

End users are typically the least complicated roles to configure for a new system because they have the fewest privileges granted. However, some complexity does come into play when we start to consider data access restrictions and analytic privileges. For this reason, it's often beneficial to treat data access restrictions separately from other privileges so that they can be mixed and matched on a specific user. When it comes to end-user data access restrictions, we will deal with this topic in detail in Chapter 11, where we'll discuss all aspects of analytic privileges.

The main thing end users need to be able to do is access data in information views. In the typical SAP HANA scenario, we will not have users directly querying SQL tables. Instead, their access should be mediated by views. This is because you cannot implement SAP HANA data access restriction on base tables.

In order to query an information view, you need SELECT access on the column view that is created when the view is activated. For all views created in the SAP HANA repository, these column views reside in the _SYS_BIC schema. Since you cannot get any data from a column view without at least one analytic privilege being granted on that model, you can generally just give end users SELECT access to the whole _SYS_BIC schema. There may be times when this is inappropriate, depending on how you have configured your models, but in general, it's a good place to start for end-user access.

In addition to querying column views, there are times when users need to execute procedures that are also stored in _SYS_BIC. This, too, is typically a safe operation because, by default, these procedures are read-only operations. If not, they should be configured for either invoker privileges or internally verify permission of the calling user before execution; otherwise, they should not be placed in _SYS_BIC.

Finally, there are several tables in the _SYS_BI schema that store metadata describing the information views deployed in the system. These tables are used by several of the frontend tools to allow a user to select a model to query from. Therefore, an end user needs SELECT access on this schema as well.

Beyond these basic rights and those granted by the built-in PUBLIC role, an end user doesn't really need any other privileges to support basic analytic scenarios with SAP BusinessObjects BI tools. Other SAP products or custom XS applications may require you to expand beyond these privileges, but that can be handled on a case-by-case basis. Therefore, a typical end-user role looks just like in Listing 2.1.

```
role examplecompany.core::user {
    catalog schema "_SYS_BIC": SELECT, EXECUTE;
    catalog schema "_SYS_BI": SELECT;
}
```
Listing 2.1 End-User Role

Because end users are not typically given access to development or QA environments, there is no need to further extend this role with additional privileges in the lower tiers.

Developer Roles

A developer needs several additional permissions beyond what an end user needs. However, developers also need to query information views. Thus, we can start by extending the basic user role when creating a developer role to avoid repeating ourselves.

Developers are also the primary candidates for a split between their development environment permissions and production permissions, depending on how restrictive your production environments are. We'll start by modeling the permissions a developer might have in production and then extend that for development environments.

A number of the permissions we might grant to a developer are optional and are likely to be used in only some scenarios. We will call these exceptions out in our examples with comments.

The primary thing that separates a developer from an end user is the ability to browse and interact with the repository. For this, the user needs EXECUTE permissions on a specific stored procedure that mediates access to the repository (SYS.REPOSITORY_REST). In order to see anything in the repository, the user needs `REPO.READ` permission to at least one package as well. Unless you want to be very restrictive, you can simply let developers have read access to the whole repository.

Finally, we suggest granting them one system privilege, `CATALOG READ`. This privilege allows unrestricted access to system views. This can be a handy way for developers to interrogate the system when debugging.

The most basic developer role for production system access can therefore be as simple as in Listing 2.2.

```
role examplecompany.core::developer
    extends role examplecompany.core::user
{
    catalog sql object "SYS"."REPOSITORY_REST": EXECUTE;
    package ".REPO_PACKAGE_ROOT": REPO.READ;
    system privilege: CATALOG READ;
}
```

Listing 2.2 Production Developer Role

This allows them to essentially be end users, except that they can browse the repository and review imported information views.

As you move into the development environment, developers obviously need several more permissions. First, they need to be able to see the base table structures on which they are tasked with building information models. This also means they need access to all data in the development environment. To provide access to all information views, a developer needs the `_SYS_BI_CP_ALL` analytic privilege. Generally, only information view modelers need this privilege.

In order to grant developers access to the schema where data is stored in your system, you need to ensure that _SYS_REPO has access to the schema as well. If you created the schema as a repository object, this is true by default. You also need to determine whether developers can modify the data in the base schema for testing purposes or if that is reserved for the ETL process. In this example, we've given the developers only read access.

In addition to access to the base tables on which to build models, they need the ability to edit and activate content in the repository in at least one package. As previously discussed, we want to limit this to the content subpackages, where they can build content for eventual deployment to production, and `system-local.private`, where they can conduct experiments.

Another important task for developers is the selection and maintenance of delivery units. Developers need to decide what content is ready for promotion to the next environment tier. In some cases, this could be a limited set of developers, in which case you could split these privileges out, but for our example, we are simply including them with the developer. The key privilege here is REPO.MAINTAIN_ DELIVERY_UNITS, which allows for creating and editing delivery unit content. There are other privileges that could also be granted here for more advanced change management features.

To grant this set of privileges, we can extend our production developer role with the following, assuming that all our data is in a schema called WAREHOUSE and that _SYS_REPO was granted access to that schema when it was created (Listing 2.3).

```
role examplecompany.core::developer_dev
    extends role    examplecompany.core::developer, {
    catalog schema "WAREHOUSE":    SELECT, EXECUTE;
    system privilege : REPO.MAINTAIN_DELIVERY_UNITS;
    catalog analytic privilege: "_SYS_BI_CP_ALL";
    package "examplecompany.public":
        REPO.EDIT_NATIVE_OBJECTS,
        REPO.ACTIVATE_NATIVE_OBJECTS,
        REPO.MAINTAIN_NATIVE_PACKAGES;
    package "system-local.private":
        REPO.EDIT_NATIVE_OBJECTS,
        REPO.ACTIVATE_NATIVE_OBJECTS,
        REPO.MAINTAIN_NATIVE_PACKAGES;
}
```

Listing 2.3 Development-Tier Developer Role

Security Admin Roles

The privileges necessary for a security administrator are not that different from those for a developer. Therefore, we can start by extending the production version of the developer role.

In addition to the basic privileges of navigating the repository, the security administrator needs to be able to manage users and roles. This means they need two key system privileges: USER ADMIN and ROLE ADMIN. However, repository-based roles cannot be granted, even by a user who has these privileges. Thus, they also need access to the granting and revoking stored procedures in the _SYS_REPO schema that we discussed in Section 2.3.2.

Finally, the security administrators are likely to be in charge of setting up and monitoring auditing for security, as well as the administration of password polices, which requires a few additional privileges. Listing 2.4 gives a good set of privileges for most security users in a production environment. Note that we have not given them the ability to edit or activate content in the repository because that should be done in the development landscape and promoted through delivery units.

```
role examplecompany.core::security_admin
    extends role examplecompany.core::developer
{
    system privilege: USER ADMIN, ROLE ADMIN;
    catalog sql object "_SYS_REPO"."GRANT_ACTIVATED_ANALYTICAL_PRIVILEGE":
EXECUTE;
    catalog sql object "_SYS_REPO"."GRANT_ACTIVATED_ROLE": EXECUTE;
    catalog sql object "_SYS_REPO"."GRANT_APPLICATION_PRIVILEGE": EXECUTE;
    catalog sql object "_SYS_REPO"."GRANT_PRIVILEGE_ON_ACTIVATED_CONTENT":
EXECUTE;
    catalog sql object "_SYS_REPO"."GRANT_SCHEMA_PRIVILEGE_ON_ACTIVATED_
CONTENT": EXECUTE;

    catalog sql object "_SYS_REPO"."REVOKE_ACTIVATED_ANALYTICAL_
PRIVILEGE": EXECUTE;
    catalog sql object "_SYS_REPO"."REVOKE_ACTIVATED_ROLE": EXECUTE;
    catalog sql object "_SYS_REPO"."REVOKE_APPLICATION_PRIVILEGE":
EXECUTE;
    catalog sql object "_SYS_REPO"."REVOKE_PRIVILEGE_ON_ACTIVATED_
CONTENT": EXECUTE;
    catalog sql object "_SYS_REPO"."REVOKE_SCHEMA_PRIVILEGE_ON_ACTIVATED_
CONTENT": EXECUTE;
// For Audit Configuration
    system privilege: AUDIT ADMIN;
// For Password Policy Management
    system privilege: INIFILE ADMIN;
    catalog sql object "_SYS_SECURITY"."_SYS_PASSWORD_BLACKLIST": SELECT,
INSERT, UPDATE, DELETE;
}
```
Listing 2.4 Security Admin Production Role

Extending the security administrator role for the development tier requires simply adding the missing privileges that allow them to create and edit the repository roles. They also need the ability to maintain delivery units, just like the developers. Therefore, you have to grant them the repository edit and activate privileges on the package set aside for security content, as well as the system privilege that allows for delivery unit management (Listing 2.5).

```
role examplecompany.core::security_admin_dev
    extends role examplecompany.core::security_admin
{
    system privilege : REPO.MAINTAIN_DELIVERY_UNITS;
    package "examplecompany.core":
        REPO.ACTIVATE_NATIVE_OBJECTS,
        REPO.EDIT_NATIVE_OBJECTS,
        REPO.MAINTAIN_NATIVE_PACKAGES;
}
```
Listing 2.5 Security Admin Development Role

System Admin Roles

Finally, we come to the system administrator roles. Configuring security for system administration is always difficult. The activities of system administrators typically require broad system access, so it's difficult to restrict their permissions to the point of safety without also preventing them from doing their jobs.

One option is give these users separate accounts—one that is quite limited and mostly has read access to monitor the system status, and a separate one that has the more elevated privileges that allows significant system reconfiguration. The breakdown of which privileges should go where in such a scenario is likely to be different for every company.

Instead of trying to answer all the possible ways you could split up system administration privileges, we will simply give a basic system admin example that points out some common privileges they need (Listing 2.6). One of the key areas we've left for the system administrator role, although it could easily be broken out into its own category, is promotion of delivery units between systems. This requires the repository import and export privileges. The other key area for system administrators is monitoring the system's health. For that, they need SELECT access to the _SYS_STATISTICS schema. Finally, there are numerous system privileges they require for managing system states and resources.

```
role examplecompany.core::system_admin
    extends role examplecompany.core::developer
{
// Delivery Unit Transport
    system privilege: REPO.EXPORT, REPO.IMPORT;
// Monitoring
    catalog schema "_SYS_STATISTICS": SELECT;
    system privilege: TRACE ADMIN;
```

```
// Backup and Restore
   system privilege: BACKUP ADMIN, SAVEPOINT ADMIN;
// Manage System and Resources
   system privilege: INIFILE ADMIN, LICENSE ADMIN,
      LOG ADMIN, MONITOR ADMIN, OPTIMIZER ADMIN,
      RESOURCE ADMIN, SESSION ADMIN, SERVICE ADMIN;
}
```

Listing 2.6 System Administrator Role

ETL Service Account Role

A core part of your security model is planning for the loading of data into the system. Depending on how you plan to manage and load data, you may have different requirements for various service accounts that will be responsible for these processes. If you are using SAP BW on SAP HANA or SAP Business Suite on SAP HANA, there are well-defined requirements for the service accounts used by SAP NetWeaver that are handled for you when those systems are set up on SAP HANA. When you are building your own data warehouse with tools like SAP Data Services, however, you have to determine the rights necessary for your ETL service accounts.

Recall from Section 2.1.4 that we have the option of either creating a user that will own the schema that holds our warehouse data or having _SYS_REPO manage the schema for us. If we are creating a dedicated user, we need to log on as that user and ensure that we grant _SYS_REPO SELECT and EXECUTE access to the schema before doing any of the other role modeling we've discussed so far.

If, on the other hand, we create the schema as a repository object owned by _SYS_REPO, we instead need to create a role that allows another service account sufficient access to the data schema to provision and load data into it. This typically requires full access to the schema, including the ability to create and drop database objects. Thus, a typical ETL service account role looks like the example in Listing 2.7.

```
role examplecompany.core::data_provisioning {
   // Read Access
   schema examplecompany.core:exampleschema.hdbschema: SELECT, EXECUTE;
   // Write Access
   schema examplecompany.core:exampleschema.hdbschema: INSERT, UPDATE,
DELETE;
   // Create, Alter and Drop Access
   schema examplecompany.core:exampleschema.hdbschema: ALTER, CREATE
```

```
ANY, DROP, INDEX, TRIGGER, DEBUG;
}
```
Listing 2.7 Example Data Provisioning Role

2.3.5 User Provisioning

Now that you have configured a set of roles that define the privileges you want your users to have, you are ready to provision user accounts in the system and allow people other than the system administrators to access the system.

Unfortunately, this is not one of SAP HANA's strong suits. It would be nice if SAP HANA had a built-in user-provisioning system similar to the authentication modules available in SAP BusinessObjects BI and other tools that allow you to automatically import users from a third-party identity management solution. Instead, SAP has gone with an approach that assumes systems will push identities into the SAP HANA system instead of SAP HANA pulling the identities in on its own. This means that, if you don't want to manually create each and every user by hand in the system's user management UI, you need to devise a solution that manages this user provisioning for you.

The mechanism SAP HANA provides for pushing user identities into the system is simply the SQL programming language, which uses CREATE statements to create a user and either the GRANT statement or the execution of the GRANT_ACTIVATED_ROLE procedure.

There are several approaches that can be taken with user provisioning, depending on the overall environment in which you are operating SAP HANA. You may have a system that already manages user provisioning globally, which can be used to push users into SAP HANA for you. An example of this is SAP Governance, Risk, and Compliance (GRC), which, in its latest editions, has built in connectors for managing SAP HANA users.

In addition to SAP GRC, if you are running the latest service packs of SAP NetWeaver 7.4 and SAP HANA is the platform database, then you can create and synchronize SAP HANA database users to match SAP NetWeaver platform users created in Transaction SU01. This would also apply to the latest editions of SAP BW on SAP HANA. Still, this isn't quite as robust a solution as provided by SAP GRC because it's specific to just one SAP NetWeaver platform instance, and it doesn't help for SAP HANA side car scenarios.

If you don't have an existing global user provisioning strategy, you need to figure out how to fit SAP HANA into your environment. First, you need to identify the system of record for user identity. This could be a system dedicated to identity management, like Active Directory or another LDAP user store. You could also use records in an HR system listing employees, or you could rely on other SAP systems in your landscape that are connecting to SAP HANA, e.g., SAP BW, SAP ERP, or SAP BusinessObjects BI.

Once you have identified from where you will get the list of user identities, you need to decide how you will synchronize information from that system into SAP HANA and how this synchronization will take place: either on a schedule or triggered immediately every time a change is made in the source system. In essence, this is no different from many other ETL process loading data into SAP HANA. You can, in fact, leverage some of the same ETL tools to help with the process, depending on the source system.

Regardless of the system you use to trigger the synchronization of users into SAP HANA, the core concepts remain the same. You need to determine for each user in the source whether an equivalent user exists in the target SAP HANA environment, and if it doesn't, you will need to issue a CREATE USER statement. In addition to mapping users into the system, you will need some method to determine which roles to grant to users after creation. This can be based on whatever properties you have attached to user records in the source system. Finally, you have to decide whether you will also manage the deletion of users that no longer exist in the source or simply deactivate the user accounts.

Restricted User Types

In SAP HANA SPS 8, a new user type was created that adds one extra decision to your provisioning logic. This new user type is the *restricted user*. The key difference between a restricted user and normal user is that the restricted user is not granted the built-in PUBLIC role and does not get a default schema created for it. Additionally, it cannot log on to the system via JDBC or ODBC connection. In general, this means it has absolutely no rights by default and must be manually granted a set of minimum rights to do anything. The use case for restricted users is mostly for web-based access to custom SAP HANA XS application scenarios.

Next, we'll walk you through the key statements for creating a user and granting it a role. We'll explain this process for both automatic user provisioning and manual user provisioning. Finally, we'll conclude with an explanation of how to grant roles to users.

Automating User Provisioning

Let's examine the key statements needed to programmatically create a user and grant it a role:

- Create a user with a given password: CREATE USER EXAMPLE PASSWORD 123456
- Create a restricted user with a password: CREATE RESTRICTED USER EXAMPLE PASSWORD 123456
- Alter a user to add a Kerberos identity and enable Kerberos access:
  ALTER USER EXAMPLE ADD IDENTITY 'example@somedomain.com' FOR KERBEROS;
  ALTER USER EXAMPLE ENABLE KERBEROS;
- Alter a user to add an SAML identity and enable SAML access:
  ALTER USER EXAMPLE ADD IDENTITY 'example' FOR SAML PROVIDER BOESAMLPROVIDER;
  ALTER USER EXAMPLE ENABLE SAML;
- Grant a catalog role to a user: GRANT ROLE EXAMPLE_ROLE TO EXAMPLE
- Grant a repository role to a user: CALL "_SYS_REPO"."GRANT_ACTIVATED_ROLE" ('saphana.security::ExampleRole','Example');

Now, let's examine the key statements needed to revoke roles and drop users:

- Revoke a repository role: CALL "_SYS_REPO"."REVOKE_ACTIVATED_ROLE" ('saphana.security::ExampleRole','Example');
- Revoke a catalog role: REVOKE EXAMPLE_ROLE FROM EXAMPLE
- Deactivate a user: ALTER USER EXAMPLE DEACTIVATE
- Drop a user: DROP USER EXAMPLE

With a combination of the above statements and the logic necessary to access your source system data, you can automate the provisioning of users so that security administrators are not forced to manually update access to the SAP HANA database for every new user.

This automation is a significant concern for SAP HANA because we need every user who consumes content to exist as a user in the database in order to enforce data access restrictions with analytic privileges. You do not want to have administrators managing this on a manual basis for large populations.

Manual User Provisioning

As much as we strongly encourage you to automate your user provisioning process, there will be times when you need to manually provision some users. You may have a small enough population that manual provisioning is a practical choice. It's also likely that system administrator accounts will be set up before a provisioning solution can be implemented. Therefore, we need to be familiar with the manual user provisioning process.

You can, of course, use the same scripting statements we just outlined above to manually provision a user by writing out the necessary CREATE and ALTER statements. This may actually be the best choice if you want the process to be repeatable in multiple environments or need to provision multiple users in a row.

However, if you opt to go with using the GUI to provision your users, you can follow the steps below. You can see an overview of the USER CREATION screen in Figure 2.24.

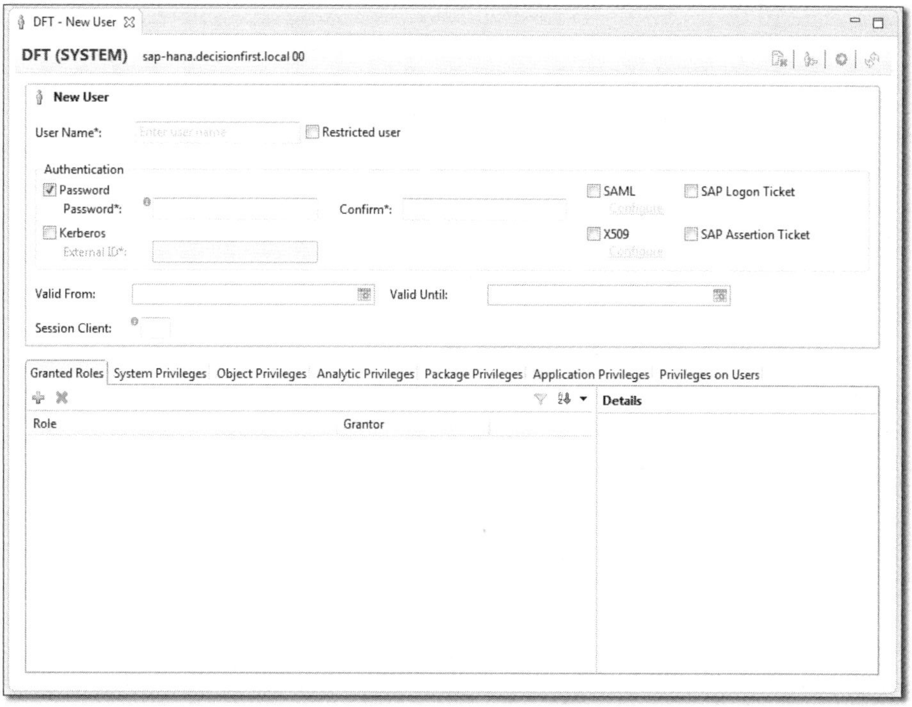

Figure 2.24 User Creation Screen

1. From the systems view in SAP HANA Studio, open the SECURITY folder.

2. Right-click the USERS folder and choose NEW.

3. The NEW USER screen is displayed.

4. Give the USER a NAME.

5. Check the RESTRICTED USER checkbox, if desired.

6. Give the user at least one authentication mechanism, e.g., a password.

7. Optionally, set a validity date range.

8. Grant NECESSARY ROLES on the GRANTED ROLES tab.

Granting Roles to Users

In this section, we'll review how you go about granting a role to a user. Granting roles can be done using the USER MANAGEMENT interface from the systems view or using SQL commands. There are some subtle differences between granting a traditional role and granting one that was created as a repository object; we will also review these.

We'll start by granting a repository role that we created. Because a role created in the repository is owned by _SYS_REPO, users can't grant access to these roles using traditional GRANT statements. Instead, we need to ensure that _SYS_REPO grants the role to users on our behalf. This is accomplished with several predefined stored procedures that are shipped with the system. These procedures can be found in the _SYS_REPO schema. See Figure 2.25 for the list of procedures used to manage repository security objects. The two most important ones are GRANT_ACTIVATED_ROLE and REVOKE_ACTIVATED_ROLE.

In order for a user to grant or revoke one of the activated repository roles, they need the EXECUTE permission on these procedures. Once you have that privilege, you can either execute the procedures directly with the CALL procedure SQL statement or grant the procedure through the user management UI, which is luckily smart enough to detect that you are attempting to grant an activated role and will call the procedures on your behalf.

To grant or revoke a traditional role in SAP HANA, you simply need the USER_ ADMIN and ROLE ADMIN system privileges. With these privileges, you can either grant the role using the SQL GRANT statement or use the USER MANAGEMENT user interface on the GRANTED ROLES tab.

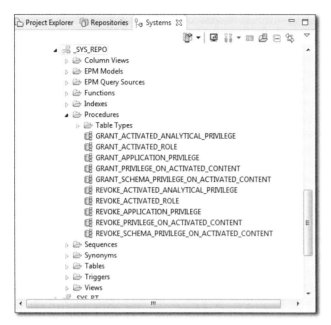

Figure 2.25 Repository Role Granting Procedures

Summary

At this point, you should have a solid starting point from which to construct a security model and system layout that will be both flexible and secure. The important thing to remember is getting this model right as early in your project as possible, which will save you the headaches of later rework.

For further reading and background information on the material covered in this section, see the SAP HANA Security Guide section on authorization:

http://help.sap.com/hana/SAP_HANA_Security_Guide_en.pdf.

2.4   SAP HANA Authentication

With your base security and content model in place, it's time to start thinking about how you will authenticate all the different users to the SAP HANA system. So far, you've been logging on to SAP HANA with system-level accounts using simple user names and passwords. This works fine for system administrators, but when it comes time to deliver a solution to a broader audience, a more sophisticated solution is in order.

Just because you've authorized a user to access an information resource doesn't mean you should allow anyone who walks up and claims to be that user to have access. You must first verify that the user requesting access really is the person they say they are by using an authentication scheme. This proof of identity is typically handled by the exchange of a *security credential*—a form of proof that the provider is who they claim to be. This verification of identity is what we mean by *authentication*.

Authentication credentials come in many forms, but the most common is, of course, the combination of a user name and a password. This proves the user's identity because only the real user should know what the password is, having never shared it with anyone or written it down somewhere others might find it.

In the modern computing world, users must access many different systems. As we all know, keeping track of a unique set of credentials for every single system that we need to access is a substantial inconvenience. This often leads to insecure practices such as writing down passwords and leaving them in plain sight or using the same password for every system we access. A common solution to this complexity is the implementation of a single sign-on (SSO) system whereby users can prove their identity once to a centralized identity management system and that verified identity can then be passed around, in a secure fashion, to each of the business systems a user must access.

The combination of all of these concerns is sufficiently complex that there are numerous computing standards that address how a system should implement authentication. SAP HANA supports several of these standards. In Table 2.3, we list the supported authentication standards available in SAP HANA, their usage for ODBC/JDBC access vs. HTTP access, and whether they are also supported by SAP BusinessObjects BI for end-to-end sign on.

SAP HANA Authentication Methods	ODBC/ JDBC	HTTP/ HTTPS	End-To-End with SAP BusinessObjects BI
Internal Authentication User Name/ Password	Yes	Yes	Yes (not recommended)[*]
Kerberos	Yes	Yes	Yes[**]
SAML	Yes	Yes	Yes (preferred method)[***]

Table 2.3 Authentication Methods Supported by SAP BusinessObjects BI and SAP HANA

SAP HANA Authentication Methods	ODBC/ JDBC	HTTP/ HTTPS	End-To-End with SAP BusinessObjects BI
X509	No	Yes	No
SAP Logon Tickets	No	Yes	No
SAP Assertion Tickets	No	Yes	No

Table 2.3 Authentication Methods Supported by SAP BusinessObjects BI and SAP HANA (Cont.)

Notes on Table 2.3

* Achieving end-to-end authentication with user names and passwords requires manual/programmatic synchronization of database and SAP BusinessObjects BI credentials.

** Kerberos works with some, but not all, applications in the SAP BusinessObjects BI platform. However, it's ideal for desktop tool access such as SAP HANA Studio and SAP Lumira.

*** Works as of SAP BusinessObjects BI 4.1. This is the preferred method because it provides the most flexible solution. It is not supported by desktop tools, so it works well in conjunction with Kerberos for desktop access.

In this section, we will look more closely at the role authentication plays in the security process. We will examine the specific types of authentication supported by SAP HANA and how those methods relate to SAP BusinessObjects BI and the integration of a total authentication solution between both platforms. In the bulk of this section, we will look at each type of authentication, covering user name/ password authentication (Section 2.4.1), Kerberos SSO (Section 2.4.2), and SAML SSO (Section 2.4.3). For completeness, we'll briefly mention the other web-based authentication methods—X509, SAP Logon Tickets, and SAP Assertion tickets—in Section 2.4.4, but, because these methods are applicable for only the XS Engine, we won't go into any detail. Finally, we'll conclude this section with a summary and some recommendations.

2.4.1   Internal Authentication with User Name and Password

Like almost all systems, SAP HANA provides support for internal authentication methods that don't rely on any external systems or additional configurations. This method leverages an internal store of user passwords. All standard system accounts are authenticated with this mechanism.

System administrators can configure the password policies for the system, setting typical conditions like minimum password length and complexity and password longevity. See Figure 2.26 for an example of the password configuration options.

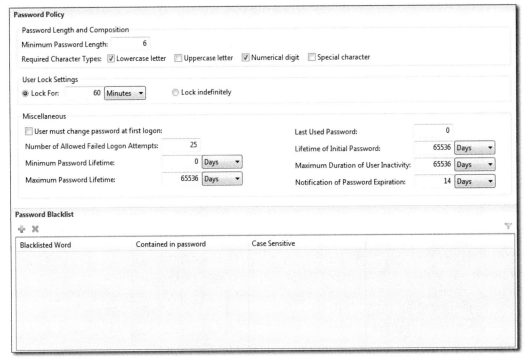

Figure 2.26 Password Policy Configuration

With this authentication scheme, users can log on with any tools, both desktop and web-based. However, the passwords for the accounts must be managed in SAP HANA. This creates yet another system of passwords to keep track of. Thus, it is not a recommended solution for anything but the basic system accounts and perhaps developer access to the SAP HANA backend. End users should be provided another mechanism.

You can achieve end-to-end authentication from SAP BusinessObjects BI to the SAP HANA database platform with this solution. This relies on a feature of SAP BusinessObjects BI that allows you to store a set of database credentials on the SAP BusinessObjects BI user account. However, there is no automatic method for setting and synchronizing those credentials. You would have to either manually keep the accounts in sync or develop a custom program that managed the setting of the SAP HANA credentials from the outside and also sets the SAP BusinessObjects BI database credentials for the equivalent user. Although you could do this, it would be a cumbersome approach and is thus not recommended.

Internal authentication is also supported by the SAP HANA XS Engine and can be used with basic or form-based logons to applications hosted in that part of the platform.

2.4.2 Kerberos Authentication

Kerberos is a network authentication protocol that comes out of work done at MIT dating back to the early days of networked computing. It's designed to be a robust protocol that protects against many forms of attack and is based on strong cryptography. Because MIT released publicly available implementations of the protocol and due to its robustness, Kerberos has been integrated in many computing systems over the years. One of the key integrations of Kerberos that has propelled its usage far and wide is the inclusion of the protocol in Microsoft's very popular Active Directory solution. This means that in almost every business environment, when you log on to your desktop, you're using Kerberos.

Kerberos relies on the principals of public/private key cryptography to achieve its robust exchange of identity information. Kerberos does rely on a central authority to manage credentials. This is known as the Key Distribution Center and, in almost all implementations in business today, it is provided by Microsoft Active Directory Services. This reliance on an external central authority can make the configuration of an end-to-end Kerberos solution somewhat cumbersome. Kerberos also was developed in the era of desktop software, so it works well in conjunction with desktop tools like SAP HANA Studio and SAP Lumira Desktop.

Kerberos can also be used for web-based SSO by way of several additional standards that integrate Kerberos into web browsers. These were first introduced by Microsoft in Internet Explorer and were later adopted by most modern browsers. SAP BusinessObjects BI has excellent support for these standards, and it is a common mechanism for implementing SSO into SAP BusinessObjects BI.

Kerberos can also be used for end-to-end solutions with SAP BusinessObjects BI. This allows SAP BusinessObjects BI to initially perform the authentication operations at the web-tier layer and then pass that authenticated identity down the stack all the way to the SAP HANA database. However, not every aspect of the platform works well with Kerberos. For example, scheduled background processes that are executing outside the scope of an authenticated Kerberos session typically don't work with Kerberos solutions. This is one of the primary reasons for the addition of dedicated SAML support for SAP HANA in SAP BusinessObjects BI 4.1. However, the platform's SAML support does not work with all desktop tools. Thus, a hybrid solution using Kerberos and SAML offers the best of both worlds.

Kerberos can also be used in conjunction with the SAP HANA XS web application to provide SSO to custom web applications developed in SAP HANA.

Additional Resources

For more technical details on Kerberos, we recommend the following resources:

▸ MIT's Kerberos Project Page (*http://web.mit.edu/kerberos/*)

▸ The Kerberos Consortium (*http://www.kerberos.org/*)

▸ Microsoft's Negotiate protocol and SPNEGO protocols (*http://msdn.microsoft.com/en-us/library/ms995329.aspx*)

▸ SAP Note 1837331: Detailed Instructions for Kerberos Configuration (*https://service.sap.com/sap/support/notes/1837331*)

▸ SAP Note 1813724: Automation Tools to Assist with Kerberos Configuration (*https://service.sap.com/sap/support/notes/1813724*)

▸ SAP Note 1631734: Configuring Kerberos Single Sign On for Business Objects (*http://service.sap.com/sap/support/notes/1631734*)

2.4.3 SAML Authentication

Security Assertion Markup Language (SAML) is a relatively new authentication standard that comes from an open-source standards body called OASIS. One of its key benefits is that the transport of authentication and security data is done via simple XML messages. This makes implementing SAML support in applications very straightforward.

SAML is somewhat different from Kerberos in that it has a much more decentralized architecture. This style of authentication solution is often referred to as a federated identity system. Although SAML isn't the only solution in this space, it's the only one adopted by SAP HANA and SAP BusinessObjects BI. The solution is called *federated* because there is a loose coupling of multiple systems that have agreed to cooperate with each other for the purpose of exchanging authentication and authorization data. Instead of a single central system that manages all identity information (as with Kerberos), SAML can support multiple *identify providers* that manage authentication of users for various parties.

When using SAML with SAP BusinessObjects BI and SAP HANA as an end-to-end authentication solution, SAP BusinessObjects BI acts as the identity provider for the interaction. This means we don't need to configure anything beyond the SAP BusinessObjects BI and SAP HANA systems to get the solution working. Additionally, because SAP BusinessObjects BI is the identity provider, any user that has successfully authenticated to SAP BusinessObjects BI by any means that SAP BusinessObjects BI supports can then access data in SAP HANA. This offers a wide degree of flexibility. You could authenticate to the SAP BusinessObjects BI platform via Kerberos, LDAP, or SAP SSO and then access data in the SAP HANA system over SAML.

SAML is also a supported SSO mechanism for SAP HANA XS web applications. An SAML identify provider other than SAP BusinessObjects BI is required for this scenario, however.

Additional Resources

For more technical details on SAML, visit the following pages hosted by the OASIS standards group that created SAML:

▶ A technical overview of SAML (*https://www.oasis-open.org/committees/download.php/27819/sstc-saml-tech-overview-2.0-cd-02.pdf*)

▶ The complete SAML specification (*http://saml.xml.org/saml-specifications*)

▶ Implementing SAML SSO from SAP BusinessObjects BI to SAP HANA, which is contained within the SAP BusinessObjects BI Administration Guide, Section 18.1.3.11 (*http://help.sap.com/businessobject/product_guides/sbo41/en/sbo41sp4_bip_admin_en.pdf*)

2.4.4 Other Web-Based Authentication Methods for SAP HANA XS

The authentication methods discussed so far are all supported with ODBC/JDBC connections, which is how SAP BusinessObjects BI and other analytic tools access data in SAP HANA, but that is not the full extent of SAP HANA's capabilities. You can provide access to either SAP-provided or custom web applications hosted on the SAP HANA XS web application platform. These applications can be authenticated with any of the above solutions plus X509, SAP Logon Tickets, and SAP Assertion Tickets. Because these methods are specific to just the XS Engine, we won't go into further detail here.

Additional Resources

For additional details on SAP HANA XS authentication, see Chapter 8 of the SAP HANA Security Guide at *http://help.sap.com/hana/SAP_HANA_Security_Guide_en.pdf*.

2.4.5 Summary and Recommendations

In SAP HANA, each user account can be enabled for any or all of the authentication methods listed above. We've already hinted at this in our discussion of combining Kerberos and SAML authentication to allow users the best of both worlds when working with a combination of desktop and web-based tools.

At this point, we feel there is just one solid approach for complete, end-to-end SSO for SAP HANA, assuming you are integrating with the SAP BusinessObjects BI platform as the primary method of analyzing your SAP HANA data. That is the integration of both Active Directory via Kerberos for desktop tool access and SAP BusinessObjects BI to SAP HANA via SAML for web-based SSO. If either of these solutions offered a complete answer on its own, there would be no need to implement both. But because desktop tools don't currently support SAML SSO and not all web-based workflows are supported by Kerberos, we feel this will give you the best overall solution.

Once you have both configurations in place, and assuming you are auto-populating your users into SAP HANA with both Kerberos and SAML identities, your users will be able to access the system from all of the SAP BusinessObjects BI web and desktop tools without issue. This includes the newer tools like SAP Lumira, which supports Kerberos on the desktop.

If the implementation of the combined solution seems daunting and you have only a small audience that is using desktop tools, then the piece you can pull back on is the Kerberos implementation. For SAP BusinessObjects BI integration to SAP HANA, at this point, SAML should be a given.

2.5   Case Study: An End-to-End Security Configuration

You should now have a complete picture of the pieces that make up an SAP HANA security solution. In this section, we will take those pieces and turn theory into practice and develop a complete model that will be used throughout the rest of this book.

In preparation for the rollout of a new BI solution based on SAP HANA and SAP BusinessObjects BI at AdventureWorks Cycle Company, the IT team has been tasked with laying out a security plan for end-to-end access. This plan needs to establish the development and administration environment in which content will be constructed, provide access to web-based analytics tools in SAP BusinessObjects BI, and support desktop access to data via SAP Lumira. In total, the security plan should provide for the following:

▸ Security should integrate with existing Active Directory structures within the corporate network. Provisioning of users should be driven by changes made in Active Directory without the need for additional manual intervention. Real-time synchronization isn't a requirement; a modest delay between user creation/change and provisioning out to all platforms is acceptable.

▸ Users logged on to the corporate network should be able to access the SAP BusinessObjects BI Launch Pad without providing additional authentication credentials.

▸ Users logged on to the corporate network should be able to access SAP Lumira Desktop and consume SAP HANA data without requiring additional credentials.

▸ There is a single development team that manages all SAP HANA development activities.

▸ Security administration is handled by a separate security team.

In this section, we'll lay out the plans to deliver on these requirements.

2.5.1   Authentication Plan

There are two key requirements affecting our authentication plan: a desire for SSO for web-based access and the need to support desktop tools like SAP Lumira. To achieve these goals, we will implement the following integrations:

▶ SAP BusinessObjects BI SSO with Active Directory via Kerberos

▶ SAP BusinessObjects BI to SAP HANA SSO with SAML

▶ SAP HANA SSO with Active Directory via Kerberos for SAP HANA Studio and SAP Lumira access

Setting Up SAP BusinessObjects BI SSO with Kerberos

Following the steps outlined in SAP Note 1631734, we will implement SSO to the SAP BusinessObjects BI environment via Kerberos. The AdventureWorks SAP BusinessObjects BI environment currently consists of one large server hosting the main SAP BusinessObjects BI platform, as well as the web application tier in Tomcat. The SAP BusinessObjects BI server name is *boe40.adventureworks.com*. However, a friendly DNS alias has been set aside for the system so that, if the environment is expanded in the future, it can be hidden from end users. The alias is *bi.adventureworks.com*. The key steps performed by the team went as follows:

1. The team created a service account named BOEKERB within the ADVENTURE-WORKS Windows domain.

2. They assigned the account the following SPNs to mark it as the service account for SAP BusinessObjects BI and to enable HTTP SSO for Kerberos:

   ▶ BICMS/boe40.adventureworks.com

   ▶ HTTP/boe40.adventureworks.com

   ▶ HTTP/boe40

   ▶ HTTP/bi.adventureworks.com

   ▶ HTTP/bi

3. The team created a KeyTab for the account with ktpass:

   ```
   ktpass -out c:\boekerb.keytab -princ BICMS/boe40.adventureworks.com
   -mapuser boekerb@ADVENTUREWORKS.COM -pass *** -ptype KRB5_NT_
   PRINCIPAL -crypto RC4-HMAC-NT
   ```

4. Using Active Directory tools, they verified that the account was trusted for Kerberos delegation.

5. The team set up Kerberos configuration files on the SAP BusinessObjects BI server.

6. The KeyTab file was copied to the SAP BusinessObjects BI Server and placed in the directory *C:/WINNT*.

C:/WINNT

Some Java programs default to looking for the Kerberos files in this directory. Testing is simpler with command-line Java tools if the default directories are used.

---

7. A *krb5.ini* file was created and stored in *C:/WINNT*:

```
[domain_realm]
.ADVENTUREWORKS.COM = ADVENTUREWORKS.COM
ADVENTUREWORKS.COM = ADVENTUREWORKS.COM

[libdefaults]
forwardable = true
default_realm = ADVENTUREWORKS.COM
dns_lookup_kdc = true
dns_lookup_realm = true
default_tkt_enctypes = RC4-HMAC
default_tgs_enctypes = RC4-HMAC

[realms]
ADVENTUREWORKS.COM = {
kdc = ADVENTUREWORKS.COM
default_domain = ADVENTUREWORKS.COM
}
```

8. A *bscLogin.conf* was created and stored in *C:/WINNT*:

```
com.businessobjects.security.jgss.initiate {
com.sun.security.auth.module.Krb5LoginModule required
debug=true;
};
com.businessobjects.security.jgss.accept {
com.sun.security.auth.module.Krb5LoginModule required
storeKey=true
useKeyTab=true
keyTab="c:/WINNT/boekerb.keytab"
principal="BICMS/boe.adventureworks.com"
debug = true;
};
```

9. The team configured the service account to run the SIA.

▶ BOEKERB was made a member of the administrators group on the SAP BusinessObjects BI server.

▶ BOEKERB was given the necessary local security polices to run a service (act as part of the operating system, log on as a batch job, log on as a service, and replace a process-level token).

▶ The SIA was configured to run as BOEKERB instead of Local System.

10. The team configured Windows AD authentication in the CMC; see Figure 2.27 for an example of this screen:

▶ Windows Active Directory authentication was enabled.

▶ *boekerb@adventureworks.com* was entered as the AD administration name.

▶ *ADVENTUREWORKS.COM* was entered as the default AD domain.

▶ Active Directory groups were mapped.

▶ Use of Kerberos authentication was enabled, and the SPN was set to match the service account `BOEKERB/ADVENTUREWORKS.COM`.

11. The team configured Tomcat for Kerberos SSO. Tomcat startup parameters were updated with Kerberos configuration files as follows:

```
Djava.security.auth.login.config=C:\WINNT\bscLogin.conf
-Djava.security.krb5.conf=C:\WINNT\krb5.ini
```

12. Next, `BILaunchpad.properties` was updated with default authentication set to `secWinAD`.

13. Next, `Global.properties` was updated with `sso.enabled` set to `true` and `vintela` properties configured, as follows:

```
sso.enabled=true
siteminder.enabled=false
vintela.enabled=true
idm.realm=ADVENTUREWORKS.COM
idm.princ=BICMS/boe40.adventureworks.com
idm.allowUnsecured=true
idm.allowNTLM=false
idm.logger.name=simple
idm.logger.props=error-log.properties
idm.keytab=C:/WINNT/boekerb.keytab
```

In Figure 2.27, we can see an example of the ACTIVE DIRECTORY CONFIGURATION screen in the SAP BusinessObjects BI Central Management Console. This is one of the key areas for configuring Active Directory SSO for SAP BusinessObjects BI.

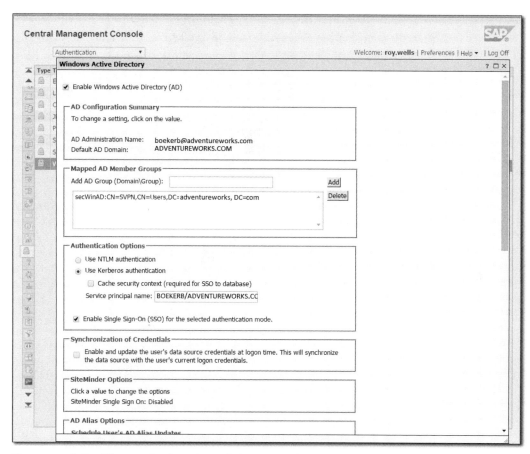

Figure 2.27 Active Directory Configuration in SAP BusinessObjects BI CMC

Once this process is complete, users can log on to the Launch Pad by simply opening their web browsers and navigating to the website URL.

Setting Up SAP BusinessObjects BI to SAP HANA SSO with SAML

Now let's establish an SSO channel from SAP BusinessObjects BI to SAP HANA. This will allow users who are signed on to the SAP BusinessObjects BI web tier to access data from the SAP HANA system without providing any additional credentials, as well as ensuring that the SAP HANA system can recognize the user's identity when it comes time to apply row-level security. The key steps from this process are the following:

1. Enable SSL on the SAP HANA server to support validation of certificates. This is done by enabling the SSL properties in the SAP HANA *indexserver.ini* file. These properties tell the SAP HANA server where to find the trust and key store files that hold the SSL certificates. Figure 2.28 shows an example configuration.

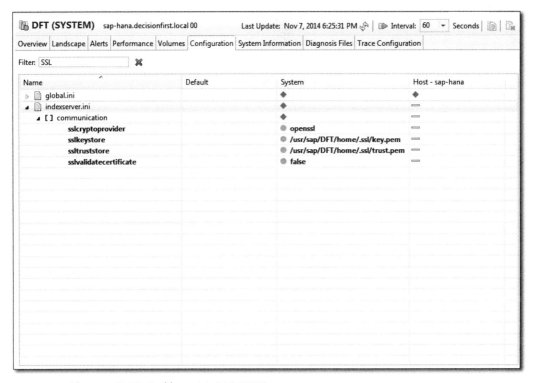

Figure 2.28 SSL Enablement in SAP HANA

2. Enable the SAP HANA SSO functionality in the Applications area of the CMC, and create an SSL certificate that identifies the SAP BusinessObjects BI server. This will be used by the SAP HANA server to verify that incoming authentication assertions are valid. Figure 2.29 has an example of this configuration step. The certificate and identity provider ID are now used by SAP HANA.

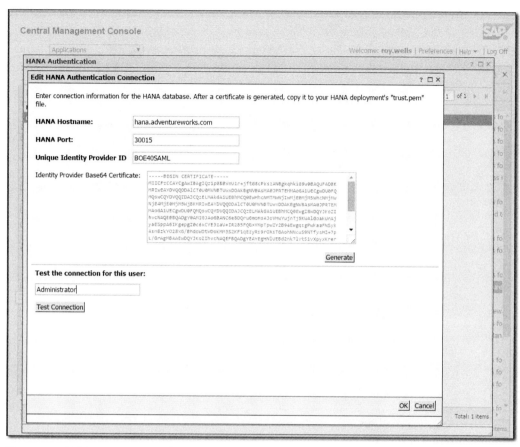

Figure 2.29 SAP HANA SAML Configuration in the CMC

3. Copy the certificate to the SAP HANA server and paste it into the *trust.pem* text file that was configured in the SSL configuration. See Figure 2.28 for reference.

4. Finally, create an identity provider entry in the SAP HANA system that you can attach SAML identities to. You must use the identity provider ID that was defined in SAP BusinessObjects BI. This is done from the SAP HANA Studio SECURITY area that you can access from the right-click menu on an SAP HANA Studio connection. See Figure 2.30 for an example of this screen.

5. From the SAML CONFIGURATION screen, you have to add a new provider with the + button and enter the identity provider name that was defined in SAP BusinessObjects BI, followed by the ISSUED TO and ISSUED BY values. For SAP BusinessObjects BI, these values always match the following, where the last entry is the identity provider name: C=CA,ST=BC,O=SAP,OU=BOE,CN=BOE40SAML.

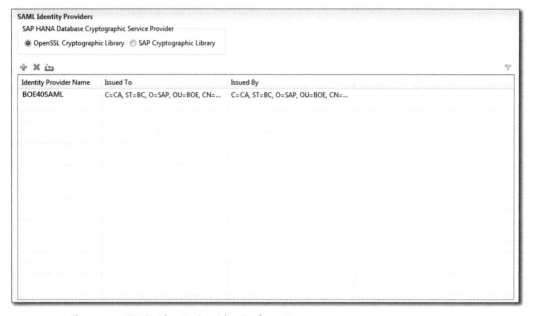

Figure 2.30 SAML Identity Provider Configuration

With these steps in place, a user that has been given an SAML credential in SAP HANA that matches their SAP BusinessObjects BI user name will be able to access SAP HANA data through SAP BusinessObjects BI.

Setting up Kerberos SSO to HANA

Now let's configure the SAP HANA platform for Kerberos authentication of users. This will allow users with Kerberos identities attached to their user accounts to access the SAP HANA system from desktop tools like SAP HANA Studio and SAP Lumira without entering any credentials, as long as they are connecting from their corporate laptops that are members of the same Active Directory domain. The key steps to this implementation are the following:

1. Define a Kerberos service account in Active Directory. The team created a service account named HANAKERB within the ADVENTUREWORKS Windows domain.

2. They assigned the account the following SPNs to mark it as the service account for SAP HANA:

   ▸ hdb/hana.adventureworks.com

   ▸ hanakerb

3. The team created a KeyTab for the account with ktpass:

   ```
   ktpass -out c:\hanakerb.keytab -princ hdb/hana.adventureworks.com
   hanakerb -mapuser hanakerb@ADVENTUREWORKS.COM -pass *** -ptype
   KRB5_NT_PRINCIPAL -crypto RC4-HMAC-NT
   ```

4. They also set up Kerberos configuration files on the SAP HANA server:

   ▸ *Hanakerb.keytab* was copied to */etc/krb5.keytab*

   ▸ The *krb5.ini* from the SAP BusinessObjects BI configuration was reused and copied to */etc/krb5.conf*

5. The SAP HANA database was restarted, and confirmation using a test user account was successful.

With these steps in place, users that have been configured with a Kerberos identity for the mapped domain will be able to access the system by setting up their desktop tools to authenticate with an operating system user instead of entering credentials manually.

We have not configured web-based SSO to the SAP HANA XS application server as part of this implementation. There are further steps required on the SAP HANA platform to enable that additional access. Because we will be accessing the system primarily from SAP BusinessObjects BI web applications, there is no need for this setup. However, if you wanted to implement custom XS applications and provide for SSO via Kerberos, you could complete those remaining steps.

2.5.2 Authorization Plan

With the SAP HANA authentication mechanisms enabled, we can begin configuring the authorization framework necessary to assign users the proper privileges to perform their tasks. We will start this section by following the best practices we outlined in Section 2.1 and configure a package structure to house our authorization roles and content. We will then use the guidelines we presented in Section 2.3 to implement our roles as repository objects to ensure easy transport between environments. Finally, we will create at least one system admin user and disable the SYSTEM account.

Setting Up the SAP HANA Package Hierarchy

The first step in the authorization scheme is creating the package hierarchy to hold all future SAP HANA development artifacts. Although we would normally recommend using your company domain name as the root package in your SAP HANA system, for the purpose of this book, we've named our root package saphana. The steps we follow to configure this package structure are as follows:

1. While logged on as the SYSTEM account, since we are setting up the initial security model, we create a package at the root of the content tree called saphana and set its properties to be a structural package to prevent any content from being created at the root.

2. We configure our SAP HANA Studio environment for SAP HANA development access, as we discussed in Section 2.4.4. This gives us the ability to create local projects and share them to the repository.

3. We create our first project as a new SAP HANA XS project and share it to the repository. We make sure that the project name matches the full path of the package in the repository, which makes it easier to manage object names within the project. This project will house all our security objects and anything else that is intended to be edited only by administrators. The project's name is SAPHANA.CORE.

4. In addition to the core package, we will go ahead and create separate projects for each of the other major subject areas we plan to deploy content to so that we can grant developers the necessary rights to these packages. This results in the following additional packages and accompanying projects:

   ▶ saphana.commonattributes

   ▶ saphana.resellersales

   ▶ saphana.internetsales

   ▶ saphana.finance

   ▶ saphana.corporatemetrics

Setting Up the Base SAP HANA Roles

Next, we will create all the necessary roles as repository objects. We will use the layering concept to build each role on top of lesser roles, limiting the amount of rework when roles need to change and minimizing the verbosity of the role definitions.

At the root of the new project, we create SAP HANA role objects following the guidelines in Section 2.3.4. This produces the following set of roles.

▶ `saphana.core::user`
The base user level that all users will be granted, allowing them to query modeled information views

▶ `saphana.core::developer`
The base developer role that developers will have in QA and Production

▶ `saphana.core.dev::developer`
The role that developers will have in the Development landscape allowing creation of new content

▶ `saphana.core::security_admin`
The base role that security administrators will have in the QA and Production landscape, allowing them to grant and revoke roles to users and manage user accounts

▶ `saphana.core.dev::security_admin`
The role that security administrators will have in the Development landscape allowing them to create new roles or edit existing ones

▶ `saphana.core::system_admin`
The role that SAP HANA database administrators will have in all landscapes allowing them to monitor and manage the database operations

With the base roles created, the rest of the system configuration can be done using regular user accounts created with the new roles. We will later configure automated user provisioning for the bulk of the user population, but for system and security administrators and core development team, it's reasonable to create the users manually.

Using the SYSTEM account, we create user IDs for each of the users and grant them the development versions of the appropriate roles. See Figure 2.31 for an example of the first system administrator user being configured.

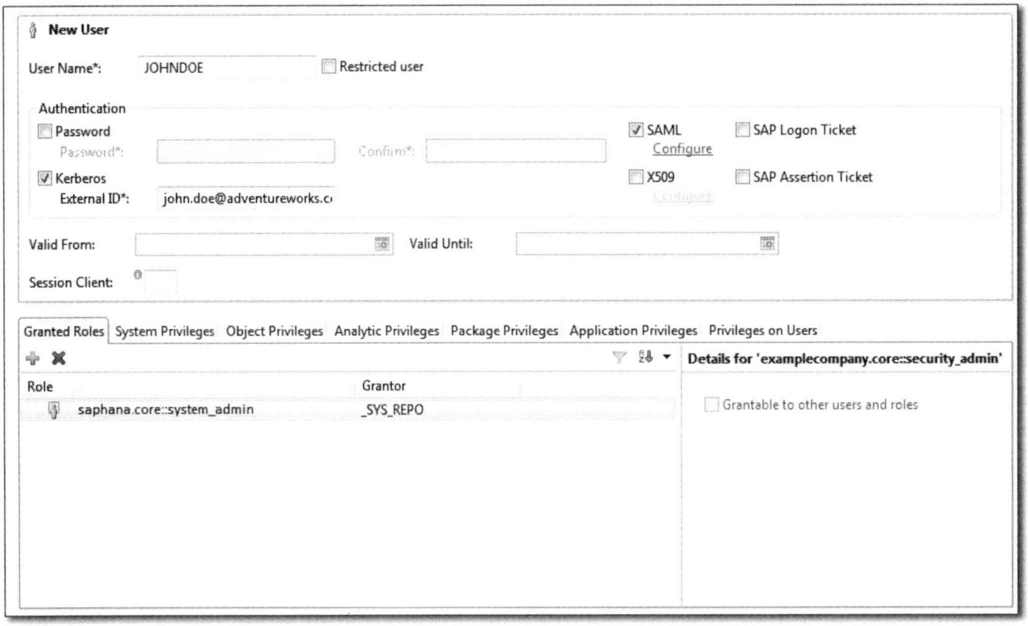

Figure 2.31 System Administrator User Creation

Disabling the SYSTEM Account

With the core SAP HANA admin team now configured, we can disable the SYS-TEM account. This will prevent users from being tempted to log on as the SYSTEM user now that they have properly assigned users for all future tasks. If we later find that there is a task that requires the SYSTEM account's authorizations, the account can be re-enabled by any user who has the USER ADMIN privilege.

In the production tier, we will turn on auditing to user account activation/deactivation so that we can see if and when someone does enable the SYSTEM account.

Disabling the SYSTEM user is simply a matter of executing an SQL statement as follows:

```
ALTER USER 'SYSTEM' DEACTIVATE;
```

2.5.3   User Provisioning Plan

With a large rollout of a reporting solution, it is unreasonable to expect the security administration team to manually provision each and every user and keep up to date with all the new hires and terminations. This process needs to be automated. We have already determined that Active Directory will be the system of record that drives user accounts for our system. This means any solution we devise will need to be able to communicate with both SAP HANA and Active Directory.

In addition to the Active Directory system, which can tell us about users and the business groups they've been assigned to, we need some extra information that will tell us how to map Active Directory group memberships to SAP HANA role assignments. This information can be easily stored in an SAP HANA table and updated by the security team when they create or alter roles in the SAP HANA platform. Therefore, we will create a table called SEC_AD_ROLE_MAPPING. The table will have only two columns: one for Active Directory group names and one for SAP HANA role names. In Figure 2.32, we show an example of what the data in the SEC_AD_ROLE_MAPPING table looks like.

	HANAROLE	ADGROUP
1	saphana.core::system_admin	CN=system_admins, OU=boe2hana, DC=adventureworks, DC=com
2	saphana.core::security_admin	CN=security_admins, OU=boe2hana, DC=adventureworks, DC=com
3	saphana.core::developer	CN=developers, OU=boe2hana, DC=adventureworks, DC=com

Figure 2.32 Example Data for SAP HANA to Active Directory Role Mappings

There are many tools we could use to communicate with Active Directory to read lists of users and groups from the system. Active Directory implements the LDAP protocol for querying the directory structure, and many programming languages have libraries for dealing with this protocol.

We also need to have the user accounts synchronized with the Active Directory system on a regular basis; thus, we need a scheduling system that can execute whatever program we decide to implement. We could use CRON on the SAP HANA platform for this, but monitoring the progress of the synchronization program would require logging on to the OS of the SAP HANA box, which is cumbersome and needs to be kept to a small audience.

The SAP BusinessObjects BI platform has a robust scheduling mechanism, and one of its lesser known features is the ability to host Java programs as schedulable objects. The program objects can be secured in a folder in the SAP BusinessObjects BI system so that only appropriate users can access them and view their history or schedule manual runs of the program. The Java programming language also has very robust support for querying and interacting with LDAP, and it can query and interact with our SAP HANA system via JDBC.

Therefore, we will implement our user provisioning automation program as a Java program hosted in SAP BusinessObjects BI. The logic of the program is straightforward and proceeds as follows:

1. Connect to Active Directory and read all the user IDs from a list of provided Active Directory groups.

2. For each user ID, also retrieve its group memberships.

3. Connect to the SAP HANA platform via JDBC as an account with the `security_admin` role.

4. For each user, synchronize their account with the SAP HANA platform, ensuring that a user account exists for each user. This is done with the following `CREATE` statements, which ensure that the user has both a Kerberos and SAML identity.

   ▶ `CREATE USER <USER_NAME> WITH IDENTITY '<USER_NAME>' FOR SAML PROVIDER BOE40SAML;`

   ▶ `ALTER USER <USER_NAME> ADD IDENTITY <USER_NAME>@adventureworks.com FOR KERBEROS;`

5. Using the data in the SEC_AD_ROLE_MAPPING table, ensure that each user has just those roles that are defined by the mappings and their current AD group memberships. This is done with the `GRANT_ACTIVATED_ROLE` and `REVOKE_ACTI-VATED_ROLE` stored procedures

With the program complete and schedules configured in SAP BusinessObjects BI, our end users' accounts will be automatically provisioned with the necessary credentials to achieve end-to-end SSO, and with their identities passed on to the SAP HANA platform, we will be able to enforce row-level security on all content they access.

2.6   Summary

This chapter offered a solid foundation in the technologies and processes needed to configure a new SAP HANA environment for access and development in a combined SAP BusinessObjects BI and SAP HANA landscape. Although this is a complex and involved topic with reliance on many third-party technologies, we hope the introduction here provides enough of a kick start to help you configure your own solutions.

With the latest versions of SAP BusinessObjects BI and SAP HANA, you can achieve an end-to-end security solution that offers SSO and row-level security on all analytic content. This combination makes for a powerful analytics development platform that is robust and manageable.

The important takeaway from this chapter should be the need to plan your security implementation carefully. It's a complex process with a number of moving pieces. It's likely an implementation that will involve collaboration among team members from multiple areas of IT, such as the Active Directory administrator, SAP HANA administrators, SAP BusinessObjects BI administrators, and network administrators, to get all of the systems talking to each other successfully.

This chapter helps you understand how data is stored most effectively in memory so you can get the best results in both compression and performance.

3 Data Storage in SAP HANA

In this chapter, we'll go into great detail on how data is stored in SAP HANA. Understanding data storage in SAP HANA is an important foundation because data storage differs from traditional database management systems in a number of ways. First, we'll start with on overview of data storage in SAP HANA to highlight these differences, and then we'll move into all of the components that make this possible (Section 3.1 and Section 3.2, respectively). We'll then discuss physical data modeling for SAP HANA in Section 3.3 to draw clear differences between traditional database systems and techniques and tools that are available in SAP HANA, and why it makes sense to actually think backward about a data model in certain cases. This chapter ends in Section 3.4 with a case study for data modeling using our sample organization, AdventureWorks Cycle Company.

3.1 OLAP and OLTP Data Storage

Storing data in SAP HANA is quite different from doing so in a traditional disk-based database. The first and most obvious point is that SAP HANA is a *relational database management system* (RDBMS), where data is stored entirely in memory, instead of relational data being stored entirely on spinning disks.

Storing data entirely in memory was once a revolutionary concept that first had its detractors making statements such as, "Data for an entire application or data warehouse structure would never all fit into memory." In fact, it was such an unconventional idea that it took some time to gain ground. However, many leading vendors now have in-memory solutions and are touting both the in-memory platform and stance for the same reason SAP sought to use this strategy in the first place—unbelievable performance. Data loaded into SAP HANA and consumed by external applications performs at an unbelievable speed—almost as if the data were staged for a demonstration. The response times are simply too fast.

SAP HANA Real-World Performance: Exhibit A

In our lab at Decision First Technologies, we took data from a customer paired with the SQL produced by an SAP BusinessObjects Web Intelligence report and placed the supporting data in SAP HANA. We then took the underlying query provided by the Web Intelligence report and ran it at the command line against the SQL Server database. The original SQL Server–based query runtime? More than an hour. The query was tuned, and the data was optimized in the SQL Server database, but the query was, frankly, quite complex, and the data volume was large. The report was critical to the customer's business, so more than an hour of runtime was simply too long to wait for the data.

As a proof of concept, we moved the data to SAP HANA for the customer, used the same exact SQL from the Web Intelligence report. We did not tune the database tables or structures for SAP HANA; we merely ported the data from SQL Server to SAP HANA. We did not tune the query. This was simply a copy-and-paste exercise. The new SAP HANA query runtime? Four seconds.

Although we did absolutely nothing to the data or the report, the runtime was immediate. Needless to say, this was a compelling story for the customer, even before we invoked the modeling techniques that exploit the storage and engine processes in SAP HANA (we'll discuss these later in this chapter).

The example in the preceding box is a real-world result that this particular customer would benefit from immediately just by porting its data to SAP HANA. These are the incredible performance benefits of in-memory computing that SAP has not been shy about touting—and rightfully so.

However, as with any great software platform, a developer must consider the needs of the platform and embrace techniques that envelop all of its strengths. This is where a gap has existed in the discussion of SAP HANA. SAP HANA simply performs so well that it allows some sloppiness in the design and still performs at an incredible pace. We believe that you can avoid this sloppiness by merely taking a step back and catering the pillars of the development effort to the needs and special characteristics native to the SAP HANA platform. As you weigh design considerations at the onset of the project, begin by considering how you want to store the data in the architecture that is unique to SAP HANA. In this section, we'll prepare you for these considerations by introducing you to the *spinning disk* problem, and then talk about how this problem can be combated with some of the unique features that SAP HANA brings to the development effort.

3.1.1   The Spinning Disk Problem

Spinning disks have been a performance bottleneck ever since they were introduced. The closer the disk is to the CPU, the faster data is rendered, searched, sorted, and processed; in SAP HANA, you take the physically spinning disk completely out of the equation to fully maximize this realization. Take, for instance, the process flow of information in a typical system and database:

1. Data is collected from an application via user input from a screen or form.

2. Data is passed to the database in a process known as an input/output (or I/O) transfer of information.

3. Data may be written to or read from a cache in memory on the database server.

4. Data is finally stored on a spinning disk.

I/O transfers performed without the use of a cache can take much longer to process. Factors that contribute to extra time include physical disk platter spinning rates, time needed to move mechanical components of the drive heads to read the disk platter, and numerous other factors that are inherent to this disk-based process and that add additional latency. This is a rather archaic process that hasn't changed greatly since the onset of computing. Conventional database systems try to improve on this by targeting specific systems that provide disk caching controllers.

Caching data is a method used to speed up this process of data access from a spinning disk, and all of the major database vendors work closely with the disk manufacturers to tune the needs and specific requirements of the database I/O processing needs. In most cases, the database vendors seek to exploit caching techniques to limit that final disk interaction as much as possible. This is simply to avoid the native issues present with disk seek and write times by using the various optimizations of the caching controllers. This is all an effort to work around the slowness of the disk, whose performance can be maximized only so far.

3.1.2   Combating the Problem

Many technologies that we rely on today were invented to work around the inherent slowness caused by the disk. Take, for instance, *online analytical processing* (OLAP) technologies (which enable faster read performance by physically restructuring the data), *online transaction processing* (OLTP) technologies (whose goal is to make writing data to disk as fast as possible), or, finally, column storage technologies (whose goal is compression to both minimize storage and increase the speed of access to the data). The important thing to keep in mind is that all of these technologies, at their core, were designed around the spinning disk and its native challenges. We'll introduce each of these technologies briefly and then talk about how they all fit into SAP HANA.

OLTP Storage Methods

An OLTP, or relational database, stores data in a normalized fashion at its core. Data is normalized to reduce redundant data and data storage patterns to optimize precious disk space and make the writing of that data to disk as fast as possible. Without techniques to minimize the storage factor, relational databases, by nature, use lots of space to store these redundant values. Consider Figure 3.1, which shows a typical normalized RDBMS table structure that's been designed to reduce redundant data storage.

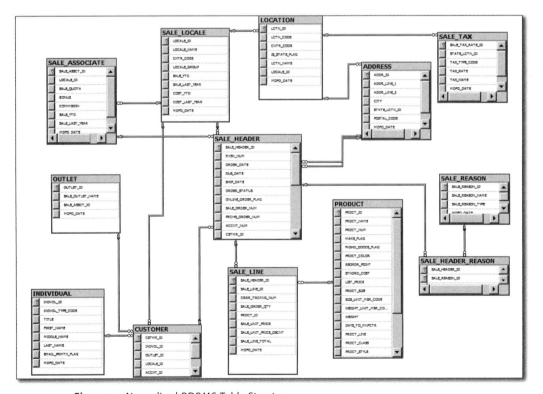

Figure 3.1 Normalized RDBMS Table Structure

Data is normalized or reduced into multiple tables so that repeating values are removed into multiple tables to store repeating values once and contain a pointer to those repeating values. For example, in Figure 3.1, SALE_HEADER records are normalized into their own table instead of just storing the columns into the SALE_HEADER table. This concept is the pinnacle of an OLTP system. This is simply the design principal on which OLTP systems are based.

There is nothing wrong with this design for inserting or storing data in *conventional* RDBMS systems. In fact, for this purpose, it's quite good. (There is a reason this methodology is the way the world stores its data!) However, there is one fundamental problem with this system: getting data out.

Retrieving data from an OLTP system requires multiple joins and combinations of various related tables. This is expensive in terms of processing in these database designs. Often, reporting in these systems is certainly an afterthought. It is problems like this one—combined with the slowness and natural speed impediment—that many technologies evolve to solve. Techniques such as OLAP technologies were invented to solve this problem.

OLAP Storage Methods

OLAP data storage methods were conceived to combat slowness caused by both data access to disk and the way that data was stored in conventional relational databases, as just described. Technologies such as OLAP data storage physically store the data in a different way because traversing a relational database on disk isn't exactly the fastest solution for reading or retrieving data. Figure 3.2 shows this alternative data storage in an OLAP database, in a typical *star schema* (named so because of the shape the related tables resemble).

In an OLAP database, data is organized into concepts called *facts* and *dimensions*. The facts and dimensions are just standard tables, but their names denote what they store. Facts are the heart of the star schema or dimensional data model. For example, FACT_SALE is the fact table in Figure 3.2. Fact tables store all of the measures or values that will be used as metrics to measure or describe facts about a business concept. Fact tables may also contain foreign keys to the date dimension tables to allow pivoting or complex date metrics. Fact tables will be arranged with differing granularities. Fact tables could have a high granularity and be at an aggregate level, aggregating measures by calendar week or a product line, for instance, or a fact table could be at the lowest level of granularity: a transaction line from a source system or combined source systems. Fact tables also contain foreign keys that refer back to dimension tables by the primary key of the dimension table. A fact is the "many" side of the relationship.

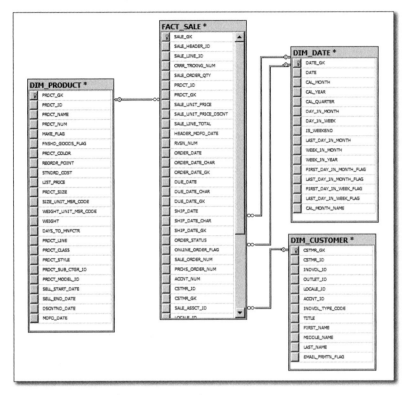

Figure 3.2 Data Stored in an OLAP Database

Dimension tables are the ancillary tables prefixed with "DIM_" in Figure 3.2. Dimension tables are somewhat the opposite of fact tables because dimensions contain descriptions of the measures in the form of accompanying text to describe the data set for analysis by labeling the data, or the dimensions are often used to query or filter the data quickly. In Figure 3.2, the DIM_CUSTOMER table provides details about customer data or attributes and is used to filter and query sales from the prospect of customer data. The same can be said for DIM_PRODUCT.

This is a dramatic solution because an entirely different table structure had to be established and created. If the modeling task symbolized in Figure 3.2 isn't enough, another element adds to the complexity: a batch-based process is created out of necessity.

A batch-based process is needed to both load and transform the data from the OLTP normalized data structure into the denormalized OLAP structure needed for fast querying. That batch process is typically called *extract, transform, and load* (ETL). An ETL process physically transforms the data to conform to this OLAP storage method.

Typical ETL Process Workflow
1. After data is extracted from one or multiple source systems, the data loads to a staging database, where multiple transformations occur.
2. Staging is a key layer where the data loses the mark of the source system and is standardized into business concepts.
3. Data is loaded into the data warehouse tables and finalized into an OLAP structure to allow for both high-performing reads and flexibility in analytical methods and ad hoc data access.

SAP's solution for ETL data integration is SAP Data Services. SAP Data Services is a fully functional ETL and data quality solution that makes building very complex processes relatively straightforward. SAP Data Services is used to extract and transform data through complex transforms with many powerful, built-in functions. Because it's the primary means to provision non-SAP data into SAP HANA, SAP Data Services plays a pivotal role in setting up data models and data storage the right way for maximum performance in SAP HANA. We'll discuss this tool's capabilities at length later in this book.

OLAP data structures like those shown in Figure 3.2 are the focus and primary use case of ad hoc analytical tools such as SAP BusinessObjects BI. The OLAP or star schema structure allows the tool to be quite flexible with the data in terms of drilling if hierarchies exist in the data or if you are using a date dimension (in the preceding example, this is DIM_DATE) to not only search and sort but also effortlessly provide running calculations or more complex, date-based aggregations. Analytic activities like these would be quite difficult to address in a fully normalized OLTP system. Certainly, this data storage and system design eases the burden placed by the slowness of the platform, as well as adding nice features for analytics.

Columnar Data Storage Technologies

One final data storage technology, and the one most relevant to SAP HANA, is the *columnar database architecture*. Columnar databases also take on the problem of working around the slowness of the disk by changing the way that data is stored on the disk. We'll walk through the SAP HANA specifics later in this chapter, but it's important to have a basic understanding of columnar architectures now.

Columnar databases have been around for quite some time, and the concept was certainly not invented with SAP HANA. Rather, this was a design methodology that was integrated into SAP HANA for the unique features and data storage aspects that a columnar database brings to the data storage equation. Columnar databases still use tables to store data as logical components, but the way that the data is laid out on the disk differs considerably from standard, row-store tables. Data values are gathered and stored in columns instead of rows. A very simple example is a product table with colors and product descriptions. In Figure 3.3, the data is stored in rows as it's represented in the logical tables in the database.

```
1, Dinner Plate , Blue  , SK001
2, Saucer       , White , SK002
3, Dinner Plate , White , SK003
4, Dinner Plate , Red   , SK004
```

Figure 3.3 Data Storage in Rows in a Table

Data is organized into rows in the physical storage of the data on disk. This is a great design for OLTP systems and is the standard for most of the world's data. So, data in a column-store table would be arranged quite differently on the disk. Data is arranged by the columns of the data in Figure 3.4.

```
1,2,3,4;
Dinner Plate, Saucer;
Blue, White, Red;
SK001, SK002, SK003, SK004;
```

Figure 3.4 Data Stored as Columns in a Column-Store Table

Notice that the repeating values are stored only once, to minimize the physical footprint of the data on the disk.

> **Note**
>
> Column-store tables can still be relational tables and data. The difference lies in the way the data is arranged on the disk.

Columnar databases have traditionally been used for OLAP applications, wherein reads are very important because data can be read much more efficiently from this type of storage structure. Data is read and presented quickly to a consuming application or report. Other challenges can arise when you insert data into disk-based column-store tables. For example, UPDATE operations are quite expensive for column-store data structures compared to their row-store cousins.

> **Inserts in Disk-Based Column-Store Tables**
>
> In our lab at Decision First Technologies, we recently ported data for a data warehouse OLAP structure from SQL Server to SAP (Sybase) IQ to take advantage of the superior compression and read technology available in columnar SAP (Sybase) IQ tables. However, we did notice some considerations that should be made in this port. These considerations are somewhat alleviated by the in-memory storage in SAP HANA, but they are still worth considering because they are in the domain of a column-based database:
>
> ► SELECT statements or reads are much faster than with a conventional row-based database. The data then loads to a staging database, where multiple transformations occur.
>
> ► Using BULK INSERT uploading data is considerably faster and should be used whenever possible, especially with large record sets.
>
> ► UPDATES or MERGE target operations are considerably slower than a conventional row-based database.
>
> ► DELETE inserts are faster when updates are needed.
>
> The main takeaway is that SELECT SQL statements or reading data for operations such as a report do not need to be altered too much, but the ETL process will most likely require INSERTS, UPDATES, and DELETES to be altered, especially for delta or change-based loads.

For reasons like these, porting an existing structure to a columnar form—while not an insurmountable task—certainly has more considerations than simply moving the data over to a different platform. As mentioned, SAP HANA mitigates some of these issues because in memory storage is so much faster. In a sense, SAP HANA masks some of these issues, but you should still consider them when you're porting very large existing data warehouse structures that require some type of ETL process with, most often, non-SAP data.

Solutions Used by SAP HANA

We've discussed OLTP, OLAP, and columnar data storage methods and the reasons they were introduced, and SAP HANA is unique in the sense that it can be a bit of a chameleon. SAP HANA can act as any of these platforms by first physically storing data in both row and column fashions; however, even more than that, it can also act as an OLAP structure and even process data by interpreting multidimensional expressions (MDX query language). It also has a common and conventional SQL interface.

In essence, SAP takes advantage of the best of all of these platforms natively. This adaptable nature has been great for SAP because it allows SAP HANA to quickly and seamlessly be addressed under many conventional applications. If a multidimensional, cube-based application, such as SAP BW or SAP Business Planning and Consolidation (SAP BPC), needs MDX to interface data, then no problem. SAP HANA has an interface layer to behave just like a cube to the application. Most applications interact with a database via SQL, and SAP HANA is just as comfortable interfacing as SQL.

It's important to note that most of these technologies were invented to combat the slowness of disk-based data access. But SAP HANA is different. Even though it can masquerade as any of these technologies, it's taking on the performance problems directly. Instead of working around the issues of the platform, SAP HANA simply changes the platform altogether. It skips the disk, and data is stored directly in memory close to the CPU, where it performs better. That SAP HANA works natively as any of these technologies is merely a product-related strategy to foster adoption of SAP HANA as a platform capable of replacing existing, underlying database technologies while offering developers new and exciting ways to both access and model data. We'll cover both accessing and modeling data in later chapters of this book.

SAP HANA goes even further in rethinking the developer's platform by moving the various data processing layers in an application so that a developer must re-envision what he or she is trying to achieve. It's truly a revolutionary platform.

3.2 Data Storage Components

To begin using SAP HANA, you must first load or provision your data into SAP HANA, but to do this, you need a *persistent layer of data storage*. This persistent layer (also known as a persistent model) is made up of basic data storage and organizational components that are actually quite common concepts to database-savvy professionals. The first two organizational components are schemas and users. From there, the components start to diverge and take on a much more SAP HANA–specific dialect: *row-store tables* and *column-store tables*.

Let's wade further into the organizational components mentioned above: schemas and users, column-store tables, and row-store tables. We'll conclude our discussion with a comparison of use cases for row- and column-store tables. All of the storage components mentioned in this chapter are found in SAP HANA Studio under the ADMINISTRATION CONSOLE and MODELER perspectives.

3.2.1 Schemas and Users

Recall that SAP HANA has many conventional components that make database administrators and database developers quickly feel at home. These are mostly organizational components that facilitate administrative tasks. At a very high level, a *user* is used to connect to and authenticate SAP HANA, and a *schema* is used to group and classify various database objects, such as tables or views. Because these aren't new concepts for SAP HANA, we will assume basic knowledge of what they mean, and will instead focus our discussion on what is required to provide a foundation for further discussion of SAP HANA–specific topics and for building the physical database-level objects for the case study examples.

Schemas

Schemas are similar to concepts that exist in other conventional database platforms. Most database platforms use schemas as a subdividing tool, and SAP HANA is no exception. In SAP HANA, schemas are used to divide the larger database installation into multiple sub-databases to organize the database objects into logical groupings. You use schemas to logically group objects such as tables, views, and stored procedures. A schema in SAP HANA is essentially a database within the larger database or catalog. (We'll go into specific details about how to create a schema in Section 3.4.1, as part of the case study for this chapter.)

Figure 3.5 shows the BOOK_USER schema in SAP HANA, from which all of the case study examples in this book will be crafted. The BOOK_USER schema is the only *user-defined* schema that is visible. The rest of the schemas visible in the figure— SYS, _SYS_BI, _SYS_BIC, and _SYS_REPO—are all default *system-generated* schemas.

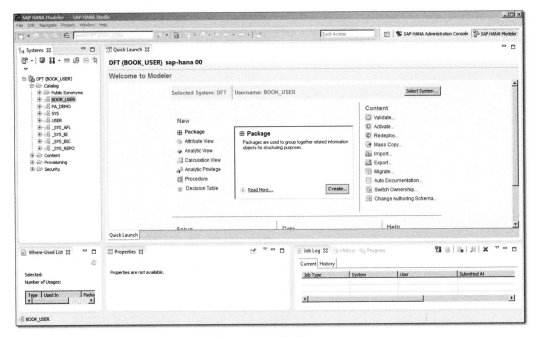

Figure 3.5 The BOOK_USER Schema in SAP HANA

Users and User Authentication

SAP HANA users are no different from users in any other conventional database in the sense that, if you want to work in SAP HANA, you must have a user name to log on to the system. After logging on to SAP HANA, your user must have privileges to perform certain tasks. Much like schemas, users feel quite standard in concept to most savvy database administrators.

SAP HANA also supports the concept of a *role*, which is a superset of privileges. Roles are granted to database users and inherit the privileges assigned to the role the user belongs to.

When SAP HANA is installed, a database user called SYSTEM is created as the default admin user. This user has superior system-level privileges to create users, access system tables, and so on. As a best practice, you should not use the system user for normal administration activities or assign roles to this user. Use the SYSTEM user to create database users with roles with the minimum set of responsibilities to perform the user's duties.

Operating System Administrator User

Aside from the SYSTEM database user, it's also important to note that an operating system administrator user (<sid>adm) is also created on the SAP HANA system upon installation. This user exists to provide a context or linkage to the base operating system in SAP HANA.

This user has unlimited access to all local system resources and owns all SAP HANA files and all operating system processes. Within SAP HANA Studio, this user's credentials are required to perform advanced operations, such as stopping or starting a database process or executing a recovery. This isn't to be confused with a database user because the <sid>adm user is concerned with the operating system on only the SAP HANA machine.

Users in SAP HANA exist only as database users to map to the privileges discussed earlier, and for internal authentication, this is the only means available.

Additional References

For additional information about user authorizations, roles, and best practices on SAP HANA security, please consult Chapter 2 and Chapter 11 of this book.

3.2.2 Column-Store Tables

Because SAP HANA is optimized, or tuned, for storing data in columns over storing data in rows, you should use *column-store tables* whenever possible. Reading data is much faster in column-based tables; from a data storage perspective, columnar storage and compression are two of SAP HANA's best offerings. In a column-store table, data simply compresses at higher rates.

As discussed earlier in this chapter, columnar storage allows repeating values to be expressed only once in storage, which allows the physical storage required to compress. In SAP HANA, this compression is due to run-length encoding or the storage of sorted data where there is a high probability of two or more values being stored contiguously or in the same spatial locale. Run-length encoding counts the repeating values as the same value, which is achieved by storing the original column as a two-column list.

This sophisticated system of reducing redundancy is an important concept of column-based storage for financial reasons. SAP HANA is licensed and priced by memory blocks, so the more memory you need to store your data, the more expensive your SAP HANA solution will be. However, pricing and cost are only one side of the equation.

Compression is also an important aspect of high-performing queries in SAP HANA. When data is compressed, it can be loaded into the CPU cache faster. The limiting factor is the distance between memory and the CPU cache, and this performance gain will exceed the additional computing needed to decompress the data. One factor that enables compression is run-length encoding, which stores values as a two-column list, while repeated values are stored only once in one column, with another column as an index or pointer to the repetitious storage. One would think this would cause a latency in performance, but the two-column list's equality check on the index column is based on a higher-performing integer value for the equality comparison—which is why proper compression can speed up aggregate operations or table scans considerably. These are the operations that stand to benefit the most from compressed data in SAP HANA.

It's easy to create a table as a column-store table in SAP HANA. To create a column-store table, just use the Administration Console perspective in SAP HANA Studio (as shown in Figure 3.6), and select Column Store under the Type menu. Now, you have a column-store table that is ready for use!

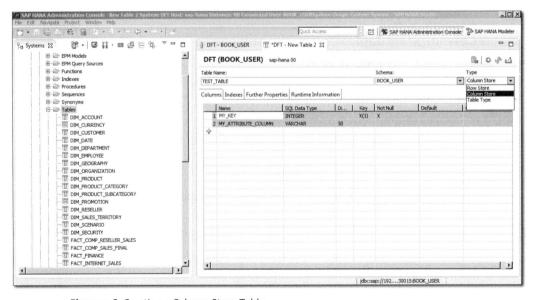

Figure 3.6 Creating a Column-Store Table

When you're deciding between a row- and column-store table, consider how the data is going to be used. For example, column-store tables are a good choice because some features, such as partitioning, are available to only column-based tables. So if partitioning is required in your application, your decision of whether to use column- or row-based tables has already been made.

You should also weigh column-based storage in terms of updates and inserts. Bulk updates, or bulk operations in general, perform well against large tables with column storage. Column-store tables are great choices for large tables with lots of read-based operations or SELECT statements—especially when you're performing aggregate operations. A number of aggregate functions exist natively in the column engine. Consider the list of SAP HANA functions that are available as native column functions by using column engine expressions as arguments. Thus, columnar tables simply perform better because they're able to use functions built directly into this column engine rather than having to switch the processing and physically move the data to the row engine.

The following functions use column-engine expressions as arguments:

▸ Numeric functions: TO_DECIMAL, TO_NUMBER, TO_BIGINT, TO_REAL, TO_DOUBLE, TO_CHAR, TO_NCHAR, TO_DATE, TO_TIMESTAMP, and BINTOHEX/HEXTOBIN.

▸ String functions: LTRIM, RTRIM, TRIM, LENGTH, SUBSTR, INSTR, and LOWER, UPPER.

▸ Date and time functions: WEEKDAY, DAYS_BETWEEN, SECONDS_BETWEEN, ADD_DAYS, UTCTOLOCAL, LOCALTOUTC, ISOWEEK, and QUARTER.

▸ Mathematical functions: LN, LOG, EXP, POWER, SQRT, SIN, COS, TAN, ASIN, ACOS, ATAN, SINH, COSH, FLOOR, and CEIL.

▸ Logic driving functions: NULLIF, NVL, NVL2, and COALESCE.

▸ Date extract function: EXTRACT (YEAR /MONTH FROM <column engine expression>)*.

Three more specific advantages to column-store tables will never be achieved in row-store tables. The first of these advantages is that columnar storage with proper compression eliminates the need for additional indexing. The columnar scans of the column-store tables, especially for run-length encoded tables, allow very high-performing reads. In most cases, these reads are fast enough that an index, with its additional overhead of metadata in terms of both storage and maintenance, is simply not necessary. It's basically an obsolete concept for a column-store table in many cases. Without having a need to index, not only does SAP

HANA gain storage due to compression, but you also don't need to account for extra storage space or time in terms of jobs and scheduled offline tasks necessary to maintain indexes to speed data retrieval as you would in a conventional database. In a sense, you're actually gaining performance while simplifying the physical model because you don't have to maintain separate index structures.

The second advantage is that the nature of the column-store structure makes parallelization possible; that is, data is already vertically partitioned into columns. With that partitioned structure of divided columns, SAP HANA easily allows parallel operations to be assigned to multiple cores on the CPU. This way, multiple columns can be searched and aggregated at the same time by different cores. The portioning that requires extra thought and maintenance—much like the indexing structures—is both redundant and unnecessary with column-store tables and column-engine processing in SAP HANA.

The final advantage is the elimination of physical aggregate data structures. Traditional BI applications and designs often call for aggregation in the database models at the presentation layer simply to deal with reporting or retrieving data against large and cumbersome record sets. This is often to work around the fact that the platform and disk-based data access bind I/O operations and simply prove negative performance implications when performing complex aggregations or queries across larger data sets. To solve this problem in a traditional RDBMS, data is physically persisted into aggregate tables that roll up the data to a higher level of granularity.

In Figure 3.7, we see an example of an aggregate table where transaction-level sales data has been aggregated to raise the granularity of the data to records totaled by period, year, and product. This table would need to be created for analysis in a traditional RDBMS if the sales transaction table contained lots of history and the analysis was mostly done at the year level of granularity. This would eliminate the performance problem while still addressing the reporting need.

PERIOD	YEAR	PRODUCT	PERIOD_QTY	PERIOD_SOLD...
1	2013	BLUE WAGON	25	250.00
2	2013	RED WAGON	30	300.00
12	2012	RED WAGON	20	200.00
NULL	NULL	NULL	NULL	NULL

Figure 3.7 Example of an Aggregate Table

Deriving this aggregate table is relatively straightforward; it's just a SUM of the quantity and amount column in the transactional source. This means that

```
Select PERIOD, YEAR, PRODUCT, QTY, SOLD_AMT From Table_A
```

would become

```
Select PERIOD, YEAR, PRODUCT, SUM(QTY), SUM(SOLD_AMT)
From Table_A
Group By PERIOD, YEAR, PRODUCT
```

This is a very simple example; the logic from moving from transactional granularity to an aggregate byproduct isn't terribly difficult to derive or design. However, you would need an ETL process to physically transform the structure and move the data over to this new structure. So, even with this one simple example, we've added quite a bit of complexity in terms of more data and more processes to be maintained.

On top of this complexity, this model introduces another problem: inherent latency. The data in the aggregate will never be real time because the aggregate will be handled by either an ETL process (by definition, a batch-based process) or the database layer (which may introduce concurrency issues with updates in terms of locking operations that could potentially block reads during rebuilds). So the important point to take away about a column-store table in SAP HANA operating using column-engine native functions is that *it isn't necessary!*

This layer can be completely removed. SAP HANA can scan the data and perform the simple or complex aggregation at runtime in memory with similar speeds as a conventional architecture performing against aggregates. This is all happening in real time against the base transaction-level data; there is no need to have a latent, batch-based process. When you have this level of performance natively, you simply don't need these additional layers. Because the data has not persisted, storage needs and costs actually diminish with the support of these column-store structures in SAP HANA.

This is a very simple example, but you can see how this might grow as the needs for multiple views of aggregated data produce more duplicated, redundant data with more processes to maintain. By removing these layers, you dramatically simplify the data model, thus simplifying the interaction of querying the data. With this single-layer model, there is no need to hop from reading an aggregate view of the data to reading the base transactional view of the data. You use the same SQL from the clause and base statement and add in function calls when necessary. This type of simplification is a major benefit of using SAP HANA and one of the ways SAP HANA is transforming the data landscape.

3.2.3 Row-Store Tables

Row-store tables are exactly what they sound like; data is stored in memory but in a row fashion. Because these tables, at the base storage level, are very similar to traditional database structures and constructs found in conventional databases, we won't go into the level of detail in this book to discuss row base-level components and data storage methodology as we did with column-store tables.

However, one item to pay particular attention to with row-store tables is that there is virtually no additional compression occurs when using a row-store table. So, what is a proper use case for a row-store table?

Row-store tables were included in the SAP HANA platform to first and foremost offer the ability for SAP HANA to be used as a valid and suitable OLTP platform (i.e., as a basis for SAP Business Suite). A large part of enabling that possibility is that row-store tables and a row engine exist to process row-by-row data access requests.

The backbone of any OLTP system that involves data entry is rapid, row-by-row access to complete or mostly complete records. These aren't cases in which one SQL statement is returning, parsing, and aggregating millions of records on just a few columns. An OLTP design requires one customer record to be looked up and written into the application layer quickly, in real time, while a sales transaction is being established in the system. This response time needs to be instantaneous, and, in most cases, the entire row of the record is needed to satisfy the application.

This type of data access is effectively the complete opposite of the OLAP style of churning through complex data sets to group, sort, and aggregate on just a few columns. Because of needs like this, SAP needed to include both platforms and engines. This inclusion of both sides (both row and column) of the data processing house makes SAP HANA truly unique, and presenting a viable row-store option fosters rapid adoption of SAP HANA as much more than a valid BI- or OLAP-serving platform. By serving the row needs, SAP HANA is the new, remarkable, multifaceted platform built and scaled to handle complex and sizable applications, such as the SAP Business Suite.

In Summary

In short, use a row-store table if you're developing a transactional interactive system, such as a row-based system or an OLTP design. Row-store tables will suit this purpose well. The bottom line is:

▸ If your table will be used mostly for getting data in through a user input–driven design, use a row-store table.

▸ If your table will mostly be used for retrieval or aggregate-based operations, use a column-store table.

It's easy to create a table as a row-store table in SAP HANA Studio. The process is much like the one outlined earlier to create a column-store table. Just use the Administration Console perspective, and select Row Store under the Type menu, as shown in Figure 3.8. After performing this step, you now have a row-store table that is ready to use.

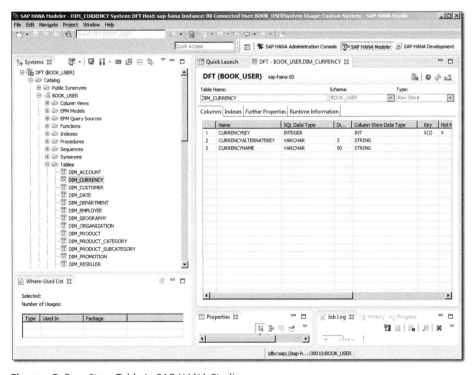

Figure 3.8 Row-Store Table in SAP HANA Studio

3.2.4 Use Cases for Both Row- and Column-Store Tables

Because they are primarily suited for most tasks in SAP HANA, column-store tables are generally the reflexive first choice for an application developer. However, as shown earlier, row stores certainly have their place for developers, as well. Though we've already touched upon some of the reasons for row- vs. column-storage, we'll conclude this section with a succinct list that will help you decide the correct type of table to create.

If you find yourself in the following scenarios, use column-based storage:

- Tables are very large in size, and bulk operations will be used against the data. There are two primary examples that fit this scenario:
  - Data warehouse tables
  - Historical tables with large record sets
- Data is primarily staged for reads or SELECT statements. There are two primary examples that fit this scenario:
  - Data warehouse tables or data mart tables for BI reporting
  - Application-based tables that will serve as the basis for reports or getting data out
- Aggregate functions will be used on a small number of columns with each SELECT or read operation.
- Table will be searched by values in one or a few columns.
- Table will be used to perform operations that require scanning the entire set of data, such as average calculations. Searches like this are quite slow, even with proper indexing in conventional or row-based structures. The columnar constructs of SAP HANA are quite good at this type of analysis.
- High compression can be achieved by large tables that contain columns with few distinct values in relation to the record count.
- Complex aggregations or calculations will be needed often on one or a few columns in the table.

If you find yourself in the following scenarios, use row-based storage:

- Table is relatively small in size or record count, making low compression rates less of an issue.
- Table will be used for returning one record quite often. A classic use case for this is an OLTP application table. This is probably the most important point and will ultimately be the best overall use case.
- Row-store tables in SAP HANA will be the backbone of the OLTP application base.
- Aggregations aren't required.

- ▸ Writing data one record at a time is required.

- ▸ Fast searching isn't required.

When considering these criteria, you'll notice clear patterns that emerge regarding which type of data is best for each storage method. If your application requires record-by-record OLTP-style data interaction, you'll need to use row-based tables. Be cautious with these tables because when they become large, they offer virtually no compression. This will bloat the licensed memory required to store the data. Column-based storage is best used for applications that have many complex read-based or SELECT operations, such as OLAP or data warehousing structures. Column-based table structures compress nicely, and properly modeled physical data structures will take advantage of all of the sophisticated functions that are available only to column-store tables.

3.3   Modeling Tables and Data Marts

When considering modeling data for SAP HANA, we'll limit our discussion to modeling the data needed to fuel and power the column-store tables and engine for maximum performance and processing. To examine row-store data modeling in this book would overlap too much with conventional data modeling books because modeling data in a row-store table follows a conventional normalized playbook. The column-store tables and the compression that is offered in the SAP HANA platform are what expand this playbook into something that exists outside of the conventional normalized data constructs.

The SAP HANA data modeling playbook offers ideas that initially seem contrary to conventional data logic and wisdom. However, this is with good reason. It's only when considering the SAP HANA platform and storage paradigm, as discussed in detail earlier in this chapter (Section 3.2.2), that these ideas begin to converge, resonate, and ultimately become conventional.

In this section, we'll review the modeling of tables and data marts that take advantage of SAP HANA-specific functionality that ultimately prepares SAP HANA for any type of data consumption. We'll start with modeling for a traditional OLAP approach and then see how this evolves for SAP HANA. We'll then move on to a discussion of how to denormalize data, which is an especially important part of the data modeling process for SAP HANA.

3.3.1 Legacy Relational OLAP Modeling

To compare and contrast data modeling techniques for SAP HANA, it's valuable to start with a basic understanding of legacy relational data modeling techniques. Legacy relational OLAP modeling is when data is arranged into a series of tables of both facts and dimensions for performance for reporting, as well as to organize data effectively into data marts. A *data mart* is a collection of one or more relational OLAP fact tables and dimensions that are unified in purpose. For this chapter, we'll use two example data marts: the first for sales data and the second for financial data.

Both structures are simplistic in nature; it's plain to see that the focal point of the design resides around speed of access to the data. The fact table in each case contains fields that are used for measuring data. Usually amounts or counts will be used as attributes in a fact table. The other fields present in a fact table will be foreign key fields related to a primary key field in a dimension.

This series of one-to-many relationships of dimensions to facts gives expansive querying abilities to the dimensions that will, in many cases, search, sort, and pivot the data effectively. The dimensions are used to describe the facts and grant a means for actively querying the facts.

It's important to remember that all of these tables are just regular database tables. Fact tables will always be the heart of the dimensional data model. Dimensions can also be conformed or shared across multiple fact tables or data marts. Conforming dimensions, which is the overlap of tables, is a common practice in relational OLAP data models. Dimensions are usually conformed because there is no need to store the table more than once; they will be used across data marts. These conformed dimensions are logically represented in a logical data model of each mart, but the data is physically persisted in only one table to reduce storage.

Figure 3.9 shows an example of a financial data mart. In this mart, you have ACCOUNT, DATE (TIME), DEPARTMENT, SCENARIO, and some type of ORGANIZATION structure dimensions—all relating to a simple fact table containing the AMOUNT values. The data is modeled into these tables because these subjects of data are commonly used concepts for financial applications. The DATE dimension allows for flexible time-based reporting, and this dimension will be conformed across the next data mart shown in Figure 3.10: the sales data mart.

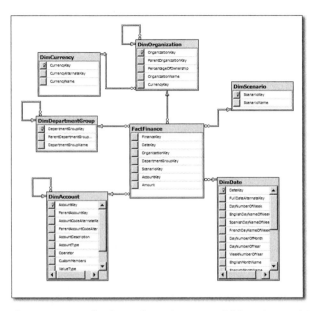

Figure 3.9 Typical Relational OLAP Data Model for a Financial Data Mart

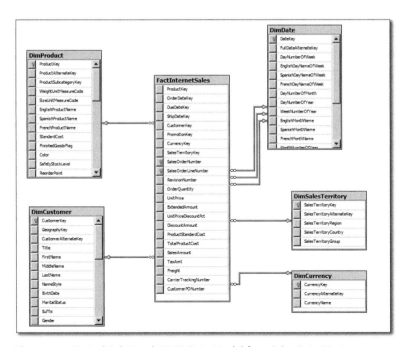

Figure 3.10 Typical Relational OLAP Data Model for a Sales Data Mart

In a typical sales data mart, you have dimensions such as PRODUCT, DATE (TIME), CUSTOMER, CURRENCY, and some type of ORGANIZATION (TERRITORY in this case)—all relating to a simple fact table containing the AMOUNT values. The DATE dimension is used for the same flexible time reporting principles outlined in the financial data mart, but all of the other dimensions represent subjects that are needed for sales analysis and reporting.

Notice that the DATE dimension and the CURRENCY dimension are repeated or shared across the two data marts. Physically, at the database level, the tables aren't repeated; there is only one DIM_CURRENCY table and one DIM_DATE table, so it's merely a logical repetition for organizational purposes. This repetition is a perfect example of a conformed dimension. We'll use conformed dimensions while building out the examples in the case study in this chapter (Section 3.4) to save on table space for the data marts in SAP HANA.

> **Note**
>
> Data marts can contain more than one fact table, but for the sake of simplicity and clear explanation of concepts in SAP HANA, we'll keep the dimensional model relatively simple.

Recall that data marts are segregated in terms of the data that they measure and describe. Considering Figure 3.9 and Figure 3.10, it's easy to see why there are two different data marts. There is little similarity with respect to the fact tables between these two data marts. The finance data mart simply has one amount field and all of the dimensional foreign keys. This allows quick pivoting and aggregations of the amount data by any of the dimensions. The sales data mart contains more complex facts because there are many more facets of a sale to measure, but the important point to note is that all sales measures are centrally located in the fact table so that all of the dimensional pivoting, querying, and sorting is done effortlessly across any or all of the dimensions. This is the primary concept that is central to a relational OLAP model.

The other concept central to a data mart is the grain of the data that is stored in the fact table or tables that make up the data mart. The grain of the data—sometimes known as the granularity of the data mart—is specific to the logical key structure of the fact table. The logical key structure is the single attribute (or combination of attributes) that makes the row of data in the fact unique.

Take, for example, the sales data mart in Figure 3.10. The FactInternetSales table has two primary key columns that make a composite key or a combined logical key: SalesOrderNumber and SalesOrderLineNumber. Data in this example is stored at the line level of the transaction; this is the lowest level of granularity, as this is at the line item of the sale. However, data is often repeated and stored in other fact tables at a higher level of granularity, such as by calendar week or product. This pre-aggregation, or materialized aggregation, is often necessary as a performance boost or method to realize a performance gain when the database platform runs out of tuning capabilities.

In this example, the fact table is at the line level, although it also contains header information in a denormalized fashion. *Denormalizing data* is merely the process of optimizing the data for reads by grouping redundant attributes together into one structure, rather than splitting the redundant attributes into multiple normalized tables. In an OLTP-normalized model, both the header-level data and the line-level data would be in two separate tables. Denormalizing occurs to ensure that one read from the FactInternetSales table obtains the necessary data, rather than reading two tables and reconstructing the data logically in the database engine with a join. This principle of denormalizing is crucial to optimizing performance in an OLAP model.

SAP HANA takes this principle of denormalizing data further to a level that at first seems contrary to performance and storage considerations; however, upon closer inspection, we find that, in many cases, denormalized data performs much faster in a column column-store table in SAP HANA using native column column-store functions than a normalized table structure in SAP HANA. In a normalized design, in many cases, SAP HANA may need to use the slower row engine to join the data. So even though this may seem counterintuitive at first, it's a core principle that will make an already fast SAP HANA system even faster!

Key Points about Data Marts

▸ Fact tables are the central element, or heart, of the data mart.

▸ Fact tables are surrounded by dimension tables.

▸ Fact tables contain only the measures and foreign keys back to the dimension tables.

▸ Dimension tables describe the facts.

▸ Denormalizing data or materializing aggregated data are techniques that are often used to boost performance when performance gains are no longer available from the database platform.

3.3.2 SAP HANA Relational OLAP Modeling

Many of the concepts and even physical structures translate over to SAP HANA directly from the conventional legacy OLAP counterparts. However, some distinctions specific to SAP HANA emerge. Let's now explore these distinctions in detail; these will drive the focus and the discussion to draw attention to the techniques to exploit SAP HANA for maximum performance benefit.

The baseline for relational OLAP modeling in SAP HANA is exactly what we've just described. It is best practice to lay out a solid relational OLAP model as a starting point for running BI operations against SAP HANA, but then a major deviation occurs: *further denormalizing*.

In SAP HANA, joins are sometimes more costly than one read against a compressed column-store data set containing the columns needed for any and all aggregate operations. Because SAP HANA has some pretty sophisticated built-in functions available in the column engine, we recommend that you flatten, or denormalize, dimensional columns into the facts so that you have data between two tables with high cardinality, or a high degree of uniqueness within the column. This way, there is one read against the table that is used to get all the data you need. (We'll go into further detail around denormalizing techniques in Section 3.3.3.)

It's true that SAP HANA can render hierarchies against denormalized or flattened data natively, but to maximize reusability in the SAP HANA analytic model, we still recommend that you keep the core attributes of a dimension in a true dimensional structure residing in a separate table. This way, if attributes from one dimension are all that is needed—for an attribute view, for example—then there is less work needed if a change needs to occur in the base table's columns. This allows for greater reusability when the base data is distributed in a more standard fashion.

Another technique that works well in an SAP HANA relational OLAP data model is adding aggregate columns directly into the fact tables rather than only storing the components of aggregations. For example, if you often multiply quantity by price to store an extended price in a fact table, consider storing the extended price as a calculation. The calculation will happen just as fast as if you stored the calculated value in a separate column. Storing the calculation is also always faster than reassembling the calculation at runtime in either the column or row engine. The final benefit of not storing the calculated data is that there is no redundant data occupying valuable space in memory in the SAP HANA database.

Of course, keep in mind that after you have calculated columns stored in SAP HANA tables, you'll need to explicitly state the columns when you need to insert data to avoid inadvertently setting the calculated columns by mistake.

Table 3.1 shows a scenario in which you have a simple example of a conventional query and table storage structure that stores the components of quantity and price as a stored, calculated value in the faster query block. This is unnecessary with SAP HANA because the calculation can be stored instead of a value that needs updates. This speeds the query because the calculation happens in real time and is always updated.

Scenario	SQL Needed
Conventional	select * from my_table where quantity * price = 100;
Faster query	select * from my_table where extended price = 100;
Supporting DDL for calculated extended_price column	alter table fact_sale add (extended_price decimal(10,2) GENERATED ALWAYS AS quantity * price);

Table 3.1 Calculated Column for a Faster Query

Paying attention to dates and time is also important for dimensional modeling in SAP HANA. For a best practice much like the denormalizing examples listed earlier, keep a date or time dimension separated from your facts for drilling or range-based date manipulation, just as with a standard dimensional model. However, SAP HANA offers built-in time dimension tables, as shown in Table 3.2.

SAP HANA Generated Time Dimension Table	Description
_SYS_BI.M_TIME_DIMENSION_YEAR	Time series with a year focus
_SYS_BI.M_TIME_DIMENSION_MONTH	Time series with a month focus
_SYS_BI.M_TIME_DIMENSION_WEEK	Time series with a week focus
_SYS_BI.M_TIME_DIMENSION	General time series generated data

Table 3.2 SAP HANA–Generated Time Dimension Tables

These tables will be shown in detail later in the analytic modeling sections. To take advantage of this built-in functionality, it's important to note that dates should be stored in your fact tables with sister `varchar(8)` columns in a format of YYYYMMDD. You'll notice in the case study at the end of this chapter that, for each date column listed in the FactInternetSales table, there are both `datefield-nameKEY` columns and `datfieldname_CHAR` columns present. The second column is simply a `varchar(8)` representation of the date, needed to facilitate joins to the `varchar(8)` fields in the M_TIME_DIMENSION tables referenced in Table 3.2. This may or may not be convenient for your data, depending on how your date columns are stored in the source data. This is very convenient for native SAP Business Suite data because this is how this data is stored in SAP. So, you can take advantage of this functionality without modification when you are running SAP Business Suite on SAP HANA, but with non-SAP data, you may very well have to transform the base date values to this `varchar()` format.

As an example value for both types of date fields, `2013-01-01 00:00:00` in your table would also be stored in a `varchar(8)` column (`20130101`) to take advantage of the built-in date and time attribute tables present in SAP HANA. Note that this functionality really serves its best use with SAP-native date formats in SAP sources. For source-agnostic BI, we recommend that you use a custom date dimension table because this adds the most flexibility and deals with dates in all formats.

A final item worth considering when you're constructing your data model in SAP HANA is the fact that you must ensure data type support for all of your aggregate operations. Take a simple example of a numeric column with a data type `Decimal(8,4)` containing a value `1111.1111`. If this number is multiplied by 10, you have a value of `11110.1111`. This value is now out of range in the base column of the SAP HANA table. You must always store your data at the greatest precision required for the max operation that will occur on that data.

This requires some thinking in advance about the types of calculations that will occur on the data you're using, even while choosing data types up front for your tables. Please keep in mind that the maximum declaration that is currently allowed is `Decimal(34,4)`. No matter what you're going to use, if you're sticking with a `DECIMAL` data type, this is the maximum value allowed. A best practice to avoid this behavior is to simply convert all decimal columns to float to handle overflow for division operations ratios; this always avoids overflow issues because SAP HANA doesn't handle the conversion automatically.

Key Points about SAP HANA–Specific Data Marts

▶ As with non–SAP HANA data marts, fact tables are the central element, or heart, of the data mart.

▶ As with non–SAP HANA data marts, fact tables are surrounded by dimension tables.

▶ As with non–SAP HANA data marts, fact tables contain the measures and foreign keys back to the dimension tables, but also specific denormalized attributes where cardinality is high between tables.

▶ SAP HANA data marts also contain a time dimension, but have dates stored both as date values and character data types for use against SAP HANA time dimension tables when SAP application data is primarily used in SAP HANA.

▶ Denormalizing data to extremes that would cripple a conventional database is often the way to get optimal performance in SAP HANA.

▶ Materializing aggregated data is simply not necessary with SAP HANA because performance is considerable in column-store tables and in the column engine.

▶ Numeric types that will be used in aggregate calculations require particular attention. You must cover the size of the resulting value from a calculation in the base numeric column. Remember that `decimal(34,4)` is the maximum allowed decimal type.

3.3.3   Denormalizing Data in SAP HANA

In column-store tables within SAP HANA, denormalized data is something that you should always find in some area of a dimensional data model. Recall our recommendation that you flatten or denormalize dimensional columns into the facts where you have data between two tables that have high cardinality or a high degree of uniqueness within the column. This is because joining data from a dimension with high cardinality is often more costly in terms of performance than just storing the attributes from the dimension that will be used often for querying or aggregations directly into the fact.

Two important principles are addressed by denormalizing data in SAP HANA. First, avoid the join in the engine and (most times) stay entirely in the column engine, where processing is much faster. Second, the penalty for the redundant data, from a storage perspective, isn't too severe because the column-store table stores only the values that repeat once, anyway, due to the nature of compression in the column-store table. Normalization is something that typically occurs in a relational database to increase performance and decrease storage; however, in columnar tables in SAP HANA, this idea is turned on its head because compression helps with both the speed of access and limiting the extra footprint of the data in memory.

Take, for instance, a product dimension and a sales fact table. These tables are often used together in SQL queries for reporting. Maybe you want to filter on attributes such as color, class, or style, or you need to see standard cost as an aggregated value to be used in calculations such as price or sold quantity. These are combinations that will occur quite often in typical sales analysis scenarios. Product data will have a high degree of uniqueness or cardinality, as well, because data is often stored at the SKU or UPC level. A record in the product dimension will be a record of unique product attributes and is the perfect candidate for denormalizing aspects of the dimension into the fact.

To start, you must identify the attributes in the table that will be the subject of querying, filtering, or aggregations. For this example, we selected the highlighted attributes from the DIM_PRODUCT table shown in Figure 3.11 to store as denormalized attributes in the fact table.

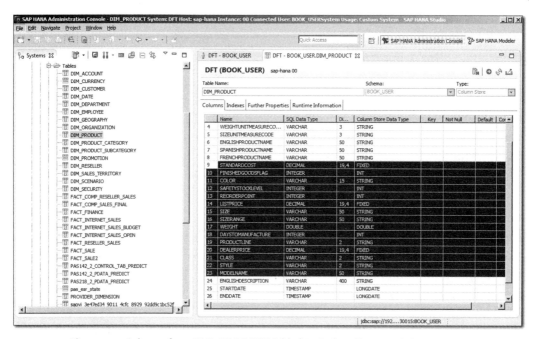

Figure 3.11 Columns from DIM_PRODUCT Added to Reduce Frequent Joins

To create the columns in the FactInternetSales table, you now need to write an ALTER TABLE SQL statement to add the new columns. Listing 3.1 shows an example of the ALTER TABLE statement that is used to add the columns to the FactInternetSales table.

SQL Used to Add the Columns to the Fact Table: FactInternetSales

```
-- Add DIM_Product columns to FACT_INTERNET_SALES
-- due to high cardinality.
-- Don Loden
-- 02.15.2013
```

```
alter table fact_internet_sales add
  (
  "DIM_PRD__STANDARDCOST" DECIMAL(19,4) CS_FIXED null,
  "DIM_PRD__FINISHEDGOODSFLAG" INTEGER CS_INT null,
  "DIM_PRD__COLOR" VARCHAR(15) null,
  "DIM_PRD__SAFETYSTOCKLEVEL" INTEGER CS_INT null,
  "DIM_PRD__REORDERPOINT" INTEGER CS_INT null,
  "DIM_PRD__LISTPRICE" DECIMAL(19,4) CS_FIXED null,
  "DIM_PRD__SIZE" VARCHAR(50) null,
  "DIM_PRD__SIZERANGE" VARCHAR(50) null,
  "DIM_PRD__WEIGHT" DOUBLE CS_DOUBLE null,
  "DIM_PRD__DAYSTOMANUFACTURE" INTEGER CS_INT null,
  "DIM_PRD__PRODUCTLINE" VARCHAR(2) null,
  "DIM_PRD__DEALERPRICE" DECIMAL(19,4) CS_FIXED null,
  "DIM_PRD__CLASS" VARCHAR(2) null,
  "DIM_PRD__STYLE" VARCHAR(2) null,
  "DIM_PRD__MODELNAME" VARCHAR(50) null
  );
```

Listing 3.1 SQL Data Definition Language (DDL) Used to Create FactInternetSales

In Figure 3.12, you can see what the FactInternetSales table looks like after you execute the SQL to add the columns. All of the denormalized columns are ready for use in the fact table. Notice that the columns were not removed from DIM_PRODUCT to foster reusability and ease maintenance for analytic modeling, as you'll see later in the book.

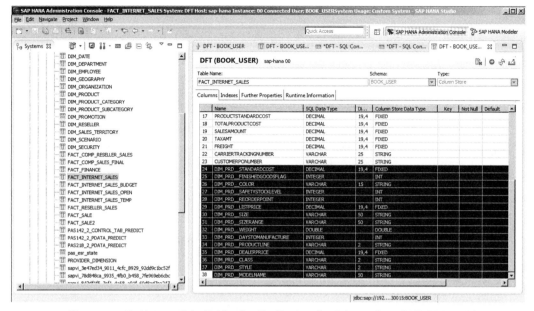

Figure 3.12 FactInternetSales Table after Replicating the Columns from DIM_PRODUCT

3.4 Case Study: Creating Data Marts and Tables for an SAP HANA Project

To illustrate various presentation options and use cases, this book uses a case study to follow a project from the ground up by starting with the data model; then provisioning the data, creating the analytic model; and, finally, fully realizing the BI capabilities with the consumption of the data using the SAP BusinessObjects BI tools. To perform all of these actions, we'll be using the sample Microsoft AdventureWorks data model for a fictitious company called AdventureWorks Cycle Company. We chose this data and model because it's a readily available sample schema with data that is familiar to many developers.

Currently, this SAP HANA system is a blank slate containing nothing but a bare install. So, first, you'll need to create a schema to house and organize the tables that you'll create. Then, you'll finally create the tables and model them to follow the best practices in an SAP HANA data model.

3.4.1   Creating a Schema for the Data Mart

Before you can begin building tables in SAP HANA Studio using SQL or a tool such as SAP Data Services, you need a schema created to house and organize your tables. To create the schema in SAP HANA, you must have a user created that can authenticate to SAP HANA. For all of the connections in the case study for this book, you'll be using the user BOOK_USER.

To create the schema using BOOK_USER, perform the following steps:

1. Open SAP HANA Studio and connect using the BOOK_USER user, as shown in Figure 3.13.

   If you're currently connected as a different user and need to change the user, you may do so in the pop-up menu. Get to this menu by right-clicking your connected SAP HANA system.

2. Open the DEVELOPMENT perspective.

3. Open the PROJECT EXPLORER view.

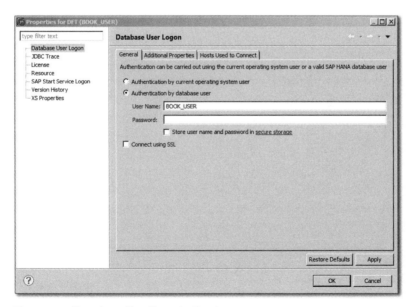

Figure 3.13 Choosing a User Name to Sign In

4. Browse in the Project Workspace to the folder where you want to create your schema definition file and right-click the folder. A menu pops up with a field

where you can specify the name of the schema. For our example, use BOOK_ USER.hdbschema. Then, choose FINISH to save the schema.

> **Caution!**
>
> If you want your schema to be a design-time object, you'll need to create the schema as a file to be saved in the repository.

5. Define the schema name by opening the file you just created in the previous step by inserting this code: `schema_name = "BOOK_USER";`.

6. Save and activate the schema file.

   ▶ Commit the schema to the repository by right-clicking the BOOK_USER schema and choosing TEAM • COMMIT.

   ▶ Activate the schema by right-clicking the BOOK_USER schema.

   ▶ Choose TEAM • COMMIT.

By performing these steps, you've now both created and activated a schema in SAP HANA, as shown in Figure 3.14. This schema is ready for use. In the next section of the case study, you'll begin to create the column-store tables. These tables will be the foundation of all the rest of the examples in this book.

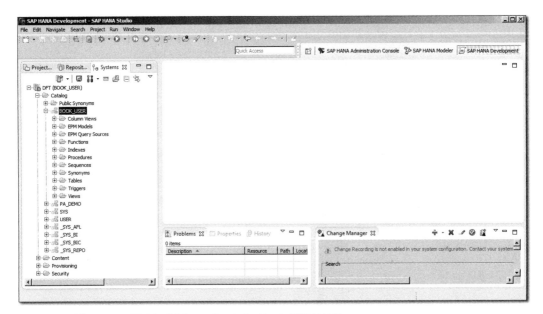

Figure 3.14 Finished Schema Ready for Use in SAP HANA

3.4.2 Creating the Fact Table and Dimension Tables in SAP HANA

We'll show you a few different ways to create the fact and dimension tables in SAP HANA, especially during the data provisioning sections using the unique features of SAP Data Services. However, for this chapter, to focus on creating the tables and the underlying model of the tables, you'll create the tables using SQL in the SAP HANA Studio.

To create the tables using SQL in the SAP HANA Studio, perform the following steps:

1. Open SAP HANA Studio and connect using the BOOK_USER user.

2. Open the MODELER perspective.

3. Open the PROJECT EXPLORER view.

4. Browse in the Project Workspace to select the tables folder under the BOOK_ USER schema that you created earlier (shown in Figure 3.14).

5. Click the SQL button, indicated by the arrow in Figure 3.15.

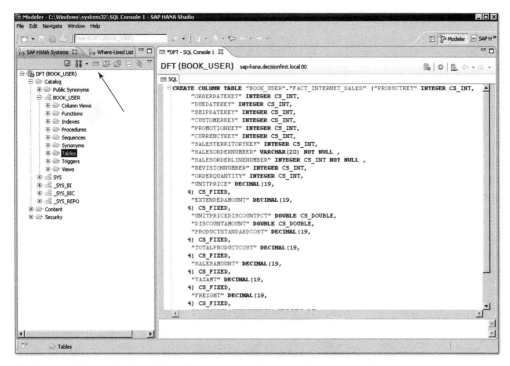

Figure 3.15 Opening the SQL Editor for the Current Session to Create the Tables

6. Type each of the following SQL statements—Listing 3.2 for FactInternetSales, Listing 3.3 for DIM_PRODUCT, Listing 3.4 for DIM_CUSTOMER, and Listing 3.5 for DIM_DATE into the SQL Editor, as shown in Figure 3.15.

Listing 3.2 is the main fact table with Internet sales measures. The only things differentiating this fact table from a standard fact table are the extra varchar() date columns for SAP HANA functions and denormalized columns from product dimension.

```
CREATE COLUMN TABLE "BOOK_USER"."FACT_INTERNET_SALES" ("PRODUCTKEY"
INTEGER CS_INT,
    "ORDERDATEKEY" INTEGER CS_INT,
    "ORDERDATE_CHAR" VARCHAR(8), --SUPPORTS HANA DATE FUNCTIONS
    "DUEDATEKEY" INTEGER CS_INT,
    "DUEDATE_CHAR" VARCHAR(8), --SUPPORTS HANA DATE FUNCTIONS
    "SHIPDATEKEY" INTEGER CS_INT,
    "SHIPDATE_CHAR" VARCHAR(8), --SUPPORTS HANA DATE FUNCTIONS
    "CUSTOMERKEY" INTEGER CS_INT,
    "PROMOTIONKEY" INTEGER CS_INT,
    "CURRENCYKEY" INTEGER CS_INT,
    "SALESTERRITORYKEY" INTEGER CS_INT,
    "SALESORDERNUMBER" VARCHAR(20) NOT NULL ,
    "SALESORDERLINENUMBER" INTEGER CS_INT NOT NULL ,
    "REVISIONNUMBER" INTEGER CS_INT,
    "ORDERQUANTITY" INTEGER CS_INT,
    "UNITPRICE" DECIMAL(19,
4) CS_FIXED,
    "EXTENDEDAMOUNT" DECIMAL(19,
4) CS_FIXED,
    "UNITPRICEDISCOUNTPCT" DOUBLE CS_DOUBLE,
    "DISCOUNTAMOUNT" DOUBLE CS_DOUBLE,
    "PRODUCTSTANDARDCOST" DECIMAL(19,
4) CS_FIXED,
    "TOTALPRODUCTCOST" DECIMAL(19,
4) CS_FIXED,
    "SALESAMOUNT" DECIMAL(19,
4) CS_FIXED,
    "TAXAMT" DECIMAL(19,
4) CS_FIXED,
    "FREIGHT" DECIMAL(19,
4) CS_FIXED,
    "CARRIERTRACKINGNUMBER" VARCHAR(25),
    "CUSTOMERPONUMBER" VARCHAR(25),
    "DIM_PRD__STANDARDCOST" DECIMAL(19,
4) CS_FIXED,
    "DIM_PRD__FINISHEDGOODSFLAG" INTEGER CS_INT,
    "DIM_PRD__COLOR" VARCHAR(15),
```

```
    "DIM_PRD__SAFETYSTOCKLEVEL" INTEGER CS_INT,
    "DIM_PRD__REORDERPOINT" INTEGER CS_INT,
    "DIM_PRD__LISTPRICE" DECIMAL(19,
4) CS_FIXED,
    "DIM_PRD__SIZE" VARCHAR(50),
    "DIM_PRD__SIZERANGE" VARCHAR(50),
    "DIM_PRD__WEIGHT" DOUBLE CS_DOUBLE,
    "DIM_PRD__DAYSTOMANUFACTURE" INTEGER CS_INT,
    "DIM_PRD__PRODUCTLINE" VARCHAR(2),
    "DIM_PRD__DEALERPRICE" DECIMAL(19,
4) CS_FIXED,
    "DIM_PRD__CLASS" VARCHAR(2),
    "DIM_PRD__STYLE" VARCHAR(2),
    "DIM_PRD__MODELNAME" VARCHAR(50),
    PRIMARY KEY ("SALESORDERNUMBER",
    "SALESORDERLINENUMBER"))
```

Listing 3.2 SQL DDL (Fact Table) for FactInternetSales

The standard product dimension describes product-level attributes. Notice that certain columns have been repeated in the fact table in Listing 3.3, yet they still exist here for reusability in the SAP HANA analytic model.

```
CREATE COLUMN TABLE "BOOK_USER"."DIM_PRODUCT" ("PRODUCTKEY" INTEGER
CS_INT NOT NULL ,
    "PRODUCTALTERNATEKEY" VARCHAR(25),
    "PRODUCTSUBCATEGORYKEY" INTEGER CS_INT,
    "WEIGHTUNITMEASURECODE" VARCHAR(3),
    "SIZEUNITMEASURECODE" VARCHAR(3),
    "ENGLISHPRODUCTNAME" VARCHAR(50),
    "SPANISHPRODUCTNAME" VARCHAR(50),
    "FRENCHPRODUCTNAME" VARCHAR(50),
    "STANDARDCOST" DECIMAL(19,
4) CS_FIXED,
    "FINISHEDGOODSFLAG" INTEGER CS_INT,
    "COLOR" VARCHAR(15),
    "SAFETYSTOCKLEVEL" INTEGER CS_INT,
    "REORDERPOINT" INTEGER CS_INT,
    "LISTPRICE" DECIMAL(19,
4) CS_FIXED,
    "SIZE" VARCHAR(50),
    "SIZERANGE" VARCHAR(50),
    "WEIGHT" DOUBLE CS_DOUBLE,
    "DAYSTOMANUFACTURE" INTEGER CS_INT,
    "PRODUCTLINE" VARCHAR(2),
    "DEALERPRICE" DECIMAL(19,
4) CS_FIXED,
    "CLASS" VARCHAR(2),
```

```
    "STYLE" VARCHAR(2),
    "MODELNAME" VARCHAR(50),
    "ENGLISHDESCRIPTION" VARCHAR(400),
    "STARTDATE" LONGDATE CS_LONGDATE,
    "ENDDATE" LONGDATE CS_LONGDATE,
    "STATUS" VARCHAR(7),
    PRIMARY KEY ("PRODUCTKEY"))
```

Listing 3.3 SQL DDL (Dimension Table) for DIM_PRODUCT

This standard customer dimension table describes customer-level attributes (Listing 3.4). The CUSTOMERKEY field has a foreign key that relates this table to the fact table.

```
CREATE COLUMN TABLE "BOOK_USER"."DIM_CUSTOMER" ("CUSTOMERKEY"
INTEGER CS_INT NOT NULL ,
    "GEOGRAPHYKEY" INTEGER CS_INT,
    "CUSTOMERALTERNATEKEY" VARCHAR(15),
    "TITLE" VARCHAR(8),
    "FIRSTNAME" VARCHAR(50),
    "MIDDLENAME" VARCHAR(50),
    "LASTNAME" VARCHAR(50),
    "NAMESTYLE" INTEGER CS_INT,
    "BIRTHDATE" DAYDATE CS_DAYDATE,
    "MARITALSTATUS" VARCHAR(1),
    "SUFFIX" VARCHAR(10),
    "GENDER" VARCHAR(1),
    "EMAILADDRESS" VARCHAR(50),
    "YEARLYINCOME" DECIMAL(19,
  4) CS_FIXED,
    "TOTALCHILDREN" INTEGER CS_INT,
    "NUMBERCHILDRENATHOME" INTEGER CS_INT,
    "ENGLISHEDUCATION" VARCHAR(40),
    "SPANISHEDUCATION" VARCHAR(40),
    "FRENCHEDUCATION" VARCHAR(40),
    "ENGLISHOCCUPATION" VARCHAR(100),
    "SPANISHOCCUPATION" VARCHAR(100),
    "FRENCHOCCUPATION" VARCHAR(100),
    "HOUSEOWNERFLAG" VARCHAR(1),
    "NUMBERCARSOWNED" INTEGER CS_INT,
    "ADDRESSLINE1" VARCHAR(120),
    "ADDRESSLINE2" VARCHAR(120),
    "PHONE" VARCHAR(20),
    "DATEFIRSTPURCHASE" DAYDATE CS_DAYDATE,
    "COMMUTEDISTANCE" VARCHAR(15),
    PRIMARY KEY ("CUSTOMERKEY"))
```

Listing 3.4 SQL DDL (Dimension Table) for DIM_CUSTOMER

The standard time dimension describes date attributes (Listing 3.5). The DATE-KEY field has a foreign key that relates this table to the fact table on multiple date attributes. The basic concept is that the date dimension will be related back on any date column in the fact table to allow for flexibility on any type of date- or time-based reporting.

```
CREATE COLUMN TABLE "BOOK_USER"."DIM_DATE" ("DATEKEY" INTEGER CS_INT
NOT NULL ,
     "FULLDATEALTERNATEKEY" DAYDATE CS_DAYDATE,
     "DAYNUMBEROFWEEK" INTEGER CS_INT,
     "ENGLISHDAYNAMEOFWEEK" VARCHAR(10),
     "SPANISHDAYNAMEOFWEEK" VARCHAR(10),
     "FRENCHDAYNAMEOFWEEK" VARCHAR(10),
     "DAYNUMBEROFMONTH" INTEGER CS_INT,
     "DAYNUMBEROFYEAR" INTEGER CS_INT,
     "WEEKNUMBEROFYEAR" INTEGER CS_INT,
     "ENGLISHMONTHNAME" VARCHAR(10),
     "SPANISHMONTHNAME" VARCHAR(10),
     "FRENCHMONTHNAME" VARCHAR(10),
     "MONTHNUMBEROFYEAR" INTEGER CS_INT,
     "CALENDARQUARTER" INTEGER CS_INT,
     "CALENDARQUARTERYEAR" VARCHAR(8),
     "CALENDARYEAR" INTEGER CS_INT,
     "CALENDARYEARMONTH" VARCHAR(15),
     "CALENDARYEARWEEK" VARCHAR(20),
     "CALENDARSEMESTER" INTEGER CS_INT,
     "FISCALQUARTER" INTEGER CS_INT,
     "FISCALYEAR" INTEGER CS_INT,
     "FISCALSEMESTER" INTEGER CS_INT,
     PRIMARY KEY ("DATEKEY"))
```
Listing 3.5 SQL DDL (Dimension Table) for DIM_DATE

7. Press F8 to execute the queries.

After executing all four SQL statements, you have one fact table and three dimension tables. These tables form the core of the data mart that will be used in the subsequent sections of the case study, and this data set will remain the base data for all of the examples present in this book. You'll also notice a financial structure consisting of the following data mart tables:

- ▶ FACT_FINANCE
- ▶ DIM_CURRENCY
- ▶ DIM_ORGANIZATION

- ▸ DIM_SCENARIO

- ▸ DIM_DATE

- ▸ DIM_ACCOUNT

- ▸ DIM_DEPARTMENT_GROUP

Note that DIM_DATE is a conformed dimension across the financial mart and sales mart. DIM_DATE references the same table that was created in this section. These financial data mart tables are created in the same manner as the sales data mart. The descriptions were given only to limit redundant descriptions for the case study.

3.5   Summary

SAP HANA is a tremendously powerful and flexible platform, in part because it truly has the ability to act as a chameleon and masquerade as multiple platforms. SAP HANA is unique in the sense that it can easily replace many of these platforms quickly because it shares the common, conventionally approved language for data access: SQL. This makes SAP HANA a plug-and-play fit for replacing the data and analytic architecture for many applications with a far more sophisticated and well-thought-out development platform. The fact that SAP HANA can also interpret MDX queries natively speaks to the same rapid integration and replacement of conventional cube-based technologies.

Native support for MDX was one reason it was no surprise that SAP undertook the task of moving SAP BW to SAP HANA so quickly. For an application such as SAP BW, moving to SAP HANA was merely another database port. This ease of movement and transport goes a long way toward SAP's no-disruption model. Now that the SAP Business Suite is also certified to run on SAP HANA, the sky is the limit in terms of possibilities on a mature and robust platform that really does do it all.

Now that you have an understanding of how SAP HANA stores data and what is needed for high-performing data in SAP HANA, we can look toward Part II of the book, which focuses on the data provisioning process. We call out the word *process* because you shouldn't just load your data into SAP HANA. Before you provision data into SAP HANA, there are some things that need to be addressed with a thorough pre-provisioning process. We'll examine this pre-provisioning in process in detail in Chapter 4.

PART II
Getting Data Into SAP HANA

Before provisioning or data loading can occur, you must perform source system analysis to see which aspects of the data need repair. Learn how to use SAP Data Services in order to provide high-quality data as a base for SAP HANA.

4   Preprovisioning Data with SAP Data Services

SAP HANA is immensely powerful and offers tremendous possibilities to your organization, but any system is only as good as the quality of its data. In this chapter, we'll explore the concept of *source system analysis*—which is, quite simply, taking a hard, detailed look at a source to really see the story behind the data.

To this end, we'll start the chapter with an explanation of the concept, including why you want to do it and what benefits you can gain from it (Section 4.1). We'll then move on to a specific discussion of performing SSA in SAP Data Services (Section 4.2) and column profiling techniques that are available in Data Services to support SSA. Finally, we'll conclude the chapter with a discussion that moves beyond the tools and talks about how to make an SSA plan for your organization, as well as tips to make SSA more successful (Section 4.3).

Having spent lots of time, effort, and money on your SAP HANA investment, you don't want to load just any data into this blank and pristine system; instead, the detailed source system analysis steps and tasks will help you closely examine the data and avoid costly mistakes. This SSA will show you the real story behind your data and help you ensure that you're not just loading fast trash into SAP HANA.

4.1   Making the Case for Source System Analysis

SSA typically begins with data profiling using a profiling tool, or even just SQL, against the base database tables. Using findings uncovered in the profiling effort, you can dig deeper into the source to uncover data realities. These realities are sometimes painful, in that they may prove or disprove stated facts or beliefs about how data is stored and represented across the enterprise.

This seems like a fairly simple concept, but SSA is very empowering for a development cycle of an SAP HANA implementation: at the core, SSA gets to the real story of what is going on with data in the enterprise, making it a very necessary step in your SAP HANA journey.

How SSA Impacted One Organization

During site visits, we often hear, "That's not possible with our data," or, "Our systems don't do that," which are often disproven empirically by profiling and analyzing the source data in detail. Although these lessons are sometimes painful for the business users, they are important for realizing a design that will truly deliver and meet functional expectations, even when the data doesn't!

Once, on an engagement, we were working with a customer and performing detailed SSA on a source that was to be used for budgeting data. After SSA, we determined that the way the accounting was being performed through classifications in the financial system was violating a core business rule, resulting in improper accounting practices and actually costing the company a great deal of money—all simply due to the way the system was set up. The data had always been behaving this way, and the business users had no idea until SSA was performed!

So why perform SSA? The answer is as simple as the task itself: SSA tells you what you need to code. ETL development generally requires transforming the data from its source form to whatever format is required by a presentation layer. That presentation layer might be a BI design with a data mart that will be consumed by BI tools, like the ones featured in the case study sections of this book, or something as different as a data migration. Regardless of the target, you're starting with a source (or multiple sources) and have to transform the data to prepare the data for the target. The rules of the business lead you to the target design, but there is still another side of the story: the source. The development effort revolves around blending the needs of both sides, and the only way that you'll acquaint yourself with the source is by analyzing with proper SSA. Considering what you find in the source compared to what is needed in the target leads you down the path of what to code.

Another positive result of proper SSA is that it allows the developer to establish all use cases at once. Instead of just going straight to code, you take the time to plan and analyze all of the permutations and scenarios that actually exist in the data at the beginning of the process. This is a key step because if you just jump straight into the code, you'll certainly address the use case in front of you, but you may miss all of the things that aren't readily present at first glance. SSA allows a break in this process cycle to create code that is more holistic and encourages you to consider the whole picture of the development effort, rather than just exploring the immediate and obvious use cases that are brought to light by the business or development effort.

Considering the entire development effort at one time is especially important with SAP HANA because it offers more flexibility in modeling typical business intelligence constructs over traditional database platforms. If a developer goes straight to code and provisions the data directly, then they may lose out on opportunities of what types of constructs to model where. For example, derived measures in a traditional landscape are often crafted in the ETL to be realized by a mart table in the data mart design. However, in SAP HANA, this may not be needed. A developer may be able to skip this step entirely, especially if all of the elements required for the calculated, or derived, measures readily exist in the source tables. If the source tables do contain all of the base elements, then the derived measures are most likely modeled in the SAP HANA information views covered in Part III of this book. This technique allows the developer to store only the base elements of the calculation or a calculated value directly in the database table. Either of these provides a more elastic solution than a rigid ETL-derived stored value. This is a much more elegant solution for an SAP HANA project, but this opportunity may be missed without proper SSA.

Mapping everything that you need to accomplish is very important for constructing modular code. You can do this by thinking in terms of objects. Using an object-oriented approach and thinking in terms of generic use cases to solve allows for reusability and ensures that your code is smarter—that is, more modular. This is necessary when you're writing object-oriented code because it avoids multiple cycles of refactoring and wasting valuable time in an SAP HANA development effort.

This may seem somewhat counterintuitive—as though time is being wasted analyzing a source and mapping logical definitions or diagrams—and prompt your team to wonder why it's necessary to perform SSA and mapping when you already know what you need to code. If it seems that just coding the use case as you see it would be much faster, consider the following example.

SSA and Mapping Example

A client had two systems that were going to be loaded from the same source into two different targets. The landing schemas for the data were the same column layout but had two different target database platforms. One target was MySQL; these tables contained fully spelled-out names, such as CUSTOMER. The other target was an IBM DB2 operational datastore whose table names were limited to eight characters. In this example, the CUSTOMER table in MySQL was equivalent to the CUST table in DB2. The other caveat is that the business logic was the same, but some of the data for DB2 required special logic to handle nulls and special characters in the ETL code.

The coding was straightforward, and we knew that we needed to address those two scenarios, but rather than going straight to the code and hoping for the best, we took the time to profile the data to get a full view of the source. We found no fewer than four more scenarios that would have created trouble in DB2!

By profiling, we were able to see what was needed at the beginning of the process rather than taking the "faster" approach and just coding before detailed examination. We were able to write good code once rather than quick code four more times!

Much can be gained from analyzing a source, both in terms of ultimate time savings in a development effort and just delivering better data to SAP HANA or a better ETL development cycle.

One thing that we always try to do during SSA is disprove business logic, not to be skeptical or cynical, but to use the business rules as the standard that the data should pass. We're effectively looking for the data to fail any of the rules. Although this seems pessimistic, it's a very good approach that is both simple and concise. Generally, you want to look for holes or gaps in the data. These could be as simple as gaps where a non-null column in the source is null in the database. Gaps happen often when application-based constraints are used. Application-based constraints are tidy from an application development perspective because they are all managed in the same layer of code and not distributed between the database and the application layer. However, because it's up to the developer to implement them consistently and properly in the database, the data that application-based constraints leave can be quite messy.

You can take even this simple example further by profiling business logic across sources or platforms. If you're merging two systems from different departments or possibly different physical instances in a global organization, the data can be even messier because application-level rules enforcement may not be possible across platforms. By analyzing the source system using a profiling tool that separates itself from the data connections, such as SAP Data Services, which is equipped with metadata capabilities, you have the power to perform this cross-platform analysis to look for patterns and sequences that would not be possible otherwise.

After seeing what is possible by analyzing a source and what can be achieved, it's easy to see why this step is very importing on your data's journey to SAP HANA. Always remember that SAP HANA is an incredible platform, but, like any system, it's only as good as its underlying data. Recall the old saying, "Garbage in, garbage out." This adage certainly holds true for SAP HANA. SAP HANA is very fast and a great solution for analyzing vast amounts of data in real time. Because complex queries or logic can be achieved on the fly in real time, there is truly no need to stage data as with traditional systems. All of this leads to the fact that speed isn't the only consideration with SAP HANA! But if you start with garbage data and then load it into SAP via ETL-based replication in SAP Data Services (as in the case study sections of this book) or with SAP Landscape Transformation (SLT) from SAP ERP, the net result will be the same: You'll merely have fast trash!

Data quality has always been a very important concept, but it may be more important than ever with SAP HANA. If SAP HANA forms the base platform of your BI or decision support system, you'll encounter any quality issues more quickly, and this could be quite costly. It's simply more important that data be correct and of high quality before it gets to SAP HANA because this will be a core platform for the organization.

Much dialogue revolves around the way that SAP HANA will alter the IT landscape and how quickly, and there are multiple case studies available to prove this and lay credibility to this claim. However, SAP HANA's real measure of success in an organization will be if the information contained is useful, but without quality data in SAP, this will be impossible. It would all be just speeds and feeds—but you would never get the right answer.

Now that we've examined why SSA is necessary in an SAP HANA development cycle and what benefits can be gained from properly analyzing a source, let's explore some of the SSA tools and techniques present in SAP Data Services to provide you with the robust profiling tools you need to accomplish proper SSA.

4.2 SSA Techniques in SAP Data Services

At a high level, SSA starts with data profiling with a profiling tool. In this book, we'll explore the built-in features of SAP Data Services, which is an ideal tool for loading data into SAP HANA. Consider all of the column metrics that are available with a simple column profile in SAP Data Services, as shown in Figure 4.1. Some are simple, such as `Min` and `Max`, while others are complex, such as the patterns of data on the far right.

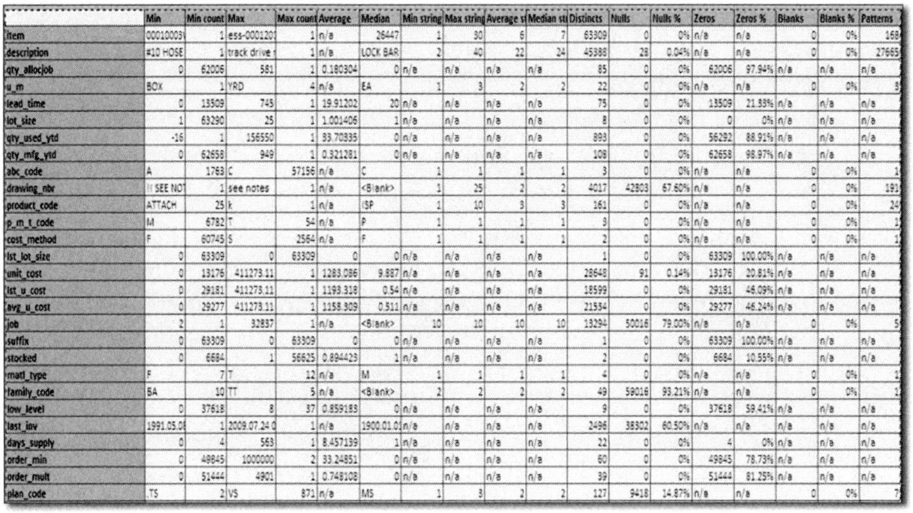

	Min	Min count	Max	Max count	Average	Median	Min string	Max string	Average st	Median st	Distincts	Nulls	Nulls %	Zeros	Zeros %	Blanks	Blanks %	Patterns
item	0001.0003	1	ess-0001207	1	n/a	26447	1	30	6	7	63309	0	0%	n/a	n/a	0	0%	168
description	#10 HOSE	1	track drive	1	n/a	LOCK BAR	2	40	22	24	45988	28	0.04%	n/a	n/a	0	0%	27665
qty_allocjob	0	62006	581	1	0.180304	0	n/a	n/a	n/a	n/a	85	0	0%	62006	97.94%	n/a	n/a	9
u_m	BOX	1	YRD	4	n/a	EA	1	3	2	2	22	0	0%	n/a	n/a	0	0%	9
lead_time	0	13509	743	1	19.91202	20	n/a	n/a	n/a	n/a	75	0	0%	13509	21.33%	n/a	n/a	3
lot_size	1	63290	25	1	1.001406	1	n/a	n/a	n/a	n/a	8	0	0%	0	0%	n/a	n/a	1
qty_used_ytd	-16	1	156550	1	33.70335	0	n/a	n/a	n/a	n/a	893	0	0%	56292	88.91%	n/a	n/a	6
qty_mfg_ytd	0	62658	949	1	0.321281	0	n/a	n/a	n/a	n/a	108	0	0%	62658	98.97%	n/a	n/a	5
abc_code	A	1763	C	57156	n/a	C	1	1	1	1	3	0	0%	n/a	n/a	0	0%	1
drawing_nbr	!! SEE NOT	1	see notes	1	n/a	<Blank>	1	25	2	2	4017	42803	67.60%	n/a	n/a	0	0%	191
product_code	ATTACH	25	k	1	n/a	ISP	1	10	3	3	161	0	0%	n/a	n/a	0	0%	24
p_m_t_code	M	6782	T	54	n/a	P	1	1	1	1	3	0	0%	n/a	n/a	0	0%	1
cost_method	F	60745	S	2564	n/a	F	1	1	1	1	2	0	0%	n/a	n/a	0	0%	1
lst_lot_size	0	63309	0	63309	0	0	n/a	n/a	n/a	n/a	1	0	0%	63309	100.00%	n/a	n/a	1
unit_cost	0	13176	411273.11	1	1283.086	9.987	n/a	n/a	n/a	n/a	28648	91	0.14%	13176	20.81%	n/a	n/a	4
lst_u_cost	0	29181	411273.11	1	1193.328	0.54	n/a	n/a	n/a	n/a	18599	0	0%	29181	46.09%	n/a	n/a	4
avg_u_cost	0	29277	411273.11	1	1158.309	0.511	n/a	n/a	n/a	n/a	21534	0	0%	29277	46.24%	n/a	n/a	4
job	2	1	32837	1	n/a	<Blank>	10	10	10	10	13294	50016	79.00%	n/a	n/a	0	0%	5
suffix	0	63309	0	63309	0	0	n/a	n/a	n/a	n/a	1	0	0%	63309	100.00%	n/a	n/a	1
stocked	0	6684	1	56625	0.894429	1	n/a	n/a	n/a	n/a	2	0	0%	6684	10.55%	n/a	n/a	1
matl_type	F	7	T	12	n/a	M	1	1	1	1	4	0	0%	n/a	n/a	0	0%	1
family_code	6A	10	TT	5	n/a	<Blank>	2	2	2	2	49	59016	93.21%	n/a	n/a	0	0%	12
low_level	0	37618	8	37	0.859183	1	n/a	n/a	n/a	n/a	9	0	0%	37618	59.41%	n/a	n/a	1
last_inv	1991.05.08	1	2009.07.24	1	n/a	1900.01.0	n/a	n/a	n/a	n/a	2496	38302	60.50%	n/a	n/a	n/a	n/a	1
days_supply	0	4	563	1	8.457139	1	n/a	n/a	n/a	n/a	22	0	0%	4	0%	n/a	n/a	1
order_min	0	49845	1000000	2	33.24851	0	n/a	n/a	n/a	n/a	60	0	0%	49845	78.73%	n/a	n/a	4
order_mult	0	51444	4801	1	0.748108	0	n/a	n/a	n/a	n/a	39	0	0%	51444	81.25%	n/a	n/a	1
plan_code	TS	2	VS	871	n/a	MS	1	3	2	2	127	9418	14.87%	n/a	n/a	0	0%	7

Figure 4.1 Column Profile Results from SAP Data Services

Some measures are available in SQL, but all of these were created at the press of a button in SAP Data Services! Column profiling in SAP Data Services results in valuable time savings for an SAP HANA initiative. Using a tool like this gives you a quick view into your source data to begin the journey of SSA.

After examining the profiling results of the tool, the analyst will use SQL to dig deeper and explore patterns in the data. This is done to see how to design the logic or extract, transform, and load (ETL) code that will guide the data through the business rules and into the reporting structures that have been modeled in SAP HANA.

SAP Data Services offers a comprehensive set of ad hoc profiling tools with no need for customization. To analyze a multitude of options right out of the box, SAP Data Services ships with two types of profiling:

▶ **Column profiling**

This type of profiling lets you profile individual column attributes. Measures include minimum, maximum, distinct values, or the amount of nulls. Pattern distribution is also available to allow a quick look into all of the patterns present in a source table column.

▶ **Relationship profiling**

This type of profiling lets you see how data is related across multiple tables.

Profiling in SAP Data Services is of an ad hoc nature. *Ad hoc profiling* is more for a developer to leverage within a development cycle. This type of profiling should not be confused with the more complex profiling that is available in SAP Information Steward, another product in SAP's enterprise information management product portfolio designed to support predictive data governance. For more on SAP Information Steward, see Appendix A.

SAP Data Services is quite flexible and operates on the concept of *metadata*. Metadata is simply data providing information about other data. In this sense, any data being analyzed is actually just an array of columns and rows. This segregation from a source or SQL connection allows SAP Data Services to profile databases, tables, flat files, and application connections in exactly the same way. The following are the different connection options for SAP Data Services profiling:

▶ Databases

- ▷ Attunity Connector for mainframe databases
- ▷ Oracle
- ▷ SAP (Sybase) IQ

- ▷ IBM DB2
- ▷ SQL Server
- ▷ Teradata

▶ Applications

- ▷ JDE One World
- ▷ Oracle applications
- ▷ SAP applications

- ▷ JDE World
- ▷ PeopleSoft
- ▷ Siebel

▶ Flat files

As you can see from this list, SAP Data Services offers many built-in connections to jump-start developers' profiling efforts. For this chapter, our focus will be on the SAP Data Services column and relationship profiling for developers. We'll limit the scope of the profiling to database tables, but do keep in mind that the examples in this chapter relate directly to these other source types because they are all just metadata to SAP Data Services. To perform our profiling tasks for loading data into SAP HANA, we'll be using the SAP Data Services Designer client application because this is where you run profiling tasks in SAP Data Services.

To launch the SAP Data Services Designer, begin at the START menu on the client computer where SAP Data Services is installed, and perform the following steps:

1. Click the START button.

2. Select SAP DATA SERVICES from the START menu.

3. Select SAP DATA SERVICES DESIGNER from the SAP DATA SERVICES START MENU group. The SAP DATA SERVICES REPOSITORY LOGIN menu pops up, as shown in Figure 4.2.

Figure 4.2 SAP Data Services Repository Logon Screen

4. Log on to SAP Data Services with a user name set up to use a local repository by clicking the LOG ON button; the repositories available to the user appear in the white dialog box. Enter the administrator logon to access the DS_RA_DEMO local repository shown in Figure 4.2.

5. Click OK to connect to the SAP Data Services local repository. The SAP Data Services Designer opens, as shown in Figure 4.3.

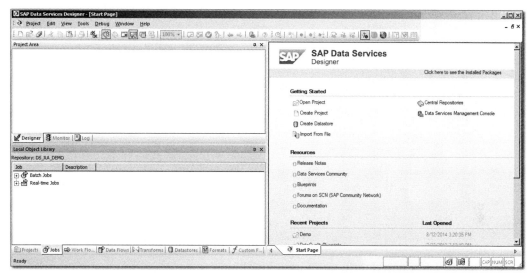

Figure 4.3 SAP Data Services Designer Client Application Ready for Use

Now that the SAP Data Services Designer is open and ready for use, let's set our focus and begin our profiling journey.

4.2.1 Column Profiling

Column profiling in SAP Data Services is exactly what it sounds like: you profile the data present in the columns of a table. This process is very simple. You instantiate a profile task from the SAP Data Services Designer and run the task interactively. After the profiling task completes, you'll have both profiling results and data at your disposal.

There are two types of column profiles: basic and advanced. We'll explore both types in detail in this section of this chapter. But before exploring the details of each type of column profile, let's discuss how to submit a column profile request.

To submit a column profile request in the SAP Data Services Designer, perform the following steps:

1. Locate the LOCAL OBJECT LIBRARY in the bottom-left corner of the SAP Data Services Designer.

2. Navigate to the Datastores tab of the Local Object Library.

3. Expand the datastore containing the table that you want to profile.

4. Right-click the table in the Local Object Library to produce the pop-up menu shown in Figure 4.4.

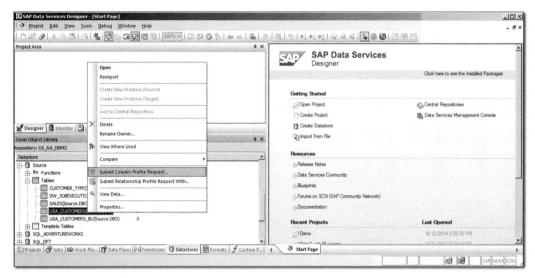

Figure 4.4 Accessing the Table to Profile

5. Select the Submit Column Profile Request option from the pop-up menu. The Submit Column Profile Request dialog box appears, as shown in Figure 4.5. This dialog box allows you to select which columns you want to use to submit detailed profile requests. This is an optional selection because detailed profiling is resource intensive, and care should be used when selecting this option.

6. In the Profiler Server Monitor dialog box that appears as shown in Figure 4.6, multiple columns are present:

   ▸ Name: Name of the profile task

   ▸ Type: Type of profiling task being executed (either column or relationship profile task)

   ▸ Status: Current status indicator field of the profile task (either Running or Done)

   ▸ Timestamp: Date and time when the profiling task was submitted

   ▸ Source: Source table or datastore connection that the profiling task was run against

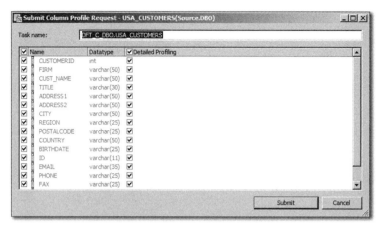

Figure 4.5 Selecting the Columns for Detailed Profiling

7. After the profiling task is done, the Status will change to Done in the Profiler Server Monitor dialog box. You may need to refresh the dialog box by clicking the Refresh button to see the status reflect Done; it doesn't always refresh automatically.

Figure 4.6 Column Profile Task Running in SAP Data Services

Now, you can see the results of the column profile by right-clicking the table in the Local Object Library and selecting the View Data option from the pop-up menu shown previously in Figure 4.4. Figure 4.7 shows the View Data dialog box that appears and displays the profile results. The pattern data in the right-hand window pane illustrates all of the patterns of data in the ADDRESS1 field from the USA_ CUSTOMERS table. It's clear to see that many patterns are available for analysis, and this display can be used to quickly toggle between viewing other patterns and the example data of the patterns in the bottom window pane. This profile data was all produced simply using the built-in column profiling task in SAP Data Services with just a few clicks! This is the true power of the column profiling task.

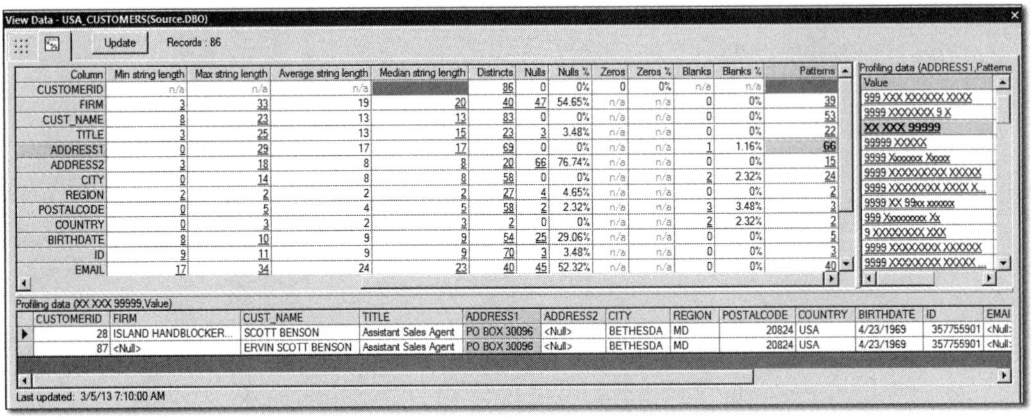

View Data - USA_CUSTOMERS(Source.DBO)

Update   Records : 86

Column	Min string length	Max string length	Average string length	Median string length	Distincts	Nulls	Nulls %	Zeros	Zeros %	Blanks	Blanks %	Patterns	Profiling data (ADDRESS1,Patterns) Value
CUSTOMERID	n/a	n/a	n/a		86	0	0%	0	0%	n/a	n/a		999 XXX XXXXXX XXXX
FIRM	3	33	19	20	40	47	54.65%	n/a	n/a	0	0%	39	9999 XXXXXXX 9 X
CUST_NAME	8	23	13	13	83	0	0%	n/a	n/a	0	0%	53	XX XXX 99999
TITLE	3	25	13	15	23	3	3.48%	n/a	n/a	0	0%	22	99999 XXXXX
ADDRESS1	0	29	17	17	69	0	0%	n/a	n/a	1	1.16%	66	9999 Xxxxxxx Xxxxx
ADDRESS2	3	18	8	8	20	66	76.74%	n/a	n/a	0	0%	15	9999 XXXXXXXX XXXXX
CITY	0	14	8	8	58	0	0%	n/a	n/a	2	2.32%	24	9999 XXXXXXXX XXXX X
REGION	2	2	2	2	27	4	4.65%	n/a	n/a	0	0%	2	9999 XX 99xx xxxxxx
POSTALCODE	0	5	4	5	58	2	2.32%	n/a	n/a	3	3.48%	3	999 Xxxxxxxx Xx
COUNTRY	0	3	2	3	2	0	0%	n/a	n/a	2	2.32%	2	9 XXXXXXXX XXX
BIRTHDATE	8	10	9	9	54	25	29.06%	n/a	n/a	0	0%	5	9999 XXXXXXXX XXXXX
ID	9	11	9	9	70	3	3.48%	n/a	n/a	0	0%	3	9999 XXXXXXXX XXXXX
EMAIL	17	34	24	23	40	45	52.32%	n/a	n/a	0	0%	40	

Profiling data (XX XXX 99999,Value)

CUSTOMERID	FIRM	CUST_NAME	TITLE	ADDRESS1	ADDRESS2	CITY	REGION	POSTALCODE	COUNTRY	BIRTHDATE	ID	EMAIL
28	ISLAND HANDBLOCKER...	SCOTT BENSON	Assistant Sales Agent	PO BOX 30096	<Null>	BETHESDA	MD	20824	USA	4/23/1969	357755901	<Null>
87	<Null>	ERVIN SCOTT BENSON	Assistant Sales Agent	PO BOX 30096	<Null>	BETHESDA	MD	20824	USA	4/23/1969	357755901	<Null>

Last updated: 3/5/13 7:10:00 AM

Figure 4.7 Column Profile Results Showing Patterns in the ADDRESS1 Field

Pattern profile attributes are quite handy tools, but notice all of the other elements available from this profiling task. You can quickly see and examine the data of NULL values, MIN values, MAX values, and numerous other measures. These types of data elements and the quick quantifications are great tools for starting the dialogue with the organization about what types of issues may be present in the data and what type of rules will be necessary to clean up data quality issues on the way into SAP HANA. Let's now go into more detail on what options are covered with both basic and advanced types of profiling tasks.

Basic Column Profiling

Let's explore the basic column profiling attributes in detail:

▶ **Min**
The minimum value present for this column.

▶ **Min count**
The number of rows that contain the minimum column value.

▶ **Max**
The maximum value present for this column.

▶ **Max count**
The number of rows that contain the maximum column value.

▶ **Average**
The average value for the column. This is present only for numeric columns and is blank for all nonnumeric columns.

▸ **Min string length**

The shortest string value in the column. This is only present for character columns and will be blank for all non-character columns.

▸ **Max string length**

The longest string value in the column. This is present only for character columns and is blank for all non-character columns.

▸ **Average string length**

The average length string value in the column. This is present only for character columns and is blank for all non-character columns.

▸ **Nulls**

The number of NULL values in this column.

▸ **Nulls %**

The percentage of rows that contain a NULL value in this column.

▸ **Zeros**

The number of zero values (0) in this column.

▸ **Zeros %**

The percentage of rows that contain a zero (0) value in this column.

▸ **Blanks**

The percentage of rows that contain a blank value (" ") in this column. This is present only for character columns and is blank for all non-character columns.

▸ **Blanks %**

The percentage of rows that contain a blank (" ") value in this column.

Basic column profiling attributes are simple measures of quality that are derived mostly by the profiling engine via SQL statements. So why use the profiling tool to derive these when they are available via SQL? Two reasons come to mind. The first is for the simplicity and convenience offered in the profiling task that offers a repeatable outcome. With just a few clicks and a submission, you can run the same set of measures against any table, providing a baseline set of quality measures for a table or series of tables. The second reason is the flexibility offered by using metadata in SAP Data Services to run this same set of measures against database tables or application connects.

In short, the true power of the tool lies in its ability to work with any type of platform or database. Basic column profiling is usually just a start, and most often you'll choose to perform advanced column profiling, as well, against a source table.

Advanced Column Profiling

Advanced column profiling offers additional attributes over the basic column profile attributes, such as the following:

▶ **Median**
The median value of this column.

▶ **Median string**
The string length of the median value for this column. This is present only for character columns and is blank for all non-character columns.

▶ **Distincts**
The number of distinct values in this column.

▶ **Distincts %**
The percentage of rows that contain distinct values for this column.

▶ **Patterns**
The number of different patterns available in this column. Numeric, non-numeric, uppercase characters, lowercase characters, and spacing are all signified and measured in the profile results.

▶ **Patterns %**
The percentage of rows that contain patterns for this column.

These attributes are particularly useful on tables with a large number of `varchar()` columns. This is the typical scenario when you choose to employ advanced column profiling.

Consider the patterns of ADDRESS1 data shown earlier, in Figure 4.7. After seeing the patterns as well as the sample data exposed in the ADDRESS1 field, you can make a few assumptions about the coding tasks that will be required. You can see via the patterns that there are P.O. box values, as well as street addresses. These are two distinct postal types; a P.O. box is a postal type, and a street address is a mailing address.

Consider a business rule example involving a manufacturer that makes a hazardous good. These goods are available for delivery only to a mailing address, so a postal address type is non-deliverable, requiring some kind of modification in the ETL code. This is a very simple example of how a quick profile task can isolate issues that require modifications and display all of the scenarios in the data that show differences that need to be handled. Examples like these demonstrate the power of the advance profile task.

So why wouldn't you run advanced profile tasks with every profile, especially because there are more options, and tables generally have at least one `varchar()` column that would benefit from this type of analysis? The answer is the simple fact that an advanced profile task is a much more expensive operation in terms of performance and processing. The processing task is much more resource-intensive on the SAP Data Services job server, and the advanced profile task runs longer. So, you must weigh the benefit of obtaining the additional character-based attributes from an advanced column profile over the performance and processing expense.

Note that, when you're running these expensive profiles, you must be cognizant of what is occurring on the SAP Data Services job server. For example, if you're running an ETL job, you don't want to kick off an advanced profile task against a large table. If the ETL job is processing a large amount of data or has long-running, resource-intensive operations, you'll probably overrun the capabilities of the SAP Data Services job server. So, be cautious about what is running on the job server before submitting the profiling tasks.

4.2.2 Relationship Profiling

Relationship profiling is important because it allows relationships to be examined and tested against two tables. This is useful if you want to see orphan records or examine whether parent-child applications are supported in the data behind the application. Great examples of this are sales headers and sales detail records; you expect to always have a header record that corresponds to the detail record because an application typically has this flow when transactions are being created.

This relationship test can be pretty easily established across multiple tables, either in one database or using some sort of database linking method in SQL. To perform this operation with SQL, you combine an outer join and look for NULL values in the outer source table. The SQL looks like this:

```
SELECT
C.*
FROM
ChildTable C
LEFT JOIN MasterTable M
ON M.ID = C.MasterID
WHERE
M.ID IS NULL
```

This task is further complicated if the tables are across multiple sources. For example, you need a customer record to create a sale in any application. However, consider what happens if you're combining two application sources into a data mart. A customer exists in a point of sales system housed in an SQL Server database and is related to sales records that are stored in this SQL Server source, but what if the business has an online point of sales system hosted in a different platform and server? The business rule is still valid because the business should still sell only to valid customer records, but the customers in IBM DB2 are difficult to compare to either customers or sales in SQL Server. The only way to perform a logical relationship test across platforms is with a profiling tool such as SAP Data Services.

Recall that SAP Data Services operates on the concept of metadata, which frees you from the confines of a source. Logical comparisons and profiles still need to be drawn as relationships across systems because business rules aren't concerned with the physical implementations of various systems. These rules operate at a logical level. Checks like these are important before coding begins when combining sources. Otherwise, assumptions are made on how data should work; if coding develops directly from these assumptions, it can lead to some very costly course corrections.

Now that we've discussed why relationship profiles are important, we'll discuss running a relationship profile task in the SAP Data Services Designer.

To submit a relationship profile request in the SAP Data Services Designer, follow these steps:

1. Locate the LOCAL OBJECT LIBRARY in the bottom-left corner of the SAP DATA SERVICES DESIGNER page.

2. Navigate to the DATASTORES tab of the LOCAL OBJECT LIBRARY.

3. Expand the datastore containing the table you want to profile.

4. Right-click the table in the LOCAL OBJECT LIBRARY to produce the pop-up menu shown in Figure 4.8.

5. Select the SUBMIT RELATIONSHIP PROFILE REQUEST option from the pop-up menu.

6. The SUBMIT RELATIONSHIP PROFILE REQUEST dialog box appears, as shown in Figure 4.9. This dialog box allows you to select which columns you want to relate for the relationship profile requests. This is laid out as two tables that appear side by side that you join with lines, just as in other conventional database graphical tools. You may relate one or more columns by dragging lines between the two tables.

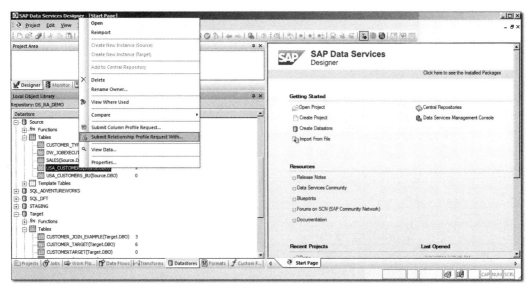

Figure 4.8 Right-Clicking the Source Table to Select Submit Relationship Profile Request

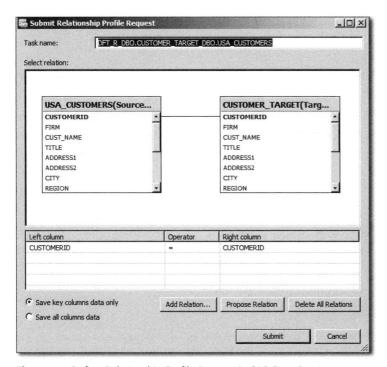

Figure 4.9 Define Relationship Profile Request in SAP Data Services

7. After you've defined the relationships, click SUBMIT to submit the relationship profile request. The PROFILER SERVER MONITOR dialog box appears, as shown in Figure 4.10. Notice the line present now to signify that a relationship profile request is running.

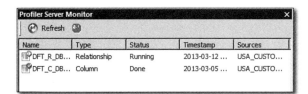

Figure 4.10 Profiler Server Monitor Screen Illustrating a Running Relationship Profile Task

8. After the profiling task is done, the status changes to DONE in the PROFILER SER-VER MONITOR dialog box (see Figure 4.10). You may need to refresh the dialog box by clicking the REFRESH button to see the status reflect DONE because it doesn't always refresh automatically.

After the profiler task is complete, you can view the results in the VIEW DATA screen shown in Figure 4.11 by right-clicking the table in the LOCAL OBJECT LIBRARY and selecting the VIEW DATA option.

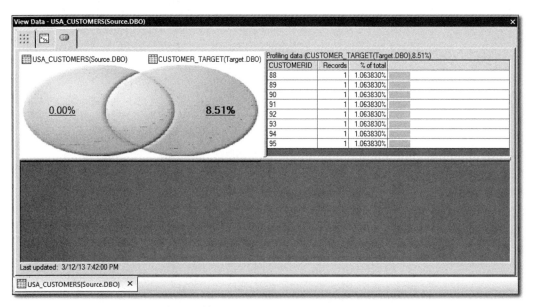

Figure 4.11 Relationship Profiles in SAP Data Services

This perfect example shows that all customers are contained in the USA_CUS-TOMERS table, but only a portion are referenced in the target table. We loaded this table so that only a subset of records are used in the target—8.51%, to be exact. You can view the results graphically in the window pane on the right, and when you select the CUSTOMERID line in the right-hand pane, the example data shows through in the gray area below. The important thing to note is that the value of 0.00% for USA_CUSTOMERS indicates that there are no orphan customer records present in the target that don't exist in the source.

After examining the profiling tools available in SAP Data Services and running both column and relationship profile tasks, you now have a great deal of information about the data that you'll load into SAP HANA. You know that you have some null columns that defy business rules and, in the customer example, a relationship that conforms to what you expect. So now what?

4.3   SSA: Beyond Tools and Profiling

Now it's time to actually look into the data at a deeper level. The profiling that we've shown with SAP Data Services happens quite rapidly. As you can see with the examples in this chapter, profiling is a point-and-click exercise—you pick the table, select the options you want to profile, and start the task. This happens very fast, and now we're ready to begin the next step of SSA: the dialogue with the business users.

To facilitate conversation with the business users, we often put together an SSA document in Microsoft Word with the following components:

▶ **Table name**
Name of the table, which is usually the fully qualified physical name of the table

▶ **Description**
Description of the logical use of the table

▶ **Record count**
Count of records at the time of the profile snapshot

▶ **Profile results**
Reference to the name of the spreadsheet that is typically used to save the pro-file results from SAP Data Services

▶ **Recommendations**
Overall summary of your review of the profile results and data in the table with your understanding of the business rules

▶ **Primary key columns**
Listing of the primary key columns in the table

The following elements also appear and repeat for each column in the table in the document:

▶ **Column name**
Column name in the table

▶ **Column data type**
Data type for the column in the table

▶ **Column foreign key**
Yes or no value to note whether the column is used as a foreign key in the table

▶ **Column text description of business rule**
Text description of the business rule of the column and how it's used in the table

▶ **SQL text for evaluating the business rule**
SQL that was used to evaluate the business rule (blank if no SQL was used)

▶ **Column recommendations**
Your judgment and recommendations of how the data conforms to the business rules and what needs to be done in the source or ETL process to correct the data

Equipped with an SSA document like the one described here, you're ready to have a full discussion, with examples of the source data in detail. It's very important to have all of this detail because you'll have many of these discussions with non-technical, functional users. These users are key to arriving at conclusions about why a source is behaving a certain way, so it's important to have as much information as possible to effectively communicate what you're seeing in a source.

When creating this document, let the profiling results be your guide. Returning to the example of NULL values that exist in a non-nullable column, you use the null violation to fill in the column text description of a business rule and column recommendations to open a conversation with the business users. Even an example as simple as this often leads to research into the system that can uncover things as far as legacy code missteps that have always been present in custom systems or simply a configuration step that was missed in an SAP source.

Note that, no matter what issues are found in the profile task or the deeper inspection of the source, the result will be additional research for functional resources, as well as the resulting business decisions of how to handle the errors. An SSA document is an important tool to share the full story of the source data with the business users.

It's a best practice to correct the source when possible. We advocate handling errors in the ETL process only if you're constrained from making changes in the source system. Let the document created from this list be the guide for the discussion with the business and functional resources to deal with the issues encountered in SSA, and strive to use the document to channel the discussion to correct issues in the source before the ETL. If that isn't possible, then use the column recommendations to describe how to handle the rule violations in the ETL process. It's paramount that these be handled before you move the data into the pristine SAP HANA environment.

Reviewing sources often involves digging into the tables that you profiled with ad hoc SQL to look beyond the profile task. After further review of the data with SQL, don't be surprised if one rule violation leads to another. It's often the case, in our experience, that the closer you look at a source, the more problems you'll find. This isn't an easy journey, and quite often it leads to some startling realizations for the business users. However, this is an incredibly important step in the SAP HANA development journey. Reassure the business users that all of the issues found and handled now will lead to a better SAP HANA system. Remember, the profile results are the starting point, and a thorough SSA is where patterns emerge and you begin to see the true color of the source.

In this section, we'll review the SSA journey in more detail by examining patterns in data (Section 4.3.1), then review how commonalities can be seen across sources (Section 4.3.2) to truly treat systems as one (Section 4.3.3). To conclude the section, we will end with a discussion of mapping data sources to the logical transformations that will occur in the ETL code on the way to SAP HANA (Section 4.3.4).

4.3.1 Establishing Patterns

Patterns are important when you're performing SSA. When looking at a source, try to look for all of the patterns present in the data. Searching for patterns is one place where you need to step beyond the established business rules to see things that haven't been disclosed. This is both an art and a science, but we'll explore some techniques that make this process easier and repeatable.

The first way to look for patterns is to search for actual patterns present in the data fields. Start with the address field example cited earlier, in Figure 4.7. This example illustrated an address pattern present in a text field using the pattern attribute of the column profile. The pattern attribute in the column profile is a good starting point for assimilating all of the patterns that exist in text fields, but you need to look more broadly into the data as well. Take nulls, for example. An easy pattern to spot is if a column is entirely null. This is very straightforward because the column was never used in the source system, and the result is obvious. What if the column were 70% percent null? At that point, you use SQL to determine if there was a date correlation to when the NULL values began occurring. Was it a particular point in time? Maybe something occurred in the application after a date exposed by a date column in the table or after an ID range maximum value? These are the types of behavior patterns that can become quite useful.

This is the inquisitive approach that is necessary to dig into the source as you should. The answers that you're looking to uncover with this type of analysis are whether the column's use changed over time, which is another type of pattern but not one that is exposed by a simple snapshot profile. Multiple profiles are needed over time, or you will most likely combine the profile results from SAP Data Services with ad hoc SQL against date columns to establish your own patterns.

Another pattern that often develops is *field misuse*, which occurs when a field, or column in a table, is used for a misleading purpose based on the name of the field in the table. With custom-developed systems, we've seen many cases where, for lack of an available field, a developer often just uses a field for a purpose that had nothing to do with the field name. Another example you'll encounter is when an application has generic fields of varying data types that are used for a variety of reasons.

Field overuse, which occurs when one field is used for multiple purposes, is another potential that should also be discussed. We often see this in code fields, when one code field is used for multiple purposes or in combination with another field. Sometimes we see that multi-character fields contain multiple code values at a specific string position of the field. This positional reference is then used in combination with the character value that the code should signify. We often see these in legacy mainframe systems, where techniques like these were used to save storage and to use every byte.

These are all examples of patterns that need to be documented and discussed with the business users. Patterns like these will lead you to questions—but not answers—on the first pass.

These are all problematic examples from an ETL or BI design, but from our experience, you'll encounter these often in source systems. Patterns are crucial for true understanding of a source. Without thorough SSA, patterns will be missed and data misinterpreted further, extending the cycle of poor data quality into SAP HANA.

4.3.2 Looking Across Sources

So far, we've described SSA as looking into a single source, but there may be times when you need to combine multiple sources. Whenever you're striving to combine multiple sources into an OLAP design for a data mart, you'll certainly need to use a profiling tool such as SAP Data Services; SQL won't take you across multiple source tables. You can use SAP Data Services relationship profiling as a tool to see and measure logical relationships across source systems and platforms.

We recommend that you use column profiling with datastore configurations to quickly run baseline profile results across multiple sources, as shown previously, in Figure 4.11. You can see where sales records don't have customers, or even whether there was supposed to be an employee attached to a sales transaction, no matter the platform. These are simple scenarios that won't be handled with SQL.

Think about the employee example. If the human resources system with employee information is hosted in the cloud but the online point-of-sale system is in an Oracle database, you'll never be able to write SQL to see if a relationship exists, even if you have the same Employee_ID field in both the human resources system and the online point-of-sales table. The only way to accomplish this is with a relationship profile in SAP Data Services. Concepts like these and tools to accomplish this type of analysis are really important for combining data from multiple sources.

4.3.3 Treating Disparate Systems as One

Treating multiple sources as one is always a challenge. By definition, most BI and data mart efforts combine multiple sources into the final OLAP data mart target. This is a challenge because when you're developing these targets, you strive to combine data from multiple sources that was never meant to be combined. This is where the business rules are very important because they serve as the guide that knits together the various systems into one story to build a comprehensive reporting solution about the business and not the various systems.

To do this effectively, you must look across sources and let the business rules be your guide. Metadata can help you do this, but not without powerful tools to help profile the data across sources. Without a tool such as SAP Data Services, you'll get lost in the weeds of one particular source and have a hard time seeing the larger picture available.

Without metadata, this would be very difficult, especially with stock SQL, because this hits only one source. Stock SQL keeps you at the database level, which, by definition, keeps you in the application, diminishing the ability to see relationships that should or should not exist between systems. Without metadata, you'll never truly be able to break out of the sources to see what the business needs. It's simply necessary for combining sources into SAP HANA.

4.3.4 Mapping Your Data

Now that you've profiled your data and exhausted the source via thorough SSA, you'll need to begin the mapping process. Mapping your data is simply a logical exercise to pre-code the ETL code before you even open SAP Data Services. You perform mapping by creating a mapping document (usually in Microsoft Excel, like the one shown in Figure 4.12) and using a TARGET section to illustrate the target table fields.

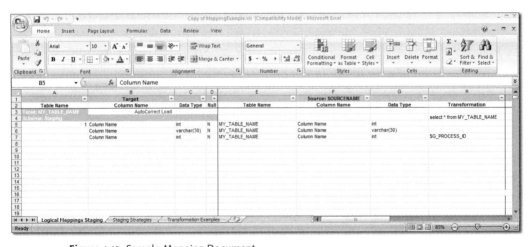

Figure 4.12 Sample Mapping Document

A Source section illustrates the fields that you're reading from in the source table. A Transformation column shows any special logic or transformations that have occurred in the ETL process.

You may be wondering why to bother with mapping when SAP Data Services is such an easy-to-use graphical tool. The first reason is simple: it's easier, faster, and cheaper to create a complete mapping document that you can throw away than to throw away code in SAP Data Services. If it seems counterintuitive at first, bear in mind that you'll actually save time in your SAP HANA development effort by spending the time to fully map your sources.

The second reason to use a mapping document and mapping process in your SAP HANA project is that the mapping document serves as a wonderful conversation piece to force a dialogue with the business users or functional consultants. The mapping document is the culmination of all of your research and SSA. It's a product of your interpretations of conversations with the business users and a final result that explicitly communicates what is going into SAP HANA and how you'll be doing it. This Excel platform provides an easily digestible format for a non-technical audience to review some rather technical things. As the last step before coding begins, this mapping phase is important to get correct the first time.

One final, often-overlooked topic should be discussed: whether to use a style in the mapping document that favors a straightforward English descriptive style or a syntactically correct style of language. Take a simple `UPPER()` function used to convert a field to uppercase. A syntactically correct style reads `UPPER(myFieldName)`. If you used an English descriptive style, then the mapping document reads "Convert `myFieldName` to upper case." This is specifically regarding the transformations section of the mapping document seen in column H in Figure 4.12. Although this may not seem like a large distinction, consider that both your development team and non-technical audience will use this mapping document. Table 4.1 shows scenarios in which each mapping document style works.

Mapping Document Style	When to Use
English descriptive style	► A small development team is used.
	► Very technical and senior developers are present.
	► Lots of interaction occurs with the business users.
	► The business users make up the main audience for the document.

Table 4.1 Mapping Document Style Comparison

Mapping Document Style	When to Use
Syntactically correct	► Many developers are involved to keep the code consistent. ► Junior developers are present in the project. ► The business users review the document, but with the help of the architect. ► The developers make up the main audience of the document, and the purpose is to keep the code uniform and succinct.

Table 4.1 Mapping Document Style Comparison (Cont.)

4.4 Summary

In this chapter, we've discussed many steps and tasks that are needed before you provision data into SAP HANA. We covered the importance of proper profiling, followed by in-depth SSA, and finally creating a mapping document to ensure that you're getting it all right before loading into SAP HANA.

SAP HANA is an immensely powerful platform, but it will be really useful only with high-quality data. Speed is helpful only if the information is worth discovering. Profiling your sources is important because it saves time and money. Using SAP Data Services for your profiling tasks is an excellent option because you get a runtime license for an enterprise-class data integration tool complete with enterprise-class profiling and SSA capabilities.

Pre-provisioning data is one step in the process that you don't want to skip. Remember that profiling is only the start of your SSA journey. You must perform thorough SSA to expose the issues to correct and then use a mapping document to guide your code through the issues. Not performing proper SSA up front in the process can lead to costly mistakes in your development cycle. Performing proper SSA shows you the real story behind your data and ensures that you're not just loading fast trash into SAP HANA. It's only after this step that you're ready to begin the process to provision your data into SAP HANA, which is the subject of the next chapter.

The design and build of the data loading process is necessary for a native implementation of SAP HANA. This can be done very effectively via SAP Data Services.

5   Provisioning Data with SAP Data Services

SAP Data Services has been SAP HANA's singular solution for non-SAP data since SAP HANA's inception and the coupling of SAP Data Services with SAP HANA's native API. With this capability, SAP Data Services is in a unique position to take advantage of options such as SAP HANA's native sophisticated bulk loading functionality, thus allowing for incredibly fast loads of very large data sets directly into SAP HANA memory. SAP Data Services can also create both columnar and row tables at runtime with a unique template table functionality, which is an important functionality for integration with SAP HANA.

The purpose of this chapter is to take a deep dive into SAP Data Services to see what it can offer to a batch method data-provisioning effort. The heart of the chapter is Section 5.1, in which we'll examine how SAP Data Services is used to load data into SAP HANA and create tables at runtime, and we'll also explore the wide palette of SAP Data Services tools, functions, and transforms that are ready and poised to enrich data on the way into SAP HANA. The focus of this section is the SAP Data Services Designer, which is our recommended tool for provisioning data for SAP HANA. However, SAP Data Services also offers another tool, SAP Data Services Workbench; we'll introduce this tool briefly in Section 5.2. Finally, although the focus of this chapter is on batch data provisioning, we'll conclude the chapter by briefly discussing some methods for real-time replication (Section 5.3).

5.1   Provisioning Data Using SAP Data Services Designer

SAP HANA customers that purchase SAP HANA in a standalone configuration are quite fortunate because they receive a runtime license of SAP Data Services, which is SAP's premier ETL solution in its information management portfolio. SAP Data

Services has a long track record of providing a quality enterprise information management (EIM) platform for both data integration and data quality, and the product is often a leader in various independent resource polls, such as Gartner's Magic Quadrant.

The heart of the SAP Data Services deployment is the SAP Data Services Designer client, wherein all of the ETL code is crafted, as shown in Figure 5.1.

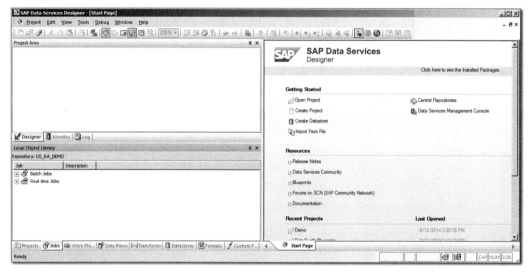

Figure 5.1 SAP Data Services Designer Client Application

Provisioning your data using SAP Data Services involves various aspects of the tool, and the goal of this section is to explain all of them. The next eight sections cover the aspects of SAP Data Services that you will use when provisioning your data to prepare it for SAP HANA:

▶ Metadata

▶ Datastores

▶ Jobs

▶ Workflows

▶ Data flows

▶ Transforms

▶ Built-in functions

- Custom functions and scripts
- File formats
- Real-time jobs

5.1.1   Metadata

Recall from Chapter 4 that SAP Data Services is quite flexible and operates on the concept of *metadata*. Metadata is simply data providing information about other data. In this sense, any data being analyzed is actually just an array of columns and rows. This segregation from a source or SQL connection allows SAP Data Services to connect to databases, tables, flat files, and application connections, as well as interact with these connections in exactly the same way. This is an important concept for SAP Data Services because a developer needs to understand and master only one interface. SAP Data Services acts as an insulating layer to the developer, and, after a developer has mastered the SAP Data Services functions, transforms, and platform, these concepts are applicable to connecting to any source database.

The development platform in SAP Data Services offers uniformity across sources, which is important for both ETL and SAP HANA because a developer will often be asked to combine multiple sources of data into SAP HANA. For SAP Data Services, these various sources and source platforms are all simply connections of arrays of data. SAP Data Services presents the developer merely with rows and columns of data that need to be handled with all of the various functionalities within the tool. SAP Data Services does the actual heavy lifting under the surface connections but automatically converts all of the native SAP Data Services functions available to the SQL syntax of the native database connections.

Consider an example in which an SAP Data Services UPPER() function is used on a varchar() column, such as a FIRST_NAME field. The function that exists in the data flow depicted in Figure 5.2 is actually converted to the SQL depicted in Figure 5.3.

This is the SQL that is presented to the database, and this functionality (known as *push down*) allows SAP Data Services to effectively push the operations or heavy lifting down to the source or target databases. Here, the developer needs to master only this one interface to the data and doesn't have to know the specifics of the syntax of the function in the source database. SAP Data Services takes care of the conversion in the OPTIMIZED SQL window shown in Figure 5.3.

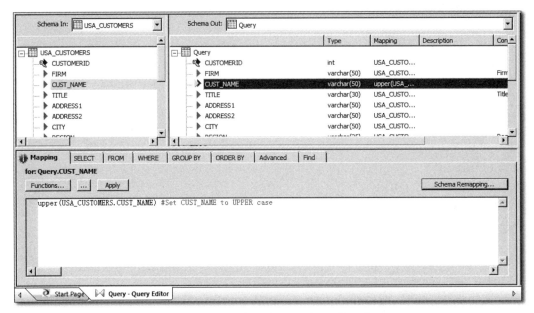

Figure 5.2 UPPER() Function in SAP Data Services Query Transform

Figure 5.3 Optimized SQL Push Down to Database via Metadata

In this example, the source database, SQL Server, happened to have the same syntax as SAP Data Services for the upper function: upper(). However, this is often not the case, especially across database platforms. If a developer were combining two sources and the syntax were different in the two database platforms, the SAP Data Services syntax in Figure 5.2 would still be the same. However, depending on the source database connection, SAP Data Services would handle the difference in the SQL to each of the varying sources! This is a great benefit that metadata brings to a development effort; it allows true standardization for a team.

If both the source and the target datastore connections are the same SAP HANA instance, it may be possible to perform full pushdown. Full pushdown for traditional database connections in SAP Data Services constructs an SQL statement like the following:

```
Insert into target_table Select * from source_table
```

For SAP HANA, full pushdown may actually not move any data at all. This is possible because SAP Data Services' tight coupling with SAP HANA allows SAP Data Services to construct analytic modeling content on SAP HANA at runtime in the form of SAP HANA views to realize the needs of the ETL code. So, there will be certain cases when ETL code does not extract or load any data to or from SAP HANA—but the transformation still occurs!

5.1.2 Datastores

Datastores are connections to databases or applications from SAP Data Services that are fully configurable. They are the physical realization of the metadata connection layer in SAP Data Services; they provide the layer of abstraction from the actual database and application connections. Configurations can be made directly to database tables or through software adapters, and they allow SAP Data Services to access metadata from a database or application and read from or write to that database or application while SAP Data Services is executing a job.

> **Note**
>
> Although it may seem unintuitive, remember that datastores don't store or hold data. They are merely a description of the connection, not the actual data stored in the table. These connections are made in the SAP Data Services Designer application.

Creating a datastore is the first step in any development effort because a connection must be made to a source and a target. The connection parameters, such as DATABASE SERVER NAME, DATABASE NAME, and PASSWORD to access the database are set in the EDIT DATASTORE configuration screen, shown in Figure 5.4.

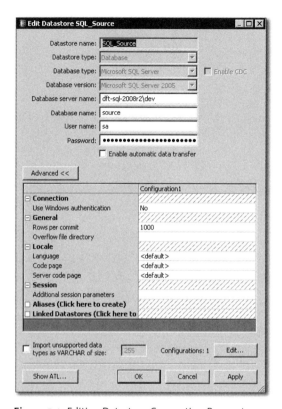

Figure 5.4 Editing Datastore Connection Parameters

Table 5.1 describes the connection parameters range from SAP Data Services settings. These are SAP Data Services settings that detail the connection to the source or target database. Keep in mind that, when you're establishing a datastore, you can't go back and change the first four configuration settings (shown with an asterisk in Table 5.1) after you've specified them, so make sure you choose these settings wisely.

Datastore Configuration Property	Description
DATASTORE NAME*	Logical name of the datastore that will be used in SAP Data Services
DATASTORE TYPE*	Type of datastore that you're creating

Table 5.1 Datastore Configuration Properties

Datastore Configuration Property	Description
DATABASE TYPE*	Type of database that you're connecting
DATABASE VERSION*	Version of database that you're connecting
DATABASE SERVER NAME	Logical name of the database server
DATABASE NAME	Logical name of the database that you're connecting
USER NAME	Database user that will be used to establish the connection
PASSWORD	Database password that will be used to establish the connection

Table 5.1 Datastore Configuration Properties (Cont.)

This is one reason it's a good idea to name the datastore after what it will be used for. If this will be the only source for your job, then you can simply call it "Source." If this is a source that will be used to load or read human resources data, you may want to call it "HUMAN_RESOURCES." Try to avoid names that are closely linked with a database or application platform because these tend to change over time. It's a best practice to keep a datastore name generic and descriptive of the task at hand.

Another important point is that these settings can be replicated across multiple configurations, so a configuration allows the same datastore to connect to different databases—or even different servers! You can create multiple configurations for a datastore, which allows you to plan ahead for different environments for your datastore, as well as limiting the level of effort when you're migrating jobs. For example, you can add a set of configurations (DEV, TEST, and PROD) to the same datastore name. These connection settings stay with the datastore during export or import. You can group any set of datastore configurations into a system configuration. When you're running or scheduling a job, you can select a system configuration and, thus, the set of datastore configurations for your current environment. This way, you can change connections at will both during unit testing and when you're scheduling a job; the net result is a very easy way to test code against multiple environments on multiple platforms. These system configurations can also have specific applications for an SAP HANA provisioning task.

Figure 5.5 shows an example of a datastore that has a DEV, TEST, and PROD configuration. Note that, even though this example has all configurations pointing to the same Microsoft SQL Server database, that needn't always be the case. These connections could be to any database, provided that the schemas for the tables are the same. The datastore configurations are a very powerful component for enabling metadata in SAP Data Services.

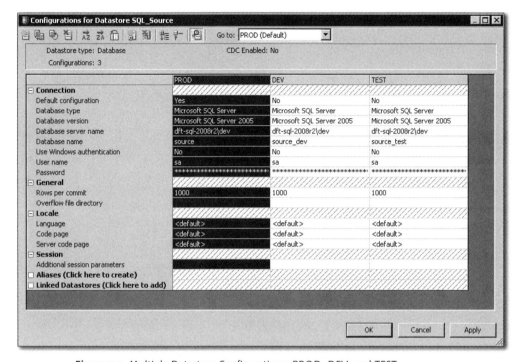

Figure 5.5 Multiple Datastore Configurations: PROD, DEV, and TEST

Provisioning Data in SAP HANA Using System Configurations

Most business intelligence (BI) initiatives using SAP HANA provision data from multiple sources into a reporting structure, which involves setting up multiple source environments. This is the precise scenario in which you want to use multiple datastore configurations, as shown in Figure 5.5. These configurations allow easy switching from environment to environment and enable you to use the same code with minimal modifications.

Instead of a connection for DEV, TEST, and PROD, you might see a connection for customer data from an SQL Server point-of-sales system, as well as a DB2 customer source from a mainframe ERP source table. As long as the customer source columns are the same, you can switch the connection at runtime from one connection to the next and use the same code to read the data. This is a very easy way to move between sources for an SAP HANA data load.

Datastores also provide a way to leverage partitioning in SAP HANA with the modern features of SAP Data Services. This allows a developer to realize extreme performance by running parallel threads of activity against the source or target database partitions independently. This is now supported in SAP HANA (SAP HANA SPS 8 running SAP Data Services 4.2 SP02 or greater) and has the potential to offer time savings on very large data loads. Take an example with five years of data and one billion records. This may take some time to load as one target with one thread, but if you could load the data in parallel and split the data into the five years with one partition per year, you could realize five loaders in a parallel fashion to SAP HANA from Data Services.

> **Note**
>
> Partitions can stand on their own, like this example, or play in concert with the discussion about workflows loading in parallel, as discussed in Section 5.1.4.

Datastores provide an important layer of isolation between objects in SAP Data Services—but they merely facilitate connections underlying source or target objects in SAP Data Services. To enable SAP Data Services to act on a connection and actually execute or perform an operation of work, you need to invoke an SAP Data Services job.

5.1.3   Jobs

A *job* is the only executable element in SAP Data Services. Without a job to execute in SAP Data Services, a datastore can't do anything. A datastore with nothing to invoke action is just metadata describing a connection—this is where a job takes over and controls the execution or the actions in SAP Data Services.

Jobs are found in the SAP Data Services Designer under the JOBS tab in the LOCAL OBJECT LIBRARY, as highlighted in the bottom left of Figure 5.6.

Batch jobs operate on a schedule and run at specified intervals dictated by the schedule. A schedule is just another object in SAP Data Services, so one job can have multiple schedules with different parameters for connections and variables. (Batch jobs are the predominant way to load data into SAP HANA; we discuss this in detail in Chapter 6.)

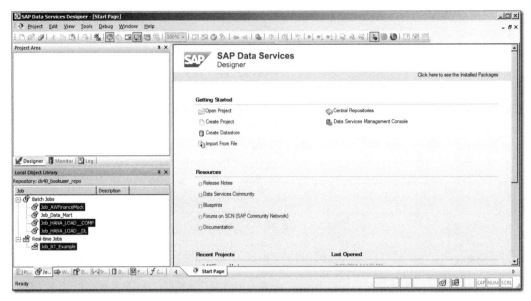

Figure 5.6 Batch and Real-Time Jobs in SAP Data Services Designer

Proper batch job form is illustrated in Figure 5.7. Best practices dictate that a batch job contain a `Try` and a `Catch` block object (see the `Try` and `End` objects at the beginning and end in Figure 5.7). The `Try` and `Catch` blocks capture errors at both the application and database levels and control process flow and interpretation of the errors.

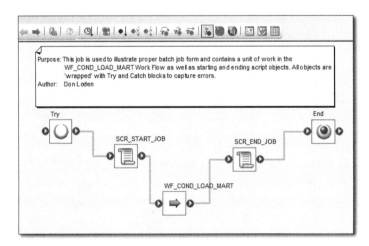

Figure 5.7 Proper Batch Job Form

Inside the `Try` and `Catch` are the script objects. The script objects are shown in Figure 5.7 as `SCR_START_JOB` and `SCR_END_JOB`, respectively. These script objects do things such as set variable values by both literal declarations and return values from database tables. The `SCR_END_JOB` script is used to finalize variable values and, most often, signify the end of the job.

Finally, the workflow icon in the center with the blue arrow is what contains the working elements of the job: the data flow. These are discussed in great detail in Section 5.1.4 and Section 5.1.5.

Jobs can also be run in real time; by definition, this doesn't require a schedule. Real-time jobs are created in SAP Data Services Designer just as a batch job is; however, they are always waiting and ready to respond to web services. They act as stateless objects, whereby an application passing data in the form of a generic XML web service gets a response back with the output of the real-time job. Real-time jobs look very similar to their batch counterparts. An example of a real-time job is shown in Figure 5.8.

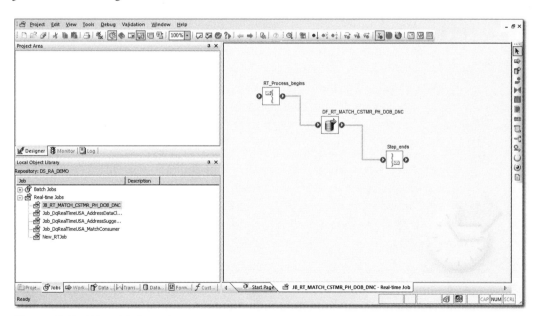

Figure 5.8 Real-Time Job Example

This type of functionality and interaction are used by applications ranging from SAP Business Suite to SAP Customer Relationship Management (SAP CRM) and SAP Master Data Governance (SAP MDG) mostly for data enhancements, such as address cleansing or matching records. It's important to note that using this functionality isn't limited to SAP applications; it can be extended to any application that can pass XML web services.

The only real difference between a batch job and a real-time job in terms of what is seen in SAP Data Services Designer is the two icons surrounding the unit of work in the middle. These are placeholder icons that show that this is a real-time job. They are placed in the real-time job by SAP Data Services upon creation, and they are non-configurable objects. Real-time jobs are also very important for provisioning data into SAP HANA because they can be used for real-time replication of data when the data needs alterations of some sort on the way into SAP HANA. Real-time jobs are discussed in Section 5.1.10.

In Figure 5.7 and Figure 5.8, we've shown and exemplified where the work happens in SAP Data Services jobs by referencing workflows and data flows. Next, let's discuss these components in detail.

5.1.4 Workflows

A *workflow* is a grouping mechanism that controls the flow of work in the job. It doesn't actually perform work on its own; it's a container object that SAP Data Services can use to layer any of the work tasks in any possible order. So, a workflow is really just an organizational component in an SAP Data Services job. The best way to think of a workflow is similar to a folder in Microsoft Windows.

Although it may not seem like workflows do very much, they actually perform some very powerful tasks in SAP Data Services. They allow parallel or series operations with some unique recovery options. Workflows also extend the object-oriented nature of SAP Data Services by extending the reusability of objects in certain cases. All of these features expand the capabilities of SAP Data Services with some very important items for SAP HANA conversions.

Next, we'll discuss three main capabilities of workflows: parallel execution, series execution, and reusability.

Parallel Execution

Workflows allow a developer to run objects or work in parallel with one another. In the example in Figure 5.9, these workflows control the work of loading the dimension tables. This is a perfect example of *parallel* operations, which occur when multiple units of work happen at the same time in an SAP Data Service job. In this example, account, employee, or customer data are all independent, with no relation to each other. Because there are no database or data dependencies on any of the tables that are being loaded, the loads can run in parallel.

By running all three data loads for DIM_ACCOUNT, DIM_CUSTOMER, and DIM_EMPLOYEE in parallel, you shorten the runtime dramatically. Let's assume for this example that loading DIM_CUSTOMER takes the longest because the organization sees more changes in customer data per day over DIM_EMPLOYEE or DIM_ACCOUNT data. So in this example, assume that DIM_CUSTOMER has a runtime of 15 minutes, while DIM_ACCOUNT and DIM_EMPLOYEE have runtimes of 5 minutes and 10 minutes, respectively. See the details in Table 5.2.

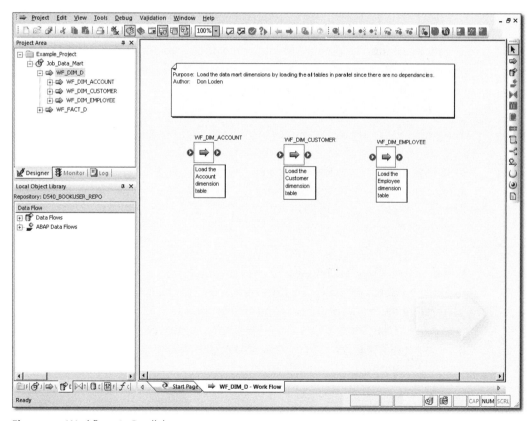

Figure 5.9 Workflows in Parallel

	Parallel Time	Series Time
Table Loaded	**Runtime**	**Runtime**
DIM_ACCOUNT	5 minutes	5 minutes
DIM_CUSTOMER	15 minutes	15 minutes
DIM_EMPLOYEE	10 minutes	10 minutes
Net Time	**15 minutes**	**30 minutes**

Table 5.2 Runtime Cut in Half with Parallel Operations

With running the three tables in a series, you have a runtime of 30 minutes because each unit of work that loads each table must complete before the next begins. If you run the units of work that load each table in parallel, you now have a longer running operation that covers the other shorter running operations. SAP Data Services is a multithreaded application that can take advantage of this parallelization. As long as the underlying database source and target can handle the requests and throughput, this is a great scenario with a much better performing outcome. By running the data in parallel for all three tables, you've now cut the runtime for all three tables in half!

This principle is very important for loading data into SAP HANA because you'll be loading very large volumes of data from your sources. Operations have long running load times, so the first thing you should consider for tuning an SAP HANA application is which operations can be run in parallel by examining the dependencies present in the data. This covers a very important process for getting data into SAP HANA and is great until something causes a failure and the job screeches to a halt.

Recovery is always an important consideration. However, now, with parallel work being done, recovery is a little more complex than it would be if you were performing the work in a linear fashion. Fortunately, SAP Data Services not only performs checkpoint recovery, but also has some nice recovery features to handle these types of situations. These situations exist more often in an SAP HANA environment requiring parallel loads to cope with extreme amounts of data.

SAP Data Services offers a robust checkpoint recovery system that is fairly intelligent. *Checkpoint recovery* monitors the job execution and keeps track of which units of work complete successfully and which don't. If any unit of work doesn't complete successfully, the job can recover the data by reprocessing the step upon the next execution of the job. You enable this feature by running the job with recovery enabled. To do this, run the job from SAP Data Services Designer by right-clicking the job and choosing EXECUTE in the project window, as shown in Figure 5.10.

This brings up the EXECUTION PROPERTIES window in SAP Data Services Designer. This window is used for many things, but if you want to enable checkpoint recovery for an SAP Data Services job at runtime, all you need to do is select the ENABLE RECOVERY checkbox, as shown in Figure 5.11.

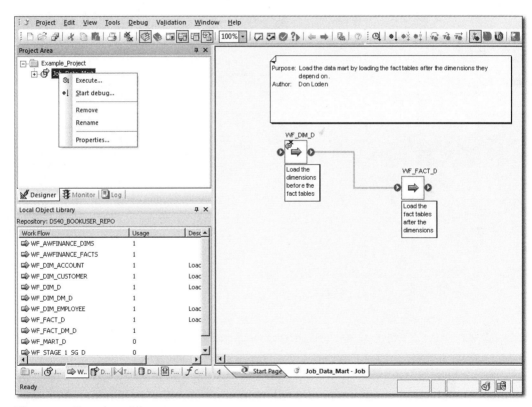

Figure 5.10 Executing a Job

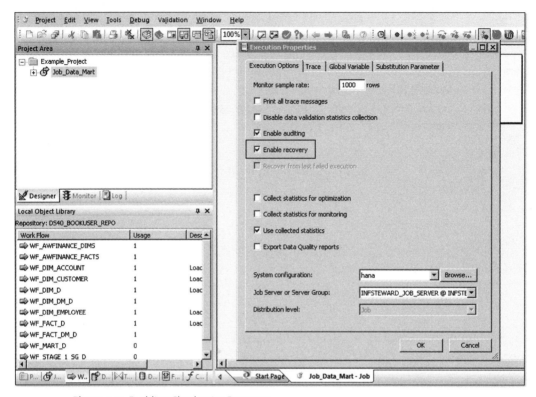

Figure 5.11 Enabling Checkpoint Recovery

This great feature works quite well when data is loaded in a singular stream. However, other challenges are introduced when you're loading data in parallel. If the tables in Figure 5.9 had a downstream dependency in the job and you needed to ensure that loading these tables was always concluded concurrently, then you could set the workflows to recover as a unit, as shown in Figure 5.12.

Recovering as a unit overrides the checkpoint recovery for any of the workflows that had finished and causes them to reprocess in the event of a failure. Sometimes, this can be dangerous, such as if the data within the tables need to be treated as a unit. If a dependency like this exists in your data, you need to create the parallel workflow to recover as a unit. When this is established, the recovery will behave as illustrated in Table 5.3.

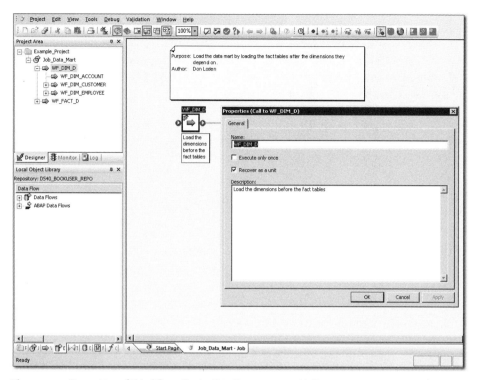

Figure 5.12 Properties of Workflow Illustrating Recovery as a Unit

Tables Loaded in Parallel	Runtime	Failed Status	Checkpoint Recovery Only	Recover as a Unit Enabled
DIM_ACCOUNT	5 minutes	Success	Skip	Reprocess
DIM_CUSTOMER	15 minutes	Fail	Reprocess	Reprocess
DIM_EMPLOYEE	10 minutes	Success	Skip	Reprocess

Table 5.3 Recovery Processing Comparing Checkpoint Only to Recover as a Unit

This works well, and there is one more level of granularity for this type of recovery scenario. You can still have all of the workflows recover as a unit, but in cases when you need the workflow to execute only once, you can use the checkbox shown in Figure 5.12. This situation usually exists where processing triggers are involved, either in this job or outside the context of the SAP Data Services job.

Example of Executing Only Once

The situation arises (albeit infrequently) when you may process the operations in a workflow only once, even on recovery. We typically see this when you need to trigger behavior in another application via depositing a file or writing to a database table.

If you have a business rule stating that a process can run only once per month, and you encounter a job failure, you don't want to re-trigger the processing with an SAP Data Services job recovery. Instead, use the EXECUTE ONLY ONCE option to force the recovery to skip the operation on recovery. This allows a much greater degree of control on what is recovered, processed, or skipped in a complex recovery situation.

Series Execution

Series execution is the most common design in SAP Data Services workflows. This design allows workflows or operations to run sequentially or in a series. One operation has to complete before the next can begin. Although this has a negative performance impact, it's a great option when dependencies arise in the data. In these types of situations, the data elements or workflows are often building blocks of logic, where step one must be completed before step two can start.

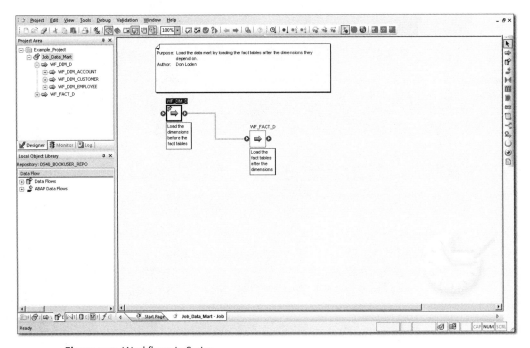

Figure 5.13 Workflows in Series

An example of this is shown in Figure 5.13, where the workflow `WF_DIM_D` builds the dimensions in the data mart in SAP HANA, and workflow `WF_FACT_D` builds the facts in SAP HANA.

By definition, you need to build the fact tables that are in the second workflow after the dimension tables because they depend on the dimensions in terms of the key structure. Fact tables always have foreign keys that reference a primary key field of a dimension table.

Consider the data example in Figure 5.14, which supports the SAP Data Services code example in Figure 5.13. To have a record in FACT_SALE, you need a product record in DIM_PRODUCT to sell. Please notice, as well, that the `WF_DIM_D` has the green icon arrow in Figure 5.13 to recover as a unit, as just discussed. All of the dimension tables may be built in parallel because there are no dependencies present, but you may want to recover all tables together in the event of a failure.

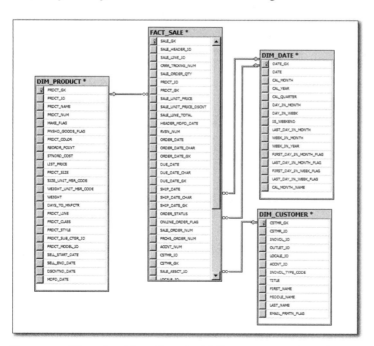

Figure 5.14 Dimensional Data Mart Model Illustrating Data Dependencies

FACT_SALE records in our SAP HANA data mart are all measures of the sales of products and customers stored at a certain level of granularity organized by a date dimension table. So, for this model to work, you have to create the primary keys in the dimension tables in the SAP Data Services job before those values can be looked up or assigned as foreign key references in the FACT_SALE table. This is the perfect example of why you need to take a hit in terms of load performance to simply meet the constraints that arise in your data model while loading SAP HANA with SAP Data Services.

To summarize, any time there is a dependency present in your job, you must design the workflows to operate in series; if there is no logical dependency, use parallel workflow designs because they operate with the highest level of efficiency and perform at the maximum level for fast loads into SAP HANA.

Series and parallel execution are two important design considerations when using workflows in an SAP Data Services job. These are the classic use cases for these container objects in SAP Data Services. However, there is one often overlooked yet important function that a workflow provides in an SAP Data Services job: reusability.

Reusability

SAP Data Services is, at its core, an object-oriented tool. We've already examined the SAP Data Services constructs—datastores, jobs, and workflows are all objects in SAP Data Services. This will continue throughout this chapter as we examine the rest of the objects used to provision your data into SAP HANA. But if these objects are reusable, the SAP Data Services reusability concept applies. Table 5.4 shows a concise list of reusable and single-use objects in SAP Data Services.

SAP Data Services Object	Object State
Workflow	Reusable
Data flow	Reusable
Query transform	Single use
Template table	Single use
Template XML	Single use
Script	Single use
Conditional	Single use
Try	Single use
Catch	Single use
Annotation	Single use

Table 5.4 SAP Data Services Objects and Reusability State

A single-use object is just as it sounds: an object that may be used only once.

In contrast, a reusable object is an object that may be used multiple times, but only one instance of that object is stored in the repository. The rest of the times that reusable object is stored, only the pointer to the object is referenced in the code, so any of the changes made to that object need to happen only once at the base level of that object. In a single-use object, any changes made to that object need to be replicated wherever the object is used. This often shows up with a script because the script's functionality often needs to be replicated in various points in an SAP Data Services job, but the script is only a single-use object. This often requires copying and pasting the contents of a script to another single-use script.

Consider the moderately complex script in Figure 5.15. Copying and pasting single-use objects works fine until a change needs to be made to the underlying logic of the script, which forces the developer to go back to each script and change the logic in each of the places. There is an easy way to reconcile this issue and transform the single-use script into a reusable object: envelop the script in a workflow!

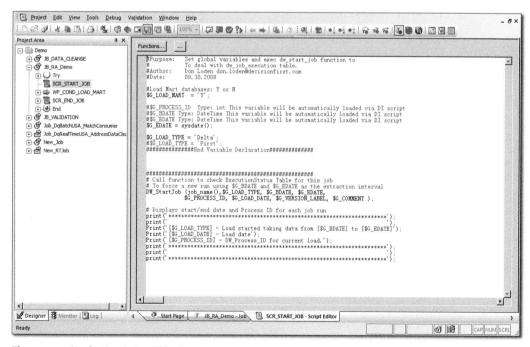

Figure 5.15 Single-Use Script Object

By doing this, you're changing the properties of the script by simply adding this script to the workflow (a reusable object). You can now treat the contents of the script as one object. If the script needs to be reused, you may now drag and drop the workflow wherever it's needed in the job. For the example in Figure 5.15, in which the script had been used multiple times, if the script is in the workflow, you need to make changes in only one place. You change the original script in the workflow, and the workflow acts as a pointer and cascades all changes wherever you used the workflow. This extension of object-oriented reusability is a huge but often overlooked benefit to using workflows in SAP Data Services. It not only saves time, but also results in more modular, flexible designs.

Workflows certainly have a very important place in SAP Data Services jobs; however, they still don't perform any work. Work and logical operations are actually performed at the data flow level in SAP Data Services, so let's turn our attention there next.

5.1.5 Data Flows

Data flows in SAP Data Services are the basic units of work. Data flows occur when data is moved from the source to your SAP HANA target tables. Data flows are where data (or even entire sets of data) is transformed at the column level. In short, data flows are where all of the action resides and the transformation logic in an SAP Data Services job happens.

This is accomplished by an extensive set of built-in *functions* and *transforms*. A function operates on a column, and a transform operates on an entire row of data; however, both significantly transform the data output. Properly designed data flows comprise both functions and transforms, and when used appropriately, they create a powerful canvas of data manipulation for loading SAP HANA. Properly designed data flows not only transform the data, but also need to be constructed in a certain order to make the best use of SAP Data Services. An example of a properly constructed data flow is shown in Figure 5.16.

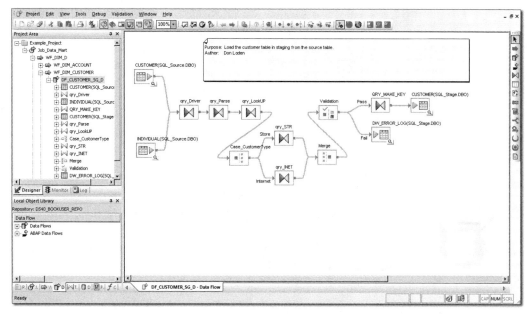

Figure 5.16 Customer Data Flow Illustrating All Stages of Processing

Having order in the data flow helps not only with delivering the logic in the data flow, but also with the performance of the data flow and the job as a whole. This order results in dividing the data flow into various processing stages. A well-constructed data flow can be separated into five main stages, which are shown in Figure 5.16:

▶ **Driver stage**
Limits the record set by pushing down all joins or restrictions to the source database.

▶ **Parsing stage**
Parses the data using SAP Data Services functions or transforms. Some of this happens in the SAP Data Services job server engine.

▶ **Lookup stage**
Looks up values for denormalization purposes or other means. This happens more often for the SAP HANA target because further denormalization is required for good base data designs (as described in Chapter 3).

▶ **Business rules validation stage**
Validates all of the work performed in the data flow against the business rules that guide the data flow; determines whether the flow performed the work it needed to perform.

▶ **Data load stage**
Loads the SAP HANA tables. The tables are bulk loaded (in most cases) and, in some cases, created in SAP HANA. Both column-store and row-store tables can be created with SAP Data Services.

Driver Stage

As shown in this list, the first stage of a properly constructed data flow is the *driver stage*, which constitutes a very important step in data flow design. This stage limits your data set with your first Query transform. Most often, data flows in an SAP HANA replication job do not process all of the data from the source with each run. The SAP Data Services job is usually constructed in such a way that it gathers only changed records to replicate over changed records. This is shown in great detail in Chapter 6, but at a high level, we'll do this by using the first Query transform to drive down the record set that SAP Data Services processes in the data flow by limiting the data with a range-based WHERE clause. Figure 5.17 illustrates the driver stage, with the first Query transform highlighted with an annotation.

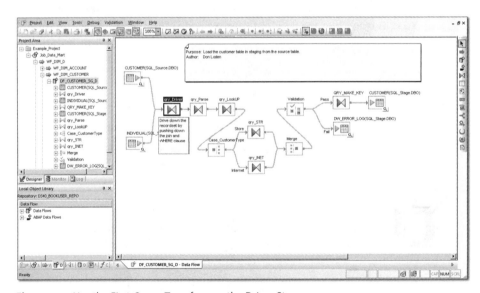

Figure 5.17 Use the First Query Transform as the Driver Stage

In this example, `qry_Driver` is used to push down a join between the CUSTOMER and INDIVIDUAL tables. This pushes down all possible operations, including the expensive WHERE clause and any joins to the source database. The database is much more efficient because the join happens natively in the database, as well as in the WHERE clause, to limit the data set. Then, the resulting set is rendered into SAP Data Services for further transformation in the next section of the code. SAP Data Services is designed with the intent of stratifying the workload between the database server and the SAP Data Services job engine, and it's this stratification that must be leveraged to create data flows using best practices.

Parsing Stage

The *parsing stage* is the next stage to occur in the data flow. Parsing usually occurs in the job server using built-in SAP Data Services transforms and functions, so you want to make sure that this occurs after the driver stage drives down the amount of data to process. The parsing stage is shown in Figure 5.18, with the `qry_Parse` Query transform highlighted.

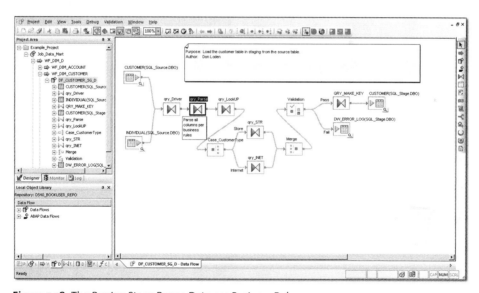

Figure 5.18 The Parsing Stage Parses Data per Business Rules

This stage may do things that are as simple as using an UPPPER() function to convert all customer names to uppercase per business rules, or as complex as if-then–type logic—using a DECODE() function or IFTHENELSE(). Some of these operations can be pushed down to the database if there is an equivalent function in the database that SAP Data Services can translate, whereas other operations will occur in the job server engine if no equivalent function exists in the database. This is why it's so important to ensure that the record set is as small as possible before invoking expensive operations in the SAP Data Services job engine. Having a smaller record set to process in the engine becomes really important in the next stage: the lookup stage.

Lookup Stage

The *lookup stage* happens almost entirely in the SAP Data Services job server engine, so it follows both the driver stage and the parsing stage. Figure 5.19 shows an example of the lookup stage in the data flow occurring after the qry_ Driver and qry_Parse.

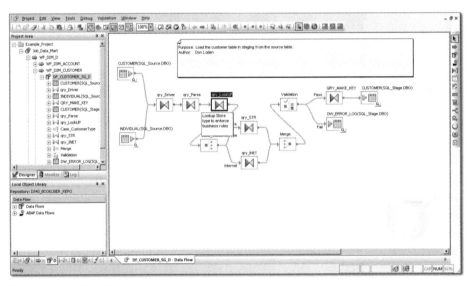

Figure 5.19 Lookup Stage in the Data Flow

Although lookups are expensive in terms of processing, they can be very powerful tools when used effectively. They are great tools for denormalizing data from normalized reference tables in OLTP systems, where data is highly normalized.

Take, for example, a customer record where you need to know for reporting purposes whether the customer is an online or in-store customer. In the source system, this information appears in two tables: CUSTOMER and CUSTOMER_TYPE. This needs to be denormalized into a simple CUSTOMER_TYPE column in the customer table in SAP HANA to avoid the join cost (as discussed in Chapter 3). To do this effi-ciently, you use SAP Data Services to look up the value either as an in-line outer join or using `lookup_ext()` functions for more tailored results. Using this function, you can pick `Max` and `Min` values if the source CUSTOMER_TYPE table contains his-tory records. Figure 5.20 shows an example of the `lookup_ext()` in action.

Notice how custom SQL is also an option for limiting a result set in `lookup_ext()` by clicking the CUSTOM SQL button in the bottom-right corner of the screen. If you use custom SQL, you can limit the comparison result set of the `Lookup` transform by typing in the SQL that directly covers all of the fields selected in the `Condition:` section and the `Output:` section in Figure 5.20. Using this feature for the example in Figure 5.20 would look like the following:

```
SELECT CUSTOMERTYPE, CUSTOMERTYPEDESC
FROM CUSTOMER_TYPE
WHERE CUSTOMERTYPEDESC = 'Online'
```

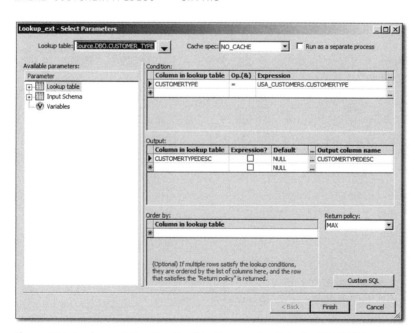

Figure 5.20 Lookup_ext Function Used to Denormalize Data for SAP HANA

This feature really is used if there is a `WHERE` clause that limits the set of data for the comparison. This example would not improve any performance because CUS-TOMER_TYPE is quite a small table, but if the table had millions of records, this feature could be quite a performance boost.

An exciting feature that has existed since SAP Data Services 4.1 allows lookups to be pushed down to the source database in certain occasions:

▶ Only in `no_cache` mode

▶ Only if the database can access source and lookup tables

▶ Only with "=" conditions

▶ Only if upstream functions and transforms don't prevent joins

Because this is such a limited list of scenarios, we still recommend that these stages be followed as a general rule with lookups coming after both the driver and parsing stages to perform lookups after data is limited and parsed. The key is to always limit the result set before evoking expensive operations in the job engine, but with these pushdown features, it's worth noting when to deviate from the norm. If the lookup meets all of the preceding conditions, then put it up front in the process at the driver stage. If all conditions are met, then the lookup will push down to the source database as an inline SELECT statement, as shown in Figure 5.21.

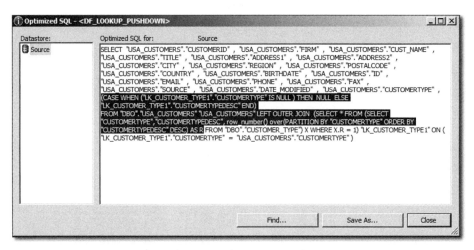

Figure 5.21 Lookup_ext SQL Pushed Down to the Source Database

Business Rules Validation Stage

Now, after all work has been performed in the driver, parsing, and lookup stages, you can validate the work that performed on the load on the way to SAP HANA with the business rules validation stage.

In the *business rules validation stage*, you validate your data using transforms such as `Validation`, `Case Logic`, and `Error Trapping`. All of these techniques are used to perform a series of logical tests to ensure that the records were transformed according to the business rules. This is shown in Figure 5.22, in the highlighted transforms: `Case_CustomerType`, `qry_STR`, `qry_INET`, `Merge`, and `Validation`.

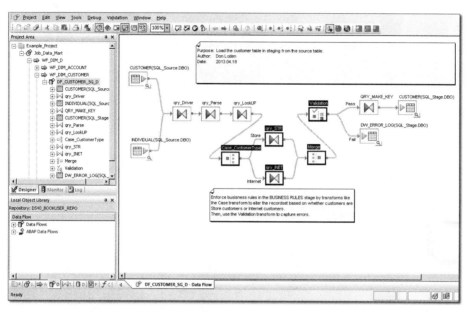

Figure 5.22 Using Validation Logic in the Business Rules Validation Stage

The `Case_CustomerType` transform is used to split the processing between customers who were either Internet customers or customers that purchased products inside the store. The `qry_STR` transform allows special transformations to occur to store customers, and the `qry_INET` Query transform allows special transformations to occur to Internet customers. This is all merged back together in the `Merge` transform, which is like a `UNION ALL` in SQL. Then, the `Validation` transform evaluates and captures statistics around whether the data passed or failed the business rules throughout the data flow. This provides metrics around the processed data because the `Validation` transform captures both pass and fail statistics and metrics around the processing. All of this occurs just because the `Validation` transform is used. `Validation` provides statistics of errors that are automatically collected in the metadata reports that are viewed in the SAP Data Services Management Console.

To access the metadata reports that are collected in the system automatically any-time a `Validation` transform is used, open the SAP Data Services Management Console and click METADATA REPORTS. The reports are a great tool to capture this extra metadata without any additional development, but to ensure that validation efforts are not lost in the metadata reports, always give your validations meaning-ful names while setting up the transforms. These reports are somewhat generic—and without proper naming conventions all of your work will just be lumped together and difficult to read—so ensure that the validation results will be read-able by using proper segregation.

Data Load Stage

The final stage of the data flow is the *data load stage*, in which you load the table structures in SAP HANA. SAP Data Services can load both row- and column-store tables in SAP HANA when you're using a regular loader. When you use the bulk loader, the default tables used are column-store tables. The bulk loader options are shown in Figure 5.23, and the regular loader options are shown in Figure 5.24.

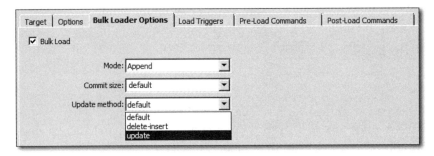

Figure 5.23 Bulk Loader Options in an SAP HANA Target Table

Notice that there are not too many controls in the bulk loader options. Because you're using the SAP HANA bulk load API, all controls go to SAP HANA. This is a very streamlined process without many controls because it's focused on the high-est performance possible. Regular loaders offer somewhat diminished perfor-mance but many more options for controlling how data is loaded into a table.

There are newer features available with the coupling of the SAP HANA API whereby bulk load need not occur only as a `Truncate` operation with inserts. By setting the Bulk Loader Options tab as shown in Figure 5.23 with the Mode field set to Append, the Commit Size field set to default, and the Update Method set to update, SAP HANA can realize a `Merge` statement (or `Upsert`) in a bulk manner. You do this by setting these exact bulk load settings on the target with the Auto Correct Load property set to YES on the Regular Load Options tab together. To achieve this bulk merge capability, you must set both the bulk load options and the regular load options this way.

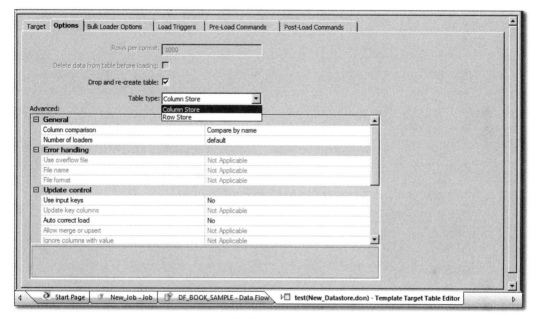

Figure 5.24 Regular Loader Options in an SAP HANA Target Table

With a regular table load, the Update control section shown in Figure 5.24 works the same way when set by itself. You can set the Auto Correct Load feature to Yes. Just this simple property setting causes SAP Data Services to change the behavior of the target table loader. Instead of just sending `INSERT` SQL statements as it would with the Auto Correct Load set to No, the setting produces `INSERT/UPDATE` pairs to test the target table to see if the records have already been loaded. Either the `INSERT` or `UPDATE` is successful.

SAP Data Services even goes a step further by pushing down an SQL `MERGE` operation to the target database if that functionality is supported in the database platform. This technique is very powerful for jobs designed around the concept of a *delta*, which processes only changed data, and for the concept of recovery. The comparison of the data can be achieved by using the native primary key of the table, or a comparison key field can be established by the software, so that a key isn't necessary.

Another important feature is the ERROR HANDLING section. You can use an overflow file to trap records that fail database constraints or data type mismatch issues. You can either write the SQL that failed or the actual data values. We find that the SQL is quite useful for troubleshooting because it allows you to run the statements individually against the target database on a native SQL client for the database for better debugging and troubleshooting database errors on loading.

The final aspect to note about the SAP HANA table loaders is that they can create either row-store or column-store tables. This simplifies the development process because the developer needs only the final result set of the data flow to produce the table structures in SAP HANA. You perform this by using the drop and re-create table functionality of a `Template Table` transform. The DROP AND RE-CREATE TABLE checkbox is shown in Figure 5.24, earlier in this section.

You can find the `Template Table` transform on the tool palette on the right-hand side of the workspace, as shown in Figure 5.25.

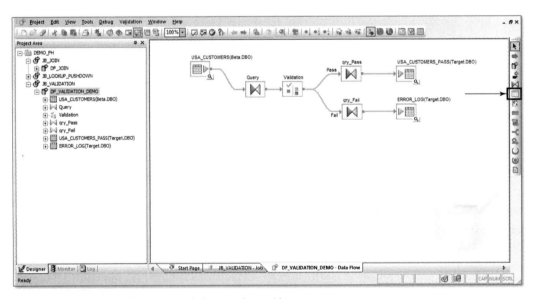

Figure 5.25 Where to Find the Template Table

To implement a template table in a data flow, just click the icon the arrow is pointing to and drop the template table where you want in the data flow.

5.1.6 Transforms

After you explore all of the processing stages of a data flow, it's clear that many things may be accomplished in a single data flow. One of the most important is the ability to create complex logic, which is generally accomplished by using the powerful transforms that SAP Data Services contains.

Transforms operate on data sets by receiving incoming data, transforming that data, and, finally, producing one or many output sets. Transforms are different from functions because they operate on sets of data or entire records where functions operate on columns within a record. SAP Data Services is packed with many powerful built-in transforms that are available from the LOCAL OBJECT LIBRARY on the TRANSFORMS tab shown in Figure 5.26.

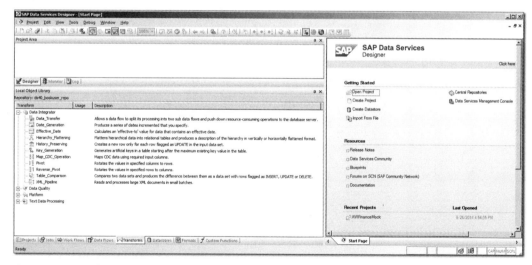

Figure 5.26 Transforms Tab with the Data Integrator Node Open

Transforms in the TRANSFORMS tab are broken into four sections: DATA INTEGRATOR, DATA QUALITY, PLATFORM, and TEXT DATA PROCESSING. The upcoming tables provide a comprehensive list of all available built-in transforms and their descriptions, by section. Data integrator transforms (Table 5.5) are available with the full SAP Data Services licensing or the Data Integrator licensing, while data quality transforms (Table 5.6) are available with the full SAP Data Services licensing or the Data Quality Management licensing. Platform transforms (Table 5.7) are always included with the product, and text data processing transforms (Table 5.8) require a separate license. If you don't have licensing for the transforms, the top-level nodes of DATA INTEGRATOR, DATA QUALITY, PLATFORM, and TEXT DATA PROCESSING are visible, but none of the transforms in Table 5.5 are available.

Transform Name	Description
Data_Transfer	Splits data flow processing between two sub-data flows to allow for better push down for resource-intensive operations. This is very useful for tuning data flows.
Date_Generation	Generates a date column as a baseline date for a user-specified range of dates.
Effective_Date	Generates an effective date column based on the specified primary key of the record.
Hierarchy_Flattening	Flattens nested relational data model (NRDM) data into relational tables; useful for transforming XML data hierarchies into parent-child relational tables in SAP HANA.
History_Preserving	Converts records flagged by the software as UPDATEs to INSERTs to preserve original values. An effective date is also specified. Useful for creating slowly changing dimensions.
Key_Generation	Generates new key values for a source. Most often used for creating a surrogate key in a data mart or data warehouse when you combine data from multiple sources.
Map_CDC_Operation	Sorts data from an input table and maps output data after resolving before and after UPDATE images; commonly used to support Oracle changed-data capture (CDC), but can be used for other database CDC support if the input requirements are met.
Pivot	Pivots the data set from columns to rows; opposite operation of a reverse pivot.
Reverse_Pivot	Pivots the data set from rows to columns; opposite operation of a pivot.
Table_Comparison	Compares an input data set to a target data set and produces the difference between them with the output records flagged as INSERTs or UPDATEs.
XML_Pipeline	Processes large XML input sets in small batches.

Table 5.5 Data Integrator Transforms and Descriptions

Transform Name	Description
Associate	Combines the result sets of two or more `Match` transforms or two or more `Associate` transforms to find matches across match sets.
Country_ID	Parses input data and identifies the country associated with the record.
Data_Cleanse	Identifies and parses name, title, firm, phone number, Social Security information, dates, and email addresses. `Data_Cleanse` transforms enhance the input data by providing gender and first names, generate match standards, and convert sources to standard formats.
DSF2_Walk_Sequencer	Adds delivery sequence information to data that can be used with presorting software to quality for walk-sequencing discounts.
Geocoder	Uses geographic location of input data to assign latitude and longitude data.
Global_Address_Cleanse	Identifies, parses, validates, and corrects global address data such as primary number, name, and type, as well as directional and secondary data.
Global_Suggestion_List	Compares input addresses to provide suggestions for possible matching addresses. Can be used for a "did you mean 'x' address?"
Match	Identifies matching records based on input sets using a complex multidimensional algorithm; outputs unique ID, best record, and grouping data.
USA_Regulatory_Address_Cleanse	Identifies, parses, standardizes, and corrects US addresses according to the US Coding Accuracy Support System (CASS).
User_Defined	Completely customizable transform using Python code; can process records individually or as sets of data.

Table 5.6 Data Quality Transforms and Descriptions

Transform Name	Description
Case	Splits data in a data flow into separated output branches of data based on input records that qualify specific conditions.
Map_Operation	Allows control over changing any SQL operation to any other SQL operation of a record against a target table. For example, `INSERT` statements can be changed to `UPDATE` statements.

Table 5.7 Platform Transforms and Descriptions

Transform Name	Description
Merge	Performs a UNION for all of two or more input streams of identical data in a data flow.
Query	Controls the read operations from one or more source tables; is similar to a SELECT statement.
Row_Generation	Generates a row of data identified by a single incrementing integer column; is useful for creating test sets of data for a target table.
SQL	Executes the SQL specified in a free-text field in the transform; blindly pushes down whatever free-form SQL is entered.
Validation	Controls and measures how well an input set performs against business rules or logic; captures and measures pass and fail statistics around the data processed.
XML_MAP	Handles complex levels of nesting present in input data. This is a finely tuned NRDM transform.

Table 5.7 Platform Transforms and Descriptions (Cont.)

Transform Name	Description
Entity_Extraction	Extracts entities and facts from any free-form text input source set.

Table 5.8 Text Data Processing Transforms and Descriptions

Depending on the licensing of SAP Data Services, there are many built-in transforms that are great time-saving aids to any development task in SAP HANA. Many of these transforms were designed around data mart activities and create proper functioning star schemas as outlined in Chapter 3 of this book. We'll highlight some of the most useful transforms in this section by examining the top five data integrator and platform transforms in terms of usefulness from a BI perspective for SAP HANA.

The Query Transform

The Query transform is the heart of a data flow. It's singularly the most used transform in SAP Data Services. The Query transform performs all portions of the SELECT statement to prepare a read of data against a source table. The Query transform controls the SELECT, FROM, WHERE, and ORDER BY clauses. Functions can be called against columns from source tables. Tables can be joined, and these joins can be pushed down to source databases to return a unified record set. Also, complex WHERE clauses can be invoked to limit or push down the WHERE clause to the source database. The Query transform is incredibly important for controlling the push down of operations, so understanding its intricacies is important for proper data flow construction. The SELECT portion of the Query transform is housed in the MAPPING tab of the Query transform shown in Figure 5.27.

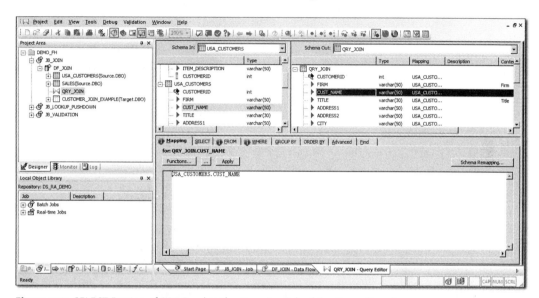

Figure 5.27 SELECT Portion of SQL Read in the Mapping Tab of the Query Transform

In the MAPPING tab of the Query transform, a field can be straight mapped where the field CUST_NAME is just read from the source table. This produces the SQL in Listing 5.1.

```
SELECT  "USA_CUSTOMERS"."CUSTOMERID"  ,  "USA_CUSTOMERS"."FIRM"  ,
"USA_CUSTOMERS"."CUST_NAME"  ,  "USA_CUSTOMERS"."TITLE"  ,
"USA_CUSTOMERS"."ADDRESS1"  ,  "USA_CUSTOMERS"."ADDRESS2"  ,
"USA_CUSTOMERS"."CITY"  ,  "USA_CUSTOMERS"."REGION"  ,
"USA_CUSTOMERS"."POSTALCODE"  ,  "USA_CUSTOMERS"."COUNTRY"  ,
"USA_CUSTOMERS"."BIRTHDATE"  ,  "USA_CUSTOMERS"."ID"  ,
"USA_CUSTOMERS"."EMAIL"  ,  "USA_CUSTOMERS"."PHONE"  ,
"USA_CUSTOMERS"."FAX"  ,  "USA_CUSTOMERS"."SOURCE"  ,
"USA_CUSTOMERS"."DATE_MODIFIED"  ,  "USA_CUSTOMERS"."CUSTOMERTYPE"  ,
"SALES"."AMOUNT"  ,  "SALES"."ITEM_DESCRIPTION"
FROM "DBO"."USA_CUSTOMERS" "USA_CUSTOMERS" INNER JOIN "DBO"."SALES"
"SALES" ON ( "USA_CUSTOMERS"."CUSTOMERID"  =  "SALES"."CUSTOMERID" )
```

```
WHERE ( "USA_CUSTOMERS"."DATE_MODIFIED"  >= '2013.05.05 00:00:00') and
( "USA_CUSTOMERS"."DATE_MODIFIED"  <= '2013.05.11 00:00:00')
```

Listing 5.1 SQL Pushed Down from the Query Transform

Notice that the SELECT portion of the SQL displayed in the USA_CUSTOMERS.CUST_ NAME field is just straight mapped with no functions applied. However, if you choose to include any functions due to business rule necessity, then they would be included in the SELECT portion of this SQL statement.

Notice the FROM clause of the SQL in Listing 5.1 and the join on the USA_CUSTOMERS table and SALES table. This portion of the SQL is handled in the FROM tab of the Query transform, as shown in Figure 5.28.

In the FROM tab of the Query transform, simple joins between two tables, such as this example, can be constructed. However, you can fashion very complex joins with mixed types: INNER joins can now be mixed with OUTER joins. All of the join specifications happen in the JOIN PAIRS section of the tab, as displayed in Figure 5.27.

The WHERE clause of the produced SQL happens in the WHERE tab of the Query transform. This is shown as a simple date range example, but the WHERE can be as complex as necessary to satisfy business rules. The WHERE tab is depicted in Figure 5.29, and the WHERE clause text is simply typed into the tab in SAP Data Services Designer.

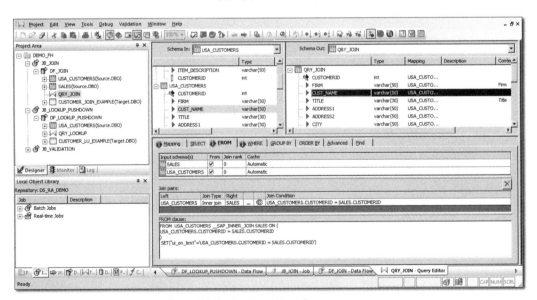

Figure 5.28 FROM Clause Tab in the Query Transform

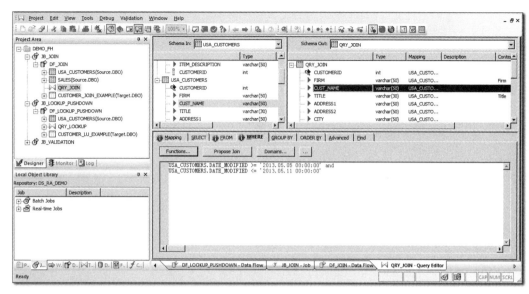

Figure 5.29 WHERE Clause Tab in the Query Transform

You've seen how complex or simple SQL can be created using a `Query` transform in SAP Data Services Designer. It can't be overstated that this transform is simply the most used transform in SAP Data Services, and it will be used extensively to design the read operations against your sources for loading data into SAP HANA.

Table_Comparison Transform

Isolating changed data in ETL development is very important for a number of reasons, and developing for SAP HANA is no different. This can be easily accomplished by using a `Table_Comparison` transform to isolate changed records in a table, as shown in Figure 5.30.

Data may change in a source, and the volume of that data loading to SAP HANA may be quite large, so it can be important to your cutover strategy to process only changed data. Another situation where detecting changes is important is for recovery operations. If the SAP Data Services job fails, the data flow quits in mid-processing, and if the data flow isn't intelligent enough to know what records already exist in the target table, then the flow fails on recovery due to duplicate `INSERT`s. Situations like these are perfect examples of when to use a `Table_Comparison` transform.

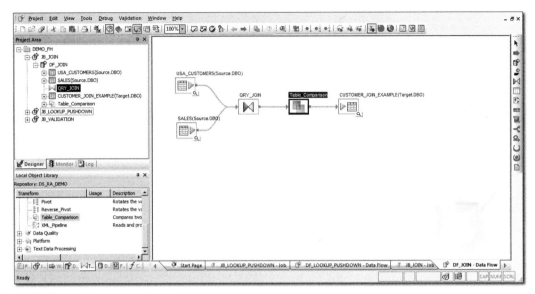

Figure 5.30 Table_Comparison Transform to Isolate Changed Data from the Target

A `Table_Comparison` transform is a drag-and-drop transform that detects whether records exist in a specified table by comparing key fields and non-key fields. If a record exists and is unchanged from the input record, then no record is sent to the target SAP HANA table. If the record isn't found in the target table, then an INSERT SQL statement is produced to insert the record into the target table. If the record exists in the target table, and the record has changed, then an UPDATE statement is produced for the target table.

You need to set a few options after dropping the transform into the data flow. Set the comparison table to the proper table to compare in the Table name field; the example table in Figure 5.31 is the CUSTOMER_JOIN_EXAMPLE table. Then, specify the input primary key field and the columns to compare in the fields: INPUT PRIMARY KEY COLUMNS and COMPARE COLUMNS, respectively.

The `Table_Comparison` transform is now ready for use. This is a very useful transform for CDC operations and is generally one of the last transforms used before the target table.

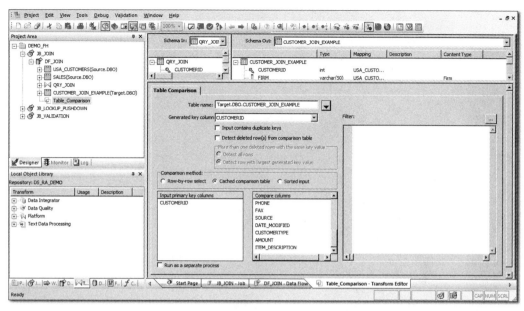

Figure 5.31 Table_Comparison Transform Options

Case Transform

A `Case` transform is another very useful transform for splitting processing tasks based on decision logic. For example, business logic may call for value substitutions only when certain conditions are met for certain fields. This would be a perfect example of when to use a `Case` transform.

Take the example data flow in Figure 5.32. This data flow uses the `Case` transform to specify different values for an Internet customer over a customer that came into a retail store.

The `Case` transform tests a `CUSTOMER_TYPE` field and splits the processing of the data into two streams: one for a `CUSTOMER_TYPE` value of `Store` and another for a `CUSTOMER_TYPE` value of `Internet`. Different values are then substituted in the two `Query` transforms: `qry_STR` for store values and `qry_INET` for Internet values. See how the `Case` transform is configured in Figure 5.33.

263

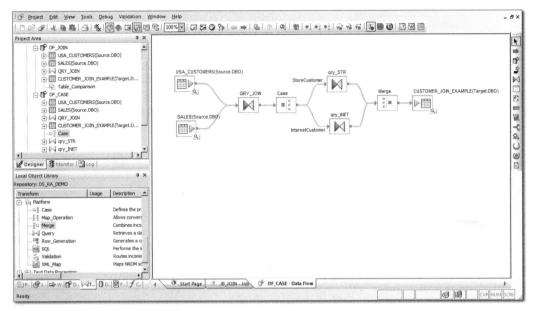

Figure 5.32 Use a Case Transform for Independent Conditional Logic

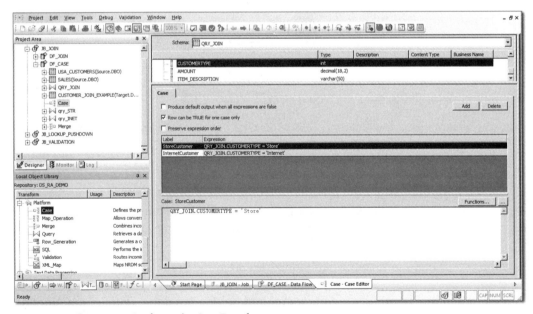

Figure 5.33 Configure the Case Transform

Map_Operation Transform

So far, we have discussed basic to advanced SQL read processing with the `Query` transform, complex CDC target comparison processing with the `Table_Comparison` transform, and conditional logic handled within the data flow with the `Case` transform. These are all powerful, complex transforms, and all are used to detect conditions in data. There is another very simple but powerful transform you can use if you know what you want to do with your data, and this is especially important for performance, which is vital for loading data into SAP HANA: the `Map_Operation` transform.

The `Map_Operation` transform is deceptively simple—it has only five fields on INPUT ROW TYPE and OUTPUT ROW TYPE, as illustrated in Figure 5.34.

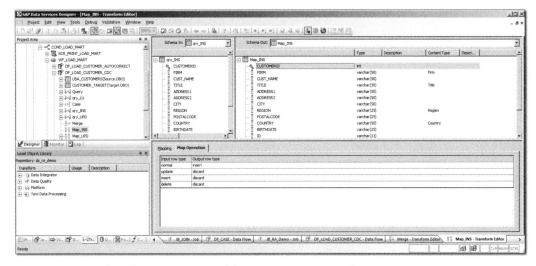

Figure 5.34 Limited Configuration Settings of the Map_Operation Transform

The following choices are available for the OUTPUT ROW TYPE for each of the five fields:

▶ NORMAL
Sets the operation of a record back to NORMAL, or just as the record was read.

▶ UPDATE
Sets the operation of the output record to an UPDATE SQL statement.

▶ INSERT
Sets the operation of the output record to an INSERT SQL statement.

▶ DELETE

Sets the operation of the output record to a DELETE SQL statement.

▶ DISCARD

Sets the operation of the output so that no statement or output is produced. In essence, the row accomplishes nothing on the target table.

This is such a simple transform that it may seem strange to mention its use as one of the top five transforms. The reason is simple: performance on loads. Performance is very important for an SAP HANA data conversion. If your code has already done the work to detect how to handle a target record, then just use this transform to set the output operations appropriately. This transform is usually used in conjunction with a Case transform and a Merge transform, as shown in Figure 5.35.

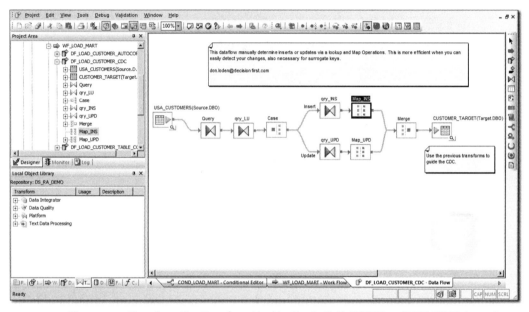

Figure 5.35 Map_Operation Transform Used to Create Both INSERT and UPDATE Statements

The Case transform splits the processing after determining, in this case, the inserts and updates. Then, the Map_Operations transform is used to convert the SQL statements to both INSERT and UPDATE statements in this example. After this, the Merge transform performs a UNION operation to merge the data streams back together before the target. Even with this simple example, you cut the workload in half from a typical auto correct load operation and still maintain the recovery. You've already determined what to issue against the target table, so the auto correct operation does twice the work with no gain because it always issues both inserts and updates.

Validation Transform

We've discussed the means to handle quite a bit of commonly processed logic with the first four commonly used transforms, but after you've performed all of the transformations, you need to ensure that your code did what you anticipated before you load your data into SAP HANA. To do this, we recommend the Validation transform.

The Validation transform simply validates your ETL code against your business rules to determine whether the transformations were successful and performed the appropriate business logic. However, the Validation transform also captures statistics that can be used to report and measure your success or failure. Just by using the Validation transform, you'll gather metrics through built-in reports on percentages of success or failure. All of this is accomplished by merely inserting the Validation transform and making a few simple configurations. You insert the transform by placing it in a data flow from the PLATFORM node of the TRANSFORMS tab, as shown in Figure 5.36.

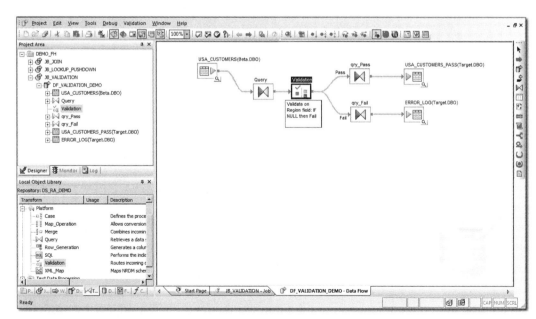

Figure 5.36 Using the Validation Transform to Check Rules and Gather Statistics

Then, double-click the Validation transform, as shown in Figure 5.36, to set the configuration of which field(s) you want to validate. You accomplish the configuration by using the controls shown in Figure 5.37. This example is quite simple — you're validating whether the field REGION is not null. If the field is NULL, it fails the condition, and the record is sent to both output paths: the USA_CUSTOMER_PASS table and ERROR_LOG table.

You can easily configure this to send only to the failure path (ERROR_LOG) by selecting a different option for the ACTION ON FAIL field. Click the EDIT button, shown in Figure 5.37, to get to the RULE EDITOR screen, as shown in Figure 5.38.

This is where all configurations for the field validations take place. You can validate as many fields as you want with as many complex validations as possible. This screen allows validations to be configured in the COLUMN VALIDATION section of this form if you create the validation rules within the Validation transform. SAP Data Services also allows for this transform to capitalize on custom validation functions that are written with SAP Data Services.

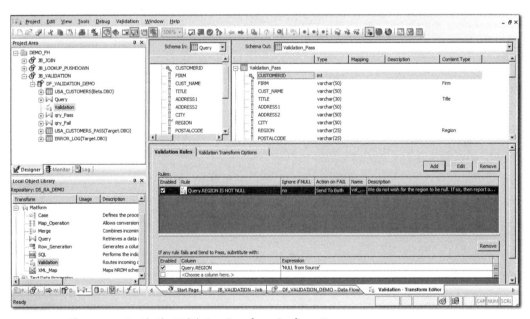

Figure 5.37 Inside the Validation Transform Configuration

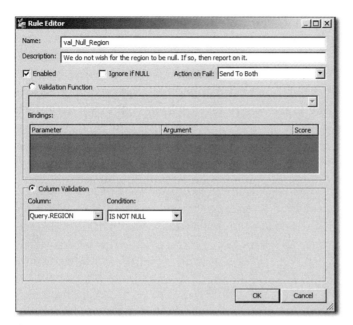

Figure 5.38 Setting Your Comparison Expression in the Validation Transform

SAP Information Steward

Another option for consuming custom validation functions is the unique capability to allow the sharing of validation rules with SAP Information Steward. SAP Information Steward is a separate product and thus requires a separate license, but, if you have it, you can also use its validation functions. This allows for a modular rules-sharing capability whereby an ETL developer for an SAP HANA migration can leverage existing business rules validation functions or SAP Information Steward functions created and approved by business users.

For more on SAP Information Steward, see Appendix A.

Data_Cleanse Transform

We've covered what we consider to be the top five data integrator and platform transforms, but there are also important data quality transforms that are also worth noting for their importance for cleansing, standardizing, and matching data on the way into SAP HANA. These data quality transforms are not included with the runtime license of out-of-the-box SAP HANA but can be added as an additional license purchase.

The Data_Cleanse transform is the first step in any data quality process for SAP HANA because it takes an input record and first breaks it into all of the record's individual logical components and then evaluates and enhances those components. Then, the Data_Cleanse transform gives an additional option of adding enhancements to the content of the data. These enhancements range from cleansing address values to comparing proper addresses or person or firm names to their standardized components. Cleansing records is more than just parsing the data with a substring and replacing functions. The Data_Cleanse transform operates on the concept of breaking a record down to evaluate the data to its standard form.

Consider the following example of cleansing a customer record to its standard forms to correct customer name discrepancies before sending it to SAP HANA. Figure 5.39 shows customer data that needs to be cleansed to fix name variations; to provide standard names for SAP HANA, you insert a Data_Cleanse transform: the EnglishNorthAmerican_Data_Cleanse transform, as shown in Figure 5.39.

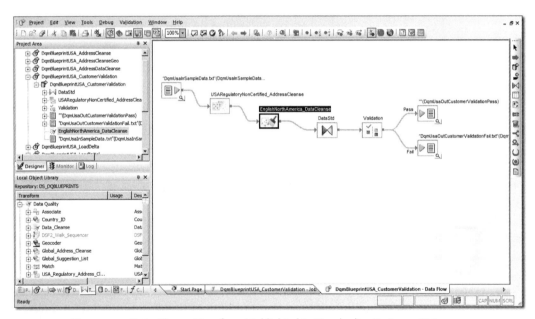

Figure 5.39 Data_Cleanse Transform Highlighted to Standardize Customer Data

This transform requires configuring both input fields to break down to their standard forms for cleansing opportunities, as well as selecting the fields from the Data_Cleanse transform's output that enhances the record by appending the cleansed fields onto the record. The configuration, or *mapping*, of the input fields is shown in Figure 5.40; this is simply a mapping of the input fields from the previous transform to the transform input fields of the `Data_Cleanse` transform.

In this example, Table 5.9 shows the input field–level mappings. The field being fed to the transform is on the right-hand side, in the INPUT SCHEMA COLUMN NAME column. The `Data_Cleanse` transform field type mapping is in the left column labeled TRANSFORM INPUT FIELD NAME.

Transform Input Field Name	Input Schema Column Name
FIRM_LINE1	ORGANIZATION
MULTILINE1	MISCELLANEOUS1
MULTILINE2	MISCELLANEOUS2
NAME_LINE1	NAME

Table 5.9 Data_Cleanse Transform Field-Level Input Mappings

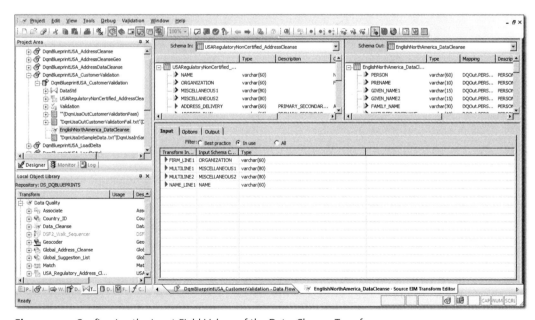

Figure 5.40 Configuring the Input Field Values of the Data_Cleanse Transform

After you've mapped the input fields, they are ready for the transform to break them down into their standard forms and evaluate the contents of the input fields. For example, the miscellaneous fields are treated as multiline information and examined as first names, last names, and both first and last names in one field. The NAME_LINE1 field is looking for customer name–specific values, and the FIRM_LINE1 field is looking for business names in any form. All of these values are evaluated against a data cleansing package for proper (language-specific) values for both person and firm data. Then, the output of this complex processing is returned from the output configuration of the transform that is shown in Figure 5.41.

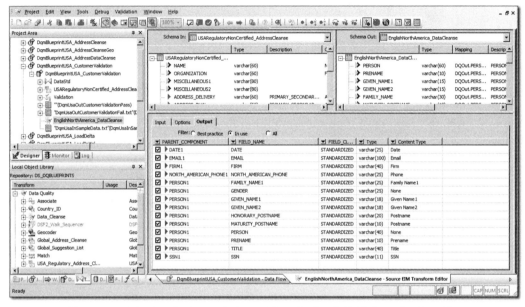

Figure 5.41 Selecting the Output Enhanced (Standardized) Fields from the Data_Cleanse Transform

Upon selecting the Data_Cleanse transform's output fields, you want to return to the record set. The record is enhanced by the addition of these cleansed fields. No field contents in the OUTPUT tab of Figure 5.41 were available to the record before the Data_Cleanse transform was used. This content of enhanced fields was returned from using the Data_Cleanse transform and the complex processing of the data in SAP Data Services, but these are the kinds of quality enhancements that are so important for avoiding fast trash data in SAP HANA.

Now that data has been effectively cleansed, the data is ready for complex matching that can be invoked by the Match transform.

Match Transform

The `Match` transform is incredibly powerful and does just what it states in the name: performs matching operations on data that is passed in as input values. This transform is used to de-duplicate data on the way into SAP HANA.

For example, if you're combining multiple customers' source data to use for reporting in SAP HANA, you can use the `Match` transform to expose and group duplicate records to have a best customer record as a single record. That record can be related to all of the individual customer records that make up that customer. Without data quality processing, this would not be possible in the SAP HANA calculation engine. In SAP HANA, you can see any type of calculation on the base repetitious customer records, but you would never know that the customers were the same customer! This is why cleansing and matching are incredibly important in SAP HANA; you are not only getting quality data in SAP HANA and avoiding fast trash, but also, with matching, you can see a full 360-degree view of your customer data.

It's important to note that, much like the `Data_Cleanse` transform we just discussed, the `Match` transform is much more than just a lookup type match or series of simple outer joins. The `Match` transform uses a complex, multidimensional algorithm to perform the matching.

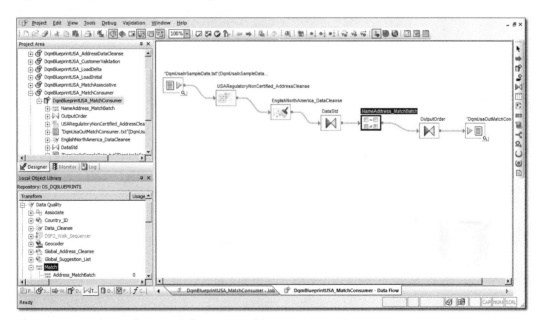

Figure 5.42 Match Transform Ready for Person and Firm Data

In the example shown in Figure 5.42, you can see that the highlighted `Match` transform (`NameAddress_BatchMatch`) is ready to receive both person and firm data for the preceding `DataStd Query` transform.

Notice that the data has been standardized using the `EnglishNorthAmerica_DataCleanse` transform right before the `Query` transform. This is the same `Data_Cleanse` transform from the previous section of this chapter, and cleansing data before matching is always a best practice. When you match, you want standardized input data fed to the `Match` transform, and the most efficient way to do that is to use the `Data_Cleanse` transform. After the data is cleansed and standardized, you use the `Match` transform to evaluate the person and firm input fields, shown in Figure 5.43, for consideration of matching in the transform.

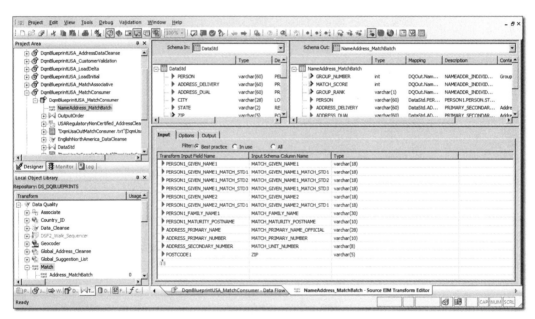

Figure 5.43 All of the Specified Input Fields for Matching Consideration

The `Match` transform uses these fields to see if the records score high enough in the processing steps to be individually considered a match based on each field's merit, and then the composite scoring of all of the fields in consideration are merged. A total score of all matching fields is used to determine whether the record is a matching record. The matching transform in this example is just matching on all candidate records that are fed from the `DataStd` transform; however, you can also compare matches against an entirely different record set. This offers a great degree of flexibility. To configure the matching scores and Match transform behavior, use the MATCH EDITOR form in Figure 5.44 exposed on the OPTIONS tab, which is the middle tab shown in Figure 5.43.

This MATCH EDITOR form is elegantly simple, yet quite powerful. This is where you specify the MATCH SCORE and NO MATCH SCORE to determine the threshold for whether or not the field scores as a matching element. The CONTRIBUTION gives the weight as a percentage of the total composite match score of the record. If the record's score is high enough, then the record is a match and grouped into a match group for the output of the transform. Let's establish definitions for each of the criteria fields shown in Figure 5.44 for more clarification:

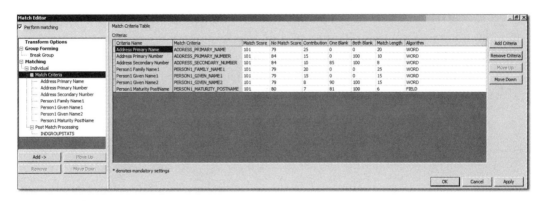

Figure 5.44 The Matching Options Overview

▶ MATCH SCORE
If the field is above this value, the field is considered a match. If the value is set to 101, then all fields are considered, even if they aren't matches.

▶ NO MATCH SCORE
If the field is below this value, the field isn't considered a match. A -1 value forces the consideration of every field regardless of whether they are matches, if desired.

▶ CONTRIBUTION
This is the percentage of the field, and it's the maximum contribution weight of the field based on the matching score of the field. All specified contribution values must add up to 100%.

▶ ONE BLANK

This makes a decision on whether to use the field or ignore it in the scoring based on blanks or nulls on *one* side of the field's comparison.

▶ BOTH BLANK

This makes a decision on whether to use or ignore the field in the scoring based on blanks or nulls on *both* sides of the field's comparison.

▶ MATCH LENGTH

This is the length of the string that is considered for the match.

▶ ALGORITHM

This is the algorithm used for matching in the transform. Can be word similarity, field similarity, geo proximity, numeric difference, or numeric percent difference based on the input field's data type.

All of these configuration settings are considered for the match; then, the `Match` transform enhances the input data much like the `Data_Cleanse` transform, discussed earlier, by appending additional fields onto the output record. These additional fields are shown in Figure 5.45.

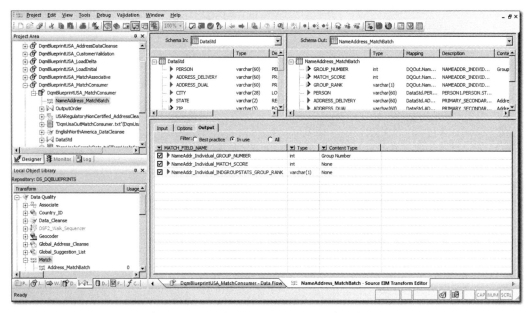

Figure 5.45 Matching Output Fields: Scores, Groups, and Ranks

The output fields in this example that get appended onto the record are NameAddr_Individual_GROUP_NUMBER, NameAddr_Individual_MATCH_SCORE, and NameAddr_Individual_INDGROUPSTATS_GROUP_RANK. These values are simply the group number for the match to be used as an identifier to cluster matching records together, the score each record received as a composite for all of the comparisons, and the ranking of the match groups, respectively. These fields can be used in numerous ways to associate records and provide relationships on records that would never have been seen before.

5.1.7   Built-In Functions

Like many software tools, SAP Data Services provides a set of built-in functions. Functions in SAP Data Services differ from transforms in that functions operate specifically on columns, while transforms operate on entire sets of data. In SAP Data Services, database and application functions, custom functions, and most built-in functions can be executed in parallel within the transforms in which they are used, but you also have the ability to run resource-intensive functions, such as lookup_ext (lookup function) and count_distinct (aggregate function), as a separate subdata flow that uses separate resources (both memory and computer) from each other. Built-in functions save development time and resources, and SAP Data Services contains a large library of built-in functionality.

SAP Data Services boasts 130 built-in functions that are ready for use. Although this is far too many to review in detail in this text, there are complete descriptions within the SAP Data Services technical manual supplied with the product. The technical manual provides a complete definition, as well as great examples of how to use each function within data flows and syntax examples. This is a very useful resource to an SAP HANA developer who may be unfamiliar with the function syntax. We'll discuss how the functions are grouped logically in the technical manuals and show an example of how the functions are used inside a Query transform.

The 130 built-in functions in SAP Data Services are grouped into 14 function categories. The categories are shown in Figure 5.46 in the SELECT FUNCTION dialog box and are described in Table 5.10.

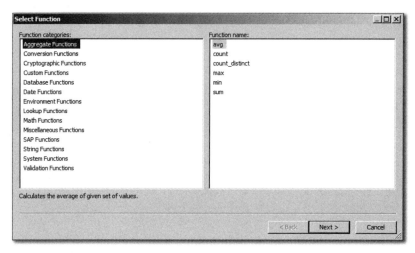

Figure 5.46 Fourteen Groups of Built-In Functions

Function Group Name	Description
Aggregate Functions	Aggregation operations such as average, sum, and count
Conversion Functions	Convert between data types, for example, dates to text, numeric to text, varchar to long, and long to varchar
Cryptographic Functions	Encryption and decryption functions
Custom Functions	Developer-built custom functions and all GUI parameters, just like any other built-in function
Database Functions	Database functions such as the SQL function to call explicit SQL statements, total rows of a table, and key generation to generate keys for a database table
Date Functions	Numerous date manipulation functions
Environment Functions	Functions specific to the SAP Data Services environment and development platform
Lookup Functions	Complex lookup functions allowing lookups to return values from any datastore connection
Math Functions	Numerous mathematical functions
Miscellaneous Functions	Function grouping for a variety of useful functions that don't fit into any of the categories
SAP Functions	SAP application-specific functions
String Functions	Numerous string manipulation functions

Table 5.10 SAP Data Services Built-In Function Groups

Function Group Name	Description
System Functions	System functions such as executing external programs and sending email
Validation Functions	Functions to validate data and field contents; all have a Boolean return

Table 5.10 SAP Data Services Built-In Function Groups (Cont.)

SAP Data Services contains many functions to aid development and speed the task of realizing data flows and complex job logic. Table 5.10 is just a starting point to explore all of the functions that are available to the developer. However, the way that the functions are used in SAP Data Services data flows is the same no matter the function. For example, to use the UPPER() function to convert a name field to uppercase, follow these steps:

1. Navigate to the column in the output schema of the Query transform where you want to use a function, as shown in Figure 5.47.

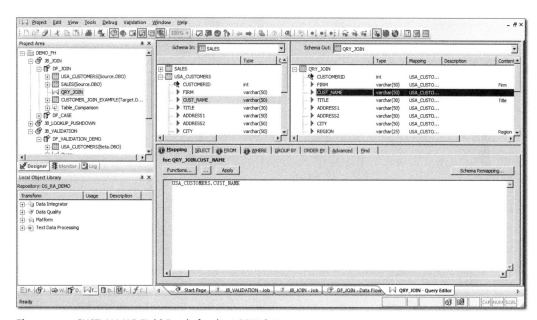

Figure 5.47 CUST_NAME Field Ready for the UPPER() Function

2. Click the FUNCTIONS button, shown in Figure 5.47, to show the dialog box to select the UPPER function under STRING FUNCTIONS (Figure 5.48).

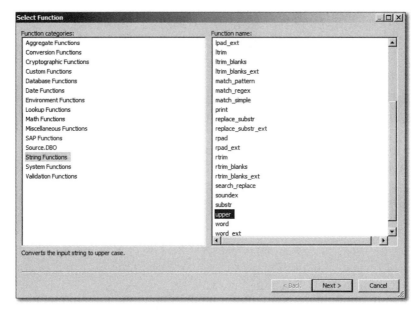

Figure 5.48 Selecting Function Dialog Box to Choose the UPPER Function

3. Click NEXT after selecting the UPPER function.

4. The DEFINE INPUT PARAMETER(S) dialog box appears, as shown in Figure 5.49. Fill in the INPUT STRING field. You may leave the INPUT LOCALE field blank because it's optional.

5. Click FINISH in the INPUT PARAMETERS dialog box to go back to the output schema of the CUST_NAME field and the fully realized function shown in Figure 5.50.

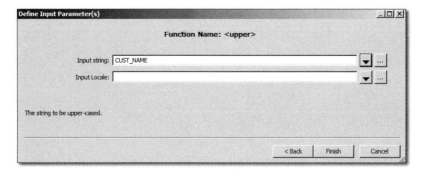

Figure 5.49 Using Define Input Parameters Input String Field to Map the UPPER Function

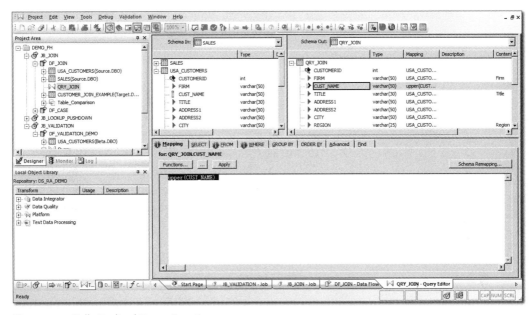

Figure 5.50 Fully Realized Upper Function

This is a very simple function example, but it's a great example of how to use the built-in function GUI. This GUI is available for any of the functions in SAP Data Services, regardless of whether they are built-in functions or custom functions that a developer creates. This way, the development team preparing the data for SAP HANA needs to be familiar with only one function syntax and interface in SAP Data Services, rather than understanding the functions present in all of the source databases from the legacy systems that are combined in SAP HANA.

After examining the built-in functions, it's clear that it's easy to accomplish many things with them, but sometimes, logic for SAP HANA data provisioning is either too complex or outside the scope of built-in functions. Fortunately, SAP Data Services allows you to create your own custom functions, as we'll discuss in the next section.

5.1.8 Custom Functions and Scripts

Custom functions are exactly as they sound: SAP Data Services allows a developer to create custom functions for reusing logic by placing that logic into a custom function container object. This allows any SAP Data Services developer to use this custom function just as you would any of the built-in functions covered in the previous section, complete with a GUI wrapper for the parameters of the custom function. This is really useful when you have a complex task or logic that needs to be used repeatedly by a team. The idea is to first create the function, and then any member of the team can use the code anywhere in the SAP Data Services jobs.

One use case that we see often is a complex job initialize script to control the CDC behavior of a source. These initialize functions can be somewhat complex, and most batch jobs that are running as *delta* jobs (or jobs that process only changed data) require some type of initialize function to control variables that set date ranges or processing ranges with a beginning and ending value to select changed data. A function, such as this initialize function, is created in a custom function SMART EDITOR window, shown in Figure 5.51.

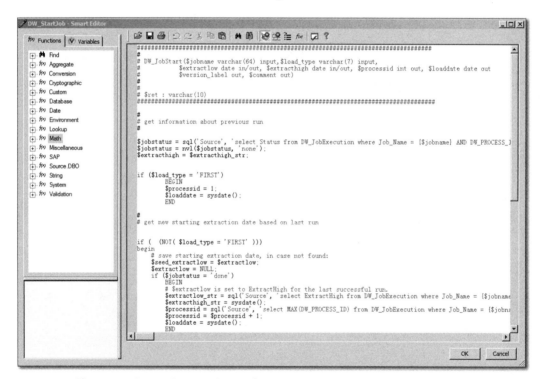

Figure 5.51 Custom Function Smart Editor

The SMART EDITOR allows a developer to free-form code any type of logical operation that is necessary in an SAP Data Services job for provisioning into SAP

HANA. The function logic looks complex, and it certainly can be! The real benefit is the reusability of the complex logic by other developers on the team that don't have to know (or even care!) about the inner workings of the function. From their perspective, the function is just a screen of input parameters, as shown in Figure 5.49. This distribution of duties in the SAP HANA project makes sure that the complex logic is correct and lends itself to a team with varying levels of development experience.

To create a new custom function and find the SMART EDITOR screen, browse to the FUNCTIONS tab in the LOCAL OBJECT LIBRARY in the bottom-left corner of SAP Data Services Designer and right-click CUSTOM FUNCTIONS. Then, select NEW from the pop-up window, as shown in Figure 5.52.

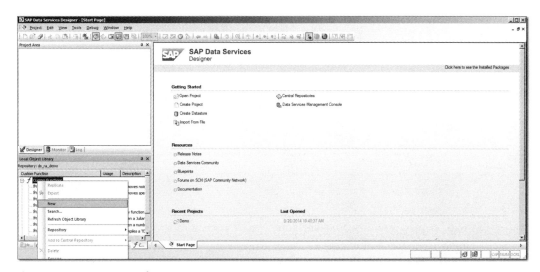

Figure 5.52 Context Menu for Creating a New Function

You then use the Smart Editor to write whatever function is needed for the task. After you have the function crafted, you can use your new function. We've already seen that functions can be called from within Query transforms, but this example of an initialize function wouldn't make sense in that context. A function in a column of a Query transform is called once for every record, or iteratively. By definition, you want to call an initialize function only once at the beginning of an SAP Data Services job. To accomplish this singular call, you need to use a script object.

A *script object* is a single-use object that is a free-form text type tool in SAP Data Services. Recall that script use cases occur when you want to call or perform steps only once. A script reads left to right, top to bottom, and performs whatever functions are called in the order that the script sees them. Scripts are highlighted in Figure 5.53; the arrow on the right shows where the script control is located.

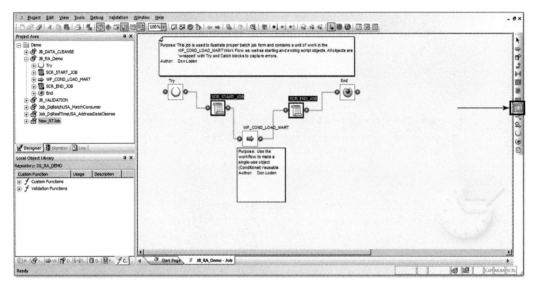

Figure 5.53 Where to Find Script Controls

The script is used to bind variables that are used as input parameters to control logic in the job. For example, the initialize script referenced in the previous examples would be placed in the script to be called only once, but also, the variable assignments would happen in the script. Both the script function call (which is highlighted) and the variable assignments (in both the highlight and the text above) are shown in Figure 5.54. Variables are preceded with $ and are needed in this format by SAP Data Services.

This way, when the script is finished executing, the custom function has performed its work and figured out the beginning and ending date values to pull the data, as cited earlier, in Figure 5.51. Then, the values of the upper- and lower-bound date are assigned to variables in the script shown in the highlighted text in Figure 5.54.

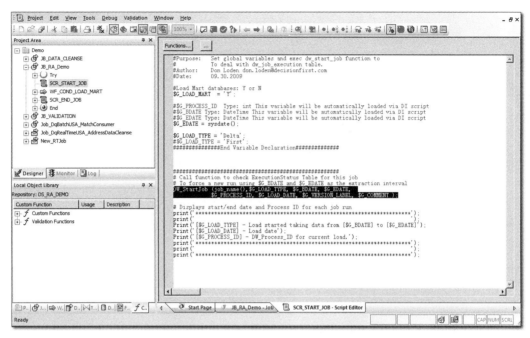

Figure 5.54 SCR_START_JOB Script Object Contents Calling a Custom Function

We've exhausted most of the SAP Data Services controls for logic in your SAP HANA data journey at this point. You've seen how there are numerous built-in functions and transforms that save time and developer effort and handle both simple and complex transformations. Then, when you need to take logical operations beyond what is included with SAP Data Services, you can use custom functions and scripts. However, with all of these examples, we've been connecting to source database tables. There may come a time when you need to load data from text files into SAP HANA, or you might need to combine the file data with data from database tables. This is certainly possible with SAP Data Services, but you need to use a file format.

5.1.9 File Formats

A *file format* is much like a datastore connection, which was covered in Section 5.1.2, except that it connects to flat files of varying types. A file format object is a multi-use object that connects to a flat file and acts as a metadata wrapper to define both the connection and characteristics of the particular file. You can find the flat file object by browsing to the FORMAT tab in the LOCAL OBJECT LIBRARY in the bottom-right corner of SAP Data Services Designer and expanding the FLAT FILES node, as shown in Figure 5.55.

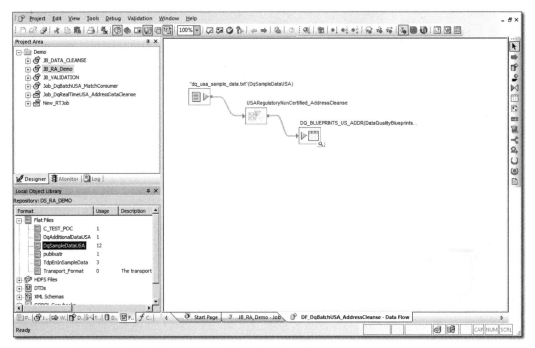

Figure 5.55 Flat File as a Source Object in a Data Flow

We've been presented with this scenario numerous times, wherein a business receives a data feed as a file from a vendor or a customer, and that data must be merged into a BI data mart structure for reporting. This is the same challenge for SAP HANA as it is for other traditional legacy database platforms. Fortunately, the file format object makes this task simple, and the flat file object ensures that this task is repeatable. To create a new flat file object, right-click the FLAT FILE node and select NEW from the pop-up menu. This brings you to the FILE FORMAT EDITOR, as shown in Figure 5.56.

The FILE FORMAT EDITOR allows for almost any imaginable combination of options for dealing with flat file connections and characteristics. Essentially, the editor is broken into three sections. The left side, or properties/values section, allows settings of various fields to drive flat-file behavior in SAP Data Services in everything from connections to delimiters. The upper-right side of the editor (the column attributes section) shows the column definitions, and the lower-right side (the data preview section) shows the data preview when data is available from the connection. If no data is available, the text No DATA appears, as shown in Figure 5.56.

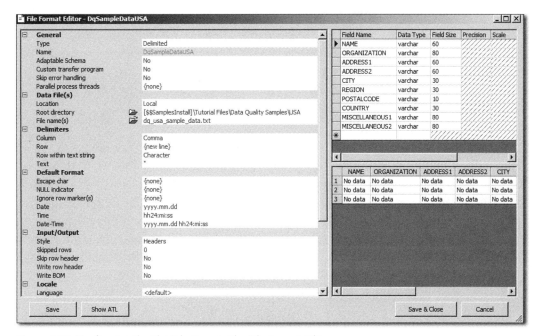

Figure 5.56 Configuring the Flat File Form in the File Format Editor

There are more options in this object than we'll cover in this chapter, but to ensure that all functionality is covered, we'll review the sections of fields present in the object. These sections are outlined in Table 5.11.

Flat File Editor Section Name	Description
GENERAL	Sets options such as whether the file is delimited or fixed width and whether to process the data in parallel
DATA FILES	Specify the connection to the flat file
DELIMITERS	Configure the type and style of the delimiter if the file is a delimited type file
DEFAULT FORMAT	Specifies escape characters or NULL indicators and date formatting

Table 5.11 Flat File Option Groups

Flat File Editor Section Name	Description
INPUT/OUTPUT	Configures whether to skip rows or use the row header as the column headers
CUSTOM TRANSFER	Specifies custom transfer protocols, if used
LOCALE	Sets language and code page settings for file interpretation
ERROR HANDLING	Handles all records that don't meet the definitions of the file; determines what happens if data fails the read of the flat file object

Table 5.11 Flat File Option Groups (Cont.)

As you can see, you can deal with just about any option for file-based connections with this object in SAP Data Services. This makes reading files quite simple. It's important to note that many of the field settings shown in Figure 5.56 can also be bound to variables, which dramatically increases the reusable nature of this connection. Take, for instance, a situation in which you are always presented with the same data structure, but the file name or location for the connection is different. In this scenario, you bind the LOCATION field, ROOT DIRECTORY field, and FILE NAME(S) field (all shown in Figure 5.56) to variables to create a reusable object. This simplifies development and makes maintenance much easier.

Another important aspect of the flat file object in SAP Data Services is that it acts as a metadata-level object and allows the same abstraction layer for flat files as is present for datastores against database tables. The flat file object connects the software to the flat file data; however, to SAP Data Services, the data that is being processed in the data flow isn't different from data from any type of database table. This abstraction layer and the ability to manage transformations on any type of data the same way is a great strength of the tool.

This simplicity of management and the power of the transformations make SAP Data Services the obvious choice for batch loads into SAP HANA. This is great for loading data in batches, but what about transforming data in real time? SAP Data Services provides this capability as well, but you need to use a real-time job to accomplish this.

5.1.10   Real-Time Jobs

SAP Data Services offers a real-time jobs platform that allows complex transformations to happen in real time from any source application that can produce a web service output. This means that any application that can produce a web service for consumption can be echoed into SAP HANA. This echo can be a direct replication of data, but more than likely, it will consist of complex transformations. Many times, these complex transformations are not just around business rules that create uniform data or get data into better structures for performance as we've discussed before. Sometimes data quality needs to be addressed on the way into SAP HANA. For instance, addresses may need to be corrected using complex data quality algorithms, or customers or vendors may need to be standardized or de-duplicated before loading to SAP HANA.

Real-time jobs in SAP Data Services are *stateless* application constructs. This means that all of the logic and functionality is encapsulated within the SAP Data Services real-time job. This way, another application doesn't have to have any knowledge of what is going to happen in the SAP Data Services real-time job. As a high-level example, a source application produces a web service in an XML format that an SAP Data Services exports to a URL hosted on the SAP Data Services job server. This process invokes the SAP Data Services real-time job to process the data, and the data is output to SAP HANA. An example of a real-time job is depicted in Figure 5.57.

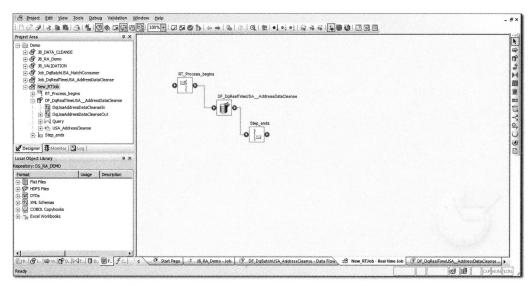

Figure 5.57 Real-Time Job

This is a very different scenario from a batch job, as we've outlined previously. Batch jobs are scheduled and executed at specific time intervals. With a real-time job, there is really nothing to execute, and the job just responds to, consumes, and processes the records as they are ready. Many times, real-time jobs do have a data quality focus, but these jobs can be used with SAP HANA anytime data needs to be significantly transformed and replicated in real time from a source application. An example of a real-time data flow that processes data from a web service is shown in Figure 5.58.

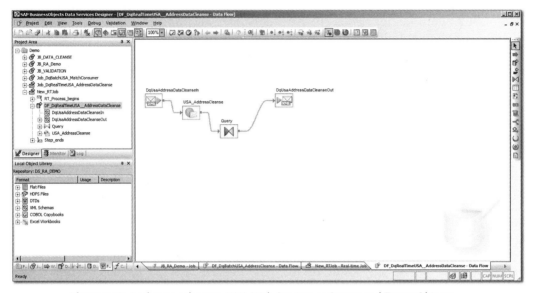

Figure 5.58 Real-Time Job Using XML Web Services as Source and Target Objects

Real-time jobs are great solutions for SAP HANA when data needs to be seen immediately, but you should never use them to load large amounts of data. They work best when data is trickled out of an application record by record. If large amounts of data need to be consumed at one time, then a batch job is a much better method to transport data.

5.2   Introduction to SAP Data Services Workbench

SAP Data Services Designer is the client development environment that has been demonstrated in most of the images in this book up until this point, and the one we recommend for provisioning data for SAP HANA. However, SAP also offers a next-generation client tool. This client tool is called the SAP Data Services Workbench, as shown in Figure 5.59.

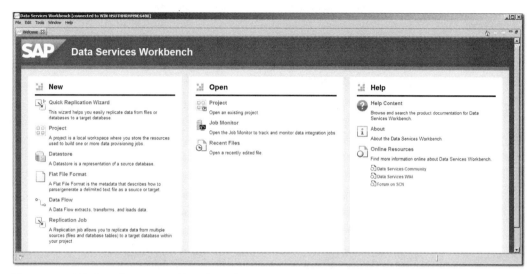

Figure 5.59 SAP Data Services Workbench: Welcome Screen

The SAP Data Services Workbench is very different from SAP Data Services Designer. The most striking difference is that it's an Eclipse-developed client application, so it looks more modern and conforms to the current SAP Business-Objects BI and SAP HANA Eclipse look and feel. This is a dramatic departure for SAP, and much work has been poured into this client tool. This is still an early iteration of the SAP Data Services Workbench, and while it contains significant core functionality, it still does not replicate all of SAP Data Services Designer in the current version. Nonetheless, there are still some compelling reasons that using the SAP Data Services Workbench makes sense, even with its limited functionality.

We'll discuss these in detail in this section of the chapter, but before examining specific features, let's examine the SAP Data Services Workbench Job Monitoring Editor, which is the SAP Data Services Designer client of the future (see Figure 5.60).

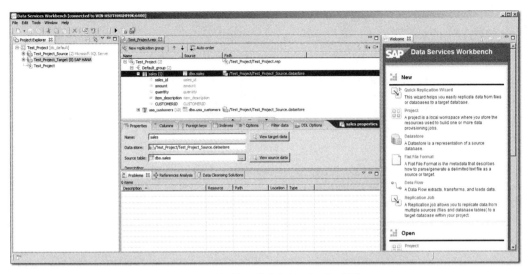

Figure 5.60 SAP Data Services Workbench Job Monitoring Editor

This client has a very different look and feel, but with this view, you're looking at a job with two connections in the source SQL Server database and two tables in the target SAP HANA system. The section in Figure 5.60 marked SALES is a context-sensitive screen pane, and thus will change after you click different sections of the TARGET pane. For instance, if you click the SALES table section, the bottom section reflects the context of the SALES load in terms of target tables, the Data Definition Language (DDL) used to create the target table in SAP HANA, and all of the other options and parameters that are used to create and load the table into SAP HANA. The same happens if you click the USA_CUS-TOMERS table.

Another major leap forward in functionality is that the SAP Data Services Workbench doesn't require a constant database connection. With the SAP Data Services Workbench, you can actively work in an offline mode. This is a great enhancement for those who have worked with SAP Data Services Designer because it requires a constant repository database connection.

Despite the look and feel and the fact that this application is useful in scenarios without a network connection, it does become apparent that many features are still missing, and we continue to recommend SAP Data Services Designer for most use cases. Nonetheless, in this section, we'll give you an overview of some of the most important functionalities in the SAP Data Services Workbench: building a data flow, moving data from an existing data warehouse, porting data, and modifying data flows and jobs.

5.2.1 Building a Data Flow

As we mentioned earlier, SAP Data Services Workbench currently has a limited feature set, although it does offer a widening degree functionality in the list of available standard transforms and functions. However, needed features like Workflow transforms are still absent from the SAP Data Services Workbench, which makes the tool appropriate only for specific use cases. Although, as we stated previously, we generally recommend SAP Data Services Designer for provisioning data for SAP HANA, we'll still briefly examine some of SAP Data Services Workbench's most important features by creating an example data flow. We will then use this data flow to create a template table in SAP HANA.

To create a data flow, first right-click the project, and a pop-up menu appears. Select NEW and choose DATA FLOW from the pop-up menu, as shown in Figure 5.61.

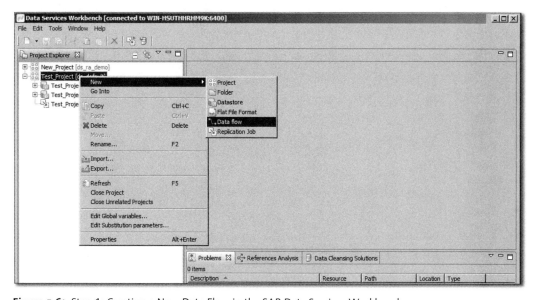

Figure 5.61 Step 1: Creating a New Data Flow in the SAP Data Services Workbench

This adds a data flow to the canvas and allows us to start creating our data flow to build the template table in SAP HANA. First, though, we must give our new data flow a name, as shown in Figure 5.62.

Figure 5.62 Step 2: Enter a Name for the New Data Flow

After naming our data flow `DF_Workbench_Example`, we start the development process by dragging our SQL Server USA_CUSTOMERS source table from the PROJECT EXPLORER on the left side of the SAP Data Services Workbench to the canvas and selecting IMPORT AS SOURCE from the pop-up menu that appears, as shown in Figure 5.63.

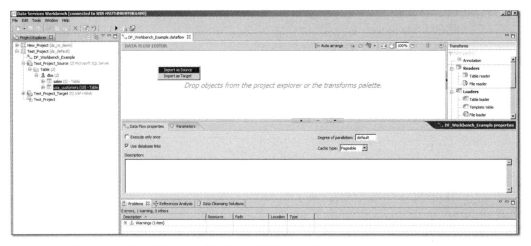

Figure 5.63 Step 3: Dragging the Source Table from the Left to Create the Source

Now, we have a source table, but just like in SAP Data Services Designer, we add a `Query` transform from the transform section on the right-hand side of the SAP Data Services Workbench screen, as shown in Figure 5.64.

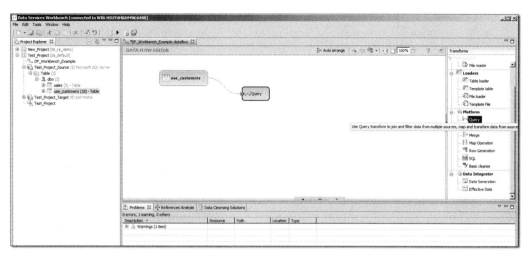

Figure 5.64 Step 4: Adding a Query Transform to the Data Flow

It is important to note that, although we are in a different development tool than the SAP Data Services Designer, the concept of the `Query` transform and processing stages (discussed in Section 5.1.5 earlier in this chapter), are synonymous, and all the same rules for job processing apply. This just happens to be a new way to create a data flow in a much more modern tool. However, although the transforms are synonymous with those in the SAP Data Services Designer, there are still quite a few missing transforms when you take a closer look at the TRANSFORMS section of the SAP Data Services Workbench, as shown in Figure 5.65.

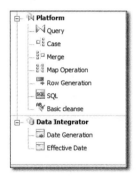

Figure 5.65 Supported Transforms (Release 4.2)

This is a much shorter list than was covered earlier in this chapter for the SAP Data Services Designer, and you can clearly see the difference when comparing Table 5.5,

Table 5.6, and Table 5.7. SAP is actively working on converting all of the SAP Data Services Designer functionality and transforms to the SAP Data Services Workbench, but as of the time of this writing, this is the current gap. This is why we still maintain the position that, for the majority of the SAP HANA data porting effort, SAP Data Services Designer is still the best choice.

However, SAP Data Services Workbench will certainly be the development console of the future. So to close out our task of building our data flow, add the Template table from the Transforms pane on the right-hand side of the SAP Data Services Workbench screen, as shown in Figure 5.66.

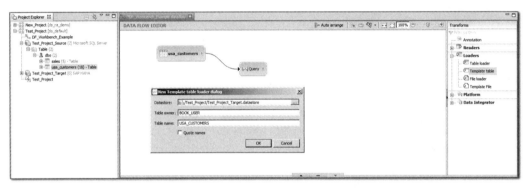

Figure 5.66 Step 5: Adding an SAP HANA Template Table to the Data Flow

Now that we have our target template table in our data flow, we can view the fully realized data flow in Figure 5.67.

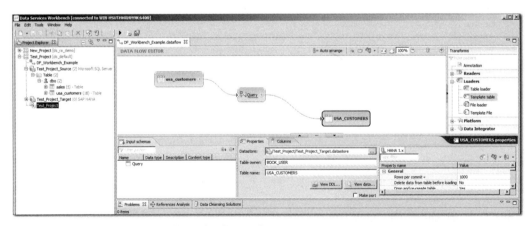

Figure 5.67 Step 6: Fully Realized Data Flow

5.2.2 Moving Data from an Existing Data Warehouse

In our experience, the current best use case for the SAP Data Services Workbench is when a customer has an existing data warehouse and wants to move the data without (many) transformations to SAP HANA, copying both the metadata (table structures, indexes, etc.) and the data. This is a complicated and laborious task involving setting up many data flows, workflows, jobs, and datastores, as well as creating the tables and indexes before loading the data. However, the SAP Data Services Workbench alleviates the work and heavy lifting required to build large numbers of data flows, substituting simple source-to-target mapping that requires little to no transformation. (In many cases, the coding process does require manual effort to handle loading changed data.) The SAP Data Services Workbench offers a brand-new interface where a user can use a wizard interface to perform the following steps:

1. Select a source system connection.

2. Select tables to be copied.

3. Select a target system connection.

4. Execute and monitor the progress of the load.

This is a simple process that makes a complicated task quite easy. You are able to turn on and off creation of indexes for one or many tables, and you can use the native bulk loaders of the target systems that are supported (now quite numerous, as we'll see in the next section, in Table 5.13). You can also examine the SQL DDL before it executes to ensure that you approve of the creation syntax. You can create column-based or row-based tables in SAP HANA, just as with the SAP Data Services Designer. Finally, you can port all of the code that is created with the SAP Data Services Workbench to SAP Data Services Designer to support all custom functions, built-in transforms, and functions that are currently not supported but will be in future releases.

5.2.3 Porting Data with the Quick Replication Wizard

SAP realized that while SAP Data Services is a great enterprise-class ETL tool, sometimes complex transformations are not immediately necessary. This is when the SAP Data Services Workbench shines. When you need to port data directly with minimal to no transformations, use the SAP Data Services Workbench. There is even a wizard to make this task very easy—reducing it to a matter of a few steps and clicks. This wizard is called the Quick Replication Wizard.

Figure 5.68 shows the first step in the Quick Replication Wizard welcome screen: assigning a name to your project. This name corresponds to the name of the SAP Data Services job that will be created by the wizard.

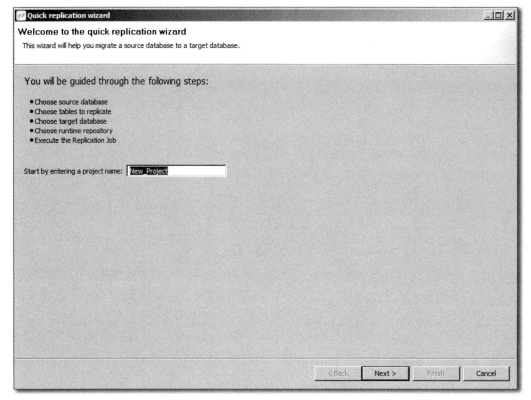

Figure 5.68 Step 1: Assigning a Project Name

The next step is to specify the source database CREDENTIALS and source database CONNECTION information, as shown in Figure 5.69.

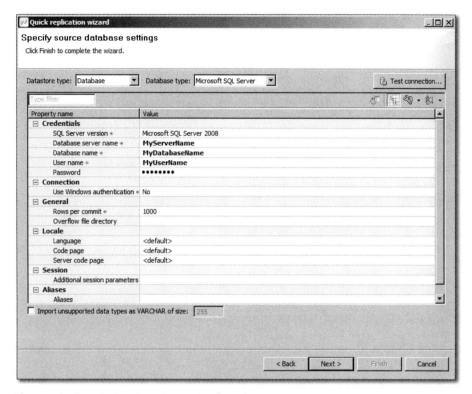

Figure 5.69 Step 2: Creating a Source Database Connection

Currently, many different sources are supported as connections for the SAP Data Services Workbench in version 4.2, as chronicled in Table 5.12.

Source Name	Source Type
Attunity Connector	Database
HP Neoview	Database
IBM DB2	Database
SAP HANA	Database
Informix	Database
Microsoft SQL Server	Database
MySQL	Database

Table 5.12 Source Database Types Supported in SAP Data Services Workbench (Release 4.2)

Source Name	Source Type
Netezza	Database
ODBC	Database
Oracle	Database
SAP (Sybase) ASE	Database
SAP (Sybase) IQ	Database
Teradata	Database
SAP Applications	Application
SAP BW	Application

Table 5.12 Source Database Types Supported in
SAP Data Services Workbench (Release 4.2) (Cont.)

The next step in the process is to select the tables that you want to move into SAP
HANA. The screen to perform this task is shown in Figure 5.70.

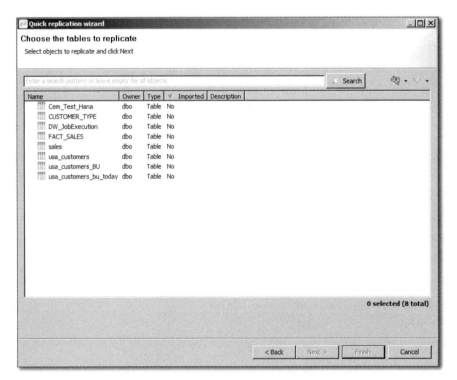

Figure 5.70 Step 3: Selecting Tables to Replicate into SAP HANA

The next step is to select your target system and specify the credentials and connection information, as shown in Figure 5.71. As of version 4.2, you can specify the following targets, as shown in Table 5.13.

Target Name	Target Type
Flat File	File
IBM DB2	Database
SAP HANA	Database
Informix	Database
Microsoft SQL Server	Database
MySQL	Database
Netezza	Database
Oracle	Database
Sybase ASE	Database
SAP (Sybase) IQ	Database
Teradata	Database
SQL Anywhere	Database

Table 5.13 Supported Targets in SAP Data Services Workbench (Release 4.2)

This is a far greater reach of supported targets since the SAP Data Services Workbench debuted with SAP Data Services 4.1. Now, a developer can obtain rapid porting of data, as described in this section of the book, for systems outside SAP HANA and SAP Sybase targets.

The next step is to set up the SAP HANA target for our data port using the SAP Data Services Workbench in Figure 5.71.

Now, you're ready to either execute the job and monitor the results from the SAP Data Services Workbench, or uncheck the EXECUTE REPLICATION JOB NOW checkbox to simply save the finished project (see Figure 5.72). This is helpful if you require further currently unsupported transformations in the future. This needs to be done in the SAP Data Services Designer, as outlined with the tools earlier in this chapter.

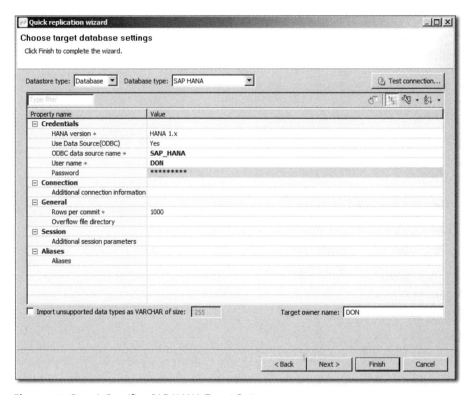

Figure 5.71 Step 4: Specifing SAP HANA Target System

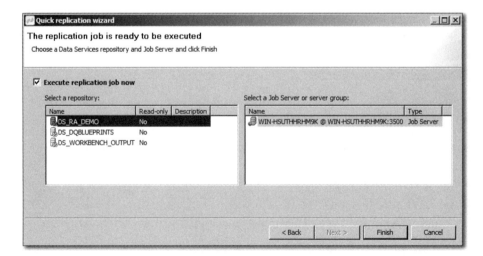

Figure 5.72 Step 5: Confirming Execution or Just Saving Code

New Options for Porting

The other option that exists in SAP Data Services Workbench is the option to move data into a target file format with the same quick porting of data that is available in the Quick Replication Wizard. When you merely select the flat file type in the Quick Replication Wizard, data is effortlessly ported to a flat file destination that the SAP Data Services Workbench server has access to. In the process, the file that is created as the target takes on whatever schema is needed to fulfill the source structure. If you select ADAPT-ABLE SCHEMA, as shown in Figure 5.73, one keystroke can build a dynamic file based on the source.

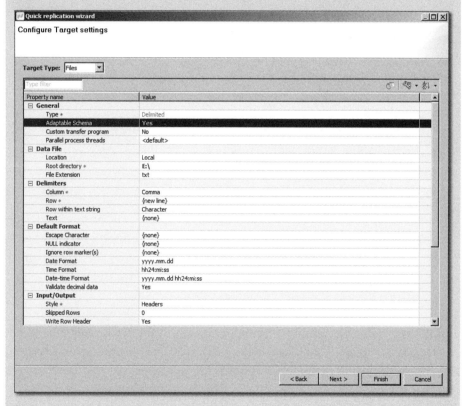

Figure 5.73 Selecting Adaptable Schema on Target File Settings

After the flat files run, you can see the results of their processing in the monitoring window in Figure 5.74.

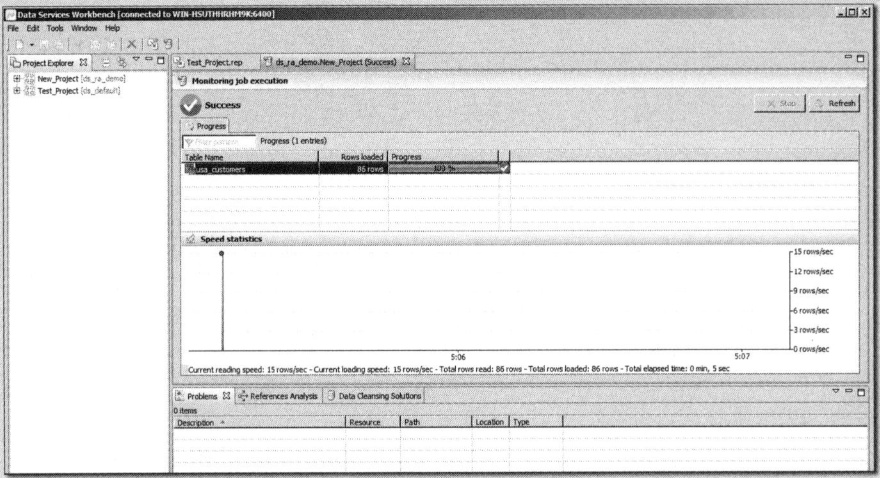

Figure 5.74 Flat File Processing Monitor Window

5.2.4 Modifying Data Flows and Jobs

If you do need to modify the SAP Data Services code created using the Quick Replication Wizard, you can do so by transporting the SAP Data Services Workbench project that you just created to an SAP Data Services repository. This is both quick and easy to do, but keep in mind that this porting to SAP Data Services Designer is currently a one-way street. After you port the code, you can't go back into the SAP Data Services Workbench! So be cautious when you do move the code, and ensure that you've received the maximum benefit of the rapid deployment that the SAP Data Services Workbench has to offer before you do any more advanced development options with the additional transforms that SAP Data Services Designer offers.

The example of the ported SAP Data Services NEW_PROJECT is found in Figure 5.75. This code is just like any that we've examined up to this point and can be modified using any of the advanced functionality available in the SAP Data Services Designer.

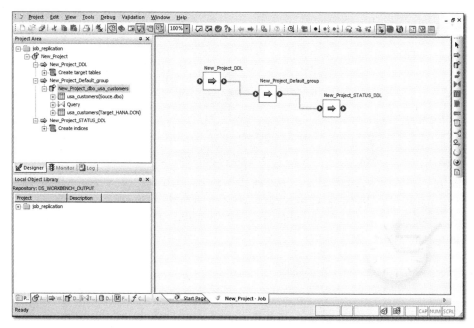

Figure 5.75 Resulting SAP Data Services Job from the SAP Data Services Workbench Quick Replication Wizard

5.3 Data Provisioning via Real-Time Replication

We've discussed the concept of replication of data into SAP HANA at length, but only with respect to transferring data via a batch method. Real-time data replication from a source system is inherently more complex than batch-based replication. The main challenge arises when data needs to be altered in quality attributes or modified in structure in real time—both of which are often the case when you create BI structures. SAP Data Services can meet those needs, but the created jobs have to contain quite a bit of intelligence coded into the effort. True real time is a challenge, because most SAP Data Services jobs are complex and write to many subject areas in an SAP HANA data model. Those subjects are called or invoked only when data is changed in the source. The problem arises because when data for one subject changes in the source, then all of the dependent objects in SAP HANA must be changed—even if they have no relationship to the source.

Because real-time use cases are usually based on source-based replication with minimal to no transformations, we consider a full discussion outside the scope of this book. Capturing an entire data warehouse load in real-time is technically possible, but expensive for a development effort and not worth the expense from a business case in most real-world scenarios.

That said, we will nonetheless briefly introduce two methods to accomplish real-time replication. The first is SAP Data Services, and the second is *SAP Landscape Transformation* (SLT).

5.3.1 SAP Data Services ETL-Based Method (ETL and DQ)

Using SAP Data Services ETL processes to denormalize, load, and create data structures in SAP HANA is what we've discussed at length in this chapter. We've covered batch jobs, but SAP Data Services also has a real-time capability. The majority of the transforms and functions are available, as along with all of the powerful data quality transforms. Cleansing data and matching records in real time is a classic use of SAP Data Services real-time jobs, and this is no different for replicating data into SAP HANA.

There are three primary situations in which to use SAP Data Services for your real-time replication choice:

▶ When you need to replicate data from multiple sources into SAP HANA in real time

▶ When you need to substantially transform the data in real time

▶ When your source data, from one or many sources, has systemic data quality issues

When you have data coming from multiple sources that requires significant transformations, the SAP Data Services real-time capabilities will likely be required. SAP Data Services allows you to design a complex ETL job that reads data from multiple sources while building the interdependency across platforms. This ensures the conformity of the data or that the data is properly merged. It's worth noting that this type of design won't be easy to code in SAP Data Services. The job that you design will be both complex and difficult to design. However, if real-time data exchange is required, then SAP Data Services is more than capable of managing the merger of data.

When the structure or form of the source data requires substantial transformation and real-time replication, SAP Data Services will prove to be the ideal solution. Data can be consumed and then transformed using the standard transforms available in the SAP Data Services suite. This occurs in real time, just before the records are provisioned within SAP HANA.

In terms of data quality, SAP Data Services contains multiple tools and options to help you clean data in real time. Developers can use both real-time matching and cleansing to standardize data while it is being provisioned within SAP HANA. The idea is that, as the data is going into SAP HANA, data is being both corrected and enhanced. Therefore, with real-time data quality, you're not only avoiding fast trash in SAP HANA, you're also doing it in real time as records are being created in the source(s).

5.3.2 SAP Landscape Transformation

We introduced the provisioning of data using SLT log-based replication in Chapter 1. Recall that it's an excellent real-time replication tool for either SAP Business Suite application data or data found in supported third-party sources. There are, however, differences in the capabilities of SLT compared to that of SAP Data Services. In general, the differences are centered on either tool's capability to transform the data as it's being replicated. In addition, the tools interface with the source using different mechanisms.

SLT provides a few basic transformation capabilities, such as filtering rows and performing in-line changes to rows. For example, you can develop an SLT job that limits sales transactions that are set to a status of complete. At the same time, you can concatenate the customer's first and last names into a new file. While this is an excellent feature of SLT, organizations often find the need to perform more complex transformations on applicable source data. In these cases, the SAP Data Services real-time capabilities will likely be required to facilitate the organization's needs.

When SLT uses an SAP Business Suite application as its source, the relationships between source tables are often very sound. This is due to the constraints that are placed in the source system that prevent incomplete or unrelated data from being captured. With that said, various pieces of information being entered are often misspelled or inconsistent. In terms of third-party sources, there is no guarantee that the information will have sound referential integrity or quality. To that end, SLT simply replicates the data into SAP HANA based on the source system's structures and quality. When the quality of your data is in question and there is a need to purify that data as it's replicated, the real-time features of SAP Data Services are required.

It's also important to understand the ways that either SLT or SAP Data Services interfaces with source system data. SLT uses remote function calls (RFCs) to interface with SAP Business Suite application data. SLT can also use direct-to-database connections to interface with third-party data. In Chapter 1, we discussed how SLT creates logging tables in the source to help it keep track of data changes. In contrast, the SAP Data Services real-time replication interface requires that the initial communication of data changes be via web service calls. These calls are made using the W3C XML schema standards. In short, the source application or data source needs to send SAP Data Services a message, via web service call, to initiate the replication of data. The data can then be transferred using either web services to transfer a data block or by using a standard batch SAP Data Services job to connect using ODBC or native middleware. If the data source doesn't support or can't provide a web services mechanism, SLT will likely be required. This also implies that SAP Data Services won't be able to easily replicate data from SAP Business Suite applications in real time. Therefore, real-time replication through SAP Data Services will likely be most appropriate for third-party data sources or custom interfaces that are integrated with SAP Business Suite applications.

5.4   Summary

In this chapter, we examined all of the methods and tools available to provision data into SAP HANA using SAP Data Services. There are certainly a variety of options for provisioning, and the choice of which to use often depends on the level of transformation needed for SAP HANA, as well as the number of sources and their complexity. That transformation can be in a structure to offer better storage and performance operations for SAP HANA, for data quality when data from the sources is suspect, or, finally, when multiple sources need to be combined for analysis. All of these scenarios are great for SAP Data Services because the built-in capabilities make these types of efforts much easier to achieve. However, if you have a single source of data, such as SAP ERP, and the quality is good, then other supported SAP HANA provisioning methods, as discussed in Chapter 1, may prove to be good options, as well. The thing to remember is that no matter your data or use case, SAP has a good provisioning solution and toolset to tackle the job.

Now that we've provided a solid overview of provisioning data into SAP HANA using SAP Data Services, we can move on to loading data into SAP HANA, covered in the next chapter.

In this chapter, we'll provide an in-depth overview of the various options for using SAP Data Services to load data into SAP HANA tables.

6   Loading Data with SAP Data Services

In the previous chapter, we discussed all of the data provisioning processes that are acceptable to prepare to load data into SAP HANA, so now we'll turn our attention to the loading process and examine it in detail. We'll start our discussions in Section 6.1 with loading data into SAP HANA in batches, which is the method used most often to combine multiple sources of data into a common BI structure for SAP HANA. In Section 6.2, we'll move on to real-time data loading, which is required by some use cases. The case studies in Section 6.3 and Section 6.4 will reflect both batch and real-time data loads, respectively, and act as concrete illustration points to begin our journey from design to realization in SAP HANA.

6.1   Loading Data in a Batch

Batch data loading is probably the single most important way to get large amounts of data into SAP HANA. It's used very often, so we'll cover this process in detail. We'll start by describing the process and proper structure for a batch job, and then complete our study with the methods available to batch load data into SAP HANA using SAP Data Services.

6.1.1   Steps

Batch data loading is loading data from an executed process on a scheduled basis. This is the most common way to load data warehouses, and SAP HANA is no exception to this process. Data is often loaded in batches to establish the basic BI data structure.

> **Note**
>
> All batch loading in this chapter is supported and illustrated using SAP Data Services, which is bundled with SAP HANA as the best means of integrating third-party (non-SAP) data.

Batch data loading is generally accomplished using an SAP Data Services job that contains four distinct steps:

1. **Initialization**
   Initialize aspects of the job by setting variables and controlling comparison logic to control loading delta records or changed data.

2. **Staging**
   Stage data to isolate sources and present data with surrogacy while denormalizing aspects for performance and storage in SAP HANA.

3. **Mart**
   Load the data into SAP HANA in structures designed for high-performing BI needs.

4. **End script**
   Close logical operators to ensure that the process is ready to begin again when the next batch is called.

These steps aren't mandatory constructs for SAP Data Services to function or even create a batch job, but this is the best-practice workflow we recommend, developed over years of development cycles. Each of these steps corresponds to workflows in Table 6.1 and Figure 6.1.

Job Step Name	Workflow Name
Initialize	WF_START_JOB
Staging	WF_STAGE_SG_D
Mart	WF_MART_D
End	WF_END_JOB

Table 6.1 SAP Data Services Job Steps and Workflow Examples

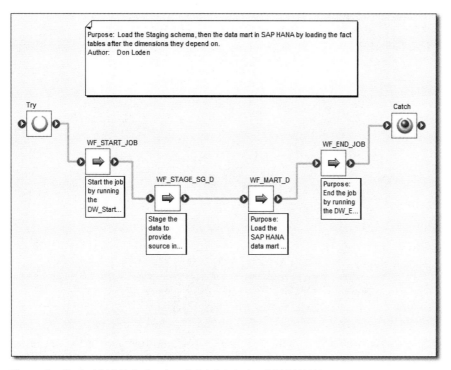

Figure 6.1 Typical SAP Data Services Batch Job to Load SAP HANA

You'll notice that there are two more objects present in Figure 6.1: the `Try` and `Catch` objects. These are designed to catch errors and perform different activities based on the errors that are trapped. We'll explore these objects in greater detail in Section 6.3.

Let's explore each of these steps in detail to see how a proper batch job is constructed in SAP Data Services to load a data mart in SAP HANA.

Initialization

The initialization stage is depicted in Figure 6.1 by `WF_SCR_JOB`, and this workflow typically contains only one object: a script. The initialization script, which is shown in Figure 6.2, performs many tasks, such as setting variables to drive certain behaviors in the job. The most important variables set controls that load the data by helping select only changed records from the source.

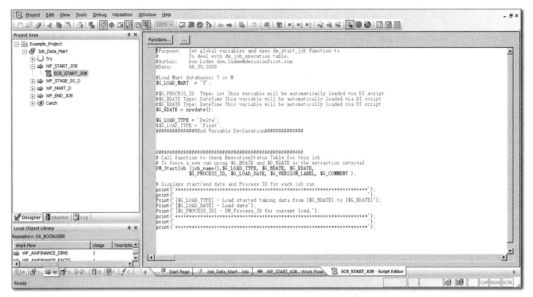

Figure 6.2 Initialization Script Containing the DW_StartJob Function

The initialization script shown in Figure 6.2 is contained inside the initialize workflow (WF_START_JOB), which is depicted in the SAP Data Services batch job in Figure 6.1. This script sets many variables, but the most important variables are the ones that the DW_StartJob sets by calling this custom function. (For more details on custom functions, please refer to Chapter 5, Section 5.1.8.) This function sets the beginning and ending date values and marks those to a DW_JobExecution table to control and bind the beginning and ending date values to a process ID or execution counter value. This way, those beginning and ending dates are used to drive the extract or read of the data from the source system.

Let's take a look at the example of a DW_JobExecution table shown in Figure 6.3.

	Job_Name	DW_Process_id	Load_Type	Status	ExtractLow	ExtractHigh	Load_Date	Remark	Version_Label	DW_Procid_Start	DW_Procid_End
	JB_RA_Demo	1	Delta	done	1900-01-01 00:00:00.000	2009-10-23 19:25:15.000	2009-10-28 19:19:38.000			0	0
	JB_RA_Demo	2	Delta	done	2009-10-23 19:25:15.000	2012-09-26 10:52:00.000	2012-09-26 10:52:00.323			0	0
	JB_RA_Demo	3	Delta	done	2012-09-26 10:52:00.000	2013-02-27 14:35:19.000	2013-02-27 14:35:19.743			0	0
	JB_RA_Demo	4	Delta	started	2013-02-27 14:35:19.000	2013-04-08 12:29:52.000	2013-04-08 12:29:52.630			0	0
▶*	NULL	NULL	NULL	NULL	NULL	NULL	NULL	NULL	NULL	NULL	*NULL*

Figure 6.3 Typical Job Execution Table in a Staging Schema

In Figure 6.3, the process ID is represented by the DW_PROCESS_ID column and is a simple incrementing integer value. The beginning and ending date range that actually drives setting the variables are the EXTRACTLOW and EXTRACTHIGH columns. These are date-time data–type columns with precision down to the millisecond. This way, with the overlap from record to record, there is no chance of missing any data or time series. The JOB_NAME column controls which job the records belong to because there may be runs from many different jobs in this DW_JobExecution table.

The final column that is really important is the STATUS column, which controls the recovery of the job by having two distinct values: STARTED and DONE. STARTED tells the DW_StartJob function to reuse the variables in the record to recover a run and reprocess the same date ranges of data in the WHERE clauses of all of the data flows present in the job. If the value is DONE, a new record is created with a process ID value, incremented by one in the new record. The new record also contains the EXTRACTLOW value set to the EXTRACTHIGH value of the previous record, and the EXTRACTHIGH value of the new record is a time stamp of the SAP Data Services job server time at the time of the run. The DW_StartJob function shown in Figure 6.2 is intelligent enough to contain all of this logic, and it uses the DW_JobExecution table in Figure 6.3 to record the return values.

The DW_JobExecution table typically exists in a staging database or schema, which may or may not exist in SAP HANA. We'll discuss the reasons for this shortly, but for now, just note that the DW_JobExecution table exists in staging because it's one of the vital logical components that will control the source-based CDC aspects of our SAP HANA job.

Staging

The staging step of the SAP Data Services job is used for all of the heavy transformations that are often needed to go from a source system to support high-performance SAP HANA application designs. It's true that, while SAP HANA outperforms traditional databases with just a mere port of the data with no transformations, recall from Chapter 3 that, when data is stored to maximize SAP HANA's strengths, both better data storage compression and better performance are realized. Figure 6.4 shows the flow of data from multiple sources to staging, where most transformations occur, and then finally to the data mart in SAP HANA, where data will be consumed by users.

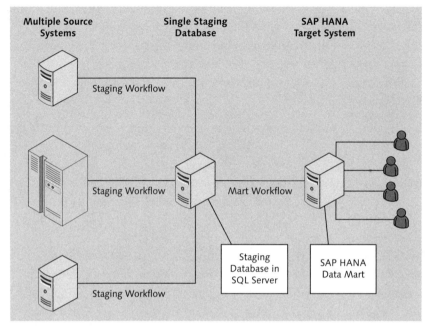

Figure 6.4 SAP HANA Data Mart Load Layout

The coding process in SAP Data Services Designer is also divided into meaningful logical sections when you develop the staging code. Not only do these sections make for more readable code, but the code that is produced is also easier to translate and share with other developers when it's organized logically. This organization also allows for the ordering of objects that need to come first in the data load process for SAP HANA. For instance, staging operations to prepare customer data for loading into a customer dimension in SAP HANA has to come first and run before the load of the data mart in SAP HANA. This process of segmentation and organization is shown in Figure 6.5.

The workflow WF_STAGE_SG_D is loaded before the data mart workflow WF_MART_D, which performs the load into SAP HANA. Workflows in SAP Data Services provide this level of both organization and order of execution.

Data compression is a key factor for maximizing the data that you can store in SAP HANA, as SAP HANA is licensed by storage size in memory. Because performance is the end goal for using SAP HANA in the first place, it makes sense to want to maximize both of these aspects in SAP HANA. All of the transformations that will occur in staging support these goals, but because staging is essentially a layer where work is performed to achieve these goals, it should exist in SAP HANA only if needed to overcome a performance burden. This staging section is shown as the workflow WF_STAGE_SG_D in Figure 6.5.

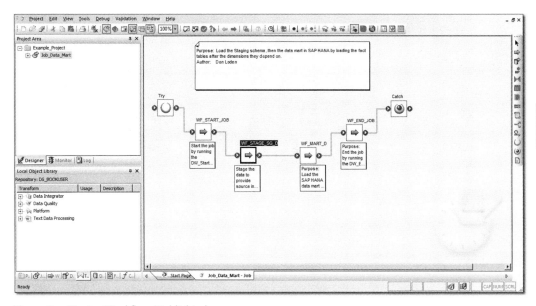

Figure 6.5 Staging Workflow Highlighted

Staging is also the primary place for combining multiple sources of data and providing surrogacy over the sources by shifting the primary key duties of the database tables to surrogate key columns in the tables. Although we won't load multiple sources of data in the case study sections of the chapter, we'll cover creating surrogate keys within the SAP Data Services ETL code to illustrate the concept. This concept is central to data warehousing, whether the data is sourced from one system or many systems.

Another point worth mentioning about staging data for SAP HANA is that staging databases or schemas are often crafted outside of SAP HANA. The simple reason for this is that SAP HANA's speed and power comes at a price, and that price escalates as more data is stored. Consequently, we recommend that you use SAP HANA to solve performance problems, which typically arise and are seen in user-facing roles. In this respect, a staging database is often not the best use of SAP HANA because it is a preparatory stage for the data. A good example of a staging database in Microsoft SQL Server is shown in Figure 6.6.

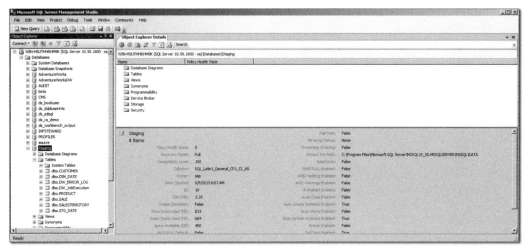

Figure 6.6 Staging Database in SQL Server

The only processes and tools to touch the system are ETL tools or system-generated devices. One exception is if the ETL process itself is performing poorly enough to get the data ready in time for presenting to the users with the SAP BusinessObjects BI reporting or exploration tools. Then, you can use the power of SAP HANA for those long-running processes to make sure that the service-level agreements for data delivery are met. However, this is a unique scenario, and we more often find only the user-facing data elements and tables in SAP HANA. These user-facing tables are generally created and/or loaded with data in the mart step of the job.

Mart

The mart step is what actually builds the data mart tables and loads the data into SAP HANA. This schema contains the data model necessary to support all of the reporting needs from the various SAP BusinessObjects BI tools, as well as the foundation to build attribute views, analytic views, and calculation views. The data mart target tables are shown in the BOOK_USER schema in Figure 6.7.

This step is segregated from the staging load to provide insulation from the schema in SAP HANA because this will be the user-facing data layer. Data will be consumed out of the SAP HANA tables listed in Figure 6.7 using the SAP BusinessObjects BI tools to present the data, so it makes sense to segregate this layer from staging to offer more freedom for development.

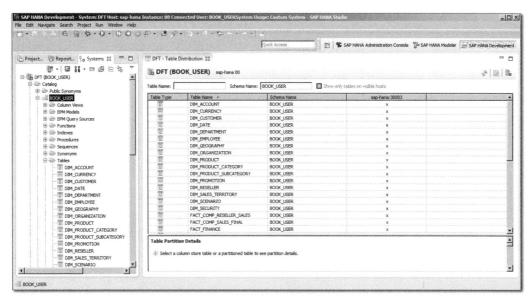

Figure 6.7 SAP HANA Data Mart Target Tables

For example, later, you may need to alter the logic of the creation and population of the data to present to SAP HANA. If the data structures are contained within one schema, then reporting will be affected with the changes as they are made in the BOOK_USER schema. But if staging is separated into a separate database or even data platform, then the changes can be made in the staging database/schema, as well as the SAP Data Services code, without affecting reports until an appropriate time for the disruption, such as after business hours.

The workflow in SAP Data Services that actually builds the data mart is shown in Figure 6.8, where the code in SAP Data Services for the data mart is segregated from the staging code. The code that loads the staging schema runs in the previous workflow, and this separation allows a split between processing the logic of staging and the data mart load to SAP HANA so that you can easily divorce both environments as needed.

After the SAP HANA data mart is loaded, there is one final task needed to close the loop, or effectively end the job: the end script.

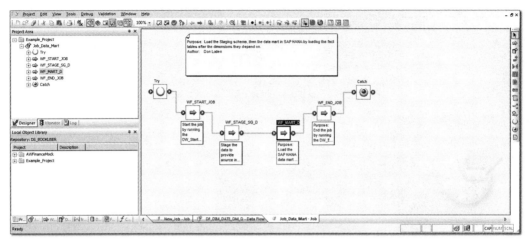

Figure 6.8 Workflow to Build the SAP HANA Data Mart

End Script

The end script step of the SAP Data Services job is the final step in a batch data load in SAP HANA. The sole purpose of this step in the batch data load is to finish tasks that the initialization section of the batch job started. For instance, earlier in this chapter, we illustrated that there is a DW_StartJob function that sets variables for ExtractLow and ExtractHigh dates for the CDC date comparisons against multiple sources. This function sets the Status in the DW_JobExecution table (refer to Figure 6.3) to Started as the job commences and clears this step.

After the job's successful execution of the staging and mart workflows, the end script closes the loop by setting the Status value in the job execution table to Done. This essentially tells the job upon next execution that all was successful from the last run and not to try to recover anything. The DW_EndJob function is shown in Figure 6.9.

The end script also returns any variable statuses back to a state of ready, if needed, and may call post-load operations such as triggering reports to run in SAP BusinessObjects BI via executables or file triggers. These types of tasks or clean-up operations are common for the end script step of a batch job.

These four steps have taken you through the batch data load process and how a typical batch data load job for SAP HANA is constructed in SAP Data Services.

Figure 6.9 End Script Call

6.1.2 Methods

There are many methods for loading data in batches into SAP HANA using SAP Data Services. In the remainder of this section, we'll focus on the following four main methods:

- Truncate and reload
- Full data set comparison target-based CDC
- Standard target-based CDC
- Source-based CDC

The primary distinction among these four methods is derived from whether you care about capturing changes within the batch load. If you care about changes or are forced to care about changes because the reload of the source data sets won't be possible in the timeframe of your load window, then you'll need to perform some sort of CDC operation. This involves the last three options. If you're able to reload the entire data set in the load time, then either the first or second method will suffice.

In the past, with traditional database architectures and technologies, you always needed some sort of CDC operation to overcome performance issues. However, that isn't always the case with SAP HANA. SAP HANA can bulk load data incred-

319

ibly fast, making it good not only for reads, but also, with the proper tuning and parallelization, for the writes, so now CDC isn't as important as it used to be.

Let's investigate each of these methods and discuss use cases for when each should be used.

Truncate and Reload

Truncate and reload is exactly as it sounds: the target table in SAP HANA is truncated and then reloaded. Data is pulled from a target, and the transformations occur in the ETL process in SAP Data Services; however, before data is loaded into the target table, the target in SAP HANA is truncated, clearing the target table of data so that all records can be extremely fast inserts. This is the easiest method to support in terms of maintenance and recovery from failures.

Figure 6.10 shows the two ways that you can perform this method in SAP Data Services and achieve the same result. With the first method, data is cleared before the ETL process begins in SAP Data Services. This usually occurs with the initialization step of the batch load process. The SAP Data Services workflow is as follows:

1. Initialization script clears all necessary target tables in one sweep.
2. ETL processing within SAP Data Services workflows and data flows occurs.
3. Tables are loaded as bulk inserts, and each of the data flows clears its respective processing tasks before inserting data with a truncate to the target table.

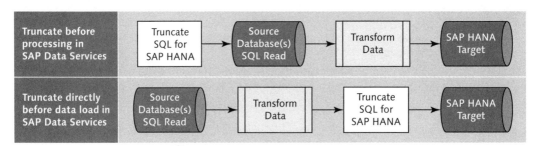

Figure 6.10 Two Types of Truncate and Reload in SAP Data Services

The second method is a little different and allows a more granular control at the SAP Data Services data flow level. In this example, the SAP HANA target table truncation actually occurs within the SAP Data Services data flows, which are scattered throughout the job. This is handled with the target table screen option shown in Figure 6.11.

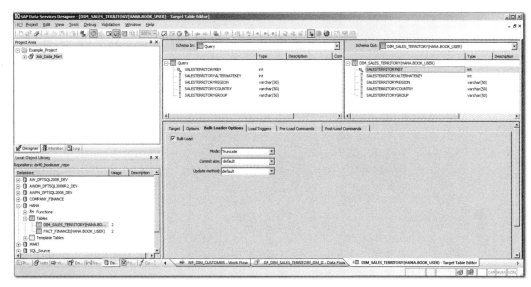

Figure 6.11 SAP HANA Bulk Loader Options

This method is typically reserved for small sources resulting in small data loads in data warehousing with traditional architectures. Even with the bulk loading capabilities of most mainstream, traditional database platforms, the performance of this method will always be a hindrance that outweighs the benefits of the ease of maintenance.

This isn't always the case with SAP HANA. There are many situations when, with proper parallelization, you can increase the speed at which SAP Data Services produces inserts for SAP HANA, removing the speed problem as an obstacle. This is a departure from traditional data warehousing, which has always relied on CDC. This will handle far more cases than a traditional data warehouse.

Full Data Set Comparison Target-Based CDC

There are times when SAP HANA certainly changes the conversation and the way things are done in terms of conventional data warehouse loading. With features available starting in SAP HANA SPS 8, as well as SAP Data Services 4.2, this is certainly the case. Certain scenarios, now with new advances in the bulk load capabilities of SAP HANA made available to SAP Data Services, will allow for auto correct loading, or merging data in bulk into SAP HANA. In short, this capability compares the full loading data set to the full target so that CDC operations are fast and effortless. This is incredible for flexibility in terms of job design; it allows the developer to fully reload sources into SAP HANA, and performance will be as fast as you can read the data, just like a truncate and reload. However, the developer is able to compare the source data against the target data in full with no real performance penalty.

Full Data Set Comparison in Practice

We were able to use full data set comparison target-based CDC functionality in practice with a customer recently to both increase the user adoption of SAP HANA and decrease the available time needed to realize BI content. The customer had an existing data warehouse in a legacy database platform that they wished to convert to SAP HANA, but as one would expect, there were many SAP Data Services data flows to convert because the data warehouse was quite large.

By using this new functionality to compare full data sets, we could craft a strategy to essentially re-provision the data into the data warehouse in bulk to fully load SAP HANA with production-ready, CDC-based data sets very quickly. This accelerated the process to BI content realization by 80% while also allowing the ETL developers time to convert the SAP Data Services code behind the scenes for the long-standing solution.

The classic approach on a migration like this is to go ahead and covert all of the data flows and run mock or test loads until the data looks correct and meets user standards through rigorous testing, which, in this case, would take 10 weeks. However, the re-provisioning process allowed us to land production-ready data in SAP HANA in two weeks. This allowed the BI development to start. Then, the ETL developers were able to finish the remaining 10 weeks of work without the business having to wait the full 10 weeks!

To perform this functionality against a target, you merely set the BULK LOADER OPTIONS on the target table as shown in Figure 6.12.

Setting the BULK LOADER OPTIONS to APPEND for the MODE and the UPDATE METHOD to UPDATE would typically tell SAP Data Services to append records to the SAP HANA target system, but you must also set another option to perform the full data set comparison delta merge. Set the AUTO CORRECT LOAD option to YES, as shown in Figure 6.13.

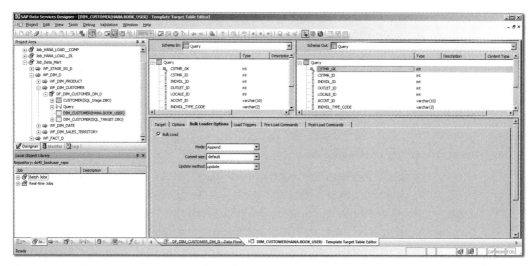

Figure 6.12 Full Data Set Comparison Bulk Loader Options

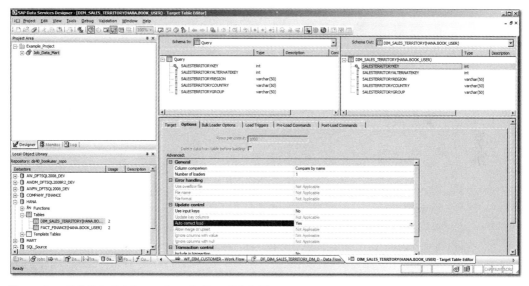

Figure 6.13 Full Data Set Comparison Options Tab Settings

This is different from how the target table options work in almost any SAP Data Services target system configuration. Typically, a developer would set either the BULK LOADER OPTIONS or the OPTIONS tab. However, for this full data set comparison scenario, you do both. Target-based CDC does not go away just because this option exists. In the real-world scenario described earlier, the CDC-enabled data flows were still converted for the customer. This new functionality merely offered a way to delay the conversion in favor of having BI content developers working in SAP HANA much more quickly. This ultimately paved the path toward a much higher adoption and end-user embrace of the new SAP HANA platform, but it did not replace true CDC operations for the customer.

Standard Target-Based CDC

In many cases, even with SAP HANA, you might need to focus on a subset of the data. Focusing on changed data is a great way to process only what you need to process, but even with the power of SAP HANA, this will be a realization under really tight data load windows or timelines. As stated in the previous section, certain scenarios—now with new advances in the bulk load capabilities of SAP HANA made available to SAP Data Services—will allow for auto correct loading or merging data in bulk. This is a great option for a true bulk delta merge that is available with modern versions of SAP HANA; however, more standard target-based CDC allows for precise comparison of target data and will always have value.

SAP Data Services offers many options for target-based CDC. In our opinion, the `Table_Comparison` transform offers one of the best means of target-based comparison for loading batch jobs into SAP HANA, as long as you don't need to perform changes in the data based on certain fields. In other words, if you're merely detecting changes and writing the same non-key attribute fields no matter whether it's an insert or an update, then a `Table_Comparison` transform is the most efficient and simplest operation.

Recall from Chapter 5, Section 5.1.6, that the `Table_Comparison` transform allows for a rapid implementation of target-based CDC. The interface is drag-and-drop, and the comparison is as easy as specifying the fields that you want to compare against either your SAP HANA target system or your staging database to the source data that you're channeling through the data flow. The `Table_Comparison` transform is shown in the product staging data flow in Figure 6.14.

The `Table_Comparison` transform in this example is comparing input data from the read of the source database in the `Query` transform to the target staging table, called PRODUCT. Each record is compared on the fields that are specified in Figure 6.15, and this captures whether records are inserts, updates, or deletes by specifying the columns to compare in the COMPARE COLUMNS window pane.

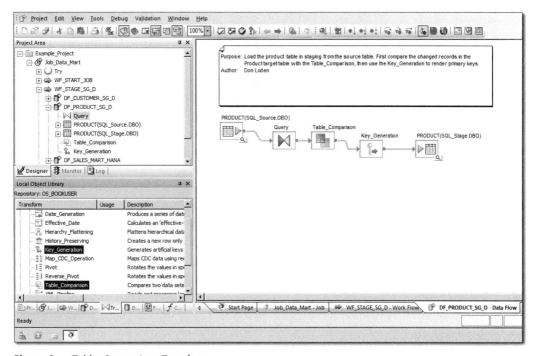

Figure 6.14 Table_Comparison Transform

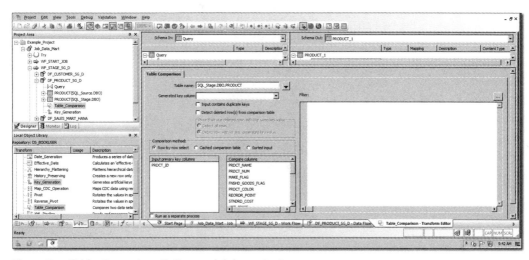

Figure 6.15 Table_Comparison Options and Columns to Compare

This way, after data has cleared the `Table_Comparison` transform, SAP Data Services has enough information about the data to provide guidance to the target table on whether to insert, update, or delete the records from the target table. If no data has changed, the records are merely discarded so that no actions occur against the target. This is very effective in comparing target tables to incoming record sets, but the processing is somewhat expensive in terms of performance.

To avoid unnecessary processing, it's best to select only records that have changed from the source using source-based CDC techniques. Let's look at these now.

Source-Based CDC

In most data warehousing scenarios, you'll have some tables that require CDC; we discussed some techniques available in SAP Data Services to handle target-based CDC in the previous section. This target-based CDC is almost always combined with source-based CDC to ensure that you're not trying to compare all of the data from the source with the target in staging for SAP HANA. You want to focus only on the changes that occurred in the source since the last time data was processed. This is usually performed by comparing a date column or a process ID indication column. In this example, a modified date is used in a source and compared to the date range of a job execution run. This date comparison is achieved by using the `Query` transform's WHERE clause to supply the date range for comparison to the source table. This is shown in the WHERE tab depicted in Figure 6.16.

Figure 6.16 WHERE Clause in the Query Transform

Using dates is typical because most source applications use this concept of a date to mark when the record was inserted or updated. The PRODUCT.MDFD_DATE (or modified date field) is used to capture a range of records from the source PRODUCT table that has been modified since the last run. The run range of dates is controlled using two variables: one for the lower bound date $G_BDATE and one for the upper bound date $G_EDATE. These date values are assigned via the initialize section of the batch job. This is done by the DW_JobExecution function returning the $G_BDATE and $G_EDATE variables from the DW_JobExecution table, which is shown in Figure 6.17.

> **Note**
>
> Make sure that you can trust your dates by performing proper source system analysis, which we covered in Chapter 4. This is crucial for using the modified date effectively and actually picking up all changed records.
>
> Don't just assume that dates are good and accurate. Make sure they are up to the task!

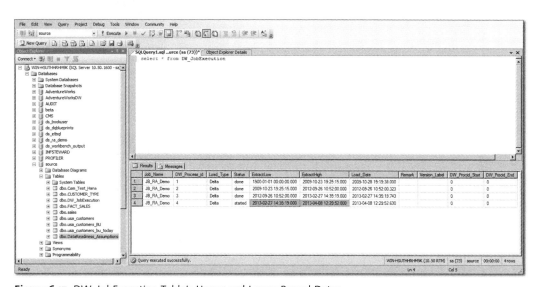

Figure 6.17 DW_JobExecution Table's Upper and Lower Bound Dates

This Query transform returns only the changed records from the source, and these records process throughout the rest of the data flow and the SAP Data Services job. In most CDC situations for loading data into SAP HANA, there will be a combination of both source-based and target-based CDC. This ensures that the batch jobs perform as efficiently as possible and don't over-process records that don't need to be touched.

6.1.3 Triggers

Batch loads require an instigating force to perform their tasks. Instigating forces can come in the form of a schedule, web service, execution command, or a third-party scheduler. We'll detail each of these methods next.

SAP Data Services Scheduling

SAP Data Services scheduling of batch jobs is probably the most typical way to instigate a batch job in SAP Data Services. This is the method that is shipped with the product and supported by the documentation as the primary means. It's handled with two different methods in the enterprise information management (EIM) landscape: the SAP Data Services scheduler and SAP BusinessObjects BI scheduler.

SAP Data Services Scheduler

The SAP Data Services scheduler is the traditional means to schedule batch jobs in SAP Data Services. It's found in the Data Services Management Console web tier application, as shown in Figure 6.18.

Figure 6.18 SAP Data Services Scheduler in the Central Management Console

This very simple, very flexible scheduler application allows scheduling by the day of the week, by days in the month, within a certain time range, and numerous other options shown in Figure 6.19. We normally see it used the majority of the time for controlling the load times of batch SAP HANA loads.

The SAP Data Services scheduler also supports one job having multiple schedules. This can be useful if you have to run the same job numerous times throughout the day, such as to pick up data and load to SAP HANA every 15 minutes. This is easily accomplished with one batch job and a schedule to run every 15 minutes. If you need the job to execute in a smarter fashion, you can create multiple schedules and bind different variables to the schedules to force different batch job behavior at different times; variable assignments can be stored with the schedules, as well as with the jobs. This flexibility offers a number of possibilities for instigating jobs.

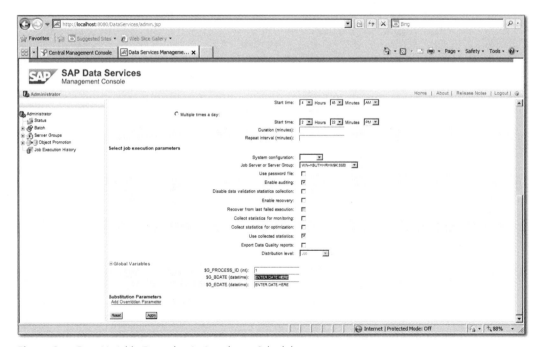

Figure 6.19 Date Variable Examples Assigned on a Schedule

SAP BusinessObjects BI Scheduler
SAP Data Services offers another option for scheduling batch jobs natively if you don't want to use the SAP Data Services scheduler: the SAP BusinessObjects BI scheduler. This is a great option if you're using SAP BusinessObjects BI for your reporting out of SAP HANA, as well as the rest of your enterprise. The SAP Busi-

nessObjects BI scheduler is wrapped within the SAP BusinessObjects BI Central Management Console (CMC), which is shown in Figure 6.20.

If you're using SAP BusinessObjects BI for this purpose, you'll already have lots of scheduled tasks to run reports in place; it makes sense to avoid scheduling tasks in SAP Data Services, because the SAP BusinessObjects BI system can be the central processing point for all of your enterprise's scheduled report tasks.

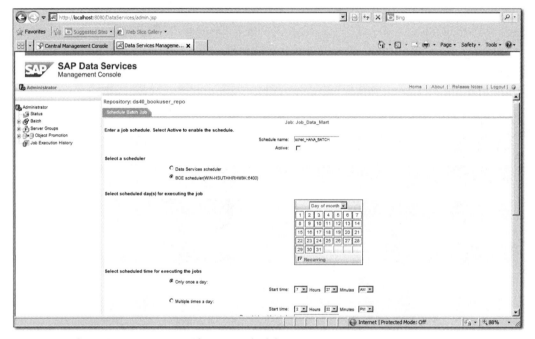

Figure 6.20 SAP BusinessObjects BI Scheduler

Using the SAP BusinessObjects BI scheduler is as easy as selecting the BOE SCHEDU-LER radio button shown in Figure 6.20. After you click the radio button, the scheduled task runs in SAP BusinessObjects BI. These are two great options that are native to SAP Data Services. However, there are two third-party scheduling options that are worth noting: integration via web services and third-party scheduling.

Integration via Web Services

Organizations use web services for a variety of purposes—everything from data exchange between applications on different platforms to stateless process execution. We've already discussed SAP Data Services real-time jobs and data flows fostering stateless real-time data exchange, but SAP Data Services batch jobs can also be triggered via web services.

This process isn't as straightforward, but it can certainly be accomplished if required by the needs of an organization. Figure 6.21 shows a real-time job calling a batch job that is instigated by a web service from an external application.

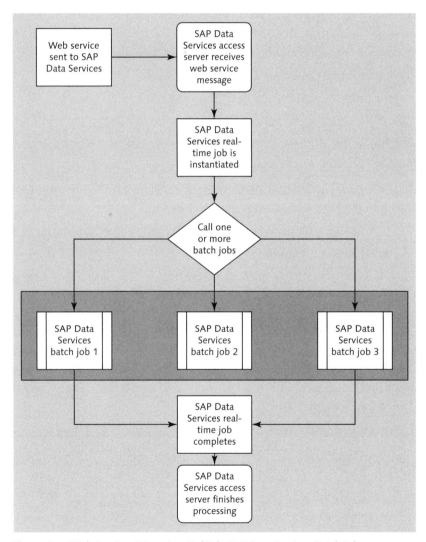

Figure 6.21 Web Services Triggering Multiple SAP Data Services Batch Jobs

Let's walk through this workflow process step by step:

1. A web service from an external application is sent to the SAP Data Services access server, which is always listening for web service requests.

2. The access server processing starts, and the web services–specified real-time job starts.

3. The SAP Data Services real-time job is configured to call another batch job instead of moving data in data flows or workflows. This is performed by an exec() function in a script object. The example in Figure 6.21 calls three batch jobs, but this number can vary depending on what is needed.

4. The batch jobs start execution.

5. All batch jobs finish execution.

6. The real-time job finishes execution.

7. The application server finishes processing and returns the web service response of completion back to the source application.

This example is reasonably complicated, but is especially useful to organizations that don't want to manage multiple scheduling systems.

Integration via Execution Commands

It is also possible to expose a batch job as an executable object. This is done by creating an execution command in the Management Console in SAP Data Services. As shown in Figure 6.22, click the ACTION column value EXPORT EXECUTION COMMAND. A screen appears that allows you to set many different options for job execution (see Figure 6.23). It's a more limited set of options than when you schedule a batch job in SAP Data Services, but you can still bind variables and run different configurations that connect to different sources to load SAP HANA. There is great flexibility when performing this function.

When you click the EXPORT button to export the execution command, two files are produced, containing execution properties in a batch file (.bat) and instructions in a text file (.txt).

Figure 6.22 The Export Execution Command

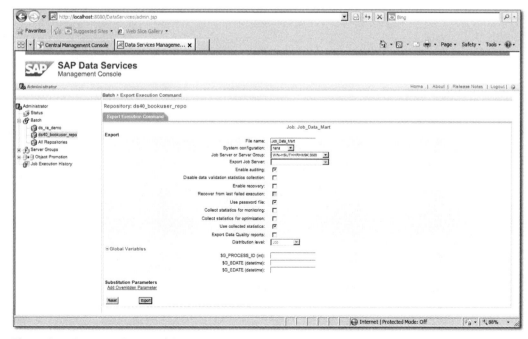

Figure 6.23 Execution Command Properties

Batch File Contents

E:\PROGRA~1\SAPBUS~1\DATASE~1/BIN/AL_RWJ~1.EXE "C:\PROGRAMDATA\
SAP BUSINESSOBJECTS\DATA SERVICES/LOG/WIN-HSUTHHRHM9K/" -W
"INET:WIN-HSUTHHRHM9K:3500" -C "C:\PROGRAMDATA\SAP BUSINESSOBJECTS\
DATA SERVICES/LOG/JOB_DATA_MART.TXT"

Text File Contents

-PLOCALEUTF8 -R"DS_BOOKUSER.TXT" -G"4D57CCC2_BFF5_481B_A7A8_A7B123F164A5"
-T5 -T14 -LOCALEGV -GV"$G_PROCESS_ID=MTAWMA;$G_BDATE=
JzIwMTMuMDYuMDUGMDA6MDA6M" -GV"DAN;" -CTBATCH
-CMWIN-HSUTHHRHM9K -CAADMINISTRATOR -CJWIN-HSUTHHRHM9K -CP3500

These files work together. The batch file is the executable component, and the text file supplies the supplementary instructions to guide the batch file to all of the values that you specified in the EXPORT EXECUTION COMMAND process.

So, when you need to call an SAP Data Services batch job, you just execute the batch file produced by this process, and the job executes with all of the logic, variables, and system configurations that have been specified in the execution command. This makes for a very simple but smart execution process.

Third-Party Scheduler

Many organizations have integrated scheduling into a third-party application that handles all job and task scheduling opportunities for the organization. SAP has made allowances for this with SAP Data Services so that loading SAP HANA can be scheduled using the same mechanisms. Essentially, this is all done with the EXPORT EXECUTION COMMAND functionality that was just chronicled in the previous section. The workflow is as follows and is shown in Figure 6.24:

1. Create your batch job to load SAP HANA.

2. Export an execution command of your completed SAP Data Services batch job that loads SAP HANA. This exports both the batch file and instruction file.

3. Ensure that your third-party scheduling application has permissions to the directory on the SAP Data Services server where this file is stored.

4. Integrate a command-line call to the batch file from your scheduling application via a UNC path: \\SAPDATASERVICESSERVER\INSTALLATIONDIRECTORY\ BATCHFILE.BAT.

5. Schedule your task in your third-party application.

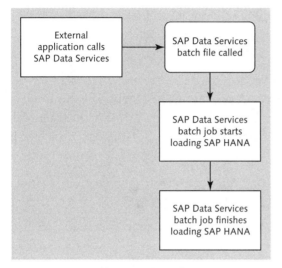

Figure 6.24 External Application Calling SAP Data Services Batch Job

6.2   Loading Data in Real Time

As you know by now, batch loading loads data and handles transformations in sets of data. For a batch operation, a transaction may be as few as 10 records or as many as 10 million records. All of the records contained in the batch load into SAP HANA need to be treated as a transaction or unit.

In contrast, real-time loading into SAP HANA is the process of echoing data into SAP HANA *as changes occur*, record by record, in a source. This means that concepts like initialization and end script, which were discussed in the context of batch loading, don't apply here; in real-time loading, there are only the records that are passed into the process from the source. You will see that this real-time process is both more condensed and streamlined. SAP Data Services is the best method to accomplish this functionality, with its massive library of transforms and functions to accomplish varied output formats, cleansing, and standardization.

Let's consider a scenario in which an online application creates a customer record, and you want to load that record in SAP HANA immediately as it's created online. The business requirement is that the sales group needs to see customer changes as they occur because research has proven that the sale is more effective knowing up-to-the-second customer information. However, there is one issue: The customer list in SAP HANA has already been cleansed and standardized to build a concise list of customers for reporting. The last thing that you want to do is see customer records for a rogue application pollute that list.

Fortunately, you can use SAP Data Services to cleanse the customer data from the application and match the record against your list in SAP HANA. This ensures that you meet the requirement and keep fast trash out of SAP HANA. An example real-time job depicting the scenario of immediately reflected customer changes is shown in Figure 6.25.

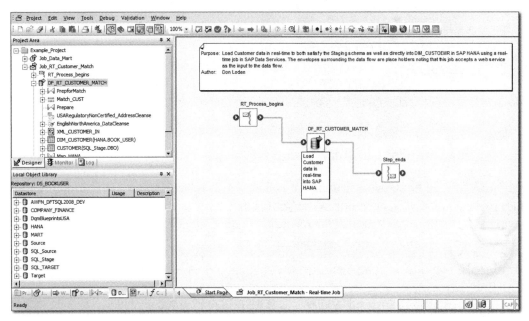

Figure 6.25 Real-Time Job to Load SAP HANA

This real-time job takes a web service input, signified in Figure 6.25 by the envelope icons that surround the data flow. (Note that these icons have no meaning or use other than to illustrate that this is a real-time job.) The data flow DF_RT_CUS-TOMER_MATCH is just a standard data flow that can be used in any batch or real-time job. This data flow is shown in Figure 6.26.

The data flow takes web services as input records and then uses a Query transform to flatten the hierarchical XML data. That flattened data is fed to an address-cleansing transform to cleanse customer address attributes from the web application that won't be used for output to the customer staging or customer dimension tables. Rather, the address data will be used as supplementary input information, along with the cleansed customer fields in the Data_Cleanse transform, to achieve a better matching result.

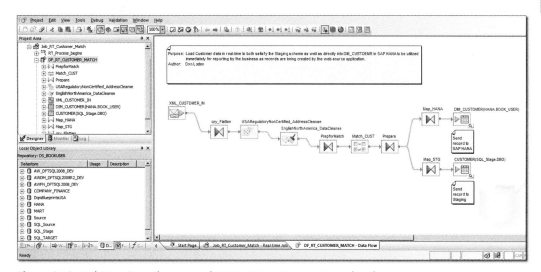

Figure 6.26 Real-Time Data Flow to Load SAP HANA as Data Is Created in the Source

After the customer-specific attributes are cleansed with the Data_Cleanse transform, matching takes place in the Matching transform using both the cleansed customer and address components. The cleansing process is important because you want to standardize not only the record elements to prepare for the match against the data in SAP HANA, but also the incoming data to the same standards and specifications that the SAP HANA DIM_CUSTOMER data has already been cleansed. After matches have occurred, the elements that you care to load into the respective customer-staging table and SAP HANA–specific table are prepared and finalized by the remaining Query transforms just before the target tables.

Table 6.2 shows this process in more detail, down to the data flow element name, the respective element type, and the description of what task each object is responsible for performing.

Data Flow Element Name	Element Type	Description
XML_CUSTOMER_IN	XML message source object	This is the XML message source from the source application. This message is in a hierarchical data format that consists of both the elements of the data, as well as the structure and data types to describe the data. SAP Data Services supports W3C standards.
qry_Flatten	Query transform	This transform is used to un-nest or flatten the hierarchy that is present in the XML data. The data must be in a flat table. A flat table consists of only rows and columns, and not relationships to other objects or constructs.
USA_RegulatoryNonCertified_ AddressCleanse	US address cleanse transform	This transform is used to both parse and correct the address elements coming from the web source application. After the address is cleansed and standardized, it's ready for use in further processing the data flow.
EnglishNorthAmerican_DataCleanse	Data cleanse transform	This transform cleanses the customer-specific attributes by using the SAP-supplied person- and firm-supporting software to parse, standardize, and correct missing or incorrect person names or firm names. This transform is also used to note the standard form of a name and provide match-standard name suggestions (e.g., William could be Bill or Billy). This yields a better match result.
PrepForMatch	Query transform	This transform organizes all of the fields that will be considered for the Match transform into a concise order and format that will be used for matching.

Table 6.2 Details of the Specific Objects in the Real-Time Data Flow

Data Flow Element Name	Element Type	Description
Match_CUST	Match transform	This is where the matching occurs. This transform performs a complex match using a multidimensional algorithm.
		Comparison fields are presented in a specified order, and each field has dozens of options that present possibilities of matches rendered individually as scores at the element level. These individual scores are aggregated up to a whole number that must meet a user-specified threshold to be considered a record level match. If the record is deemed a match, it's placed into a group with its respective matching record and given a score that can be used for later processing.
Prepare	Query transform	This transform prepares the output by selecting only the fields that are needed to satisfy both output tables. Because the schema and columns are different between SAP HANA and staging, this transform must contain all of the columns to satisfy both.
Map_HANA	Query transform	This transform selects only the columns that are specific to SAP HANA DIM_CUSTOMER for the insert or update.
Map_STG	Query transform	This transform selects only the columns that are specific to the CUSTOMER staging table for the insert or update.
DIM_CUSTOMER	Target table: SAP HANA	Target table in SAP HANA: DIM_CUSTOMER. We're using the Auto_Correct option to determine whether the record is an insert or update to the target SAP HANA table.
CUSTOMER	Target table: staging	Target table in staging: CUSTOMER. We're using the Auto_Correct option shown to determine whether the record is an insert or update to the target staging table in SQL Server.

Table 6.2 Details of the Specific Objects in the Real-Time Data Flow (Cont.)

> **W3C Standards**
>
> *W3C standards* define the standard that XML schemas should maintain and define. Various vendors have their own methods and flavors, but these standards make up the basic components of XML structures. SAP Data Services supports these; more information on these standards can be found at the W3C website: *www.w3.org/XML/Schema.*

The data flow is complex but not too extreme when broken down to its individual elements. The important thing to note here is that this real-time data loading example with SAP Data Services is the perfect example of what is possible in terms of complex transformations that could never be accomplished with SAP HANA information views. Information views can handle complex aggregations, but we're maintaining and creating master data in SAP HANA with our complex cleansing and matching process. This is the type of data-quality operation that will ensure that our data in SAP HANA is trustworthy, as well as not contributing to fast trash in SAP HANA.

This is a great example of supplementing the batch load process that we've detailed in this chapter with real-time information in SAP HANA that includes complex transformations. Both batch and real-time loading often work together in a fully realized deployment of native SAP HANA.

6.3   Case Study: Loading Data in a Batch

The AdventureWorks Cycle Company has recently implemented a new BI platform based on SAP HANA, SAP Data Services, and SAP BusinessObjects BI. Using SAP Data Services, its BI resources were able to successfully extract, translate, and load the supporting Internet sales dimension and fact tables into an SAP HANA schema using a batch approach.

This section of the chapter outlines this process and cites specific examples of the build of the SAP Data Services job, transformations contained in the job, and mechanisms to build the tables in SAP HANA.

This first case study details the batch job that loads and creates the following tables in SAP HANA:

- DIM_PRODUCT
- DIM_CUSTOMER

- DIM_SALES_TERRITORY

- DIM_DATE

- FACT_INTERNET_SALES_RETAIL

> **Note**
>
> We'll be discussing the build process of only five of the tables of the data mart. The data mart contains many more tables than this, but these five tables were selected because they cover the primary scenarios needed to illustrate the development process. To minimize redundancy in the build process, we won't show the other tables.

To create these tables, you'll construct a batch job in SAP Data Services that first loads a staging database, as described in Chapter 5, per best practices, and then load these tables.

For the purpose of our examples in the batch job case study, the staging database is in Microsoft SQL Server 2008R2. Any number of database platforms can be used, but we wanted to select a staging database platform that is readily available to customers and most likely in their enterprise.

> **Downloadable Code Information**
>
> The extended code used to create this case study exists in a downloadable format on the SAP PRESS page for this book (*http://www.sap-press.com/3703*) and can be downloaded and installed in your environment.
>
> The code was developed on these versions of the software, and you must use these versions:
>
> - Staging database: Microsoft SQL Server 2008R2
> - SAP Data Services 4.2
> - SAP HANA SPS 8
>
> This code is a sample to construct basic structures and examples from this case study, but further work and review may be needed to fully realize a sandbox system.

The first step is to structure the SAP Data Services job, which is shown in Figure 6.27. Recall from Section 6.1.1 that this job is comprised of four steps:

- Initialization

- Staging

- ▶ Mart

- ▶ End script

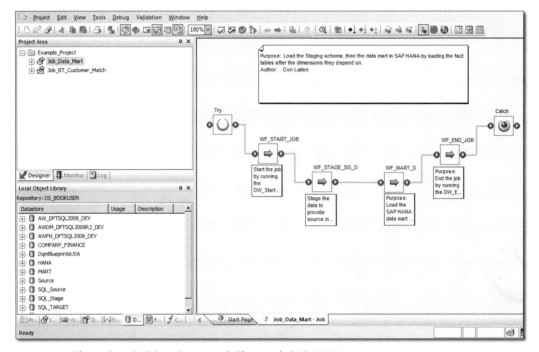

Figure 6.27 SAP Data Services Job That Loads SAP HANA

Before we dive into the first step, though, it's important to mention the `Try` and `Catch` objects that capture and respond to processing errors for recovery purposes. The `Try` and `Catch` objects shown in Figure 6.27 wrap the workflows and are generally referred to as a block. This block of objects performs all of the error trapping, halts to the job, and notifications to the users in the event of a problem. The `Try` object is just a placeholder object for noting that error trapping has begun for all workflows or data flows placed after the `Try`. The `Catch` object has all of the design-making power; this object can trap many types of errors, as shown in Figure 6.28.

Any of the errors shown in Figure 6.28 will cause SAP Data Services to execute the code contained in the script object `SCR_HALT_NOTIFY`. This script object contains the code provided in Listing 6.1 that will both halt the job and send out an email notification to any specified user that there is a problem.

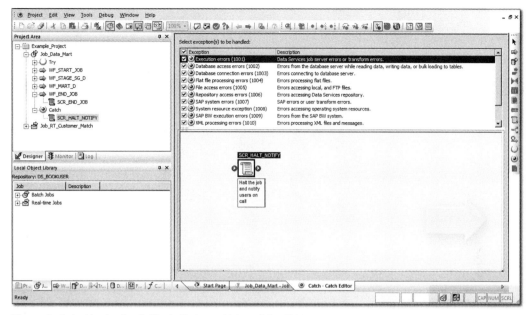

Figure 6.28 Inside the Catch Block: Script to Halt and Email Users

```
#### HALT THE JOB ###
#
#Raise Exception for the log and to denote failure for recoverability.
raise_exception(job_name( ) || ' terminated due to error');

##### Email users
#
#First parameter is the list of emails
#Second is the email subject
#Third is text for the email body
#Fourth and fifth are line counts of how much of the SAP Data Services
logs to include
#
smtp_to('don.loden@decisionfirst.com','SAPHANA_Mart_Job Failed',
'SAPHANA_Mart_Job Failed.', 10, 10);
```

Listing 6.1 Halting the Job in the Event of an Error

Without further ado, let's dive into the details of our four main steps for loading data in a batch.

6.3.1   Initialization

After clearing the `Try` and entering the `Try/Catch` block section of the code, you now enter the initialization stage of the SAP Data Services code. The initialization phase is pretty simplistic because this workflow (`WF_START_JOB`) contains only one object: `SCR_START_JOB`. `SCR_START_JOB`'s function is twofold: to set the variables that will control the logic of the job and to execute the `DW_StartJob` function to control the `ExtractLow` and `ExtractHigh` dates for source-based CDC operations. The `SCR_START_JOB` script object is shown in Figure 6.29.

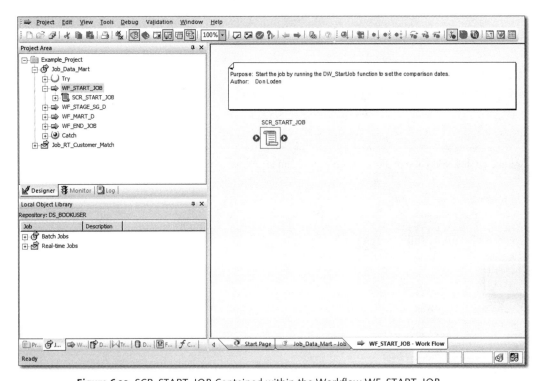

Figure 6.29 SCR_START_JOB Contained within the Workflow WF_START_JOB

The script contains the code shown in Listing 6.2.

```
#Purpose:   Set global variables and exec
# dw_start_job function to
# deal with dw_job_execution table.
#Author:    Don Loden don.loden@decisionfirst.com
#Date:    09.30.2012
```

```
#Load Mart databases: Y or N
$G_LOAD_MART  = 'Y';

#$G_PROCESS_ID  Type: int This variable will be automatically loaded
via DI script
#$G_BDATE Type: DateTime This variable will be automatically loaded via
DI script
#$G_EDATE Type: DateTime This variable will be automatically loaded via
DI script
$G_EDATE = sysdate();

$G_LOAD_TYPE = 'Delta';
#$G_LOAD_TYPE = 'First';
###############End Variable Declaration##############

# Call function to check ExecutionStatus Table for this job
# To force a new run using $G_BDATE and $G_EDATE as the extraction
interval
DW_StartJob (job_name(),$G_LOAD_TYPE, $G_BDATE, $G_EDATE,
        $G_PROCESS_ID, $G_LOAD_DATE, $G_VERSION_LABEL, $G_COMMENT );

# Displays start/end date and Process ID for each job run
print('****************************************');
print('                        ');
Print('[$G_LOAD_TYPE] - Load started taking data from [$G_BDATE] to
[$G_EDATE]');
Print('[$G_LOAD_DATE] - Load date');
Print('[$G_PROCESS_ID] - DW_Process_ID for current load.');
print('****************************************');
print('
   ');
print('****************************************');
```

Listing 6.2 Code to Set Variables and Call DW_StartJob in the Script

6.3.2 Staging

After you clear the initialization stage of the job, it's time for the real work to begin in the staging stage of the SAP Data Services batch job. This step performs many tasks, including the following important ones:

- Creating surrogate keys
- Establishing source independence
- Standardizing data
- Performing CDC against the source
- Transforming for denormalization for SAP HANA

> **Note**
>
> We're loading only a single source in this batch job into SAP HANA, but the examples of surrogacy still hold true whether you have one data source or ten.

The staging workflow (WF_STAGE_SG_D) is depicted in Figure 6.30. This workflow performs all of the tasks previously mentioned to properly prepare data for high performance in SAP HANA.

You start the journey to SAP HANA by creating surrogate keys, as described in Section 6.1.1, to divorce the data source constraints from the key structures needed for SAP HANA. This will be done in staging, which is used to build the tables and provide independence from the source system database constraints; this makes no sense when multiple sources are combined in SAP HANA. We'll examine this in detail and show how this process is executed in each of the four staging table builds. These fields result in a naming convention shift from "_ID" to "_GK". Fields ending in "ID" will be the native source primary keys, where *GK* stands for *generated key*. GK fields are the surrogate keys that encompass all source relationships.

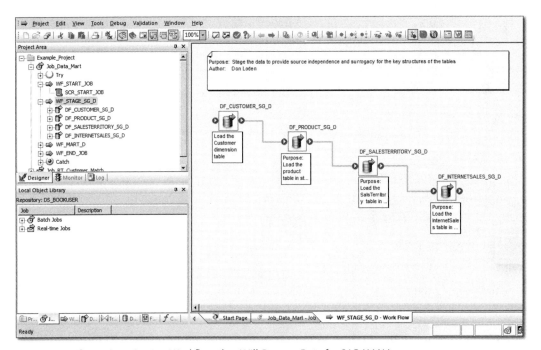

Figure 6.30 Staging Workflow that Will Prepare Data for SAP HANA

Source independence will also be shown in staging by using a column to identify where records are coming from as they make their way to SAP HANA. This is particularly important when there are multiple sources, but in any data mart or data warehouse construct, it's best practice to include these columns. Because you never know when you'll encounter more sources, it's always prudent to plan ahead and assume that you'll have them. The source column for staging and SAP HANA is the same among all of the tables and is called DW_SOURCE.

Data standardization is another theme that remains central throughout the staging process. You're taking data from a transactional source system in this case study and standardizing it for use in SAP HANA. Again, because there is only one source, this isn't as crucial, yet it's still important that standards are followed so that reports from SAP HANA consume data of high quality. There isn't one specific example of this, but this theme remains constant throughout the staging transformation layer of the SAP Data Services batch job.

Source-based CDC is something else that is also quite prevalent in staging. In these examples, assume that you're not performing an initial load from the Adventure-Works transactional system with every batch data load. You'll use the concepts discussed earlier of driving data with a range of modified date values from the respective source tables. This will be performed by using variables for an ExtractLow date, as well as an ExtractHigh date in the WHERE clause of our various data flows in the staging level of the SAP Data Services batch job.

Finally, we'll illustrate denormalization into one staging table that will be used to load a fact table in SAP HANA, which we discussed in Chapter 3. This concept is crucial for maximum performance of SAP HANA, especially across two tables with high cardinality, such as for the sales header and sales detail source tables. There are other cases of mild denormalization for the dimension table loads in staging, but this fact sales table, called Internet Sales in Staging, is the classic SAP HANA denormalization example.

Now, let's discuss the details of the next four table builds—customer, product, sales territory, and Internet sales.

Customer

The CUSTOMER staging table is the first staging table build that we'll explore, and it's also the most complicated of the staging tables because there were unique requirements around CUSTOMER for the AdventureWorks Cycle Company. For instance, certain values needed to be substituted depending on customer type; also, an alternative method of performing target-based CDC is required. With these extra requirements, the data flow becomes quite complex, as you can see in Figure 6.31.

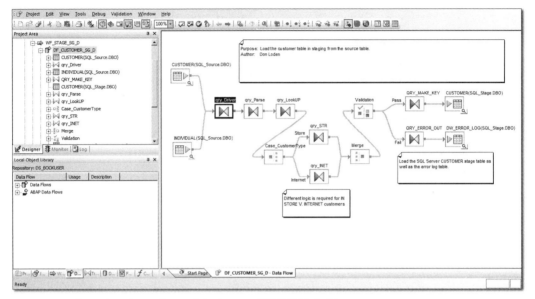

Figure 6.31 Driver Stage of the Staging CUSTOMER Build

This example covers the main stages of a data flow:

- Driver stage
- Parsing stage
- Lookup stage
- Business rules validation stage

Driver Stage

The build of this data flow starts with the driver stage, shown as `qry_Driver` in Figure 6.32. This shows a properly constructed join that will be pushed down to the source database. Figure 6.33 depicts the `WHERE` clause using two variables, `$G_BDATE` and `$G_EDATE`; these two variables obtain their values from the `DW_JobExecution` function in the "Initialization" subsection of Section 6.1.1 and are used throughout the remaining staging table driver sections.

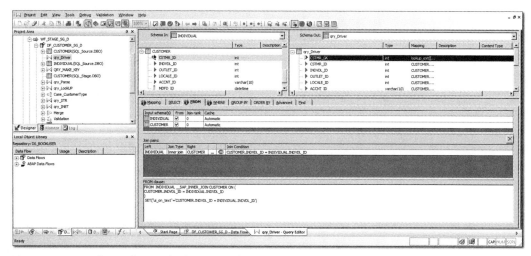

Figure 6.32 Join That Will Be Pushed Down to the Source Tables

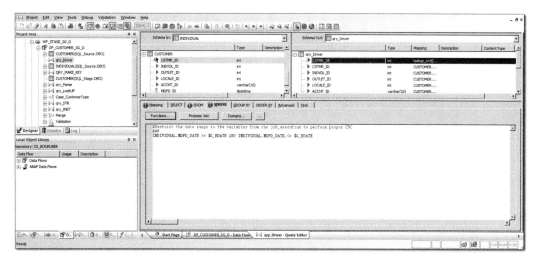

Figure 6.33 CDC WHERE Clause to Only Capture Changed Data from the Source

One last item makes the CUSTOMER build's driver section unique. To show an alternative method of target-based CDC in this CUSTOMER load, a `lookup_ext` function was included to return the primary key values from the CUSTOMER table if they exist. This is shown in Figure 6.34.

If the value exists, the `GK` (CUSTOMER primary key) value is returned. Otherwise, a `NULL` value is returned. This `NULL` is handled in the parsing section of the data flow.

Figure 6.34 Lookup_Ext Function Syntax Performed Inline

The lookup syntax isn't trivial, so it may be best to code it in the SAP Data Services GUI that is shown in Figure 6.35. Both of these methods perform the same task, so developers are able to pick whichever method they desire.

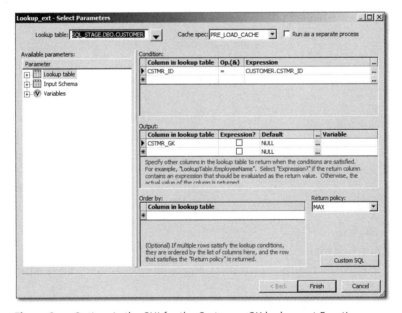

Figure 6.35 Options in the GUI for the Customer_GK lookup_ext Function

Parsing Stage

Next, we'll explore the parsing stage of the CUSTOMER staging data flow per business rules. This is shown in `qry_Parse` in Figure 6.36. This occurs after the record set is driven down with the source-based CDC performed in the driver stage.

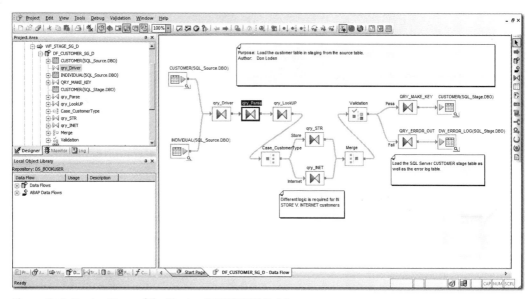

Figure 6.36 Parsing Stage of the Staging CUSTOMER Build

This parsing stage of the CUSTOMER build is actually quite simple in that the only values that need to be parsed are the NULL GK values returned by the `lookup_ext` function in the previously covered driver stage. This is accomplished by an NVL() function that replaces NULL values with any specified values, as shown in Figure 6.37.

This function works with `lookup_ext` to produce primary key values for new records. If you didn't do this, new records or inserts would fail the lookup and have a NULL value because they wouldn't be found in the CUSTOMER target table. Thus, you pair the NVL() function with a `Key_Generation` function to produce the necessary key values. This is an alternative method to the `Table_Comparison` transform that you'll use for the remaining staging tables.

NVL() + Key_Generation Function Syntax

```
nvl( qry_Driver.CSTMR_GK, key_generation('SQL_Stage.DBO.CUSTOMER',
'CSTMR_GK', 1))
```

Figure 6.37 NVL() Function Producing Key Values for New Records

Lookup Stage

After the parsing stage of the CUSTOMER staging data flow finishes, it's time to begin the lookup stage. This is the qry_Lookup shown in Figure 6.38.

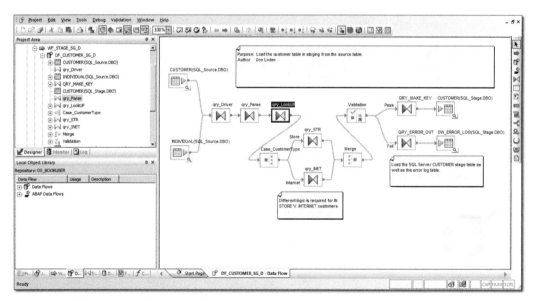

Figure 6.38 Lookup Stage of the Staging CUSTOMER Build

In terms of performance, lookups are expensive and, consequently, should be limited to this stage of the data flow where possible. The target-based CDC operation illustrated earlier is one exception: parsing needed to occur after that lookup to replace NULL values with newly created primary key values using the NVL function. You'll use the lookups in this section to drive business logic by looking up whether a customer is an Internet customer or came in and purchased a bicycle in a store.

Lookups can be performed in-line, as you saw earlier in this section with the difficult-to-read syntax, but they also may be inserted as function calls. This is the case for the ONLINE_ORDER_FLAG field that you need to return from the SALES_HEADER table from the source system. The function call method is shown in Figure 6.39; the lookup_ext function in the GUI is shown in Figure 6.40.

Figure 6.39 Lookup_ext Functions Inserted as Function Calls Not Inline

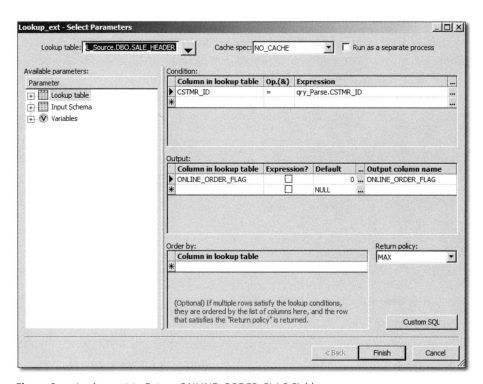

Figure 6.40 Lookup_ext to Return ONLINE_ORDER_FLAG Field

A final item in the lookup stage is assigning two very important columns to the CUSTOMER table: a source indictor column (DW_SOURCE) and a process ID column (DW_PROCESS_ID). These are shown in Figure 6.41.

The DW_SOURCE column acts as an identifier to tell the users where the records came from. Of course, because we have only one source, this isn't as important for our case study example, but data warehousing applications in SAP HANA frequently combine multiple sources, so this column always should be used. Notice that a variable $G_SOURCE is used to set this column. This is done for code flexibility so that this method can be used everywhere to avoid hard-coding source values in the data flow. This best practice makes the data flow modular and allows for greater reuse.

The other column that is set in a similar manner with a variable is the DW_PROCESS_ID column. This is a crucial column that exists in every table in staging as well as in SAP HANA because it serves an important purpose. This is the ID value, which is a numeric value that signifies the number of the execution or job run. So, when the job runs, all of the data that is produced by the date range from the source system is stamped with this value. This concept provides a platform for recovery. You can recover the job; dates have been removed from the equation because, with our process ID value, the transaction is just that ID. The ID transaction of today may have pulled 50,000 customers, but it's still execution number 1,000 in the DW_PROCESS_ID column. This allows you to recover as a unit should a failure occur. Process ID also plays a very important role in the mart batch job section of the code for loading to SAP HANA, which we'll cover in Section 6.3.3.

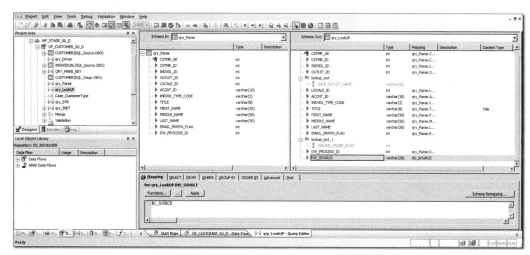

Figure 6.41 Setting the Source Field with a Variable for Flexibility

Now that you've used the `lookup_ext` functions to know which ones are Internet customers and which are in-store customers, you can use a combination of `Case`, `Query`, and `Merge` transforms to perform the field substitutions needed to fulfill the business requirements shown in Figure 6.42.

First, you need to use the `Case` transform to act upon the values returned from the lookup. You'll use the `Case` transform to drive the data into one query transform or another. If the ONLINE_ORDER_FLAG is 0, then guide the records to the `qry_STR` transform, or if you know the customer must be an Internet customer, you can also drive the records to the `qry_STR`. The options in the CASE tab to guide the data in this manner are shown in Figure 6.43.

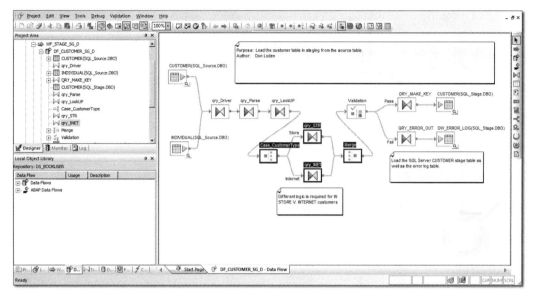

Figure 6.42 Complex Case Logic and Merging the Staging CUSTOMER Build

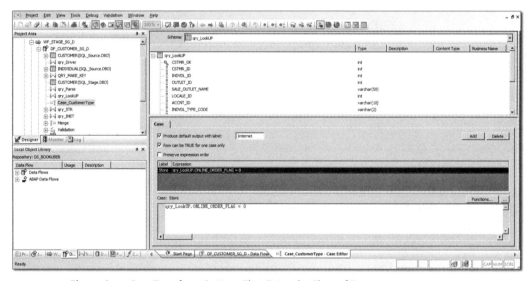

Figure 6.43 Case Transform Options That Drive the Flow of Data

After the data has been driven into the appropriate `Query` transform, the value substitutions occur as shown in Figure 6.44 and Figure 6.45, showing brick-and-mortar and Internet settings, respectively.

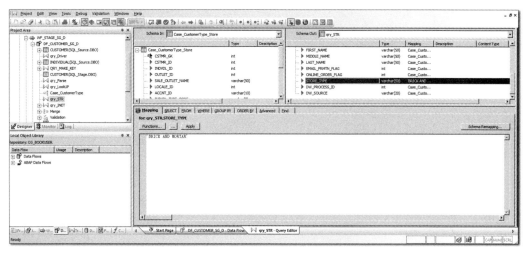

Figure 6.44 Setting the Brick-and-Mortar Value

Figure 6.45 Setting the Internet Store Value

The record sets, which are identical in structure, are merged back together using a `Merge` transform, as shown in Figure 6.46.

This is a very simple demonstration of case logic, but a good example of how `Case`, `Query`, and `Merge` transforms work together. The important thing to keep in mind is that this is where you perform value substitutions, even with complex logic such as lookups or decode functions. The complexity doesn't matter, but the field's structure is important.

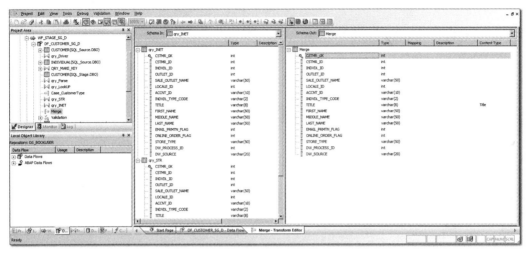

Figure 6.46 Merging the Two Record Sets Back Together

> **Note**
>
> For the merge to be performed, the field names and order in both Query transforms must be identical.

Business Rules Validation Stage

Now that all of the transformations from the CUSTOMER data flow have been performed and the data is almost ready to write to the staging CUSTOMER table, you need to validate your work in the validation stage shown in Figure 6.47.

The validation stage is a combination of the Validation transform and the DW_ERROR_LOG table. This section of the code captures failures of the business rules that need enforcement post-transformations. Common examples include primary and foreign key (orphan records) enforcement across sources, but you can really measure any fields.

In this case, the Validation transform measures both orphans and custom transformations recently produced with the case logic, specifically the following:

- Ensuring Internet versus in-store values were set correctly
- Checking for customer orphan records
- Checking for individual orphan records
- Checking for outlet orphan records

The validation property settings to produce this result are shown in Figure 6.48.

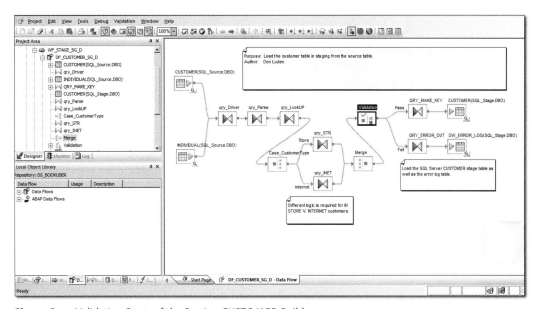

Figure 6.47 Validation Stage of the Staging CUSTOMER Build

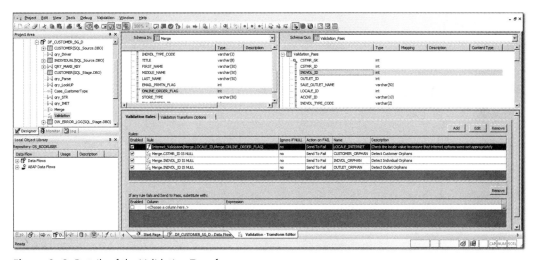

Figure 6.48 Details of the Validation Transform

Notice the validation function in comparison to the field validations. This validation function can also come from SAP Information Steward.

If all of the logic tests in the `Validation` transform succeed, then the record is sent to the CUSTOMER target through the `QRY_MAKE_KEY` transform, as shown in Figure 6.49.

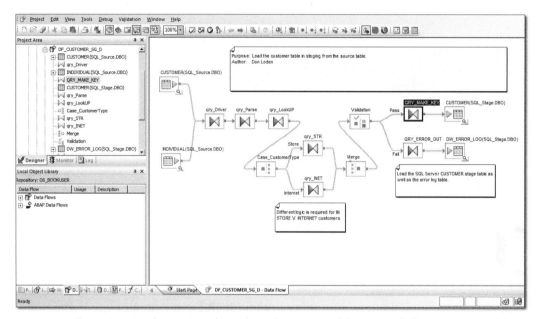

Figure 6.49 Final Query Transform Aligns the Output Field Names with the CUSTOMER Table

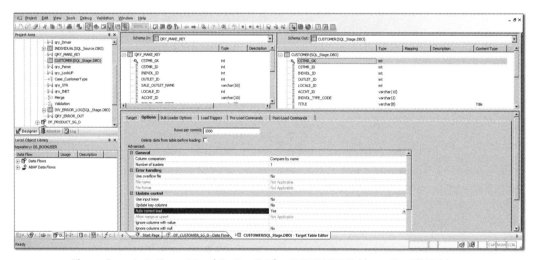

Figure 6.50 Auto Correct Load Option Set for CUSTOMER Table on the GK Field

Then, the records are written to the CUSTOMER table using the auto correct load functionality described in Chapter 5. The auto correct load functionality provides insert records if the record isn't detected in the target table, and update records if the record is detected in the target. As you see in Figure 6.50, this is easily accomplished with the selected property field.

> **Note**
>
> The update occurs against the CSTMR_GK field because this is the primary key field with the primary key icon in Figure 6.50. If you need this functionality against a table that doesn't have any keys, you can use the USE INPUT KEYS setting after declaring one or more fields as key in the previous Query transform.

In the event that records did not meet the conditions of the Validation transform, they are routed to the QRY_ERROR_OUT transform, as shown in Figure 6.51.

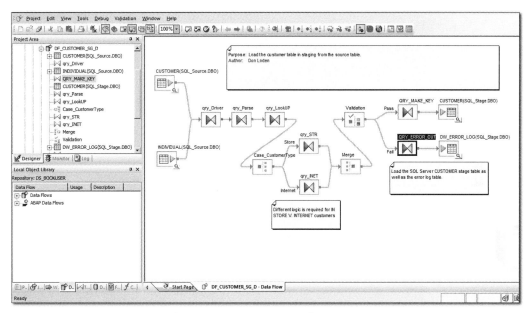

Figure 6.51 Error Trapping Stage of the Staging CUSTOMER Build

This error-trapping logic is something that you *can't* do in SAP HANA. This is something that can occur only in SAP Data Services. With a properly constructed SAP Data Services batch load job, you can perform complex error substitutions, as shown in Figure 6.52.

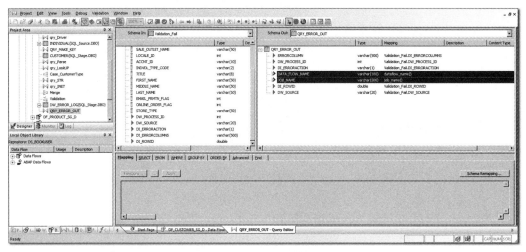

Figure 6.52 Specific Fields Routed to Error Log Table

You're capturing both data errors and statistics that SAP Data Services captures about the processing. This is a great deal of information that—because you're putting the data into a table—will be easy to report using one of the SAP BusinessObjects BI tools. After the `Query` transform, you'll use the AUTO CORRECT LOAD property setting to control the inserts and updates in the target table, as shown in Figure 6.53.

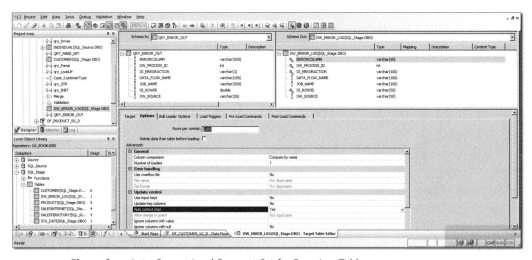

Figure 6.53 Auto Correct Load Property Set for Error Log Table

This completes the CUSTOMER staging table, so let's move on to the next table in staging: PRODUCT.

Product

In comparison to the complexity of the CUSTOMER table, the PRODUCT staging data flow is quite simple. The data in the table from the source was already quite good for reporting, and the business rules didn't require any further transformations past the typical data warehousing constructs detailed in the CUSTOMER section. Note the relative simplicity of the data flow in Figure 6.54.

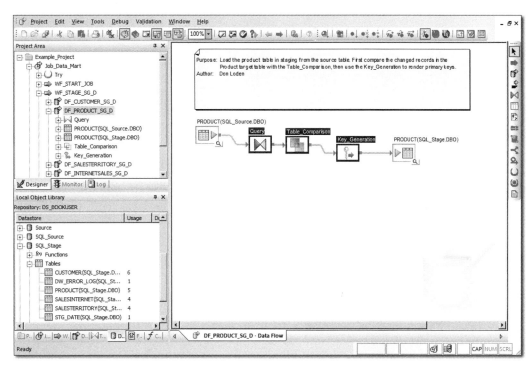

Figure 6.54 Simplicity of Product Load with Unique CDC Mechanisms

The data flow and the introduction of the `Table_Comparison` transform are simple. You'll see how this transform takes the place of many of the transforms that you used in the CUSTOMER flow: the `Table_Comparison` transform is quite powerful. However, before exploring the capabilities of the `Table_Comparison`, let's look at the first `Query` transform to see that the same `$G_BDate` and `$G_EDate` variable values and `WHERE` clause are used in Figure 6.55.

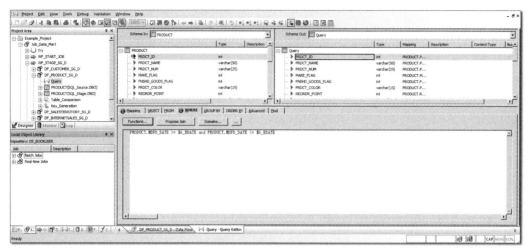

Figure 6.55 Driver Stage of the Product Load Showing the Source-Based CDC

The WHERE clause is exactly the same because you still want to process only changed data from the source that is marked with a modified date (MDFD_DATE). However, not many transformations are occurring in the SCHEMA OUT section (on the right) because the Table_Comparison transform handles many of the operations that require the use of other transforms. It should also be noted that the GK will be handled later by a different method, but first, you must deal with the target CDC and handle the update controls of the target using the options in Figure 6.56.

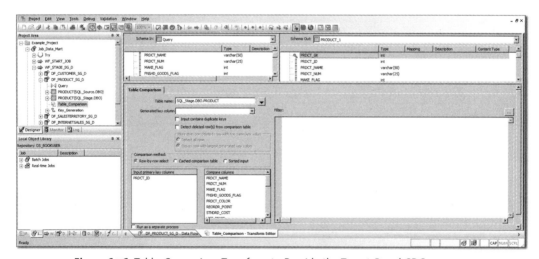

Figure 6.56 Table_Comparison Transform to Provide the Target-Based CDC

The PRDCT_ID is used in the INPUT PRIMARY KEY COLUMNS box in the screen, and all of the attribute fields selected in the COMPARE COLUMNS box are used to compare the fields from the Query transform in the data flow with the PRODUCT target table. If the record is found using these comparison columns, the output of the Table_Comparison transform produces an UPDATE SQL statement. If the record isn't found, then an INSERT SQL statement is produced. This sounds much like auto correct load, but there is one important difference: if there is no change in a record, the table comparison discards the record in order not to touch the target table in the event of no net change. The auto correct load setting always produces an update and touch of the target with every record. The Table_Comparison won't do this.

After the Table_Comparison is finished handling all of the CDC duties, use a Key_Generation transform, as shown in Figure 6.57.

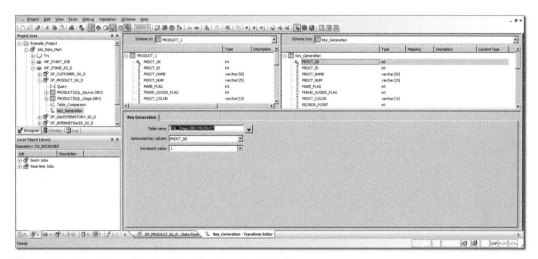

Figure 6.57 Key_Generation Function Creating the GK Column

The Key_Generation transform is quite simple. You merely point the transform to the target table and set the field you want to cast the key values against. Then, the final property is the level to increment the value. The default value is 1, and this is typically what is required.

> **Note**
>
> The Key_Generation transform is a direct equivalent of the Key_Generation function that you used in the CUSTOMER data flow. This is simply another way to accomplish the same task and is typically used with Table_Comparison due to the output row types that Table_Comparison produces.

The final step of loading the table is to take a look at the options present in the PRODUCT table. Note that all options are default, and Auto Correct Load is set to No. Because `Table_Comparison` has performed all of the heavy lifting and figured out exactly what is needed for the target load, no loader options are required, and the data is ready as is (see Figure 6.58).

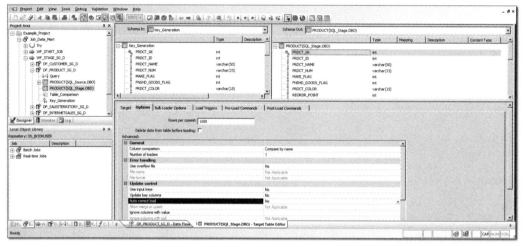

Figure 6.58 Default Target Table Options with No Auto Correct Load

With PRODUCT complete, you're now ready to focus on loading the SALESTERRITORY table.

Sales Territory

The SALESTERRITORY table is much like the PRODUCT table. This simple table is shown in Figure 6.59.

`Table_Comparison` and `Key_Generation` transforms are used for the target-based CDC comparisons, just like in the PRODUCT flow. Also, you'll again always use the `MDFD_DATE` field to focus only on reading the changed records into the data flow for processing. Notice that the WHERE clause tab in Figure 6.60 is very similar to PRODUCT. There aren't any transformations in the Schema Out section of the `Query` transform.

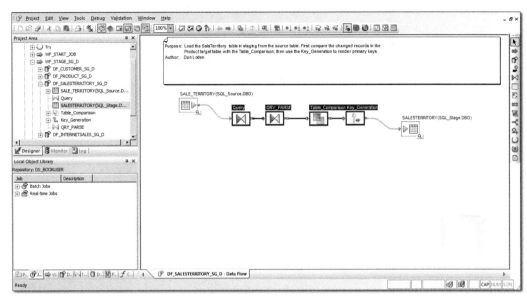

Figure 6.59 Sales Territory Using Table_Comparison for CDC

Figure 6.60 Source-Based CDC in the Driver Stage Query Transform

An additional `Query` transform is required in Figure 6.61 to map some of the fields to fields that have different names in the target table of SALESTERRITORY. It's critical to perform this before the `Table_Comparison` in Figure 6.62.

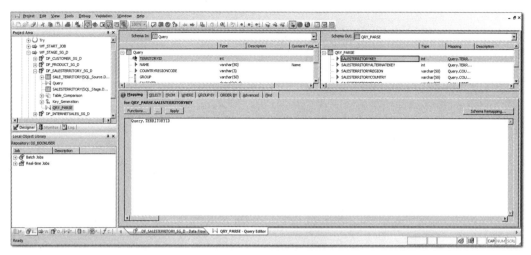

Figure 6.61 The Parsing Stage Query Transform Remapping Field Names

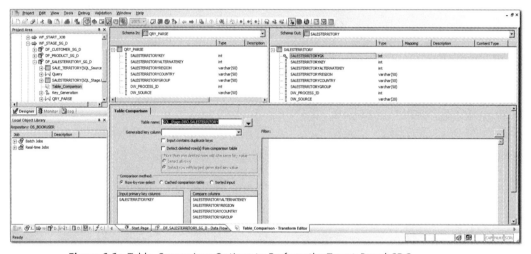

Figure 6.62 Table_Comparison Options to Perform the Target-Based CDC

> **Note**
>
> Table_Comparison for SALESTERRITORY has the same options as in PRODUCT. The same target CDC functionality is needed.

Then, after the CDC operations are handled by the Table_Comparison, use the Key_ Generation function in Figure 6.63 to assign the GK field for SALESTERRITORY.

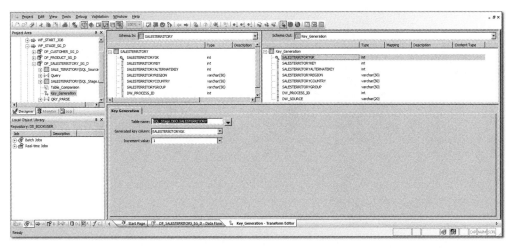

Figure 6.63 Key_Generation Function Creating the GK Column

Finally, the target table is loaded just as PRODUCT was, with no options; for example, there is no AUTO CORRECT LOAD property set. All target table options are the defaults shown in Figure 6.64. They are simply not needed with the `Table_Comparison` transform.

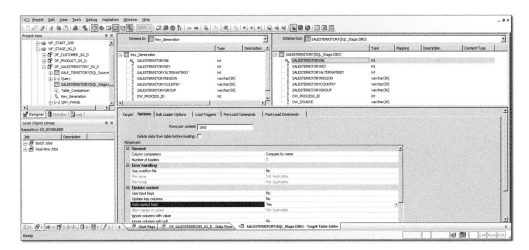

Figure 6.64 Default Target Table Options

Internet Sales

All of the staging tables that will form all of the dimension tables in SAP HANA are now complete with the finalization of SALESTERRITORY. It's now time to construct the table that will form the baseline of one of the central tables for this book: FactInternetSales. FactInternetSales will derive directly from the staging table INTERNET_SALES, so we'll go into great detail on how this table is constructed.

> **Note**
>
> Another fact table that will be mentioned quite often in Part IV of the book is FACT_RESELLER_SALES. We won't cover the build of this fact table because it would be redundant after the coverage of the INTERNET_SALES table.

The first important thing to note is that we'll do something quite different with INTERNET_SALES that is specific for SAP HANA. In a traditional data warehouse on a traditional hardware and database platform, you would construct two fact tables: one for header and one for detail. For SAP HANA, that isn't the case; you denormalize the two tables into one table called SALESINTERNET. This causes the header values to repeat.

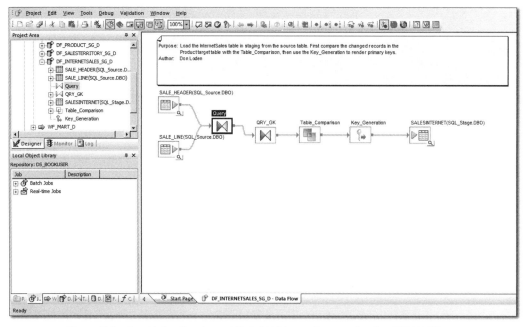

Figure 6.65 Combining Header and Detail Tables to Denormalize for SAP HANA

In a traditional structure, this would be bad both in terms of data storage and performance. But in SAP HANA, because of its columnar table data storage, compression, and run length encoding, this isn't a problem—in fact, it's preferable. You'll achieve better performance, as well as have no penalty in terms of data storage. For these reasons, you'll denormalize the data in the data flow depicted in Figure 6.65.

Notice in Figure 6.65 that two source tables—SALE_HEADER and SALE_LINE—are joined to combine the results. The first `Query` transform contains the join to combine tables and is shown in Figure 6.66.

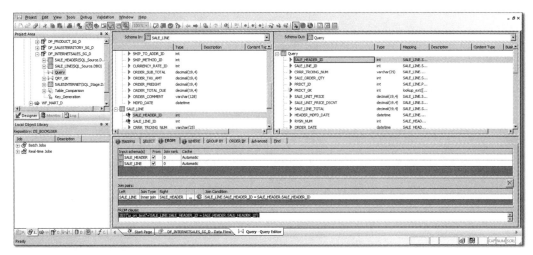

Figure 6.66 Join to Be Pushed Down to the Source Database

The same `WHERE` clause is used in the `Query` transform to produce only changed records from the source system (see Figure 6.67).

Figure 6.67 Driver Stage WHERE Clause to Perform the Source-Based CDC

You'll then use a `Lookup_ext()` function (much like before) to look up the GK values in the target tables to see whether the record exists. There is one difference with the SALESINTERNET table: because it will be the basis for a fact table, it will be the center of the star in the star schema. This means that you'll need foreign key relationships for all of the related dimension tables—which is precisely what all of the `lookup_ext()` functions are performing in Figure 6.68.

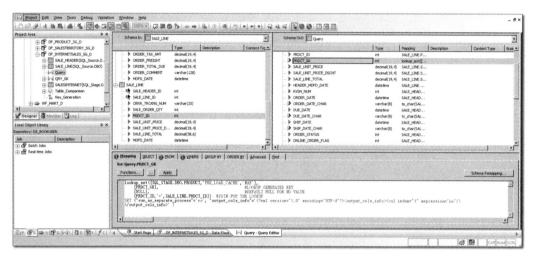

Figure 6.68 Lookup_Ext Example to Provide the Foreign Key Values for Sales-Based Tables

Now that you've handled the foreign keys, you can assign the DW_PROCESS_ID and DW_SOURCE columns in Figure 6.69.

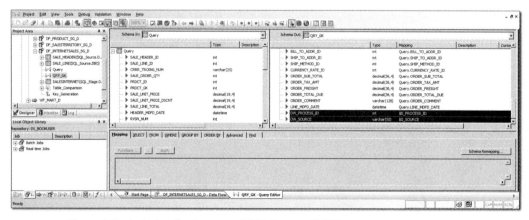

Figure 6.69 Assigning the Source and DW_Process_ID Values

The `Table_Comparison` transform then provides all of the standard target-based CDC operations on SALESINTERNET, as it did for all of the base dimension tables in Figure 6.70.

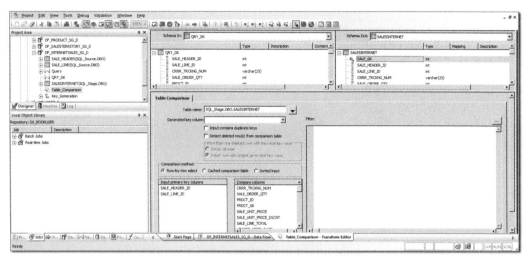

Figure 6.70 Table_Comparison Transform to Provide the Target-Based CDC

Then, the `Key_Generation` transform performs its work by assembling the GK values for the SALESINTERNET table's primary key (Figure 6.71).

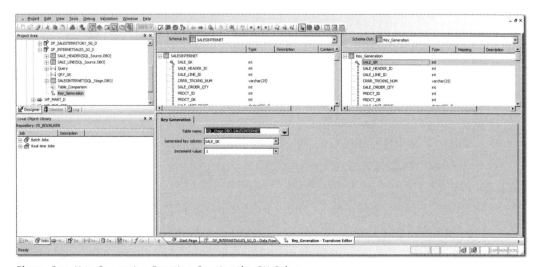

Figure 6.71 Key_Generation Function Creating the GK Column

Finally, the SALESINTERNET target table options are generic because the `Table_Comparison` transform has handled the rest, as shown in Figure 6.72.

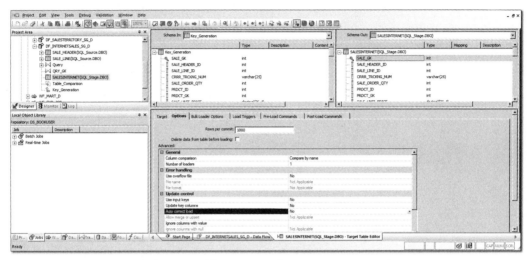

Figure 6.72 Default Target Table Options with No Auto Correct Load

This completes the loading process of the various staging tables. You're now ready to begin loading data into SAP HANA. Because data has been properly prepared per best practices, the data flows that load SAP HANA are actually quite simple. All of the more complex logic has been performed in staging.

6.3.3 Mart

There are two sub-steps that occur as part of the mart step: building the dimension tables and building the fact table. We'll discuss each next.

Build Dimension Tables in SAP HANA

The data mart workflow used to load SAP HANA is depicted in Figure 6.73. As you'll see in this section, this flow is somewhat different from the staging flows.

Order is very important at a higher level for the build of the tables in SAP HANA. Dimension tables must be loaded before the fact tables are loaded, as shown in Figure 6.74. The workflows are used to organize the parallel load of the dimension tables in Figure 6.75.

> **Note**
>
> Parallel loading of SAP HANA is important for extreme performance. It's possible because all of the order and dependencies were met by the organization of the staging load. All primary keys and foreign keys are intact and ready to process into SAP HANA as fast as possible.

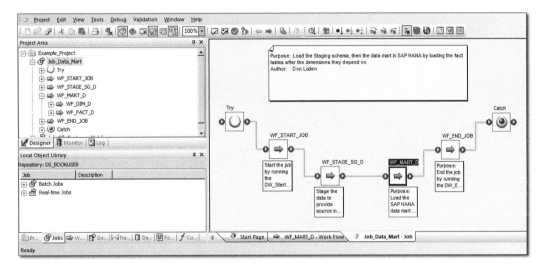

Figure 6.73 Mart Workflow That Loads Data into SAP HANA

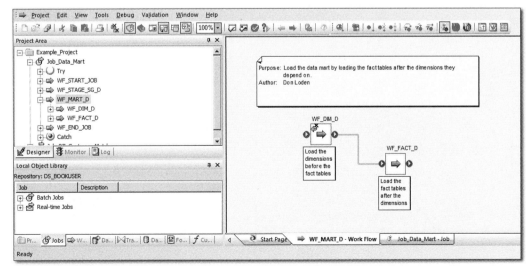

Figure 6.74 Mart Workflow Detailed with Dimension and Fact Builds

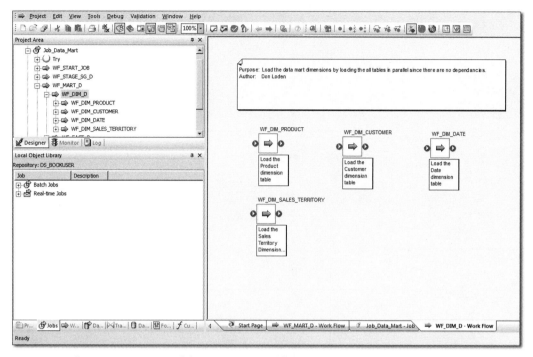

Figure 6.75 Contents of the Dimension Workflows within the Mart Workflow

You need to load data into SAP HANA in a certain order, which is dictated by the data via dependencies. For instance, dimensions need to be loaded before facts because they will be referenced in the fact loads. Hence, load data in the following order:

1. Dimension tables: All tables will be loaded in parallel.

2. Fact table: Load this in order because the foreign keys must reference values that already exist in the dimension tables.

With a basic understanding of the order of execution of the dimensions and fact table, you can start the build process for each of the tables.

DIM_PRODUCT

Upon first glance at the data flow for DIM_PRODUCT in Figure 6.76, you discover that the data flow is simple. This flow is intentionally even simpler than the simplest data flows in staging. The reason for the simplicity is that these flows should load SAP HANA as fast as possible.

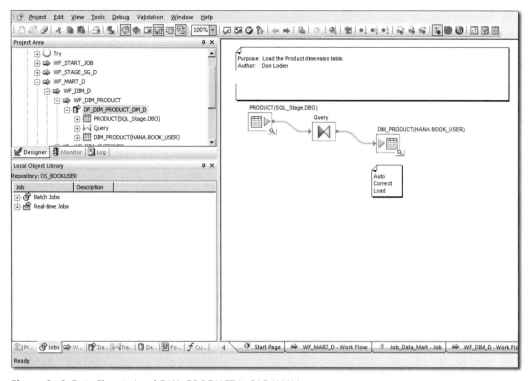

Figure 6.76 Data Flow to Load DIM_PRODUCT in SAP HANA

CDC is important for loading into SAP HANA, but you can't perform this operation by using date comparisons because staging contains many different sources with many different modified dates. This is where the concept of the DW_PROCESS_ID column takes effect. You use this to insulate the CDC processing from the needs and requirements of any of the source-modified date columns. The idea is that whatever was loaded or touched in staging should be moved to the data mart in SAP HANA by a very simple WHERE clause, as shown in Figure 6.77.

The best practice is to perform all of the transformations in staging, so after this, no transformations are present in the Query transform. Staging is complete, so you're essentially just moving the data in its current state to SAP HANA. You'll be using similar options for the target tables for the target-based CDC, such as AUTO CORRECT LOAD, as shown in Figure 6.78.

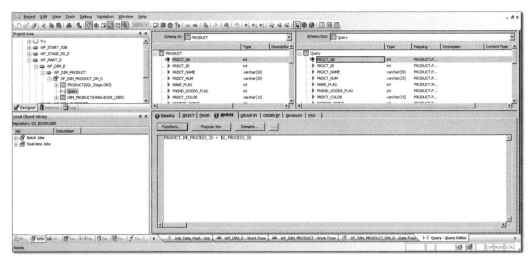

Figure 6.77 Source CDC from Staging Handled via a Process ID Comparison

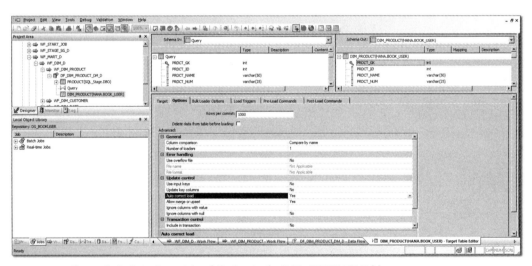

Figure 6.78 Auto Correct Load Option in the DIM_PRODUCT Table

Because you're loading small amounts of changed data in this example, the inefficiency of auto correct load won't hurt the performance objectives—but it will make recovery quite simple.

> **Note**
>
> Many target options exist in SAP Data Services for SAP HANA load performance. We detailed bulk loading options in Chapter 5 that can be used in the right use case.
>
> The example in this case study focuses on small data sets narrowed by a date range in the source. If large data sets are involved, then you have to employ a different approach using the bulk loader capabilities in SAP HANA.

DIM_CUSTOMER

DIM_CUSTOMER is much like DIM_PRODUCT in that it's simple and requires no transformations. AUTO CORRECT LOAD is again used against the DIM_PRODUCT target table. The only piece of logic that is distinctive is the DW_PROCESS_ID comparison against the product table. Aside from comparing against a different table, all of this functionality works the same way as in the DIM_PRODUCT table, so we won't go to that same level of detail in DIM_CUSTOMER. The data flow for DIM_CUSTOMER is shown for reference in Figure 6.79.

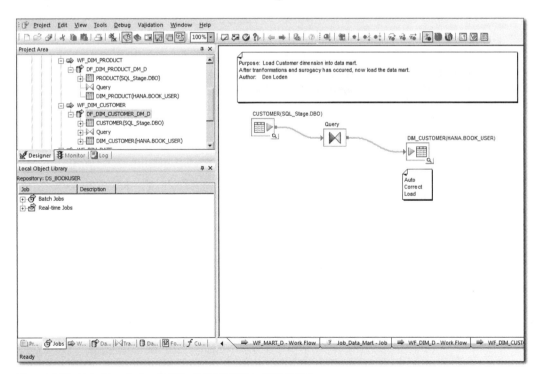

Figure 6.79 Data Flow to Load DIM_CUSTOMER in SAP HANA

DIM_SALES_TERRITORY

Again, DIM_SALES_TERRITORY is much like DIM_PRODUCT and DIM_CUSTOMER; it, too, is simple and requires no transformations. AUTO CORRECT LOAD is used, as well, against the DIM_SALES_TERRITORY target table. The only piece of logic that is distinctive is the DW_PROCESS_ID comparison against the product table. All functionality works the same way as in the DIM_PRODUCT and DIM_CUSTOER tables, so we won't go to that same level of detail in DIM_SALES_TERRITORY. The data flow for DIM_SALES_TERRITORY is shown for reference in Figure 6.80.

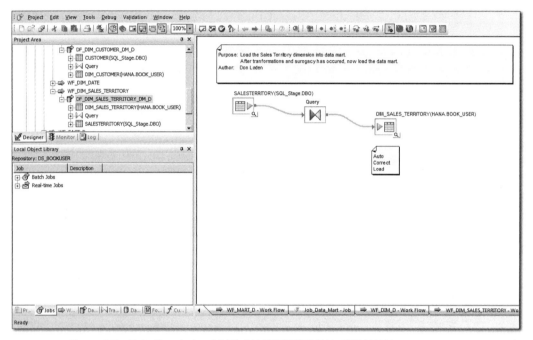

Figure 6.80 Data Flow to Load DIM_SALESTERRITORY in SAP HANA

DIM_DATE

The data flow for DIM_DATE is somewhat unique for a few different reasons:

▶ It has no source table. DF_DIM_DATE_DM_D is sourced from a Date_ Generation transform that only produces a generated date.

▶ All of the columns that are generated from the Date_Generation transform are manufactured entirely from transformations within the data flow.

▶ This data flow constructs the date dimension table DIM_DATE primarily in the SAP HANA data mart, but it also writes back to a date table in staging that possibly can be used for other ETL processing and transformation needs in staging.

The DIM_DATE table in SAP HANA is the foundational table for the date reporting and visualization operations that will be shown in subsequent sections of the case study. We'll show its build here. The data flow that builds DIM_DATE is shown in Figure 6.81.

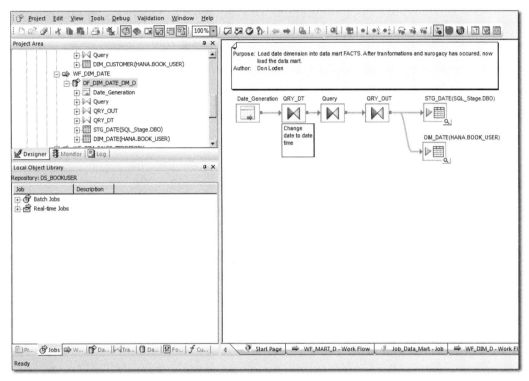

Figure 6.81 Data Flow to Load DIM_DATE into SAP HANA

Notice the difference in the data source for the data flow in Figure 6.81. Recall that this is an SAP Data Services transform! There is no true data source—just a transform that is quite flexible in terms of generating dates from a specified range. The options that control this behavior are shown in Figure 6.82.

This transform looks and is quite simple; there aren't many options to set, and it produces only a generated date column to read. So what makes it so special? The answer is that with all of the date functions present in SAP Data Services, you can use this column as the baseline to create sophisticated date dimension tables. Consider, for example, all of the columns that are being derived in Figure 6.83; although this is a pretty simple date dimension, there are quite a few columns.

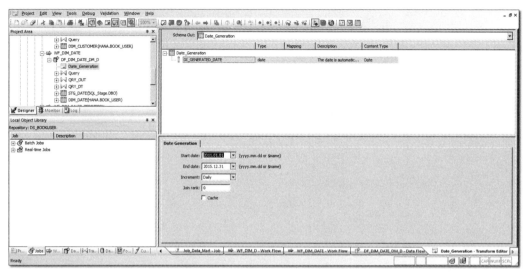

Figure 6.82 Date_Generation Transform Detailed with Options

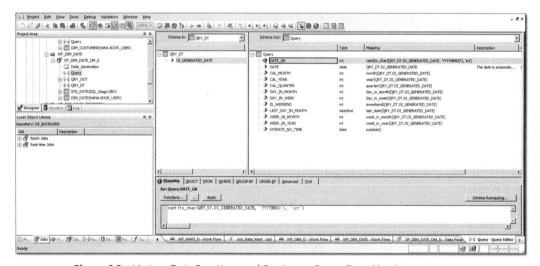

Figure 6.83 Various Date Functions and Parsing to Create Date Metrics

We've used this technique hundreds of times in real-world examples to create almost any date metric imaginable. The built-in functions can be combined in just about any way possible, but we wanted to keep the example simple for the AdventureWorks Cycle Company to demonstrate the basic possibilities. See Table 6.3 for the syntax of the various functions.

Column	Function	Syntax	Description
DATE_GK	CAST() and TO_CHAR()	cast(to_char(QRY_DT.DI_GENERATED_DATE, 'YYYYMMDD'), 'int')	Creates the GK value in the format of YYYYMMDD to make the value more usable.
CAL_MONTH	MONTH()	month(QRY_DT.DI_GENERATED_DATE)	Integer of the month number of the calendar year.
CAL_YEAR	YEAR()	year(QRY_DT.DI_GENERATED_DATE)	Integer of the year number of the calendar year.
CAL_QUARTER	QUARTER()	quarter(QRY_DT.DI_GENERATED_DATE)	Integer of the quarter number of the calendar year.
DAY_IN _MONTH	DAY_IN _MONTH()	day_in_month(QRY_DT.DI_GENERATED_DATE)	Integer of the day of the calendar month.
DAY_IN_WEEK	DAY_IN _WEEK()	day_in_week(QRY_DT.DI_GENERATED_DATE)	Integer of the day of the week.
IS_WEEKEND	ISWEEKEND()	isweekend(QRY_DT.DI_GENERATED_DATE)	Flag for whether the day of the week falls on a weekend; value of 1 for the weekend days and 0 for weekdays.
LAST_DAY_IN _MONTH	LAST_DATE()	last_date(QRY_DT.DI_GENERATED_DATE)	Date value of the last day of the month; useful for setting flag values.
WEEK_IN _MONTH	WEEK_IN _MONTH()	week_in_month(QRY_DT.DI_GENERATED_DATE)	Integer of the number of the week in a calendar month.
WEEK_IN _YEAR	WEEK_IN _YEAR()	week_in_year(QRY_DT.DI_GENERATED_DATE)	Integer of the number of the week in a calendar year.
SYSDATE _NO_TIME	SYSDATE()	sysdate()	Returns a date time value of the system date in a date-time() data type. This column was cast in the data flow into a date data type to truncate the time value returned by the sysdate() function.

Table 6.3 Details of the Various Date Functions and Definitions for Usage

As you can see, there are many ways to derive useful date information, and this is only a small fraction of what is possible. Sometimes, it's necessary to break out of the stock function returns and build upon a value that is produced by the function, and Figure 6.84 shows this in the building of date flags (see the boxed sections in the figure). The date flags will be used to signify the first and last days of the month and week and to sum operations in the SAP HANA mart tables.

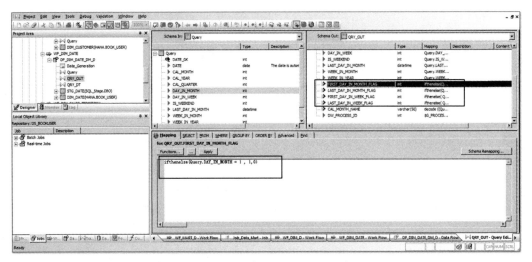

Figure 6.84 Date Flag Construction in the QRY_OUT Transform

Consider Table 6.4 for a more detailed view of the syntax of the functions.

Column	Function	Syntax	Description
FIRST_DAY _IN_MONTH _FLAG	IFTHENELSE()	ifthenelse(Query.DAY_IN_ MONTH = 1 , 1,0)	Flag the first day of the calendar month as a 1; otherwise, 0.
LAST_DAY _IN_MONTH _FLAG	IFTHENELSE()	ifthenelse(Query."DATE" = Query.LAST_DAY_IN_ MONTH, 1,0)	Flag the last day of the calendar month as a 1; otherwise, 0.
FIRST_DAY _IN_WEEK _FLAG	IFTHENELSE()	ifthenelse(Query.DAY_ IN_WEEK = 1,1,0)	Flag the first day of the calendar week as a 1; otherwise, 0.
LAST_DAY _IN_WEEK _FLAG	IFTHENELSE()	ifthenelse(Query.DAY_ IN_WEEK = 1,1,0)	Flag the last day of the calendar week as a 1; otherwise 0.

Table 6.4 DIM_DATE SAP Data Services Date Functions and Column Definitions

Staging is now complete, and all of the dimensions are in place in SAP HANA. We've taken the time to ensure that all logical dependencies are met by running all flows in order and in sequence and performing staging. We can also take some performance liberties in the dimension builds in the data mart in SAP HANA by running the work in parallel. With all of this accomplished, we're now ready to build the final table in the data mart: FACT_INTERNET_SALES.

Build Fact Table

The fact table, like many of the dimension tables, isn't a very complex build in the SAP HANA data mart. All of the denormalization transformations were completed in the staging data flow for INTERNETSALES, so the movement of the data into SAP HANA follows the precedent of the dimensions and is quite simple. The workflow that houses the data flow to build the table FACT_INTERNET_SALES_ RETAIL is housed within the WF_FACT_D workflow and runs after all of the dimensions are built in parallel in WF_DIM_D (see Figure 6.85).

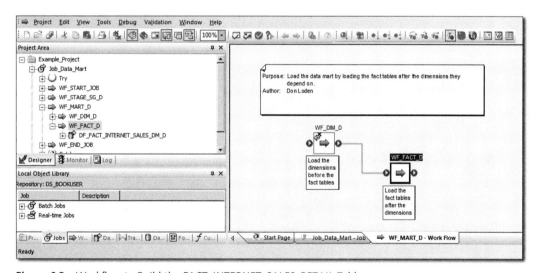

Figure 6.85 Workflow to Build the FACT_INTERNET_SALES_RETAIL Table

There is only one table, and therefore one data flow in the WF_MART_D workflow that contains the data flow FACT_INTERNET_SALES_DM_D. As mentioned earlier, this data flow is quite simple, as shown in Figure 6.86.

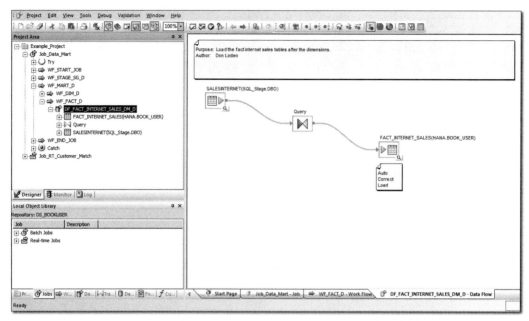

Figure 6.86 Data Flow to Construct FACT_INTERNET_SALES in SAP HANA

There is a read from the staging table INTERNETSALES that was previously denormalized and then standardized to SAP HANA best practices, so all that is left to do is to perform the source-based CDC on DW_PROCESS_ID in the WHERE clause, as shown in Figure 6.87.

Figure 6.87 Source CDC from Staging Handled via Process ID Comparison

Now, you're merely left to write data to the FACT_INTERNET_SALES table using the AUTO CORRECT LOAD functionality that was described earlier in this chapter and is also shown in Figure 6.88.

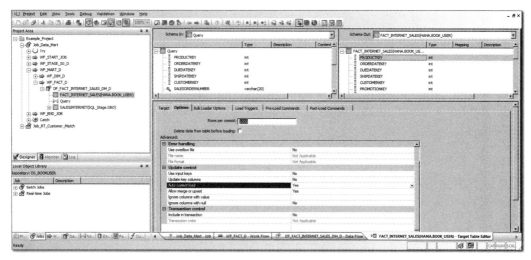

Figure 6.88 Auto Correct Load Options in the FACT_INTERNET_SALES Table

With the entire list of the data mart tables in SAP HANA now loaded, you're almost finished with the batch job to load the data mart. There is only one task left to complete. You started the load process in the installation phase; now, to close the loop that you opened in the DW_JobExecution table, you run the end script as described next.

6.3.4 End Script

The end script section of the job is as simple as the initialize script section of the job, and they have mutually exclusive purposes. The initialize script starts the load process by creating the DW_JobExecution record and setting the STATUS value to STARTED. The end script simply sets the value of the STATUS field in the DW_JobExecution record to DONE to begin again with the next run. The workflow and script object are shown in Figure 6.89 and Figure 6.90, respectively.

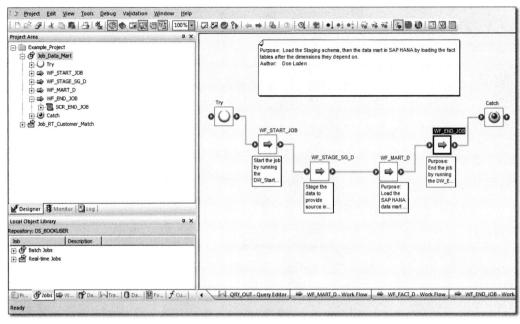

Figure 6.89 End Script Workflow to End the Job

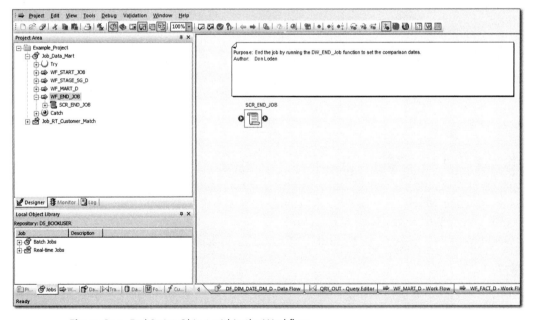

Figure 6.90 End Script Object within the Workflow

The idea is quite simple. By placing the end script at the end of the job, no further logic needs to be built into the function or call of the function. If the job makes it to the end to call the script, then it's complete. If there were a problem with the job, then the Try Catch block would have caught the error and halted the job. The job would never have made it to the end script to close the loop and set the STATUS field in the DW_JobExecution to DONE. Because the loop would have remained open with the DW_JobExecution value set to STARTED, the next run of the job would have recovered all of the variable values and reprocessed them until it completed.

This is how the end script section of code works together with the initialization section of code. It's only with these two working together that you can ensure that all of your data made it successfully to SAP HANA.

The contents of the end script are as follows:

```
# Updates job status with a value of 'done'
DW_EndJob(job_name());

#Write to Trace Log when you are finished...
print( 'Finished - ' || job_name() || ' at ' ||
to_char(sysdate(),'dd/mm/yyyy hh24:mi:ss') || '.' );
```

6.4   Case Study: Loading Data in Real Time

Data has now been loaded in batch in SAP HANA, and the process has worked well for the AdventureWorks Cycle Company. The batch process that was coded and designed in Section 6.3 runs once a day, and this has met the majority of the business needs. The analysts at AdventureWorks are able to access data with unprecedented speeds.

However, upon further analysis of both business and supporting data needs, the BI team determines that certain aspects of sales data need to be loaded in real time to support the analysis of Internet sales transactions. Particularly, sales attributes and customer attributes need to be refreshed as sales transactions are entered in the online sales system. This allows the sales associates to have up-to-the-minute customer and sales transactional information in SAP HANA as a supplement to the data mart data that is being loaded once a day in batch.

This problem can be solved via the use of web services. Data can easily be triggered as web services because this is a native communication platform of the company's web-based sales system. As these web services are rendered, portions of the data are loaded into SAP HANA to support the sales staff with changed data throughout the day. This meets the business need for up-to-the-second sales information, but doesn't necessitate an entire refresh of the data warehouse during the day in real time. With this method, AdventureWorks Cycle Company can meet its needs without disrupting its batch load or the design of the batch-based system for data loading and transformation.

In this section, we'll review the design process and build of the real-time data flows for the sales data, as well as how the AdventureWorks team can reuse certain aspects of the SAP Data Services data flows. (Note: This section won't go into nearly the detail of Section 6.3 because real-time loads are merely a subset of the batch load.)

When designing a real-time solution to meet stated business needs, the IT team at AdventureWorks constructed two different components:

▸ A new real-time job

▸ A new batch job exposed as an executable

The real-time job is a web services–triggered job that is very similar to the customer master data cleansing job described earlier in this chapter (Section 6.2). The job has a similar name, but its purpose is very different. This real-time job is just an execution mechanism that can be called from a generic web service from the AdventureWorks online sales system. The job is quite simple, as shown in Figure 6.91.

This real-time job is only the first step in the process of loading the customer and sales data into SAP HANA. To see why, open the data flow DF_RT_SALES_START, shown in Figure 6.92.

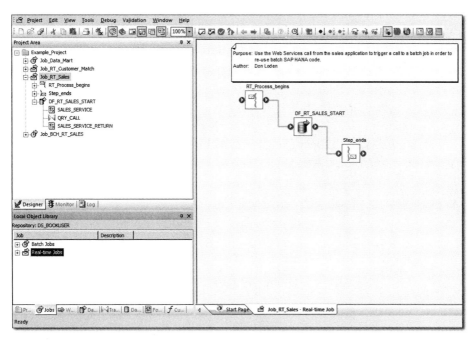

Figure 6.91 Real-Time Sales Job Acting as an Execution Object for a Batch Job

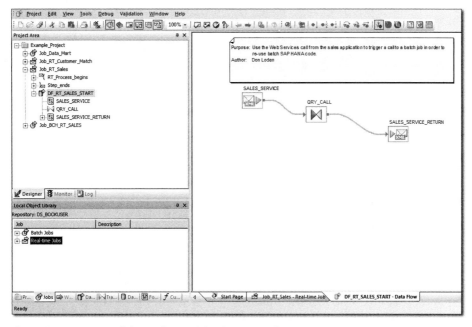

Figure 6.92 Contents of the Real-Time Sales Start Data Flow

Everything looks quite similar to earlier examples, with a web service call coming from the online sales application. The XML message request to represent this in Figure 6.92 is called SALES_SERVICE. There is also one Query transform, but its usage isn't for data transformations. Instead, you'll use the Query transform to call another SAP Data Services job. To do this, you'll use a very flexible SAP Data Services exec() function. This function is capable of triggering *.exe* or *.bat* files from anywhere that the SAP Data Services service user has rights to see. To keep this example simple, a batch file is executed that launches the SAP Data Services batch file, which is stored on the local job server, as shown in Figure 6.93.

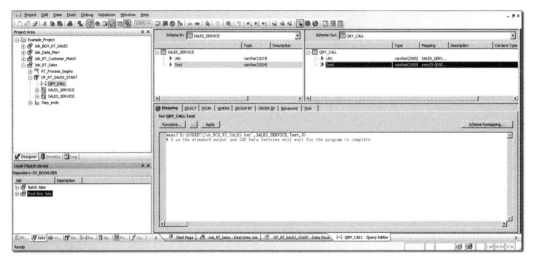

Figure 6.93 Exec Function Call in the Query Transform

The exec function calls the batch file that starts the SAP Data Services batch job with the first parameter, and arguments can be passed with the second parameter. This example passes the XML message text as the argument because it's formatted appropriately. If additional formatting were needed for the string, you could perform the string transformations using other built-in SAP Data Services functions. The third parameter is the output of the function. Choose the output option of 0 because this is the standard output.

This option also forces the SAP Data Services real-time job to wait for the execution of the batch file/SAP Data Services batch job to complete, making the real-time job act as a wrapper for the call to the executable to instantiate the SAP Data Services batch job. The real-time job won't report success or failure back to the web-based sales system supplying the call until the SAP Data Services batch job processing is complete. The following is the entire syntax to call the batch job:

```
exec('E:\DSEXEC\Job_BCH_RT_SALES.bat',SALES_SERVICE.Text,0)
# 0 is the standard output, and SAP Data Services will wait for the
program to complete
```

Create the batch file that is called by this `exec()` function by exporting an execution command of an SAP Data Services batch job that was detailed earlier in this chapter, in Section 6.1.3. After the process to create the execution command is complete, both the *.bat* file and *.txt* instructions file are produced, and they have been moved to the local job server directory *E:\DSEXEC* (see Figure 6.94).

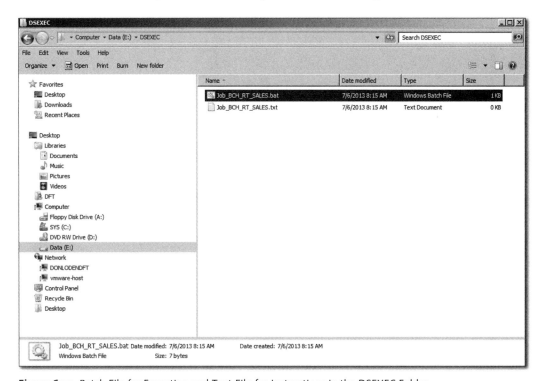

Figure 6.94 Batch File for Execution and Text File for Instructions in the DSEXEC Folder

These two files have all of the components needed to call the batch job that has been created to reuse existing SAP HANA and staging data flows for the following tables that were created in the first case study:

▶ Staging.CUSTOMER

▶ HANA.BOOK_USER.DIM_CUSTOMER

▶ Staging.INTERNETSALES

▶ HANA.BOOK_USER.FACT_INTERNET_SALES

The batch job is called JOB_BCH_RT_SALES (see Figure 6.95) and is a pared-down version of the batch job created in the previous case study.

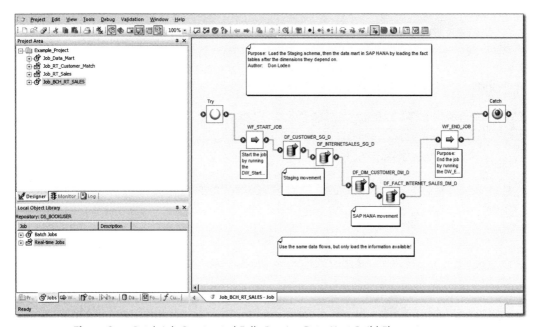

Figure 6.95 Batch Job Constructed Fully Reusing Data Mart Build Elements

This job reuses the data flows as well as the scripts, so there is no need to walk through the job in its entirety. By reusing SAP Data Services, you've successfully met the needs of the business for real-time data by reusing 100% of the data flows created to move the data into SAP HANA! This means that, when a change happens from the business for a table or column, you'll need to make that change in only one place because the object is the same for both real-time and batch.

This is a perfect example of harnessing the power of best practices in object-oriented code design with SAP Data Services. Because we won't walk through the entire job in this section due to the redundancy of the data flows, we've provided Table 6.5, which lists the first case study sections where the build of the job elements occurs.

Real-Time Job Element	Batch Job Section
WF_START_JOB	Section 6.3.1, Initialization
DF_CUSTOMER_SG_D	Section 6.3.2, Staging Workflow: Customer
DF_INTERNETSALES_SG_D	Section 6.3.2, Staging Workflow: Internet Sales
DF_DIM_CUSTOMER_DM_D	Section 6.3.3, Build Dimension Tables in SAP HANA: DIM_Customer
DF_FACT_INTERNET _SALES_DM_D	Section 6.3.3, Build Fact Table: FACT_Internet_Sales_Retail
WF_END_JOB	Section 6.3.4, End Script

Table 6.5 SAP Data Services Real-Time Job Components

6.5   Summary

Now that data has been loaded into SAP HANA, you have the data foundation. You've successfully set the stage for a data platform that can be loaded in a variety of different ways, as well as provided the properly designed data tables for the SAP HANA data mart. Data is modeled into a best-practice, denormalized structure in columnar tables that are still heavily based on a traditional star schema. This approach will both unleash the power of SAP HANA's performance and exploit the capabilities of the SAP BusinessObjects BI suite of tools.

You're now ready to explore the data in the next section of this book. You'll leave the data layer and move into some of the most exciting elements that SAP HANA has to offer in terms of multidimensional modeling. These capabilities are where SAP HANA really shines, and thus are most often reviewed and highlighted in all discourse from SAP. However, this platform can be fully realized only by a properly prepared and constructed data foundation layer. Because you now have this foundation, you're ready to move on to the next step.

PART III
Multidimensional Modeling in SAP HANA

7   Introduction to Multidimensional Modeling

The true value of data to an organization comes in many forms. It can be measured through its depth, its quality, and its ability to effectively explain occurrences within an organization. There is no doubt that businesses and organizations have accumulated vast amounts of data with the emergence of information systems and software applications that manage their daily operations. However, for data to have true value, it must be structured and organized in a way that is intuitive and easy to understand. In addition, the data must be able to quickly, accurately, and securely answer the questions that are posed by analysts, managers, and executives. In this regard, the goal of multidimensional modeling is just that—to help answer questions that bring insight and value to the questioner.

SAP HANA was designed with this very principle in mind. It's capable of storing data in a platform that was designed to provide secure and easy access to a wealth of data. In addition, it has built-in mechanisms to facilitate intuitive and easily understood multidimensional data models—or, as these multidimensional models are called in SAP HANA, *information views*. The multidimensional modeling capabilities built directly into SAP HANA were developed to organize data into categories or structures that can explain the movement of processes or transactions throughout time or across the hierarchy of facets that characterize the attributes of each data record.

In previous chapters, we discussed at length the ability of SAP Data Services to manage and combine data from multiple sources. The combined data was then stored in a data model that was both comprehensive and optimized to provide fast access to the data. We also discussed the importance of data quality and how SAP Data Services can be used to manage it. This chapter introduces you to the concepts of multidimensional modeling and how these concepts can be used to create value for your organization and users of the SAP BusinessObjects BI reporting tools.

7.1 Understanding Multidimensional Models

Before we begin our coverage of SAP HANA's multidimensional capabilities, let's review the basics of the *multidimensional model*. The foundation of the multidimensional model is the *transaction*. Transactions are stored in rows that contain multiple columns. Each column represents a characteristic of the row. As multiple rows are stacked together, these columns begin to form common groups. The groups are then capable of providing dimensionality to the rows. In traditional online analytical processing (OLAP), these groups are called *dimensions*. Dimensions are then paired with *measures* to explain how often, when, or where dimensional values are expressed. Dimensions and measures can be attributed to *hierarchies* that highlight both the macro and micro perspectives of aggregated data. Hierarchies also contain paths that can be followed to help properly explain the results of aggregated data.

The basic multidimensional model illustrated in Figure 7.1 shows the basic relationships between dimensions and transactions. This logical relationship between dimensions and transactions is commonly referred to as the *star schema*. Dimensions are derived from each Internet sales transaction and grouped into logical areas, such as customers, dates, products, and shipping addresses. Measures are derived from the Internet sales transactions by aggregating items such as sales amount, tax amount, and quantity sold.

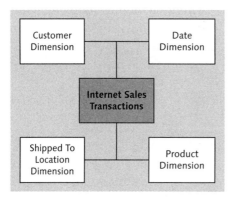

Figure 7.1 Internet Sales Multidimensional Model Diagram

Each dimension is comprised of one or more attributes that can be used for sorting, grouping, or filtering. The attributes of a dimension are derived from the transaction and other master data sources both internal and external to an organization. In Figure 7.2, you can see that attributes such as age, name, and gender are all components of customers. After these attributes are combined with the Internet sales transaction's measures, you can easily answer basic questions, such as, "Which age group places the most orders over the Internet?" You can also combine attributes from other dimensions with the customer dimension to answer more complex questions, such as, "What were the top products sold last year, by country?"

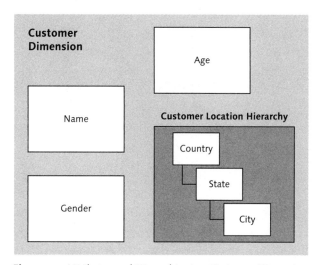

Figure 7.2 Attributes and Hierarchies in a Customer Dimension

Dimensions are also the basis for deriving hierarchies. A hierarchy can be defined from the customer's country, state, and city, as shown in Figure 7.2. Hierarchies are derived from the natural parent-child relationships that exist in the attributes of a dimension. For example, the relationship among country, state, and city is naturally derived from the customer's address. Based on the hierarchy in Figure 7.2, a sales manager can easily identify the top country for sales, drill into the states to find the top state, and finally, drill into city to identify the top city.

Hierarchies are also used to provide a concentric set of roll-up levels or subtotaling levels in reporting tools. Hierarchies based on dates can, for example, provide subtotals for the year, month, and week, as shown in the calendar date hierarchy in Figure 7.3. Dimensions can contain one or more hierarchies; in Figure 7.3, the two hierarchies are the retail date hierarchy and the calendar date hierarchy.

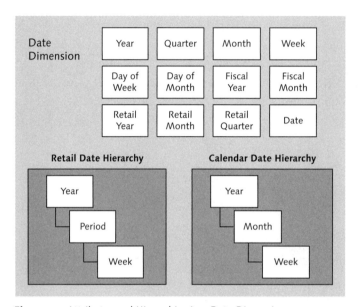

Figure 7.3 Attributes and Hierarchies in a Date Dimension

Although hierarchies aren't required in dimensions, they are a key feature of multidimensional analysis based on many of the reasons stated previously. Dimensions that don't contain hierarchies are considered flat but are still very useful in grouping, filtering, and sorting data.

With the basic building blocks in a multidimensional model, simple and complex questions can be answered. Developers create multidimensional models to define relationships between transactions and their attributes. These relationships create a new set of information about the data that is commonly referred to as *metadata*. Dimension names, attribute names, and their long text descriptions are also considered metadata. All of this metadata is stored in the model and used to describe both the relationships between attributes and additional information to help consumers locate and use the appropriate attributes.

Many OLAP tools on the market use these basic components and the actual supporting data to create a proprietary storage medium called a *cube*. The cube is a combination of both the source data and the defined metadata. When both the data and metadata are stored in this special database, it's widely referred to as *multidimensional OLAP (MOLAP)* storage. MOLAP is preferred in most products because it contains special indexes or aggregated data to help optimize the performance of queries executed against the multidimensional model.

Many tools on the market also support *relational OLAP* storage (ROLAP). ROLAP is similar to MOLAP, but only the metadata is stored in the cube, while the actual source data remains in the supporting relational database. ROLAP is preferred in situations when either the time required to create or update the cube is extensive or real-time access to the data is required.

In comparison to MOLAP, ROLAP is generally slower at answering queries with traditional relational databases and cubes. This isn't true in every circumstance, but when large quantities of data are concerned, MOLAP almost always produces faster results. Traditionally speaking, ROLAP is slower largely because of the inefficiencies of the underlying relational databases. SAP HANA uses a storage mechanism similar to ROLAP. However, SAP HANA's underlying columnar in-memory relational database is exceptionally fast, making ROLAP storage a viable solution for multidimensional analysis. In short, the SAP HANA appliance has the unique capability to offer the benefits of both MOLAP and ROLAP in a single platform.

The usefulness of a multidimensional model depends largely on the quality of the source data, definition of the model, and tools that are used to access it. In Chapter 8 and Chapter 9, we'll discuss the tools and components that are essential to creating valuable SAP HANA multidimensional models.

In the previous chapters, we used SAP Data Services to produce both quality data and meaningful data models. As you'll discover in the chapters that follow, the data models that are produced using SAP Data Services play a very important role in aiding the SAP HANA models. This is true even when we consider the multidimensional capabilities of SAP HANA. In subsequent chapters, we'll also discuss the role that SAP BusinessObjects BI plays in designing visual analytics based on either the columnar tables or multidimensional model. For the multidimensional model to provide value, the reporting and analytic tools that access the models must be able to use its metadata to produce quality results. Quality tools should provide consumers the ability to slice, dice, drill, roll up, and pivot the data. In addition, the tools must facilitate the answering of both simple and complex questions.

> **The Role of SAP HANA Models**
>
> Before venturing too deep into the topic of multidimensional modeling, it's important for you to understand the role of SAP HANA models in the overall context of the SAP BusinessObjects BI platform and solution we describe in this book.
>
> In Part II of the book, we introduced you to SAP Data Services. SAP Data Services serves as the engine to consolidate, clean, manage, and load data from one or more sources into the SAP HANA columnar tables. The design of these SAP HANA columnar tables is based on well-established data modeling best practices. SAP Data Services is also required, at times, to denormalize or restructure the source data when SAP HANA cannot or should not.
>
> After the data is stored in the SAP HANA columnar tables, special views can be created to express the data in SAP HANA's multidimensional models, known as information views—and this is the focus of Part III of the book. Of course, the information views themselves can't answer questions or visualize the data without a tool to analyze, explore, or generate reports. This is a job for the SAP BusinessObjects BI tools, which are the focus of Part IV of the book.

7.2   Benefits of SAP HANA Multidimensional Modeling

Although subsequent chapters will go into great detail about the actual process of creating SAP HANA information views, it makes sense to consider why you might want to do it in the first place. In this section, we'll discuss the benefits that SAP HANA information views offer to business users or other consumers of the models. In addition, we'll cover the benefits that SAP HANA offers to an IT department in terms of solution and management. In some cases, the benefits are based on the capabilities of the platform in conjunction with the SAP HANA modeling capabilities.

7.2.1   Business Benefits

If we truly believe that the purpose of BI is to transform raw data into meaningful and informative decision-making tools, we must provide users and other consumers of the data a capable platform and solution. SAP HANA is at the center of this solution. It's not just a database—it's a decision-making platform. SAP HANA has many of the same characteristics of a database, but it also has many unique features that are centered on the best practices of BI. In total, these unique features deliver a solution that adds value to organizations, including those that aren't conducting commercial business. SAP HANA's benefits are universal for many departments and organizations. For example, government agencies, non-profits, medical research firms, customer service companies, accounting firms, manufacturing companies, and other entities can gain value from SAP HANA.

This section discusses the five main benefits that the SAP HANA platform provides to the direct end users of an SAP HANA platform: simple and complex analytics, operational data, metadata, centralized business logic, and data processing.

Simple and Complex Analytics

A staple of any sound BI platform is the ability to facilitate both simple and complex data analysis tasks. Organizations need a means to measure and analyze trends, KPIs, leading indicators, lagging indicators, and goals. They also need a sound platform that can facilitate predictive analysis, statistical analysis, and multidimensional analysis.

Through the use of information views, SAP HANA can facilitate all of these tasks while delivering value to its users in a single platform. On its own, SAP HANA is simply the engine to facilitate these needs. In the context of this book, both SAP BusinessObjects BI and SAP Data Services play a key role in the overall solution, as well. SAP Data Services is responsible for managing the structure and quality of the data. SAP BusinessObjects BI provides the tools that users use to visualize and analyze the data. In this regard, SAP HANA is the core engine that facilitates both simple and complex analysis. As we'll discuss, SAP HANA supports multiple query languages and statistical libraries that transform it from an ordinary database into an extraordinary analytics platform.

Operational Data

Organizations use BI not only to analyze data, but also to bolster operations, business processes, and real-time performance management. Many organizations use data for their day-to-day operations. Operational reporting is one of the most common and legacy forms of BI. As opposed to generating analytics, operational reporting is more focused on the detailed transactions that are occurring throughout the day or the transactions that occurred in the recent past. For example, an inventory manager can use a listing of currently open orders to understand the impact fulfilling those orders would have on his current inventory and staff. In addition, a customer support center manager can see the number of calls currently in the call queue, allowing him or her to add additional capacity. In general terms, operational reporting focuses on the here and now and less on the long-term past or future. The supporting data is often obtained directly from online transaction processes (OLTP) sources.

SAP HANA has several features that facilitate real-time operational reporting needs for organizations. Real-time access to data is something that many organizations require. It can be used to provide knowledge where immediate action is required. It adds benefits to organizations that need to react to information before it becomes unusable. Because the SAP HANA information views do not physically store the data, they are able to facilitate real-time access to the underlying tables. The models act as a middle layer that simply adds metadata and consistent access to the underlying SAP HANA tables.

Solutions such as SAP Business Suite on SAP HANA or sidecar implementations of SAP Business Suite are perfect examples of where SAP HANA can provide true real-time operational access to the data. When real-time solutions are not required, SAP Data Services can also be utilized to create near real-time solutions capable of accommodating operational reporting needs.

In situations when analytical processing isn't needed, data can be accessed directly from the base SAP HANA tables using SQL statements or the SAP HANA SQLScript language. In short, using information views isn't a requirement for data access in the SAP HANA platform. As we've established, SAP HANA can support both analytical and operational needs in the same platform. This adds value to most organizations because a single platform can be used to facilitate either need.

Metadata

Metadata is often referred to as information about information. Organizations can amass large volumes of data from the multitude of systems they use to manage their day-to-day operations. As we've already established, this vast quantity of data will add value to an organization after it has been massaged into a solution that is intuitive and easy to understand.

SAP HANA can facilitate the benefits of metadata through its information views. The data relationships, hierarchies, attribute names, measures, and attribute descriptions are all components of metadata. Metadata can be used to provide consumers and external applications with information about the data stored in

SAP HANA. This, in turn, adds value to the data because it makes the data easier to analyze and understand.

Centralized Business Logic

All sound BI solutions are centered on the need to provide consumers a single version of the truth. Without this single version of the truth, organizations will find it difficult to make the correct strategic decisions, largely due to lack of faith in the data or lack of access to a central repository of information. For data to bring value to an organization, the data must be readily available and trusted.

SAP Data Services is the starting point for providing a single version of the truth. Data is extracted, translated, cleansed, and loaded into tables that create a single source for quality information. SAP HANA adds value to this data by providing a central repository of metadata, calculations, and data relationships in the form of its information views. Poorly implemented BI strategies often focus on department- or subsidiary-level solutions wherein each is the master of the data they manage. This typically creates a scenario wherein each unit establishes disjointed master data repositories and subjective business rules to govern its analytical calculations. In these situations, it's often impossible for executives to find a single source and version of the truth. SAP Data Services and SAP HANA can solve this problem through sound data governance and through the proper implementation of each tool.

Data Processing

While SAP HANA's information views are a very important aspect of SAP HANA's capabilities, we must also remember that SAP HANA is a powerful platform for processing data. SAP HANA is a fusion of both software and hardware. The software is highly optimized to take advantage of modern hardware capabilities, such as in-memory storage, multicore central processing units, and 10 GB Ethernet networks.

Because of this marriage between software and hardware, data processing is accelerated in the SAP HANA platform. The exact technical details of how this marriage works is beyond the scope of this book. However, organizations will find that SAP HANA is capable of managing billions of rows of data, complex calculations, and operational data at incredible speeds. Consumers will find tremendous benefit in the response times that SAP HANA offers compared to traditional magnet disk-based platforms.

7.2.2 Technology Benefits

In addition to the benefits that SAP HANA provides to organizations as a whole, there are also several technology benefits SAP HANA can offer as a solution. SAP HANA is unique in that it offers several capabilities in a single platform.

We've established that SAP HANA is more than just a database and how it benefits the needs of an organization, so let's examine five specific technical reasons this is true: support for industry-standard drivers; OLAP analysis with MDX; relational analysis with SQL; integration with Predictive Analysis Library (PAL), Business Function Library (BFL), and R language; and aggregate table elimination.

Industry-Standard Drivers

For an application to access data in a given database, it needs to speak the language of that database. If we assume that each database has its own unique set of features and options, we must also assume that each database speaks its own language. However, if every database and application on the market today spoke its own language, it would be incredibly difficult for applications and databases to communicate with each other. To solve this problem, many database and application venders adopted the use of standard drivers or application programing interfaces (API) to facilitate the communications between applications and databases. These drivers act as an interpreter, allowing supporting applications to communicate using a universal language.

SAP HANA supports Open Database Connectivity (ODBC), Java Database Connectivity (JDBC), and Object Linking and Embedding Database for OLAP connectivity (OLE DB for OLAP). Because SAP HANA supports these industry-standard drivers, application vendors and BI developers will find it easier to communicate with SAP HANA. These drivers are made available through the SAP HANA client. In Chapter 12, we will discuss some of the use of these drivers and the SAP HANA client in more detail.

OLAP Analysis with MDX

SAP HANA provides support for the multidimensional expression language (MDX). MDX is a well-established query language that has been used by organizations and analysts for decades. It's a specific language designed to support data that is stored in OLAP cubes. Its unique qualities make it ideal for querying multidimensional models.

From a technology perspective, SAP HANA has incorporated the support of MDX directly within its platform. After an information view is activated in SAP HANA, users can query the model using the MDX language with tools that support the SAP HANA Object Linking and Embedding Database for OLAP (OLE DB for OLAP) driver. Because MDX is a well-known query language, organizations will find it easy to adopt SAP HANA.

With SAP HANA, there is no need to load data into a cube. The information views of SAP HANA always access their data directly from columnar tables in a schema. This technical benefit can help with the overall load times associated with the solution. Data only needs to be replicated or batch loaded into SAP HANA columnar tables. After data is loaded into the tables, any of the associated models are usable. This benefit can reduce organizations' overall daily data processing times.

Relational Analysis with SQL

SAP HANA provides support for SQL, which is a well-established query language that was designed to support access to data that is stored in an RDBMS. SQL has a standard structure that has been adopted by many RDBMS vendors. As a result, many analysts, developers, and DBAs have SQL coding experience. Knowledge from one vendor's RDBMS can be easily applied to another system. Because SAP HANA supports the use of SQL, organizations will find it easy to adopt SAP HANA. SAP HANA provides support for SQL using the industry-standard ODBC or JDBC drivers.

> **Quick Tip: Using SQL to Access the SAP HANA Models**
>
> The information views in SAP HANA can be queried using SQL. In the _SYS_BIC schema, for example, every active information view has one or more corresponding column views. These column views can be queried using standard SQL SELECT statements. Column views associated with OLAP-based analytic views can be queried using SQL, but each SQL statement must aggregate a measure column and also contain a GROUP BY clause. This is a unique characteristic of SAP HANA in that OLAP-style sources can actually be queried using standard SQL statements.

Integration with PAL, BFL, and R

SAP HANA has built-in Predictive Analysis Library (PAL) functions, Business Function Library (BFL) functions, and support for the open-source R statistical languages. Because these languages and functions are directly integrated into the SAP HANA platform, there is no need to extract the data from SAP HANA to perform the desired analysis. While there are several vendors that support these libraries and functions, most of them require that the data be extracted from an RDBMS and placed into an application layer for processing. These processes can lead to several performance bottlenecks and also increase the complexity of the BI architecture. With SAP HANA, they are integrated directly into the platform, which means that the data can be processed using the hardware and software benefits of SAP HANA. This will substantially increase the performance of such advanced calculations while allowing organizations to react quickly. In addition, the data will remain in the SAP HANA system during processing, reducing the footprint of the BI architecture required to support these types of calculations.

In Chapter 13, we'll discuss this capability in more detail. For now, though, we'll only advise that this direct integration, coupled with the power of SAP HANA, can greatly benefit an organization.

Aggregate Table Elimination

Due to the hardware and software benefits of the SAP HANA platform, large quantities of data can be processed without the need to create aggregate tables. When large quantities of data are stored in a traditional RDBMS, aggregate tables are often created to help reduce the overall impact that analytic queries tend to have on large tables and indexes. SAP HANA doesn't need to maintain aggregate tables to achieve faster query response times. As a result, the overall data load and data storage footprint is reduced.

Aggregate tables also have the tendency to remove valuable attributes from the data. The process of aggregating results into smaller tables requires that detailed transactions or rows be substituted for summaries. In many cases, this process can reduce the effectiveness of the data being analyzed and lead to incorrect analysis. SAP HANA can provide organizations the full value of their data due to its overall architecture and design.

Embedded Application Server

Since the release of SAP HANA SPS 5, there is an embedded application server in the SAP HANA landscape. The *SAP HANA Extended Application Services* or *XS*

Engine is an application and web server that is directly embedded into the SAP HANA platform. This application server allows you to directly embed applications into the SAP HANA platform. Because these services are embedded directly in the SAP HANA landscape, you can develop code that directly leverages the SAP HANA database without transferring data between the database and application tiers. This advantage enables you to define HTML5-based and JavaScript-based visualization applications that can directly leverage the information views, stored procedures, and columnar tables in the SAP HANA platform. Because the application code in the XS Engine is running on the same landscape as the SAP HANA appliance, you can push more work to the SAP HANA engines for processes.

In addition to these technical performance capabilities, you'll find it beneficial that the development workbench for the XS Engine is directly embedded in SAP HANA Studio. This is advantageous because the full development lifecycle can be managed in a single tool. You can create the information views, stored procedures, HTML5, JavaScript code, and other dependent coding parts with a single tool. In addition, SAP HANA Studio supports the use of a central code repository that facilitates standard lifecycle management, versioning, and the transportation of code between environments.

> **Additional References**
>
> A complete listing of the capabilities and features of the SAP HANA XS development platform is beyond the scope of this book. For more information on SAP HANA XS, visit *http://scn.sap.com/* and search for "SAP HANA Extended Application Services."
>
> You can find additional development information on the SAP HANA appliance software site at *http://help.sap.com/hana_appliance*.

7.3   Summary

For data to have true value, it must be structured and organized in a way that is intuitive and easy to understand. Multidimensional modeling is one way we can give data value. In this chapter, we've just touched the surface of multidimensional modeling in SAP HANA. In the next chapters, we will go into further detail about how we construct information views within SAP HANA.

The first step in data modeling is understanding the tools at your disposal.

8   Tools and Components of Multidimensional Modeling

In this chapter, we'll explore the basic tools and core components of SAP HANA multidimensional models, often referred to as *information views*. We'll start by introducing you to your main tool for creating information views within SAP HANA: SAP HANA Studio. In Section 8.1, we'll walk you through the MODELER perspective and how it helps us to create multidimensional models within SAP HANA. In the remainder of the chapter, we'll introduce you to two core components that heavily impact the creation of SAP HANA information views: schemas (Section 8.2) and packages (Section 8.3).

When explaining the basic components of the multidimensional model, we used terms such as *dimensions*, *hierarchies*, *measures*, and *cubes*. SAP HANA has incorporated many of these same basic components into its multidimensional modeling tools, but SAP has chosen to name its basic components a little differently. While the names might not be the same, the principles and features are similar, if not identical.

8.1   SAP HANA Studio

The first step in creating information views in SAP HANA requires the installation and configuration of SAP HANA Studio. SAP HANA Studio is a client tool that is installed on an SAP HANA developer or administrator's workstation. It's built on the Java-based Eclipse 3.6 platform.

Whether you're installing SAP HANA Studio or upgrading SAP HANA Studio, we recommend that the installed version match that of the SAP HANA appliance that is used for development. Each patch version of SAP HANA Studio supports either a full installation or an update of an existing SAP HANA Studio installation. As a result, only one download and installation is required for the first installation to support the appropriate version of the SAP HANA appliance that is being used. As of the time of this writing, SAP HANA Studio supports the operating systems listed in Table 8.1.

Supported Operating Systems	Version
Windows XP	32 bit and 64 bit
Windows Vista	32 bit and 64 bit
Windows 7	32 bit and 64 bit
Red Hat Enterprise Linux (RHEL) 6.5	64 bit
SUSE Linux 11 x86	64 bit

Table 8.1 Supported Operating Systems for SAP HANA Studio

Because SAP HANA Studio runs in a Java Virtual Machine (JVM), the Java 1.6 or 1.7 Java Runtime Environment (JRE) must be installed prior to the SAP HANA Studio installation. If you plan to install the 32-bit version of SAP HANA Studio, you must download and install the 32-bit version of the JRE. If you plan to use the 64-bit version of SAP HANA Studio, you must download and install the 64-bit version of the JRE.

Additional References

The installation of SAP HANA Studio is beyond the scope of this book. For more information on the installation of SAP HANA Studio, please download the *SAP HANA Database: Studio Installation Guide* from *http://help.sap.com/hana_appliance#section2*.

In addition, the installation instructions for installing a JVM are beyond the scope of this book. For more information on installing the Oracle JRE, please visit *www.java.com*.

SAP HANA Studio provides several *perspectives*, depending on the nature of the work that you're attempting to complete. Perspectives are essentially a set of predefined layouts or views for the Eclipse *workbench*. The workbench is effectively a user's local space in SAP HANA Studio. To access a perspective in SAP HANA Studio, select WINDOW • OPEN PERSPECTIVE • OTHER from the FILE menu bar. Figure 8.1 shows the perspective that can be used.

Figure 8.1 The SAP HANA Studio Open Perspective Window

Perspectives are simply predefined or custom collections of views within the SAP HANA Studio Eclipse workspace. Each view provides one or more operations specific to SAP HANA administration, SAP HANA modeling, or other supported SAP HANA features. SAP HANA Studio includes the SAP HANA DEVELOPMENT, MODELER, DEBUG, and ADMINISTRATION CONSOLE perspectives by default; these are listed in Table 8.2, along with a description of when you should use them. The other listed perspectives in Figure 8.1 are standard to the Eclipse workspace.

Perspective	Best Use
MODELER	The MODELER perspective is best used for the management and development of SAP HANA information views. This perspective also provides many of the same views of the ADMINISTRATION CONSOLE perspective, but primarily it contains the views specific to development. The MODELER perspective contains a handy QUICK LAUNCH screen that lists the main components of modeling with a brief description of their uses. In addition, the QUICK LAUNCH screen allows you to create or manage various aspects of SAP HANA development tools, lifecycle management, and data provisioning interfaces.

Table 8.2 SAP HANA Studio Perspectives

Perspective	Best Use
ADMINISTRATION CONSOLE	The ADMINISTRATION CONSOLE perspective contains the basic views that are needed to administer the SAP HANA appliance. This perspective doesn't contain the main views implemented to aid in the development of modeling content. Administrative tasks include creating users, creating roles, managing system settings, and executing Structured Query Language (SQL) statements. It's best used by SAP HANA appliance administrators.
DEVELOPMENT	The DEVELOPMENT perspective contains many of the same features or views found in the MODELER perspective. However, this perspective also contains support for the SAP HANA repository and SAP HANA Extended Application Services (SAP HANA XS) projects. This perspective is best used by more advanced or experienced application developers utilizing SAP HANA to build applications.
DEBUG	The DEBUG perspective is used to debug code developed within SAP HANA Studio. This perspective is best used by more advanced or experienced SAP HANA application developers.
TEAM SYNCHRONIZING	The TEAM SYNCHRONIZING perspective contains various menus and views necessary to aid developers in the process of synchronizing local workspace objects with the SAP HANA repository.

Table 8.2 SAP HANA Studio Perspectives (Cont.)

From this point forward, we'll focus primarily on the MODELER perspective. This perspective contains all of the features necessary to explain the components of SAP HANA models. When the MODELER perspective is active, there are two main areas that can be used to create the components of SAP HANA information views. The first is the SYSTEMS view, which is located on the far-left side of the perspective. Figure 8.2 shows an example SYSTEMS view in SAP HANA Studio. You'll also see the QUICK LAUNCH welcome screen located to the right in the MODELER perspective, which we'll discuss in more detail shortly.

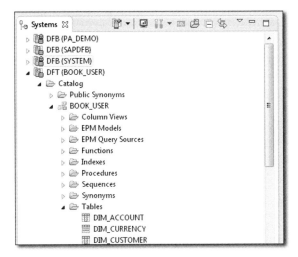

Figure 8.2 The Systems View in the SAP HANA Modeler Perspective

8.1.1 Systems View

The SYSTEMS view contains one or more hierarchies that each start with the system objects. The system object contains the connection details for a defined SAP HANA appliance and an associated user account. To log on to SAP HANA and develop content, you must first define a system by right-clicking anywhere in the SYSTEMS view and choosing ADD SYSTEM.

To define a system, you need to know the following information:

▸ The SAP HANA appliance host name

▸ The SAP HANA appliance system number

▸ The user name and password to access the SAP HANA appliance

After the system is defined, a view appears, similar to that previously shown in Figure 8.2. There are three main areas listed under each system in the SYSTEMS view:

▸ CATALOG
The CATALOG area provides access to the PUBLIC SYNONYMS (links to system procedures) and the database schemas. We'll discuss schemas in more detail in Section 8.2.

▶ SECURITY

The SECURITY area is used primarily by administrators to manage access to the SAP HANA appliance. From a developer's standpoint, this area is used to grant permissions to other users or roles that might want to access their content.

▶ PROVISIONING

The PROVISIONING area is used to set up, monitor, and configure Smart Data Access or federated connections to a supported remote RDBMS system. Developers can also import federated tables as virtual tables within this area.

▶ CONTENT

The CONTENT area is used predominantly during the information view development life cycle to create and manage the main components of SAP HANA modeling. In the CONTENT view, you find a hierarchy of objects specific to SAP HANA modeling. We'll discuss these objects in more detail in subsequent chapters of the book.

8.1.2 Quick Launch View

As mentioned earlier, there is a second area that you can use to create SAP HANA information views. Located on the right-hand side of the MODELER perspective is the QUICK LAUNCH view. Figure 8.3 shows what you typically see in this view.

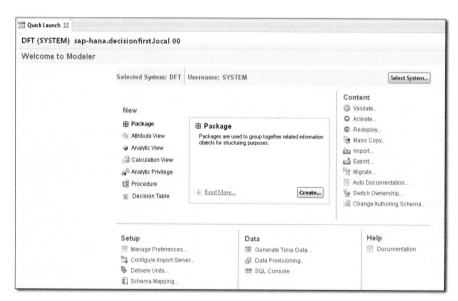

Figure 8.3 The Quick Launch Modeler Welcome Screen

The Quick Launch view contains five main sections. Each section contains one or more links that launch functions or wizards specific to an SAP HANA development task.

► New
Contains links to create the various components of SAP HANA information views. As each item is selected, a helpful message is displayed to the right that includes a summary of the object's purpose, a Read More link, and a button to launch a wizard to create the selected object.

► Content
Contains links to various development-related tasks. After the link is clicked, a wizard appears to guide you through the selected task.

► Setup
Contains links to tools that can set up specific functions, such as promotion of content or the importing of schema DDL from third-party databases.

► Data
Contains links to tasks specific to the importing of data using SAP Landscape Transformation (SLT) or Sybase replication, the creation of the SAP HANA built-in date-time table, or the launching of the SAP HANA Studio SQL Editor.

► Help
Contains a link to the SAP HANA documentatión area on *http://help.sap.com/in_memory*.

Many of the links in the Content, Setup, and Data areas are only available through the Quick Launch view. However, many of the options under the New area are also available in the Systems view discussed earlier. As you use SAP HANA Studio, the availability of each function and its location will become more apparent. The majority of information view creation takes place in the content Systems view after you become more familiar with the components of the SAP HANA models. For new developers, the Quick Launch view provides basic help as they start the development process. As we discuss the remaining components of SAP HANA modeling throughout this chapter, we'll delve into more detail about the options for creating each object type.

In summary, SAP HANA Studio is a desktop application that is used to administer the SAP HANA appliance, as well as develop information views. Three main perspectives available in SAP HANA Studio offer a view specific to either administrators or developers. Developers can create each component of an information view using either the content SYSTEMS view or the modeler QUICK LAUNCH view in the MODELER perspective.

8.2   Schemas

While the schema isn't a direct component of the multidimensional modeling features in SAP HANA, it's a vital component of the overall process. Schemas are logic storage containers in a relational database; they are often referred to as subdatabases within a relational database management system (RDBMS). They are used to logically store key database components such as tables, views, procedures, functions, triggers, and other items. Developers can manage schemas from the MODELER perspective in the CATALOG section of the SYSTEMS view.

Figure 8.4 contains a fully expanded view of the CATALOG section where schemas are managed in SAP HANA. The schema BOOK_USER contains several subfolders that each represents a specific component type that will be logically stored in a schema. SAP HANA also contains several default system schemas. As shown in Figure 8.4, the SYS, _SYS_BIC, _SYS_REPO, and other _SYS schemas are used by the SAP HANA appliance for managing repository content, multidimensional metadata, and other content essential to the operation of SAP HANA. In general, any schema that is prefixed with _SYS can be considered a system-managed schema.

From the perspective of multidimensional modeling, the TABLES component in a schema is essential to the overall design process. Once expanded, the TABLES component lists the row or columnar tables associated with the schema. Tables defined as the columnar type are used directly by information views.

Recall from earlier chapters that SAP HANA tables are also used to manage the relational data that is loaded and stored in the SAP HANA appliance with SAP Data Services. Tables are key components where data is logically stored and organized in SAP HANA. Without tables, the multidimensional models in SAP HANA would not be able provide data results to users querying the models.

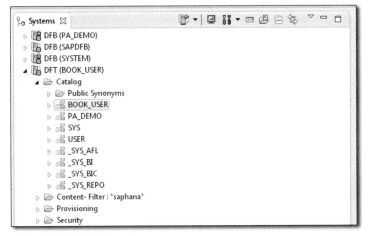

Figure 8.4 The Catalog Section in the Systems View and Modeler Perspective

As mentioned earlier, the schema contains several components that are listed beneath it on the screen. Some of these components can be used directly by information views. There are several components listed under a schema. Only a limited number are used by developers when creating SAP HANA information views. Table 8.3 outlines important components that are available from the MODELER perspective and their relationships to the SAP HANA information views. You will find that there are additional components listed under a schema; however, they are not necessarily vital to the modeling process and, therefore, will not be discussed in this section.

Schema Component	Relationship to Multidimensional Models
Tables	Tables are the physical components that store data in SAP HANA. They can be defined as either row or columnar type. Tables are a fundamental component of SAP HANA information views. Many of the SAP HANA information views directly reference one or more tables.
Views	Views are logical objects that can be developed to act as a virtual table. Views are compiled using simple or complex SQL statements that can join, filter, sort, or rank data from one or more tables or views. Views can't be used directly in the graphical multidimensional modeling components, but they can be used in script-based calculation views or procedures that are referenced by calculation views.

Table 8.3 Objects Created in a Schema (When in Modeler Perspective)

Schema Component	Relationship to Multidimensional Models
Procedures	Procedures allow for the development of complex transactional SQL code that is appropriate when the basic use of table joins and filtering isn't sufficient to properly express a result set. Procedures use the SAP HANA SQL and R languages and support higher levels of application-style programming. In the context of information views, procedures can be used only indirectly in SAP HANA calculation views.
Column Views	Column views are a special type of view unique to SAP HANA. In general, they act as virtual database tables, but they have characteristics that are different from tables or views. In the _SYS_BIC schema, they provide multidimensional model metadata to external reporting or visualization tools.
	Column views should not be confused with database SQL views. Unlike database views, column views don't contain any compiled SQL `SELECT` statements or transactional SQL code. They are compiled using a coding language specific to SAP HANA.
	Column views are also created with procedures that return a result set when executed. Procedural columns views can be used by SAP HANA calculation views or other external reporting tools and act as virtual tables.

Table 8.3 Objects Created in a Schema (When in Modeler Perspective) (Cont.)

Tables in a schema are used by information views as the source for all data, making them an important component of the overall process. Procedures in a schema can also be used by information views, but in a more limited capacity. As we'll discuss in more detail, columnar tables can be used directly within the components of the SAP HANA information views such as the attribute views, analytic views, and calculation views. In addition, procedures can be used in calculation views in situations when more complex data processing or complex calculations are required. In Chapter 9, we'll discuss the role of attribute views, analytic views, and calculation views in more detail.

SAP HANA Schema Security and SQL Privileges

Remember that each component of the multidimensional model is committed to the SAP HANA repository by the _SYS_REPO system user, and therefore, the _SYS_REPO user must have `SELECT` or `EXECUTE` access to every schema object that you will use in a model. Refer back to Chapter 2 for a discussion of the _SYS_REPO user and the specific rights that are required for it to access tables stored in a schema.

8.3 Packages

Packages are another key component of SAP HANA information views. Each component of the multidimensional model must be stored in a user-defined package. These are the parent objects of each information view that is developed in SAP HANA Studio. Packages can have sub-packages, which facilitate arrangement in a logical hierarchal order. As a result, package privileges can be established to limit other SAP HANA Studio users or developers from viewing, editing, activating, or maintaining packages and their child objects. The package hierarchy also allows developers and administrators to arrange packages and their child objects in a logical order that facilitates reusability and promotes a logical organization for a shared development environment. Packages can also be arranged into delivery units that are used to transport modeling content from one SAP HANA system to another. In many ways, the package hierarchy acts as a repository for content that is developed and stored within SAP HANA. In fact, many refer to this package hierarchy as the *SAP HANA repository*.

To access packages in SAP HANA Studio, choose the MODELER perspective by selecting WINDOWS • OPEN PERSPECTIVE • MODELER. As shown in Figure 8.5, on the left side of the MODELER perspective is the SYSTEMS view. Expand the CONTENT folder to view existing packages, or right-click the CONTENT folder and select NEW to create a new package. If there are multiple packages, developers can right-click and choose FILTER PACKAGES to limit the results. To modify a package, right-click an existing package and choose EDIT.

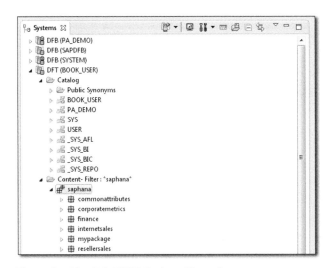

Figure 8.5 The SAP HANA Package Hierarchy

As an alternative to using the SYSTEMS view, you can use the MODELER perspective QUICK LAUNCH view to create a new package. To create packages this way, choose the MODELER perspective by selecting WINDOWS • OPEN PERSPECTIVE • MODELER. The QUICK LAUNCH view should now appear as the prominent window or view, as shown in Figure 8.6. In the QUICK LAUNCH view, click the PACKAGE icon, and click the CREATE button located in the white box that appears to the right. A wizard appears to walk you through the processes of creating a package.

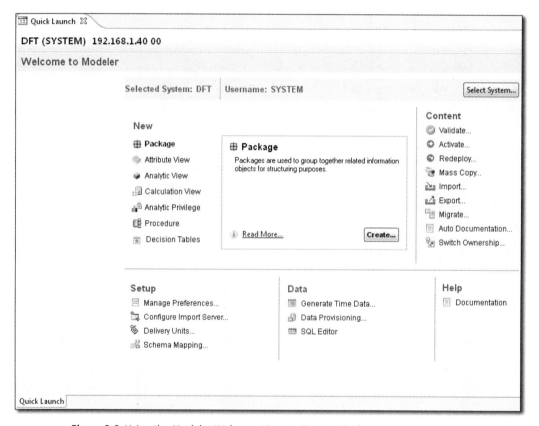

Figure 8.6 Using the Modeler Welcome View to Create a Package

Table 8.4 outlines the properties that can be established when creating a package or modifying an existing package.

Package Property	Description of Property
NAME	The NAME field reflects the name of the package. Each package name must be unique in its respective level. A sub-package can have the same name of its parent, but it can't have the same name as its sibling. Sub-package names are created by appending a period and the sub-package name to the parent. Each subsequent sub-package will be prefixed with a period—for example, `acme.department.finance.gl`. Only the following characters are allowed: lowercase letters (a–z), numbers (0–9), hyphens (-), and up to nine nonconsecutive periods (.).
DESCRIPTION	The DESCRIPTION field should be used to fully explain the purpose of the package. It can also be used to provide useful metadata to users and developers.
DELIVERY UNIT	The DELIVERY UNIT is a special object that allows one or more packages to be grouped into a common unit for exportation or transportation to another SAP HANA system. Packages that contain dependencies to each other should be grouped together.
STRUCTURAL	The STRUCTURAL option allows you to configure a package so that it can contain only sub-packages. If the option is set to YES, then only a sub-package can be created in the package. If the option is set to No, then the package can contain sub-packages and modeling objects as well. This option is best used to prevent you from creating modeling content in a designated package. You can find the STRUCTURAL option only after creating a package and then accessing the edit package option. To edit a package, right-click the package in the systems hierarchy and choose EDIT.
ORIGINAL LANGUAGE	The ORIGINAL LANGUAGE field defines the language of the package.
PERSON RESPONSIBLE	The PERSON RESPONSIBLE field reflects the SAP HANA user account that is responsible for the package.
LOGON LOCALE	The LOGON LOCALE is the locale that is established when defining the SAP HANA system within SAP HANA Studio. Generally, the LOGON LOCALE and ORIGINAL LANGUAGE properties should be the same during the development process.
TRANSLATION	Click the TRANSLATION button, located at the bottom of the NEW PACKAGE window, to define text translation options for the package name.

Table 8.4 Available Properties When Creating or Editing a Package

After a package has been created, developers or administrators can't change the name of the package. Therefore, it's important that you thoroughly develop a proper naming convention and package hierarchy before creating any multidimensional modeling components. This step is especially important before external reporting tools, such as SAP BusinessObjects BI, begin using the content.

Packages play an important role in helping developers and administrators organize, secure, and distribute each component of the SAP HANA multidimensional model. They are also used to organize content and code related to custom applications developed for use in the SAP HANA XS Engine. Before developers can create and maintain components of the model, a package must be created, and the appropriate privileges must be granted to the developer's user account or role. As we discuss the remaining components of the SAP HANA models in the subsequent sections of this chapter, it's important to understand that a package is the starting point of the process.

SAP HANA Package Security and Package Privileges

While we discussed security in detail in Chapter 2, we wanted to take a moment to remind you of the following two items:

▸ SAP HANA platform users who require development access to information views need to be assigned roles or privileges to access a package or their child components in the SAP HANA appliance.

▸ By default, members of the MODELING role and CONTENT_ADMIN role have full access to the root package or top-level package. In most cases, it's recommended that these default roles are never assigned to a user and that custom roles be established by the organization.

8.4   Summary

In this chapter, we introduced you to the core pieces and parts of SAP HANA that you'll need to understand before creating SAP HANA information views. We walked you through the elements of SAP HANA Studio that you'll use, and then introduced you to the core concepts of schemas and packages. In the next chapter, we'll dive into the heart of SAP HANA multidimensional modeling by introducing you to the different SAP HANA information views.

The heart of SAP HANA multidimensional modeling lies in its information views.

9 Creating SAP HANA Information Views

To add value to data we need to express it in a way that is easy for data consumers to understand. With that goal in mind, SAP HANA multidimensional models—otherwise known as *information views*—provide consumers with value by formatting data elements into easy to understand business centric objects. They provide metadata-rich access to data by clearly defining their role and purpose.

In order to construct information views, you must understand the different types that can be developed in SAP HANA: attribute views, analytic views, and calculation views. In this chapter, we will explore these in more detail.

9.1 Attribute Views

In SAP HANA, an *attribute view* is another name for what is commonly referred to as a *dimension*. As we discussed in Chapter 7, dimensions are an important component of multidimensional modeling. They contain one or more values that are used to describe a transaction or quantifiable measure. In many cases, the combination of values in a dimension forms a hierarchy that can be used to provide drilling, aggregation levels, or navigation paths.

In the example shown in Figure 9.1, there are five columns of data. The first column, PRODUCT ID, represents the *primary key* of the table and is used predominantly to join to other tables in the model. The remaining columns are used to describe an attribute of the product ID. In this case, the PRODUCT NAME and PRODUCT NUMBER will likely be unique values just like the PRODUCT ID, but the PRODUCT COLOR and PRODUCT LINE values will have duplicate values. Because these values repeat from record to record, a natural hierarchy can be defined based on the values in these columns. In our example, a PRODUCT LINE, PRODUCT COLOR, and PRODUCT NAME hierarchy can be defined based on the three columns, meaning that the top level of the hierarchy is the PRODUCT LINE, followed by PRODUCT COLOR, and finally, PRODUCT NAME.

Product ID	Product Name	Product Number	Product Color	Product Line
989	Mountain-500 Black, 40	BK-M18B-40	Black	M
990	Mountain-500 Black, 42	BK-M18B-42	Black	M
991	Mountain-500 Black, 44	BK-M18B-44	Black	M
992	Mountain-500 Black, 48	BK-M18B-48	Black	M
993	Mountain-500 Black, 52	BK-M18B-52	Black	M
984	Mountain-500 Silver, 40	BK-M18S-40	Silver	M
985	Mountain-500 Silver, 42	BK-M18S-42	Silver	M
986	Mountain-500 Silver, 44	BK-M18S-44	Silver	M
987	Mountain-500 Silver, 48	BK-M18S-48	Silver	M
988	Mountain-500 Silver, 52	BK-M18S-52	Silver	M
980	Mountain-400-W Silver, 38	BK-M38S-38	Silver	M
981	Mountain-400-W Silver, 40	BK-M38S-40	Silver	M
982	Mountain-400-W Silver, 42	BK-M38S-42	Silver	M
983	Mountain-400-W Silver, 46	BK-M38S-46	Silver	M

Figure 9.1 Example Product Dimension Columnar Table in an SAP HANA Schema

What's in a Name?

Because SAP HANA uses the term *attribute view* to describe the traditional multidimensional modeling term *dimension*, we'll refer to dimensions as attribute views from this point forward.

Attribute views are the logical modeling components in SAP HANA that allow you to define attributes and hierarchies to describe a series of transactions or quantifiable measures in a set of data. Based on the example data set in Figure 9.1, imagine that this table was joined with another table that contained sales transactions. For each transaction, you can use the products table to identify which product was sold. In addition, you can use the PRODUCT COLOR and PRODUCT LINE columns to identify its product color and line. You can use filters and aggregates to identify the number of Mountain-500 Black, 40 products that were sold and the amount of revenue they generated. You can also use the PRODUCT COLOR column to identify the most popular colors by product line. By definition, attribute views can be considered the modeling component that is used to describe a series of transactions or measures.

There are four main concepts of an attribute view that we need to review. First, how do we create an attribute view? Second, what properties can we define for an attribute view? Third, how do we create hierarchies? Finally, how do we save and activate an attribute view? As you read over the next few pages, you will learn the answer to these questions.

9.1.1 Creating an Attribute View

To create an attribute view in SAP HANA Studio, use the MODELER perspective by selecting WINDOWS • OPEN PERSPECTIVE • MODELER from the FILE menu bar. When the MODELER perspective is activated, there are two options for creating an attribute view:

▶ **Quick Launch view**
Select the ATTRIBUTE VIEW icon, and click the CREATE button located in the white box that appears to the right. This launches a wizard that walks you through the processes of defining an attribute view.

▶ **Systems view**
In the SYSTEMS view, expand the CONTENT folder to view the packages. If no packages are present, create a package to store the attribute view. Right-click the appropriate nonstructural package and choose NEW • ATTRIBUTE VIEW. This launches a wizard allowing you to define a new attribute view.

Both options result in the appearance of a wizard (see Figure 9.2). Table 9.1 outlines the six main properties that must be defined in the wizard.

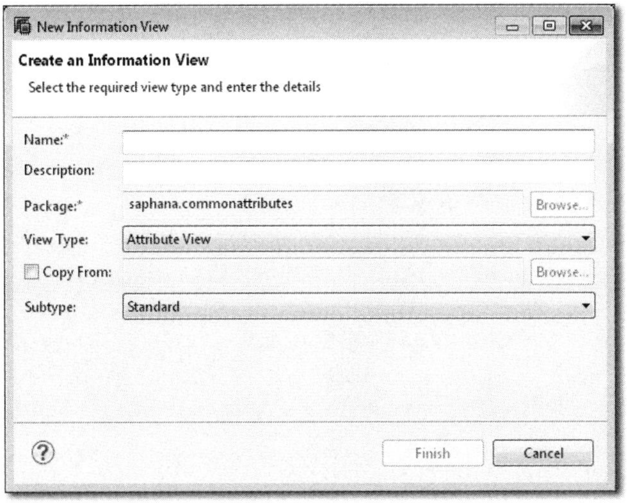

Figure 9.2 The New Attribute View Wizard Window

Property	Description
NAME	The name of the attribute view.
	This is a required property that can't be changed after the attribute view is saved and activated. It's important to establish a standard attribute view naming convention before starting a development project in SAP HANA. Only the alphabet characters *Aa–Zz*, numbers 0–9, and underscore (_) are allowed in the name.
DESCRIPTION	The description of the attribute view.
	This property can contain a free-text description of the attribute view and should be used to add additional metadata to the view or a thorough description that other developers can use to identify the purpose of the attribute view.
PACKAGE	The package that the attribute view will be assigned to.
	Only nonstructural packages can be used as the parent object for an attribute view. If you're using the QUICK LAUNCH view to create the attribute view, a package must be selected. If using the SYSTEMS view, the package that was right-clicked is automatically selected.
VIEW TYPE	The view type that allows you to identify the information view as either an attribute view or analytic view.
	This can be confusing depending on the workflow that was selected to create the attribute view. While you might assume that the workflow creates only an attribute view, the wizard allows you to select another modeling component called an *analytic view*. We'll discuss analytic views in more detail in Section 9.2. Assuming that you intend to create an attribute view, select the default selection of ATTRIBUTE VIEW from the dropdown.
COPY FROM	Checkbox that allows you to effectively copy the definition of an existing attribute view to create a new attribute view based on an existing attribute view.
	After an attribute is copied, the new copy has no association with any existing attribute views.
SUBTYPE	The subtype that can be defined with each attribute view.
	The following list describes each of the three subtypes:
	▶ STANDARD: Standard attributes are those that you use when you intend to define each facet of the attribute. This includes the various table joins, output columns, filters, calculated columns, and hierarchies.
	▶ TIME: Choosing the time-based attribute subtype invokes the wizard to automatically generate a date- and time-based attribute view. The attribute view is based on the system tables that are found in the _SYS_BI schema, starting with M_TIME_DIMENSION*.

Table 9.1 Main Properties of an Attribute View and Their Purpose

Property	Description
	▸ DERIVED: A derived attribute is an attribute view that is based on an existing attribute view. However, this isn't the same as the COPY FROM option listed in this table. A derived attribute is simply an alias of an existing attribute. Any changes made to the master attribute view are automatically implemented in the derived attribute. Derived attributes are used in situations when an attribute view must be joined to an analytic view's DATA FOUNDATION node more than once.

Table 9.1 Main Properties of an Attribute View and Their Purpose (Cont.)

9.1.2 Defining Properties of an Attribute View

When designing an attribute view, the developer interface is comprised of two main nodes: the DATA FOUNDATION node and the SEMANTICS node. After successfully creating an attribute view using the wizard, you see a design window similar to that in Figure 9.3.

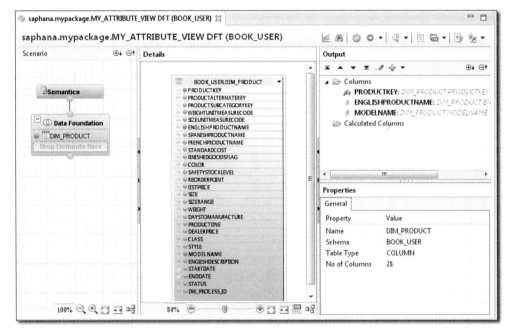

Figure 9.3 The Data Foundation and Semantics Nodes of an Attribute View

On the far left side of the design window are two nodes that can be selected to invoke their respective properties. Clicking the DATA FOUNDATION node invokes all necessary panes to manage the attribute view's DATA FOUNDATION node. Clicking the SEMANTICS node invokes the necessary panes to manage the semantics options for the attribute view.

The Data Foundation Node

The DATA FOUNDATION node is used to define the relationship between two or more tables and for defining output columns, filters, and calculated columns. An attribute view can be based on one or more tables. It can also be modeled on the joining of two or more tables in a fashion that is very similar to joining tables in SQL, where you can you join two or more tables to produce a more complete set of results; for example, you can join a customer table to an address table to produce a single result set that contains both a customer's name and address. You can incorporate a similar technique in an attribute view.

The amount of joining that is required in an attribute view depends greatly on the physical structure of the underlying tables or the overall structure of the data model that is stored in the source schema. In the context of this book, we generally try to reduce the number of joins in an SAP HANA attribute view by using the powerful SAP Data Services engine to model a table that is fully denormalized. In short, we do most of the modeling and denormalization in SAP Data Services before we prevision the table in SAP HANA. This methodology not only simplifies the processes of creating an attribute view, but also increases the overall performance of the model by eliminating expensive table joins.

When joining two or more tables in the DATA FOUNDATION node of an attribute view, you can use one of the five types of joins outlined below:

▸ **Inner**

When joining two tables by using the inner join option, the values in the adjoining columns from both tables are evaluated. The resulting data set is limited to only those records for which the adjoining columns match. If the values don't match in either column, their associated records are effectively filtered from the results. The inner join is always evaluated, even when there are no output columns associated with one table or the other.

It's best to use an inner join when the referential integrity of the adjoining column is known to be sound. Another way of saying this is that we need to make sure the column value exists in both tables; otherwise, the record is excluded from the results.

- **Left outer**

  When you join two tables by using the left outer join option, all values in the leftmost table are evaluated and compared to those in the rightmost table. The resulting data set contains all records from the leftmost table, and only those that match the adjoining columns in the rightmost table. If no match is found in the rightmost table, NULL values are returned for any output columns associated with the rightmost table.

  The left outer join is best used when values in the leftmost table are known to not always have a match in the rightmost table.

- **Right outer**

  When you join two tables using the right outer join option, all values in the rightmost table are evaluated and compared to those in the leftmost table. The resulting data set contains all records from the rightmost table and only those that match the adjoining columns in the leftmost table. If no match is found in the leftmost table, NULL values are returned for any output columns associated with the leftmost table.

  The right outer join is best used when values in the rightmost table are known to not always have a match in the leftmost table.

- **Referential**

  The referential join type is the default join type in any SAP HANA modeling component. Referential joins are similar to inner joins in that the values in the adjoining columns from both tables can be evaluated. The resulting data set is limited to only those records for which the adjoining columns match. However, if a query fails to reference columns in both tables, only the tables that contain the requested columns are included in the results. This effectively removes the unreferenced table from the join equation and eliminates the need to perform any expensive matching between the two tables. Referential joins can be called *smart joins* because they automatically remove unnecessary join processes from the SAP HANA engines. Referential joins can lead to issues, however. Tables that don't have sound referential integrity can produce unpredictable results. Given that the inner joins are evaluated only when a query references columns in each table, an orphaned value in either table can lead to the inclusion or exclusion of records.

  Therefore, it's best to use the referential join only when adjoining values exist in both tables. In terms of this book, you should use SAP Data Services to validate the data and referential integrity before you provision the tables in an SAP HANA schema.

▶ **Text**

A text join is unique to SAP HANA. Text joins allow you to join two tables wherein one contains characteristics and the other contains the characteristic in a specific language. They were developed specifically to work with SAP ERP tables and the SPRAS fields to provide automatic translation of characteristics or columns.

Text joins act as inner joins, meaning that they restrict the results based on matching records. There is also a special dynamic language parameter that is defined in the join definition. This parameter is automatically processed with the join to filter the language table, producing a record wherein the specified column returns text in a specific language. This parameter is evaluated based on the locale of the user querying the attribute. In short, text joins are used to provide automatic multi-language support in query results for attributes.

You can also define calculated columns and filters in the attribute view DATA FOUNDATION node. Calculated columns are those that are derived on the basis of one or more existing output columns in the DATA FOUNDATION node tables. Calculated columns can be developed using SAP HANA–specific syntax and functions. However, most developers will find that the syntax is similar to functions utilized when developing SQL scripts or procedures.

Calculated columns allow developers to create a calculated column that concatenates a customer's last name and first name into a single string. You can also create a calculated column that derives a customer's current age in years based on the customer's birthday and today's date. Again, the use of calculated columns depends greatly on the needs to further transform or derive data stored in the source table. If you're using SAP Data Services to provision your tables in SAP HANA, you can perform the same calculation in your SAP Data Services code and further simplify the attribute view design. In many ways, using SAP Data Services to generate the calculated columns is beneficial. Calculated columns have the potential to move the processing of queries from the SAP HANA OLAP engine into the SAP HANA calculation engine. In Chapter 12, we'll discuss these engines in more detail, but for this chapter, it's important to understand that calculated columns can have an effect on the performance of queries, so they should be used with caution.

You can also filter tables in the attribute view's DATA FOUNDATION node. Filtering is another modeling technique that can be used to limit the records that are returned from an attribute view. There is a wide range of reasons that you might want to filter the attribute view, including the need to denormalize the data to the need to remove null records from the table. Regardless of the reason, it's important to understand that you can create filters to restrict the data set in an attribute view. In the context of this book, we generally use SAP Data Services to filter the data before provisioning the table in SAP HANA. However, there are legitimate situations where filtering should be implemented only in the attribute view based on the way it will be used. For example, you might want to use a columnar table containing product details to accommodate two different requirements, one where a group of users wants to see expired products and one where another groups only wants to see active products. Having the ability to define filters within the attribute view allows you to accommodate both groups. You can create a logical attribute view that shows expired products using a filter on the product status column, and then another logical attribute view that only shows active products with a slightly different filter defined on the same product status column.

The goal of an attribute view is to produce a result set that contains a key column and one or more attributes columns to describe the key column. In the attribute view's DATA FOUNDATION node, it's the developer's responsibility to identify the columns that will be used for output and those that will represent key columns. It's important to understand the role of the key columns when you're designing an attribute view. The key columns are used to join an attribute view to the analytic view's DATA FOUNDATION node. We'll discuss the role of the analytic view's DATA FOUNDATION node in more detail in subsequent sections of this chapter. However, you should define a key column if you intend to use the attribute in an SAP HANA model. The key column should be assigned to one or more columns that represent the uniqueness in your foundation table.

Key columns are important because they relate to creating measures and other aggregates in the overall model. If you join an attribute view to an analytic view's DATA FOUNDATION node and the adjoining column isn't unique in the attribute view, there is a possibility that any resulting aggregation will be overstated. This is similar to the typical SQL traps that are created when you join two tables and aggregate their results. If there are two identical product ID values in the `Product ID` field, any records in the transaction table that reference them in the attribute view are repeated and overstated. If you're not careful in this regard, the reliability of your model might come into question. Therefore, it's important that you not only define the key column in your attribute view, but also profile the results to ensure that each column is unique. In the context of this book, we generally validate that each key column is unique during the processes of provisioning tables using SAP Data Services. This further simplifies the process of creating an attribute view and also increases the overall reliability of the model.

In addition to defining output columns and key columns in our attribute view's DATA FOUNDATION node, you can also configure columns using the properties described in Table 9.2. You can establish the properties of a column by selecting the column in the OUTPUT window. Just below the OUTPUT window, you will find a list of options on the GENERAL tab of the PROPERTIES window.

Property	Description
NAME	This is the technical name of the output column.
	This generally matches the name of the source column, but it can be changed to make it more intuitive.
LABEL	This is an alternative name for the column.
	This is a secondary field that can be used to further enhance the attribute view's overall metadata. Generally, it's used to create a more user-friendly and longer-text version of the output column name.
MAPPING	The mapping property describes the technical source path of the column in terms of schema name, table name, and column name. The property is read only and very useful when the developer needs to locate the source of the column.
LENGTH	Depending on the source column's data type, the length column displays the maximum allowed length of values within the column. For example, a `varchar` column with a defined length of 25 cannot contain more than 25 characters. This is a read-only column, and the property cannot be changed.
SCALE	Depending on the source column's data type, the scale defines the number of decimal places available to store numbers. For example, a column defined as `decimal (10,2)` will have a maximum length of 10 digits with a maximum of 2 decimal places. This is a read-only column, and the property cannot be changed.
DATA TYPE	This property defines the data type of the column. Every column in an SAP HANA table has a defined data type. This property describes the types of data that can be stored in the column.
KEY ATTRIBUTE	If set to YES, the column is defined as a key attribute or key column. If set to No, the column is considered a standard output column.

Table 9.2 Output Column Properties in an Attribute View Data Foundation Node

Property	Description
Drill Down Enabled	This property can be used to indicate that the object is a member of a drill group. It also affects the presentation or organization of attributes in some reporting tools, such as SAP BusinessObjects Analysis for OLAP. In general, only reporting or visualization tools that support this property can use it, and how it affects the reporting tool varies from tool to tool.
Label Column	This property allows you to define a surrogate column to be used in place of the actual column. For example, the Product Key column can be configured to always display the product SKU text. Using a label column is preferred when the selected Output column values have no meaning to the user consuming the model's data.
Hierarchy Default Member	In MDX, a hierarchy default member is used to define the default value within a hierarchy column that should be visible or selected. However, this column property is not well defined in any publicly available documentation. It is most likely used by the MDX engine, but we are unable to confirm its exact use.
Semantic Type	Semantic types allow the developer to define additional metadata for the column that can be utilized by client tools to define the appropriate use or format of the column. The following semantic types are available: ▶ Amount with Currency Code ▶ Quantity with Unit of Measures ▶ Currency Code ▶ Unit of Measure ▶ Date ▶ Date—Business Date From ▶ Date—Business Date To ▶ Geo Location—Longitude ▶ Geo Location—Latitude ▶ Geo Location—Carto ID ▶ Geo Location—Normalized Name After a semantic type is selected, additional properties are visible, allowing further definition. For example, if there is an attribute column named Sales Amount that contains sales data and another attribute named Currency Type that contains a currency format, you can assign the Currency Code semantic type to the Currency Type attribute and assign the Amount with Currency Code semantic type to the Sales Amount attribute column.

Table 9.2 Output Column Properties in an Attribute View Data Foundation Node (Cont.)

Property	Description
HIDDEN	This property allows you to define a column in the output of the model but suppress it from being used by the user consuming the models data.
	It's best used in situations when the column needs to be used for calculations but suppressed from output.

Table 9.2 Output Column Properties in an Attribute View Data Foundation Node (Cont.)

The Semantics Node

The second main node of the attribute view is the SEMANTICS node, which is used to manage the output columns identified in the DATA FOUNDATION node and any hierarchies that need to be defined in the attribute view. Figure 9.4 shows an example of the column and hierarchy view that are visible after you select the SEMANTICS node in the ATTRIBUTE VIEW MANAGEMENT view.

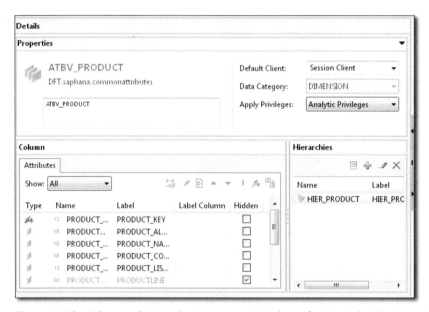

Figure 9.4 The Column and Hierarchy Management Windows after You Select the Semantics Node

The column configuration pane is shown on the left side of Figure 9.4. In the column section of the SEMANTICS node view, you can specify the column type. The COLUMN TYPE field allows you to specify whether the column is a key attribute or standard attribute. A similar option was available in the DATA FOUNDATION node, as well, but it was set using a TRUE/FALSE dropdown.

There are also options for specifying the LABEL column and a checkbox to indicate whether the objects should be HIDDEN. Again, these are the same options that were available in the DATA FOUNDATION node. The SEMANTICS view appears to provide you with a more intuitive and graphical alternative of setting these properties.

9.1.3 Creating Hierarchies

The HIERARCHIES design pane is shown on the right-hand side of Figure 9.4. You can use this pane to create or define hierarchies in your attribute view. To create a new hierarchy, select the plus sign icon on the icon bar. A new window appears that allows you to define the properties for the hierarchy (see Figure 9.5).

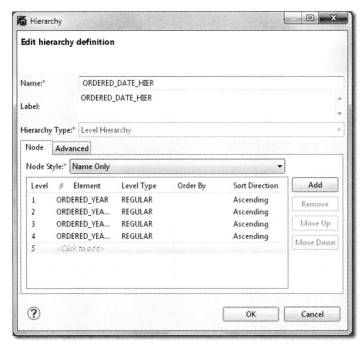

Figure 9.5 Hierarchy Configuration Window

Table 9.3 outlines the six basic options that can be defined in reference to the hierarchy.

Property	Description
NAME	The technical name of the hierarchy. This is a mandatory field, but it can be changed at any time.
LABEL	An alternative name for the hierarchy. This is a secondary field that can be used to further enhance the attribute view's overall metadata. Generally, it's used to create a more user-friendly and longer-text version of the hierarchy name.
HIERARCHY TYPE	Two types of hierarchies are available: ▶ LEVEL HIERARCHY: This hierarchy can be derived from one or more output columns. It's assumed that there is a natural order to the values in a column selected for this type of hierarchy. For example, YEAR, QUARTER, MONTH, WEEK, and DAY can be used to derive a calendar date hierarchy. ▶ PARENT-CHILD HIERARCHY: This hierarchy can be derived by a recursive self-join in the data foundation table. For example, the employee foundation table might contain a column that contains the employee's supervisor. A supervisor might have multiple employees in the same table. SAP HANA can generate a hierarchy by recursively joining the table to itself until a flattened parent-child relationship is established. It's important to note that, after a hierarchy type is established, it can't be changed.
NODE	The NODE tab contains options and buttons used to define the node style, node attributes, and node levels.
NODE STYLE	Defines the composition of the hierarchy level name. Because hierarchy level names need to be unique, these options allow you to define three different options to achieve this uniqueness: ▶ LEVEL NAME: The unique node value is composed of the level name and node value—for example, [Level 1].[USA]. ▶ NAME ONLY: The unique node value is composed of the node value only—for example, USA. ▶ NAME PATH: The unique node value is composed of the result node name and the names of all ancestors, apart from the (single physical) root node—for example, [USA].[GEORGIA].

Table 9.3 Hierarchy Configuration Window Properties

Property	Description
HIERARCHY LEVEL LIST	Allows you to define the parent-child relationships between the columns in the hierarchy.
	With level hierarchies, one or more attribute columns can be added to represent the natural hierarchy that can occur in an attribute view's DATA FOUNDATION node. The columns should be placed in logical order based on the relationship of the values in the selected columns. With a parent-child hierarchy, only the parent and child columns are available for selection. SAP HANA then parses these columns recursively to produce a hierarchy. Both columns and calculated columns can be defined as hierarchy levels.

Table 9.3 Hierarchy Configuration Window Properties (Cont.)

Table 9.4 lists the advanced options found on the advanced tab depicted in Figure 9.5. Many of the advanced options are subjectively interrupted depending on the BI tool and protocol used to access the information view. For example, tools that connect through the MDX driver will likely interpret these hierarchy options differently than tools that access the same hierarchy through the JDBC driver. It is important to remember this as you read through the listed options.

Property	Description
AGGREGATE ALL NODES	Specifies whether each level of the node should include its own measure value in any aggregate.
	If it is set to TRUE, the value of the parent is aggregated with the values of the child members. If it is set to FALSE, the child values are aggregated independently of the parent level. This doesn't affect the overall results of the model because only the SAP HANA multidimensional expression (MDX) engine interprets this setting.
DEFAULT MEMBER	Currently not defined by SAP.
ORPHAN NODE	This option specifies how the BI tool should manage orphaned nodes. Orphaned nodes are nodes that have no defined parent. The following options establish how the BI tool should treat orphaned nodes.
	▶ ROOT NODE: Treats orphaned nodes and root nodes.
	▶ ERROR: Stops processing the hierarchy and returns an error.

Table 9.4 Hierarchy Configuration Window Advanced Properties

Property	Description
	▶ IGNORE: Ignores the issue and continues to process the hierarchy.
	▶ STEPPARENT: Assigns the orphaned node to a defined surrogate parent node. You must then define the ID of the stepparent node.
STEPPARENT	Used in conjunction with the ORPHANED NODE option STEPPARENT. The ID defined in this column is used as a surrogate for ORPHANED NODE.
ROOT NODE VISIBILITY	This option indicates whether the BI tool should or should not display a root node. ADD ROOT NODE: This option adds a root node with an ID of ALL. DO NOT ADD ROOT NODE: This option suppresses the root node when selected.
MULTIPLE PARENT	This checkbox should be checked when a child attribute value is known to have multiple parents. For example, calendar weeks can often span two months. Countries can often span multiple regions.

Table 9.4 Hierarchy Configuration Window Advanced Properties (Cont.)

Previewing a Hierarchy in SAP HANA Studio

It's important to note that there is no OLAP-style interface in SAP HANA Studio to preview or see a hierarchy in action. However, you can query the column view that is created in the _SYS_BIC schema after the attribute view is saved and activated in the repository. This column view returns a fully flattened tabular representation of the hierarchy.

This is an excellent way to troubleshoot hierarchy parsing issues when querying the raw hierarchy level data defined by its column view. If there are design issues with the hierarchy definition, queries against this column view fail to execute.

You can find this column view in the _SYS_BIC schema using the naming convention *package.subpackage/ATTRIBUTE_NAME/hier/HIERARCHY_NAME*.

9.1.4 Saving and Activating the Attribute View

After you define all of the options in both the DATA FOUNDATION and SEMANTICS nodes of an attribute view, it is standard practice for the attribute view to be saved and activated in the repository. This must be done before the attribute view can be previewed or rendered usable in the model. As we discuss the remaining components of SAP HANA modeling, you'll discover that they need to be saved and activated, as well.

There are two ways to save and activate an attribute view. The first option is to locate the green icon on the top-right of the attribute view design window. Hover over the icon that contains a white arrow pointing to the right. The hover text should read, SAVE AND ACTIVATE. Click the icon to initiate the save and activate process. The second option for saving and activating the attribute view is to right-click the attribute view in the NAVIGATOR window and choose the ACTIVATE option. If the ACTIVATE option is grayed out and the REDEPLOY option is active, the attribute view has already been verified and activated. In this state, it can only be redeployed. The redeployment process is similar to the activation process.

In either case, a JOB LOG window or tab appears to display the status and outcome of the activate process. If the process completes successfully, the job action name remains black with black text. If there are any errors, the job action name turns red. You can double-click the job action name to reveal the job details and review details of the activate process.

There is also an option to allow you to save and validate the attribute view. The SAVE AND VALIDATE option can be executed in a similar fashion. However, its icon is green with a white checkmark. This option only saves and then validates the code for correctness. Unlike with activation, it doesn't make the attribute view available for use or publish it to the repository.

Remember, attribute views are effectively the dimensions of the SAP HANA information views. It's quite common for there to be dozens, if not more, attribute views in a package. The number of attribute views that are needed for a project depends greatly on the type of data that is being modeled. Attribute view are used to describe a transaction or quantifiable records in a table. In SAP HANA, an attribute view can comprise one or more joined tables to produce a single logical modeling object. You can use joins, filters, and calculated columns to produce a logical dimension. In subsequent sections of this chapter, we'll discuss how attribute views are combined with analytic views to produce the complete information view.

> **Security Required for Viewing the Results of an Information View**
>
> When attribute views or any of the information views in SAP HANA are saved and activated, one or more column views are created in the _SYS_BIC schema. For you to query column views in the _SYS_BIC schema, you must have the correct SQL privileges and analytic privileges.
>
> At a minimum, you need the `SELECT` and `EXECUTE` privilege on the _SYS_BIC schema. However, more granular object security can also be defined on specific column views. If you're using the built-in time data attributes, you also need the `SELECT` privilege on the _SYS_BI schema. In addition to these SQL privileges, you need analytic privileges to view the application data in an information view.
>
> Developers require elevated privileges to develop, save, and activate information views. For reference, view the privileges setup within the default MODELER role to determine the rights required to develop information views.
>
> In addition to these SQL privileges, you need analytic privileges to query an information view. We discuss analytic privileges in more detail in Chapter 11.

9.2 Analytic Views

As we've already discussed in this chapter, attribute views are the modeling components used to describe a transaction or other quantifiable data in a table. But before you can match attribute views to a transaction table, the transaction table must be configured in an *analytic view*. Analytic views are the second type of information view available in the SAP HANA platform, and they are used to define both measures and the relationship between their attributes. Measures are defined by aggregating quantifiable columns in a table. For example, if you have a sales transaction table that contains a column for quantity sold, you can define a measure on that table that summarizes all values in the table. If you were to summarize all of the rows in the table for quantity sold, you would have the grand total of all transactions in the table.

However, to add value to this measure, you need to assign characteristics to the measure to produce dimensionality or subtotals. For example, you can add a product attribute view to the measure to allow the consumer to see the quantity sold per product. You can also add a sale date attribute view to this measure to show both the quantity of products that were sold and the days, weeks, months, or years in which they were sold. You can add a customer attribute view to the measure to see the number of products sold by customer region, as well.

> **What's in a Name?**
>
> While an attribute view is another term for what is commonly called a dimension, an *analytic view* is used in SAP HANA in place of the traditional multidimensional modeling term *cube*.

We hope you're now beginning to visualize the potential that adding dimensionality to a set of quantifiable transactions can achieve. With SAP HANA, the analytic view can best be described as the modeling component that allows you to define both measures and their relationships between one or more attributes. Technically speaking, the primary goal is to define the logical star schema depicted in Chapter 7, Figure 7.1.

There are three main concepts of an analytic view that we need to review. First, how do we create an analytic view? Second, what properties can we define for an analytic view, and where do we define them? Third, how do we save and activate an analytic view? As you read over the next few pages, you will learn the answers to these questions.

9.2.1 Creating an Analytic View

There are two ways to create an analytic view in SAP HANA Studio. As with attribute views, you can use either the SYSTEMS view or the QUICK LAUNCH view.

To create an analytic view using the QUICK LAUNCH view, open the MODELER perspective by selecting WINDOWS • OPEN PERSPECTIVE • MODELER from the FILE menu bar. On the right-hand side of the screen, we should now see the QUICK LAUNCH view, similar to what is displayed in Figure 9.6. Select ANALYTIC VIEW, and click the CREATE button in the white box that appears to the right. This launches a wizard that walks through the processes of defining an analytic view.

The second option for creating an analytic view is to use the SYSTEMS view located on the left side of the MODELER perspective. In the SYSTEMS view, expand the CONTENT folder to view the packages. If no packages are present, create a package to store the analytic view. Right-click the appropriate nonstructural package and choose NEW • ANALYTIC VIEW. This launches a wizard enabling you to define a new analytic view, as shown in Figure 9.7. You'll define the five main properties in the wizard outlined in Table 9.5.

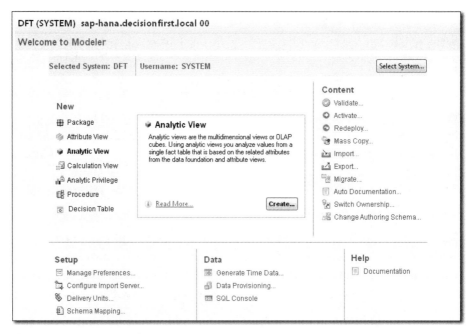

Figure 9.6 Creating an Analytic View in SAP HANA Studio

Figure 9.7 The New Analytic View Wizard Window

Property	Description
NAME	The name of the analytic view.
	This is a required property that can't be changed after the analytic view is saved and activated. It's important to establish a standard analytic view naming convention before starting a development project in SAP HANA. Only the alphabet characters *Aa–Zz*, numbers 0–9, and underscore (_) are allowed in the name.
DESCRIPTION	The description of the analytic view.
	This property can contain a free-text description of the analytic view and should be used to add additional metadata to the view or a thorough description that other developers can use to identify the purpose of the analytic view.
PACKAGE	The package that the analytic view will be assigned to.
	Only nonstructural packages can be used as the parent object for an analytic view. If you're using the QUICK LAUNCH view to create the analytic view, a package must be selected. If you're using the SYSTEMS view, the package that was right-clicked is automatically selected.
VIEW TYPE	The view type that allows you to identify the information view as either an attribute view or analytic view.
	This can be confusing depending on the workflow that was selected to create the analytic view. While you might assume that the workflow creates only an analytic view, the wizard allows you to select either an ANALYTIC VIEW or ATTRIBUTE VIEW. Assuming that you intend to create an analytic view, select the default selection of ANALYTIC VIEW from the dropdown menu.
COPY FROM	Checkbox that allows you to effectively copy the definition of an existing analytic view to create a new analytic view based on an existing analytic view. After an analytic view is copied, the new copy has no association with any existing analytic views.
SUBTYPE	This option is not applicable. Analytic views do not currently have a subtype.

Table 9.5 The Initial Properties of an Analytic View and Their Purposes

9.2.2 Defining Properties of an Analytic View

An analytic view comprises three main nodes: the DATA FOUNDATION node, LOGICAL JOIN node, and the SEMANTICS node. After successfully creating an attribute view using the wizard, you should see a design window similar to that shown in Figure 9.8. As you click each node found on the left side of the analytic view user interface (UI), a different set of panes appears to the right-hand side DETAILS pane. Each set of panes is unique to the selected node.

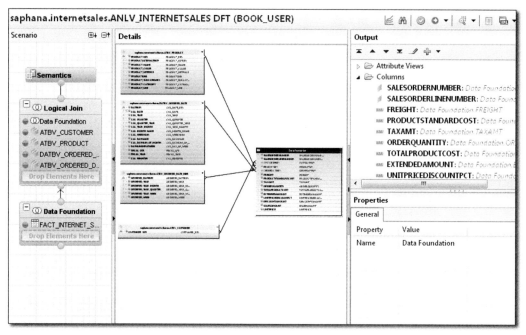

Figure 9.8 Three Main Nodes of an Analytic View

As mentioned earlier, the main purpose of the analytic view is to allow you to define both measures and their relationships between attributes. However, before you can define a measure, you must identify the transaction table where they are stored.

The Data Foundation Node

The DATA FOUNDATION node, in an analytic view, is the area in which you define these base tables. Figure 9.9 shows an example screenshot of the DATA FOUNDATION node UI. Similarly to attribute views, you can define one or more tables in the analytic view's DATA FOUNDATION node. If you have more than one table, the tables need to be joined in a manner similar to joining tables in SQL. Technically speaking, you can join your transaction table in this node to other column tables that contain attributes. However, these attributes aren't reusable with other analytic views, and you can't define hierarchies in an analytic view. Therefore, it's best to build attribute views for the purpose of reusability and hierarchies.

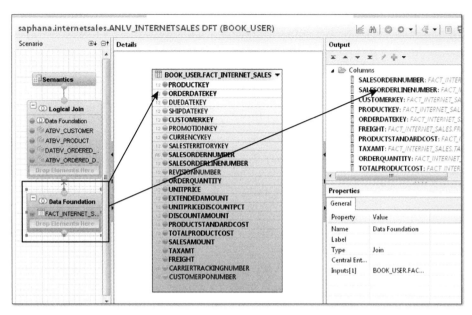

Figure 9.9 The Data Foundation Node User Interface

Joining Multiple Transaction Tables in the Analytic View Data Foundation Node

While it's possible to join multiple transaction or fact tables in the analytic view DATA FOUNDATION node, you should make note of three items:

▸ Make sure that the cardinality isn't adversely affected when you join two or more transaction tables in this node. If the adjoining columns produce duplicate measureable rows, the resulting aggregation is overstated. This leads to incorrect results in the model. As we'll discuss shortly, calculation views are capable of solving aggregation issues like this. However, you'll need to define an individual analytic view for each transaction or fact table to solve this problem with a calculation view.

▸ If you join two or more large transaction tables in the analytic view's DATA FOUNDATION node, the model's performance is likely affected. In many cases, the cost of joining the two multi-million row tables slows the response of the query. We recommend that you use the powerful SAP Data Services engine to model all required data into a single fact or transaction table before it's provisioned into an SAP HANA schema. This eliminates the need for the SAP HANA engines to join the two tables and likely increases the performance of the query.

▸ Each attribute view can be joined only to one physical table in the DATA FOUNDATION node.

In addition to managing the foundation table, the DATA FOUNDATION node is also used to identify the output columns that are used in the LOGICAL JOIN and SEMAN-TICS nodes. The columns that are specified for output in this node are represented in a logical table in the subsequent node. Effectively, you use the DATA FOUNDA-TION node to physically join one or more tables and to specify each column that will be needed throughout the remaining nodes of the analytic view.

The Logical Join Node

The LOGICAL JOIN node, in an analytic view, is the area in which you define the logical joins between existing attribute views and the output of the DATA FOUN-DATION node. In addition, additional output columns can be defined in the LOGI-CAL JOIN node to further enhance the model. The joins are logical because only the output columns of the analytic data foundation table are joined to one or more existing attribute views. At this stage, you're not joining physical tables.

To logically join an attribute view to the output of the DATA FOUNDATION node, you must add one or more existing attribute views to the LOGICAL JOIN node detail section. As shown in Figure 9.10 in the DETAILS pane, we've joined an attribute view to the output columns defined in the DATA FOUNDATION node.

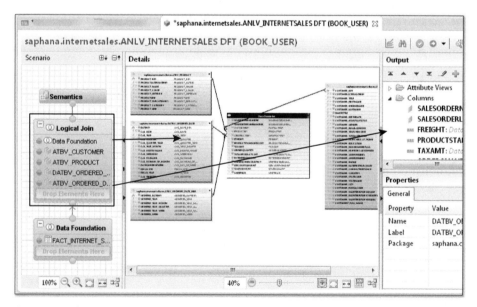

Figure 9.10 The Logical Join Node

While both objects appear to be tables, they are, in fact, only a logical representation of either the attribute view you designed in Section 9.1 or the outputs defined in the analytic view DATA FOUNDATION node.

Once added, you can define the join relationship between the attribute view and analytic data foundation table using the attribute view's key column and one or more output columns defined in the analytic view DATA FOUNDATION node. There are six supported join types, which are listed in Table 9.6.

Join Type	Description
Inner join	When you join attribute views to the analytic data foundation table using the inner join option, the values in the adjoining columns from both logical tables are evaluated. The resulting data set is limited to only those records wherein the adjoining columns match. If the values don't match in either column, their associated records are effectively filtered from the results. The inner join is always evaluated between the two logical tables, even if values from the attribute view aren't selected during the query process.
Left outer	When you join attribute views to the analytic data foundation table using the left outer join option, all values in the data foundation table are evaluated and compared to those in the attribute view. The resulting data set contains all records from the data foundation table and only those that match the adjoining columns in the attribute view. If no match is found in the attribute view, NULL values are returned for any output columns associated with the attribute view. The left outer join is best used when values in the data foundation table are known to not always have a match in the attribute view.
Right outer	When you join attribute views to the analytic data foundation table using the right outer join option, all values in the attribute view are evaluated and compared to those in the data foundation table. The resulting data set contains all records from the attribute view and only those that match the adjoining columns in the data foundation table. If no match is found in the data foundation table, NULL values are returned for any output columns associated with the data foundation table. The right outer join is best used when all values in the attribute view must be returned even when there are no associated transactions in the data foundation table.
Referential	The referential join type is the default join type in any SAP HANA modeling component. Referential joins are similar to inner joins in that the values in the adjoining columns, from both logic tables, can be evaluated. The resulting data set is limited to only those records wherein the adjoining columns match.

Table 9.6 The Supported Join Types between an Analytic View Data Foundation Table and an Attribute View

Join Type	Description
	However, if a query fails to reference columns in an attribute view, only the attribute views that contain the requested columns are included in the join calculation. This effectively removes the unreferenced attribute view from the join equation and eliminates the need to perform any expensive matching between the two logical tables. Referential joins can be called smart joins because they automatically remove unnecessary join processes from the SAP HANA engines.
	Referential joins can lead to issues, however. Logical tables that don't have sound referential integrity can produce unpredictable results. Given that the inner joins are evaluated only when a query references columns in both logical tables, an orphaned value in either table can lead to the inclusion—or, conversely, the exclusion—of records or aggregated results. Therefore, it's best to use the referential join only when the adjoining values exist in both tables. In terms of this book, we recommend that you use SAP Data Services to validate the date and referential integrity before the tables are provisioned in an SAP HANA schema.
Text	Text joins are unique to SAP HANA. They are special join types that allow you to join two tables wherein one contains characteristics and the other contains the characteristic in a specific language. Text joins were developed specifically to work with SAP ERP tables and the SPRAS fields to provide automatic translation of characteristics or columns. Text joins act as an inner join, meaning that they restrict the results based on matching records.
	There is also a special dynamic language parameter in the join definition. This parameter is automatically processed with the join to filter the language table, producing a record wherein the specified column returns text in a specific language. This parameter is evaluated based on the locale of the user querying the attribute. In short, text joins are used to provide automatic multi-language support in query results for attributes.
Temporal	Temporal joins are available only when you're joining an analytic view foundation to attribute views. It's a special referential join type that allows you to define a series of join conditions whereby the attribute value is time dependent on the record in the analytic foundation table. A temporal column from the data foundation table is compared to a FROM column and To column in that attribute view to return an attribute value that is time dependent. There are also temporal conditions that can be defined in this join type to manipulate how the between join is executed.

Table 9.6 The Supported Join Types between an Analytic View Data Foundation Table and an Attribute View (Cont.)

In addition to creating joins, you can also define calculated columns, restricted columns, and input parameters in the LOGICAL JOIN node. Each item that is created in the LOGICAL JOIN node is available as an output column. As we'll discuss shortly, each output column can then be defined as a measure or private attribute in the model. In addition to the logical output columns, all columns from the adjoined attribute views are also available as shared output columns. This includes the calculated columns and the hierarchies that were defined in the attribute view. You can't make changes to an attribute view in the LOGICAL JOIN node, but you can see each supported item in the OUTPUT pane by expanding the ATTRIBUTE VIEW folder.

Calculated columns in the LOGICAL JOIN node are similar to those that can be created in the attribute view. The calculated columns can be developed using the SAP HANA SQL syntax and functions. However, in the LOGICAL JOIN node, you can define calculations that incorporate columns from one or more attribute views. These cross–attribute view calculations allow for more sophisticated calculations to be performed. For example, you can define a flag value that indicates customers in a particular region who purchased products from a particular product line. This type of calculated column evaluates values in both the customer attribute view and products attribute view.

As with attribute views, the use of calculated columns can negatively affect the performance of the final model. In many cases, the use of calculated columns forces the model to be processed in the SAP HANA calculation engine. The use of this engine can slow the processing of the query. As we recommended before, it's best to define calculated columns using SAP Data Services when possible. Admittedly, there are some calculations that can only be defined in an SAP HANA information view. In these cases, it's important to know that the impact of calculated columns will likely invoke the use of the SAP HANA calculation engine. In Chapter 12, we'll discuss the role of the SAP HANA calculation engine in more detail.

Restricted columns can be used to create conditional aggregates. For example, a restricted column can be developed to return the sales amount when the ordered year is equal to 2010. Later, in the SEMANTICS node, you can convert this into a measure so that only transactions that were ordered in 2010 are summarized in this column. The conditions in a restricted column are built using a graphical user interface (GUI) and dropdown lists. Neither complex formula language nor SAP HANA SQL code can be used to derive restricted measures; therefore, they are limited to basic filtering criteria. However, restricted measures provide faster processing than measures executed on calculated columns.

Input parameters can be used to define a runtime parameter or list of values for a runtime parameter. An input parameter can be defined in all three nodes of an analytic view. The node you choose to create the input parameter within has no bearing on how it functions or how it's used. On their own, input parameters have little bearing on the overall analytic view. They must be used in a calculated column as a placeholder for a runtime value before they have an effect on the model results. For example, you might define a formula in a calculated column to multiply the sales amount by a user-provided percentage. Input parameters aren't used for filtering. As we'll discuss shortly, you can use variables for dynamic runtime filtering, a feature that greatly enhances the usability of any model.

In the context of an analytic view, parameters can be defined as one of the five types outlined below:

▶ **Direct**
A direct input parameter can be used to provide a runtime value to the model for calculation purposes. It's also used in the processes of converting currencies at runtime. It's best used in instances when a single, static value is used to manipulate the output of a column.

▶ **Column**
A column-based parameter derives its list of values from an existing column in the model. It's best used when an input parameter requires a large list of possible input values, and these values can be derived from an existing column in the model.

▶ **Derived from table**
A derived-from-table parameter derives its list of values from an existing column found in a table. The values don't need to be in the model and can be derived from any existing table in a schema. It's best used when an input parameter requires a large list of possible input values, and these values can be derived from an existing table in the database.

▶ **Static list**
A static list parameter derives its list from a user-defined list stored in the parameter. If the values in the list require updating, you have to modify the list and reactivate the model. It's best used when an input parameter requires a large list of possible input values, and these values can't be derived from an existing table or attribute.

The Semantics Node

The final node of the analytic view is the SEMANTICS node. In the SEMANTICS node, you can define both local and shared output columns. Figure 9.11 shows the SEMANTICS node UI. LOCAL output columns are those that were created in the LOGICAL JOIN node. SHARED output columns are those that are automatically included with the adjoined attribute views.

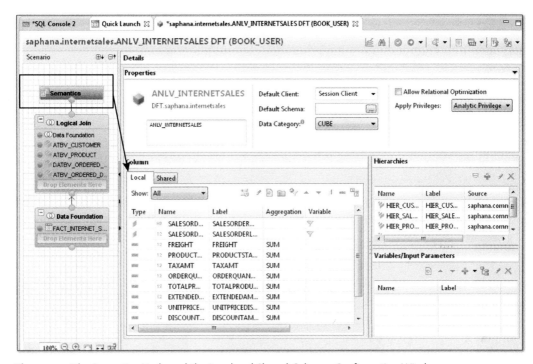

Figure 9.11 The Semantics Node and the Local and Shared Columns Configuration Window

In the COLUMN pane, there are two tabs. The first tab is labeled LOCAL. The LOCAL tab is used to define each output column in the analytic view. Output columns can be defined as either an attribute or measure type. To change the output column type, click the cell in the TYPE column, and a dropdown list appears.

To define a column as a measure, choose the MEASURE type. Measures are the output columns that will be aggregated in the model. SAP HANA supports only the SUM, MIN, MAX, and COUNT aggregation functions in an analytic view.

To change the aggregation function, click the cell in the AGGREGATION column, and a dropdown appears, containing a list of the available aggregation functions. The SUM, MIN, and MAX aggregates can be defined only for numeric output columns. The COUNT function can be used with any column type.

In the LOCAL tab of the COLUMN pane, you can also configure the output column as an attribute type. Attributes defined in the LOCAL column tab were referred to as private attributes in previous revisions of SAP HANA. As of SAP HANA version 45 (SPS 5), they are simply called *local attributes*. Local attributes are the values in the data foundation table that can be used to describe each transaction. They are similar to the attributes found in an attribute view, but they are defined explicitly in the analytic view and based on the data foundation table. They can't be reused in other analytic views without being explicitly redefined in that analytic view.

Depending on the SAP Data Services data modeling strategy, it's possible that the fact or transaction table contains several local attributes. As mentioned during the SAP Data Services discussions, joins are very expensive in a columnar store database. Therefore, it's sometimes better to include attributes in the fact or transaction table than to store them in a separate dimension table. This isn't a strict rule, but rather a suggestion that can sometimes increase the performance of the overall analytic view.

You can configure a LABEL COLUMN to serve as a surrogate value for any local attribute. To configure an attribute column's LABEL COLUMN, simply click the cell in the LABEL COLUMN, and a dropdown list appears, containing existing output columns that serve as a substitute.

Finally, you can also define a variable for any attribute type output column. Variables are created in the SEMANTICS node and can be used to create runtime filters.

For both measures and attributes, you can configure each output column as HIDDEN. Hidden output columns can be used in the model for processing but are excluded from the analytic view results. There is also a LABEL column that can be used to provide an alternative name for any output column. This column should not be confused with the LABEL COLUMN column. LABEL COLUMN columns are based on other columns in the model; they change the columns' output. However, a label is a static value that is used to name the column, and it has no effect on the column's output values.

The second tab in the Column pane is labeled Shared. The Shared tab contains a listing of all columns associated with attribute views defined in the analytic view model. You can configure three options for each column in the Shared tab:

- **Change the name of the attributes or columns**
  To change the name, click in the desired cell of the Name column, and enter a new name.

- **Associate a variable with one or more columns**
  Variables can be used to create a runtime filter and prompt a list of values for the analytic view. To associate a variable to a column, click the desired cell in the Variable column. A dropdown list appears, allowing you to select an existing variable. As we'll discuss shortly, variables are defined in a separate pane found in the Semantics node.

- **Hide a column from the final model**
  The Hidden column contains a checkbox. Any column that has this boxed checked is hidden from the results of the analytic view. However, the column can be used in the model for processing.

In the Semantics node of an analytic view, you can also define variables and input parameters. The ability to create input parameters in this node is redundant. You can also create the same input parameters in the Logical Join node and Data Foundation node. The types of input parameters that were discussed previously also pertain to input parameters created in this node.

Variables, on the other hand, can be defined only in the Semantics node. On the far right side of the Semantics node interface is a pane labeled Variables/Input Parameters. On the menu bar in this pane, there is a plus sign and a dropdown arrow. To create a variable, select the plus sign icon. Note that clicking the down arrow to the right of the plus sign allows you to choose between a variable and an input parameter.

The primary purpose of a variable is to filter rows based on a runtime parameter. Variables are associated with an existing attribute to define a pick list or list of values. They are also assigned to an attribute for filtering purposes. When you're creating variables, a wizard appears. In this wizard there are eight different configuration options, as outlined in Table 9.7.

Option	Description
NAME	The name of the variable is presented to the user during runtime. It's best to name a variable so that those users understand its purpose at runtime. The variable name can't contain spaces or certain special characters. Only the alphabet characters *Aa–Zz*, numbers 0–9, and underscore (_) are allowed in the name—for example, `Select_A_Product_For_Filtering`.
LABEL	The label can be used to provide a free-text description of the variable. This metadata can be used to fully describe the purpose of the variable.
ATTRIBUTE	This is the associated attribute that contains the values that populate the pick list or list of values for the variable at runtime. This doesn't assign the variable to the attribute for filtering.
SELECTION TYPE	This is the type of filter or operator that is used to restrict the rows of data at runtime. The following selection types are supported in a variable: ▸ SINGLE VALUE: Used when only a single value is required. This assumes the use of the operator equal (=), and the operator can't be changed. ▸ RANGE: Used when the selected value operator needs to be defined at runtime. This assumes the use of the operators =, `between`, <, >, <=, >=, `is null`, or `isn't null`. ▸ INTERVAL: Used when all values that exist between a specified starting and ending value are required. This assumes the use of the `between` operator, and the operator can't be changed.
MULTIPLE ENTRY	The MULTIPLE ENTRY checkbox allows you to specify whether a variable can be used multiple times at runtime. For example, a user can select products sold in year 2010 and products sold between 2006 and 2008. Each entry is assumed as an OR condition.
DEFAULT VALUE	This is the default value for the variable. If a variable is often used with a particular value, you can configure this value and store it with the variable. At runtime, the variable is automatically prepopulated with this default value.
IS MANDATORY	The IS MANDATORY checkbox allows you to require a value for the configured variable at runtime. In short, this prevents the value from remaining blank.
ATTRIBUTE ASSIGNMENT	This is the attribute assigned to the variable for filtering purposes. A variable can be assigned to one or more attributes for filtering at runtime.

Table 9.7 Configuration Options for a Variable Defined in an Analytic View

Located at the top of the SEMANTICS node windows, you will find a series of properties and options:

▶ DEFAULT CLIENT

If the analytic view is based on data from an SAP application, this setting allows the analytic view to be rendered using either the session client or a cross client. When the option is set to SESSION CLIENT, the client number defined with the SAP HANA user is utilized to filter the MANDT or client columns found in tables used in the model. When the option is set to CROSS CLIENT, no filters are applied based on the SAP HANA user's session.

▶ DEFAULT SCHEMA

The default schema option can be used to specify the default schema for database objects used in the definition of the analytic view.

▶ DATA CATEGORY

When this option is set to CUBE, reporting tools see the published analytic view. When it is set to blank, most reporting tools do not list this analytic view as an available data source.

▶ ALLOW RELATIONAL OPTIMIZATION

This checkbox enable automatic optimization of SQL statements with a specific syntax. If the SQL statement is written as `SELECT COLUMN, SUM(COLUMN) FROM (SELECT * FROM TABLE) GROUP BY COLUMN`, then the SAP HANA optimizer rewrites the statement as `SELECT COLUMN, SUM(COLUMN) FROM TABLE`. By eliminating the `SELECT * FROM` statement from the syntax, the query will likely execute faster.

▶ APPLY PRIVILEGES

This option can be utilized to disable or enable the need to apply analytic privileges on the analytic view. When it is set to blank, analytic privileges are not required to query the analytic view. (For more on analytic privileges, see Chapter 11.)

9.2.3 Saving and Activating the Analytic View

Just as with attribute views, it's standard practice to save and activate the analytic view in the repository after defining all of the options in an analytic view. The process for doing this is the same as with an attribute view; see Section 9.1.4 for details.

After saving and activating the analytic view, a complete information view is available for external consumption. We'll discuss other components of the SAP

HANA information views shortly, but the analytic view is the core of any model. The analytic view is a combination of attribute views and transactions tables that contain quantifiable columns. The attribute views are used to describe the *what, how, when, where,* and *why* characteristics of each transaction. Because analytic views allow for the definition of measures, you can aggregate the quantifiable columns to any level defined in an attribute view or local attribute column.

You've now taken the first steps in assigning real value to the data that is being stored in the underlying SAP HANA tables. The remaining modeling components can be used to expand upon the capabilities of the analytic view. As we'll discuss, they can provide scenarios whereby more advanced calculations are required. (In addition, there are components to aid in the implementation of data-level security, which we discuss in Chapter 11.)

9.3 Calculation Views

In cases when more advanced processing or advanced data mining is required, SAP HANA provides *calculation views*. Calculation views can be used to model complex aggregations into a comprehensive and accurate data set.

Calculation views are used in situations when an analytic view or attribute view is unable to properly express a calculation or business requirements dictate a more advanced layering of processing logic. Calculation views can't be used to physically manipulate data because they are considered read-only views. A calculation view can be used to express the same functionality as an analytic view, but calculation views are more appropriately used in situations when an analytic view is unable to facilitate a desired query.

Previously, we discussed how an analytic view should be limited to a single class of transactions. Attempting to join sales transactions and inventory movements into the same foundation results in incorrect results. This is one of many scenarios when a calculation view can be developed to solve a common aggregation issue. Calculation views do this by first aggregating the sales transactions and products to produce a product summary, which then produces a similar summary using products and inventory movements. Finally, you can then combine the results of both summaries using the product attributes as the merger point. Because both results were aggregated independently and then combined post-aggregation, the final results are calculated correctly. For purposes of data mining, calculation views can be used to identify correlations, intersections, trends, and other common mining tasks.

Calculation views can be built in two main ways: via a GUI or via a script. In this section, we'll start by introducing you to the initial creation of a calculation view. We'll then introduce you to the concepts involved in defining both a graphical calculation view and a script-based calculation view.

9.3.1   Creating a Calculation View

There are two way to create a calculation view in SAP HANA Studio. As with other information views, you can use either the SYSTEMS view or the QUICK LAUNCH view.

To create a calculation view using the QUICK LAUNCH view, open the MODELER perspective by selecting WINDOWS • OPEN PERSPECTIVE • MODELER from the FILE menu bar. On the right-hand side of the window, the QUICK LAUNCH view appears (see Figure 9.12). In the QUICK LAUNCH view, select the CALCULATION VIEW button, and then click the CREATE button located in the white box that appears to the right. This launches a wizard that walks you through the processes of defining a calculation view.

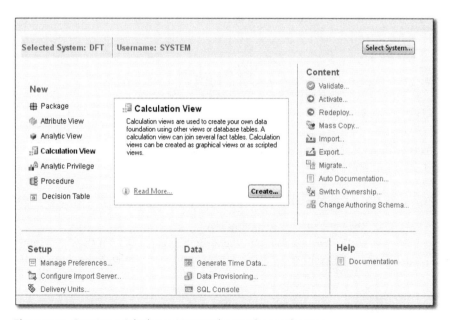

Figure 9.12 Creating a Calculation View in the Quick Launch View

The second option for creating a calculation view is to use the SYSTEMS view located on the left side of the MODELER perspective. In the SYSTEMS view, expand the CONTENT folder to view the packages. If no packages are present, create a package to store the calculation view. Right-click the appropriate nonstructural package, and choose NEW • CALCULATION VIEW. This launches a wizard allowing you to define a new calculation view.

Figure 9.13 shows the wizard that is launched as a result of both methods.

Figure 9.13 The New Calculation View Wizard Window

The CALCULATION VIEW wizard window offers you 10 options to be configured or selected, as outlined in Table 9.8.

Property	Description
NAME	The name of the calculation view.
	This is a required property that can't be changed after the calculation view is saved and activated. It's important to establish a standard calculation view naming convention before starting a development project in SAP HANA. Only the alphabet characters *Aa–Zz*, numbers 0–9, and underscore (_) are allowed in the name.

Table 9.8 Calculation View Configuration Options

Property	Description
LABEL	The label or description of the calculation view.
	This property can contain a free-text description of the calculation view and should be used to add additional metadata to the view or a thorough description that other developers can use to identify the purpose of the calculation view.
PACKAGE	The package that the calculation view will be assigned to.
	Only nonstructural packages can be used as the parent objects for calculation views. If you're using the QUICK LAUNCH view to create the calculation view, you must select a package. If you're using the SYSTEMS view, the package that was right-clicked is automatically selected.
VIEW TYPE	This option allows you to define the type of information view that you wish to create. By default, it selects the calculation view type, assuming that you followed a workflow specific to creating a calculation view.
COPY FROM	Choose the COPY FROM option when there is a need to create a new calculation view that is a copy of an existing calculation view. Select the BROWSE button to select an existing calculation view. All content from the source calculation view is copied into the new view.
SUBTYPE – GRAPHICAL	Choose the VIEW TYPE – GRAPHICAL option to create a calculation view using graphical objects and workflows. This option doesn't require you to use SQL code or the SAP HANA calculation engine functions.
SUBTYPE – SQLSCRIPT	Choose the VIEW TYPE – SQLSCRIPT option to create a calculation view using SQLScript code or SAP HANA calculation engine functions. This option should be used by experienced developers who need to define complex calculations and developers with a thorough understanding of the SAP HANA calculation engine functions.
DATA CATEGORY – CUBE	The CUBE category classification automatically adds an `Aggregation` transform just before the SEMANTICS node within the calculation view's design window. It is also an indication that the calculation view is used for analytic purposes. Calculation views used for analytic purposes aggregate measures to their constituent attributes.
DATA CATEGORY – DIMENSION	The DIMENSION category classification automatically adds a `Projection` transform just before the SEMANTICS node within the calculation view's design window. It is also an indication that the calculation view should be treated like an attribute view and that no aggregations will occur. This is a required setting for any calculation view containing a `Star Join` transform.

Table 9.8 Calculation View Configuration Options (Cont.)

Property	Description
WITH STAR JOIN	When this is checked, the calculation view's design window automatically contains the `Star Join` transform. The `Star Join` transform is a special-use transform that allows the calculation view to act as if it were an analytic view. However, the star join calculation view is processed entirely within the calculation engine.
	The `Star Join` transform can manage only two types of objects. First, you must add an incoming transform containing the transactional data. The incoming transform can be only a single `Projection`, `Aggregation`, or `Union`. The process is similar to adding a table to an analytic view's DATA FOUNDATION node. Second, you can add only calculation views defined using the dimension category. These views effectively act as an attribute view within the final model. You then join the dimensional calculation views to the incoming transactional table. This process is similar to the logical join foundation of an analytic view.

Table 9.8 Calculation View Configuration Options (Cont.)

Calculation views essentially allow you to choreograph the movement of data sets through a gauntlet of logical transformations, until the desired result set is produced. In some ways, calculation views can be used to transform data similarly to the ways SAP Data Services can transform data.

As we'll discuss in Chapter 10, calculation views contain fewer transformations than SAP Data Services. They can be defined using a GUI or scripts. However, in either case, the general workflow is the same. Figure 9.14 contains a workflow diagram that illustrates an example calculation view's workflow.

In the example workflow in Figure 9.14, five major steps and components are used to transform two analytic views into a single comprehensive information view. For this example, we'll assume that the goal of the calculation view is to produce a combined information view that displays the product, year, and month attributes. In addition, we'll associate two measures representing the quantity sold and quantity of products returned. If we assume that returned products are a KPI, this information view can be used to identify products that are defective or unsatisfactory.

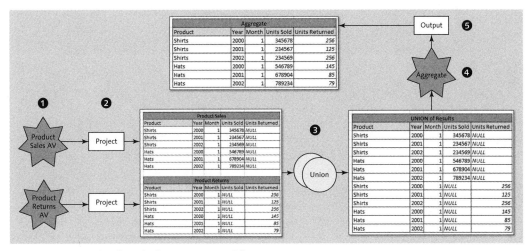

Figure 9.14 Example of a Calculation View Workflow

Let's walk through the steps now:

❶ Using an existing products-sold analytic view and a products-returned analytic view, obtain the needed attributes and measures from each view.

❷ Using the `Projection` transformation, select the desired components from each analytic view. If you assume that each analytic view contains several attributes and measures, then projecting the results to the needed components can increase the performance of the overall calculation view. In addition, you can use the `Projection` transformation to add new calculated columns filters. (We'll discuss all of the features of the `Projection` transformation in Section 9.3.2.)

❸ Using the `Union` transformation, combine the two projected analytic views into a single logical result set. This transformation works similarly to the SQL function union. At this point, the results have not been fully combined. There are records for the products returned and the products sold.

❹ Using the `Aggregation` transformation, fully combine the results of each analytic view. This `Aggregation` transformation works similarly to the SQL GROUP BY function. Because you're aggregating the two measures against the three attribute columns, rows for products that were sold are combined with rows of products sold.

❺ The final output is a comprehensive result set that contains a row for each product, year, month, quantity sold, and quantity returned. You can define each output column as either an attribute or measure in the `Semantics` transformation.

9.3.2 Defining a Graphical Calculation View

As mentioned before, SAP HANA supports the development of calculation views using either a GUI or custom-developed scripts. Each interface has different options and capabilities. The GUI is the easiest for a developer to use. As its name suggests, all of the development in this interface is conducted by placing objects on a canvas and using drag-and-drop principles to connect and choreograph their relationships.

Figure 9.15 contains an example of the graphical calculation view design window. The TOOLS PALETTE pane appears on the left side within the SCENARIO window, and the DETAILS and OUTPUT panes appear on the right. The panes on the right-hand side contain properties that appear depending on the object that is selected from the graphical design area of the SCENARIO window. In some cases, objects also contain a secondary OUTPUT pane, allowing you to manage the logical output of the transformation.

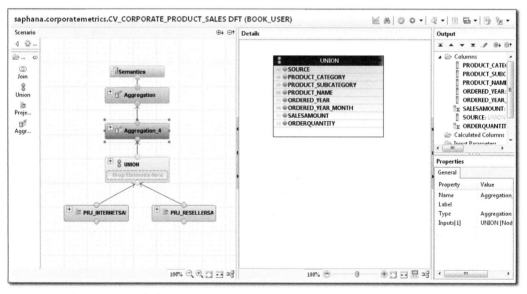

Figure 9.15 A Calculation View Design Window in the Graphical User Interface

The TOOLS PALETTE and SCENARIO window are the main graphical design areas within the calculation view design screen. Various data sources and transformations can be added to the SCENARIO window. Lines can be created to connect objects and express their workflow of transformation. The starting point of a calculation view begins with the addition of data sources to the SCENARIO window. One or more analytic views, attribute views, stored procedure column views, or tables can be used as data sources for a calculation view.

After the data sources are added to the graphical SCENARIO window, five additional transformations can also be added from the graphical TOOLS PALETTE window. Each transformation has a unique purpose, as outlined below:

▸ **Join**

The Join transformation enables you to query one or more supported data sources to generate a new logical result set. After the object is added to the SCENARIO window and selected, the DETAILS and OUTPUT panes appear to the right. The DETAILS pane allows you to graphically join data sources connected to the Join transformation.

You can graphically maximize or minimize the transform by clicking the plus or minus sign found in the top-left corner. When minimized, the constituent data sources are not visible within the node. When maximized, the constituent data sources are listed within the node.

You also select one or more data source columns in the DETAIL pane and assign them as output columns. The OUTPUT pane allows you to specify the output column name and generate calculated columns. Finally, you can select existing input parameters or create new input parameters.

▸ **Projection**

The Projection transformation allows you to manipulate a supported data source to generate a new logical result set. The manipulations include the ability to select a subset of columns from the source, create calculated columns, define filters, and define input parameters. After the object is added to the SCENARIO window and selected, the DETAILS and OUTPUT panes appear to the right. Select one or more data source columns in the DETAIL pane and assign them as output columns.

You can graphically maximize or minimize the transform by clicking the plus or minus sign found in the top-left corner. When minimized, the constituent data sources are not visible within the node. When maximized, the constituent data sources are listed within the node.

The Output pane allows you to specify the output column name and generate calculated columns. You can select existing input parameters, defined in any connected analytic views, or create new input parameters and define filters to limit the results of the connected data source.

► **Union**

The Union transformation allows you to merge two or more data sources into a single logical result set. The merger doesn't combine rows, but simply stacks them one on top of another. After the object is added to the Scenario window and selected, the Details pane appears to the right. The Details pane allows you to graphically connect columns from each data source to a common target column. Columns from the source are placed in the target area using standard drag-and-drop techniques. The connection points are used by the Union transform to identify which columns should be aligned when the two data sources are combined. The combined columns must share the same data type and precision. Any column that isn't linked to a target column outputs a NULL value for the unassigned data source.

► **Aggregation**

The Aggregation transformation allows you to summarize measureable columns into groups of attributes. The functionality is similar to using a GROUP BY statement in an SQL statement. The transform supports the aggregation functions SUM, MIN, and MAX.

You assign a measure column to the output by right-clicking a column found in the Details pane and then choosing the option ADD AS AGGREGATED COLUMN. Conversely, you can assign an attribute column by right-clicking and choosing the option ADD AS OUTPUT.

Using the Scenario window GUI and standard drag-and-drop principles, you can design a workflow that connects both data sources and transformations together to produce a comprehensive result set. Typically, these workflows are designed from the bottom up.

In the Scenario window on the left side of Figure 9.16, you can see an example of how two analytic views are being transformed into a single logical data set. The workflow starts with two analytic views, contained within separate Projection transforms, at the bottom of the Scenario window. The results of each Projection transform are then combined using a Union transform. The results of the Union transform are then aggregated to produce a summary. In the final Semantics transform, the summarized results are converted into attributes, measures, and hierarchies within the SEMANTICS node.

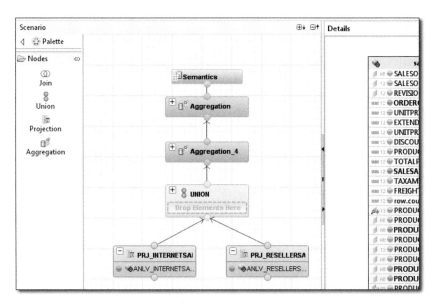

Figure 9.16 Calculation View Workflow

You connect objects in the SCENARIO window by dragging the small circle located on the top or bottom of the object to the small circle located on the adjoining object. Each line represents the movement of a logical data set from one object to the next. Lines connected on the bottom of the object are considered the incoming connection. Lines protruding from the top of the object are considered the outgoing connection. The assumption is that the incoming data is changed, using the supported logic of the transformation, and then passed along to the next object for additional transformation or final output.

Objects can be connected in a variety of configurations, but they should be connected in the most logical order. For example, the Join and Union transformations typically contain two or more incoming connections and a single outgoing connection. However, you can create two or more outgoing connections for many of the objects, as well. While you can output more than one logical data set, all branches of the workflow must inevitably coincide with a single SEMANTICS node for final output. In other words, all objects and workflows must eventually connect to a single output. Therefore, the most efficient workflow is one that performs the least amount of transformations and calculations while producing the desired output. After the workflow is completed, the calculation view can be saved and activated to allow consumers to query the results.

The final step of a calculation view is the configuration of the final transformation and SEMANTICS node. The final transformation node can be either an `Aggregation` transform or `Projection` transform, depending on the type of calculation view needed. In many ways, these two final nodes work in tandem. For example, changing a column to a measure in the SEMANTICS node also changes the column to an aggregate output column in the AGGREGATION node. However, there are a few differences between the two nodes.

If the calculation view will be utilized predominantly for aggregating results, we should place an `Aggregation` transform just before the SEMANTICS node. The final AGGREGATION node works like all `Aggregation` transforms. Columns are selected for output as an aggregate, measure, or attribute. Columns defined as attributes are used to group the data set. Columns defined as measures are aggregated by each attribute. In addition to the standard output columns, we can also define other object types. In total, there are five objects that can be created in this pane:

▶ **Attribute columns**
Columns can be created as either attributes or measures.

Attributes are the columns that will be used for grouping, sorting, filtering, and ranking the results of the calculation view. They incorporate many of the features described in the sections pertaining to attribute view columns, but they are defined explicitly in the calculation view.

You assign attributes to this pane by right-clicking columns in the details pane virtual table and selecting ADD TO OUTPUT. The attribute columns are then present within the COLUMNS node of the OUTPUT window.

▶ **Measure columns**
Measures represent the columns that will be summarized or aggregated in the calculation view. Calculation view measures support the `SUM`, `MIN`, and `MAX` aggregation functions. They incorporate many of the same features that were described in the sections pertaining to analytic view measures.

You assign measures to this pane by right-clicking columns in the details pane virtual table and selecting ADD AS AGGREGATED COLUMN. The measure columns are then present within the COLUMNS node of the OUTPUT window.

- **Calculated columns**

  Calculated columns are columns that are derived from one or more columns in the calculation view. They are designed using the SAP HANA SQL syntax. They incorporate many of the features described in the sections pertaining to attribute view calculated columns, but they are defined explicitly in the calculation view.

  You assign calculated columns to this pane by right-clicking the CALCULATED COLUMN section and selecting NEW CALCULATED COLUMN.

- **Counters**

  Counters can be used to create a count distinct aggregate and measure. They are based on attributes defined in the calculation view. At this time, only a count distinct and a single attribute can be configured in each counter's options.

  You assign counters to this pane by right-clicking the CALCULATED COLUMN section and selecting NEW COUNTER.

- **Restricted columns**

  Restricted measures can be utilized to create a conditional aggregation. This is a measure that aggregates only when an associated attribute's value matches a defined value. You define them by selecting an output measure and then assigning a simple filter based on one or more output attributes. Both the measure and attribute columns must be defined in the COLUMNS node before they can be selected within the restricted column definition.

  Restricted columns are automatically defined as a measure type, and their aggregation function is the same one defined on the base measure used in their definition. If the base measure is defined as a SUM, then the restricted measure is also defined as a SUM.

- **Input parameters**

  Input parameters can be used to define a runtime parameter or a list of values for a runtime parameter. Input parameters can be used in calculated columns and calculated measures to facilitate runtime manipulation of the data. They can be defined in multiple calculation view transforms, as well. In addition, input parameters can be inherited from source analytic views used in the definition of the calculation view.

  Input parameters can be assigned in the Join, Projection, Aggregation, and Semantics transforms. In all areas, you assign them by right-clicking the INPUT PARAMETERS section and choosing NEW. There is also an option to manage the inherited input parameters labeled MANAGE MAPPINGS.

471

If the calculation view will be used in a `Star Join` transform or if the results should not be aggregated, we need to place a `Projection` transform in the workflow just before the Semantics node. The `Projection` transform described earlier allows us to define output columns, calculated columns, filters, and input parameters. Because the output columns are all assumed to be attributes, no aggregations or measures can be defined within the output of the calculation view. It is most appropriately used when the calculation view is configured with the data category of Dimension.

The Semantics node is the final node in a calculation view. We use this node to finalize the output columns and define hierarchies, variables, and input parameters. As depicted in Figure 9.17, when we select the Semantics node, four new windows appear on the right-hand side, within the details frame: the Properties window, Columns window, Hierarchies window, and Variables/Input Parameters window.

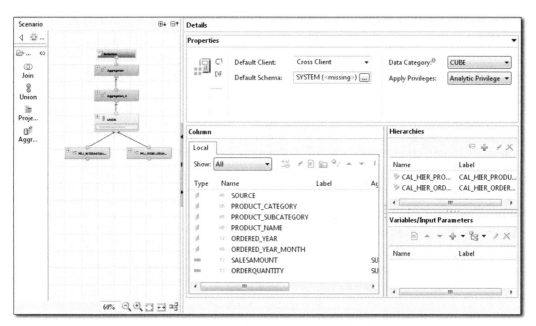

Figure 9.17 Details Pane after You Select the Semantics Node of a Calculation View

Each of these windows contains options that allow us to define the final output of the calculation view. Table 9.9 contains a description of how we might use each of these windows.

Window	Description
PROPERTIES	The PROPERTIES window contains options that allow us to manage the default client, default schema, data category, and how analytic privileges are applied:
	▸ DEFAULT CLIENT is a setting used specifically with SAP data. When a user is provisioned within SAP HANA, a default client can be defined. Tables that contain the SAP-specific client number field (MANDT) are automatically filtered when the session client option is selected.
	▸ DEFAULT SCHEMA represents the schema that should be assumed as the owner of any table used in the mode.
	▸ DATA CATEGORY represents a setting that is used to manage the visibility of the calculation view in terms of reporting tools. When a blank value is selected from the dropdown list, the view is not visible within most reporting tools. When CUBE or DIMENSION is selected, the view is likely visible in most reporting tools. The DIMENSION setting is also used to define a calculation view that is similar to an attribute view. However, when this setting is selected, the calculation view can be useful only within the `Star Join` transform.
	▸ APPLY PRIVILEGES is a setting used to define how the calculation view utilizes analytic privileges.
COLUMN	Within the COLUMN window, we can define columns as attributes or measures. We can also hide columns, define a column label, specify the aggregation function for measures, define label columns, and assign variables.
	If the calculation view's data category is set to dimension, only attributes and key attributes can be defined in this window. Key attributes should represent the primary key of the dimensional calculation view. This also assumes that the preceding transform is of the type `Projection`.
	If the calculation view's data category is set to cube or blank, then attributes and measures can be defined in this window. This also assumes that the preceding transform is of the type `Aggregation`.
HIERARCHIES	Hierarchies can be created directly in a calculation view. They are designed using one or more of the attributes defined in the calculation view. Unlike attribute views, hierarchies in a calculation view can span columns that exist naturally in disparate attribute views.
	You assign hierarchies to this pane by right-clicking the HIERARCHIES section and selecting either a parent-child or level hierarchy.

Table 9.9 Semantics Node Windows

Window	Description
VARIABLES / INPUT PARAMETERS	As with analytic views, variables can be used to create a runtime filter and prompt list of values for the calculation view. They can be configured using the same options listed previously in Table 9.7 in Section 9.2.2. You assign variables to this pane by right-clicking the VARIABLES section and selecting NEW.

Table 9.9 Semantics Node Windows (Cont.)

After the calculation view is activated, SAP HANA converts the graphical workflow of the transformation into highly optimized code that maximizes the use of the hardware capabilities of the SAP HANA appliance.

Calculation views should not be confused with stored procedures in the SAP HANA appliance. Although both mechanisms are capable of transforming data to produce robust analytics, stored procedure logic is generally more expensive to execute than calculation view logic. Stored procedures rely heavily on orchestration logic and procedural SQL statements. They can be characterized by the use of costly row-by-row operations that evaluate records in a loop. They can also be characterized by the need to calculate data in a series of rigid steps. Calculation views incorporate a different technique in the processing of data. If designed correctly, they use declarative logic to minimize the cost of processing data. They work more efficiently analyzing data in sets, using logic that can be parallelized in the SAP HANA engines. Calculation views can be characterized by their ability to efficiently process multiple calculations at the same time. Because of this, calculation views are ideal for producing complex analytical models, which are based on high-cardinality tables, each possessing complex relationships to other tables. With that said, calculation views invoke the use of the SAP HANA calculation engine. In situations when the query can be satisfied using the standard star schema analytic view, calculation views aren't recommended.

9.3.3 Defining a Script-Based Calculation View

Calculation views can also be composed using scripting language for situations when the GUI has limitations or complex procedure logic is required. Script-based calculation views can be defined using standard SAP HANA SQL statements or a special SQLScript language and *CE_functions*. The CE_ functions are the preferred choice for developers when creating SQLScript-based calculation views. CE_ functions are directly executed in the SAP HANA calculation engine and can be better optimized for parallel execution by the SAP HANA engine. Script-based calculation views can contain a mixture of either standard SQL statements or CE_ functions. However, we don't recommend that you mix these scripting languages in the same calculation view because, in many cases, intermixing can have an adverse effect on the calculation view's performance.

> **Note**
>
> While CE_ functions currently offer the best performance within scripted calculation views, we expect that SAP will enhance its engine optimizers in future releases. These enhancements will likely allow developers to utilize standard SQL statements or other SAP HANA SQLScript statements to develop scripted calculation views without the risk of performance issues. If the SQL statement optimizer is enhanced, it will likely be unnecessary to use CE_ functions purely for the basis of performance.

Figure 9.18 shows an example of the script-based calculation view design window. The Scenario pane appears on the left side; the Details pane, containing the scripting interface, appears in the center; and the input parameters, output parameters, and output columns generated for the script appear on the far-right side. The output columns aren't automatically generated from the script, so you must define them manually by clicking the green plus sign icon in the Output window.

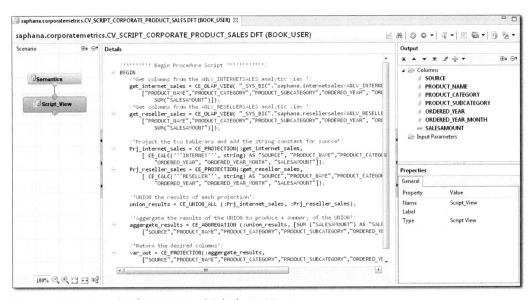

Figure 9.18 An Example of a Script-Based Calculation View

The SCENARIO pane contains only two nodes:

▸ The SCRIPT_VIEW node is used when writing the script, defining output columns, and defining input and output parameters.

▸ The SEMANTICS node is used to define attributes, measures, hierarchies, variables, and additional input parameters based on the output of the script. There are also properties such as default schema, data category, and apply privileges that can be established after the SEMANTICS node is selected.

To activate a node, click the node object, and its DETAILS panes appear to the right-hand side.

The scripting process is conducted using many of the same principles we discussed regarding the graphical calculation view design process. The goal of the script is to choreograph the movement of a data set through a series of transformations until the desired results are produced. While the methodology may be the same, the process is implemented using a specific code language, and not graphical objects.

In comparison to the GUI, the scripting interface is considerably more complex. However, increased complexity brings more control and features. For example, the scripting interface can accommodate situations when stored procedures are needed to transform data sets or predictive analysis functions need to be used in the calculation view.

To help you better understand script-based calculation views, let's review the example workflow that was shown earlier, in Figure 9.14. The graphical calculation view combined both Internet sales and reseller sales into a single result set. Because the Internet sales and reseller sales transactions were maintained in two separate transaction tables, we were unable to develop a sole analytic view to properly query and aggregate the combined sales transactions. Using a graphical calculation view, we were able to orchestrate the processing of data and solve the issues related to aggregating results from two different transaction tables.

Listing 9.1 contains an example calculation view script. The script is the equivalent of the graphical example displayed in Figure 9.16. The exact semantics of the SAP HANA SQLScript language are beyond the scope of this book, but we offer this example to illustrate how a calculation view can be devised using hand-written SAP HANA SQLScript code. In addition, this example script incorporates the use of the highly optimized CE_ functions. Though this is subject to change, CE_ functions are currently a faster alternative to standard SQL statements or stored procedure logic.

```
/********* Begin Procedure Script ************/
 BEGIN
/**Step 1**/
/**Get columns from the ANLV_INTERNETSALES analytic view **/
get_internet_sales = CE_OLAP_VIEW( "_SYS_BIC"."saphana.internetsales/
ANLV_INTERNETSALES/olap",["PRODUCT_NAME","PRODUCT_CATEGORY","PRODUCT_
SUBCATEGORY","ORDERED_YEAR", "ORDERED_YEAR_MONTH",SUM("SALESAMOUNT")]);
/**Get columns from the ANLV_RESELLERSALES analytic view **/
get_reseller_sales = CE_OLAP_VIEW( "_SYS_BIC"."saphana.resellersales/
ANLV_RESELLERSALES/olap",["PRODUCT_NAME","PRODUCT_CATEGORY", "PRODUCT_
SUBCATEGORY", "ORDERED_YEAR", "ORDERED_YEAR_
MONTH",SUM("SALESAMOUNT")]);

/**Step 2**/
/**Project the two results to add the string constant for source**/
Prj_internet_sales = CE_PROJECTION( :get_internet_sales, [ CE_CALC(
'''INTERNET''', string) AS "SOURCE", "PRODUCT_NAME", "PRODUCT_
CATEGORY", "PRODUCT_SUBCATEGORY", "ORDERED_YEAR", "ORDERED_YEAR_MONTH",
"SALESAMOUNT"]);
Prj_reseller_sales = CE_PROJECTION( :get_reseller_sales, [ CE_
CALC('''RESELLER''', string) AS "SOURCE", "PRODUCT_NAME", "PRODUCT_
CATEGORY", "PRODUCT_SUBCATEGORY", "ORDERED_YEAR", "ORDERED_YEAR_MONTH",
"SALESAMOUNT"]);

/**Step 3**/
/**UNION the results of each projection**/
union_results = CE_UNION_ALL (:Prj_internet_sales, :Prj_reseller_
sales);

/**Step 4**/
/**Aggregate the results of the UNION to produce a summary**/
aggergate_results = CE_AGGREGATION (:union_results, [SUM
("SALESAMOUNT") AS "SALESAMOUNT"], ["SOURCE", "PRODUCT_NAME", "PRODUCT_
CATEGORY", "PRODUCT_SUBCATEGORY", "ORDERED_YEAR", "ORDERED_YEAR_
MONTH"]);

/**Step 5**/
/**Return the desired columns**/
 var_out = CE_PROJECTION(:aggergate_results, ["SOURCE", "PRODUCT_NAME",
"PRODUCT_CATEGORY", "PRODUCT_SUBCATEGORY", "ORDERED_YEAR", "ORDERED_
YEAR_MONTH", "SALESAMOUNT"]);

END
/********* End Procedure Script ************/
```

Listing 9.1 Example SAP HANA SQLScript that Incorporates CE_ Functions

> **Additional References**
>
> For more information on the SAP HANA SQLScript language and a complete listing of the available CE_ functions, please review the SAP HANA SQLScript reference guide found at *http://help.sap.com/hana_appliance#section7*.

Calculation views are powerful information views that allow you to solve complex aggregation problems or perform complex data-mining tasks. In simple terms, they allow for the orchestration of a data set for the purpose of complex analysis. Calculation views add value to the SAP HANA platform by allowing you to formulate queries when standard multidimensional analysis can't accommodate your requirements.

9.4   Summary

In this chapter, we offered a comprehensive explanation of the heart of SAP HANA multidimensional modeling: the attribute, analytic, and calculation information views of SAP HANA. With this information, you're now ready to move into a practical discussion of real-world multidimensional modeling.

With the basics described in the past few chapters, you're now ready to get your hands dirty and dive into real-world modeling with SAP HANA.

10   Multidimensional Modeling in Practice

In the last several chapters, we have focused largely on the tools and options used to model analytics in SAP HANA. We'll now take a moment to examine the capabilities of SAP HANA modeling in the context of how data can be stored in the SAP HANA tables and fields. In Section 10.1, we'll discuss normalized and denormalized data, which are the two main types of data that can exist in SAP HANA. In addition, we'll discuss the effects that each format can have on the SAP HANA system. Then, in Section 10.2 and Section 10.3, we'll use two case studies that walk you through the process of creating real-world models in SAP HANA. The first case study guides you through the creation of a simple analytic view. The second case study guides you through a more complex scenario in which a calculation view is required to produce the desired result.

10.1   Data Processing in SAP HANA

In Chapter 3 of this book, we explained many of the concepts behind data storage in SAP HANA, including OLTP and data denormalization. Because and understanding of these concepts are also necessary for multidimensional modeling, we want to briefly review them here.

With any RDBMS, there are specific database field and table design techniques that application developers use to eliminate data storage redundancy. These design techniques are also used to optimize the processes that application code uses to insert and update data in a database. This design technique is referred to as *database normalization,* and it's often incorporated into the data model design of databases used for OLTP. On the other hand, BI applications often work better when accessing data that has undergone a *denormalization* process. This denormalization process can be incorporated directly into the data model design of data warehouses or data marts, but it can also be accomplished on the fly using RDBMS-stored procedures, scripts, or functions. At their core, both of these data modeling techniques are mutually exclusive concepts. Normalized data models work best with OLTP applications, whereas denormalized data is better suited for BI applications. With the SAP HANA appliance, either data model scenario can exist in its tables. Therefore, it's important that we discuss the challenges and benefits associated with both denormalization techniques. In this section, we'll explore the issues associated with modeling normalized data in SAP HANA. We'll also differentiate the terms *data modeling* and *analytic modeling*. To conclude, we'll discuss the specific solutions SAP HANA offers for managing normalized data.

What Is Online Transaction Processing (OLTP)?

Although we discussed OLTP in Chapter 3, here's a brief refresher: OLTP is often used to describe applications, systems, or databases that are used for transactional data input and retrieval. Most organizations use software applications to facilitate their daily operations by tracking occurrences or transactions. These transactions are then stored in a database for future reference. For example, a sales agent records all of the details of a telephone sales order into an ordering system. This data can later be retrieved by the shipping department to fulfill the order. The data can also be periodically updated with an order status that allows the customer to view the status over the Internet and receive email notifications until the order is shipped. With this in mind, the primary purpose of an OLTP application and database is to manage each transaction.

10.1.1 Normalized Data versus Denormalized Data

In this section, we'll define normalized and denormalized data. In addition, we'll discuss the difference between the logical denormalization and the physical denormalization of data. These terms and concepts are important for SAP HANA information view developers to understand because they relate to the capabilities and scalability of such solutions.

Database normalization is an issue inherent in data that is replicated into SAP HANA from an OLTP system in its native format. The SAP HANA platform, coupled with SAP Data Services, SLT, or SAP (Sybase) Replication Services, has the capability of processing data in real time or near-real time. When data is replicated into SAP HANA without any further transformation, it will likely be replicated in its native normalized formats or in the format that the business application uses. In Part II of this book, we discussed in detail the role that SAP Data Services can play in not only replicating the data from one or more sources, but also transforming data from a normalized structure into a star schema (legacy relational OLAP model) or modified star schema denormalized structure (SAP HANA relational OLAP model) (see Chapter 3). While real-time replication isn't a topic of this book, it's important to understand the scenarios in which normalized data is replicated into SAP HANA. It's also important that we discuss the impact that normalized data can have on the SAP HANA platform.

While database normalization is an optimal field and table design technique for applications, it presents several challenges to BI solutions that focus on multidimensional modeling. Database normalization techniques typically encourage table and field design techniques that force individual attributes into their own tables. For example, a customer table might contain the customer's first and last name, but the address, city, state, and country fields exist as only foreign key fields referencing other tables that contain the address, city, state, and country information. In other scenarios, a customer's attributes might be stored in a table where each attribute is represented by a separate record in the database. For example, the customer's contact information might exist in a customer contact table, where each phone number is stored as an individual row. In a fully denormalized structure, the same customer information exists as a single row with each telephone number attribute stored as a column in the row. To query the normalized structure, you must join multiple tables and possibly pivot the contact information using complex scripts to eliminate future cardinality issues. In contrast, to query the denormalized structure, the query needs to reference only a single table.

Keep in mind that normalized data must be denormalized before it can be presented to users in a physical or logical start schema. When you create information views in SAP HANA, you're effectively transforming data into a logical start schema. However, there are some cases where normalized data can be challenging in a multidimensional model, as described below:

▶ **Excessive joins**
Normalized data stores related attributes in multiple tables. When you create information views, these attributes often need to be combined in a single attribute view to support hierarchies and make the attributes more intuitive for users. The process of combining these attributes is often achieved using table joins. The table joining processes aren't very challenging unless the cardinality between the tables creates duplicate rows for each distinct attribute. These

duplicate rows can create aggregation issues when joined to the analytic view DATA FOUNDATION. Excessive joining can also lead to performance issues in the SAP HANA information views.

▶ **Data pivots**
Normalized data can often be stored so that each attribute is stored as a separate record. In contrast, a denormalized structure stores each attribute as a separate column. In an attribute view, this scenario creates cardinality issues and subsequent aggregation issues for the model. However, if the data is transformed from multiple rows into a single row with multiple columns, the issue can be eliminated. This type of transformation is often referred to as a data pivot. While the concept of pivoting data is easily understood, the coding required to achieve the transformation in an attribute view is very difficult. In terms of an SAP HANA attribute view, there aren't many options for solving this problem on the fly. Technically speaking, this type of transformation can be achieved in a stored procedure and subsequently incorporated into a calculation view. However, the use of stored procedures in calculation views can lead to both performance and scalability issues.

▶ **Audit history**
In OLTP application databases, you'll often find situations in which an application keeps track of transaction changes by recording each attribute change as a separate record. For example, a customer table might contain multiple records for the same customer, where each record represents a small change to a column in that record. This is a common technique used in applications wherein an audit trail is required for each data change. However, in its native format, this, too, can create a cardinality issue in an SAP HANA attribute view. To solve the problem, SAP HANA developers need to logically reduce the table to a single record for each unique attribute. In many cases, this can be solved with a simple filter. However, in other cases, there is insufficient information in the table to identify the correct record for the attribute view. In the more complex scenarios, this situation has to be solved in a calculation view and stored procedure. However, the use of stored procedures in calculation views can lead to both performance and scalability issues.

▶ **Multiple sources**
Many organizations have multiple systems for managing their daily operations. In some cases, these systems can overlap in terms of product, customer, or other types of attribute and analytical information. When you replicate normal-

ized data into an SAP HANA schema from two or more sources, there are times when the data needs to be merged from each source to form a single, comprehensive information view. While one could argue that this issue isn't directly the result of normalized data, developers will find it difficult to model data from multiple sources into a single comprehensive information view. This is especially true when the data is replicated in a normalized format. SAP HANA calculation views provide limited options for merging data and de-duplicating attributes, but there are cases in which stored procedures are again required to properly merge and transform the data. However, the use of stored procedures in calculation views can lead to both performance and scalability issues.

▶ **Hierarchical data**
Hierarchical data is often stored in a normalized relational database table in a format that is problematic for reporting. For example, an employee table might contain a self-referential column for the employee's manager. This self-referential column contains a reference to another record in the same table. In some situations, this self-referencing can lead to a complex matrix of parent-child relationships wherein parent records can have parent records themselves. As these parent-child relationships are formed, levels are also formed. Application designers prefer the normalized approach to storing hierarchical data because there are no limits to the number of levels that can be stored in the table. However, from a BI standpoint, developers often need to flatten this data into a single record to prevent cardinality issues and subsequent aggregation issues. SAP HANA attribute views contain options allowing this data to be represented in an attribute hierarchy. However, there are few options to flatten this data into columns in an attribute view. Stored procedures can be developed to flatten the data and then incorporate it into a calculation view, but there are both performance and scalability issues associated with the use of stored procedures.

In the context of BI applications and RDBMS, two main methodologies for denormalizing normalized data into a star schema have arisen: logically or physically. In either case, BI developers need to logically or physically restructure normalized data into a star schema when creating information views.

The process of logically or physically modeling the structure of data to support multidimensional queries is referred to as data *denormalization*. Logically redesigning the structure implies that the process is accomplished using stored procedures, scripts, or views whereby the physical source structure is never permanently manifested into a persistent and reusable structure. Physical denormalization implies that the process is accomplished by extracting, transforming, and loading the data into a new set of well-defined, permanent tables.

Physical denormalization is the process that best describes traditional data modeling—the use of SAP Data Services and ETL-based loading of SAP HANA whereby well-defined dimension and fact tables are transformed in a star schema. With physical denormalization, the major workload is executed only once per batch ETL job. Subsequent queries to the physical denormalized tables result in little or no workload because the excessive joins and other complex transformations have already been completed and permanently stored in the table. In contrast, direct replication of data, followed by the use of SQL statements, information views, or stored procedures, best describes the *logical denormalization* of data. Logical denormalization also implies that the denormalization work is repeated each time the information is queried from the model.

If we assume that logical denormalization results in complex and repetitive work, we must also assume that the work is executed at a higher overall CPU and memory cost in the SAP HANA landscape. In database terms, high-cost denormalization can affect the overall performance of the database or the individual execution time of any given query. Work is required each time the model is queried and is repeated each time the same model is queried. Add to this that multiple users can access these models at the same time, and the cost of logical denormalization can accrue exponentially. Also remember that your total SAP HANA license cost can increase when excessive amounts of RAM are required to manage all of the computations of logical denormalization. This is because the RAM used for computation is included in the cost of each SAP HANA license unit.

Logical denormalization isn't unique to SAP HANA. Since the invention of the relational database, organizations have struggled with this issue. Some organizations use complex scripts and procedures to denormalize their data on the fly, while others choose to build physical denormalized tables in a data mart or warehouse. In most cases, the physical denormalization approach proves to be the most economical. This is largely based on the limitations of legacy relational databases. With SAP HANA, this might not be the case. Both physical and logical denormalization may prove viable because of the power of the SAP HANA platform. However, it's our opinion that physical denormalization is the most sustainable and scalable methodology for SAP HANA. This isn't necessarily based on the need to maximize the performance of the SAP HANA models; there are other issues that need to be considered, as well. Data quality, master data management, the centralization of business rules, the need for advanced functions, the limitations of SAP HANA scripts, and data governance practices are all examples in which physical denormalization using SAP Data Services provides advantages.

It's also wise to remember that SAP HANA can be used to manage data from any source, not just data from SAP applications. SAP has solutions such as SAP HANA Live that focus on real-time replication and logical denormalization. Because SAP HANA is powerful, this solution works well for SAP application data. However, not all source data is structured and managed like the data in an SAP application. Therefore, physical denormalization is often a better option for third-party data sources.

Normalized data can create many challenges when you're designing information views. In SAP HANA, there are two options for denormalizing data to facilitate multidimensional modeling. You can choose to logically denormalize the data using scripts, information views, and stored procedures. You can also leverage SAP Data Services to denormalize the data before it's physically stored in SAP HANA. In either case, careful consideration should be given to determine the best option to support the reporting and analytic needs of the organization.

10.1.2 Data Modeling versus Multidimensional Modeling

We just addressed the differences between logical denormalization and physical denormalization. To the same regard, there is also a difference between data modeling and SAP HANA's multidimensional modeling. Although the SAP HANA modeling components are often referred to as data modeling tools, it's more appropriate to describe them as *virtual multidimensional modeling* tools. The models are considered virtual because no data is stored in the SAP HANA information views. This is sometimes referred to as a ROLAP solution. Multidimensional modeling tools create logical views and semantics that present data in an intuitive format that facilitates analysis and reporting. In contrast, data modeling is a process whereby a new multidimensional-optimized database schema is devised and subsequently loaded using ETL tools such as SAP Data Services. Because the data isn't physically moved into a new schema, the capabilities of the SAP HANA information views are best described as virtual multidimensional modeling.

When discussing the capabilities of SAP HANA, it's important to understand the difference between physical data modeling and virtual multidimensional modeling. There are three main reasons this distinction is important:

▶ **Performance**
The performance of SAP HANA can be negatively affected if the solution relies predominantly on the information views and scripting capabilities of SAP HANA to transform the data. It's better to use SAP Data Services to transform the source data into a star schema that is optimal for multidimensional analysis. This simplifies the information view development processes and increases the overall performance of SAP HANA. Admittedly, the SAP HANA platform is incredibly efficient and powerful, regardless of the state of the data. In many cases, this recommendation might yield response times that are just a few seconds faster. With that said, if your goal is to maximize the performance of your queries, transforming your data into a physical star schema while loading data into SAP HANA will result in the best possible performance.

▶ **Manageability**
It's very difficult to develop and subsequently manage stored procedures and scripts to achieve transformation. In addition, impact analysis, lineage, and business logic are very costly and difficult to manage when layers of code are imbedded in the SAP HANA system. In contrast, SAP Data Services relies predominantly on graphical data flows and metadata to transform the data. Impact analysis and lineage are automatically generated with each data flow. In addition, relationships and dependencies between coding elements are easily visualized. Future versions of SAP HANA will include some of these same features, but at the moment, it doesn't contain a mature tool set to help manage metadata.

▶ **Capabilities**
Developers need to be realistic about the capabilities of SAP HANA to manage the common and complex transformations that are needed when you're working with normalized data. SAP HANA's information views are limited to a basic set of native transformations. When complex transformations are needed, stored procedures are required. However, stored procedures aren't easily developed and maintained. In addition, stored procedures can lead to performance degradations. In contrast, SAP Data Services has a well-established set of transformations that were created to address the common needs associated with creating star schemas, data marts, data warehouses, and multidimensional models.

Being able to distinguish between the analytic model and data modeling is important when you're developing solutions based on the SAP HANA standalone appliance. SAP HANA offers several technological benefits that can easily disguise bad solution design. This might be acceptable for some organizations because the performance of the SAP HANA solution will likely be superior to solutions based on their legacy RDBMS. However, it's our opinion that a developer should always follow best practices when designing solutions on SAP HANA to maximize the organization's investment. If your source data requires significant transformation, it's wise to leverage SAP Data Services and an optimal data model for your solution. If your source data requires little or no transformation or real-time access to data, SAP HANA's information views will likely be able to manage and facilitate the multidimensional analytic modeling without consequence.

While we might agree that performing more of the denormalization work within SAP Data Services yields the best performance, we also need to consider the goals of our SAP HANA implementation before deciding how best to model our data. For example, if the goal of the SAP HANA implementation is to provide real-time access to data, we will need to predominantly transform the data using information views. Relying on SAP Data Services to transform the data will likely add latency to the availability of data. This is because the batch ETL loading process takes time to execute. In contrast, replicating data to SAP HANA using tools like SAP Landscape Transformation offers a near-zero latency solution. Because SAP HANA's information views are virtual, they, too, do not add any latency to the availability of the data. This process is often referred to as extract, load, and transform (ELT). It is a process whereby the data is loaded in its raw format and then virtually transformed into an appropriate business centric model. With this in mind, we sometimes have to leverage SAP HANA information views to provide a true real-time solution.

10.1.3 Managing Normalized Data in SAP HANA

While we've largely focused on the challenges associated with creating information views on normalized data, we'll now explore the areas where SAP HANA can natively transform normalized data. Table 10.1 outlines the main transformation options available in SAP HANA and provides a description of each option and the areas where they can be implemented.

Option	Description	Implemented Within
Table joins	Joining tables in SAP HANA information views and stored procedures is a fundamental component of modeling. Assuming that there are no cardinality issues attributed to joining the tables, joining tables is an appropriate technique for managing normalized data in the SAP HANA information views.	▸ Attribute views ▸ Analytic views ▸ Calculation views ▸ Stored procedures
Static filtering	Creating static filters is also a fundamental component of modeling. In situations when tables need to be filtered to denormalize the results, SAP HANA accommodates static filters in all information views and stored procedures.	▸ Attribute views ▸ Analytic views ▸ Calculation views ▸ Stored procedures
Dynamic filtering	Dynamic filters are similar to static filters. However, dynamic filters change based on input parameters. They are supported in analytic views and calculation views as variables. In stored procedures, input parameters can be created to provide dynamic filtering.	▸ Analytic views ▸ Calculation views ▸ Stored procedures
Derived columns	Derived columns are instrumental in transforming columns in a table. They support type conversions, concatenations, string functions, date functions, and many other types of columnar transformations.	▸ Attribute views ▸ Analytic views ▸ Calculation views ▸ Stored procedures
Aggregation	SAP HANA supports aggregations using the SUM, MIN, and MAX functions in analytic views. In addition to these, calculation views also support counters or count distinct aggregations. Stored procedures support the full array of aggregation functions, as well. Aggregations aren't directly used to denormalize data, but they are the basis for measures in information views.	▸ Analytic views ▸ Calculation views ▸ Stored procedures
Union	The union function can be used to merge data sets into a single comprehensive set. There are several denormalization and calculation techniques that benefit from the union transformation. Calculation views and stored procedures support the use of a union function.	▸ Calculation views ▸ Stored procedures

Table 10.1 Options for Managing Normalized Data in the SAP HANA System

Option	Description	Implemented Within
SQL functions	Generically speaking, functions are implemented in derived columns, calculation views, or stored procedures. Functions provide a variety of capabilities that are useful in transforming or denormalizing data.	▸ Attribute view ▸ Analytic views ▸ Calculation views ▸ Stored procedures
Stored procedures	Stored procedures can be embedded directly into calculation views or executed directly from reporting tools. Stored procedures offer the most flexibility in managing normalized data, but they can also introduce performance and scalability penalties.	▸ Calculation views
SQLScript	SQLScript code can be used in calculation views and stored procedures. SQLScript provides several options for managing normalized data. Assuming that the CE_ functions are used for the SQLScript, the performance will be exceptional. However, when mixed with SQL statements or recursive procedure logic, performance will likely be degraded.	▸ Calculation views ▸ Stored procedures
SQL statements	SQL statement code can be used in calculation views and stored procedures. It provides several options for managing normalized data. Compared to using SQLScript and CE_ functions, it generally results in slower performance.	▸ Calculation views ▸ Stored procedures

Table 10.1 Options for Managing Normalized Data in the SAP HANA System (Cont.)

By now, you should have a better understanding of how SAP HANA provides options to manage normalized and denormalized data. You should also understand that different methodologies are utilized based on the requirements of the users. For example, a real-time solution will require more use of the SAP HANA information views, while a high-performance solution will require more traditional data modeling and ETL coding.

In the next two sections, we will walk you through two cases studies. The first case study introduces you to the use of attribute and analytic views. The second case study looks at calculation views and provides a real-world example of when one might choose to use them.

10.2   Case Study 1: Modeling Sales Data to Produce Robust Analytics

The AdventureWorks Cycle Company has recently implemented a new BI platform based on SAP HANA, SAP Data Services, and SAP BusinessObjects BI. Using SAP Data Services, the company's BI resources were able to successfully extract, transform, and load the supporting Internet sales dimension and fact tables into an SAP HANA schema using a best-practices approach.

Now that the required data is available, the Internet sales management team has requested access to this data. The sales management team's requirements were that the solution be simple and easy to use. In the past, the Internet sales team had to rely on multiple IT resources to compile data into reports and analytics. Given the capabilities of its SAP BusinessObjects BI platform, the team is requesting that IT develop a solution that grants the Internet sales manager access to the data without having to engage IT resources on a daily basis.

The BI team at AdventureWorks Cycle Company has determined that SAP BusinessObjects Explorer, SAP Lumira Desktop, and SAP BusinessObjects Analysis, edition for Microsoft Office, are the best end-user tools to accommodate the requirements. However, they must first develop an SAP HANA analytic view to support access to the requested data. The sales managers have requested the ability to analyze Internet sales transactions by customer, order date, and product.

Based on these requirements, let's walk through the processes of creating the attribute views and analytic views required to facilitate the requirements of the Internet sales managers. Please remember that the concepts of creating information views were discussed in detail in Chapter 9, and refer back to that chapter as necessary.

10.2.1   Creating the Supporting Attribute Views

The first step is to produce four attribute views based on the SAP HANA tables listed in Table 10.2. These tables exist in the BOOK_USER schema in our example:

- "BOOK_USER"."DIM_CUSTOMER"
- "BOOK_USER"."DIM_PRODUCT"
- "BOOK_USER"."DIM_DATE"

To design attribute views, you must first open SAP HANA Studio and configure an SAP HANA system.

Defining an SAP HANA System

If your SAP HANA system is already defined, proceed to the next step. If not, perform these steps to configure a system in SAP HANA Studio.

1. Launch the SAP HANA Studio application.

2. Switch to the MODELER perspective. From the FILE menu bar, choose WINDOW • OPEN PERSPECTIVE • MODELER.

3. On the left side is the NAVIGATOR window. Right-click in the NAVIGATOR window and choose ADD SYSTEM.

4. In the SYSTEM window, fill in the following fields, as shown in Figure 10.1:

   ▸ HOSTNAME: Enter the fully qualified domain name of the SAP HANA server.

   ▸ INSTANCE NUMBER: Enter the instance number of your SAP HANA system.

   ▸ DESCRIPTION: Enter a description as needed.

   ▸ LOCALE: Select your design-time language.

5. Click the NEXT button to proceed to the next step.

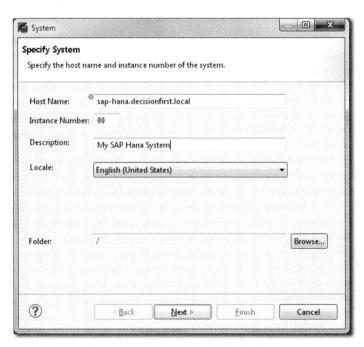

Figure 10.1 Configuring Properties in an SAP HANA System

6. In the CONNECTION PROPERTIES window, enter the database user name and password assigned by your SAP HANA administrator, as shown in Figure 10.2.

7. Click the FINISH button.

Figure 10.2 The Authentication Options When Defining a System Connection in SAP HANA Studio

Creating the Root Packages and Subpackages

> **Note**
>
> In Chapter 2, we provided instruction for creating the root package (saphana) and subpackage (internetsales). However, in the event that you need to create them again, please review the following instructions.

Because AdventureWorks Cycle Company will develop multiple models over time, start by creating a root package (saphana) and two subpackages (commonattributes and internetsales) to better organize the information views.

Follow these steps to create the root packages:

1. Using the MODELER perspective, expand the system listed in the NAVIGATOR window located on the left side by clicking the arrow next to the system name.

2. In the system hierarchy, expand the CONTENT node.

3. Right-click the CONTENT node and choose NEW • PACKAGE.

4. In the NAME field, enter the package name "saphana".

5. In the DESCRIPTION field, enter a description of the package.

6. Specify the person responsible. This should be your SAP HANA database user account.

7. Choose the package's original language. This language should match the locale specified in the screen shown in Figure 10.1.

8. Click OK to save the package.

9. Right-click the SAPHANA package, and choose EDIT.

10. Change the STRUCTURAL option from No to YES to prevent any modeling content from being created directly in the root package.

You now need to create two subpackages in the saphana root package. The subpackage commonattributes will store attributes that are reusable across multiple information views, and the subpackage internetsales will be used to store analytic views and calculation views pertaining to Internet sales. Follow these steps to create the two subpackages:

1. Right-click the saphana root package, and select NEW • PACKAGE.

2. Enter the subpackage name "commonattributes". The subpackage name should be prefixed with "saphana." to indicate that it's a child of the saphana root package.

3. Enter the requested information for the remaining fields.

4. Right-click the saphana root package and select NEW • PACKAGE.

5. Enter the subpackage name "internetsales". The subpackage name should be prefixed with "saphana." to indicate that it's a child of the saphana root package.

Creating Attribute Views

Now that you've created the desired package hierarchy, you can begin the process of developing the attributes. To better organize and identify your attributes, adopt a standard attribute view naming convention in which standard attribute views are prefixed with ATBV_ and derived attribute views are prefixed with DATBV_.

Defining the ATBV_BASE_DATE Attribute View
Follow these steps to create the first attribute view:

1. Right-click the `commonattributes` subpackage and choose NEW • ATTRIBUTE VIEW.

2. Using Table 10.2 and Figure 10.3 as references, define the properties for the attribute view.

Property	Value
NAME	ATBV_BASE_DATE
DESCRIPTION	The base date attribute view.
PACKAGE	`saphana.commonattributes`
VIEW TYPE	ATTRIBUTE VIEW
COPY FROM	Unchecked
SUBTYPE	STANDARD

Table 10.2 Properties for the ATBV_BASE_DATE Attribute View

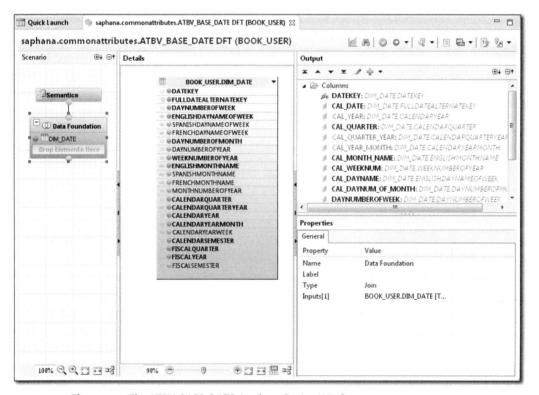

Figure 10.3 The ATBV_BASE_DATE Attribute Design Window

3. Click the DATA FOUNDATION node located on the left side of the attribute view design window.

4. In the DETAILS pane, right-click the white space and choose ADD.

5. Using the provided search field, enter "DIM_DATE". Once this is found, click the DIM_DATE object listed in the MATCHING ITEMS window. Click OK to add the table to the DETAILS pane.

6. Highlight the columns, using Table 10.3 as reference. To select multiple columns, hold down the ⌈Ctrl⌉ key and click each column.

7. Right-click the highlighted columns and choose ADD TO OUTPUT.

8. Using the OUTPUT pane on the far-right side of the attribute design window, click each column and update its name and label using the mapping values listed in Table 10.3. To update the attribute name and label, click each OUTPUT column. Using the PROPERTIES pane located below the OUTPUT pane, edit the NAME and LABEL fields.

Database Column Name	Attribute Name	Attribute Label
DATEKEY	DATEKEY	CAL_DATE_KEY
FULLDATEALTERNATEKEY	CAL_DATE	CAL_DATE
CALENDARYEAR	CAL_YEAR	CAL_YEAR
CALENDARQUARTER	CAL_QUARTER	CAL_QUARTER
CALENDARQUARTERYEAR	CAL_QUARTER_YEAR	CAL_QUARTER_YEAR
CALENDARYEARMONTH	CAL_YEAR_MONTH	CAL_YEAR_MONTH
ENGLISHMONTHNAME	CAL_MONTH_NAME	CAL_MONTH_NAME
WEEKNUMBEROFYEAR	CAL_WEEKNUM	CAL_WEEKNUM
ENGLISHDAYNAMEOFWEEK	CAL_DAYNAME	CAL_DAYNAME
DAYNUMBEROFMONTH	CAL_DAYNUM_OF_MONTH	CAL_DAYNUM_OF_MONTH
DAYNUMBEROFWEEK	DAYNUMBEROFWEEK	CAL_DAY_OF_WEEK
FISCALQUARTER	FISCAL_QTR	FISCAL_QTR
FISCALYEAR	FISCAL_YEAR	FISCAL_YEAR

Table 10.3 Column Mappings for ATBV_BASE_DATE

9. On the left side of the attribute design window, click the SEMANTICS node located in the SCENARIO pane.

10. In the COLUMN pane, locate the CAL_YEAR, CAL_QUARTER_YEAR, and CAL_
YEAR_MONTH columns. In the HIDDEN properties column, check the box to
hide each column. We'll design a separate attribute view for these columns at
a later time.

11. In the COLUMN pane, click the DATE_KEY column. Using the TYPE column on
the far left, set the DATE_KEY to the type KEY ATTRIBUTE.

12. When this is complete, save and activate the attribute view by clicking the
SAVE AND ACTIVATE button on the top-right toolbar, as shown in Figure 10.4.

In the toolbar, locate the green icon containing a right-pointing arrow. Each
icon in the toolbar produces hover text when you place your mouse pointer
over the icon. You can use this hover text to also identify the SAVE AND ACTI-
VATE icon.

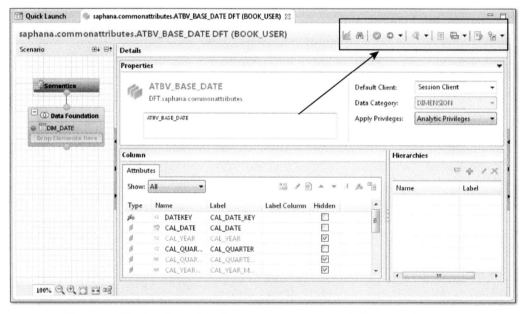

Figure 10.4 The Locations of the Save and Activate, Save and Validate, and Save and Activate
All Icons

Defining the ATBV_PRODUCT Attribute View

Follow these steps to create this attribute view:

1. Right-click the `commonattributes` subpackage and choose NEW • ATTRIBUTE VIEW.

2. Using Table 10.4 as a reference, define the properties for the attribute view.

Property	Value
NAME	ATBV_PRODUCT
DESCRIPTION	The products attribute view.
PACKAGE	`saphana.commonattributes`
VIEW TYPE	ATTRIBUTE VIEW
COPY FROM	Unchecked
SUBTYPE	STANDARD

Table 10.4 Properties for the ATBV_PRODUCT Attribute View

3. Click the DATA FOUNDATION node on the left side of the attribute view design window.

4. In the DETAILS pane, right-click the white space and choose ADD.

5. Using the provided search field, search for the following tables:

   ▸ DIM_PRODUCT_CATEGORY

   ▸ DIM_PRODUCT_SUBCATEGORY

   ▸ DIM_PRODUCT

   Once these are found, add each table to the MATCHING ITEMS pane. Click OK to add the tables to the DETAILS pane.

6. In the DETAILS pane, join the three tables using the information listed in Table 10.5, which contains two distinct join configurations. To create each join, right-click the white space in the DETAILS pane and choose CREATE JOIN. Once this is completed, the DETAILS pane should appear like the example in Figure 10.5. As an alternative, you can join the tables graphically using the drag-and-drop method.

Join	Property	Option
JOIN 1	Left Table	DIM_PRODUCT_SUBCATEGORY
	Left Column	PRODUCTSUBCATEGORYKEY
	Right Table	DIM_PRODUCT
	Right Column	PRODUCTSUBCATEGORYKEY
	Join Cardinality	(1:N)
	Join Type	Referential

Table 10.5 Join Conditions for the ATBV_PRODUCT Attribute View

Join	Property	Option
JOIN 2	Left Table	DIM_PRODUCT_CATEGORY
	Left Column	PRODUCTCATEGORYKEY
	Right Table	DIM_PRODUCT_SUBCATEGORY
	Left Column	PRODUCTCATEGORYKEY
	Join Cardinality	(1:N)
	Join Type	Referential

Table 10.5 Join Conditions for the ATBV_PRODUCT Attribute View (Cont.)

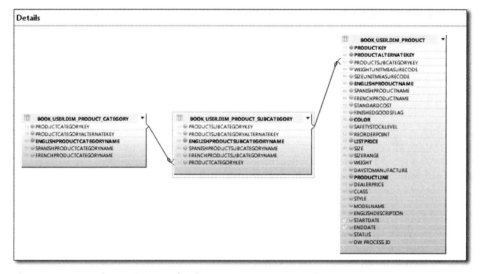

Figure 10.5 Example Join Diagram for the ATBV_PRODUCT Attribute View

7. Highlight the columns, using Table 10.6 as reference. To select multiple columns, hold down the ⌐Ctrl⌐ key and click each column.

8. Right-click the highlighted columns and choose ADD TO OUTPUT.

9. Using the OUTPUT pane on the right-hand side of the attribute design window, click each column, and update its name and label using the mapping values listed in Table 10.6. To update the attribute name and label, click each output column. Using the PROPERTIES pane located below the OUTPUT pane, edit the NAME and LABEL fields.

10. Create a calculated column for the product line attribute. Right-click the CAL-CULATED COLUMN node in the OUTPUT pane. Choose NEW.

11. In the data, the product line field is sometimes NULL. You need to create a calculated measure to convert the NULL values into a static alpha value X.

Define the PRODUCT_LINE calculated column using the options listed in Figure 10.6 using the following formula: if(isnull("PRODUCTLINE"),'X',"PRODUCTLINE").

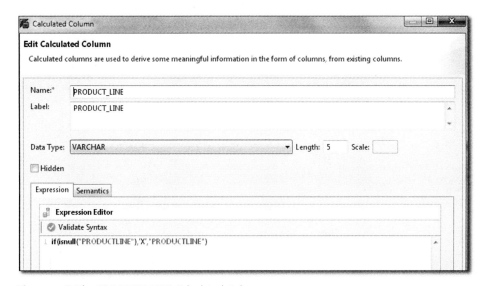

Figure 10.6 The PRODUCT_LINE Calculated Column

Column Name	Attribute Name	Attribute Label
DIM_PRODUCT.PRODUCTKEY	PRODUCT_KEY	PRODUCT_KEY
DIM_PRODUCT.PRODUCTALTERNATEKEY	PRODUCTALTERNATEKEY	PRODUCT_ALTKEY
DIM_PRODUCT.ENGLISHPRODUCTNAME	PRODUCT_NAME	PRODUCT_NAME
DIM_PRODUCT.COLOR	PRODUCT_COLOR	PRODUCT_COLOR
DIM_PRODUCT.LISTPRICE	PRODUCT_LISTPRICE	PRODUCT_LISTPRICE
DIM_PRODUCT.PRODUCTLINE	PRODUCTLINE	PRODUCTLINE

Table 10.6 Column Mappings for ATBV_PRODUCT

Column Name	Attribute Name	Attribute Label
DIM_PRODUCT_SUBCATEGORY. ENGLISHPRODUCTSUBCATEGORYNAME	PRODUCT_ SUBCATEGORY	PRODUCT_ SUBCATEGORY
DIM_PRODUCT_CATEGORY. ENGLISHPRODUCTCATEGORYNAME	PRODUCT_ CATEGORY	PRODUCT_ CATEGORY

Table 10.6 Column Mappings for ATBV_PRODUCT (Cont.)

12. On the left side of the attribute design window, click the SEMANTICS node located in the SCENARIO pane.

13. In the COLUMN pane, locate the PRODUCT_LINE column. In the HIDDEN PROPERTIES column, check the box to hide the column.

14. In the COLUMN pane, click the PRODUCT_KEY column. Using the TYPE column, set the PRODUCT_KEY to the type KEY ATTRIBUTE.

15. In the HIERARCHY pane, select the green plus sign to create a products hierarchy. Define the hierarchy using the options listed in Figure 10.7.

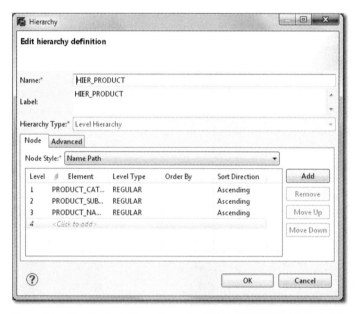

Figure 10.7 The Product Hierarchy in the ATBV_PRODUCT Attribute View

16. Define the properties for the product hierarchy. When defining each level of the hierarchy, use the green plus sign to add each level.

17. When this is complete, save and activate the attribute view by clicking the SAVE AND ACTIVATE button in the toolbar.

Defining the ATBV_ORDERED_DATE_HIER Attribute View

Next we'll outline the steps for creating the ATBV_ORDERED_DATE_HIER attribute view. This attribute view will be used to define the specific elements required for the ordered date hierarchy. While we could have used the ATBV_BASE_DATE attribute view to manage this hierarchy, in subsequent steps, we'll use the ATBV_BASE_DATE attribute view as the basis for creating a derived attribute. In our testing, we've found that hierarchies in a derived attribute aren't compatible with some of the SAP BusinessObjects BI tools. As a result, we've decided to develop dedicated ordered data attribute views to manage each data hierarchy. To do so, follow these steps:

1. Right-click the `commonattributes` subpackage and choose NEW • ATTRIBUTE VIEW.

2. Using Table 10.7 as a reference, define the properties for the attribute view.

Property	Value
NAME	ATBV_ORDERED_DATE_HIER
DESCRIPTION	The ordered date hierarchy.
PACKAGE	`saphana.commonattributes`
VIEW TYPE	ATTRIBUTE VIEW
COPY FROM	Unchecked
SUBTYPE	STANDARD

Table 10.7 Properties for the ATBV_ORDERED_DATE_HIER Attribute View

3. Using Table 10.8 as a guide, develop the attribute view.

Column Name	Attribute Name	Attribute Label
DIM_DATE.DATEKEY	ORDERED_DATEKEY	ORDERED_DATEKEY
DIM_DATE.CALENDARYEAR	ORDERED_YEAR	ORDERED_YEAR
DIM_DATE.CALENDARYEARMONTH	ORDERED_YEAR_MONTH	ORDERED_YEAR_MONTH

Table 10.8 Column Mappings for ATBV_ORDERED_DATE_HIER

Column Name	Attribute Name	Attribute Label
DIM_DATE. CALENDARQUARTERYEAR	ORDERED_YEAR_QUARTER	ORDERED_YEAR_QUARTER
DIM_DATE. CALENDARYEARWEEK	ORDERED_YEAR_WEEK	ORDERED_YEAR_WEEK

Table 10.8 Column Mappings for ATBV_ORDERED_DATE_HIER (Cont.)

4. In the Semantics node, configure the ORDERED_DATEKEY as a Hidden column.

5. In the Column pane, click the ORDERED_DATEKEY column. Using the Type column on the far left, set the ORDERED_DATEKEY to the type Key Attribute.

6. Using Figure 10.8 as a guide, develop the ORDERED_DATE_HIER hierarchy.

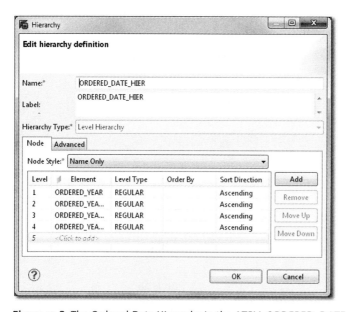

Figure 10.8 The Ordered Date Hierarchy in the ATBV_ORDERED_DATE_HIER Attribute View

7. When this is complete, save and activate the attribute view by clicking the Save and Activate button on the toolbar.

Defining the ATBV_CUSTOMER Attribute View
Follow these steps to create the ATBV_CUSTOMER attribute view:

1. Right-click the `commonattributes` subpackage and choose New • Attribute View.

2. Using Table 10.9 as a reference, define the properties for the attribute view.

Property	Value
NAME	ATBV_CUSTOMER
DESCRIPTION	The products attribute view.
PACKAGE	saphana.commonattributes
VIEW TYPE	ATTRIBUTE VIEW
COPY FROM	Unchecked
SUBTYPE	STANDARD

Table 10.9 Properties for the ATBV_CUSTOMER Attribute View

3. Click the DATA FOUNDATION node on the left side of the attribute view design window.

4. In the DETAILS pane, right-click the white space and choose ADD.

5. Using the provided SEARCH field, search for the tables listed below:
   ▶ DIM_CUSTOMER
   ▶ DIM_SALES_TERRITORY
   ▶ DIM_GEOGRAPHY

   Once these are found, add each table to the MATCHING ITEMS pane. Click OK to add the tables to the DETAILS pane.

6. In the DETAILS pane, join the three tables using the information listed in Table 10.10, which contains two distinct join configurations. To create each join, right-click the white space in the DETAILS pane and choose CREATE JOIN.

Join	Property	Option
JOIN 1	Left Table	DIM_GEOGRAPHY
	Left Column	GEOGRAPHYKEY
	Right Table	DIM_CUSTOMER
	Right Column	GEOGRAPHYKEY
	Join Cardinality	(1:N)
	Join Type	Referential

Table 10.10 Join Conditions for the ATBV_CUSTOMER Attribute View

Join	Property	Option
JOIN 2	Left Table	DIM_SALES_TERRITORY
	Left Column	SALESTERRITORYKEY
	Right Table	DIM_GEOGRAPHY
	Right Column	SALESTERRITORYKEY
	Join Cardinality	(1:N)
	Join Type	Referential

Table 10.10 Join Conditions for the ATBV_CUSTOMER Attribute View (Cont.)

7. Using Table 10.11 as a guide, develop the attribute view.

Column Name	Attribute Name	Attribute Label
DIM_CUSTOMER. ADDRESSLINE1	CUSTOMER_ ADDRESSLINE1	CUSTOMER_ ADDRESSLINE1
DIM_CUSTOMER. ADDRESSLINE2	CUSTOMER_ ADDRESSLINE2	CUSTOMER_ ADDRESSLINE2
DIM_CUSTOMER. BIRTHDATE	CUSTOMER_ BIRTHDATE	CUSTOMER_ BIRTHDATE
DIM_CUSTOMER. COMMUTEDISTANCE	CUSTOMER_ COMMUTEDISTANCE	CUSTOMER_ COMMUTEDISTANCE
DIM_CUSTOMER. CUSTOMERALTERNATEKEY	CUSTOMERALTERNATEKEY	CUSTOMERALTERNATEKEY
DIM_CUSTOMER. CUSTOMERKEY	CUSTOMER_ KEY	CUSTOMER_ KEY
DIM_CUSTOMER. DATEFIRSTPURCHASE	CUSTOMER_ DATEFIRSTPURCHASE	CUSTOMER_ DATEFIRSTPURCHASE
DIM_CUSTOMER. EMAILADDRESS	CUSTOMER_ EMAILADDRESS	CUSTOMER_ EMAILADDRESS
DIM_CUSTOMER. ENGLISHEDUCATION	CUSTOMER_ EDUCATION	CUSTOMER_ EDUCATION
DIM_CUSTOMER. FIRSTNAME	CUSTOMER_ FIRSTNAME	CUSTOMER_ FIRSTNAME
DIM_CUSTOMER. GENDER	CUSTOMER_ GENDER	CUSTOMER_ GENDER

Table 10.11 Column Mappings for ATBV_CUSTOMER

Column Name	Attribute Name	Attribute Label
DIM_CUSTOMER. HOUSEOWNERFLAG	CUSTOMER_ HOUSEOWNERFLAG	CUSTOMER_ HOUSEOWNERFLAG
DIM_CUSTOMER. LASTNAME	CUSTOMER_ LASTNAME	CUSTOMER_ LASTNAME
DIM_CUSTOMER. MARITALSTATUS	CUSTOMER_ MARITALSTATUS	CUSTOMER_ MARITALSTATUS
DIM_CUSTOMER. MIDDLENAME	CUSTOMER_ MIDDLENAME	CUSTOMER_ MIDDLENAME
DIM_CUSTOMER. NAMESTYLE	NAMESTYLE	NAMESTYLE
DIM_CUSTOMER. NUMBERCARSOWNED	CUSTOMER_ NUMBERCARSOWNED	CUSTOMER_ NUMBERCARSOWNED
DIM_CUSTOMER. NUMBERCHILDRENATHOME	CUSTOMER_ NUMCHILD_AT_HOME	CUSTOMER_ NUMCHILD_AT_HOME
DIM_CUSTOMER. PHONE	CUSTOMER_ PHONE	CUSTOMER_ PHONE
DIM_CUSTOMER. TITLE	CUSTOMER_ TITLE	CUSTOMER_ TITLE
DIM_CUSTOMER. TOTALCHILDREN	CUSTOMER_ TOTALCHILDREN	CUSTOMER_ TOTALCHILDREN
DIM_CUSTOMER. YEARLYINCOME	CUSTOMER_ YEARLYINCOME	CUSTOMER_ YEARLYINCOME
DIM_GEOGRAPHY.	CUSTOMER_ COUNTRY	CUSTOMER_ COUNTRY
DIM_GEOGRAPHY. CITY	CUSTOMER_ CITY	CUSTOMER_ CITY
DIM_GEOGRAPHY. POSTALCODE	CUSTOMER_ POSTALCODE	CUSTOMER_ POSTALCODE
DIM_GEOGRAPHY. STATEPROVINCECODE	CUSTOMER_ STATECODE	CUSTOMER_ STATECODE
DIM_GEOGRAPHY. STATEPROVINCENAME	CUSTOMER_ STATENAME	CUSTOMER_ STATENAME
DIM_SALES_TERRITORY. SALESTERRITORYCOUNTRY	CUSTOMER_ SALESTERRITORYCOUNTRY	CUSTOMER_ SALESTERRITORYCOUNTRY

Table 10.11 Column Mappings for ATBV_CUSTOMER (Cont.)

Column Name	Attribute Name	Attribute Label
DIM_SALES_TERRITORY. SALESTERRITORYGROUP	CUSTOMER_ SALESTERRITORYGROUP	CUSTOMER_ SALESTERRITORYGROUP
DIM_SALES_TERRITORY. SALESTERRITORYREGION	CUSTOMER_ SALESTERRITORYREGION	CUSTOMER_ SALESTERRITORYREGION

Table 10.11 Column Mappings for ATBV_CUSTOMER (Cont.)

8. In the SEMANTICS node, configure the NAMESTYLE as a HIDDEN column.

9. In the COLUMN pane, click the CUSTOMER_KEY column. Using the TYPE column on the far left, set the CUSTOMER_KEY to the type KEY ATTRIBUTE.

10. Define the CUSTOMER_FULL_NAME calculated column as a `varchar(250)` type using this formula:

```
"CUSTOMER_LASTNAME" + ', ' + "CUSTOMER_FIRSTNAME" + ' ' +
"CUSTOMER_MIDDLENAME"
```

11. Define the properties for the customer location hierarchy using Figure 10.9 as a reference.

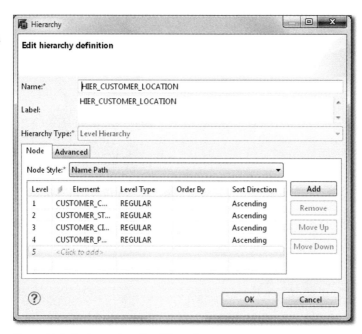

Figure 10.9 Customer Location Hierarchy

12. Define the properties for the product hierarchy using Figure 10.10 as a reference.

Figure 10.10 The Customer Sales Territory Hierarchy

13. When this is complete, save and activate the attribute view by clicking the SAVE AND ACTIVATE button on the toolbar.

Creating the Derived Attribute View DATBV_ORDERED_DATE

This section will outline the steps required to create a derived attribute view based on the ATBV_BASE_DATE attribute view.

1. Right-click the commonattributes subpackage, and choose NEW • ATTRIBUTE VIEW.

2. Using Table 10.12 as a reference, define the properties for the attribute view. When this is complete, click OK.

Property	Value
NAME	DATBV_ORDERED_DATE
DESCRIPTION	The derived ordered date attribute.

Table 10.12 Properties for the DATBV_ORDERED_DATE Derived Attribute View

Property	Value
PACKAGE	saphana.commonattributes
VIEW TYPE	ATTRIBUTE VIEW
COPY FROM	Unchecked
SUBTYPE	DERIVED
DERIVED FROM	Select the BROWSE button and search for "saphana.commonattributes.ATBV_BASE_DATE"

Table 10.12 Properties for the DATBV_ORDERED_DATE Derived Attribute View (Cont.)

3. No additional changes are required. With the derived attribute design window open, save and activate the derived attribute view by clicking the SAVE AND ACTIVATE button on the toolbar.

10.2.2 Creating Analytic Views

Now that you've developed and activated the required attribute views, you can begin the process of designing an analytic view. In the analytic view, you'll define the foundation table, join the foundation to attributes, and define measures to facilitate the aggregation of the results.

Designing the Data Foundation Node

Follow these steps to create an analytic view and define the DATA FOUNDATION node:

1. Right-click the internetsales subpackage and choose NEW • ANALYTIC VIEW.

2. Using Table 10.13 as a reference, define the properties for the attribute view.

Property	Value
NAME	AV_INTERNETSALES
DESCRIPTION	The Internet sales analytic view.
PACKAGE	saphana.commonattributes
VIEW TYPE	ANALYTIC VIEW
COPY FROM	Unchecked
SUBTYPE	N/A

Table 10.13 Properties for the ATBV_BASE_DATE Attribute View

3. Click the DATA FOUNDATION node located on the left side of the analytic view design window, as shown in Figure 10.11.

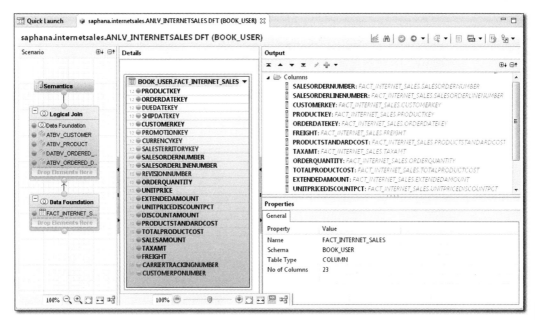

Figure 10.11 Analytic View Design Window

4. In the DETAILS pane, right-click the white space, and choose ADD.

5. Using the provided SEARCH field, enter "FACT_INTERNET_SALES". Once this is found, click the FACT_INTERNET_SALES object listed in the MATCHING ITEMS pane. Click OK to add the table to the DETAILS pane.

6. Highlight the following columns. To select multiple columns, hold down the ⌨Ctrl key and click each column:

   ▸ FACT_INTERNET_SALES.SALESORDERNUMBER

   ▸ FACT_INTERNET_SALES.SALESORDERLINENUMBER

   ▸ FACT_INTERNET_SALES.CUSTOMERKEY

   ▸ FACT_INTERNET_SALES.PRODUCTKEY

   ▸ FACT_INTERNET_SALES.ORDERDATEKEY

   ▸ FACT_INTERNET_SALES.FREIGHT

   ▸ FACT_INTERNET_SALES.PRODUCTSTANDARDCOST

- ▸ FACT_INTERNET_SALES.TAXAMT
- ▸ FACT_INTERNET_SALES.ORDERQUANTITY
- ▸ FACT_INTERNET_SALES.TOTALPRODUCTCOST
- ▸ FACT_INTERNET_SALES.EXTENDEDAMOUNT
- ▸ FACT_INTERNET_SALES.UNITPRICEDISCOUNTPCT
- ▸ FACT_INTERNET_SALES.DISCOUNTAMOUNT
- ▸ FACT_INTERNET_SALES.SALESAMOUNT
- ▸ FACT_INTERNET_SALES.UNITPRICE

7. Right-click the highlighted columns, and choose ADD TO OUTPUT.

Designing the Logic Joins

Follow these steps to define the logic joins between an analytic view and existing attribute views:

1. Click the LOGIC JOIN node located on the left side of the analytic view design window.

2. In the DETAILS pane, right-click the white space and choose ADD.

3. Using the provided SEARCH box, search for the following attribute views:
   - ▸ ATBV_CUSTOMER
   - ▸ ATBV_PRODUCT
   - ▸ ATBV_ORDERED_DATE_HIER
   - ▸ DATBV_ORDERED_DATE

   Click OK to add each attribute view to the LOGICAL JOIN pane.

4. Join each attribute view to the DATA FOUNDATION table by right-clicking the white space in the DETAILS pane and selecting CREATE JOIN.

5. Using Figure 10.12 as a reference, create the join between the DATA FOUNDATION table and the ATBV_CUSTOMER attribute view.

6. Using Figure 10.13 as a reference, create the join between the DATA FOUNDATION table and the ATBV_PRODUCT attribute view.

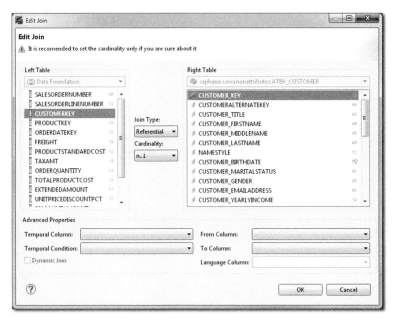

Figure 10.12 The Join between the Data Foundation Table and the Customer Attribute View

Figure 10.13 The Join between the Data Foundation Table and the Product Attribute View

7. Using Figure 10.14 as a reference, create the join between the DATA FOUNDA-TION table and the ATBV_ORDERED_DATE_HIER attribute view.

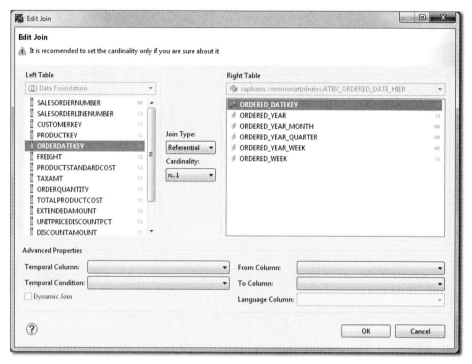

Figure 10.14 The Join between the Data Foundation Table and the Ordered Date Hierarchy Attribute View

8. Using Figure 10.15 as a reference, create the join between the DATA FOUNDA-TION table and the DATBV_ORDERED_DATE-derived attribute view.

9. Update the alias name for the columns in the derived attribute view ordered date. Because a derived attribute acts as an alias of an existing attribute view, it's recommended that each of the columns in a referenced derived attribute view be aliased as well.

10. In the LOGICAL JOIN node, locate the OUTPUT pane on the right-hand side. Expand the ATTRIBUTE VIEW • DATBV_ORDERED_DATE node.

11. Click each column in this node, and locate the PROPERTIES pane.

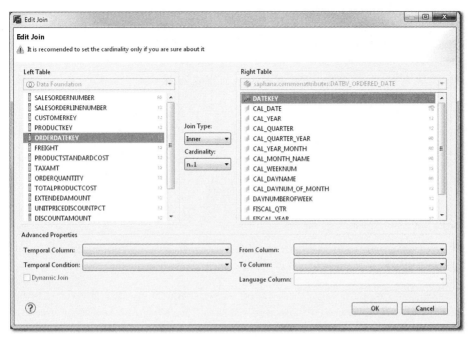

Figure 10.15 The Join between the Data Foundation Table and the Ordered Date–Derived Attribute View

12. In the PROPERTIES pane, locate the ALIAS NAME and ALIAS LABEL fields. Using Table 10.14 as a reference, update both alias fields with the same value.

Attribute View Column Name	Alias
DATEKEY	ORDERED_DATE_KEY
FULLDATEALTERNATEKEY	ORDERED_DATETIME
CALENDARYEAR	
CALENDARQUARTER	ORDERED_CAL_QTR
CALENDARQUARTERYEAR	
CALENDARYEARMONTH	
ENGLISHMONTHNAME	ORDERED_CAL_MONTH
WEEKNUMBEROFYEAR	ORDERED_CAL_WEEKNUM
ENGLISHDAYNAMEOFWEEK	ORDERED_CAL_DAYNAME

Table 10.14 The Alias Name and Alias Label Cross-Reference Table

Attribute View Column Name	Alias
DAYNUMBEROFMONTH	ORDERED_CAL_DOM
DAYNUMBEROFWEEK	ORDERED_CAL_DOM
FISCALQUARTER	ORDERED_FISCAL_QTR
FISCALYEAR	ORDERED_FISCAL_YEAR

Table 10.14 The Alias Name and Alias Label Cross-Reference Table (Cont.)

Note that for CALENDARYEAR, CALENDARQUARTERYEAR, and CALENDAR-YEARMONTH, the columns don't need an alias because they are hidden.

Designing the Semantics Node

In the SEMANTICS node, we'll finalize the configuration of the analytic view by defining attributes and measures. We'll also hide columns.

1. Click the SEMANTICS node located on the left side of the analytic view design window. Figure 10.16 contains an example of the window you should now see.

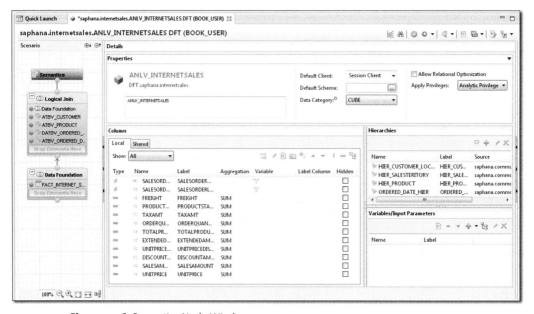

Figure 10.16 Semantics Node Window

2. Locate the COLUMNS pane just below the DETAILS pane.

3. Click the LOCAL tab in the COLUMN pane.

4. Configure the SALES ORDER NUMBER and SALES ORDER LINE NUMBER output columns as attributes. Using the Ctrl key, highlight both columns. In the COLUMNS pane, locate the ATTRIBUTE icon on the right-side header. Click the icon to convert the highlighted columns into attributes.

5. Configure the remaining columns as measures. Using the Ctrl key, highlight the remaining columns. In the COLUMNS pane, locate the MEASURE ICON on the right-side header. Click the icon to convert the highlighted columns into measures.

6. Click the SHARED tab in the COLUMN pane. This pane allows you to manage the columns returned from the connected attribute views.

7. Locate the NAMESTYLE, PRODUCTLINE, CAL YEAR, CAL QUARTER YEAR, and CAL YEAR MONTH columns. To the right of each column, locate the HIDDEN column. Place a checkmark in the provided box to hide these columns.

8. When complete, save and activate the analytic view by clicking the SAVE AND ACTIVATE button on the toolbar.

9. Preview the analytic view using the DATA PREVIEW (small magnifying glass image overlooking a table) icon located to the right of the SAVE AND ACTIVATE icon.

The analytic view and attribute views are now ready for consumption by the SAP BusinessObjects BI tools. In Part IV of the book, we'll examine how each SAP BusinessObjects BI tool connects; the analytic view will be the main connection point to the Internet sales data in SAP HANA. Users will be able to use this information view to analyze their Internet sales transactions by product, customer, and ordered date.

Let's consider another case study that better explains why you need calculation views to facilitate multidimensional analysis. In the next case study, we'll walk you through both the requirements and solution for solving a common query issue using a calculation view.

10.3 Case Study 2: Building Complex Calculations for Executive-Level Analysis

The Internet sales managers at AdventureWorks Cycle Company have been using the self-services BI solution powered by SAP HANA, SAP Data Services, SAP

Lumira, and SAP BusinessObjects Explorer for a few weeks. They have found it to be a perfect self-service solution for analyzing their Internet sales transactions without waiting for IT developers to create reports.

AdventureWorks Cycle Company sells directly to customers via its website and directly to resellers or local bike shops. In its technical landscape, it uses two different applications to manage these sales transactions: one system is hosted in the cloud and used to manage Internet sales, and the other system is based on a legacy ordering application that is hosted in the main office data center. The CEO needs to see the reseller sales transactions in the SAP HANA information view, as well as the Internet sales. He also has a requirement to view both sources in a single, comprehensive model. Having the transactions aggregated and combined into a single model will enable the CEO to analyze sales for the entire company.

The BI team at AdventureWorks Cycle Company has determined that they can incorporate the reseller sales information into their existing Internet sales SAP HANA landscape. Using SAP Data Services, they will add a new reseller sales fact table and update the existing dimension tables to include the relevant information for both Internet sales and reseller sales. In SAP HANA, they will build new attribute views, analytic views, and analytic privileges to support new analytic models. To directly address the requirements for the CEO, they will create a calculation view that intuitively combines the measures from the Internet sales analytic view and the reseller sales analytic view.

Based on these requirements, let's walk through the process of creating the calculation view to support the requirements of the CEO. We'll assume that the reseller sales analytic view and supporting attribute views have already been created by IT. This case study will focus predominantly on the process for creating the calculation view that combines both the Internet sales and reseller sales data. Again, please remember that the concepts of creating information views were discussed in detail in Chapter 9.

10.3.1 Creating the Package

> **Note**
>
> In Chapter 2, we provided instruction for creating the `corporatemetrics` subpackage. However, in the event that you need to create it again, please review the following instructions.

As with any information view, calculation views must also be stored in a package. We've decided to store the CEO's calculation view in a common package named `corporatemetrics`. This package will be used to store any future information views that manage information across different business lines. This decision is purely subjective, meaning that there are no technical requirements for organizing information views this way. The IT department has simply decided that this will be the best way to organize the information views.

Follow these steps to create the package:

1. Launch the SAP HANA Studio application.

2. Switch to the MODELER perspective. From the FILE menu bar, choose WINDOW • OPEN PERSPECTIVE • MODELER.

3. Right-click the `saphana` package and choose NEW • PACKAGE.

4. Using Figure 10.17 as a guide, enter the name "corporatemetrics" following the `saphana` package name. This creates a subpackage in the existing package.

5. Using Figure 10.17 as a guide, enter the remaining information. If your user account isn't BOOK_USER, choose the appropriate account as the owner of the package.

6. Click OK to save the package.

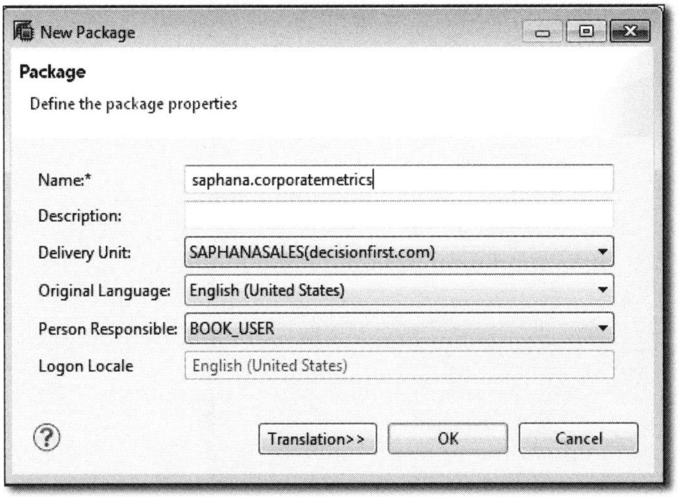

Figure 10.17 Creating the corporatemetrics Package

10.3.2 Creating the Calculation View

Now, let's create the calculation view. Because the process of combining the Internet sales and reseller sales is very basic, a graphical calculation view is sufficient to produce the desired results.

Follow these steps:

1. Launch the SAP HANA Studio application.

2. Switch to the MODELER perspective. From the FILE menu bar, choose WINDOW • OPEN PERSPECTIVE • MODELER.

3. Right-click the `saphana.corporatemetrics` package and choose NEW • CALCULATION VIEW.

4. Using Figure 10.18 as a guide, enter the calculation view name of "cv_corporate_product_sales". You're creating a new calculation view using the graphical view type.

5. Click FINISH because you'll define the remaining parts of the calculation view manually.

Figure 10.18 Creating the Calculation View

After clicking the FINISH button, you now see a blank calculation view design window like the one shown in Figure 10.19.

There are three main areas to focus on when designing a calculation view:

▶ **Palette pane (far left)**
The PALETTE pane, on the far left, contains transformations used in the design of the graphical calculation view. Just to the right of the PALETTE pane is the graphical design window. You use this area to choreograph and design data transformation workflows, which make up the core code of the calculation view.

▶ **Details pane (center)**
This pane contains the details of any object that is highlighted in the design area of the SCENARIO pane. You use this area to configure the selected transformation or design element.

▶ **Output columns (far right)**
This area allows you to configure the output of a selected aggregation or projection transformation.

▶ **Properties window (bottom far right)**
This area is present when an aggregation or projection transformation is selected. The PROPERTIES window content changes as different elements in the DETAILS or OUTPUT pane are selected.

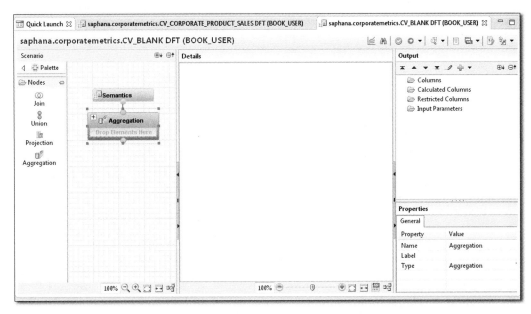

Figure 10.19 An Undefined or Blank Calculation View

10.3.3 Defining the Calculation View

We'll now walk through the processes of defining a graphical calculation view. At this point, you should have completed the case study in Section 10.2 and imported the AdventureWorks sample content discussed in the appendix. The ANLV_RESELLERSALES analytic view is assumed to already exist at this point.

Adding the ANLV_INTERNETSALES and ANLV_RESELLERSALES Analytic Views

Starting with your bank calculation view design window, add the ANLV_INTERNETSALES and ANLV_RESELLERSALES views to the SCENARIO pane design window by following these steps:

1. In the SAP HANA MODELER perspective, expand the NAVIGATOR window on the far-left side of Figure 10.20. Expand both the `internetsales` and `resellersales` packages to expose the ANLV_INTERNETSALES and ANLV_RESELLERSALES analytic views.

2. Drag and drop the ANLV_INTERNETSALES and ANLV_RESELLERSALES analytic views from the SYSTEMS view to the SCENARIO design window pane.

   As shown in Figure 10.20, you now have two analytic views located below the `aggregation` transform in the SCENARIO design window pane.

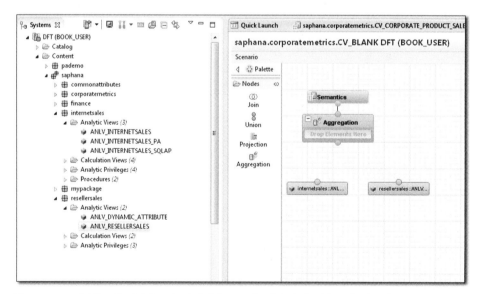

Figure 10.20 Adding the Existing Analytic View to the Calculation View Tools Palette

Projecting the Analytic Views

Using the transformations listed in the Palette window, drag two `Projection` transformations to the calculation view workflow. You then drag each analytic view to its own `Projection` transform (two analytic views means two `Projection` transforms) and select common columns from each analytic view. Follow these steps:

1. Drag a `Projection` transformation from the Palette window to the Scenario design area, as shown in Figure 10.21. This adds the `Projection` transformation to the Scenario design window pane. Add a second `projection` transformation to this same area.

2. Drag the ANLV_INTERNETSALES analytic view into the first projection transform and drop it in the area labeled Drop Elements Here.

3. Repeat this process for the ANLV_RESELLERSALES analytic view. Make sure that you place the ANLV_RESELLERSALES analytic view in the second `Projection` transformation, as shown in Figure 10.21.

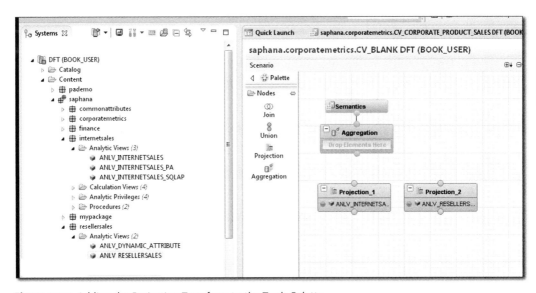

Figure 10.21 Adding the Projection Transform to the Tools Palette

4. Highlight the `Projection` transformation located above the ANLV_INTERNETSALES analytic view.

5. Right-click the `Projection` transformation and choose Rename. Rename the projection "PRJ_INTERNETSALES".

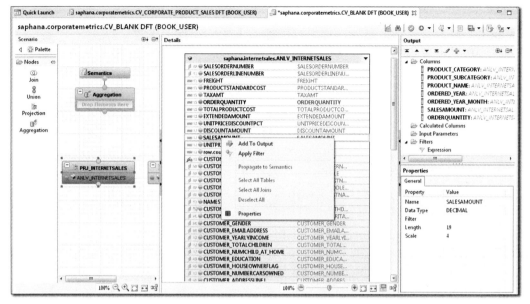

Figure 10.22 Adding Columns to the Output of the Projection Transform

6. Using the Details pane, as shown in the middle of Figure 10.22, right-click the below columns and choose Add to Output:

  ▸ PRODUCT_CATEGORY

  ▸ PRODUCT_SUBCATEGORY

  ▸ PRODUCT_NAME

  ▸ ORDERED_YEAR

  ▸ ORDERED_YEAR_MONTH

  ▸ SALESAMOUNT

  ▸ ORDEREDQUANTITY

7. Using Figure 10.23 as a guide, create a calculated column by right-clicking the Calculated Column folder in the Output pane and choosing New.

8. Using Figure 10.24 as a guide, create a calculated column named Source. This column will be used in the final model to identify the source of the data. The formula is a string literal. Enter "'INTERNET'", as shown in the Expression Editor area of the screen.

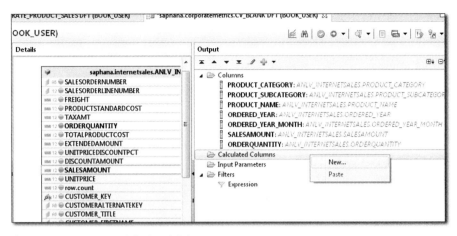

Figure 10.23 Creating a Calculated Column

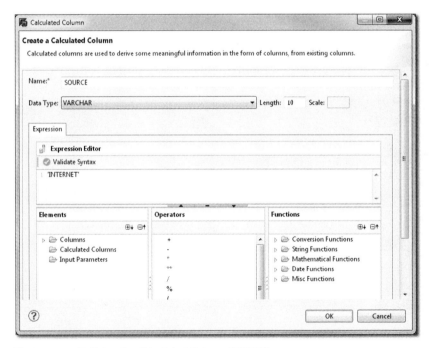

Figure 10.24 Defining the Calculated Column SOURCE

9. Highlight the `Projection` transformation containing the ANLV_RESELLER-SALES analytic view.

10. Right-click the `Projection` transformation and choose RENAME. Rename the projection "PRJ_RESELLERSALES".

11. Using the DETAILS pane, right-click the below columns and choose ADD TO OUTPUT:

- ▶ PRODUCT_CATEGORY
- ▶ PRODUCT_SUBCATEGORY
- ▶ PRODUCT_NAME
- ▶ ORDERED_YEAR
- ▶ ORDERED_YEAR_MONTH
- ▶ SALESAMOUNT
- ▶ ORDEREDQUANTITY

12. To create a calculated column, right-click the CALCULATED COLUMN folder, located in the OUTPUT pane, and choose NEW.

13. Using Figure 10.25 as a guide, create a calculated column named SOURCE.

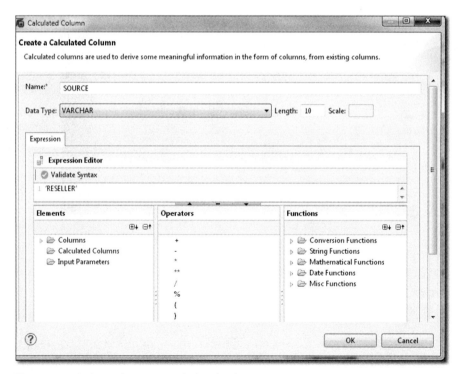

Figure 10.25 Defining the Source Calculated Column

This column will be used in the final model to identify the source of the data. The formula used in the EXPRESSION EDITOR is a string literal. Enter "'RESELLER'" surrounded by single quotes.

Combining the Results with a Union

Now that you've selected or projected the appropriate columns from each analytic view, you must combine their results into a single logical data set using a union transformation. Follow these steps:

1. Using Figure 10.26 as a guide, drag the Union transformation from the PALETTE pane to the SCENARIO design area.

2. Place the Union transformation above the PRJ_INTERNETSALES and PRJ_RESELLERSALES projections.

3. Using the drag-and-drop method, join PRJ_INTERNETSALES and PRJ_RESEL-LER-SALES to the Union transformation. Drag the circle from the top of each Projection transform to the circle at the bottom of the Union transform.

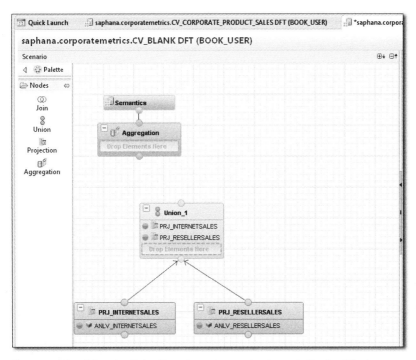

Figure 10.26 Adding the Union Transformation to the Scenario Design Window

4. After the objects are joined, highlight the `Union` transform named UNION_1, right-click, and choose RENAME. Change the name to UNION.

5. With the UNION object highlighted, notice that the DETAILS pane contains two SOURCE items on the left side. On the right-hand side of Figure 10.27, there is a TARGET pane, where you'll map the columns from each source.

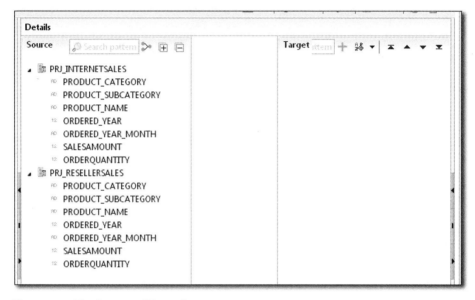

Figure 10.27 The Source and Target Panes

6. There are two options for mapping the columns.

   ▶ You can manually drag and drop the columns from the PRJ_INTERNET-SALES source and place them in the TARGET pane. Then, using drag and drop again, you can map the same column from PRJ_RESELLERSALES to its equivalent output column in the TARGET pane. Make sure to drop the source column over the existing TARGET column to properly complete the mapping. A line appears, depicting a connection between each merged column.

   ▶ You can allow the union design window to guess based on the column names from each source. Locate the AUTO MAP BY NAME icon on the top-right side of the source pane search box. This generates an output similar to what is depicted in Figure 10.28.

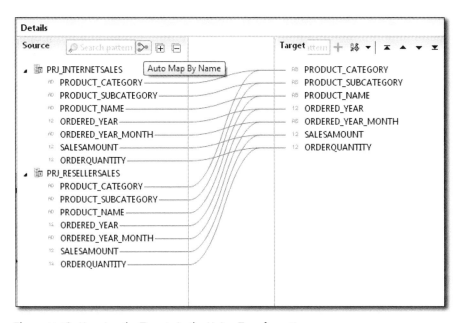

Figure 10.28 Mapping the Targets in the Union Transformation

Aggregating the Results of the Union

Now that you've combined the projections of each analytic view, you need to aggregate the results of UNION to produce a summary of sales by product and ordered year. The aggregation will effectively transform the results to appear as a single, combined source. Follow these steps:

1. Using Figure 10.29 as a guide, join the `Union` transform to the existing `Aggregation` transformation.

2. Drag the circle, located at the top of the `Union` transform, to the circle located at the bottom of the `Aggregation` transform.

3. With the `Aggregation` transform highlighted, notice that the DETAILS pane contains the output of the `Union` transform. See Figure 10.29 for an example.

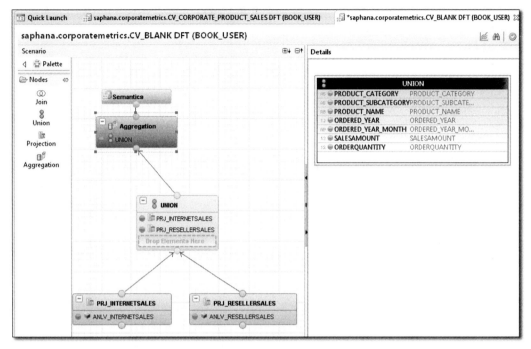

Figure 10.29 Adding the Aggregation Transformation to the Tools Palette

4. Right-click the columns listed below and choose ADD TO OUTPUT. The columns defined as output only will be used as the GROUP BY columns in the aggregation engine:

  ▶ SOURCE

  ▶ PRODUCT_CATEGORY

  ▶ PRODUCT_SUBCATEGORY

  ▶ PRODUCT_NAME

  ▶ ORDERED_YEAR

  ▶ ORDERED_YEAR_MONTH

5. Right-click the SALESAMOUNT and ORDEREDQUANTITY columns and choose ADD AS AGGREGATED COLUMN. These columns will be summarized based on the output columns listed in the table.

Once this is complete, the Output pane should look similar to the screen shown in Figure 10.30.

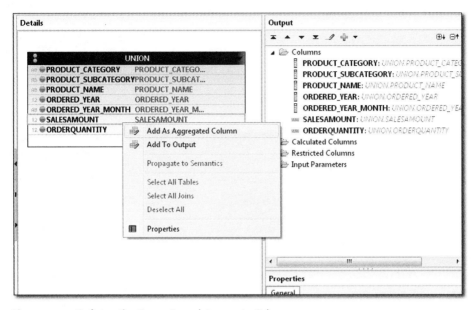

Figure 10.30 Defining the Group By and Aggregate Columns

Defining the Final Output of the Calculation View

In the final phase of the calculation view development process, you'll finalize the output within the Semantics transform. In the Semantics transform, you'll define attributes, measures, hierarchies, counters, calculated columns, calculated measures, variables, and input parameters. Follow these steps:

1. The Semantics transform should already be joined to the Aggregation transform based on the type of calculation view we selected during the first few steps.

2. Using Figure 10.31 as a guide, select the Semantics transformation found in the Scenario design area. Once this is selected, a new series of windows appears within the Details pane. Notice the Column, Hierarchies, Variables/Input Parameters, and Properties windows.

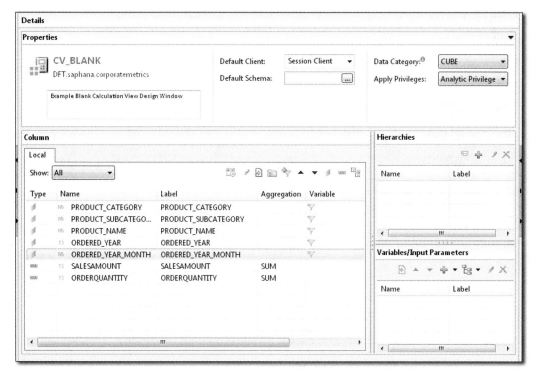

Figure 10.31 Defining the Final Output of the Calculation View

3. In the Column window, make sure that the below columns are configured as attributes:

   ▸ SOURCE

   ▸ PRODUCT_CATEGORY

   ▸ PRODUCT_SUBCATEGORY

   ▸ PRODUCT_NAME

   ▸ ORDERED_YEAR

   ▸ ORDERED_YEAR_MONTH

   Click within the cell located in the Type column. A dropdown menu appears. Change the column type to Attribute. The Attribute type is prefixed with the blue icon.

4. Repeat the above process for the two measures SALESAMOUNT and ORDERE-DQUANTITY. Because we defined them as measures within the `Aggregation` transform, they are most likely already configured as measures. If they are not, click the TYPE cell and choose MEASURE.

5. In the HIERARCHIES window, click the green plus sign to create a new level hierarchy.

6. Using Figure 10.32 as a guide, define the products hierarchy. To add levels to a hierarchy, click the green plus sign icon to add each level. Use the MOVE UP and MOVE DOWN buttons to arrange the order of the levels.

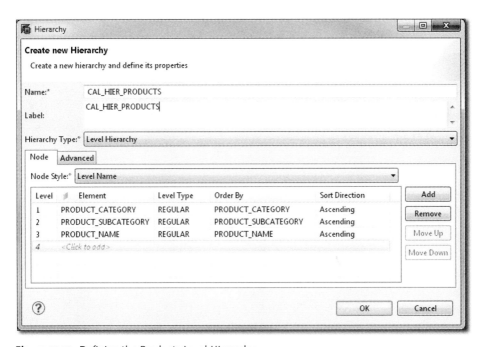

Figure 10.32 Defining the Products Level Hierarchy

7. Using Figure 10.33 as a guide, define the ordered date hierarchy.

8. Once completed, your output columns and hierarchies should be configured similarly to what is depicted in Figure 10.34.

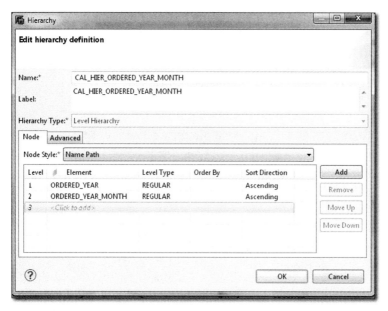

Figure 10.33 Defining the Ordered Date Hierarchy

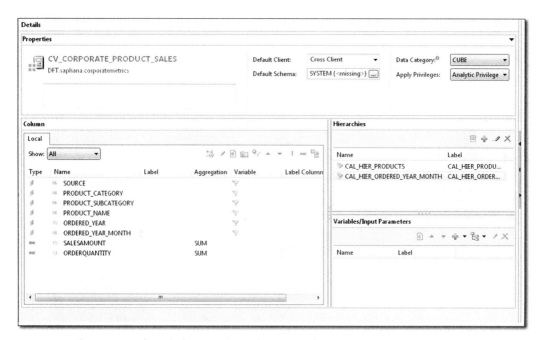

Figure 10.34 The Calculation View Final Output Columns

9. When this is complete, save and activate the calculation view by clicking the green SAVE AND ACTIVATE button on the toolbar.

10. Preview the calculation view using the DATA PREVIEW icon (small magnifying glass image overlooking a table) located to the right of the SAVE AND ACTIVATE icon.

The calculation view should now be available for consumption by the SAP BusinessObjects BI tools. Because the view was able to combine the Internet sales and reseller sales transactions by product and date, the CEO now has the means to produce a comprehensive metric. In addition, because the calculation view uses highly optimized SQLScript functions to combine the results, the view makes the most use of the SAP HANA appliance hardware.

10.4 Summary

To truly assign value to data, that data must be structured and organized in a way that is intuitive and easy to understand. As you've seen in this chapter, you can transform complex data into intuitive data using the modeling components in SAP HANA. In terms of performance and manageability, we discussed the differences between the processing of normalized and denormalized data in the SAP HANA system. We explored the differences between physically denormalizing the data using SAP Data Services and logically denormalizing the data using the SAP HANA information view tools and components. Finally, we concluded with two detailed case studies that showed SAP HANA multidimensional modeling in practice.

Ensuring proper data security in a complex environment is one of the key factors for a successful analytics solution.

11 Securing Data in SAP HANA

In almost every organization, it is a given that users require their data access to be filtered by a set of business rules that ensure that each user has access to only the data that is appropriate for their role in the organization. Often, these rules for restricting data carry the force of law in the form of Sarbanes-Oxley or HIPAA compliance. Ensuring the proper enforcement of these rules is an absolute requirement for a working analytics platform.

In most analytics applications on the market today, the enforcement of this form of security is left up to the reporting and analytics platform that sits on top of a dumb database. This does not mean that other database platforms don't offer options to enforce data security in the database, but these options are seldom used, due to unfamiliarity, complexity, or lack of support from analytics tool vendors.

In contrast, SAP HANA makes data security in the database a first-class citizen, putting the database front and center in your data security strategy. In addition, SAP BusinessObjects BI has tight integration with SAP HANA, allowing it to take full advantage of the data security enforcement that SAP HANA offers. This combination ensures a single place to define business rules that affect data security and guarantees that the data is always secure, no matter how it is accessed.

This philosophical approach to data security follows from the broader SAP strategy of using SAP HANA as more than just a database, but as a complete application development platform. Thus, SAP HANA collapses the formerly complex stack of interacting applications down to a single, central hub that provides all the necessary functionality for a complete data solution.

In this chapter, we will cover an overview of the tools used in the SAP HANA database to enforce data security (Section 11.1), and then review in detail the methods for creating and managing analytic privileges (Section 11.2). We will follow this with a discussion of the interaction of analytics privileges on information models (Section 11.3), and finally, we will wrap up this chapter with a specific case study applying analytic privileges to models that you created in the previous chapters on analytic modeling (Section 11.4).

11.1 Introduction to Analytic Privileges

We first mentioned analytic privileges in Chapter 2. In this section, we will go deeper into the concepts of analytic privileges and how they help us implement data security in SAP HANA. We will start with a general overview of what analytic privileges are and how they affect security, cover the different types of analytic privileges that exist (repository vs. SQL-based), and introduce you to the concepts of dynamic vs. static value restrictions.

11.1.1 What are Analytic Privileges?

As we introduced in Chapter 2, analytic privileges are a type of object created by developers that expresses a business rule restricting data returned by an information model. They are not themselves information models. They don't define relationships between tables, nor do they define calculated fields or values. Their sole purpose is to define which information models a user or role can access and which rows of data from an information model those users or roles can access.

One of the key points in that definition is, "data returned by an information model." Analytic privileges cannot be used to restrict a user's access to data stored in base tables or catalog views in a schema. This fact leads to the conclusion that all data access in SAP HANA should be mediated by information models if you wish to enforce data security in the SAP HANA platform and not at an application tier sitting on top of SAP HANA.

Because analytic privileges are assigned to either users or roles in the system, it is crucial that all user access to data in SAP HANA be done with a unique, authenticated user account that maps to a real-world person and not a generic account that is shared among many users. This is one of the key elements to achieving data security in SAP HANA. We talked at length about the importance of user provisioning in Chapter 2 for just this reason.

Another key aspect of analytic privileges in SAP HANA is that they are not optional. A user cannot access data from an information model at all unless they have at least one analytic privilege that references that information model. This is in addition to the requirement that the user have a SELECT privilege on the runtime version (column view) of the information model stored in the _SYS_BIC schema.

Each analytic privilege has the option to define restrictions on the columns of its referenced information models. These restrictions determine which rows of data are returned to a user who has been granted the analytic privilege in question. For example, if an analytic privilege defined a restriction on a sales territory that required only Western region data to be returned, then the users granted this analytic privilege would see only data about the Western region. Restrictions can be placed on multiple columns, in which case users will receive only data for which all restrictions are satisfied. Restrictions can also be omitted completely, in which case a user receives all data.

So far, we've been talking about the properties common to all analytic privileges. However, there are multiple ways to create analytic privileges, and those different approaches have properties that are distinct to each. In the next section, we will introduce you to these different types of analytic privileges.

11.1.2 Types of Analytic Privileges

There are two types of analytic privileges currently available in SAP HANA. The original analytic privilege, which we will refer to as a *traditional* analytic privilege, was introduced with the earliest editions of SAP HANA. A new kind was introduced with more recent service packs, which we will refer to as *SQL-based* analytic privileges.

These two types are predominately distinguished by how they are created. Traditional analytic privileges are created as modeled repository objects using a graphical user interface (GUI) that can be accessed from either the SAP HANA Studio Modeler perspective or the new SAP HANA Development perspective. SQL-based analytic privileges, as their name implies, are created using SQL CREATE statements.

These different approaches have a significant effect on the life cycle of the created analytic privileges. Traditional analytic privileges, being repository objects, are owned and managed by the _SYS_REPO user like all repository content. This means they can be transported between SAP HANA landscapes as part of a delivery unit and tested and transported as a unit, along with the information models they refer to. In contrast, SQL-based analytic privileges, being created with SQL statements, are owned by the user who executes the SQL statement that creates them and can therefore be granted to users or roles only by the same user who created them. This makes the transport and management of SQL-based privileges between environments significantly more complex.

Despite the added complexity that SQL-based analytic privileges have, they still have a useful place in the SAP HANA landscape. Specifically, it's much easier to automate the creation of the privileges from an outside source if they can be managed with simple SQL statements. Also, as we'll see later when we look at the steps for creating privileges, SQL-based privileges have more flexible options for defining data restrictions than traditional analytic privileges.

This new type of analytic privilege is clearly aimed at the dedicated application on top of an SAP HANA scenario, i.e., SAP BW or SAP Business Suite on SAP HANA, and it is in SAP BW that we see the first usage of this new type of analytic privilege. In SAP BW 7.4 SP5+ on SAP HANA, a new security synchronization feature was added that allows SAP BW to push down its security model to SAP HANA so that users can query information models that are generated by SAP BW directly, yet maintain an equivalent security structure. SAP BW achieves this by creating SQL-based analytic privileges for you.

It will be interesting to see how these SQL-based analytic privileges evolve over the next several SAP HANA releases. Perhaps they will gain better support for transport and management across landscapes. For now, though, most scenarios outside of SAP BW utilize the traditional analytic privilege because of its better manageability.

In addition to the two types of analytic privilege, there are generally two approaches to defining the restricted values for attributes in an analytic privilege. In the next section, we'll review these approaches and when they are likely to be used.

11.1.3 Dynamic vs. Static Value Restrictions

Defining which values should be restricted in an information model is the core purpose of an analytic privilege. For both traditional and SQL-based analytic privileges, these restrictions come in two forms: either static or dynamic.

When we say *static restrictions*, what we mean is that the restricted value defined at the time of the creation of the analytic privilege stays fixed for the life of that privilege. When you grant an analytic privilege to a user or role that has static value restrictions, you know exactly which values you are granting that user access to. Static privileges are the easiest to define, but they are not necessarily the easiest to manage in the long term.

If there are many distinct, valid values for a restricted column or unique combinations of values when multiple columns are being restricted, then the number of analytic privileges you need to create increases drastically. This can make keeping track of or updating this many objects a significant maintenance headache for the security team.

For example, if you want to secure sales data to the individual sales person responsible for a transaction and you have 1,000 sales people, then you likely need a unique analytic privilege for every sales person, leading to the maintenance of a 1,000 objects. This is not a tenable situation.

It is for exactly this type of scenario that the option to define dynamic restriction values was added. With dynamic restrictions, the restricted value is not set at the time the analytic privilege is created. Instead, the designer expresses a rule about where the restricted values for a given user can be found. Then, when a user goes to actually retrieve data, the rule is applied, and the specific restriction values for that user are retrieved and applied. This means that, when dynamic restrictions are used, you can typically have just a few analytic privileges defined, and the bulk of the configuration about which users is assigned to which values is externalized.

This, of course, means that the configuration of the analytic privilege with dynamic restrictions is quite a bit more complex at the start because you need some external mechanism to store the user-to-data relationship. This is typically achieved with one or more tables dedicated to just that purpose. The upside to this approach is that it is typically much easier to manage the relationship between user and data as an entity in a table than as a native object like an analytic privilege. Data in tables can be exposed to applications and be distributed to the business for maintenance. It can also be loaded into SAP HANA from external systems where this relationship may already exist, removing the need for dual maintenance of business rules.

Therefore, in all but the simplest use cases, you will typically find yourself gravitating toward the analytic privilege with dynamic restrictions.

In the next sections, we'll cover the specific steps used to create each of the types of analytic privileges, as well as both static and dynamic restriction scenarios for each.

11.2 Creating Analytic Privileges

In this section, we will cover the specific steps required to create an analytic privilege for each of the two types. We will start with the traditional analytic privileges created with the MODELER perspective (Section 11.2.1) with both static and dynamic restrictions applied. We will follow that with a section on creating SQL-based analytic privileges (Section 11.2.2), again with both static and dynamic restriction values.

Because analytic privileges are constructed in reference to information models, you must first create at least one information model. We will be using some of the same information models we created in the previous chapters on multidimensional modeling as the basis for our example analytic privileges here.

11.2.1 Traditional Analytic Privileges

To start the process of creating a traditional analytic privilege, you need to be in either the SAP HANA MODELER perspective or the SAP HANA DEVELOPMENT perspective. You can create traditional analytic privileges either directly in the repository using the SYSTEMS view or as part of a project in the PROJECT EXPLORER view, and then commit them to the repository for activation. Because the specific steps for creating the privilege remain the same regardless of which view you use, we will present the steps from the SYSTEMS view.

In the SYSTEMS view, you expand the CONTENT folder to view the packages, and right-click the package in which you wish to create the analytic privilege. From the right-click menu, you choose NEW • ANALYTIC PRIVILEGE. This launches a wizard allowing you to define a new analytic privilege. Figure 11.1 shows an example of what the NEW ANALYTIC PRIVILEGE screen looks like.

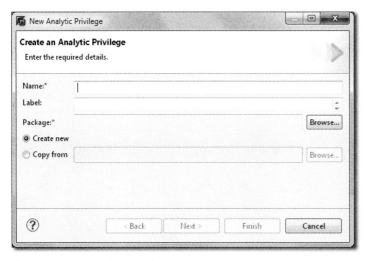

Figure 11.1 New Analytic Privilege

Table 11.1 outlines the five options that can be configured or selected in this wizard.

Property	Description
NAME	The name of the analytic privilege.
	This is a required property that cannot be changed after the analytic privilege is saved and activated. It's important to establish a standard analytic privilege naming convention before you start a development project in SAP HANA. Only the alphabet characters *Aa–Zz*, numbers 0–9, and underscore (_) are allowed in the name.
LABEL	The label or description of the analytic privilege.
	This property can contain a free-text description of the analytic privilege and should be used to add additional metadata to the analytic privilege or a thorough description that other developers can use to identify the purpose of the analytic privilege.
PACKAGE	The package that the analytic privilege will be assigned to.
	Only nonstructural packages can be used as the parent object for an analytic privilege. If you selected a package at the start, this is automatically populated, but you have the option to change it here.
CREATE NEW	Choose the CREATE NEW option when you're developing a new analytic privilege to define the analytic privilege from scratch.

Table 11.1 Options to Configure When Creating an Analytic Privilege

Property	Description
COPY FROM	Choose the COPY FROM option when you need to create a new analytic privilege that is a copy of an existing analytic privilege. Click the BROWSE button to select an existing analytic privilege. All content from the source analytic privilege is copied into the new analytic privilege.

Table 11.1 Options to Configure When Creating an Analytic Privilege (Cont.)

Naming Conventions
It's a good practice to have a common naming convention for all object types. This way, they are easily identifiable in the repository view. For analytic privileges, we typically use a prefix of AP_ in the name, followed by the subject area—like sales—and ending with a summary of the rules applied, i.e., AP_INTERNETSALES_SE for an analytic privilege that grants access to Internet sales data for the Southeast sales region.

For now, we will use the CREATE NEW option so that we can see what it looks like to create an analytic privilege from scratch. When you click FINISH on the NEW ANALYTIC PRIVILEGE screen, your analytic privilege is created, and a new ANALYTIC PRIVILEGE EDITOR window opens. This window is broken down into several different sections; you can see its initial state in Figure 11.2. In Table 11.2, we'll review the attributes and purpose of each section.

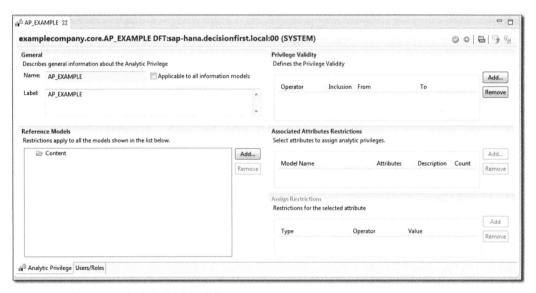

Figure 11.2 Analytic Privilege Editor

Section	Description
GENERAL	This section contains the analytic privilege name and description that you set in the NEW ANALYTIC PRIVILEGE screen. You can change the description but not the name of the privilege here. In addition to these general properties is a checkbox labeled APPLICABLE TO ALL INFORMATION MODELS. Activating this checkbox causes the analytic privilege to grant access to all information models, regardless of the models selected in the REFERENCE MODELS section. This is essentially never used, except by the system-provided _SYS_BI_CP_ALL analytic privilege which allows developers access to all information models.
PRIVILEGE VALIDITY	In this section, you have the option of defining a privilege validity date range. This limits the period of time during which the privilege has an effect on the system. In theory, you could use this to promote a changed privilege to production but have it take effect at some future date. Date ranges can be defined by the following operators combined with FROM and TO dates: ▶ Equal (=) ▶ Between (<>) ▶ GreaterThan (>) ▶ GreaterEqual (>=) ▶ LessThan (<) ▶ LessEqual (<=)
REFERENCE MODELS	The REFERENCE MODELS section is where you select the set of information models that this analytic privilege will grant access to. Models not referenced here are not affected by this analytic privilege. An analytic privilege serves no purpose unless it applies to at least one information model. You can choose any combination of attribute, analytic, or calculation views as the reference models for an analytic privilege. A privilege does not have to apply to just one model. Instead, you can combine multiple models in one analytic privilege and define any shared restrictions at the same time. We'll discuss later the detailed interactions of multiple information views in a single analytic privilege. Using the ADD and REMOVE buttons to the right of the REFERENCE MODEL pane, you can associate one or more information views to the analytic privilege.

Table 11.2 Analytic Privilege Editor Window Sections

Section	Description
	A user who is granted this analytic privilege is able to access data from all the referenced information models. If no attribute restrictions are defined, the user has access to all data in the models. Otherwise, the user has access to data limited by the attribute restrictions.
	If users or roles have multiple analytic privileges defined for the same information view, the least restrictive option takes precedence. Analytic privileges are combined using an OR operator, meaning either can be true.
ASSOCIATED ATTRIBUTE RESTRICTIONS	In this section, you have the option of defining which attributes in an information model determine the visible rows of data for a user.
	Using the ADD and REMOVE buttons located on the right of the ASSOCIATED ATTRIBUTE RESTRICTIONS pane, you can select one or more attributes or columns based on the information views that were defined in the REFERENCE MODELS pane.
	When you assign multiple attributes or columns, the combined restrictions use an AND operator internally to restrict the information view. This implies that all defined attribute or column restrictions conditions must be true.
	This is an optional setting. If no attributes or columns are specified in this section, the analytic privilege grants full access to the associated information views.
ASSIGN RESTRICTIONS	If you define an associated attribute restriction on an information model, you must then define the set of values that can be retrieved by users who are granted this analytic privilege. This can be done as either a static list of values or a dynamic list of values. There is a separate set of restricted values for each associate attribute restriction.
	Using the ADD and REMOVE buttons to the right of the assign restrictions pane, you can define one or more restrictions for the column that is highlighted in the ASSOCIATED ATTRIBUTE RESTRICTIONS pane.
	When you assign multiple restrictions to the same attribute or column, the restrictions use an OR operator internally to filter the attributes or columns. This implies that each individually defined restriction can be true without affecting the others. To define a restriction, you must select each attribute or column individually in the associated attribute restrictions pane and subsequently define its restrictions.

Table 11.2 Analytic Privilege Editor Window Sections (Cont.)

Section	Description
	The TYPE property for the restriction determines whether the values are provided statically at design time (FIXED) or dynamically at run time. Dynamic values are provided by way of a stored procedure that returns the proper values for the user. The procedures can be defined as CATALOG PROCEDURES in a schema or as REPOSITORY PROCEDURES. The OPERATOR property determines how the values are interpreted; you have the following options: ▸ Equal (=) ▸ Between (<>) ▸ GreaterThan (>) ▸ GreaterEqual (>=) ▸ LessThan (<) ▸ LessEqual (<=) ▸ Contains Pattern (like) ▸ Is Null ▸ Is Not Null If you select FIXED values, a list of values pane can be invoked in the VALUE column, allowing you to select or search from all values associated with the attribute. If you select CATALOG PROCEDURE or REPOSITORY PROCEDURE, the VALUE column provides a selector for an existing procedure in the system.

Table 11.2 Analytic Privilege Editor Window Sections (Cont.)

With the basics of creating analytic privileges out of the way, let's dive into a discussion of how to build analytic privileges with both static and dynamic value restrictions.

Building Analytic Privileges with Static Value Restrictions

Using static values is a relatively straightforward process and can be summarized with the following steps:

1. Create the analytic privilege in the NEW ANALYTIC PRIVILEGE screen, giving it a name and description.

2. Select one or more information models that will be affected by the privilege in the REFERENCED MODELS section of the ANALYTIC PRIVILEGE EDITOR.

3. Optionally, define a limited date range during which the privilege will take effect.

4. Optionally, define one or more attributes of the information model that will be restricted in the ASSOCIATED ATTRIBUTE RESTRICTIONS section.

5. Select a set of values that users will be limited to in the ASSIGN RESTRICTIONS section.

Creating an analytic privilege with dynamic value restrictions is a somewhat more complex process. The analytic privilege itself is not that different; the steps are nearly identical to the above summary. The only thing that changes is the last step, whereby you select the values to restrict the user to. Instead of picking an explicit list of values, you must instead pick a named, stored procedure from the system. That is easy enough from the NEW ANALYTIC PRIVILEGE screen, but where does the stored procedure come from? The answer to that question is that you have to build it, and there are some specific requirements that the stored procedure must live up to. We'll review in detail the process for creating a stored procedure for this purpose in the following section.

Building Analytic Privileges with Dynamic Value Restrictions

Dynamic analytic privilege values come to our rescue when the complexity of the security model makes setting up static restrictions impractical. This happens in a great number of cases because simply combining restrictions on two separate attributes where each attribute has five distinct values would result in 25 unique analytic privileges to satisfy all combinations, assuming all combinations are valid and not worrying about users who have unrestricted access. Adding one more restricted attributes with five more distinct values would turn 25 into 125.

With dynamic restrictions, we don't have to hard code the values for the restrictions into the analytic privilege. Instead, restricted values for an attribute are retrieved at runtime on a per-user basis. This does require that we have a data structure that stores the relationship between a user and their restricted values in our SAP HANA database, but maintaining that type of data structure is typically much easier than managing many analytic privileges. With this type of scenario, instead of 25 or 125 unique analytic privileges, we are likely to have just one.

Expressing the relationship between a user and their restricted values to the analytic privilege is done by creating an SAP HANA stored procedure that returns the restricted values for the current user. We can achieve this dynamically by using a system variable SESSION_USER inside our stored procedure, which allows us to determine which user we are retrieving values for.

The output of the stored procedure is defined by the operator we wish to use it with. In most scenarios, this is the IN operator, which expects us to return a list of values the current user is allowed to access for the restricted attribute. Other operators, like Equal or GreaterThan, expect to retrieve a single output parameter that defines the comparison value. The Between operator requires the procedure to return two output parameters, and the Is Null and Is Not Null operators are not supported with dynamic restriction values because their values are implied by the operators. The data types of all returned output parameters, regardless of operator, must match the data type of the attribute we are restricting.

There are some additional restrictions that the procedure must also adhere to. First, it cannot accept any input parameters as it is being executed behind the scenes by the system. Second, the procedure must execute with elevated privileges so that it can access all values for all possible users. You do this by setting the procedure to execute with DEFINERS RIGHTS. It's up to the procedure author to make use of the SESSION_USER variable to ensure that only data for the current user is returned. Finally, the procedure must be free of side effects. This is achieved by marking the procedure as Read-Only.

This concept can best be explained with an example. For this, we will use one of the models we created in the previous chapters, ANLV_INTERNETSALES. Let's assume we need to have user's data restricted by product category. Let's also assume that we are managing the relationship between users and products in a table named PRODUCT_CATEGORY_SECURITY. The table has two columns, USER_NAME and PRODUCT_CATEGORY. Users should be able to access data for only the product categories for which they have a record in the table. The logic for the stored procedure that retrieves the list of valid product categories for a user might look like the following:

```
SELECT PRODUCT_CATEGORY
FROM PRODUCT_CATEGORY_SECURITY
WHERE USER_NAME = SESSION_USER
```

The trick then is to get this logic into a stored procedure that conforms to the requirements we discussed above. To do that, we will need to construct a new procedure. The first decision, then, is what type of procedure to create: catalog or repository. This is an easy question to answer because repository procedures are really the only good choice. The benefits of repository object management and transportability with delivery units, as well as the lack of any offsetting benefit to catalog procedures, makes repository procedures the de facto choice.

There are two ways to build a repository stored procedure. You can start from the SYSTEMS view in the content area or create them in a project in the PROJECT EXPLORER. For the time being, there are some differences between the editors you are presented with when creating procedures in the SYSTEMS view vs. the PROJECT EXPLORER view. The SYSTEMS view editor is, in our opinion, somewhat easier to use, so we recommend that approach for now. We expect SAP to further harmonize these editors over time. So, this recommendation could change in the future.

To start the process, right-click a specific package and select NEW • PROCEDURE. You are presented with the NEW SQL PROCEDURE screen. In Figure 11.3, you can see an example of the NEW PROCEDURE window. In Table 11.3, we'll review the options you have to make from this window.

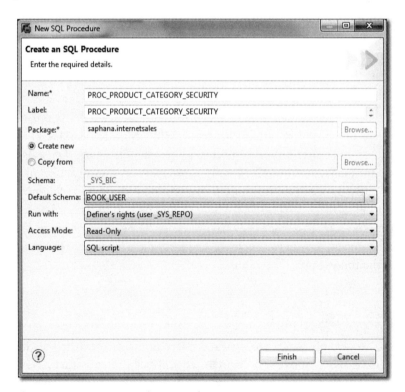

Figure 11.3 New SQL Procedure Wizard

Property	Description
NAME	Procedures should have unique names given to them. This is the unique identifier of the procedure you will later select when applying it to an analytic privilege.
	Following from our example scenario, we have named this procedure `PROC_PRODUCT_CATEGORY_SECURITY`.
LABEL	In the LABEL field, you have the option of giving the procedure a plain-text description that better explains to other developers its purpose.
PACKAGE	This is the package in the repository where your procedure is created. This is set for you based on the package you clicked on to create the procedure in the first place.
CREATE NEW/ COPY FROM	You have the option of creating a new procedure from scratch or copying an existing procedure as a starting point.
SCHEMA	This is the schema in which the procedure's runtime version is created. Like all repository objects, this is _SYS_BIC.
DEFAULT SCHEMA	This should be set to a schema containing any tables that you need to reference inside the stored procedure. Setting this eliminates the need to fully qualify the table names inside the procedure's SQL code. For example, we are setting this to the BOOK_USER schema where our PRODUCT_CATEGORY_SECURITY table resides.
RUN WITH	This option defines whose security is used to determine authorizations for access during procedure execution. As we stated earlier, for use in analytic privileges, this must be definer's rights.
ACCESS MODE	This option determines whether the procedure can alter any data during its execution. This, too, has only one option for analytic privilege scenarios, which is read-only.
LANGUAGE	This is the language with which you are going to define the logic of the stored procedure. Again, there is only one choice: SQLScript.

Table 11.3 New SQL Procedure Options

With these properties defined, you can click FINISH, and then your new procedure object is created and a new PROCEDURE EDITOR window opens. You can see an example of this editor in Figure 11.4. The screen is divided into three main sections: the SCRIPT VIEW, OUTPUT pane, and INPUT pane. We will describe each of these areas in Table 11.4.

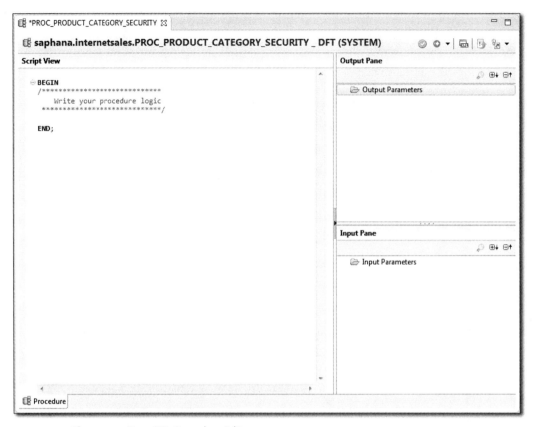

Figure 11.4 New SQL Procedure Editor

Section	Description
SCRIPT	In this section of the editor, you write the SQLScript logic that defines the process that the procedure uses to retrieve the restricted values for a user. SQLScript is similar in syntax to other stored procedure languages that you may be familiar with.
OUTPUT	In the OUTPUT pane, you define any output parameters that are returned by the stored procedure. Recall that, for the different operators available in the analytic privilege, we have to define a specific set of output parameters: either a table type parameter for the In operator or a single/pair of single values for the other types.

Table 11.4 New SQL Procedure Editor Sections

Section	Description
INPUT	In the INPUT pane, you can define any input parameters that are passed into a procedure to alter its behavior at runtime. Recall that, in order to be used in an analytic privilege, that procedure cannot have any input parameters. Thus, for our purposes, you can ignore this section of the editor.

Table 11.4 New SQL Procedure Editor Sections (Cont.)

Now that you have a new procedure open in the editor, the first thing to do is define the output parameters that we will return back to the analytic privilege where your procedure will be used. In our current example, we are assuming that a user should have access to any product categories for which they have a record in the PRODUCT_CATEGORY_SECURITY table. This implies that our analytic privilege restriction uses the In operator. The In operator covers the vast majority of all dynamic restriction scenarios. Also, recall that the returned values need to match the data type of the attribute we are restricting—in this case, the PRODUCT_CATEGORY field of the ANLV_INTERNETSALES analytic view.

Therefore, we need to create a single output parameter that is a table type with a single column whose data type is equal to that of the PRODUCT_CATEGORY, which happens to be VARCHR(50).

To create this output parameter, follow these steps:

1. Create the new output parameter by right-clicking the OUTPUT PARAMETERS folder icon in the OUTPUT pane and selecting NEW.

2. This opens the DEFINE OUTPUT PARAMETERS window, where you define the new table type that your procedure will return. The new type is defined in the _SYS_BIC schema. Your table type needs a name, but anything will do. We will use var_out.

3. After assigning a name to your table type, you need to define the single column that this table will contain. Click in the NAME column of the DEFINE COLUMNS area and give the column a suitable name, such as PRODUCT_CATEGORY.

4. Assign the DATA TYPE and LENGTH to match the target attribute. In this case, enter values of "VARCHAR" and "50", respectively.

5. Click OK to complete the definition of your parameter.

You can see an example of a fully filled-in output parameters definition in Figure 11.5.

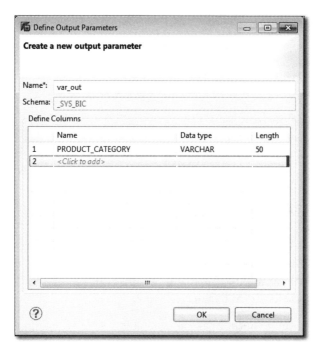

Figure 11.5 Output Parameter Definition

At this point, you can include the SQL to retrieve the necessary values from the security tables based on the current logged-in user name by way of the SESSION_ USER value. In SQLScript, to output a table of values from a procedure, you set the output parameter (var_out) equal to the results of the select statement that retrieves the required values. Each statement in SQLScript must be terminated with a semicolon (;). Thus, the final stored procedure code inserted in the SCRIPT view would look like the example shown below:

```
BEGIN
var_out =
    SELECT PRODUCT_CATEGORY
    FROM PRODUCT_CATEGORY_SECURITY
    WHERE USER_NAME = SESSION_USER;

END;
```

With the procedure logic completed, you can activate the new procedure object by clicking the ACTIVATE button in the PROCEDURE EDITOR toolbar. This creates the runtime object in _SYS_BIC. We now have a fully functional procedure that can be used in an analytic privilege to retrieve restricted values dynamically based on the current logged-in user at runtime.

Let's go back to the Analytic Privilege Editor and complete our example. We'll start by creating an empty analytic privilege with the New Analytic Privilege screen, as we described earlier. We will name this privilege AP_INTERNETSALES_ PRODUCT_CATEGORY_SEC and place it in the same package as the ANLV_INTER-NETSALES analytic view that it is based on, i.e., saphana.internetsales.

With the empty analytic privilege created, we need to add ANLV_INTERNETSA-LES to the list of reference models. To do that, we need to click the Add button in the Reference Models section, and from the pop-up window, navigate to the saphana.internetsales package and select the ANLV_INTERNETSALES analytic view. You can see an example of the reference model selection process in Figure 11.6.

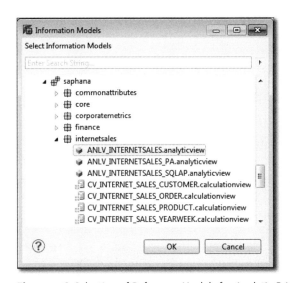

Figure 11.6 Selection of Reference Models for Analytic Privilege

With the reference model selected, we can define our attribute restriction. To do that, click the Add button in the Associated Attribute Restrictions area, and then select Product Category from the Select Object pop-up window. You can see an example of this selection process in Figure 11.7.

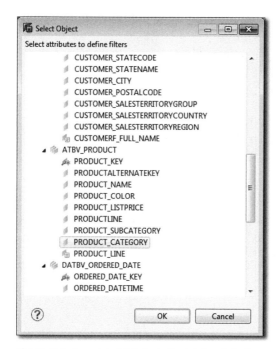

Figure 11.7 Associated Attribute Restriction Selection

With the attribute selected, we can now define the restricted values using the stored procedure we created. We do this by clicking the ADD button in the ASSIGN RESTRICTIONS area. This adds a new row to the Assign Restrictions table. We then select REPOSITORY PROCEDURE from the TYPE column, In from the OPERATOR column, and finally, the procedure name in the VALUE column. To that, we are presented with an object FIND window. Simply start typing the name of the procedure we created, and the tool searches the repository for us. Once the object is found, select it and click OK.

You can see an example of the object search process in Figure 11.8.

Your analytic privilege is now fully defined and ready for activation. Any user who is granted this analytic privilege is able to query the ANLV_INTERNETSALES analytic view, but can see only records for which PRODUCT_CATEGORY matches a value that they have assigned to their user name in the PRODUCT_CATEGORY_SECURITY table. In Figure 11.9, we have an example of the complete analytic privilege with all elements filled in.

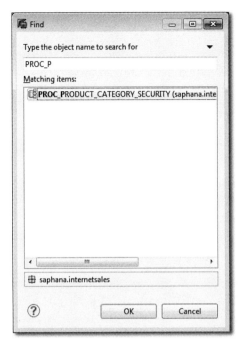

Figure 11.8 Selecting the Analytic Privilege Procedure

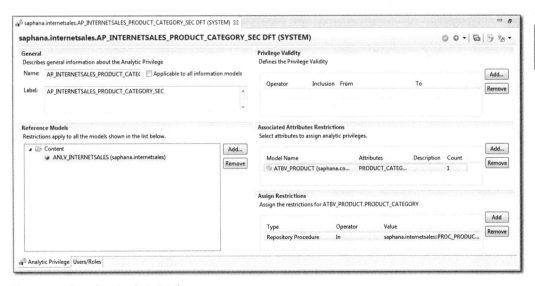

Figure 11.9 Complete Analytic Privilege

> **Analytic Privilege Summary**
>
> You should now be familiar with the basics of creating an analytic privilege to restrict data. The example we've given is rather simple, and you may find that the real-world logic of your dynamic restriction stored procedures can be a lot more complex. However, you have the full power of the SQLScript language to express that complexity, which is typically more expressive than trying to configure a GUI application.

11.2.2 SQL-Based Analytic Privileges

Unlike the traditional repository-based analytic privilege that we've just introduced you to, the newer SQL-based analytic privileges are not modeled in the repository. They are not transportable between systems using delivery units, and there is no user interface provided for creating or managing them. So why do they exist at all?

The main goal of SQL-based analytic privileges is to allow an external system that already has a user interface for defining data restriction logic to push that logic down to SAP HANA. A primary example of this scenario is the latest version of SAP BW on SAP HANA. In this new system, the restrictions defined in SAP BW are pushed down to SAP HANA using a program that executes in SAP BW and invokes the necessary SQL statements and database updates to transfer the logic to SAP HANA.

If you were building a custom application on SAP HANA and wanted to provide a mechanism for users to create and manage dynamic restrictions from within the application, then SQL-based analytic privileges would be the ideal solution. The one significant advantage that SQL-based privileges provide, in addition to being amenable to script-based creation, is that they offer arbitrarily complex conditions that can combine any set of logical AND/OR conditions on any number of restricted columns.

Before we begin reviewing the steps necessary to create an SQL-based analytic privilege, there are some prerequisites. Because you will be creating these objects outside of the repository activation process, you need a dedicated system account to perform these actions. Only the account that creates the privilege can grant others access to it. In addition, there are certain system privileges required to perform these actions. Specifically, you need CREATE STRUCTURED PRIVILEGE to create the analytic privilege in the first place, and you need STRUCTURED PRIVILEGE ADMIN to grant the privilege to users and roles. To create the column view we will use for testing, you need CREATE SCENARIO. For repository objects, like traditional analytic privileges, it is the _SYS_REPO user who has these rights.

Issue with SQL-Based Analytic Privileges
Currently, our testing with SQL-based analytic privileges on top of modeled information views in SAP HANA SP8 has shown some issues. Specifically, setting the information views to use SQL-based analytic privileges in the modeler UI doesn't seem to work. However, creating information models manually in SQLScript with the necessary settings does work. We believe this indicates a fairly simple UI bug in SAP HANA Studio, which will hopefully be rectified soon. As a result, all examples given here use manually created column views in SQLScript, which is not a common or recommended practice. This is not something you have to worry about if you encounter SQL-based privileges in SAP BW on SAP HANA because all the hard work is done for you.

The column view we will use for our examples can be created with the following statement. It generates a custom view on top of the same base analytic model as ANLV_INTERNETSALES. For reference, this is what the _SYS_REPO user is normally doing for you as part of the view activation step.

Column View Creation Script

```
CREATE COLUMN VIEW "BOOK_USER"."ANLV_INTERNETSALES_SQLAP" TYPE
CALCULATION WITH PARAMETERS ('PARENTCALCINDEXSCHEMA'='_SYS_BIC',
'PARENTCALCINDEX'='saphana.internetsales/ANLV_INTERNETSALES',
'PARENTCALCNODE'='finalAggregation', 'REGISTERVIEWFORAPCHECK'='0')
STRUCTURED PRIVILEGE CHECK;
```

The key points from the above code are the last line, where the REGISTERVIEW-FORAPCHECK is set to false (0), which disables normal analytic privileges, and the STRUCTURED PRIVILEGE CHECK, which enables the SQL-based analytic privilege enforcement.

Like traditional analytic privileges, SQL-based privileges can have their filter conditions set statically when the privilege is created, or the filter conditions can be read from a table at runtime. Regardless of how the values are defined, the bulk of the creation statement is the same. The basic form of the statements is in five parts:

▶ The Create statement itself that identifies the type of object being created—in this case, a structured privilege

▶ The name we are giving to the analytic privilege that will be used to uniquely identify it

▶ The type of action the privilege grants, which can only be SELELCT

▶ The identifier of the column view the privilege is granting access to

▶ The definition of the restricted values

It is only the last part that differs between privileges with static values and those with dynamic values. Next we will look at specific examples of each type.

Creating SQL-Based Analytic Privilege with Static Restrictions

It's easiest to start by looking at the code for the analytic privilege creation statement and then breaking down what it does. We will create a privilege that allows a user to retrieve data from the column view we created above, but only if the data is for the Bikes product category and the customer is in the Southeast sales territory.

Analytic Privilege Creation Script

```
CREATE STRUCTURED PRIVILEGE SQLAP_INTERNETSALES_BIKES_SE FOR SELECT
ON "BOOK_USER"."ANLV_INTERNETSALES_SQLAP" WHERE PRODUCT_CATEGORY =
'Bikes' and CUSTOMER_SALESTERRITORYREGION = 'Southeast';
```

As we described above, the statement has five parts. We identify that we are creating a structured privilege named SQLAP_INTERNETSALES_BIKES_SE that enables the user to SELECT data from the column view ANLV_INTERNETSALES_SQLAP, but only where the PRODUCT_CATEGORY = 'Bikes' and the CUSTOMER_SALESTERRITO-RYREGION = 'SouthEast'. This should be fairly clear from the statement's syntax.

The key to the statement's restriction of data with static values is the WHERE clause. In this WHERE clause, you can express any condition as long as it references only static, inline values. You cannot use a sub-select or reference data in any tables as you might if you were writing a SELECT statement WHERE clause, but within those bounds, the WHERE clause can be as complex as needed with any number of nested AND/OR clauses with parentheses for control of order of evaluation. You can use any of the following operators in your condition definitions: =, <=, <, >, >=, LIKE, BETWEEN, and IN. The key omissions from that list are any negation operators.

With the privilege defined, you can grant the privilege to a user or role with the following statement.

SQL-Based Analytic Privilege Grant Statement

```
GRANT STRUCTURED PRIVILEGE SQLAP_INTERNETSALES_BIKES_SE TO SOMEUSER;
```

Creating SQL-Based Analytic Privilege with Dynamic Restrictions

To implement a dynamic set of values in an SQL-based analytic privilege, we must create a stored procedure that returns the WHERE clause portion of the restriction as a string at runtime. The stored procedure must adhere to the following restrictions:

- It must have security mode DEFINER.
- It must be a read-only procedure.
- It must be executable by SYS_REPO.
- It must have no input parameters.
- It must have one output parameter of type NVARCHAR(256) or VARCHAR(256).

As you can see, the limit of 256 characters for the output string can be a limiting factor in the complexity of the analytic privilege, especially if a user should have access to a long list of values in an IN clause.

For this example, assume we are trying to achieve the same logical outcome as the static example and that the same column view exists. Because we are returning a text representation of the WHERE clause for the restriction dynamically, we need somewhere to get that representation from. There are many ways this information could be stored and retrieved. For simplicity, we will assume a single table with a user name column and a VARCHAR(256) column holding the representation of the restriction.

The following code creates our stored procedure to return the dynamic WHERE clause.

Dynamic Where Clause Stored Procedure Creation Script

```
CREATE PROCEDURE "BOOK_USER"."SQLAP_PROVIDER"(OUT OUT_FILTER
VARCHAR(256)) LANGUAGE SQLSCRIPT SQL SECURITY DEFINER READS SQL DATA AS
BEGIN
SELECT "FILTER" INTO OUT_FILTER FROM "BOOK_USER"."SALES_FILTERS" WHERE
USER_NAME = SESSION_USER;
END;
```

The above procedure has the required output parameter of Type VARCHAR(256). We use the SELECT INTO syntax to populate the output parameter of the stored procedure and now-familiar SESSION_USER variable to ensure that we get only the value for the current logged-in user at runtime.

To achieve an equivalent restriction to the one used in our static data example, we need a value in the SALES_FILTERS table that matched the following.

Example dynamic filter value

```
(PRODUCT_CATEGORY = 'Bikes' AND CUSTOMER_SALESTERRITORYREGION =
'Southeast')
```

In order to use the newly created procedure in an analytic privilege, we need to satisfy the last condition and ensure that _SYS_REPO has the authority to execute the procedure. This can be achieved with the following GRANT statement.

Granting of Procedure Execution to _SYS_REPO

```
GRANT EXECUTE ON "BOOK_USER"."SQLAP_PROVIDER" TO _SYS_REPO;
```

Finally, we can create the actual analytic privilege using a command very similar to the one we used in the static data example.

Dynamic Analytic Privilege Creation Script

```
CREATE STRUCTURED PRIVILEGE SQLAP_SALES_FILTERS FOR SELECT ON "BOOK_
USER"."ANLV_INTERNETSALES_SQLAP" CONDITION PROVIDER "BOOK_
USER"."SQLAP_PROVIDER";
```

As you can see, the difference between this and the static example is fairly minimal and is limited to the last piece, where we identify how to restrict the values.

Instead of an explicitly defined WHERE clause, we list a CONDITION PROVIDER and give the name of our stored procedure. At runtime, our stored procedure is executed, and the dynamically generated WHERE clause is used as if it had been defined statically.

As with the static example, we can grant the privilege to a user or role with the same grant statement syntax we used previously.

> **SQL-Based Analytic Privilege Summary**
>
> You should now be familiar with the required syntax for creating SQL-based privileges. Although there are some complexities in using these privileges for the time being—and for most scenarios, it is best to stay with the traditional approach—it is interesting to see how this feature evolves over the next several SAP HANA service packs. I can see leveraging the scriptable nature of this approach as a way to further automate security management or integrate it into broader enterprise solutions outside the scope of SAP HANA. Time will tell.

11.3 Applying Analytic Privileges

So far, we have provided you examples of analytic privileges in the context of individual information models, with fairly straightforward restrictions. In the real world, you will be working with multiple models of all types: attribute, analytic, and calculation. In this section, we will examine some of the more complex interactions that can take place when we encounter more realistic scenarios.

We will start with an overview of the application of analytic privileges to information models in Section 11.3.1. Then, in Section 11.3.2, we will recap the interaction that occurs between multiple analytic privileges assigned to a user, as well as multiple attribute restrictions within an analytic privilege. Finally, we will follow that with a deep dive into the interactions of multiple information models in conjunction with analytic privileges in Section 11.3.3.

11.3.1 Applying Analytic Privileges to Information Views

When an information model is created, the developer must choose whether the view will enforce analytic privileges, and if so, what kind of analytic privilege (either traditional or SQL-based).

The developer can define the privilege enforcement in the SEMANTICS node of any modeled information view. In the PROPERTIES panel of the SEMANTICS node is a dropdown selection labeled APPLY PRIVILEGES. In the dropdown list, there are three choices available: BLANK, ANALYTIC PRIVILEGE, and SQL ANALYTIC PRIVILEGE. Figure 11.10 shows an example of applying the analytic privilege choice to an information view.

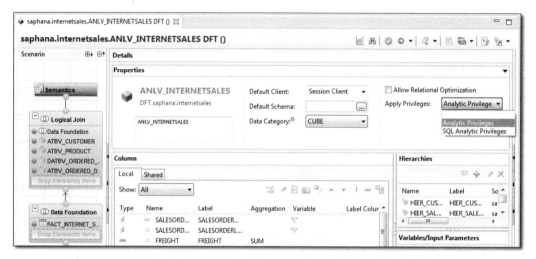

Figure 11.10 Setting Analytic Privilege Enforcement on an Information Model

If the developer opts not to apply any analytic privileges by selecting the blank value from the dropdown, then all users with the SELECT object privilege to the view's runtime object are able to access all records from this information view.

If a view does not contain any sensitive information and all users are granted access to all the records, then choosing blank can have a small to moderate performance improvement over defining an analytic privilege that grants wide open access. The system performs one fewer check at query runtime when analytic privileges are not applied, and your overall security model is simpler. This is a common scenario for attribute views on unsecured dimensions.

If the view contains data that does need to be secured to specific users, then the developer chooses either the analytic privilege choice or the SQL analytic privilege choice based on the type of analytic privileges you plan to use. In either case, access to this view now requires a user to have at least one analytic privilege that grants access to the content of this view before being allowed to query data from it. This is in addition to the requirement that the user have `SELECT` object privilege on the runtime view created for this model in the _SYS_BIC schema.

> **Views Enforce Only One Type of Analytic Privilege**
>
> Each information view can enforce only one of the two types of analytic privilege. You cannot mix and match privileges from both types.

11.3.2 Interaction of Multiple Analytic Privileges and Multiple Restrictions

We've touched on this subject in the description of the analytic privilege creation process, but it is sufficiently important that we take a moment and ensure that the interactions between analytic privileges are clear. We have three types of interactions to contend with:

▸ Multiple analytic privileges, which affect the same information model assigned to a single user

▸ Multiple attribute restrictions on an information model in a single analytic privilege

▸ Multiple restriction values for a single attribute in a single analytic privilege

These three types of interactions can be combined to achieve a desired security outcome. In conjunction, they give you the option to have restrictions combined with `OR` (least restrictive) and `AND` (most restrictive) operations. Depending on your desired outcome, you may need to leverage one, two, or all three of these interactions.

Let's review what happens in each of the combination scenarios listed above in Table 11.5.

Combination Type	Outcome
Multiple analytic privileges assigned to the same user	The user receives the restricted values of both analytic privileges combined with an `OR`. This produces the least restrictive output for the user. If either privilege allows the user to see a record, then that record is returned to the user.

Table 11.5 Types of Analytic Privilege Interaction

Combination Type	Outcome
Multiple attribute restrictions on one information model	The defined restrictions are combined for each row with an AND operator. This produces the most restrictive output for the user. All conditions must evaluate to `true` for a record to be returned.
Multiple restriction values for a single attribute	Like with multiple analytic privileges, the user receives all records that match any of the restricted values; thus, the restrictions are combined with an `OR`, and the user receives the least restricted set.

Table 11.5 Types of Analytic Privilege Interaction (Cont.)

These different forms of restriction can be combined. Let's take a sales example wherein sales people are responsible for specific product lines in specific sales territories. A particular user should see data only if the sales territory and the product line both match their assigned area of responsibility. For that, we need an AND rule on two attributes, and thus, we need multiple attributes restricted in a single analytic privilege.

However, users may wear multiple hats and cover more than one territory. Therefore, you can combine multiple values on a single attribute, like territory, which gives the desired OR rule.

Finally, you may have two alternate ways of securing the data: one based on the territory a user is currently assigned to manage and another based on all sales where a user was historically the sales person assigned to the transaction. This latter attribute is distinct from the current sales territory and product line. If we combine it in the same analytic privilege, it falls under the rule of multiple attribute restrictions on one model and results in an AND operator that we don't want. Instead, we'll need a second analytic privilege that enforces a restriction only on the sales person, and we will grant both analytic privileges to our users, thus achieving the total desired outcome.

11.3.3 Interaction of Multiple Information Views with Analytic Privileges

In contrast to the interactions described above, in this section, we will describe the interactions that occur when multiple information models are used in an analytic privilege, when information models refer to each other, and how that affects analytic privilege design.

Quite often, one information view will reference another. This happens with attribute views that are reused in multiple analytic views and analytic views used in multiple calculation views. In these scenarios, the application of analytic privileges to secure access to data can be applied at various levels, and interaction of those levels does not always have intuitive outcomes.

The simplest case of applying analytic privileges to an information model occurs when a single model is being queried directly and relies on no other models for information. Examples of this scenario would be an attribute view queried directly for master data reporting or a calculation view modeled directly on base tables. The only evaluation that has to be made is the definition of any restrictions in analytic privileges that are in effect.

Things get more complex when models are built on top of other models, particularly because not all model interactions are the same. When you build a calculation view that references other views, either calculation or analytic, the resulting execution plan creates a hierarchy of view access wherein the base views are queried and their results passed on to the operations contained in the top-level view.

In this scenario, if the base views enforce analytic privileges, a user needs analytic privileges that grant access to all the referenced views, as well as the top-level view, which references those views. The resulting data output is the combination of all restrictions on the base data, plus any additional restrictions placed on the top-level view. Thus, the restrictions will be combined with a logical AND. Effectively, views that reference other views only ever see the data that the lower-level views pass on to them. If a restriction on those lower levels prevented the top-level view from seeing the data in the first place, it doesn't matter if there is an analytic privilege that grants the user access to the data from that view because the data was never there in the first place.

This sort of scenario can come into play when you have a calculation view that unions two or more base analytic views together.

In contrast, analytic views that reference attribute views work quite differently because analytic views do not form a runtime hierarchy of execution plans. Instead, the logic contained in the attribute views is embedded into the generated analytic view execution model at view activation time. Thus, an analytic privilege that restricts access to an attribute view but does not also reference a dependent analytic view has no effect on the data retrieved from the analytic view. This can be very surprising to developers unfamiliar with this behavior.

For the same reason, an analytic privilege that grants access to data in an analytic view is all that is required. A user does not need any specific analytic privilege–granting access to the attribute views that were used in the construction of the analytic view in order to access the data via the analytic view. However, if you want the user to also be able to directly query the attribute view for master data purposes, they will need explicit granting of access to the attribute view.

Things can be even more confusing when an analytic privilege grants accesses to multiple analytic views that share a common set of attribute views. If you add a restriction to limit data for an analytic view based on a shared attribute from an attribute view, it restricts data for all analytic views that are referenced in this analytic privilege that also make use of the common attribute.

This behavior leads to a common practice of grouping multiple analytic views and their referenced attribute views into a single analytic privilege that controls access to all the views simultaneously. This has the advantage of limiting the number of times you need to express the restrictions but requires that you build larger analytic privileges that set permissions on multiple analytic views in the same definition that more tightly couples changes together.

A final level of confusion can enter into the process when you have calculation views that reference the analytic views, which reference the attribute views on which you have placed restrictions. You might assume that, as with the analytic views described above, if you simply add your calculation view to the combined analytic privilege containing your analytic and attribute views, the restriction placed on the attribute view is sufficient. Unfortunately, the calculation view does not recognize the restriction on the attribute view as granting access to data in the calculation view, and your users cannot to access data in the calculation view.

There are a couple of ways to work around this issue with calculation views. If there are additional restrictions that need to be placed on the calculation view that don't pertain to the underlying analytic views, then simply adding those restrictions is sufficient to allow access to the data of the calculation view. This combines with the already-restricted data coming from the analytic view to give you the total restriction. However, if you don't need any additional restrictions, you can either grant access to the calculation view in an analytic privilege of its own or simply disable analytic privilege checks on the calculation view because all the data is filtered at the analytic view level.

Conversely, if you only need only for users to query the calculation view, you can set the lower-level views not to enforce analytic privileges, only grant the user access to SELECT from the calculation view, and define all your restrictions on the calculation view exclusively.

The interaction of analytic privileges and multiple information views can be quite complex. Table 11.6 summarizes the various scenarios for configuring analytic privileges.

Scenario	Privilege Configuration
Single view, no dependencies	A single analytic privilege grants access to the view.
Multiple analytic views with shared attribute views	A single combined analytic privilege referencing all analytic views. Attribute views should be unsecured or added to the analytic privilege.
Calculation view with dependent analytic views, no additional restrictions on calculation view	Same as above, but either disable analytic privilege checks on the calculation view or create a second analytic privilege that grants access to just the calculation view, but with no restricted attributes.
Calculation view with dependent analytic views, with additional restrictions on calculation view	Same as multiple analytic views, but add the calculation view and its restrictions to the combined analytic privilege.

Table 11.6 Scenarios for Configuring Analytic Privileges

Effective Analytic Privileges

To help you quickly identify the effective analytic privileges assigned to a user, there is a database view stored in the SYS schema called EFFECTIVE_PRIVILEGES. Using the following example query, administrators can quickly identify the effective analytic privileges assigned to a user:

```
SELECT * FROM "SYS"."EFFECTIVE_PRIVILEGES" WHERE USER_NAME = 'BOOK_
USER' AND OBJECT_TYPE = 'ANALYTICALPRIVILEGE'
```

The administrator simply replaces the 'BOOK_USER' string in the WHERE clause with the user name to review (for example, USER_NAME = '<your user>').

11.4   Case Study: Securing Sales Data with Analytic Privileges

In this case study, we will review a complete data security strategy for all of the core information models that we have created so far for the AdventureWorks Cycle Company. We will start with an overview of the information models in question and the key attributes that we will use for security. We will then discuss the overall strategy we will follow for the security model, and finally, we will present specific implementation examples from that strategy.

11.4.1 Overview and Requirements

The SAP HANA analytics platform is coming along nicely for AdventureWorks. We have loaded our data warehouse with sales and finance data. We have developed attribute, analytic, and calculation views on top of that data that exposes the information in a consumer-friendly form, and now we will configure those views for secure consumption by end users.

The package structures we've created so far organize our models into meaningful groupings. In Table 11.7, let's start reviewing that structure and the key models contained in it to determine what our requirements for a security policy will be.

Package	Description
Commonattributes	This package contains shared attribute views that are used in various other packages. We are not concerned with securing the data in these views for now because there is no sensitive data in the master data.
Corporatemetrics	This package contains cross-functional aggregates and virtualized rollups of the core sales and finance data. All models in this package are based on top of other, lower-level models.
Finance	This package contains the financial reporting models, all of which are based on a core analytic view, ANLV_FINANCE.
Internetsales	This package contains models that report on the subset of sales data that is transacted through our website. Like with Finance, all the models in this section stem from one core analytic view, ANLV_INTERNETSALES.
Resellersales	This package is the sister to Internetsales and contains models that report on the subset of sales transacted through licensed resellers. Again, a single analytic view forms the core of this package.

Table 11.7 Package Structure Overview

To secure the data in these packages, the business has given us several restrictions that they want to enforce on this data. The key data areas that drive these restrictions are the finance models and, separately, the Internet sales and reseller sales—there are separate teams managing those sales processes.

Finance model security is driven by the key attribute of the parent organizational unit (PARENTORGANIZATIONKEY). Specifically, there are four main business units that need their data secured: European operations, North American operations, Pacific operations, and US operations. In addition, there are corporate office team members who should simply have access to all data.

The Internet sales management team is organized around product data because customers come in from all over the world and there is no tight tie to sales territory. This is secured at the product category level, in the PRODUCT_CATEGORY column. Like with Finance, corporate office team members need access to all data.

The reseller sales data is the most complex to secure because there are two parts to it. Individual reseller representatives need access to all sales they are responsible for based on the (EMPLOYEEKEY) attribute, whereas territory managers need access based on (SALESTERRITORY_REGION), and as usual, corporate office members need access to all data.

11.4.2 Implementation Strategy

Based on the requirements listed above and the structure of our views and data, we can define a strategy for the security for each package and its information models. We'll review the detailed plan for each package in Table 11.8. In general, we will apply security by way of traditional modeled analytic privileges so that we can take advantage of delivery units for transportation to test landscapes. In areas where the number of uniquely secured values is small and relatively static, such as finance and Internet sales, we will create analytic privileges with static restriction values. For reseller sales for which the security is more complex and the number of unique values is larger, we will use analytic privileges with dynamic restriction values.

Package	Strategy
Commonattributes	► No need to secure master data. ► Ensure that all users can access content by setting APPLY PRIVILEGES to false on all models. ► No need to create analytic privileges.

Table 11.8 Security Implementation Strategy

Package	Strategy
Corporatemetrics	▸ Models are constructed on top of finance and sales models. ▸ No additional security above and beyond that defined for base models. ▸ Will rely on base model security by setting APPLY PRIVILEGES to false on all models.
Finance	▸ ANLV_FINANCE is the base model that requires security. ▸ Four analytic privileges with static values will be created, one for each organization unit. ▸ One analytic privilege that grants unrestricted data access will also be created. ▸ Calculation views and attribute views will have APPLY PRIVILEGES set to false.
Internetsales	▸ ANLV_INTERNETSALES is the base model that requires security. ▸ Three analytic privileges with static restrictions will be created, one for each product category. ▸ One analytic privilege that grants unrestricted data will also be created. ▸ All other calculation and attribute views will have APPLY PRIVILEGES set to false.
Resellersales	▸ ANLV_RESELLERSALES is the base model that requires security. ▸ Two security management tables will be created and loaded with data, one for territory managers and one for reseller reps. ▸ Two analytic privileges will be created that use dynamic restrictions based on these tables. ▸ One analytic privilege that grants unrestricted access will also be created.

Table 11.8 Security Implementation Strategy (Cont.)

11.4.3 Implementation Examples

In this section, we will present examples from the above implementation strategy that demonstrate the overview of tasks necessary to turn this strategy into reality.

To confirm that our changes are having the desired effect, we will test as we go using a test account. The account will be given the minimum-security role of a base user (SELECT access to _SYS_BIC/_SYS_BI). Then, as we create and alter analytic privileges and make model changes, we can execute `SELECT` statements against the models as this user to see if we get the expected result.

Common Attributes

The first and easiest implementation step is allowing users to perform master data reporting without concerns for data access restrictions in the `commonattributes` package. We will achieve this by disabling the enforcement of analytic privileges on all of the attribute views in this package. In Figure 11.11, we show an example of this step wherein we have set the APPLY PRIVILEGES selection to blank on the product attribute view (ATBV_PRODUCT). This step is repeated for all views in this package.

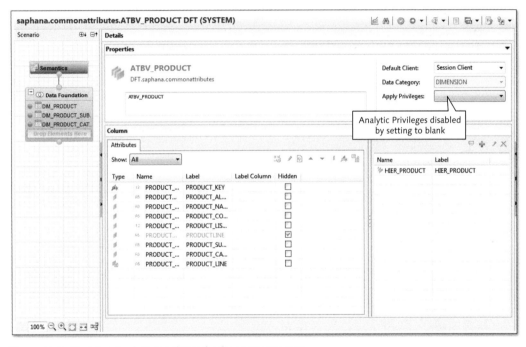

Figure 11.11 Disabling Analytic Privilege Checks on Master Data

Using our test account to confirm that we can now execute master data queries without restriction, we run the following SQL command, and as expected, it returns all records from the product attribute view, even though we have not created or granted any analytic privileges.

```
SELECT *
FROM "_SYS_BIC"."saphana.commonattributes/ATBV_PRODUCT"
```

Corporate Metrics

In the corporatemetrics package, we have a number of calculation views that aggregate data from base analytic views. As we explained in Section 11.3.3, if you do not need to further secure the data in a calculation view and it is based on one or more analytic views that are already secured, then you can disable analytic privilege checks in your calculation view. This is the plan we will follow for the corporatemetrics views because they are all based on either the ANLV_FINANCE view or one of the two sales analytics views.

In Figure 11.12 we have an example screen where, again, we have set the APPLY PRIVILEGES attribute to blank, this time on one of the calculation views.

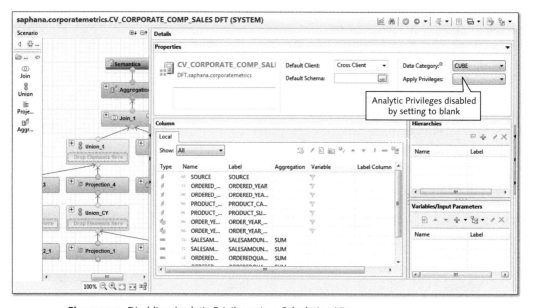

Figure 11.12 Disabling Analytic Privileges in a Calculation View

We can now test our change using our test account. You might mistakenly think that at this point the user is able to access data from this calculation view. However, we have not yet granted the user access to the base analytic views that are referenced by this calculation view. Until we do that, we get an authorization error when we attempt to query the view. This proves that security on the base views is still applied. The test query can be seen below.

```
SELECT *
FROM "_SYS_BIC"."saphana.corporatemetrics/CV_CORPORATE_COMP_SALES"
```

The result of executing this SQL statement is a COLUMN STORE ERROR [2950] USER IS NOT AUTHORIZED. This is exactly the outcome we expect. We will re-execute this test statement after we complete the rest of the security changes, at which point we should start getting data for our user.

Finance

The finance security is relatively straightforward to configure because there is only one analytic view with only a small number of attribute values to secure. The Finance package does, however, have some local attribute views and calculation views specific to finance. These views will follow the same pattern as commonattributes and corporatemetrics above so that only the base analytic view will need to enforce security.

To secure ANLV_FINANCE, we will create a series of analytic privileges. As we discussed in our implementation strategy, we will have four analytic privileges, one for each organizational unit of the business and one global access analytic privilege for corporate office finance members who can see all data.

We will start by creating the global access privilege because it requires the fewest steps, which you can follow below:

1. We will store the analytic privileges for finance along with the models they reference in the finance package. Thus, we right-click the finance package and choose NEW • ANALYTIC PRIVILEGE.

2. We fill in the NEW ANALYTIC PRIVILEGE screen so that it looks like Figure 11.13.

3. With the privilege defined, we add the ANLV_FINANCE view to the referenced models section using the ADD button. This results in an analytic privilege that looks like Figure 11.14. Because there are no filters to define, this privilege is complete.

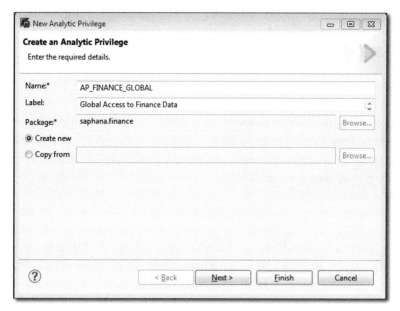

Figure 11.13 Finance Global Access Privilege

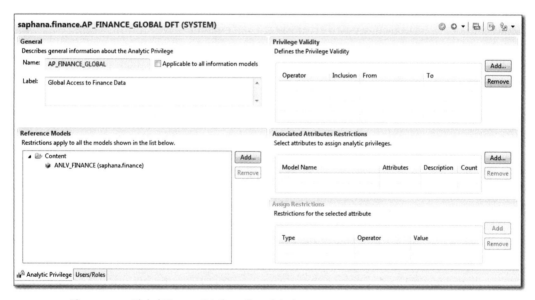

Figure 11.14 Global Finance Privilege Completed

We can now test our global access privilege by assigning the analytic privilege to our test user from the user management screen and executing the following test SQL statement. We should receive access to all records in the ANLV_FINANCE view.

```
SELECT *
FROM "_SYS_BIC"."saphana.finance/ANLV_FINANCE"
```

As expected, all results are returned when we execute this statement, confirming that our analytic privilege is now working.

With the global filter in place, we can add the four restricted filters by starting from a copy of the global filter, using the following steps:

1. Right-click the finance package and choose NEW • ANALYTIC PRIVILEGE.

2. Fill in the NEW ANALYTIC PRIVILEGE screen, selecting COPY FROM instead of CREATE NEW this time. See Figure 11.15 for a completed example for North American operations.

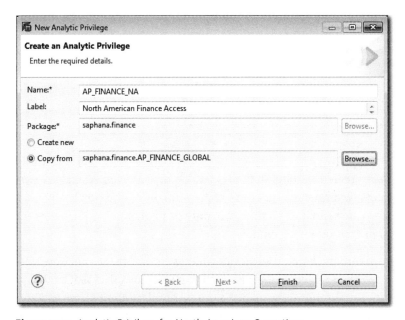

Figure 11.15 Analytic Privilege for North American Operations

3. This gives us the analytic privilege with ANLV_FINANCE already configured in the REFERENCED MODELS area.

4. Add `PARENT_ORGANIZATIONKEY` to the Associated Attribute Restrictions, and add a static restriction value using the `Equal` operator. The value for North America is `2`.

5. With the restriction value set, we can save and activate the analytic privilege. You can see the full analytic privilege configuration in Figure 11.16.

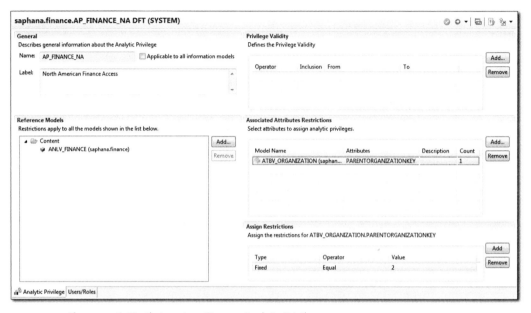

Figure 11.16 North American Finance Analytic Privilege

With this privilege created, setting up the remaining ones is even easier. We simply need to create new ones with the Copy From option using the North American privilege as a template so that, each time, the only thing that has to change is the value in the assign restrictions column.

With all of our finance analytic privileges created, we can test the outcome with our test user, using the same test SQL statement we used for the global privilege, but first grant the North American finance analytic privilege to the user and take away the global privilege. With this done, we should receive data for North American organization units only. Note that with this scheme, the US is treated separately, so North America is only the Canadian division.

Internet Sales

For the configuration of analytic privileges for Internet sales, we can essentially replicate what was done for `Finance`, except that we are replacing `PARENT_ORGA-NIZATIONKEY` with `PRODUCT_CATEGORY`. This results in the creation of four analytic privileges, one for global access and three for specific product categories. You can use the same steps from the "Finance" section to configure these privileges

Reseller Sales

The requirements for the configuration of reseller sales are somewhat more complex than the other business areas; we are also dealing with a larger list of unique attribute values that need to be secured. Thus, we intend to use dynamic restriction values for these analytic privileges.

The first step, like with finance and Internet sales, is to disable analytic privilege checks on any attribute views and calculation views other than the base analytic view ANLV_RESELLERSALES. With that step out of the way, we can begin configuring our analytic privileges.

Also like finance and Internet sales, we need one privilege that grants global access to ANLV_RESELLERSALES. Follow the same steps we laid out in the "Finance" section to create this initial analytic privilege. We will then use that as the starting point for other privileges by using the COPY FROM feature.

Before we can proceed with the rest of the analytic privileges, we need to configure the tables that will manage our security relationships. Recall that we intend to have two tables: one for managing the mapping of reseller rep employee IDs to users and one for territory managers. Eventually, we will need to configure SAP Data Services loading scenarios to update these tables or create user interfaces using SAP HANA's native development capabilities so that the business users can manage this mapping data. For now, we will simply insert test records into the table to confirm that our model is working properly for our test user.

The following code examples can be used to create the tables we require.

```
CREATE COLUMN TABLE "BOOK_USER"."RESELLERREP_USER_MAPPING"
(
 "EMPLOYEEKEY" INTEGER,
 "USER_NAME" VARCHAR(20)
);
```

Listing 11.1 Reseller Rep Mapping Table

```
CREATE COLUMN TABLE "BOOK_USER"."TERRITORY_MANAGER_SEC"
(
 "SALESTERRITORY_REGION" VARCHAR(50),
 "USER_NAME" VARCHAR(20)
);
```

Listing 11.2 Territory Manager Security Table

With the tables to store security mapping data, which assigns values to users in place, we can start creating the stored procedures necessary to retrieve data from these tables for use by the analytic privileges. Both of these procedures use the same form from which we select those records from the table where the user name column matches the currently logged user, as defined by the SESSION_USER variable. We will create and store these procedures in the same package with the analytic view and privileges, i.e., resellersales.

The following steps create the procedure for reseller reps. You can follow essentially the same steps with different table names to create the procedure for territory managers.

1. Right-click the resellersales package and choose NEW • PROCEDURE. Fill in the NAME, LABEL, and other properties to match the example in Figure 11.17.

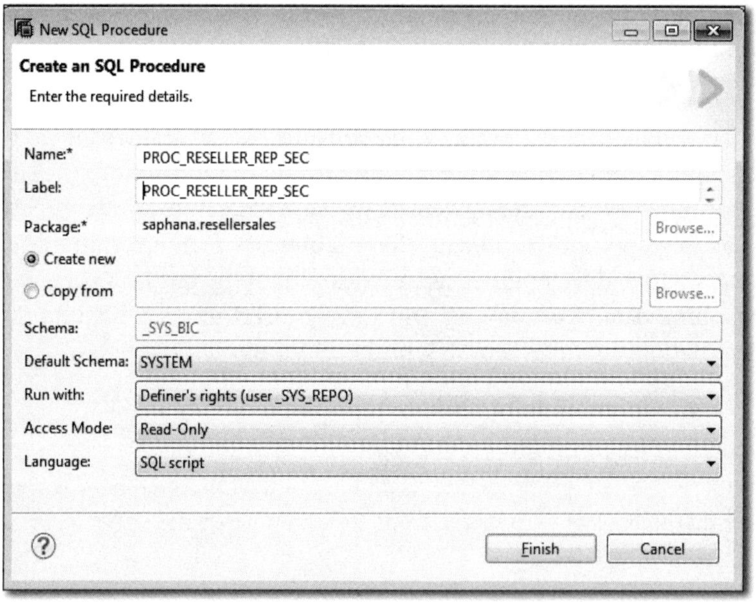

Figure 11.17 Creation of the Reseller Rep Security Procedure

2. Configure the output table to return the reseller rep's EMPLOYEEKEY, and add the SQL statement to retrieve the data. You can see a completed version in Figure 11.18.

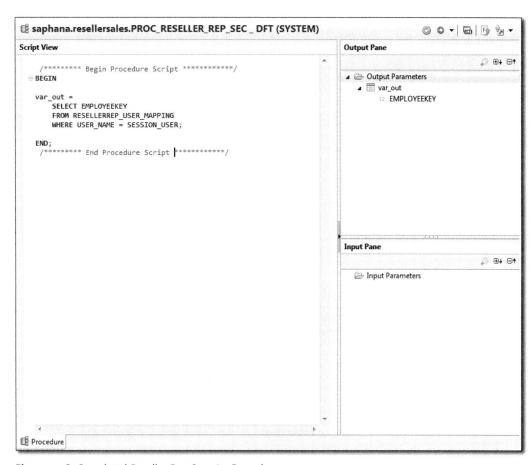

Figure 11.18 Completed Reseller Rep Security Procedure

You can create a nearly identical procedure to handle the territory manager scenario.

With the procedures in place, we can construct the analytic privileges that will use these procedures. Follow these next steps to set up the reseller rep security privilege:

1. Right-click the resellersales package and choose New • ANALYTIC PRIVILEGE.

2. Create the privilege by copying the global reseller sales privilege we created earlier, as we've shown with the other examples.

3. Add the EMPLOYEEKEY attribute to the list of ASSOCIATED ATTRIBUTE RESTRICTIONS, and configure the ASSIGN RESTRICTIONS value to use the repository procedure we just finished creating. The final analytic privilege can be seen in Figure 11.19.

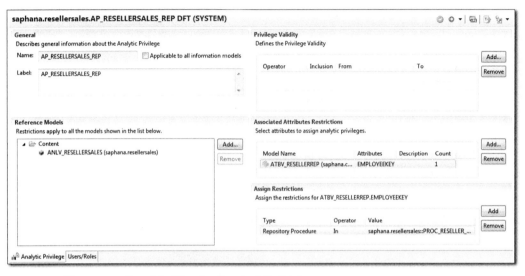

Figure 11.19 Completed Reseller Rep Analytic Privilege

Again, you can follow the same steps to configure the territory manager privilege by simply swapping out the attribute and referenced procedure name.

In order to test these newly create privileges, we'll need to enter some test data into our security mapping tables for our test user and then take turns granting each of the two analytic privileges to the test user and executing our select statements. Always remember to remove other analytic privileges before adding new ones when testing so that you are sure you are only testing one thing at a time.

The following SQL statements can be used to create test records in the mapping tables.

```
INSERT INTO "BOOK_USER"."RESELLERREP_USER_MAPPING"
VALUES (272, 'BOOK_CONSUMER1');
```

```
INSERT INTO "BOOK_USER"."TERRITORY_MANAGER_SEC"
VALUES ('France', 'BOOK_CONSUMER1');
```
Listing 11.3 Test Data

With the test data in place, we can test our new privileges using a select statement against ANLV_RESELLERSALES. The following example SQL can be used.

```
SELECT *
FROM "_SYS_BIC"."saphana.resellersales/ANLV_RESELLERSALES"
```
Listing 11.4 Reseller Sales Test SQL

This SQL, when executed while we have the reseller analytic privilege applied, should return data only for Representative 272, and when we switch to the territory manager privilege, we should receive data only for France.

With the final pieces of our security model in place, there is one final test: to go back and retry our corporate metrics test query from earlier while our test user is granted the analytic privileges for global Internet sales and global reseller sales data. With these privileges applied, the user should be able to query all data from our corporate rollup views.

Assigning Privileges to Roles

With our model fully unit tested, we can now roll it out for assignment to users. We do not want to manage the assignment of analytic privileges to users directly the way we have with our test user. Instead, we want to map the privileges into roles that the security management team can assign out. Refer back to Chapter 2 if you need a refresher. In general, our analytic privileges can be mapped one to one on to new roles; however, the global access privileges can probably all be combined into a single corporate office user role.

11.5   Summary

This chapter offered a solid foundation in the processes needed to configure a data security strategy with SAP HANA. Although this is a complex topic, we hope the introduction here provides enough of a kick start to help you configure your own solutions.

The advantages offered by securing data at the base platform level in SAP HANA will pay off in the long term because you now have a single, central, secure data-store that any and all reporting tools, including SAP BusinesinessObjects BI and possible third-party tools, can take advantage of. No longer are you reliant upon the application server sitting on top of your database to enforce security, and, therefore, no longer do you have to go throughout your system landscape redefining security logic in multiple systems.

At this point, you should have a solid idea of how to provision data to an SAP HANA system using SAP Data Services, prepare that data for consumption with information views, and, now, secure that data in preparation for consumption by end users. In Part IV of the book, you'll learn how to further prepare the data for consumption by using SAP BusinessObjects BI reporting tools and creating rich semantic layers with the SAP BusinessObjects BI universe design tools.

PART IV
Integrating SAP HANA with SAP Business Intelligence Tools

This chapter provides an overview of the semantic layer built into SAP BusinessObjects BI and how it is used to provide access to data within SAP HANA.

12 Building Universes for SAP HANA

Before SAP acquired Business Objects, the semantic layer, known as the *universe*, was the center point for many of the Business Objects reporting and analysis tools. Although SAP has since devised alternatives to support its own legacy reporting and analysis tools that don't require a developer to define universes for native SAP application data sources, many organizations still design the universe to provide an intuitive, central, and secure point of access to their third-party data sources.

The universe is designed to make the report design process easy for average business users when they access data in an RDBMS. It shields report designers from the complexities of designing SQL statements, identifying database objects, and resolving complex SQL traps. As opposed to writing SQL statements, consumers can design queries against the universe, using a graphical user interface (GUI). Database objects such as tables, fields, joins, filters, and aggregates are embedded in the universe. They are then presented to the consumer in a graphical, object-oriented, multidimensional format that is rich in metadata. With a universe, users don't need to consult a data dictionary or have intimate knowledge of the data model to work with and identify database objects. Universe objects can be defined with full-text names and descriptions to help users quickly identify the object's purpose. In addition, the universe can be configured with technical metadata that provides the reporting tools information necessary to properly process complex queries.

Once completed, the universe effectively serves as a multidimensional model, much like the SAP HANA information views.

If you're familiar with the new SAP BusinessObjects BI environment, you've likely noticed that there are two types of universes and universe design tools available in the platform. This can sometimes be confusing for both legacy and new adopters of the SAP BusinessObjects BI platform. However, SAP's choice to include both the legacy format and the new format was a wise decision; it allows an organization to easily adopt the SAP BusinessObjects BI platform without having to make radical changes to their development processes. From the perspective of connecting to SAP HANA, both universe types are supported, and there are few differences concerning SAP HANA.

The legacy universe is developed in the *Universe Design Tool* (UDT) and produces a universe object with a file extension of UNV. When we mention a UDT- or UNV-based universe, we are referring to the legacy universe format. The *Information Design Tool* (IDT) is new in the SAP BusinessObjects BI platform. It produces universe objects with a file extension of UNX. When we mention an IDT- or UNX-based universe, we are referring to the new universe format.

In general, the principles in this chapter apply to both UNX and UNV universes. The one major exception is the ability to automatically generate a universe using the UDT. The UDT does not support this functionality. However, a UDT universe can be manually developed, using the same principals, against an SAP HANA source. There are other minor differences, as well; for example, the UNV universe doesn't have a separate data foundation layer or a business layer. Instead, the UNV Universe Designer combines these layers into a single design canvas. In addition, the UNV universe doesn't support multiple connections or multiple data sources.

In this chapter, we'll discuss the basic concepts of the UNX universe, including when you need a universe to access data in SAP HANA and how to connect universes to SAP HANA (Section 12.1). We'll then spend the rest of the chapter teaching you how to work with UNX and SAP HANA: manually building universes for SAP HANA (Section 12.2), automatically generating universes for SAP HANA (Section 12.3), and explaining how the SAP HANA engines affect universe design (12.4). To conclude the chapter, we'll walk you through a case study to demonstrate the process of creating a universe to access SAP HANA (Section 12.5).

Note

The goal of this chapter is not to make you an expert in universe design, but to give you a primer on the elements that are especially relevant for SAP HANA. For additional information about universe design, we recommend the following:

> ‣ The SAP training courses BOID10 and BOID20
>
> ‣ The book *Universe Design with SAP BusinessObjects BI: The Comprehensive Guide* (Ah-Soon, Mazoué, Vezzosi, SAP PRESS, 2014)
>
> ‣ SAP's guides at *http://help.sap.com/bobip#section5*. Here, you'll find the *Information Design Tool User Guide* and the *Universe Design Tool User Guide*.

12.1   SAP HANA and the Universe

In many ways, the capabilities of the information views in SAP HANA and in an SAP BusinessObjects BI universe are very similar. The intent of both semantic layers is to provide consumers an intuitive, multidimensional representation of their data. Both tools act as a *semantic layer* that shields the consumer from the complexities of the underlying data model and database coding languages. Data objects and semantics are represented as graphical business objects. This is all achieved while providing organizations with a central layer that adds metadata, applies data security, and centralizes business logic.

Much like the SAP HANA information views, data objects in a universe are represented as attributes and measures. However, in a universe, the terms *dimensions* and *measures* are used to describe these same objects. Universes also contain other objects, such as *details* and *conditions*, that can be used to further simplify access to the underlying data model. There are several other features of the SAP HANA information views and SAP BusinessObjects BI universe that are similar as well; for example, derived columns, calculated measures, runtime filters, and hierarchies are supported in both tools.

There are also several profound differences between these tools. To list a few, the SAP BusinessObjects BI universe is designed to support multiple vendor-specific relational database management systems (RDBMS), and not just the columnar tables in SAP HANA. Universes support the coding languages of their source RDBMS, while the SAP HANA models support only the coding languages embedded within the SAP HANA platform. SAP HANA models are configured to leverage the powerful hardware specifications of the SAP HANA appliance, while the universe relies on the performance capabilities of its source RDBMS. SAP HANA models can take advantage of coding libraries such as SQLScript, Predictive Analysis Library (PAL), R language, and Business Function Library (BFL), while the universe is limited to SQL or, in some cases, multidimensional expressions (MDX).

It can also be argued that some of the more powerful features of the universe are enacted only in the SAP BusinessObjects Web Intelligence reporting engines. In contrast, the SAP HANA calculation views can perform complex calculations directly in the SAP HANA calculation engine. Take, for example, cross-fact aggregation and data synchronization. Based on definitions in the universe, SAP BusinessObjects Web Intelligence executes multiple SQL statements and then synchronizes the results in its engine to create a merged view of the dimensions and measures. The SAP HANA calculation views can produce the same results without needing an external reporting tool engine.

Because the SAP HANA calculation view is embedded directly in the SAP platform, all supported tools can access these calculation views. Table 12.1 provides an outline of the major feature comparisons between an SAP BusinessObjects BI universe and the SAP HANA information views. Please note that there are additional similarities or differences; this table focuses on the high-level comparison.

Major Feature Comparison	SAP BusinessObjects BI Universe	SAP HANA Information View
Acts as a semantic layer?	Yes. Developers can define dimensions, measures, business friendly names, descriptions, hierarchies, and so on.	Yes. Developers can define attributes, measures, business-friendly names, descriptions, hierarchies, and so on.
Supports complex calculations?	Yes. Complex calculations might require reporting tool engines. Features may vary by underlying database.	Yes. Information views can produce complex calculations while directly leveraging the SAP HANA appliance engines. Complex calculations are reporting tool agnostic.
Supports calculated columns?	Yes. Using the coding syntax of the underlying data source, universe dimensions, and measures can be designed to manipulate the source data.	Yes. Using the SAP HANA SQL syntax, developers can produce calculated columns and measures in information views.
Directly access data from multiple sources?	Yes. Using the Data Federator plugin, an IDT universe can access data from multiple supported data sources.	Yes. Using the Smart Data Access feature, virtual tables can be added to a schema and modeled in an SAP HANA calculation view or procedure.

Table 12.1 High-Level Feature Comparison between a Universe and SAP HANA Model

Major Feature Comparison	SAP BusinessObjects BI Universe	SAP HANA Information View
Leverages relational OLAP?	Yes. Application data is never stored in a universe. The universe and reporting tools generate only SQL or MDX code, and data is retrieved from the underlying data source.	Yes. Application data is never stored in an information view. Code is executed to retrieve the data from the underlying columnar store tables.
Provides a row-level security mechanism?	Yes. There are multiple ways to implement row-level security in a universe.	Yes. Information views can be configured with analytic privileges to implement row-level security.
Column-level security?	Yes. Columns can be restricted or suppressed based on logon credentials.	No. Information views are currently limited to the view and row level via analytic privileges.
Dynamic filters?	Yes. Universes support dynamic runtime filtering using prompts.	Yes. Analytic views and calculation views support dynamic runtime filters using variables.
Native support for R, PAL, and BAL libraries?	No. Universes support only the SQL and MDX languages based on their underlying data source.	Yes. Calculation views and stored procedures support the R, PAL, and BAL libraries.
Supports hierarchies?	Yes. Hierarchies are based on one or more dimensions and are used predominantly for SAP BusinessObjects Web Intelligence drill-down analysis.	Yes. Hierarchies can be defined from flat sources or parent-child sources. They are used predominantly for expand and collapse functionality in pure play OLAP or MDX-based reporting tools.
Native support for currency conversion?	No. This can be achieved using complex prompt functions and custom currency tables, but it's not a native feature of the universe. Functionality is limited.	Yes. The information view leverages tables and fields from the SAP Business Suite applications to easily and seamlessly convert currencies.
Native support for application data translation?	No. This can be achieved using complex prompts and custom language tables, but it's not a native feature of the universe. Functionality is limited.	Yes. The information view leverages tables and fields from the SAP Business Suite applications to easily and seamlessly display application data in the appropriate user locale.

Table 12.1 High-Level Feature Comparison between a Universe and SAP HANA Model (Cont.)

Major Feature Comparison	SAP BusinessObjects BI Universe	SAP HANA Information View
Provides a dedicated object that acts as a predefined filter?	Yes. The universe supports the creation of *conditions* or reusable filters that can be subjectively applied to reporting tool queries.	No. Filters are hard coded into the information view as either static filters or variables.
Delegated measures or smart measures?	Yes. Measures that calculate averages and ratios can be flagged as delegated. This informs the reporting tool that the database must aggregate and calculate the column to prevent the report engine from producing incorrect results.	No. Measures can't be delegated or flagged to prevent the reporting tools from producing incorrect results.

Table 12.1 High-Level Feature Comparison between a Universe and SAP HANA Model (Cont.)

Before we dive into the specifics of universe design for SAP HANA, let's focus on two important concepts: when it's appropriate to use a universe with SAP HANA and how to connect universes to SAP HANA. Although there is a degree of functionality overlap between the SAP HANA information views and the SAP BusinessObjects BI universe, a universe is still required for some of the tools in the SAP BusinessObjects BI platform when you're connecting to SAP HANA. In this section, we'll explain when you need to use a universe, and how to make the connection to SAP HANA.

12.1.1 When to Use a Universe with SAP HANA

Many of the SAP BusinessObjects BI tools are capable of accessing an SAP HANA information view without the need for a universe. In some cases, the tool can also push down all of its operations to the powerful SAP HANA engines. When operations are pushed down to SAP HANA, the data stays in SAP HANA and does not need to be transferred to the reporting tool. Ultimately, only the information required to populate the visualization or visual table is transferred between SAP HANA and the tool. This is a powerful feature that represents the benefits of the integration between SAP HANA and SAP BusinessObjects BI. However, not every tool is capable of pushing down its operations fully to SAP HANA. In addition, there are cases in which we might not want to push down operations to SAP HANA.

Table 12.2 outlines each SAP BusinessObjects BI tool and indicates when it supports a universe to access SAP HANA, when it requires a universe to access SAP HANA, and when it can query an SAP HANA information view. We will also indicate when the tool is capable of fully or partially pushing its operations down to SAP HANA.

Tool	Uses a Universe?	Requires a Universe?	Queries an SAP HANA Information View?	Pushes Operations to SAP HANA?
SAP BusinessObjects Web Intelligence	Yes	Yes	Yes (via a universe)	Partially
SAP Crystal Reports 2013	Yes (UNV)	No	Yes	Partially
SAP Crystal Reports for Enterprise	Yes (UNX)	No	Yes	Yes (OLAP)
SAP BusinessObjects Explorer	Yes	No	Yes	Fully
SAP BusinessObjects Analysis for OLAP	No	No	Yes	Fully
SAP BusinessObjects Analysis for Microsoft Office	No	No	Yes	Fully
SAP BusinessObjects Design Studio	Yes	No	Yes	Fully
SAP Lumira	Yes	No	Yes	Fully

Table 12.2 SAP BusinessObjects BI Tools, When They Need a Universe, and When They Can Directly Connect to SAP HANA

Why do we currently require a universe to connect to SAP HANA with some tools, and when might the universe be a better option based on the end user's requirements? The following list outlines the primary reasons the universe is currently relevant, even though SAP HANA has built-in models that function like a universe:

▶ Sometimes, you need to use a universe to support the requirements of the users based on the functionality of the SAP BusinessObjects BI tools. Accounting for the fact that many of the SAP BusinessObjects BI tools were originally developed to support legacy third-party RDBMSs and that they are efficient in generating standard SQL statements based on metadata in the universe, some of the SAP BusinessObjects BI tools currently have more available options when using a universe.

▸ Organizations can have diverse reporting needs, so having the ability to choose between the functionality of a universe and the functionality of the SAP HANA information view can be an advantage. While there are several overlapping features between the two sources, there are also a few items that are very different. For example, the universe contains delegated measures, predefined conditions, and detail objects. These objects aren't currently available in SAP HANA models. With this in mind, the universe might be a better choice, depending on the organization's requirements.

▸ Universes can be easily converted to support SAP HANA as a source, so customers that are already running SAP BusinessObjects BI on a third-party RDBMS will find it easier to adopt SAP HANA. From the perspective of the developers and the users, little will change because they will continue to support and use a universe.

12.1.2 Connecting Universes to SAP HANA

On their own, the SAP BusinessObjects BI tools or universe can't connect to the SAP HANA appliance without the use of database *middleware*. Middleware is software developed to provide an application access to a database (e.g., an RDBMS). It helps to ensure that both the application and database speak the same language. Practically every RDBMS today requires the use of middleware or software code to provide access to the database. The same is true for any application that requires access to SAP HANA. The special piece of software or middleware is called the *SAP HANA client*. The SAP HANA client must be installed on both the SAP BusinessObjects BI server and an SAP BusinessObjects BI developer workstation to provide the reporting and analysis tools access to the SAP HANA appliance.

The SAP HANA client provides industry-standard drivers, such as ODBC, JDBC, and OLE DB for OLAP. The SAP BusinessObjects BI tools primarily use either ODBC or JDBC to access the SAP HANA appliance. The SAP HANA client is available in both 32-bit and 64-bit distributions. It currently supports the operating systems (OSs) listed in Table 12.3.

Operating System	CPU Support	OS Versions
IBM AIX	RS/6000 64 bit	5.2, 5.3, 6.1, 7.1
HP UNIX	Intel Itanium 64 bit	11.31
Linux Red Hat	x86 64 bit	EL5, EL6
Linux SUSE 11	x86 64 bit	SLES10, SLES11
Linux SUSE 11	x86 32 bit	SLES11
IBM OS/400	POWER	V7R1
Solaris	SPARC 64 bit	10, 11
Solaris	x86 64 bit	10, 11
Microsoft Windows	x86 32 bit	Win7, XP, VISTA, 2008
Microsoft Windows	x86 64 bit	Win7, VISTA, 2008, 2008 R2

Table 12.3 Operating Systems Supported by the SAP HANA Client

Additional Information

The installation of the SAP HANA client is beyond the scope of this book. In many cases, the installation of the SAP HANA client varies by OS. For complete instructions on the installation of the SAP HANA client, please review the information available at *http:// help.sap.com/hana_appliance*. Look for the *SAP HANA Client Installation Guide*.

After the SAP HANA client is installed, you'll need to configure either the ODBC or JDBC clients to support the SAP BusinessObjects BI universe.

Configuring ODBC

Most OSs can be configured to recognize a data source name (DSN) using a configuration file or ODBC utility. This section will walk you through the processes of configuring the ODBC DSN on the Microsoft Windows OS. Please note that the IDT requires the use of a DSN configured using the 32-bit ODBC Data Source Administrator. However, the SAP BusinessObjects BI server requires the use of a DSN configured using the 64-bit ODBC manager.

To configure a 32-bit ODBC to support the SAP BusinessObjects BI client tools, follow these steps:

1. If you're running a supported 32-bit or 64-bit Windows OS, download and install the 32-bit SAP HANA client to support the IDT or other client tools. The SAP BusinessObjects BI client tools are compiled with 32-bit binaries.

2. If you're configuring the ODBC DSN for the IDT, launch the 32-bit ODBC Data Source Administrator to configure the DSN. For Windows 64-bit OSs, this can typically be launched using the *C:\Windows\SysWOW64\odbcad32.exe* executable. For native 32-bit OSs, this can typically be launched using the *C:\Windows\System32\odbcad32.exe* executable or the ODBC manager found in the CONTROL PANEL.

3. Figure 12.1 shows an example of what you should see after launching the ODBC Data Source Administrator. Click the ADD button to create an ODBC DSN.

Figure 12.1 The ODBC Data Source Administrator

4. As shown in Figure 12.2, select the SAP HANA ODBC driver. The driver name is HDBODBC. The driver version should match that of your SAP HANA server. The COMPANY column contains the name SAP AG.

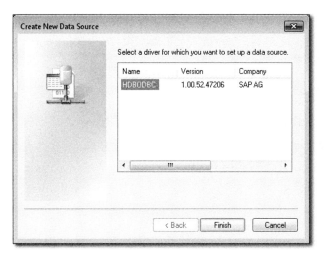

Figure 12.2 The SAP HANA ODBC Driver When Creating a New Data Source

5. After selecting the HDBODBC driver, you must configure the data source name, description, fully qualified hostname, and TCP/IP port of the SAP HANA appliance.

The data source name and description can be anything you prefer, but they should be defined so that the DSN is easily identified. In the Server:Port field, the hostname you enter must resolve to the SAP HANA appliance's client network IP address. The port number is in the format of the 3<INSTANCE>15, where <INSTANCE> is the two-digit instance number of your SAP HANA instance. As shown in Figure 12.3, the value you enter for the Server:Port field should be a concatenation of the SAP HANA host and port number.

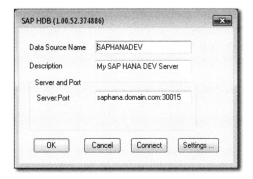

Figure 12.3 Configuring the SAP HANA and Port in an ODBC DNS

> **Note**
>
> Make sure your corporate firewall allows access from your client PC to the SAP HANA host and port.

6. To configure SSL or other special properties for the connection, click the SETTINGS button shown in Figure 12.3.

7. Click the CONNECT button to validate and test the connection details.

8. Using Figure 12.4 as a guide, enter your SAP HANA USER NAME and PASSWORD. Select the CONNECT USING SSL checkbox if your connection requires SSL encryption.

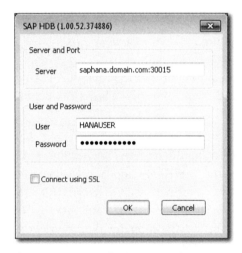

Figure 12.4 Testing the SAP HANA Connection while Creating the ODBC DSN

Assuming that your information was entered correctly, you'll receive a CONNECTION SUCCESSFUL! message, as depicted in Figure 12.5.

Figure 12.5 Connection Successful Message

1. Click OK to close the message.

2. Click OK to save your ODBC DSN.

3. If you receive an error during the connection test, please contact your SAP HANA DBA.

To configure a 32-bit and 64-bit ODBC to support the SAP BusinessObjects BI server, when you create an ODBC DSN on your workstation and subsequently configure a universe and universe connection based on an ODBC DSN, it's assumed that the same ODBC DSN will also exist on the SAP BusinessObjects BI server. In short, you must also create a matching ODBC DSN on the SAP BusinessObjects BI servers. Because there are multiple services that can interact with the SAP HANA appliance on the SAP BusinessObjects BI platform, we recommend that you configure the same ODBC DNS on all SAP BusinessObjects BI nodes used for report processing.

The process of configuring the ODBC DNS on the Windows servers is similar to that of the Windows workstation. However, there are a few items to note. The following instructions will guide you in configuring the ODBC DNS on a Windows 2008 R2 server and provide special notes when appropriate.

1. The SAP BusinessObjects BI platform is a mix of 64-bit and 32-bit services, so download and install both the SAP HANA 64-bit client and SAP HANA 32-bit client for Windows on each SAP BusinessObjects BI node.

2. If you're configuring the ODBC DSN for SAP BusinessObjects BI 32-bit processes, launch the 32-bit ODBC Data Source Administrator to configure the DSN. For the Windows 2008 R2 server OS, this can typically be found in the *C:\Windows\SysWOW64\odbcad32.exe* executable.

3. If you're configuring the ODBC DSN for the SAP BusinessObjects BI 64-bit processes, launch the 64-bit ODBC manager, which is typically located in *C:\Windows\System32\odbcad32.exe* or in the Windows 2008 R2 control panel.

   We recommend that you configure both the 32-bit and 64-bit ODBC each time a new DSN is created. This will make the management processes easier in the long term. From this point forward, the process of configuring an ODBC DNS is the same as what is listed earlier.

4. After you launch the ODBC Data Source Administrator, click the ADD button to create an ODBC DSN.

5. Select the SAP HANA ODBC driver. The driver name will be HDBODBC. The driver VERSION should match that of your SAP HANA server. The COMPANY column will contain the name SAP AG.

6. After selecting the HDBODBC driver, you must configure the data source name, description, fully qualified hostname, and TCP/IP port of the SAP HANA appliance. The data source name and description can be anything you like, but they should be entered so that the DSN is easily identified. In the SERVER:PORT field, the hostname you enter must resolve to the SAP HANA appliance's client network IP address. The port number is in the format of 3<INSTANCE>15, where <INSTANCE> is the two-digit instance number of your SAP HANA host. The value you enter for the SERVER:PORT field should be a concatenation of the SAP HANA host and port number. Again, make sure your corporate firewall allows access from your client PC to the SAP HANA host and port.

7. To configure SSL or other special properties for the connection, click the SETTINGS button.

8. Click the CONNECT button to validate and test the connection details.

9. Enter your SAP HANA user name and password. Select the CONNECT USING SSL checkbox if your connection requires SSL encryption.

10. If your information is entered correctly, you receive a CONNECTION SUCCESSFUL! message.

11. Click OK to close the message.

12. Click OK to save your ODBC DSN.

13. If you receive an error during the connection test, please contact your SAP HANA DBA.

Let's turn our attention from configuring ODBC to configuring JDBC.

Configuring JDBC

As an alternative to using ODBC, developers and administrators can configure their SAP BusinessObjects BI platform and its client tools to support the SAP HANA JDBC driver. JDBC is an industry-standard, Java-based driver that allows applications running within a Java Virtual Machine (JVM) to interact with an RDBMS. For SAP HANA, the installation of the SAP HANA client includes the

JDBC library file. Unlike ODBC, JDBC doesn't have a central configuration GUI or configuration file. Each connecting application must be made aware of the connection information for SAP HANA and the path to the SAP HANA JDBC library file. The SAP HANA library file is named *ngdbc.jar*. It's located in the SAP HANA client root installation directory. On a 64-bit Windows OS, this is typically located under *C:\Program Files\sap\hdbclient*. The installation path for UNIX or Linux will vary based on the installation path information provided during the UNIX SAP HANA client installation.

In many cases, the JDBC client is easier to manage in environments that are using UNIX or Linux to run their SAP BusinessObjects BI environment. With JDBC, there is no need for the SAP BusinessObjects BI administrator to create an identical ODBC DSN on server nodes. The JDBC connection details are read directly from the SAP BusinessObjects BI universe connection objects. The administrator needs only to update a few configuration files, one time, on each SAP BusinessObjects BI server node to indicate the path to the *ngdbc.jar* file. In addition, there are no special considerations for 32-bit versus 64-bit OSs. Many of the SAP BusinessObjects BI tools are preconfigured with either a 32-bit or 64-bit JVM. Because the *ngdbc.jar* is compiled to support the JVM, it's effectively OS and CPU independent.

To configure JDBC support for the SAP BusinessObjects BI universe, follow these steps, which apply to both the client workstation and the SAP BusinessObjects BI server:

1. Install the SAP HANA client. We recommend that you install a 32-bit SAP HANA client on your workstation in the event that you need ODBC support, but technically, the *ngdbc.jar* can be obtained from either installation. For the server, we recommend that you install both the 32-bit and 64-bit SAP HANA client.

2. Locate the installation directory of your SAP HANA client. The 32-bit client installation directory is typically located at *C:\Program Files (x86)\sap\hdbclient*. Likewise, the 64-bit client installation directory is located at *C:\Program Files\ sap\hdbclient*.

3. Copy the *ngdbc.jar* file to the following path: *[Business-Objects Install Path]\ SAP BusinessObjects Enterprise XI 4.0\dataAccess\connectionServer\jdbc\drivers\ newdb*.

4. Note that the NEWDB folder might not exist. If the folder isn't available, create it.

5. Each time you update your SAP HANA client version, you'll need to copy the *ngdbc.jar* file from the client installation directory to the *newdb* directory. The JDBC driver version number should match that of your SAP HANA appliance.

You'll need to follow these same steps on each SAP BusinessObjects BI server node. No additional configuration is required to support JDBC.

12.2   Manually Building UNX Universes for SAP HANA

We'll now turn our attention to the process of manually building a UNX universe to support access to data in SAP HANA. Pay close attention to the concepts that are discussed here, and keep in mind that they also apply to the legacy UNV universe.

The IDT can be found in the Windows START menu under the path START • ALL PRO-GRAMS • SAP BUSINESS INTELLIGENCE • SAP BUSINESSOBJECTS BI PLATFORM 4 CLIENT TOOLS • INFORMATION DESIGN TOOL. The IDT runs as a 32-bit process, but it can be installed on a supported 64-bit Windows OS. Because it's compiled in 32 bit, it will works only with locally installed middleware that is also complied in 32 bit. This is important for developers who want to construct and test a universe using their locally installed database drivers or middleware. Because it's a 32-bit application, it will work only with 32-bit middleware. Therefore, we need the 32-bit SAP HANA client to work with SAP HANA within the IDT. To test both the client and server connection to SAP HANA, there is an option in the IDT to also use the SAP BusinessObjects BI server's middleware, which we'll discuss in more detail later in Section 12.2.3.

> **Configuring the Information Design Tool to Support Windows Active Directory Authentication**
>
> By default, the IDT doesn't support Windows authentication unless the *krb5.ini* and *bsclogon.conf* files have been installed and configured on your Windows OS. If you are using active directory single sign on with SAP HANA, you need to log on to the IDT using your AD credentials. For instructions for configuring Windows Active Directory authentication support for the IDT, please refer to SAP Note 1621106.

In this section, we'll provide you with the basic information and best practices for manually configuring an IDT universe based on SAP HANA as a data source. We'll discuss the steps required to create a relational connection and an OLAP connection, and then the steps required to test these connections. We'll then discuss the steps required to create a project, data foundation, and business layer. To help you understand the design concepts specific to SAP HANA, we'll highlight both the data foundation and business layer options specific to SAP HANA. Finally, we'll conclude with details about publishing a universe.

12.2.1 Creating Relational Connections

The first step in designing an IDT universe requires that you create a relational connection to your SAP HANA data source. However, you must also first install the SAP HANA client that was discussed in Section 12.1.2. The relational connection is used by the majority of the SAP BusinessObjects BI tools when accessing SAP HANA. Relational connections are created in the REPOSITORY RESOURCES window visible in the default IDT workspace, as shown in Figure 12.6.

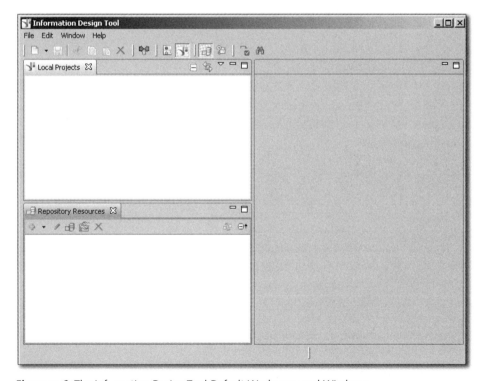

Figure 12.6 The Information Design Tool Default Workspace and Windows

Before creating a repository relational connection, you must authenticate with the SAP BusinessObjects BI platform and generate a session. To create a session, click the green plus sign located on the top-right side of the Repository Resources window or the windows depicted in Figure 12.7, and choose Insert Session.

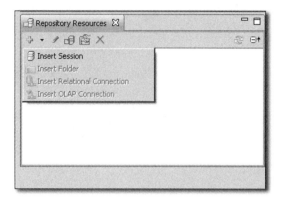

Figure 12.7 Inserting or Creating an SAP BusinessObjects BI Session

The Open Session window appears, allowing you to authenticate with your SAP BusinessObjects BI platform. As shown in Figure 12.8, enter the host or cluster name of your SAP BusinessObjects BI system in the System field. You can then enter your SAP BusinessObjects BI user name, password, and authentication type to create the session.

Figure 12.8 Authenticating with SAP BusinessObjects BI

After successfully authenticating, you should have a session in the REPOSITORY RESOURCES window. Expanding the session object reveals all existing connections and universes available to the authenticated user. Figure 12.9 shows the expanded session in the REPOSITORY RESOURCES window.

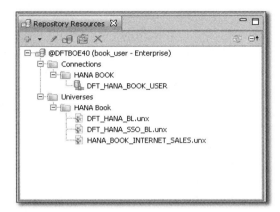

Figure 12.9 Viewing Universes and Connections in the Repository Resources Window

To create a relational connection, use Figure 12.10 as a guide, and right-click a location under the CONNECTIONS folder, where your user account has the appropriate rights to create a connection. Choose INSERT RELATIONAL CONNECTION from the context menu.

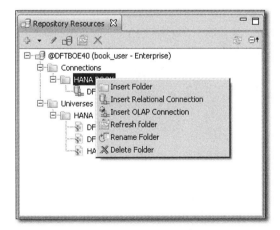

Figure 12.10 Creating a Relational Connection

The NEW RELATIONAL CONNECTION wizard appears, as shown in Figure 12.11. Enter the desired relation connection name in the RESOURCE NAME field and the desired description in the DESCRIPTION field. Because relational connections can be reused by multiple universes, we recommend that you create a name that is generic and appropriate for use in multiple universes. We also recommend that you add a description to indicate the system and appropriate use of the connection. After you've entered the desired name and description, click the NEXT button.

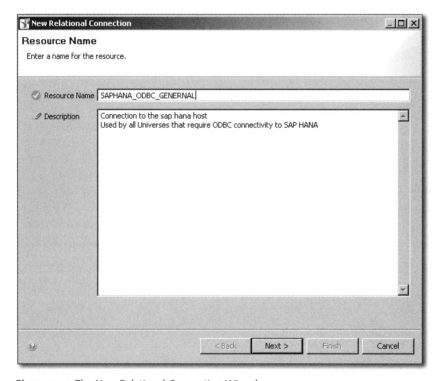

Figure 12.11 The New Relational Connection Wizard

In the DATABASE MIDDLEWARE DRIVER SELECTION screen shown in Figure 12.12, expand the SAP node, and then expand the SAP HANA DATABASE 1.0 node. Choose the ODBC DRIVERS option, and click NEXT. You can also choose the JDBC DRIVERS option if you want to use JDBC. For the purposes of this section, first configure the connection using the ODBC middleware driver.

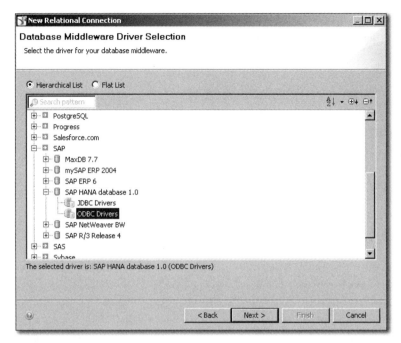

Figure 12.12 Choosing the SAP HANA Middleware and Driver

In the parameters for the SAP HANA DATABASE 1.0 connection window shown in Figure 12.13, specify the authentication mode, user name, password, and ODBC DNS data source name.

There are two authentication modes available for SAP HANA ODBC connections. The first option is labeled USE SPECIFIED USERNAME AND PASSWORD. With this option, the user name and password are coded and stored with the connection option. Tools that access universes based on this connection will always send these credentials to the SAP HANA appliance to authenticate the connection.

As an alternative, you can choose the USE BUSINESSOBJECTS CREDENTIAL MAPPING option. Tools that access the universes based on this connection will send the alternative credentials that are stored with each SAP BusinessObjects BI user account. Individual credentials will be sent to the SAP HANA system based on those mapped to the SAP BusinessObjects BI user account. The second option is best used when analytic privileges are used in SAP HANA information views to restrict access to specific data. However, credential mapping requires that the SAP BusinessObjects BI administrator maintain alternative database credentials for each SAP BusinessObjects BI user.

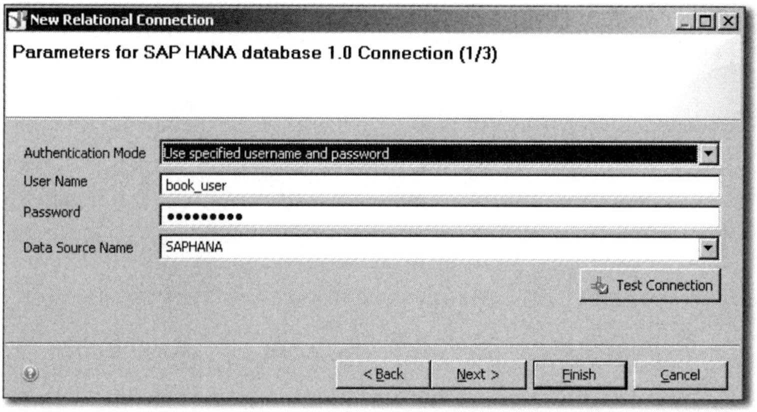

Figure 12.13 ODBC Parameters for the SAP HANA Database

When you configure the JDBC parameters for the SAP HANA database 1.0 connection, there are only two main differences. The AUTHENTICATION MODE, USER NAME, and PASSWORD options are similar, but as opposed to choosing an existing ODBC DSN, with JDBC, you must specify the fully qualified SAP HANA hostname and TCP/IP port in the SERVER (HOST:PORT) field. The hostname and port should be separated with a colon.

There is also an additional AUTHENTICATION MODE option called USE SINGLE SIGN-ON WHEN REFRESHING REPORTS AT VIEW TIME. With this option, the SAP HANA Kerberos and SAP BusinessObjects BI Kerberos configuration is leveraged, and Kerberos tickets are transferred between the SAP BusinessObjects BI system and the SAP HANA system to authenticate the user. For implementations for which single sign-on (SSO) to the SAP HANA database is required, this option should be selected. This option also allows the solution to leverage individual SAP HANA user rights when analytic privileges are set up to restrict access to data in SAP HANA information views. Unlike the USE BUSINESSOBJECTS CREDENTIAL MAPPING option, there is no need for the SAP BusinessObjects BI administrator to manage alternative credentials for each SAP BusinessObjects BI user account.

As shown in Figure 12.14, click the TEST CONNECTION button to verify that your SAP HANA credentials and parameters are set up properly. If they are, a TEST RESULT window appears, as shown in Figure 12.15. Click the SHOW DETAILS button to expose the details view. This window and view provide details about the SAP HANA client build and the location of the various SAP BusinessObjects BI connection configuration files. If the connection test fails, double-check your connection parameters, network access to the SAP HANA host, or the configuration of your

SAP HANA client. Click CLOSE to exit the TEST RESULT window and return to the screen shown in Figure 12.14. Click NEXT to proceed to the next step.

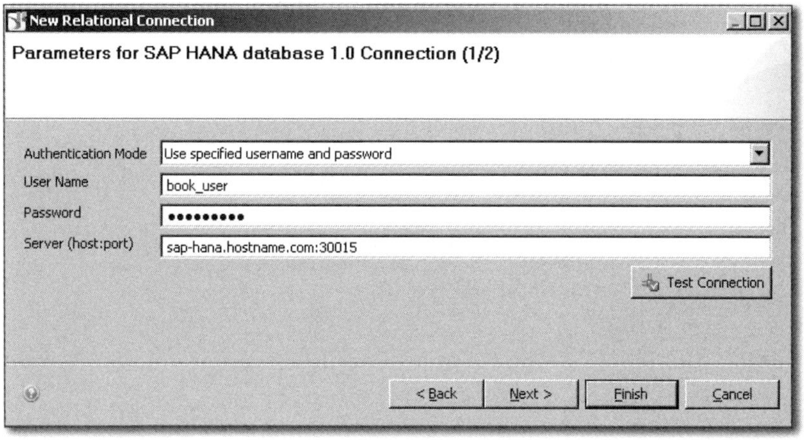

Figure 12.14 JDBC Parameters for the SAP HANA Database

Figure 12.15 The IDT Universe Connection Test Result Window

An additional parameters window appears, as shown in Figure 12.16, which lets you configure additional connections pool options. In most cases, the default values are acceptable for most implementations and solutions. However, it's possible to manipulate these connection pool options to increase or decrease the overall reporting performance under specific scenarios. The creation of a database connection in the SAP BusinessObjects BI platform is an expensive process. If the pool settings are too aggressive, a user's reporting experience can be slowed. Table 12.4 outlines the various connection pool options and provides a description of how each option affects reporting users.

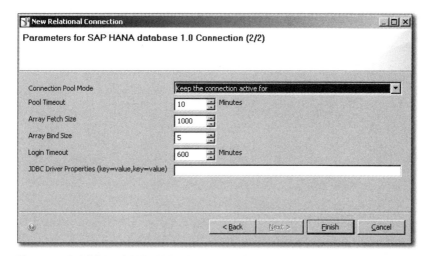

Figure 12.16 Additional SAP HANA Connection Options

Option	Description
CONNECTION POOL MODE • KEEP THE CONNECTION ACTIVE FOR	This is the default connection pool mode and should be used in most use cases. Each database connection is maintained for the specified timeout in anticipation that a subsequent request for a connection will be issued. Setting the value too low negatively affects users because new connections have to be created more often. Setting the value too high results in excess connection on the SAP HANA database. In most cases, 10 minutes is sufficient.
CONNECTION POOL MODE • DISCONNECT AFTER EACH TRANSACTION	This connection pool mode isn't recommended for normal reporting use. A new connection is created for each report transaction. If there are a list of values and multiple queries in your reports, this option results in poor overall report performance. Traditionally, this option is used only with an RDBMS that is limited in its support of connections based on security or software licensing. SAP HANA isn't licensed by connection or user. Therefore, there is no need to use this option.

Table 12.4 Connection Pool Options for SAP HANA

Option	Description
CONNECTION POOL MODE • KEEP THE CONNECTION ACTIVE DURING THE WHOLE SESSION (LOCAL MODE ONLY)	This connection pool mode is applicable only for local mode universe usage or use with client tools. The connection to the database remains open until the client tool is closed. This should be used only if the developer is frequently querying the SAP HANA system and doesn't want to create a connection for each attempt.
POOL TIMEOUT	When the KEEP THE CONNECTION ACTIVE FOR option is selected, this parameter specifies the desired timeout before the connection is closed. It's closed only when the connection has been idle for the specified time.
ARRAY FETCH SIZE	This option specifies the number of records that are retrieved from an SQL query per request. If the value is set to 1,000 and the query returns 10,000 records, the processing server requests 1,000 records from the database 10 times until the total number of records are transferred. Setting this value too low slows the performance of the query because there are too many requests and round trips required to process the records set. Setting the value too high results in network latency or saturation. In addition, setting the value too high can increase the CPU and RAM use on the SAP BusinessObjects BI platform. Ironically, setting the value too high can also result in slower report performance. In most cases, the default value is acceptable. However, if you have the resources to manage a larger number of records concurrently, increasing the value might result in faster processing times.
ARRAY BIND SIZE	This option specifies the size of the bind array before it's sent in a single request to the SAP HANA database. This option is most often used for inserting data with `INSERT` statements, but it can also apply to `SELECT` statements. The default value of 5 is acceptable for universes based on SAP HANA.
LOGIN TIMEOUT	The amount of time (in minutes) that can pass before a connection is closed. If your query runs for longer than the specified time, the query fails.

Table 12.4 Connection Pool Options for SAP HANA

In general, customizations to these connection pool settings should be tested thoroughly when changed from the default. An important component of your testing should include the testing of the settings under high concurrent load, and not just testing them with one user or request. The default settings are a well-balanced combination that addresses both individual-user and multiple-user concurrencies.

After you've established these connection pool settings, click the FINISH button to save the connection to the SAP BusinessObjects BI repository.

12.2.2 Creating OLAP Connections

There are two types of connections in the SAP BusinessObjects BI repository. The *relational connection* is used to provide access to standard relational database sources. There is also an *OLAP connection* that can be used to access traditional OLAP sources, such as SAP BW or Microsoft's SQL Server Analysis Services. In most cases, the relational connection manages the issuing of SQL statements to the RDBMS. OLAP connections manage the issuing of MDX statements to the OLAP source.

For those familiar with the capabilities of SAP HANA, this might be confusing. SAP HANA provides SQL access and MDX access to its information views, and its information views mimic the capabilities of OLAP in several ways. However, when establishing SAP HANA connectivity to the SAP BusinessObjects BI tools, you'll use the relational connection in almost all instances. The one exception is the use of the SAP BusinessObjects Analysis for OLAP client tool. For the SAP BusinessObjects Analysis for OLAP tool to access SAP HANA as an OLAP source, you must create an OLAP connection and store it in the SAP BusinessObjects BI repository. The IDT allows you to create an OLAP connection and save it to the repository for most OLAP sources. However, you can't use the IDT to create an SAP HANA OLAP connection. As an alternative, you can use the SAP BusinessObjects Central Management Console (CMC) to create an SAP HANA OLAP connection.

To create an SAP HANA OLAP connection, you must have access to the CMC and the rights to create a connection, and then follow these steps:

1. Open your browser and access the CMC using the URL provided by your SAP BusinessObjects BI administrator. Typically, the URL is constructed as follows: *http://<SAP BusinessObjects Host>:8080/BOE/CMC*.

2. Log on to the CMC using the appropriate credentials.

3. On the CMC home page, locate the OLAP CONNECTIONS link found at the bottom of the ORGANIZE list.

4. In the CMC OLAP Connections Manager, locate the folder you want to save the connection in and highlight it.

5. Click the green connection icon (third icon from the left) on the toolbar to create a new OLAP connection, as shown in Figure 12.17.

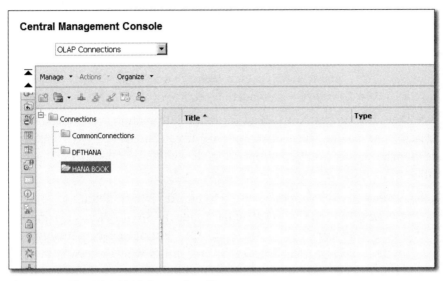

Figure 12.17 The CMC OLAP Connections Manager

6. Select the SAP HANA provider first to enable the remaining fields that need to be completed, as shown in Figure 12.18.

Figure 12.18 Configuring an OLAP Connection to Access SAP HANA

7. In the NAME field, enter the desired name of the connection.

8. In the DESCRIPTION (OPTIONAL) field, enter the desired connection description. Note that the DESCRIPTION field is optional.

9. In the SERVER INFORMATION field, enter the host name of the SAP HANA SERVER and the TCP/IP PORT that represents the instance of SAP HANA.

10. Click the CONNECT button to select a specific information view to act as the desired OLAP source. This is also optional. If you choose to bypass this step, the user can choose a desired information view when creating an SAP BusinessObjects Analysis for OLAP report.

11. In the AUTHENTICATION dropdown list, select the desired authentication option. The PRE-DEFINED option allows you to hard code the SAP HANA user name and password. The PROMPT option forces the SAP BusinessObjects Analysis for OLAP users to specify their SAP HANA credentials when accessing the SAP HANA source.

12. Click the SAVE button to save and close the connection window and return to the OLAP connection manager in the CMC.

12.2.3 Testing Connections Using the Local or Server Middleware

Another key option of the IDT is the ability to choose between the preference of testing connections and accessing data using either locally installed middleware or the middleware that is installed on the SAP BusinessObjects BI server.

With most organizations, installing and maintaining database middleware on client workstations are time-consuming tasks. With the IDT, users have the option to use the middleware installed on the SAP BusinessObjects BI server. When this option is chosen, the IDT communicates all connection attempts through the SAP BusinessObjects BI platform by using its connection libraries to access the desired data source. To change this preference, you need to access the IDT preferences by choosing WINDOW • PREFERENCES in the IDT FILE menu bar. In the PREFERENCES window, locate the option by expanding the INFORMATION DESIGN TOOL • SECURED CONNECTIONS option.

Figure 12.19 shows the two available options. Choose SERVER MIDDLEWARE to leverage the SAP BusinessObjects BI server for all SAP HANA connection attempts. Choose LOCAL MIDDLEWARE to leverage the middleware installed on your local workstation.

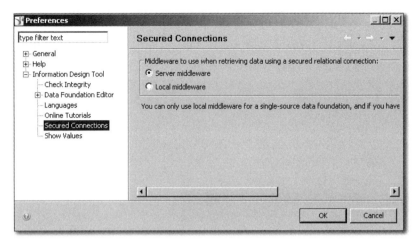

Figure 12.19 Choosing between the Local and Server Middleware

Server middleware can be useful in many ways (for example, when you need to ensure that the server's middleware is set up properly or when you need to ensure that the SAP HANA connections work when executed from the server). If connection attempts fail using this option, then they will likely also fail when interacting with SAP BusinessObjects BI reports and web-based tools. This option is also useful when you're unable to obtain or install the SAP HANA client on your local workstation.

12.2.4 Creating Projects

After creating a relational connection to an SAP HANA system, you're ready to start the processes of designing a universe. However, before you can begin designing a universe, you must define a local *project* in the IDT. Projects are used to organize the local versions and individual components of an IDT universe. This is a new universe design concept that was first implemented with the IDT. Projects are stored and maintained only on the developer's workstation. They aren't stored with universes published to the SAP BusinessObjects BI repository.

While projects are represented as logical folders in the IDT, they are also physically stored on the developer's workstation in their OS user profile directory. To access your local IDT project files outside of the IDT, browse to *%userprofile%\ .businessobjects\bimodeler_14\workspace*. Remembering this path's location is useful when you need to recover project files from another user's profile or manage the project files independently of the IDT.

Follow these steps to create a project in the IDT:

1. Launch the IDT from the Windows START menu.

2. Ensure that you're using the IDT default display. If you're unsure, locate the RESET option under the FILE menu by selecting WINDOW • RESET TO DEFAULT DIS-PLAY.

3. Locate the NEW icon on the icon toolbar (first icon on the left). Click the arrow to the right of the NEW icon to activate the dropdown menu, as shown in Figure 12.20.

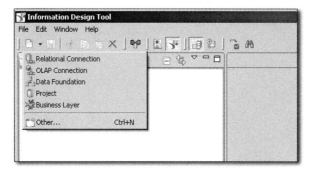

Figure 12.20 Activating the New Item Dropdown Menu

4. Choose PROJECT from the dropdown to create a new project and display the NEW PROJECT window.

5. Enter the desired name for your project, as shown in Figure 12.21. Remember that projects are used only to store the local components of the IDT universe. The name of your project won't be visible to other users or stored in the SAP BusinessObjects BI repository.

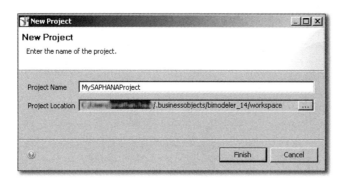

Figure 12.21 Configuring the Project Name

6. Click the FINISH button to save and create the project. Your project is now listed in the LOCAL PROJECTS window, as shown in Figure 12.22.

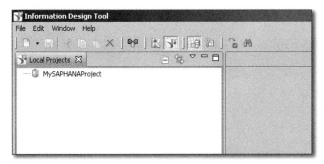

Figure 12.22 Viewing Your Project in the Local Projects Window

All universes require a connection object to properly interact with schema information and data stored in an RDBMS. The first step in creating a universe requires that you define a connection object in your project. There are two types of connection objects that can be assigned to a project: *local connection* objects and *repository connection* objects.

Local connections can be created and used in a local project library. They were originally useful only in instances when a developer needed to test connectivity to an RDBMS without the need to publish the universe or connection object to the SAP BusinessObjects BI repository. However, in SAP BusinessObjects BI 4.1, a local connection is required to automatically generate a universe based on an SAP HANA information view. In Section 12.3.1, we will walk you through the process of creating a local connection.

Repository connections are first created in the SAP BusinessObjects BI repository. This procedure was outlined in Section 12.2.1 earlier in this chapter. They should then be referenced within a local project. When using a repository connection in a local project, you must define the connection as a *relational connection shortcut*. This means that the repository connection won't physically exist in the local project, but rather logically exists as a shortcut.

If the universe needs to be accessible to any user or developers, you need to store it in the repository first. You then have to share it with your local project. To create a relational connection shortcut in your project, follow these steps:

1. In the REPOSITORY RESOURCES window, create a session, or log on to an existing session.

2. Locate the repository connection object that you want to use in your project. If one does not already exists, please refer to the instructions in Section 12.2.1.

3. Right-click the connection, and choose the CREATE RELATIONAL CONNECTION SHORTCUT option, as shown in Figure 12.23.

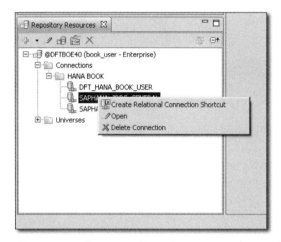

Figure 12.23 Selecting a Relational Connection Shortcut for Use in a Local Project

4. The SELECT A LOCAL PROJECT window appears. Select a local project to store the relational connection shortcut, as shown in Figure 12.24. Click OK to save the shortcut. Accept the message to commit the shortcut to your local project.

Figure 12.24 Selecting a Local Project

You now have instructions for creating a connection and referencing it as a connection shortcut in your IDT project.

12.2.5 Designing the Data Foundation

Before we discuss the concepts of the data foundation that are unique to SAP HANA, you must first understand the basics of the data foundation and how they are created.

The *data foundation* is the next logical component of the IDT universe. Data foundations rely on one or more connection objects that reside in a local project. Data foundations can be designed using either a single source or multiple sources. Single-source connections use the database middleware associated with the connection object. For example, a single-source universe uses the SAP HANA client to interact with the SAP HANA appliance. Multisource data foundations use the SAP Business-Objects Data Federator engine that is built in to the SAP BusinessObjects BI platform to interact with one or more RDBMSs. For example, a multisource data foundation can be used to merge data from SAP HANA with data found in a flat file.

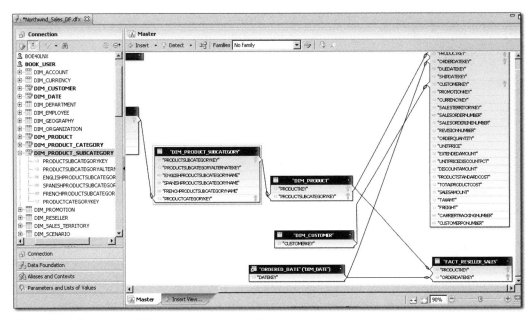

Figure 12.25 An Example IDT Universe Data Foundation

The data foundation component is used to describe the relationship between tables and their adjoining columns. Much like the data foundations found in an SAP HANA attribute view or analytic view, the defined relationships should be configured to produce the elements of a multidimensional model. However, the universe foundation is used to describe all of the possible joins and relationships that might exist between tables in a database or between databases. This includes both tables that contain transactions and tables that describe those transactions.

Figure 12.25 contains an example IDT universe data foundation. The left side of the figure contains the schemas and tables that reside in the assigned connection object. The right side contains a canvas where you define the join relationships between tables to produce a multidimensional model.

Next, we'll explore the steps required to create a data foundation in a local project, where it's both created and stored. To create a data foundation, follow these steps:

1. Right-click your project, as shown in Figure 12.26. Choose NEW • DATA FOUNDATION.

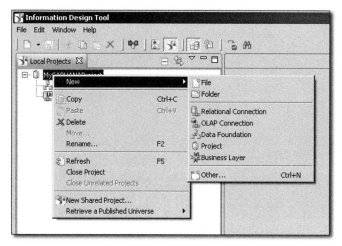

Figure 12.26 Creating a Data Foundation

2. In the NEW DATA FOUNDATION window, enter the name of the data foundation and a description (see Figure 12.27). Click the NEXT button to continue.

3. Using Figure 12.28 as a guide, select the SINGLE SOURCE data foundation option if you intend to connect to only a single RDBMS, or choose MULTISOURCE-ENABLED if you intend to build a single data foundation on two or more data sources. In this case, click SINGLE SOURCE and the NEXT button to continue.

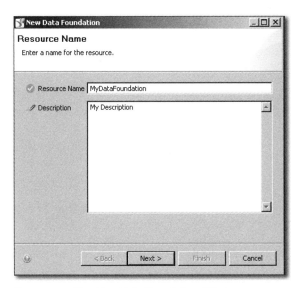

Figure 12.27 The New Data Foundation Window

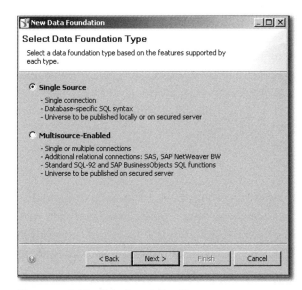

Figure 12.28 The Data Foundation Type

4. Place a checkmark beside the connection that is configured to access SAP HANA, as shown in Figure 12.29. Click the FINISH button to complete the process.

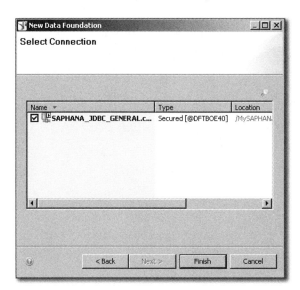

Figure 12.29 Selecting a Connection for a Single-Source Data Foundation

Now that we've discussed the basic concepts of a data foundation and the steps required to create a data foundation, we'll discuss universe design concepts that are unique to SAP HANA; specifically, concepts about information views, columnar tables, optimization, and aggregates. As stated before, the goal of this chapter isn't to make you an expert IDT universe designer. However, this chapter *is* designed to give experienced IDT universe designers information relevant to building a universe on SAP HANA.

Information Views

As we discussed in Chapter 9, SAP HANA has built-in multidimensional models—more commonly known as *information views*—that are developed and then published to the SAP HANA repository for consumption by reporting and analysis tools, such as those found in SAP BusinessObjects BI. In many cases, those tools require the use of a universe to interact with the SAP HANA data. When you activate an SAP HANA information view, a column view is created in the _SYS_BIC schema. These column views then become a possible source for the IDT universe data foundation.

When designing a universe data foundation on an SAP HANA system, you can choose to leverage the information views in the _SYS_BIC schema. To locate the _

SYS_BIC schema, expand the connection object located in your data foundation. Figure 12.30 contains an example of a _SYS_BIC schema and the paginated list of column views that are available for use in the data foundation. From the perspective of an IDT universe designer, these column views appear as a typical table and can be used as such in the data foundation.

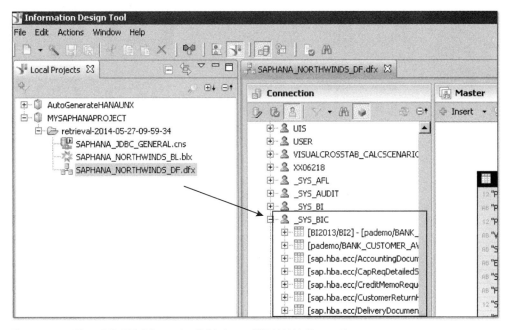

Figure 12.30 The _SYS_BIC Schema Available in an SAP HANA Connection

Figure 12.31 contains an example of how these information views are presented to the IDT developer in the data foundation. Each column view is named in the PACKAGE.SUBPACKAGE/INFORMATION_VIEW format. For example, if you have a package named saphana, a subpackage named internetsales, and an analytic view named ANLV_INTERNETSALES, then the full name would be SAPHANA.INTERNETSALES/ANLV_INTERNETSALES/OLAP. There is also a unique icon associated with each type of column view. For example, analytic views have an icon that depicts a table overlaid by an orange cube. On the icon bar, there is also a drop-down menu located under the filter icon. This menu contains all of the possible types of SAP HANA column views that can exist. This filtering option allows you to limit the list to a specific type of column view, standard view, or table.

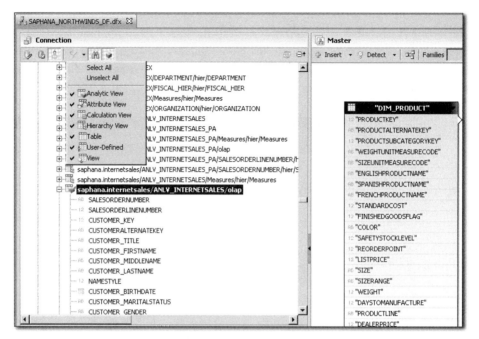

Figure 12.31 The SAP Information Views Available as Tables in the IDT Data Foundation

There are several reasons to use an information view as the basis of a data foundation:

▸ Information views effectively perform similar functions as a universe data foundation. You can either re-create the concepts of the information view in the data foundation or leverage the work that was completed in SAP HANA Studio to reduce the design cost of the universe. In short, it's quicker to use an information view than redefine the table and join relationships.

▸ The organization is using SAP BusinessObjects BI tools that directly access the SAP HANA information views without the need for a universe. In this case, the organization might not want to maintain both a standard model universe data foundation and an information view. For these organizations, it's better to leverage the information view as the central source of analytic modeling.

▸ Using an analytic view can result in better query performance than using the underlying columnar tables. This will be discussed in more detail when we address the various SAP HANA processing engines that are found in the SAP HANA index server.

▶ If you need to leverage the analytic privilege applied to an information view, you have to define the universe using the information views, represented as columns views, in the _SYS_BIC schema. This is an appropriate design consideration when SSO to the SAP HANA appliance has been set up in the SAP BusinessObjects BI environment.

▶ Starting with SAP BusinessObjects BI 4.1, the IDT can automatically generate a universe data foundation and business layer based on SAP HANA information views. This streamlines the process of creating a universe based on an SAP HANA information view.

In addition to these reasons, there are also four types of information views that you can select from in the _SYS_BIC schema: analytic, calculation, hierarchy, and attribute views. Proper identification of the different column views is important when you're defining an IDT universe data foundation on SAP HANA. Let's outline the types of information views that can be selected from the _SYS_BIC schema and the rules applicable to their use in the IDT data foundation.

Analytic Views

An analytic view is a specific type of column view in the _SYS_BIC schema. Fortunately, an IDT universe data foundation configured with an SAP HANA connection depicts each column view type with a different icon. Analytic view icons portray an image of a table with a small cube in the bottom-right corner. The icon is very small but can be identified by the distinct orange color of the cube. Figure 12.32 shows an example image containing analytic views and their associated icons.

Figure 12.32 Identifying Analytic Views in the _SYS_BIC Schema

The analytic views are depicted in both the listing windows and search results window below. Analytic views adhere to one of the two following standard naming conventions: either PACKAGE.SUBPACKAGE/ANALYTIC_VIEW_NAME OR PACKAGE.SUBPACKAGE/ANALYTIC_VIEW_NAME/OLAP.

There is a good reason that the _SYS_BIC schema contains two different naming conventions for analytic views. If an analytic view contains a calculated column, the system automatically generates two information views. The first is the base analytic view; it has the */OLAP* appended to the end. The second is a calculation view. The reasons for this will become clearer when we discuss calculation views in the next section. However, an analytic view will always have the distinct orange cube icon.

When you're choosing a column view from the _SYS_BIC schema, analytic views are the best overall choice. Analytic views should never be joined to other tables or information views for performance reasons and based on best practices. Analytic views have strict rules about how they can be queried. Every query that is produced from the IDT data foundation, based solely on an analytic view, must contain either a SELECT DISTINCT or GROUP BY and an aggregate function. Although they do typically result in the best overall performance, it can be difficult to automatically force a SELECT DISTINCT or GROUP BY statement into the queries that a report developer will likely produce. Later in this section, we'll discuss how aggregate awareness can be used to mitigate these problems.

Calculation Views

A calculation view produces a column view in the _SYS_BIC schema that contains an icon portrayed as a table with a small calculator in the bottom-right corner. Figure 12.33 shows an example image containing calculation views and their associated icons.

Calculation view can exist in two forms. The first form is the result of a user-defined calculation view. These calculation views are deliberately developed in SAP HANA Studio as calculation views. The second are those automatically generated by the system. When activating an analytic view that contains calculated columns, the system automatically creates two types of information views: the analytic view mentioned earlier and the calculation view based on that analytic view. Because calculated columns require the use of the SAP HANA calculation engine, the SAP HANA system automatically produces both the analytic view to manage the base star schema processing and a calculation view to manage the calculated columns. Those generated by the developer have the following naming convention: PACKAGE.SUBPACKAGE/CALCULATION_VIEW_NAME. Those automatically generated by the system to support calculated columns in an analytic view have the following naming convention: PACKAGE.SUBPACKAGE/ANALYTIC_VIEW_NAME. In either case, the icon is exactly the same.

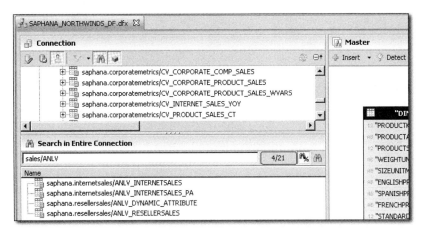

Figure 12.33 Identifying Calculation Views in the _SYS_BIC Schema

Calculation views are also acceptable to use in the IDT universe data foundation. As with analytic views, they should not be joined to other tables or information views in the data foundation. Again, this is based on both performance and best practices. With that said, calculation views are necessary when the universe needs to be based on a calculation view developed in SAP HANA Studio. In other cases, they are necessary when you need to access the calculated columns that are defined in an analytic view. Calculation views don't require the use of a SELECT DISTINCT or GROUP BY in their SQL query. As a result, they are easier to incorporate into the data foundation and overall universe design.

Calculation views are also important when the universe foundation needs to leverage the statistical and predictive scripting languages embedded in the SAP HANA platform. Script-based calculation views can use these languages and then be presented to the IDT data foundation for consumption.

Calculation views often impose additional layers of processing in the SAP HANA engines. These additional layers can slow performance, but they are often necessary to facilitate an organization's requirements. Calculation views can invoke multiple SAP HANA engines depending on the design techniques used in their development. For example, a script-based calculation view that uses a mixture of standard SQL statements, columnar tables, analytic views, and CE_ functions invokes the SAP HANA join engine, SAP HANA OLAP engine, and SAP HANA calculation engine. Therefore, it's important to study the execution plans of a calculation view to ensure that an alternative or less costly option isn't available. These alternatives might include redevelopment of the calculation view or the use of columnar tables in the foundation. These concepts will become more apparent when we discuss the various engines used to process queries in the SAP HANA system.

Hierarchy Views

A hierarchy view produces a column view in the _SYS_BIC schema that contains a distinct icon portraying a table with a hierarchical folder structure in the bottom-right corner. Figure 12.34 contains an example listing of these information views in the IDT data foundation.

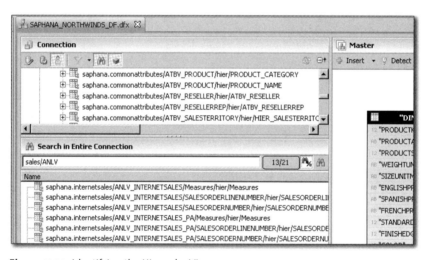

Figure 12.34 Identifying the Hierarchy Views

You can identify hierarchy views based on the use of the term *hier* in their names. Hierarchy views have the following naming convention: PACKAGE.SUBPACKAGE/ INFORMATION_VIEW_NAME/HIER/COLUMN.

Hierarchy views have limited use in an IDT data foundation. They typically return only metadata specific to the creation of hierarchy groupings in supported reporting and analysis tools. Future functionality might use these information views in the universe, but at this time, they aren't useful in the data foundation or universe.

Attribute Views

An attribute view produces a column view in the _SYS_BIC schema and contains a distinct icon, as well. Its icon portrays a table with a series of joined tables covering the base of the icon. Figure 12.35 contains an example listing of these information views in the IDT data foundation.

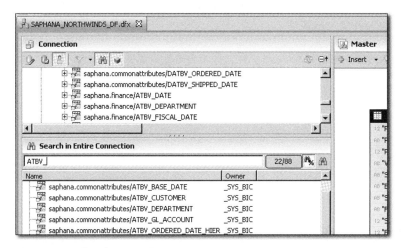

Figure 12.35 Identifying Attribute Views

Attribute views have the following naming convention: PACKAGE.SUBPACKAGE/ ATTRIBUTE_VIEW_NAME.

Attribute views should have limited use in an IDT universe. It's not recommended that you join an information view to other tables or column views. Because only a single information view should be designed in the data foundation, advanced universe design concepts are no longer applicable. For example, contexts require that there be one or more tables joined in the data foundation. Without joins, there is no means by which to create contexts. Index awareness, aliases, and join paths are also not applicable when best practices are followed.

You should now have a greater understanding of the four types of column views that exist in the _SYS_BIC schema. Recall that the column views are representative of the various information views that are developed in SAP HANA Studio. The analytic view and calculation view representatives are the most appropriate for use in the IDT data foundation. Analytic views represent the best-performing option but must be accessed using specific SQL statements.

Columnar Tables

As an alternative to using the column views in the _SYS_BIC schema, you can leverage columnar tables located in any schema. Recall Chapter 9, when we used columnar tables to define the foundation of each information view. If you choose to define your universe data foundation using columnar tables, you could argue that you're performing a similar task. For those experienced with universe design based on a traditional RDBMS, this process will be very familiar. When you use columnar tables, all standard universe design techniques are applicable.

There are six situations when it's appropriate to choose to develop your IDT foundation on columnar tables:

▶ The universe will be predominantly used for operational reporting needs. Universes used in this capacity make little use of measures and are most often used to list information based on strict filter criteria. Because analytic views require the use of GROUP BY statements and aggregate functions, it's difficult to force users to include a measure in every query.

▶ Some organizations will find it easier to adopt SAP HANA as a data mart solution if their existing universes can be quickly converted to use SAP HANA as a source. This is because the use of columnar tables in the data foundation is fundamentally the same as using row tables from a traditional RDBMS.

▶ If the organization needs to take advantage of traditional universe features, building the universe on columnar tables allows these features to be easily implemented. Take, for example, the use of contexts, index awareness, derived tables, aggregate awareness, access restrictions, and row-level security. When an information view is used in the data foundation, some of these features will be obsolete, incompatible, or difficult to implement.

▶ The organization doesn't have the skill set to create information views using SAP HANA Studio. If we assume they have adequate skill sets to design universes, this will likely be the easiest path for implementing SAP HANA with SAP BusinessObjects BI.

▶ The use of columnar tables outperforms the use of calculation views in the data foundation. In some circumstances, querying a calculation view might require excessive processing and result in slower response times. This is especially true when the calculation view returns more columns than necessary to satisfy a user's ad hoc query. Universes based on columnar tables request only columns used in the reporting tool queries. This is particularly important because of the nature of the SAP HANA in-memory columnar store database.

▶ The use of SAP HANA information views is not practical given their design or quantity. In some cases, the information view design might not be conducive for universe design principles. In other cases, there are too many views to choose from. This is often the case with the predefined SAP HANA information views delivered with SAP HANA Live content. With SAP HANA Live, many of the information views were created to act as either a building block for subsequent views or a unique query to address a specific business question. It is our experience that it is often easer to simply create a universe against the base columnar tables than try to reuse the SAP HANA Live calculation views in a universe for ad hoc reporting purposes.

While there are legitimate reasons to use columnar tables as the basis for the data foundation, there are also reasons that this is less than optimal. When you're using columnar tables as the basis, the reporting tools effectively issue standard ANSI SQL92 statements to the SAP HANA system. These types of statements predominantly use the SAP HANA join engine to processes queries. In many cases, this engine is slower than the OLAP engine that is invoked with the use of analytic views and some calculation views. With that said, the performance differences correlate directly with the design of either the calculation view or universe. This is especially true when you compare the performance of calculation views, executed in the calculation engine, to column tables used in the IDT data foundation. We should also note that, starting with SAP HANA SPS 6, calculation views can be configured to execute in the SQL engine. This effectively converts the calculation view into a large SQL statement. It is then subject to the SQL optimizer, much like the SQL that would be produced by a universe. In these cases, there is virtually no execution difference between an SQL engine calculation view and a universe based on the base columnar tables.

Optimization

When you're developing a universe on SAP HANA, there are a few optimization strategies that you can implement to increase the performance of queries and the

SAP HANA reporting tools. The following list outlines these optimization tips and provides a description of their use:

▶ Use information views that contain filter-based input parameters to increase the performance of queries. These filters are pushed to SAP HANA engines and reduce the volume of data that SAP HANA has to process. The SAP BusinessObjects BI universe will detect input parameters used for filtering the information view. It then automatically generates a prompt and list of values based on the input parameter definition defined in SAP HANA.

▶ Include a mandatory universe-based filter and prompts. This is not as optimal as the native input parameter option mentioned above, but it will help to reduce the volume of records transferred between SAP HANA and the connected SAP BusinessObjects BI reporting tool.

▶ Avoid joining information views or column views in the _SYS_BIC schema to each other. This includes joining them to other columnar tables or other column views. This process will likely invoke multiple SAP HANA engines and slow their performance. As an alternative, push the joins back into the information view by designing more complete models in SAP HANA Studio.

▶ When you're using information views as the basis of your data foundation, try to use analytic views instead of calculation views. Analytic views are processed by the SAP HANA OLAP engine, which offers the best overall processing performance. Later in this section, we'll discuss the use of aggregate awareness as a solution to automatically force the use of GROUP BY and aggregate functions. Without this automation, users need to always include a measure in queries based on a universe that uses an analytic view in its data foundation.

▶ When establishing your SAP HANA connection, experiment with larger array fetch sizes to determine the best overall fetch size for your environment. In some cases, increasing the array fetch size can increase the response times of reports and queries.

▶ If you are creating a standard universe based on native SAP HANA tables, use the columnar table type when you define the data foundation. Avoid using row tables and joins between row tables and other SAP HANA columnar tables or information views. Row tables have to be converted to columnar tables on the fly in SAP HANA computation memory before they can be joined to other columnar tables.

▶ In some cases, the use of native SAP HANA tables in the data foundation will actually outperform the use of complex calculation views that rely on the SAP HANA calculation engine.

▶ The use of index awareness can result in fewer joins between tables when you define a traditional data foundation using columnar tables. It can also enable filtering on key columns versus large `varchar` columns.

Aggregate Awareness

Aggregate awareness is a feature of the SAP BusinessObjects BI universe that allows you to define alternative query paths against pre-aggregated tables. Historically, this technique required that special, pre-aggregated tables be created in the source RDBMS schema. These pre-aggregated tables were designed as a smaller and better-optimized source for aggregate queries. The process is dynamic and automatic, meaning that the queries are rewritten automatically to leverage the most aggregated table, depending on the objects used in the report QUERY panel.

As we established in Chapter 7, there is no need to create aggregate tables when using SAP HANA. This is because its architecture can produce fast results without the need to pre-aggregate data. With that said, SAP HANA offers a unique opportunity to take advantage of its different engines with the use of aggregate awareness. If you substitute the pre-aggregated tables with analytic views in the _SYS_BIC schema, you can design a universe that takes advantage of both the underlying columnar tables and the well-optimized information views at the same time. In many ways, this technique provides an opportunity to leverage the features of building a standard universe with the performance optimizations of an analytic view. As we mentioned before, querying an analytic view in the _SYS_BIC schema requires the use of the GROUP BY statement or an aggregate function. Given how aggregate awareness works, designing your universe with this functionality automatically rewrites queries to access an analytic view properly.

When you're defining an analytic view to support this functionality, we recommend that you keep a few items in mind:

▶ To define aggregate awareness, you must create an analytic view that contains the same underlying columnar tables as those defined in your universe data foundation. This is recommended to ensure that no discrepancies exist between the two foundations.

▶ The analytic view should be modeled to return the same results as those defined using columnar tables in the IDT data foundation. Make sure your joins are set up the same between the tables in the IDT data foundation and the tables in the analytic view foundations. This is also true for any attribute view used in the analytic view.

▶ You don't need to include every possible column from your columnar tables in the analytic view. In short, design your analytic view as if you were developing an aggregate table. Define only the columns that are commonly used in aggregate queries.

▶ Use the aggregate awareness function on both measures and dimensions. The mixture of both dimensions and measures in queries is the key to properly leveraging this functionality.

▶ Make sure to establish aggregate incompatibilities using the Aggregate Navigation Wizard. Dimensions and measures that don't incorporate the @Aggregate_ Aware function should be marked as incompatible with the analytic view's column view.

▶ Be mindful that a query that uses only dimensions can fail if all of the dimensions are aggregate aware and the query contains no other objects. This is because aggregate awareness will try to query the analytic view without the use of an aggregate function or GROUP BY function.

▶ Test your queries thoroughly, and view the generated SQL to make sure aggregate awareness is working properly.

Additional Information

A complete description of the implementation of aggregate awareness is beyond the scope of this book. For additional information, please review to the aggregate awareness chapters in both the *Information Design Tool User Guide* and the *Universe Design Tool User Guide* (*http://help.sap.com/bobip#section5*).

The case study located at the end of this chapter will walk you through a few basic examples in the context of designing the universe against SAP HANA, but it won't outline every possible aspect of aggregate awareness.

12.2.6   Designing the Business Layer

The *business layer* is the next logical layer of the IDT universe to develop after the data foundation is complete. The business layer is the layer visible to both SAP

BusinessObjects BI developers and ad hoc report developers who use the universe. In the business layer, classes, dimensions, measures, conditions, and detail objects are created. The objects should be named and organized so that users can easily identify the object in business terms. This is similar to the Semantics node design considerations we discussed in Chapter 9.

To create a business layer, right-click your project folder, and choose New • Business Layer. Choose the Relational Data Foundation option as the universe type, and click Next. Enter the desired name of the business layer, and choose Next again. Select the corresponding data foundation by clicking the three dots to the right of the Data Foundation field. In the Select a Data Foundation window, select the desired data foundation. Check the Automatically Create Folders and Objects option if you want to have the IDT automatically generate the business layer and objects. Click Finish to complete the process.

Regardless of the types of columnar tables or information views used in the data foundation, the business layer setup is the same. Dimensions should be organized into common classes, and measures should be developed using SAP HANA aggregate functions. Figure 12.36 shows an example of the various objects that are created in the IDT business layer. The objects are listed on the left side of the workbench.

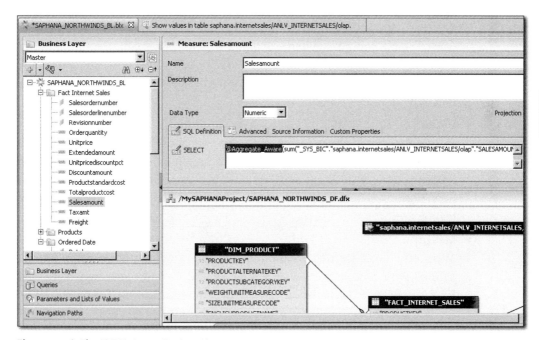

Figure 12.36 The IDT Universe Business Layer

The organization, creation, and naming of objects within the IDT business layer is important because this is the layer where users directly interact with a universe. The business layer is directly depicted within most SAP BusinessObjects BI reporting tools and its structure is used to aid users in the process of selecting the right data elements. Universe developers should always strive to make the process easier for users and report developers, so the organization and naming of objects is important. In addition, it's important to configure the business layer settings and measure objects for optimal performance.

Let's take a look at five different areas within the business layer to see how they affect our SAP HANA implementation.

Organizing Objects

Five types of objects can be defined in the business layer. It is important that we understand how these objects relate to those found in an SAP HANA information view. While there might be some overlap, there are also areas where there are differences.

▶ **Dimension**
Dimensions are used for grouping, sorting, filtering, and displaying information. Each dimension represents a column in a table or a formula based on one or more table columns. When combined with a measure, dimensions are used to group the measures at the query and possibly the reporting tool level. Dimensions are similar to attribute columns defined in an SAP HANA information view.

▶ **Detail**
Details are used for grouping, sorting, filtering, and displaying information. At the query level, they perform the same function as the dimension. In some reporting tools, they act as detail objects that disable the report-level aggregation. This object does not have an equivalent object within an SAP HANA information view.

▶ **Measure**
Measures are objects that are used to aggregate columns. Measures should be defined with both a query-level aggregate and a report-level aggregate. SAP HANA analytic and calculation views also contain measures. They are used for the same purpose.

► **Condition**

Conditions are objects used to house predefined filters. Typically, they are created to perform complex filters that aren't easily developed by the user. They aren't mandatory in a query, but they can be set up as mandatory in any query that uses specific objects. SAP HANA information views do not have a similar object. This is unique to the SAP BusinessObjects BI universe.

► **Class**

Classes are folders that are used to organize like objects into easy-to-identify groupings. For example, a customer class contains objects that return a customer's information and measures specific to customers. There is nothing currently within an SAP HANA information view that relates to a class.

When you're organizing the objects, it's best that dimensions of the same type are placed into the same class. When creating the business layer, the IDT offers to automatically create the objects and classes for you. Each table is converted into a class, and the columns in that table are converted into objects.

This is an efficient option when a traditional data foundation is designed. However, when you're creating a business layer on a data foundation that uses an SAP HANA information view, there will likely be only one table. When this type of data foundation is used to generate the business layer, only a single class, containing all columns as objects, is generated. If you're following best practices, these objects should be reorganized into classes that represent a common set of objects. For example, if your information view contains customer, date, and product columns, it's best to create a customer, date, and product class and then move related objects into each class. There are no technical requirements to perform this extra step, but it's advisable to help users locate the objects in a universe. In many ways, the universe business layer adds value to the SAP HANA information view by allowing additional metadata to be defined.

Naming Objects

When naming objects, it's best to represent them using a convention that is easy for the average business user to understand. In addition, it's important to add descriptions to the objects to help communicate the use of the objects to all types of report developers.

Setting Query Options

When you're designing a business layer, there are a few query options that you must establish to ensure the proper function of the final universe. Query options are located on the right-hand side of the business layer after you select the top-most node of the object hierarchy. The top node represents the entire universe and is located just above the top-level classes.

Figure 12.37 contains an example business layer in the IDT. On the left side, you'll find the object hierarchy. Click the universe object in the object hierarchy to activate the universe properties on the right. Click the QUERY OPTIONS tab to display the options depicted on the right-hand side of Figure 12.37.

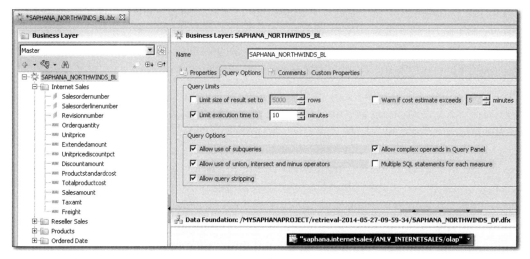

Figure 12.37 Setting the Query Options in the Business Layer

By default, these options might be set lower than expected or produce unexpected results. In the QUERY LIMITS section, you should generally disable the LIMIT SIZE OF RESULT SET TO checkbox. The LIMIT EXECUTION TIME TO option is often set to the default limit of 10 minutes. This prevents long-running queries from being executed with the reporting tools. However, if your reports are scheduled, a high value might be appropriate.

There are also specific query options that can be enabled or disabled based on the intended use of the universe. For example, you can prevent users from defining sub-queries in the reporting tool QUERY panel. Starting with SAP BusinessObjects BI 4.1, query stripping is an available option in the business layer. This feature intelligently rewrites SQL statements by eliminating unused columns from the SELECT statement. In many cases, this increases the performance of the SQL query and any reporting tool using the business layer where this option is enabled. Query stripping can greatly increase the response times of queries executed against SAP HANA columnar tables or information views.

Creating Measures

When defining a business layer, you'll likely have several objects that can be converted into measures. Measure objects are used to aggregate columns. For example, you can create a measure for total sales, tax, or quantity sold. In addition to defining the object as a measure, it's important that you also add an SAP HANA aggregate function to the object definition. For example, if the column is ORDERS.SALES, you should update the definition to SUM(ODERS.SALES).

Placing the aggregate function around the measure definition is extremely important. Failure to define the objects with an aggregate function significantly degrades the performance of reports that use the universe. Properly defined measures invoke an aggregation at the query level. If the measure object definition doesn't contain an aggregate function, then the resulting query won't contain a GROUP BY statement.

The GROUP BY statement is critical to reducing the number of records transferred between the SAP HANA system and the SAP BusinessObjects BI reporting tool. Take, for example, a query that returns YEAR and TOTAL SALES. If you define the measure correctly using an aggregate function, the generated SQL statement looks like this:

```
SELECT YEAR, SUM(TOTAL SALES)
FROM TABLE
GROUP BY YEAR
```

Table 12.5 contains the example output of query that uses a properly defined measure. This query returns only a record for each year and a summary of all records making up that year.

YEAR	TOTAL SALES
2009	56,456,345
2010	65,657,123
2012	66,890,234
2013	59,345.134

Table 12.5 Correct Query Results

When the measure isn't properly defined, the following SQL query is generated:

```
SELECT YEAR, TOTAL SALES
FROM TABLE
```

Table 12.6 contains an example of the results when the measure object is incorrectly defined. This query returns all records from the source database and causes the reporting tool to manage the result set.

YEAR	TOTAL SALES
2009	6,456
2009	5,657
2009	6,890
2010	9,345
2010	9,345
2010	9,345

Table 12.6 Incorrect Query Results

With this in mind, it's important that you convert all measurable columns into measure objects defined with the proper aggregate function. This is especially important when you're using an information view as the data foundation source. Analytic views can be queried only if a GROUP BY aggregate function or SELECT DISTINCT operation is used in the query. Failure to define the measures with an aggregate function prevents the use of analytic views as a possible data foundation source.

Optimization

Consider the following tips for optimizing a universe based on SAP HANA:

▶ As mentioned in the previous section, it's important that a measure's definition contain an aggregate function to reduce the number of records transferred between the SAP HANA appliance and the SAP BusinessObjects BI reporting tool.

▶ Use aggregate awareness functions in the business layer objects when the data foundation contains both columnar tables and information views.

▶ Use the universe parameter JOIN_BY_SQL to push SAP BusinessObjects Web Intelligence data synchronization to the SAP HANA appliance for processing. When this parameter is enabled, SAP BusinessObjects Web Intelligence generates a single SQL statement that queries each source as an inline view. It then performs a full outer join to merge the results. This, too, can increase the performance of reports by moving data synchronization to the SAP HANA appliance for processing.

▶ Avoid defining dimensions with formulas. When a calculated column is used in a GROUP BY statement, the performance of the query can be significantly degraded. In the context of this book, it's best to perform these types of operations using SAP Data Services before loading the data into SAP HANA. This recommendation will help with defining both the universe and the SAP HANA information views.

▶ Always check the integrity of your objects before publishing the universe to the SAP BusinessObjects BI repository. Keep in mind that analytic views might not parse correctly because the integrity checker doesn't know to use a GROUP BY, aggregate function, or SELECT DISTINCT when validating these objects. For other column views or tables, this is important because it identifies any potential issues with the design of the universe.

▶ Enable query stripping in the business layer. This allows an increase in the query response time by removing columns not used in the report from the SQL SELECT clause.

▶ The tasks performed in the universe business layer can have an impact on how SAP HANA performs, so it's also important to organize your universe objects in a fashion that is easy for ad hoc users to identify these data elements.

12.2.7 Publishing the Universe

After completing the design of the business layer and checking the integrity of the objects, you're ready to publish the universe to the SAP BusinessObjects BI repository. Before the reporting tools can access the universe, the universe must be published to the repository. When publishing the universe to the repository, the IDT offers to perform an integrity check on each object. Ordinarily, this is a proper course of action. However, as mentioned in the previous section, objects-based analytic views might not parse correctly.

To publish a universe to the repository, follow these steps:

1. In the LOCAL PROJECTS area, locate the business layer object.

2. Right-click the business layer object, and choose PUBLISH • TO A REPOSITORY, as shown in Figure 12.38.

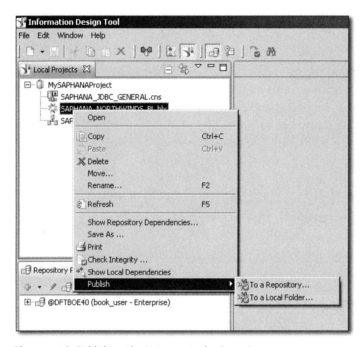

Figure 12.38 Publishing the Universe to the Repository

3. As shown in Figure 12.39, the CHECK UNIVERSE INTEGRITY wizard appears. Select the elements you want to validate, and click the CHECK INTEGRITY button. To skip the integrity check, click NEXT.

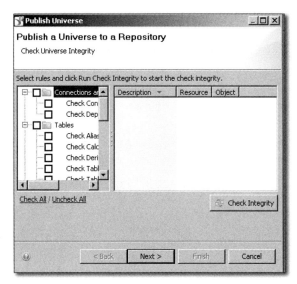

Figure 12.39 Checking the Integrity of the Universe before Publishing to the Repository

4. In the next window, shown in Figure 12.40, select an existing universe repository folder or create a new folder to store your universe. Select the desired folder, and click FINISH to publish the universe.

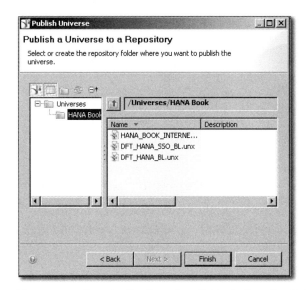

Figure 12.40 Choosing the Repository Folder to Store the Universe

12.3 Automatically Generating UNX Universes for SAP HANA

In Section 12.2, we learned the basic concepts related to manually developing a universe against SAP HANA. Beginning with SAP BusinessObjects BI 4.1, developers now also have an option that allows the IDT to automatically generate a universe based on one or more SAP HANA information views. This option greatly reduces the development life cycle when you're producing universes based on SAP HANA information views. For organizations that have invested effort into building SAP HANA analytic views and attribute views, this option will help them leverage those development efforts without the need to endure an additional significant development effort.

> **Note**
>
> Calculation views are also supported, but the IDT does not effectively interpret a calculation view's SAP HANA metadata.

In this section, we'll walk you through the process of automatically generating a universe in the IDT, which involves three main steps: creating a local connection, selecting information views, and reviewing the data foundation and business layer. Finally, we'll discuss how SAP HANA's metadata impacts the process of automatically generating a universe.

12.3.1 Creating a Local Connection

The first step in generating this universe requires that you create a local connection within an IDT project. When you manually generate a universe against SAP HANA, you start with a relational connection shortcut. However, the automatic generation process requires that you start with a local connection.

To create a local connection in your project, right-click your project in the LOCAL PROJECTS window and choose NEW • RELATIONAL CONNECTION, as shown in Figure 12.41.

Enter a name in the RESOURCE NAME field, as seen in Figure 12.42. This is the name of the connection objects. You can also enter a message in the DESCRIPTION field. Once everything is entered, click the NEXT button to continue.

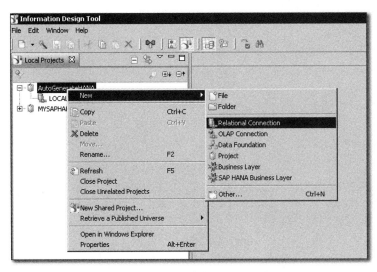

Figure 12.41 Creating a Local Relational Connection

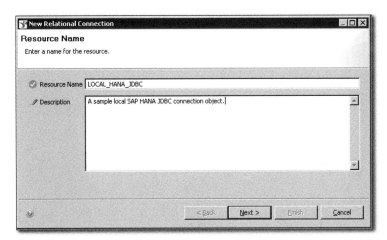

Figure 12.42 Naming Your Local Relational Connection Object

In the DATABASE MIDDLEWARE DRIVER SELECTION window, expand the SAP • SAP HANA DATABASE node and select JDBC DRIVERS as your database middleware. Figure 12.43 contains an example of this window. Click NEXT to enter additional SAP HANA connection details. Please note that, as of the writing of this book, only the SAP HANA JDBC driver is supported for the automatic SAP HANA-based universe generation feature.

Figure 12.43 Choosing the SAP HANA JDBC Driver

In the PARAMETERS FOR SAP HANA DATABASE 1.0 CONNECTION (1/2) window, specify the appropriate authentication mode, user name, password, host name, and instance number for your SAP HANA instance. Figure 12.44 contains an example based on our SAP HANA lab. Click NEXT to configure additional connection parameters.

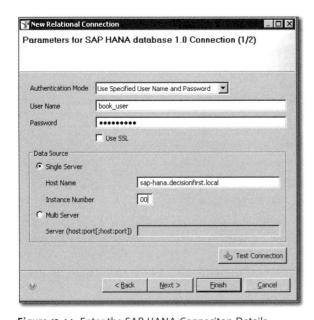

Figure 12.44 Enter the SAP HANA Conneciton Details

In the PARAMETERS FOR SAP HANA DATABASE CONNECTION (2/2) window, review the default settings and make changes as needed. Typically, the default settings depicted in Figure 12.45 are sufficient. Click FINISH to complete the connection wizard.

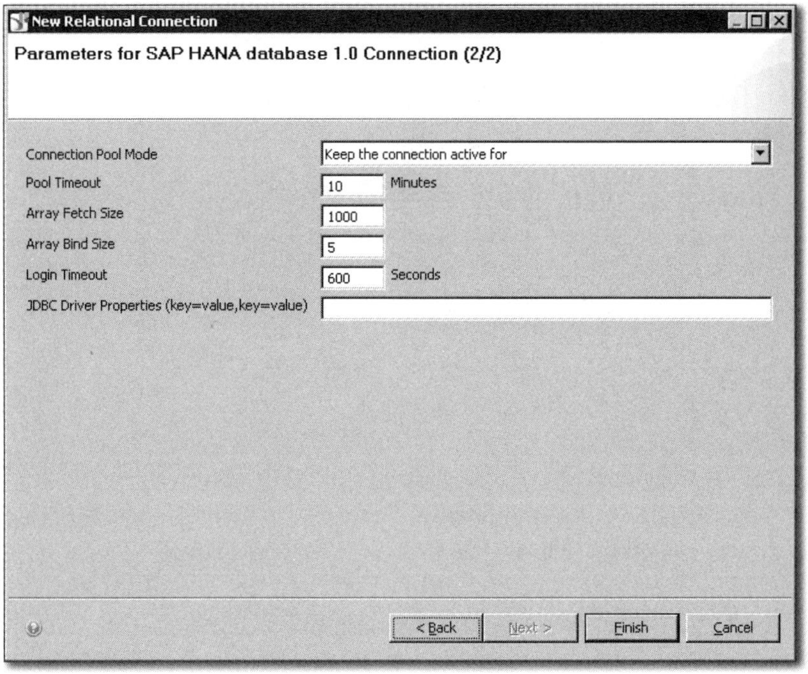

Figure 12.45 Adjusting SAP HANA Connection Settings as Needed

You should now have a JDBC-based SAP HANA local connection in your IDT project. We can now proceed to generating the universe based on an SAP HANA information view.

12.3.2 Selecting Information Views

Prior to selecting the individual SAP HANA information views, we need to invoke the SAP HANA Business Layer wizard. Highlight your IDT project and right-click. In the right-click menu, choose NEW • SAP HANA BUSINESS LAYER. FIGURE 12.46 contains an example of the right-click menu.

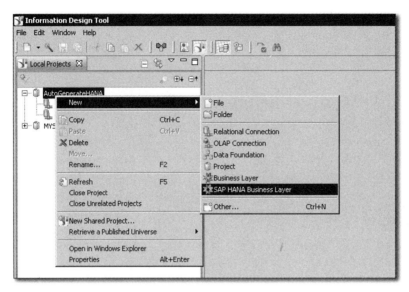

Figure 12.46 Generating an SAP HANA Business Layer

In the RESOURCE NAMES window, enter a name for the business layer and data foundation. You can also enter additional text in the DESCRIPTION field. Figure 12.47 contains an example. Click NEXT to proceed to the next step.

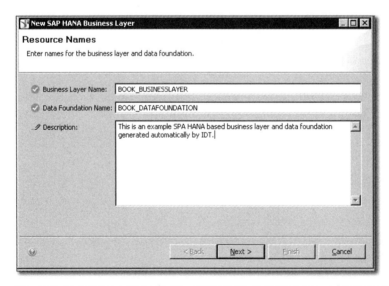

Figure 12.47 Entering a Name for Your SAP HANA Business Layer and Data Foundation

In the SELECT SAP HANA CONNECTION window, choose the desired JDBC connection object. This list contains only local connection objects that are stored in the parent IDT project. To choose the desired connection, place a checkmark in the box located to the left of the connection objects. Figure 12.48 depicts the process of selecting the desired connection object.

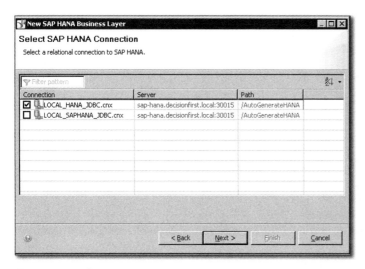

Figure 12.48 Selecting an SAP HANA JDBC Connection

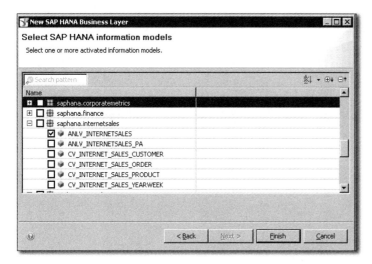

Figure 12.49 Selecting One or More SAP HANA Information Views

In the SELECT SAP HANA INFORMATION MODELS window, select one or more information views from the SAP HANA package hierarchy. Place a checkmark in the box located to left of the desired information views. Figure 12.49 depicts the process of selecting the information view named ANLV_INTERNETSALES. Click FINISH to complete the process. The IDT now automatically generates a data foundation and business layer based on the selected information views.

12.3.3 Reviewing the Data Foundation and Business Layer

Now that we have automatically generated the business layer and data foundation, it's time to review how the IDT sets up these layers. This is an important step in the process. In many cases, we need to make a few naming convention changes in the business layer. We might also want to create a custom list of values, filters, and measures objects to further enhance the universe.

As depicted in Figure 12.50, your local project should now contain a new data foundation and business layer object. The data foundation object contains each individual information model that was selected during the automatic generation process. The business layer object contains all of the universe-specific dimensions, measures, and folders that were extrapolated from the SAP HANA information view metadata. With this information in hand, let's explore how each layer was created using the automatic generation wizard.

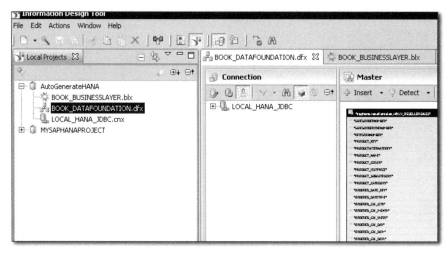

Figure 12.50 The Automaticaly Generated Data Foundation Based on an SAP HANA Information View

Data Foundation

When we first examine the structure of the automatically generated data foundation, you will notice that each information view appears as an independent table. For experienced universe designers, this should stand out as abnormal and potentially a problem. In a normal universe, tables in the data foundation are joined together based on the need to produce denormalized results. However, SAP HANA information views do not represent independent normalized or partially normalized tables. Information views depict a fully denormalized multidimensional model. From the perspective of the universe designer, each table or information view contains multiple attributes and measures that are already denormalized within the SAP HANA model. Therefore, there is no need to repeat that process within the universe data foundation. Although this might alleviate universe designers from their typical, tedious task of joining tables, it does present them with challenges. Specifically, how do you prevent the data foundation from producing a Cartesian product? A Cartesian product produces a result set for which the sum total of records from one table is multiplied by the sum total of records in another. In a normal universe data foundation, unjointed tables are prone to producing a Cartesian product. Because Cartesian products often create extreme performance segregations on the RDMS, universe designers try to prevent them from occurring.

To work around this issue, the automatically generated process starts by creating a self-restricting join or self-referencing filter on each information view table. A self-referencing filter is one wherein a particular column is expressed as being equal to itself. In SQL terms, an individual column is always equal to itself. Therefore, this filter has no effect on the result set when expressed in an SQL query. To view the expression, locate the FILTER icon on the left side of a column within the information view table. Choose EDIT FILTER to view the expression. Figure 12.51 contains an example of what the FILTER icon and right click menu should look like. When the expression is displayed, you should notice that the column in question is set equal to itself.

While the IDT depicts this object as a self-referencing filter, it can also be considered a join. Because it is a join, the IDT can configure it as a member of a specific context. If the foundation option of multiple SQL statements for each context is also enabled, we can avoid a Cartesian product. This is specifically applicable to SAP BusinessObjects Web Intelligence, and means that any referencing of SAP BusinessObjects Web Intelligence can avoid the problem by generating a separate

SQL statement for each context. If every information view in the foundation is configured with a self-restricting join and in its own unique context, then a separate SQL statement is generated for each information view. The results are then synchronized in a way that no additional query problem is exhibited within the SAP BusinessObjects Web Intelligence report.

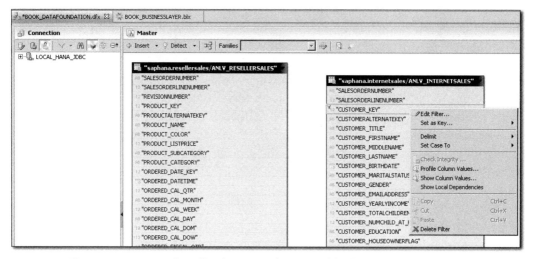

Figure 12.51 Viewing the Self-Referencing Filter Created by the Automatic SAP HANA–Based Universe

To view the context created by the auto-generation process, locate the ALIAS AND CONTEXTS accordion menu located on the left side of the IDT data foundation window depicted in Figure 12.52. As you click on each context, you will notice that each self-restricting join is included in that context, and all remaining self-restricting joins are marked as NATURAL.

In addition to the setup of the contexts, there are two additional critical settings that must be implemented for this methodology to work properly. You must ensure that a separate SQL statement is generated for each context and that no Cartesian products are possible. To locate these settings, follow these steps:

1. Within the data foundation window, locate the DATA FOUNDATION button within the accordion menu located on the left side.

2. After you click the data foundation button, a hierarchy that includes joins and tables should be present, as depicted in Figure 12.53.

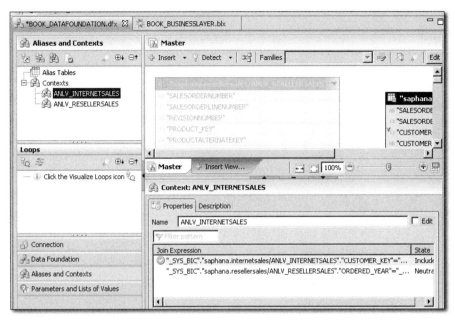

Figure 12.52 Viewing the Universe Contexts Created by the Auto-Generation Process

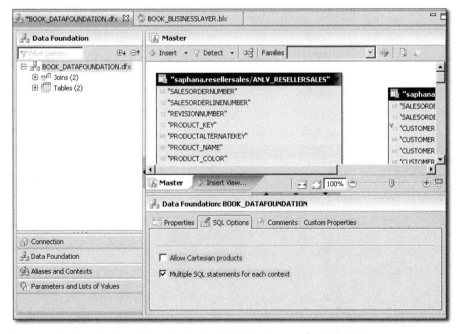

Figure 12.53 Viewing the Option for Multiple SQL Statements for Each Context

Click the top node of the hierarchy, which should represent the name of the data foundation file. Once this is selected, a series of tabs should be present in the bottom-right-side frame. Click the SQL OPTIONS tab to locate the two critical settings. The ALLOW CARTESIAN PRODUCTS checkbox should be unchecked. The MULTIPLE SQL STATEMENTS FOR EACH CONTEXT checkbox should be checked. Assuming that these two options are properly configured, the universe foundation settings will ensure that SQL issues are produced.

Business Layer

After reviewing the data foundation of an automatically generated SAP HANA–based universe, we must examine the business layer to discover how it is set up to aid in the process. We need to pay close attention to how this layer is set up because the automatic generation process is directly correlated with how the metadata in the SAP HANA information view is architected.

As we learned in Chapter 9, SAP HANA information views can be constructed using attribute views, analytic views, and calculation views. In many ways, the attribute view is a basic building block of the analytic view. One or more reusable attribute views are linked to transactions in the logical foundation of the analytic view. This is the basis of a star schema. Because we find that attribute views are often reused in multiple analytic views, we will find that many of the same attribute columns are repeated in different analytic views. Because the metadata is apparent and available to the IDT tool's automatic generation engine, it has the opportunity to consolidate repeated attributes into a single universe dimension object. At first glance, this is likely not noticed, but if we take the time to examine the folder structure and dimension object definition, we will see that an efficient design was instituted.

The first item we should notice in the IDT business layer is that folders are organized by the underlying metadata found in the SAP HANA information views. Figure 12.54 contains an example based the Internet sales and reseller sales information views we created in Chapter 9. Attribute views and their corresponding attribute columns are grouped into folders. Private attribute columns are organized each into their own folder. This is because private attribute columns are defined in the foundation of the analytic view and not within a reusable attribute view. In some ways, they are treated as independent and non-reusable attributes in the universe business layer. Measures are grouped into folders based on their corresponding SAP HANA analytic views. You will notice that the analytic view's corresponding name is listed between the square brackets.

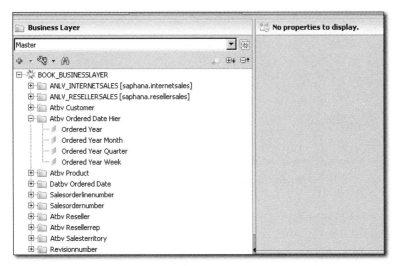

Figure 12.54 A View of How IDT Interprets Metadata from SAP HANA Analytic and Attribute Views

The second item we should notice is that the reusable dimensions contain an aggregate-aware function in their SQL definitions. Reusable dimensions occur when the same attribute view and attribute column are defined within one or more analytic views. The IDT engine recognizes that this is the same underlying object in the SAP HANA information view. To avoid creating multiple copies of the object within the business layer, the IDT auto-generation engine uses the aggregate awareness function to force how the SQL is generated. Effectively, it allows the SQL generation to target the correct attribute column in one of the underlying analytic views defined in the data foundation.

The third item we should notice is that measures and aggregate navigation also play a key role in the setup. For each underlying analytic view, a folder and measures are generated within the business layer. Figure 12.55 depicts an example of how IDT generates measures from the Internet sales and reseller sales SAP HANA analytic views.

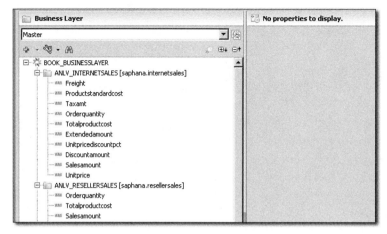

Figure 12.55 Measures Created Based on Their Definitions in Each Analytic View

We now need to examine how aggregate navigation is also used in conjunction with the aggregate awareness function defined on reusable dimensions. To view this, we then need to access the set aggregation navigation window. You can bring up this window within the business layer by accessing ACTIONS • SET AGGREGATION NAVIGATION on the IDT file menu bar. As depicted in Figure 12.56, the AGGREGATE NAVIGATION window should now appear.

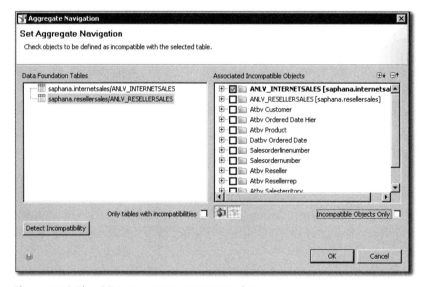

Figure 12.56 The IDT Aggregate Navigation Window

To ensure that each dimension's aggregate awareness function correctly generates SQL, the IDT engine forces the measures from one SAP HANA information view to be incompatible with the other. As you click on each data foundation table, located on the left side of Figure 12.56, you will notice that incompatible objects on the right-hand side are checked and highlighted with bold text. Because the measures are incompatible from one information view to the next, the aggregate-aware dimensions will know which underlying information view is the correct source based on the selection of the object in the SAP BusinessObjects BI QUERY panel. Without this incompatibility, the aggregate-aware dimensions would not know how to construct the proper SQL when measures from multiple information views are defined in a single SAP BusinessObjects BI QUERY panel.

For experienced universe designers, the setup in the data foundation and business layer should help you to understand one efficient way to work with SAP HANA information views. The use of context, aggregate awareness, and aggregate incompatibilities shields the report developer from the complexities of navigating and locating repeated business layer objects from each underlying SAP HANA attribute view.

12.3.4   How SAP HANA Metadata Impacts the Process

You should now have a better understanding of how the constituent components of the automatically generated universe, based on SAP HANA information views, work together to deliver a solution. With that information in mind, we need to understand how the information view's design within SAP HANA impacts the business layer that is automatically generated.

IDT's ability to efficiently create reusable dimensions within the business layer is directly correlated to the use of attribute views within our analytic view model. Without the use of attribute views, all attributes would be assumed as private attributes. As we mentioned previously, private attributes are each placed in their own independent business layer folder. Because there is insufficient source metadata, IDT is unable to set up private attributes in a reusable fashion. The end result, within the business layer, is that all private attribute columns will be repeated. If a single analytic view is used to define a universe, this might not be a significant issue. However, if your data foundation is based on multiple analytic views, each consisting of private attributes, you will discover a significant proliferation of objects within the business layer. You would then need to manually reorganize the objects or attempt to manually implement what IDT easily does automatically.

You also have to consider how metadata is interpreted from calculation views. Calculation views can comprise code that utilizes multiple analytic views. If these analytic views comprise attribute views, one might assume that this metadata will be utilized by IDT. Unfortunately, the IDT is unable to extrapolate attribute view metadata from calculation views when constructing the universe business layer. This means that calculation view attributes will most likely be represented similarly to how private attributes are represented. However, we have found that calculation view hierarchy metadata is properly interpreted. If a hierarchy is defined in the semantic layer of the calculation views, each hierarchy and its attributes will be organized into a business layer folder.

Most will find that the automatic generation process works best when the SAP HANA information views are composed solely of analytic views. These same analytic views should also be based solely on reusable attribute views. Unfortunately, most SAP HANA information view developers will find this impossible to comply with. This is because they often need private attributes or calculation views to satisfy the end user's requirements. This is why it is important for universe developers to understand how the automatic process works. In most cases, manual adjustments to the business layer will be required to help facilitate fluid ad hoc reporting against the automatically generated content. In other cases, it will likely be easier to build the universe from scratch, without utilizing the automatic building process within IDT. Despite some of its limitations, the automatic generation process does outline a very interesting solution.

12.4   The SAP HANA Engines in Universe Design

When it comes to universe design, there are several ways to query the data that is stored in SAP HANA. As with any universe, you can define the relationships between the standard columnar tables that are defined in an SAP HANA schema. However, you can also define your universe on information views. Recall from previous sections of this chapter that there are different engines in the SAP HANA index server that are used to processes queries depending on the information views or SQL queries that are executed. When you design a universe—or even when you define an SAP HANA information view—it's important that you understand the capabilities of each engine and the circumstances in which each engine is used.

In SAP HANA Studio, you can use the Plan Visualization tool found in the SQL query console to identify the engines that are invoked with the queries generated by the universe. Simply copy and paste your generated SQL statements into SAP HANA Studio's SQL query console, highlight the contents of the statement, right-click the highlighted text, and choose Visualize Plan. The initial plan visualization provides a high-level overview of the processing workflow. Figure 12.57 is an example of the initial Visualized Plan window that appears.

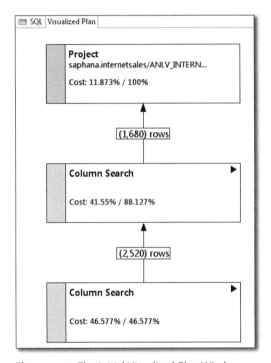

Figure 12.57 The Initial Visualized Plan Window

To view the details of each node, right-click the visual blocks and choose Execute to calculate the full execution plan. Figure 12.58 contains an example of the detail that can be seen after executing the plan and expanding the visual blocks.

In the SAP HANA index server, there are three main engines that are used to process analytical queries. The join engine, OLAP engine, and calculation engine are used to processes queries produced by a universe and the SAP BusinessObjects BI tools. When reviewing the Visual Plan details, items that are prefixed with "JE" indicate processing with the join engine, items that are prefixed with "BW" indicate processing with the OLAP engine, and items prefixed with "CE" indicate processing with the calculation engine. We'll now discuss these engines in more detail and provide information about how different universe design techniques invoke the different engines.

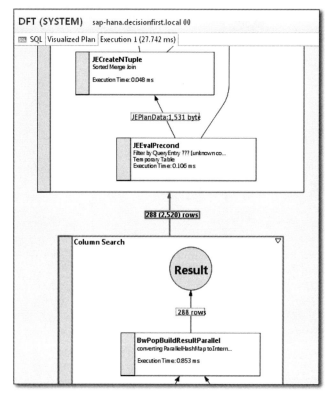

Figure 12.58 Details of the Visualized Plan

12.4.1 SAP HANA Join Engine

The join engine is used to process standard SQL queries. These are the queries that follow the ANSI standard by incorporating the use of the SELECT, FROM, WHERE, GROUP BY, or ORDER BY statements. If your SQL statement contains joins between two or more columnar tables, the join engine is used to process the query. In addition, if you query an attribute view's column view in the _SYS_BIC schema, the join engine is also used. However, the join engine can also be invoked in a script-based calculation view that uses ANSI SQL, stored procedures, or joined multiple information views in the universe data foundation.

In most cases, the join engine's performance is superior to that of a traditional RDBMS. This is because the engine is able to leverage the in-memory and column store features of SAP HANA. However, the join engine isn't as well optimized as the OLAP engine and, in some cases, the calculation engine. In real-world testing, the join engine experiences performance degradation when processing multiple concurrent joins or joins between large tables. With that said, its performance is still superior to that of a traditional, disk-based RDBMS.

When you develop a universe, it's important to understand that the use of columnar tables in the data foundation will likely be processed by the join engine. The join engine can also be invoked when you join a columnar table to an information view, when you use non-aggregate functions when querying an information view, or when you join an information view to another information view. When joining information views to other items, it's important to understand that the join engine is used at the tail end of the processing to merge the results of the information view to the other items.

The same is true when you use non-aggregate functions when querying an information view. From a processing standpoint, this can add significant overhead to the index server as it manages the temporary results of each information view and then attempts to join them or manipulate their results. In most cases, it's best to make sure your queries are processed by only one engine. In the case of the join engine, this can be achieved if you use only columnar tables in the data foundation or if your queries use a single information view in the SQL FROM clause.

12.4.2 SAP HANA OLAP Engine

The OLAP engine is the most optimized engine in the SAP HANA index server. It's designed to process star schema queries or queries with one or more attribute tables that have a one-to-many relationship with a transaction or fact table. The OLAP engine is able to process joins and calculations in parallel to better leverage the hardware platform of SAP HANA. In terms of multidimensional processing, this is the optimal engine to use.

Analytic views are designed to use the OLAP engine. When you define an analytic view in SAP HANA Studio, you're effectively designing a logical star schema by joining attribute views to an analytic foundation table. When developed correctly, this produces the required one-to-many joins that are efficiently processed in the OLAP engine.

Not all analytic views are processed entirely by the OLAP engine. Analytic views that contain calculated columns can invoke the use of the calculation engine during the processing of related queries. This includes the use of attribute views with calculated columns in the analytic view.

In reality, this process isn't automatic. The process occurs outside the query execution plan. When you activate an analytic view that contains calculated columns, two information views or column views are created in the _SYS_BIC schema. One information view is the pure analytic view version. The second is the calculation view version of the analytic view. The calculation view version must be used to process the calculated columns defined in the analytic view. The pure analytic view versions represent the base logical star schema, which will be processed in the OLAP engine. The calculation view is built upon the analytic view to process the calculated columns. In short, it's up to the universe designer to determine which view is chosen when defining the data foundation of the universe. If the designer chooses the analytic view, the calculated columns will be absent from its column view in the _SYS_BIC schema.

In terms of universe design, avoid invoking non-aggregate functions in SQL queries based on an analytic view. For example, if your SELECT statement uses the function substr() on an attribute in the analytic view, the join engine is also used to process this extra calculation. To translate this in universe design terms, you should avoid using functions in the definition of dimensions. Functions used in measures don't have this effect, assuming that the universe measure is defined on a column that is also defined as a measure in the analytic view. In these situations, it's best to move these functions to the SAP Data Services ETL process to optimize both the analytic view and universe.

12.4.3   SAP HANA Calculation Engine

The calculation engine is used to process calculation views. Calculation views can use several different types of objects as their source. When you define a calculation view using only analytic views as the source, the OLAP engine is used to process each analytic view in the calculation view definition. After each analytic view has been processed in the OLAP engine, the results are sent to the calculation engine to perform the additional calculations and transformations.

You can also use columnar tables as the source of the calculation view. In this instance, portions of the query leverage the OLAP engine if the query optimizer determines that it's possible to enhance performance. The calculation engine and join engine will also be used. With script-based calculation views, you can leverage columnar tables, stored procedures, and other information views. Because the developer has free range to define the script as needed, script-based calculation views have the potential to invoke multiple engines. If the script is defined using only CE_ functions and analytic views, only the OLAP engine and calculation engine are used. However, if the script uses ANSI SQL statements or stored procedures, the join engine can also be invoked. To fully understand the engines used in a calculation view, it's best to analyze SQL statements using the Plan Visualization tool in SAP HANA Studio. While the examples just described are correct for the stated scenario, each calculation view should be analyzed to fully understand the engines that are invoked. For the purposes of this section, understand that calculation views often invoke the calculation engine and other engines when processing related queries.

As with analytic views, if you define additional functions in universe objects, additional layers of processing are invoked to facilitate the complete execution plan. Again, avoid using functions in universe business layer objects to avoid this extra processing. In the context of this book, it's best to push this process back to SAP Data Services. However, don't assume that every calculation can be pushed back to SAP Data Services. In many cases, the calculation view is used to process queries and calculations that can be expressed only at runtime. This is why the calculation engine and calculation views are needed in most SAP HANA BusinessObjects BI solutions.

In terms of calculation view performance, analytic views are faster at processing data than calculation views. However, in the context of this book, the performance difference can be negligible. This is mostly due to the fact that SAP Data Services is performing the majority of the data denormalization and transmutation before SAP HANA is provisioned. However, calculation views can sometimes perform much slower than an analytic view, depending on their design and the structure of the data. In terms of the join engine, there is no set rule regarding which is faster at processing multidimensional queries. The performance of a calculation view depends greatly on the way it's designed. The same is true of standard ANSI SQL queries executed in the join engine. From a universe design standpoint, you need to understand the impact of your design as it relates to the various options for configuring a universe against SAP HANA.

12.5 Case Study: Designing a Universe to Support Internet Sales Data

The AdventureWorks Cycle Company has recently implemented SAP HANA and has decided to use SAP Data Services to extract, transform, load, and cleanse data from multiple sources while provisioning columnar tables in SAP HANA. The company recently created several information views using SAP HANA Studio to support analysis of the Internet sales data. The views are now fully tested and ready for use with the SAP BusinessObjects BI platform.

The IT department at AdventureWorks Cycle Company has received a request to create several dashboards and provide ad hoc reporting access to the business users. To facilitate this request, the IT department needs to develop an SAP BusinessObjects BI universe. Because they are new to the SAP BusinessObjects BI platform and need to support direct binding queries in SAP BusinessObjects Dashboards, they have decided to design a UNX universe using the IDT.

The lead universe developer has studied the Internet sales information views and determined that he needs to develop a universe that leverages both the columnar tables provisioned with SAP Data Services and the information views produced by the SAP HANA information views. To implement this universe correctly, the lead developer will use aggregate awareness to allow the universe to automatically switch between the universe-modeled columnar tables and the Internet sales analytic view. This is an important design technique that allows the universe to support both operational reporting and analytical reporting in a single solution.

12.5.1 Creating the Universe Connection and Project

This step involves leveraging the existing step-by-step instructions already outlined in the beginning of this chapter, in Section 12.2. Here, we'll supply additional information and object names:

1. Using Section 12.2.1 as a guide, create a JDBC relation connection named SAPHANA_JDBC_DEV. This connection will be used to connect to the SAP HANA system. Connections are typically named in reference to their system and environment.

2. Using Section 12.2.4 as a guide, create a project named InternetSales in the IDT.

3. Using Section 12.2.1 as a guide, create a relational connection shortcut in the INTERNETSALES project.

12.5.2 Designing the Data Foundation

You must now create a data foundation that facilitates the use of both columnar tables and the column views found in the _SYS_BIC schema. This workflow was discussed in detail in Section 12.2.5. For the case study, we are going to add the SAP HANA analytic view that represents the Internet sales. This view was created in SAP HANA Studio and published to SAP HANA in Chapter 9. Follow these steps to create this data foundation:

1. Create a data foundation in your local project.

2. Right-click the local project named INTERNETSALES, and choose NEW • DATA FOUNDATION (see Figure 12.59).

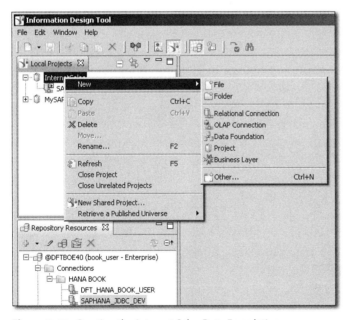

Figure 12.59 Creating the Internet Sales Data Foundation

3. As shown in Figure 12.60, name the data foundation INTERNETSALES_DF, and include a description to help others identify the data foundation. Click NEXT to proceed to the next window.

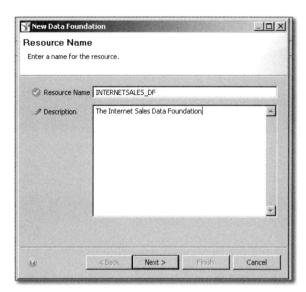

Figure 12.60 Naming the INTERNETSALES_DF Data Foundation

4. Select SINGLE SOURCE as the data foundation type, as shown in Figure 12.61. In this example, you're connecting to only a single instance of SAP HANA. Click NEXT to proceed to the next window.

Figure 12.61 Select the Data Foundation Type

5. As shown in Figure 12.62, select the connection name SAPHANA_JDBC_DEV, and choose FINISH. An undefined data foundation window appears.

Figure 12.62 Selecting a Connection for the Data Foundation

6. In the INTERNETSALES_DF.DFX DATA FOUNDATION tab, add the following tables to the MASTER design window located on the right-hand side of Figure 12.63:

- ▸ DIM_CUSTOMER
- ▸ DIM_PRODUCT
- ▸ DIM_PRODUCTSUBCATEGORY
- ▸ DIM_PRODUCTCATEGORY
- ▸ DIM_DATE
- ▸ INTERNETSALES_FACT

7. To add tables to the master design window, expand the SAPHANA_JDBC_DEV connection in the leftmost CONNECTION window shown in Figure 12.63. Expand the BOOK_USER schema containing the listed columnar tables. One at a time, highlight the listed tables and move them to the MASTER design window using the standard drag-and-drop technique.

8. Join the table to produce a multidimensional data foundation. This is a foundation where the tables prefixed with "DIM_" (short for "dimension") are each joined to the FACT_INTERNET_SALES table. The relationship between each DIM_ table and the FACT_INTERNET_SALES table must be one-to-many.

665

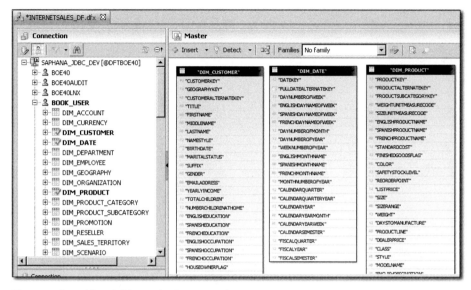

Figure 12.63 Adding Tables to the Data Foundation

9. To join a table, choose INSERT • INSERT JOIN from the dropdown menu in the MASTER window (see Figure 12.64). The join definition window should now appear.

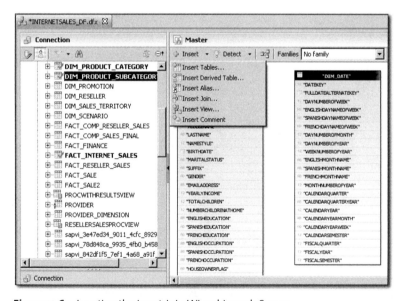

Figure 12.64 Locating the Insert Join Wizard Launch Screen

10. As shown in the left side of Figure 12.65, choose the DIM_CUSTOMER table from the dropdown list. In the center of the screen, choose the = option. On the right-hand side of the screen, choose FACT_INTERNET_SALES. Located near the bottom, set the CARDINALITY option to 1,N. Click OK to save the join definition.

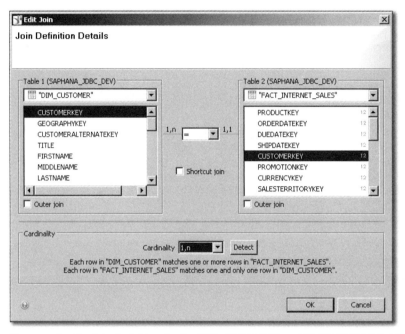

Figure 12.65 The Join Definition for the DIM_CUSTOMER and FACT_INTERNET_SALES Tables

11. Define the join definition between DIM_DATE and FACT_INTERNET_SALES, as shown in Figure 12.66.

12. Using Figure 12.67 as a guide, define the join definition between DIM_PRODUCT and FACT_INTERNET_SALES.

13. Define the join definition between DIM_PRODUCT and DIM_PRODUCT_SUBCATEGORY, as shown in Figure 12.68. In this join definition, you're not joining to FACT_INTERNET_SALES. This join is required to provide a product subcategory for each product. Notice that you're still maintaining a one-to-many join relationship between the two tables.

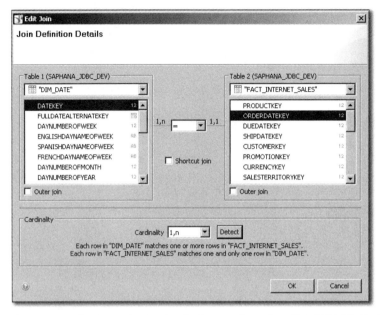

Figure 12.66 The Join Definition for the DIM_DATE and FACT_INTERNET_SALES Tables

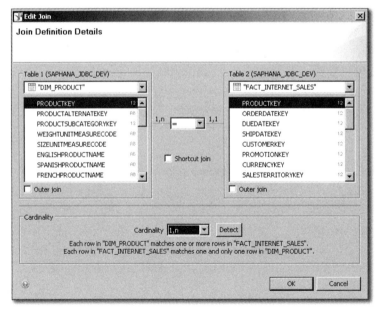

Figure 12.67 The Join Definition for the DIM_PRODUCT and FACT_INTERNET_SALES Tables

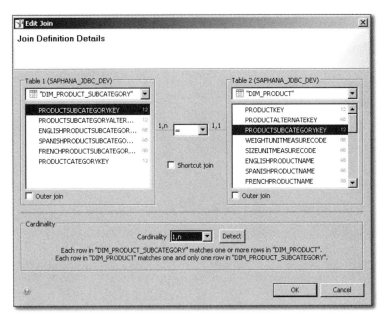

Figure 12.68 The Join Definition for the DIM_PRODUCT and DIM_PRODUCT_SUBCATEGORY Tables

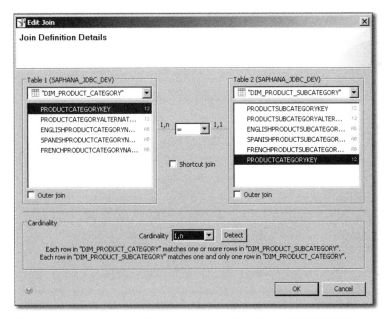

Figure 12.69 The Join Definition for the DIM_PRODUCT_SUBCATEGORY and DIM_PRODUCT_CATEGORY Tables

669

14. Using Figure 12.69 as a guide, define the join definition between DIM_PRO-DUCT_CATEGORY and DIM_PRODUCT_SUBCATEGORY.

15. To automatically arrange your table in the MASTER design window, click the AUTO-ARRANGE button on the MASTER design window icon bar, which is boxed in Figure 12.70.

16. Add the Internet sales analytic view to the data foundation, but don't join it to any tables. Later, you'll reference this column view in the business layer where you define @aggregrate_aware functions. Figure 12.71 shows an example of this analytic view in the CONNECTION window under the _SYS_BIC schema.

17. Drag the table named saphana.internetsales/ANLV_INTERNETSALES/olap to the MASTER design window canvas just below the tables that are joined.

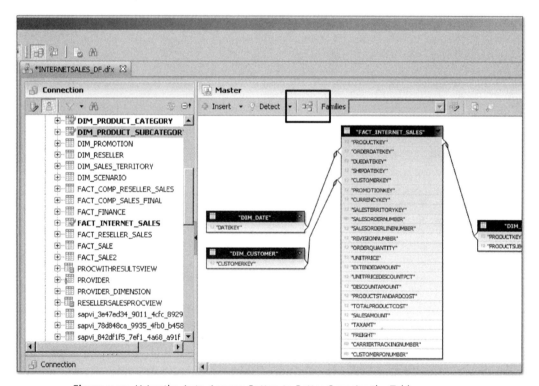

Figure 12.70 Using the Auto-Arrange Button to Better Organize the Tables

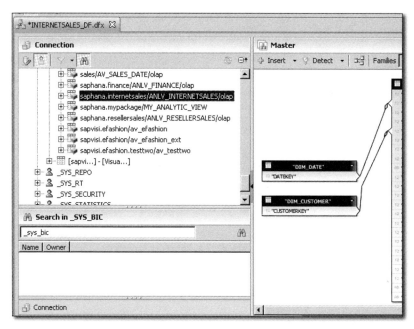

Figure 12.71 Adding the Internet Sales Column View from the _SYS_BIC Schema to the Data Foundation Master Design Window

18. Save the data foundation in the local project workspace by pressing `Ctrl`+`S`.

12.5.3 Designing the Business Layer

The next step in the design process is the definition of the business layer. In this layer, you define the dimensions, measures, and classes using the columnar tables and Internet sales analytic view. In some cases, you delete objects, rename objects, or reorganize them to help simplify the universe.

Because the Internet sales analytic view isn't joined to the columnar tables, you define some of the universe objects with aggregate awareness. These concepts were discussed in the "Optimization" subsection in Section 12.2.6. This allows the universe to automatically switch between querying an analytic view and the columnar tables based on the definition of reporting tools queries. To create the business layer, follow these steps:

1. Right-click the project named INTERNETSALES, and choose NEW • BUSINESS LAYER, as shown in Figure 12.72.

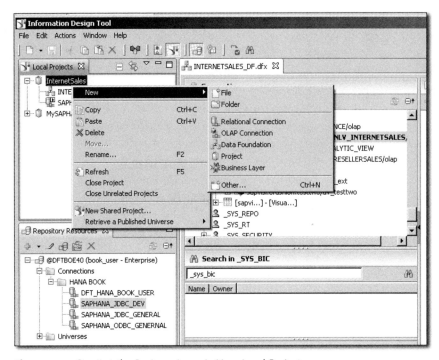

Figure 12.72 Creating the Business Layer in Your Local Project

2. When the NEW BUSINESS LAYER window appears, choose the RELATIONAL DATA FOUNDATION option, and click NEXT (see Figure 12.73).

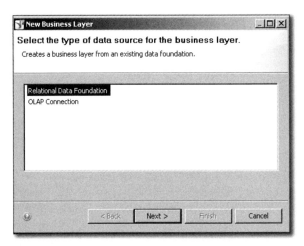

Figure 12.73 Selecting the Relational Data Foundation Option

3. When the RESOURCE NAME window appears, enter the name "INTERNET-SALES_BL", and click NEXT to continue, as shown in Figure 12.74.

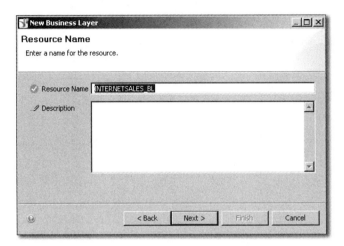

Figure 12.74 Naming the Business Layer in the New Business Layer Wizard

4. When the SELECT DATA FOUNDATION window appears, click the ellipsis, and select the INTERNETSALES_DF.DFX data foundation that is stored in the INTERNETSALES local project. Make sure the option AUTOMATICALLY CREATE FOLDERS AND OBJECTS is selected, as shown in Figure 12.75. Although you'll change the auto-generated objects later, selecting this option saves time, compared to creating them individually. Click FINISH to close the wizard.

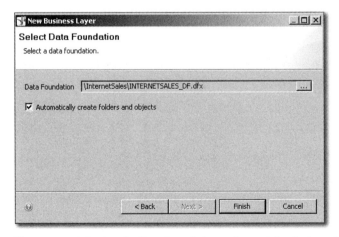

Figure 12.75 Selecting the Data Foundation to Support the Business Layer

5. The business layer should not be visible in the IDT workspace. Figure 12.76 contains an example of this business layer. On the left side is the Business Layer design window, in which the objects and classes that were automatically generated by the New Business Layer window appear. The right-hand side contains two windows. The top of the rightmost window contains the options for any highlighted object. The bottom window contains an image of the referenced data foundation.

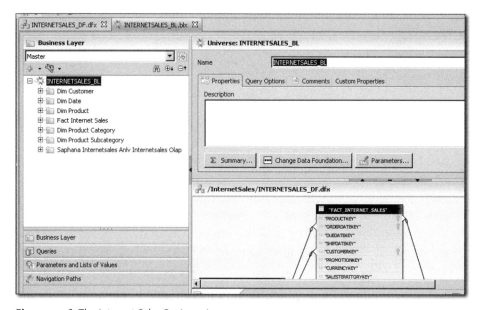

Figure 12.76 The Internet Sales Business Layer

6. Because you chose to have the business layer automatically generate folders and objects, you must now remove or rename objects to make the universe more user friendly.

Renaming Objects

Follow these steps to rename objects in the Business Layer windows:

1. Locate the object and highlight it to activate the options window on the right-hand side. In the options window for the selected object (see the fields boxed in Figure 12.77), locate the Name field.

2. Expand each class or folder, and rename the objects to be more user friendly. The process of renaming the objects is the same as the one described earlier for renaming classes. Later, figures are provided to help you create the suggested object names.

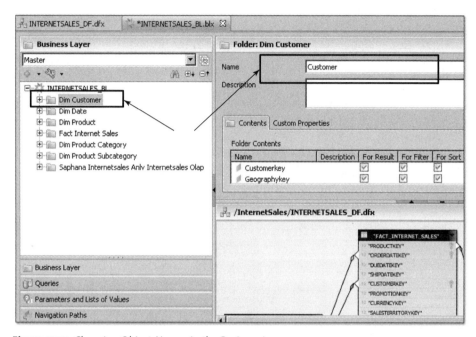

Figure 12.77 Changing Object Names in the Business Layer

3. Rename each folder or class as listed in Table 12.7.

Auto-Generated Class Name	New Class Name
DIM CUSTOMER	CUSTOMER
DIM DATE	ORDERED DATE
DIM PRODUCT	PRODUCTS
FACT INTERNET SALES	INTERNET SALES TRANSACTIONS AND MEASURES
DIM PRODUCT CATEGORY	PRODUCT CATEGORY
DIM PRODUCT SUBCATEGORY	PRODUCT SUBCATEGORY

Table 12.7 Renaming the Internet Sales Business Layer Classes

Deleting Objects

Delete the Saphana Internetsales Anlv Internetsales Olap class and objects from the business layer. These objects can't be referenced directly in the business layer without generating a database Cartesian product. To delete this class and its objects, right-click the class and choose Delete. Confirm the deletion by selecting the Yes option. Later, you'll define existing objects to reference the underlying Internet sales analytic view using aggregate awareness.

Delete objects that won't be used by users or the universe designer. To delete an object, right-click the object and choose Delete.

Hiding Objects

Hide objects that should not be made available to users but need to remain available to the universe designer. The outputs of these objects don't have any meaning to a user because they are used by the database for joining or other purposes in the data model. However, the universe designer might find them useful when designing the universe. Follow these steps to hide objects:

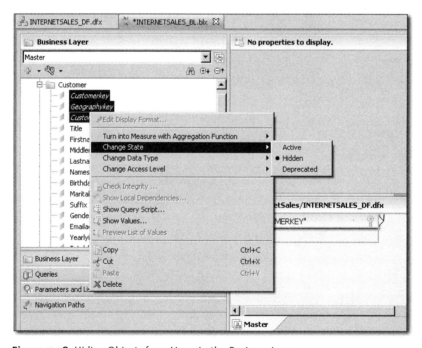

Figure 12.78 Hiding Objects from Users in the Business Layer

1. Click each object in the BUSINESS LAYER window. To select multiple objects, hold down the ⟨Shift⟩ key while selecting each.

2. Right-click the object or objects and choose CHANGE STATE • HIDDEN, as shown in Figure 12.78. Figures are provided later to suggest objects to hide.

Moving Objects

You can move an object from the top level so that it's nested in existing classes. Because the product subcategory and product category are effectively attributes of the product class, follow these steps to move them to the product class to help the user easily identify them:

1. Highlight the PRODUCT SUBCATEGORY class and place it in the PRODUCT class using the drag-and-drop method. This can be a tricky process at first.

2. To ensure that you're dropping the class into the correct location, hover over the PRODUCTS class until it expands.

3. Release the mouse button to move the product subcategory class and its objects. Once this is complete, move the PRODUCT CATEGORY class into the PRO-DUCTS class, as well.

Adding Objects

Add objects or classes to the business layer to enhance the user experience. In some cases, you'll want to create subclasses or folders to organize your objects. To add an object, follow these steps:

1. To add an object, right-click the parent class or folder and choose NEW, as shown in Figure 12.79.

2. A window appears allowing you to choose from various object types. To create a subclass, choose the FOLDER option.

Defining Dimensions and Measures

The next part of the business layer design process is to define the relevant dimensions and business measures. Follow these steps to do so:

1. Ensure that your CUSTOMER class, subclasses, and objects appear as depicted in Figure 12.80. Rename the objects and create the subclasses shown. Note that the CUSTOMER NUMBER references the Customerkey field.

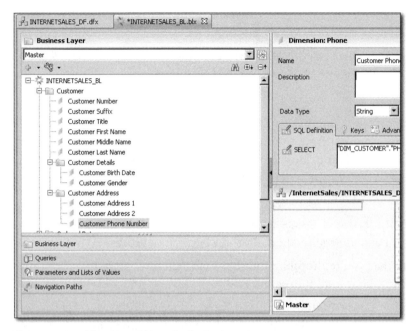

Figure 12.79 Adding New Objects in the Business Layer

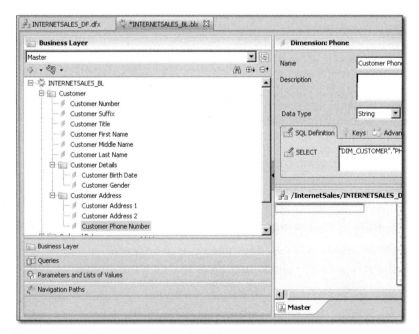

Figure 12.80 The Customer Class and its Objects

Note

In cases in which English, Spanish, or French language columns appear, choose the column appropriate to the users of the universe throughout this section. In this example, we chose the English version.

2. Ensure that the ORDERED DATE class appears as depicted in Figure 12.81. Notice that the Datekey field is hidden.

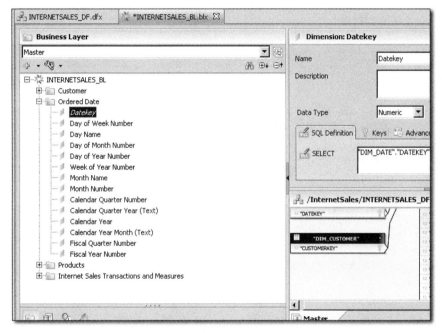

Figure 12.81 The Ordered Date Class and its Objects

3. Ensure that the PRODUCTS class appears as depicted in Figure 12.82.

4. Convert dimensions into measures and add the SUM() function to the object's definition. To convert an object or objects, highlight the dimensions. To select multiple dimensions, use the [Shift] key while highlighting. Right-click the highlighted measures and choose TURN INTO MEASURE WITH AGGREGATION FUNCTION • SUM, as shown in Figure 12.83.

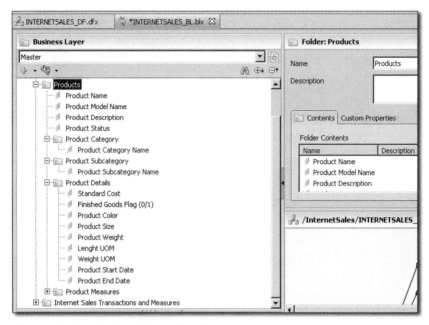

Figure 12.82 The Products Class and Its Objects

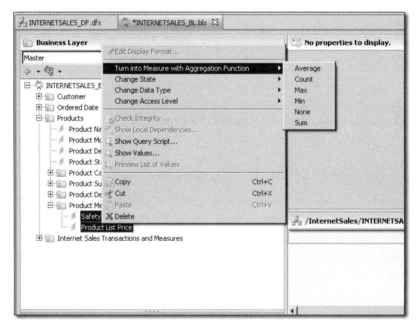

Figure 12.83 Converting Dimensions into Measures

5. Create the PRODUCT MEASURES class, move the objects listed in Figure 12.84 into the class, and convert them to measures with a SUM() function.

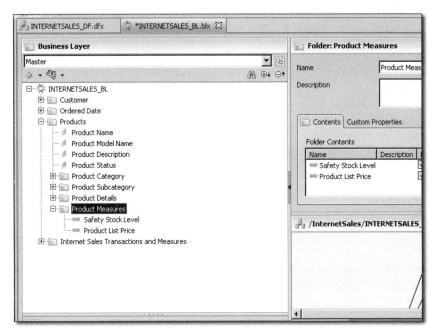

Figure 12.84 The Product Measures Class and Its Objects

6. Define the INTERNET SALES TRANSACTIONS AND MEASURES class as depicted in Figure 12.85. Convert the DIMENSIONS into MEASURES with the SUM() function as shown, and delete any objects not defined in the screen.

7. Review the definition of each measure. Highlight each measure, and look at its definition in the rightmost windows. Notice the SELECT field. In this field, the underlying columnar table column appears. The syntax of this field is the SQL syntax of SAP HANA. Notice that the standard SUM() function has been added to each object. Later, when you define aggregate awareness, you'll include additional universe-specific syntax to the SELECT field.

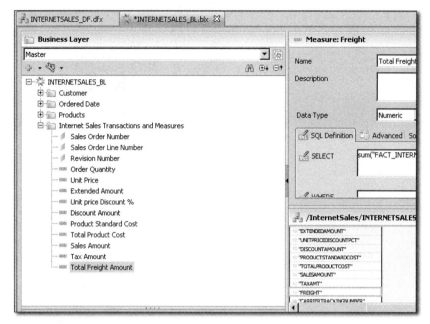

Figure 12.85 The Internet Sales Transactions and Measures Class and Its Objects

Configuring Aggregate Awareness

In this section, we'll walk you through the processes of implementing aggregate awareness, which involves modifying dimensions and measures by incorporating the universe function @Aggregate_Aware() in the object definition. This function must have a minimum of two input parameters, each separated with a comma. In the classic universe based on a legacy RDBMS, there can be multiple aggregate tables defined in the source schema. With SAP HANA, we expect there to be only one aggregate table or analytic view. In the context of using this method with SAP HANA, each input parameter represents one object in the columnar tables and a corresponding object in the analytic view.

The objects should be defined in the input parameters working from left to right, as follows: the corresponding analytic view column should be defined as the first input parameter. If the object is a measure, make sure to wrap the function SUM() around the column. The second input parameter should be the corresponding column in the columnar table. Again, make sure to wrap the column in the function SUM() if it's a measure.

The same process is true for each dimension object. However, with dimension objects, aggregate functions should not be included in the object definition. Figure 12.86 contains an example of how this function is defined on the ORDER QUANTITY measure. Figure 12.87 contains a closer view of the syntax.

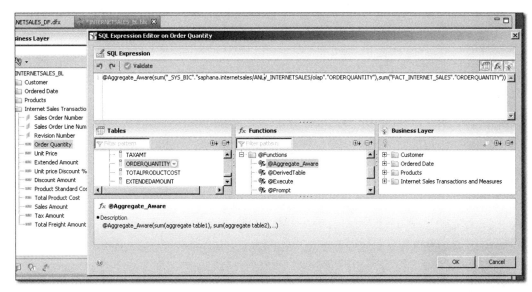

Figure 12.86 Updating Objects to Use Aggregate Awareness

Update the objects outlined here to incorporate aggregate awareness into the case study universe. The instructions will contain screenshots of each object's SELECT field, located in the rightmost window of the BUSINESS LAYER tab.

1. Update the ORDER QUANTITY measure using the syntax shown previously in Figure 12.87. Click the SQL ASSISTANT button, to the right of the SELECT field, to activate the editor that is shown.

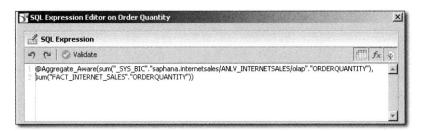

Figure 12.87 Defining Aggregate Awareness on a Measure

2. Update the SALES AMOUNT measure using the syntax shown in Figure 12.88.

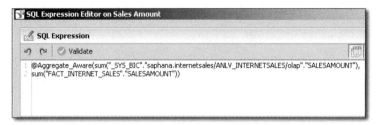

Figure 12.88 Defining Aggregate Awareness on the Sales Amount Measure

3. Repeat the process on the remaining measures. In each case, define the column from the Internet sales analytic view as the first parameter and the column from the columnar table as the second. Because they are measures, each input parameter column should contain the SUM() function.

4. Update dimensions to include aggregate awareness. Dimensions defined in the analytic view and columnar tables must also be made aggregate aware.

5. Update the calendar year dimension in the ordered date class to include the aggregate-aware function. Figure 12.89 contains the required syntax. Notice that the analytic view column is in the first parameter, and the columnar table column is in the second parameter. In addition, notice that the SUM() function isn't included with the dimension objects.

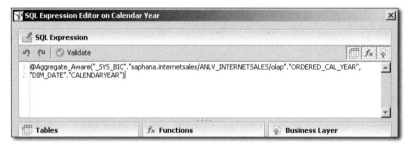

Figure 12.89 Updating the Calendar Year Dimension in the Ordered Date Class

6. Update the remaining dimensions to use aggregate awareness. Note that only dimensions that exist in both the analytic view and the defined dimension list should be included. In addition, this process is necessary only for objects that are commonly used in analytical queries. Please also note that, with SAP

HANA, dimension objects will fail validation. The IDT validation engine doesn't take into account that the analytic view objects must be tested with a measure to meet the minimum requirements of querying an analytic view.

7. Save the business layer.

8. Set aggregate incompatibilities using aggregate navigation. The Aggregate Navigation wizard is located under ACTIONS • SET AGGREGATE NAVIGATIONS.

9. In this wizard, select DETECT INCOMPATIBILITIES at the bottom of the screen. This is a vital step that informs the universe concerning which combination of objects can be combined and used against the analytic view and which objects are incompatible with aggregate awareness. If an incompatible object is used in a universe query, the SQL syntax is updated to use only the columnar tables and joins. Failure to complete this step results in a Cartesian product for most queries. Therefore, it's extremely important that aggregate incompatibilities be defined.

10. Save the business layer.

Setting Query Options

Before publishing the universe to the SAP BusinessObjects BI repository, you need to review and establish a few options for the universe. These options control several important features of the universe and should be reviewed. The following steps outline the processes of accessing these options and changing the critical options to facilitate a properly designed universe.

1. To access the query options in the IDT business layer, locate the topmost node of the universe class and object hierarchy located in the left side of the business layer. Highlight the top node, which represents the entire universe. On the right-hand side, a new window appears that contains four tabs. Click the QUERY OPTIONS tab. Figure 12.90 contains an example of the expected view, found in the IDT business layer.

2. Take note of the QUERY LIMITS and QUERY OPTIONS areas.

3. Change the option LIMIT SIZE OF RESULT SET TO. By default, the business layer options restrict the universe to 5,000 rows. For most organizations, this number is too low and should be either disabled or increased. To disable this option, uncheck it. To increase the number of rows, change the value to a more

suitable number. Note that restricting to a specific number of rows might result in partial results in reports. Based on firsthand experience, this can lead users to incorrect conclusions. Granted, the reporting tool indicates partial results, but the warning isn't apparent to most users. Query limits should be restricted by time and not by number of records.

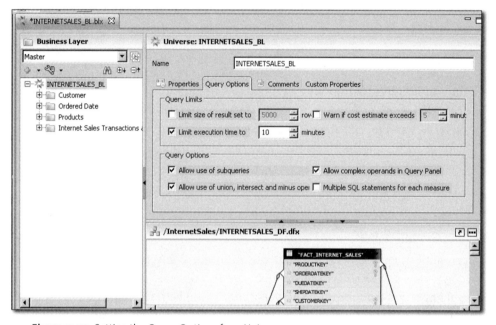

Figure 12.90 Setting the Query Options for a Universe

4. Change the option MULTIPLE SQL STATEMENTS FOR EACH MEASURE. When enabled, a separate SQL query is generated by the reporting tool to facilitate each measure. This can lead to access queries and slow performance. It's best to disable this option when dealing with star schemas in the data foundation.

Setting Universe Parameters

In addition to setting the query parameters, you can also establish or change parameters that affect the way SQL statements are generated by following these steps:

1. To access the query options in the IDT business layer, highlight the top node, and a new window appears. Click the PROPERTIES tab. Figure 12.91 contains an example of the expected view found in the IDT business layer.

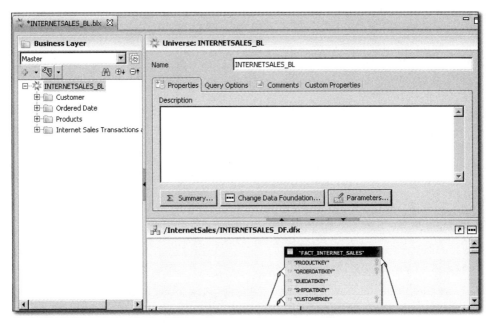

Figure 12.91 Setting the Properties and Parameters for a Universe

2. Click the PARAMETERS button to launch the universe properties window. Figure 12.92 contains an example of the EDIT QUERY SCRIPT PARAMETERS window.

3. To change a parameter, highlight the parameter in the list. Click the VALUE column to enable the dropdown list. In the dropdown list, select the desired value for the parameter.

4. To add an additional parameter, locate the dropdown at the bottom of the window. This dropdown contains the ADD, DELETE, and DEFAULT VALUE buttons.

5. In the dropdown, locate the JOIN_BY_SQL parameter. Click the ADD button to add this parameter to the list. The JOIN_BY_SQL parameter moves SAP BusinessObjects Web Intelligence data synchronization from the report engine to SAP HANA for processing. In most cases, this option results in increased performance. (Note: This only works for SAP BusinessObjects Web Intelligence.)

6. Change its value from the default No to YES. Click OK to save your changes.

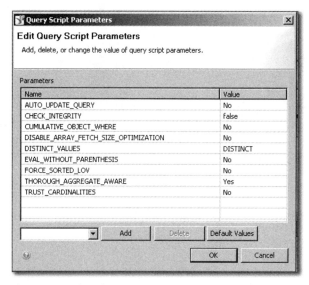

Figure 12.92 The Edit Query Script Parameters Window

12.5.4 Publishing the Universe

After all objects have been updated, you can publish the universe to the SAP BusinessObjects BI repository. This step, which is outlined in Section 12.2.7, is required to allow the SAP BusinessObjects BI reporting tools to access the universe.

Now that the design process is complete, AdventureWorks Cycle Company has a universe that can support many of the SAP BusinessObjects BI tools. This universe was designed to support all types of queries. The universe foundation is designed with both columnar tables and analytic views to facilitate both operational and analytic reporting. This design decision helps facilitate both features that are unique to the universe semantic layer and those that are unique to SAP HANA's information views. The business layer is organized and contains named objects to help users identify their use. In addition, aggregate awareness, which automatically rewrites queries to use the most efficient SAP HANA object, is incorporated into the definition of objects.

12.6 Summary

Since the inception of Business Objects, the universe has played a key role in providing report developers and ad hoc report designers a business-centric representation of their organizations' data. SAP HANA, too, shares this concept in the form of its information views. Although there is functional overlap between these two layers, you must still use the universe to fully integrate SAP HANA and SAP BusinessObjects BI.

When designing a universe against an SAP HANA source, you need to pay close attention to the different options you can use to access data in SAP HANA. Depending on the options you choose, different SAP HANA engines are used to process universe-generated SQL queries. Each engine has different capabilities in terms of performance and scalability. For you to fully analyze queries and understand the engines they invoke, SAP HANA Studio provides a utility to visually analyze the execution plan of queries.

You should now have a better understanding of the rules and concepts that are specific to creating a universe against SAP HANA. In the rest of the chapters in this part of the book, we'll explore the different SAP BusinessObjects BI tools and how they leverage either the universe or the SAP HANA information views directly. Regardless of the requirements, the SAP BusinessObjects BI tools are able to deliver unparalleled flexibility, speed, and performance.

Recognizing the need for organizations to tap into insights in their operational data, SAP has developed several tools that integrate with SAP HANA to run predictive algorithms on very large data sets.

13   Predictive Analytics with SAP HANA

In the past several years, the practice of BI has begun a slow shift from reporting and visualizing to identifying insights and performing causation analysis. Users have traditionally had the ability to drill down within traditional BI reports to derive the causes of trends, but an emerging need is the ability to use the rich historical data stored in an organization's data warehouse to determine what may happen in the future. Traditional statistical tools are often siloed and difficult to integrate into production environments, but SAP HANA has several features and companion tools that make the data manipulation, extraction, prediction, and model integration processes more seamless than ever before.

The toolset for predictive analysis in SAP HANA includes three main components: predictive functions available in SAP HANA through the Predictive Analysis Library (PAL), the capability to integrate SAP HANA with an external Rserve host to run open-source R algorithms efficiently, and the visualization and predictive user tool SAP Predictive Analysis, which incorporates all of the functionality of the SAP Lumira visualization tool and includes predictive functionality to run R and PAL predictive functions on SAP HANA.

> **SAP InfiniteInsight**
>
> In addition to SAP Predictive Analysis, SAP has acquired another tool for predictive analysis: SAP InfiniteInsight (formerly KXEN). Because SAP InfiniteInsight does not currently integrate natively with SAP HANA, we do not cover it in this chapter. However, the future roadmap calls for SAP InfiniteInsight algorithms to be added into the PAL as native SAP HANA functions.

In addition to summarizing features, implementation, and architecture of the SAP HANA predictive analysis tools listed previously, this chapter will include an overview of the predictive analysis process itself and common business problems for which predictive tools can provide solutions (Section 13.1) and several integration scenarios for implementing predictive algorithms in an SAP BusinessObjects BI environment running on SAP HANA (Sections 13.2 and Section 13.3). Finally, we'll include two use cases for our AdventureWorks retail firm to integrate predictive models into its operational practices (Section 13.4 and Section 13.5).

13.1 Predictive Analysis and SAP HANA: The Basics

At the most basic level, *predictive analysis* is focused on developing a way to determine the expected future result of some action or decision. This allows the business to evaluate alternative paths and select the most profitable option. A *predictive model* is an algorithm, or set of rules, used by an organization to generate this expected outcome based on known input characteristics. The predictive model can simply be a collection of existing business rules or management decisions, but to develop the most accurate and statistically valid predictions, organizations are now often relying on statistical techniques to develop the predictive model equation and values based on error-minimization techniques.

After the predictive model has been developed, an organization can use the prediction algorithm to evaluate the expected results of alternative business strategies and determine how best to allocate scarce resources, such as marketing funds, research and development budget, and labor hours.

Predictive algorithms can be used in many areas of an organization, including advertising, marketing, product development, customer service, operations, and human resources. Consider a few common applications of predictive analytics in an organization:

▶ Marketing response or uplift models that predict the likelihood of response (or incremental response) from customers reacting to a specific marketing stimulus (e.g., email, direct mail, text message, or promotional offer)

▶ Product suggestion models to influence customers to increase their purchase size by cross-selling or up-selling complementary products

▶ Customer segmentation methodologies to categorize customers who behave or transact similarly and therefore may continue to transact or respond similarly in the future

▶ Fraud models for transactions, interactions, or claims to predict which events are most likely to merit further investigation or require confirmation prior to processing

Let's break this list down. One common source of confusion is differentiating between the common business applications in the preceding list and the actual predictive algorithms used to solve them. This list includes some common business applications for predictive solutions, but for each of these business problems, a number of different algorithms can be used. For example, a firm wanting to estimate the likelihood of a binary outcome (e.g., will a customer churn use of a service) could use a number of different algorithms, including a decision tree model; a logistic regression model; a Naive Bayes classifier; or even an unsupervised learning algorithm, such as clustering. Selecting the most accurate and appropriate algorithm (or combination of several algorithms) for the business problem requires a balance of analytics experience, business knowledge, and trial and error; this is where predictive analytics is more art than science.

In this chapter, we use the term *predictive analysis* to include a broad set of analytical methods and tools for extracting insights and implementing better decision making in a BI environment. However, there are many related terms that you may be familiar with, as well. Many of these overlap or are used interchangeably with each other and the broader predictive analysis term. Let's define and differentiate several popular terms used within the analytics industry:

▶ **Predictive analytics**
This is one of the most popular analytics-related terms often used to refer to both predictive and descriptive analysis. It is often used interchangeably with *data mining* and *advanced analytics*.

▶ **Data mining**
This is a broader term that covers any method of extracting insights from large data sets. Data mining includes the discovery of both descriptive and predictive insights based on either statistical or machine learning methods.

▶ **Advanced analytics**
Largely a marketing term, this phrase is typically used to distinguish any analysis that uses statistical or machine learning algorithms from analyses relying only on simple database queries and manual examination of different slices of data. *Advanced analytics* also often refers to the analysis of unstructured data and text analysis.

▸ **Descriptive analytics**

Often bundled into the *predictive analytics* umbrella term, descriptive analytics focuses on exploring or profiling existing relationships and characteristics of the data, rather than predicting future outcomes, like predictive analytics. Descriptive analytic techniques are often used to prepare or explore data prior to developing predictive models.

▸ **Business analytics**

This refers to the application of analytic methods to business environments. Common sub-classifications include marketing, risk, fraud, customer, operations, and HR analytics. *Business analytics* may refer to the use of predictive or advanced analytical techniques or more straightforward reporting-type analysis.

▸ **Statistical models**

Statistical models are formal mathematical equations showing the relationship between input variables and results (e.g., linear regression), which are differentiated from models built on business rules, knowledge, or machine learning algorithms.

▸ **Knowledge discovery**

Synonymous with *data mining*, knowledge discovery is simply the process of uncovering patterns, trends, or relationships in large data sets.

▸ **Machine learning**

As a specific set of algorithms based on artificial intelligence principles, machine learning algorithms use data to learn about relationships. Popular tools that fall into the machine learning category include neural networks and support vector machines.

Predictive algorithms and statistical learning methods are often employed to synthesize, better understand, and extract actionable insights from large data sets. These tools have become especially attractive to organizations that are amassing vast repositories of data, including transaction history, web browsing patterns, sensor readings, and even social media chatter. Predictive models are already in use in many customer-serving organizations, influencing items suggested to customers, determining what types of promotional offers are extended, and even specifying how quickly a customer may be connected to a call center representative. Predictive models help organizations realize a return on the investment of collecting and maintaining their data repositories; extracting actionable insights from this data helps organizations better understand and serve their customers and ensure that scarce resources are used to target customers most effectively.

At its core, a predictive model determines a mapping between input data (e.g., demographic information such as age, gender, household information, or purchase history) and a predicted output, such as whether customers will respond to an offer, make a transaction, or discontinue their relationship with the company.

Predictive models can be divided into the following two categories:

- **Supervised learning algorithms**
  These models have two sets of input data: inputs and outputs. Supervised algorithms attempt to determine the effect of the inputs on the related outputs for each input scenario. The inputs are assumed to be at the beginning of the causal chain and the outputs at the end. While supervised learning has the advantage of defining a model based on the actual output prediction that is desired, it does require that a sufficient quantity of accurate output data be available. For example, if an organization wants to predict which customers are most likely to respond to a particular marketing offer, it must have a sample of response records from a representative portion of its customer base. This might mean running a preliminary pilot program to gather response data or using data from a similar prior marketing campaign to build the model. Well-known and commonly used supervised learning algorithms include classification algorithms, such as decision trees, all regression models (including linear, logarithmic, logistic, and exponential regression), time series models, neural networks, linear discriminant analyses, support vector machines, and association algorithms.

- **Unsupervised learning algorithms**
  These models have only one set of input data and assume that the input observations are at the end of a causal chain of latent variables. Unsupervised learning algorithms can typically develop into larger, more complex models than supervised algorithms because the complexity of trying to find a connection between two sets of observations increases exponentially with each increase in the number of steps between the observations, while the complexity of an unsupervised learning algorithm increases only proportionally with each intermediate step. Popular unsupervised learning algorithms include clustering and some types of neural network learning algorithms.

The main difference between supervised and unsupervised learning is how the classifications are determined. In supervised learning, the known output class value (e.g., did customer respond to offer) for each input scenario is already determined prior to modeling, whereas one of the outputs of the unsupervised algorithm is actually the classification for each input observation.

To further explain, in the example of trying to determine whether a customer responded, the supervised learning method takes in the customer input characteristics (e.g., how long has it been since the customer's last transaction, where does the customer live, customer demographic characteristics), as well as the output (e.g., Customer 1 responded, Customer 2 did not, etc.) and extracts a mathematical relationship between the inputs and outputs. The unsupervised learning method takes in only the inputs and divides the customers into some number of similar groups based on these input characteristics. The unsupervised learning algorithm effectively creates groups of like customers, under the assumption that if demographically similar customers have similar behaviors, the groups determined by the clustering algorithm will have different response rates.

One consideration in determining which algorithm to use is the availability and reliability of data. Because unsupervised learning methods don't require known result data, they may be more attractive; however, there is no way to know if they are effectively differentiating customers. It's still necessary to have known output data to validate the effectiveness of the unsupervised algorithm model.

After you have fitted and validated a predictive model, your organization can effectively accept that the insights extracted from the historical data can be generalized to predict the future.

In this section, we'll give an overview of the predictive analysis development process and discuss some motivations for implementing predictive analytics in an organization. We'll conclude with a discussion of the predictive tools available in SAP HANA.

13.1.1 The Predictive Analysis Process

Developing a predictive model includes many different steps, including strategic planning (e.g., what predicted output would help my business? What data do I have to build this model?), technical execution in obtaining the modeling data set, and the statistical and analytical process to iterate through possible models and evaluate each one. Finally, the best model must be implemented and made available for business processes and decisions to take action on the results.

Here we've broken the modeling process down into six steps, some of which may be repeated more than once:

1. Identify the modeling strategy.

2. Select an appropriate modeling tool.

3. Perform data discovery and develop the modeling data set.

4. Develop the model.

5. Implement the selected model.

6. Maintain and update the model as needed.

Each of these steps may be performed by different teams of resources that include stakeholders from several business units and technical resources. Steps 1, 2, 3, and 6 may require budgeting and strategic approval from an executive team and the commitment of a team of cross-functional resources from the business, analytic, and IT departments to develop the modeling data set and implement the final model.

Let's walk through each of these steps in more detail.

Step 1: Identifying the Modeling Strategy

While it may seem straightforward, setting the strategy for an analytic project is critical to ensuring that the project finishes in a timely fashion and all parties receive the output they expect.

Too often, analytical projects start with unrealistic expectations and too broad of a focus, causing analysts to become overwhelmed with summarizing and examining the vast amounts of data available. Further, the timeline for analytical projects can easily be extended if, each time the analyst brings a presentation of the findings to date, the team comes back with additional suggestions, such as, "Why didn't you look at factor X or break results down by customer group Y?" While this is often unavoidable, having all of the stakeholders in the room at the beginning of the project can help identify all of the angles for analysis up front, and there should be general agreement on the dimensions and scope (including detail, complexity, and depth) of the analysis at the beginning of the project to ensure that the timeline is met.

To avoid this analysis paralysis and the never-ending cycle of re-analysis, a team that includes both the analysts completing the work and the managerial team should develop a few goals for the analysis with actionable results and quantifiable business benefits. Rather than asking broad, open-ended questions, this analytical and executive team should drill down to the most pressing questions. Table 13.1 shows examples of how extremely broad questions might be shaped into analytical projects with actionable results.

Business Goal or Question	Analytical Project Goals	Actionable Implementation
Why are my customers leaving?	▸ Which customers are most likely to defect? ▸ Is there a preceding event that commonly occurs immediately before a customer defects?	▸ Customer outreach: Evaluate the impact of an outreach campaign in decreasing the defect rate. Alternatively, reduce investment in customers most likely to defect. ▸ Business process evaluation: If there are transactions that are likely causing defection, examine them for friction points or gaps that lead to defection.
How can I increase my sales?	▸ Which customers are most likely to respond to the sales offer? ▸ Which product offering is most likely to result in the highest purchase amount/profit/lifetime value?	▸ Reduce marketing costs by contacting only customers most likely to respond. ▸ Optimize product offerings to suggest the goal-maximizing product for each sales opportunity.
How can I reduce the cost of fraud to my business?	▸ Which transactions are most likely to be fraudulent? ▸ Which transactions are likely to result in the highest recoverable fraud amount?	▸ Reduce fraud investigation costs by targeting investigations to only those transactions above a fraud value threshold.

Table 13.1 Sample Analytical Project Scoping

A final consideration during the strategic planning process for an analytics project is the data available. While it's not necessary to dive deep into specifics at this point, the strategic discussion should include team members familiar enough with the organization's data to know whether there is data available for performing the analysis. For example, an organization that wants to build models to select customers for marketing campaigns but has never kept records of its previous marketing efforts may have to limit its initial analytic goals because the company won't have specific data available to train a response model (though it may still be able to perform some basic customer segmentation). Unfortunately, this portion of the strategic planning is often skipped, and time and effort are wasted with the ultimate revelation that there is insufficient data to build the agreed-upon models.

Step 2: Select an Appropriate Modeling Tool

After the analytical goals have been determined at a high level, the analytic team must select the appropriate statistical tool or tools for the project. To select a tool, the analytic team must consider its needs across seven key areas of the tool. Table 13.2 includes a summary of several key features users should consider when selecting a predictive modeling tool.

Feature	Questions to Ask
Data access	▸ How is data imported into the tool?
	▸ Where is my data coming from, and can the tool access it directly?
	▸ How can data be extracted from the modeling tool? Can it write data directly back to the database?
Data manipulation	▸ Can the tool facilitate simple data manipulations (e.g., grouping values, calculations, and value changes for minor cleansing)?
	▸ How much manipulation of the data do I want to do in the tool?
Capacity and processing power	▸ How much data will be processed by the tool?
	▸ What runtime for predictive algorithms am I willing to accept?
User interface and skill level	▸ What is the skill level (technical and statistical) of the users for this software?
	▸ Will the users be able to work in a code-based tool, or do they require a graphical user interface?
	▸ How much support and explanation of statistical terms do the users require?
Available predictive algorithms	▸ Based on the long-term goals of the organization, what is the breadth of algorithms that may be needed in the long term?
	▸ Specifically, which algorithms are most likely to be important to the organization?
Model evaluation	▸ What automated visualizations and model accuracy comparison metrics are built into the tool?

Table 13.2 Tool Evaluation Dimensions

Feature	Questions to Ask
Model implementation and maintenance	▶ How will models developed by the tool be integrated back into the operational systems? ▶ What maintenance features are available (e.g., version control, archival, shared objects between users)?

Table 13.2 Tool Evaluation Dimensions (Cont.)

Because predictive tools are generally expensive and require an investment in infrastructure, talent, training, and integration, in addition to the software costs, selecting a tool is most likely a rare event in an organization and should be undertaken with great care. Prior to selecting a tool, the organization should think about its long-term analytics strategy and what type of tool will fit these needs.

For example, an organization that expects to need very complicated predictive models for a variety of different operational areas might want to consider a full-function tool that has a wide variety of highly configurable statistical algorithms that can be employed. However, these tools are often quite expensive and require a technically savvy analyst with statistical experience to operate them. In contrast, an organization that just wants to experiment with one particular approach, such as customer clustering, might select a tool that is specialized to that one area, costs less, and has built-in visualizations or model-evaluation tools specific to that particular model or business area.

Evaluating SAP Predictive Analysis and SAP HANA

So how does SAP's predictive tool for SAP HANA, SAP Predictive Analysis, rate in each of these tool assessment categories? We've assigned a letter grade based on the current and expected functionality, as we'll describe in the following list:

▶ **Data access: A**
SAP Predictive Analysis can access data directly from SAP HANA and many other popular databases, as well as flat files and SAP BusinessObjects BI universes. Combined with SAP Data Services, data from nearly any source can be ported to SAP HANA for use in SAP Predictive Analysis.

▶ **Data manipulation: B**
In SAP HANA online mode, data can be manipulated in SAP HANA information views or during loading with SAP Data Services, but the data must be fully manipulated and assigned as an attribute or measure outside the predictive tool. In offline mode, SAP Predictive Analysis has tools for basic data manipulation, such as calculation, grouping, and joining multiple data sets.

- **Capacity and processing power: A**
  When paired with SAP HANA, SAP Predictive Analysis can handle extremely large data sets with impressively fast processing times.
- **User interface and skill level: A+**
  The SAP Predictive Analysis interface is easy to understand, and even an inexperienced user can easily construct a predictive workflow. This is likely to improve further through modules that help guide business users though the predictive process.
- **Predictive algorithm availability: B**
  The current PAL and included R algorithms cover basic popular statistical algorithms, and you do have the ability to create custom R transforms in SAP Predictive Analysis. This allows a technical user to program any algorithm in the tool and share the custom transform with a wider audience.
- **Model evaluation: C**
  Currently, model evaluation is limited; while some algorithms have fit statistics in the raw result printout, there are currently few fit visualizations, and many of those don't support large data sets.
- **Model implementation and maintenance: A (implementation)/C (maintenance)**
  Current and expected features allow easy integration of predictive results and scoring algorithms, including exporting PAL-based models directly to SAP HANA and the ability to write predictive data directly back to the SAP HANA database. However, model versioning, archival, and comparison features don't currently exist.

Step 3: Perform Data Discovery and Develop the Modeling Data Set

Data discovery is the process of evaluating all available data elements and determining which elements should be included in the analysis. This includes inspecting all elements for completeness and accuracy and evaluating the likelihood and validity of a relationship between the modeled outcome and each potential predictor. This initial data discovery should reveal which predictors are correlated with the desired outcome and narrow down the list of predictors that will be considered during the modeling process.

This process is often iterative because insights gleaned from the initial data discovery push the analyst back to the data source to pull other data that might reveal additional trends or change the data to increase or decrease complexity. The result of the data discovery process should be a finalized modeling data set and an understanding of all of the potential predictors.

Step 4: Develop the Model

After completing the data discovery process and constructing the modeling data set, you'll test different predictive algorithms and variables to determine the best fit and result for the organization.

To accurately and independently evaluate a model, you need to divide the initial modeling data set into two sets: one used to fit or train the model, and another as an independent validation set. This data division ensures that the model that is developed accurately reflects the impact of the true influencing factors within the environment, and not simply compensating for the specific, random variation in one single data set, which is called *over fitting*.

While evaluating different models, analysts must consider not only the accuracy of the prediction, but also the complexity of the model and the impact on implementation. To rerun or score the model later and generate predicted results for new records, the same fields that were used during fitting must be pulled, generated, or calculated. Minimizing the number of predictors in the model not only reduces complexity in terms of data preparation for rescoring, but also reduces the variance in the predicted values. Balancing complexity with accuracy is a difficult process that requires the modeler to evaluate the organization's needs, costs, and technical capabilities.

Step 5: Implement the Selected Model

After the final model has been selected and approved for implementation, the analytical team must work with the systems team to make either model scores or the procedure for generating a model score for a given set of inputs. Simply writing calculated scores from the modeling engine back to a database is the easiest method of model implementation. However, to have immediate, real-time scoring of new records, the modeling algorithm must be available within the database. The organization's use of the predictive model dictates the implementation process and determines whether implementation consists of only scores written back to a database from the modeling tool and whether the model algorithm is implemented within a database or application.

Step 6: Maintain and Update the Model as Needed

Predictive models require maintenance just like any other business rules, targets, and operational procedures. Model predictions may degrade with time due to either operational or technical changes that change the quality or meaning of input data, or even environmental shifts, such as economic changes, product changes, competitive marketplace changes, or changes in consumer trends. Therefore, a model must be monitored regularly to ensure that predictions are still accurate and that the input data remains relevant and accurate.

If the accuracy of the model begins to degrade, you should either refit (recalculate new coefficients based on a more recent set of data) or rebuild (reconsider the list of predictor variables included in the model) the model. Rebuilding a model is a longer process, but it can allow an organization to add new predictors that may not have been available when the original model was developed. A general rule of thumb is that model maintenance should be performed whenever accuracy begins to degrade, as well as any time there has been a significant change to the input data, in terms of quality, composition, or availability.

13.1.2 When to Use Predictive Analytics

Because predictive analytics is often used in areas with major revenue streams, the business case for developing better insight into trends and customer behavior is often quite strong. In this section, we'll first discuss the general foundation for typical business cases around predictive analytics and then walk through a brief example of calculating the financial impact of implementing a presales selection model to decrease the acquisition cost of prospective leads.

Predictive analytics is typically focused on generating more accurate predictions, so the savings is generated through reducing waste or increasing the likelihood of sales. In addition, applying statistical algorithms to develop these models allows the development of more accurate predictive methods without the extensive manual analysis that would be required to identify these trends without predictive models. Finally, predictive models provide an objective and consistent evaluation methodology, rather than allowing inspectors or marketers to make their own judgments, which tend to be biased by past outliers.

Let's revisit some common business benefits and metrics that are impacted when you implement popular predictive models:

▶ **Product suggestion**
   A model to suggest which product customers are most likely to purchase results in an increased purchase amount, manifesting as either an increase in the bas-

ket or purchase size during the initial purchase, or an increase in the number of purchases for each customer, depending on when the suggestion is made.

Even a small increase in the purchase basket has direct impact on profitability; for example, when an online retailer immediately suggests another product to be added to the purchase basket prior to completion of the order, the additional cost of sales is essentially zero. Increasing the purchase rate on these suggestions not only increases the purchase basket amount, but also improves customer satisfaction by displaying products the customer is interested in.

▶ **Customer clustering or segmentation**
A clustering model allows customers to be divided into groups that are expected to act similarly. Therefore, if you have a model that divides customers into three segments and have determined the lifetime value of the three segments to be different, you may invest more in attracting or acquiring the most valuable customer group than the less valuable customer groups.

Over time, this strategy can lead to a more valuable customer population, effectively increasing the value of the organization. Metrics for this improvement might include increased customer tenure, decreased customer defection, larger purchase or profit margins per customer, and other related impacts.

▶ **Marketing response model**
The ability to better predict which customers are most likely to respond to a marketing offer allows you to target only customers most likely to respond to expensive sales calls, mail pieces, or promotional offers. With this additional predictive intelligence, customer acquisition cost should decrease, and so should the response rate on marketing campaigns. This decrease in acquisition cost allows a reallocation of the marketing budget savings to other programs and, ideally, results in higher overall sales levels with the same marketing budget.

▶ **Retention or churn model**
Identifying customers who are most likely to churn (or defect) from an organization allows customer-saving resources to be allocated to customers most likely to need them and enables organizations to react proactively and prevent defection rather than retroactively trying to reacquire defected customers. With predictive models identifying those most likely to defect and strategic programs to mitigate these defections, organizations can realize significant reduction in churn rates and related increases in tenure and customer-value metrics.

▶ **Fraud likelihood prediction**
Organizations that implement fraud models can realize benefits in two main ways: fraud avoidance and fraud cost reduction. As a proactive technique, *fraud models* can be used prior to processing a transaction and require additional identification or authorization to be processed. Retroactively, identifying likely fraudulent transactions or claims allows investigation resources to be deployed efficiently to the transactions most likely to result in a denial or recovery. A successful fraud model results in a lower rate of fraud within the organization, as well as reduced fraud prevention and investigation costs.

▶ **Clinical decision support models**
Decision support models result in an automated suggestion or likelihood of diagnosis based on input data. These can help caregivers review the likelihood of diagnosis or suggested treatment based on symptom and diagnostic inputs. These models are also often used to identify patients most likely to be stricken with debilitating conditions and suggest preventative treatment. Used in these two ways, clinical models should reduce the time to diagnosis, improve treatment outcomes, and reduce occurrence of many preventable conditions, such as heart disease and diabetes. Often, the preventative care and speed of diagnosis leads to a reduction in hospital stays and medical expenses such as prescriptions.

Finally, let's walk through the actual financial impact of one case, which can be used as an example of how to approach the financial impact of predictive modeling for a marketing acquisition model.

Let's say you work in the marketing department at a large financial-services company that is promoting a new loan product. The sales force has a large prospect database, but the cost of contacting each prospect and going through the sales process is quite high, and only a portion of prospects are eligible for the loan product.

The executive management team has requested a methodology to identify prospects most likely to be eligible for the loan product so that the marketing team can focus limited resources on customers most likely to be eligible.

The following details become apparent:

▶ Total prospect database: 1.2 million prospects available

▶ Experience: 36.6% eligible for product, with seven known demographic variables

▶ Cost per contact: $15

▶ Current effective cost per eligible prospect: $15/36.6% = $41

▶ Value per eligible prospect: $45

A decision tree model was built that is able to identify a portion of the database that has 71% eligibility. The full impact of expending marketing expenses on this portion of the prospect base is shown in Table 13.3.

	No Model	Decision Tree
Prospects to contact	1,200,000	495,000
% eligible	36.6%	70.7%
Total marketing cost	$18,000,000	$7,400,000
Cost per eligible prospect	$41	$21
Total prospect value	$19,764,000	$15,748,411
Net prospect value	$1,764,000	$8,323,639
% improvement		371.9%

Table 13.3 Business Case for Eligibility Decision Tree Model

Now that we've discussed the process for creating predictive models, let's take a look at the specific predictive tools available for use with SAP HANA.

13.1.3 Predictive Tools Available in SAP HANA

SAP HANA has three tools available to run predictive algorithms. The first two (the SAP HANA Application Function Libraries and SAP HANA-R integration) allow SAP HANA users to run predictive algorithms in the SAP HANA environment through code written and executed in SAP HANA Studio. The last, SAP Predictive Analysis, is a companion product from SAP installed on the user's workstation. It allows users to visualize data stored on SAP HANA and access the first two predictive toolsets through a graphical user interface (GUI).

Let's take a closer look at these tools.

SAP HANA Application Function Libraries

The SAP HANA *Application Function Libraries* (AFL) are collections of algorithms available to users and applications that run on SAP HANA. These libraries are dynamically linked to the SAP HANA database kernel, offering excellent performance. In the AFL, functions are grouped by topic into individual libraries. The AFL includes two libraries that are useful for predictive analytics: the BFL and the PAL.

The *Business Function Library* (BFL) contains functions implemented in C++ and makes available common business functions that are fully compliant with the SAP HANA calculation engine. The BFL enables significant performance improvement and application programming simplification by leveraging the calculation engine for complex functionality and allowing the use of SQLScript to call these complex, predefined functions. The BFL includes many financial functions, such as depreciation, cash flow discounting, present value and rate of return calculations, and forecasting, as well as several averaging algorithms. These functions are particularly useful for predictive analyses that require time series forecasting, such as budget setting by month, or financial analysis, such as discounting cash flows.

The *Predictive Analysis Library* (PAL) also includes functions that can be called using SQLScript; however, the PAL includes commonly used data mining algorithms. As of the time of this writing, six categories of algorithms are available in the PAL, with a total of 23 algorithms represented:

▶ **Clustering**
Unsupervised learning algorithms that accept only numerical data to group similar observations or detect anomalies and divide a data set into discrete groups.

▶ **Classification**
Supervised learning algorithms that accept categorical or numeric data, including the popular decision tree, regression (linear, logistic, and other forms), Nearest Neighbor algorithms, and the Support Vector Machine algorithm.

▶ **Association**
Includes the Apriori algorithm for determining correlations, patterns, and causal structures within a set of items, such as within transactions.

▶ **Preprocessing**
Commonly used in conjunction with the other categories to manipulate or adjust the data prior to modeling, including grouping, scaling, and sampling, as well as others.

▶ **Time series**
Used for forecasting time-dependent data series and includes Exponential Smoothing algorithms (single, double, and triple). Most recently, the ARIMA algorithm was added to this group.

▶ **Statistics algorithms**
Includes basic univariate and multivariate statistical calculations (mean, median, standard deviation, correlation) and Chi-Square tests for independence and fitness, and a variance equality test. Most recently, algorithms for distribution fitting and sampling, CDF, and quantile calculations were added.

▶ **Social Network Analysis algorithms**
One algorithm for predicting which nodes in a network are most likely to have missing links.

▶ **Miscellaneous**
Includes two algorithms for grouping observations based on user-defined weights, allowing organizations to quickly apply business rules to their existing inventory or customer data.

SAP HANA Application Function Modeler for the Application Function Libraries

Starting with SAP HANA SPS 6 (version 60 and later), the Application Function Modeler became available within SAP HANA Studio to facilitate the use of the Application Function Library (PAL and BFL) functions without having to manually generate code to call the PAL function. An example of using the Application Function Modeler is included in the PAL Apriori case study in Section 13.5.2. The Application Function Modeler significantly increases the usability of PAL algorithms within SAP HANA Studio; however, it does not include any visualization or model evaluation tools and still requires a thorough knowledge of the specific algorithm requirements and input and output structure. SAP Predictive Analysis, which we'll discuss later in this chapter, provides a superior user interface, but the Application Function Modeler is a great advantage over coding PAL functions in SAP HANA Studio if SAP Predictive Analysis is unavailable.

SAP HANA R Integration

In addition to the PAL algorithms, SAP HANA includes an integrated R client in the calculation engine. This allows SAP HANA to submit R code to an `Rserve` instance on an affiliated Linux host.

R is an open-source programming language that is very popular with mathematicians and statisticians. Originally used primarily within the academic community, R has surged in popularity for business users in the past few years. R stores all data, objects, and definitions in memory and performs its own memory management to ensure that the workspace is appropriately sized.

Typically, R is run using a command-line interface; however, several editors and Integrated Development Environments (IDEs), such as R Studio, are available. One of the main benefits of R is the wide range of predictive algorithms available. R's predictive functionality is available in packages that are submitted by users to the Comprehensive R Archive Network (CRAN). These packages are subject to some review and testing prior to submission, but much of the functionality is user tested. Popular packages are well tested and reliable; more obscure algorithms may be less reliable. No formal support is available for R packages.

R was a natural choice for integration with SAP HANA because it both complements the in-memory architecture of SAP HANA and is freely available and has extensive predictive functionality, essentially allowing SAP HANA to run thousands of predictive algorithms. Rserve is a TCP/IP server that supports remote connection, authentication, and file transfer and allows integration of R functionality into other applications. Rserve is called by the R client in the SAP HANA calculation engine. While there is some cost to marshaling data between the SAP HANA server and the Rserve host, this is minimal because both systems hold data in memory, eliminating the need for writing to disk, and also because the SAP HANA calculation engine's matrix primitives are similar to R's data frame structure. The transfer between R and SAP HANA is in binary format, minimizing the quantity of data transferred across the network. While Rserve is supported on most operating systems, SAP currently officially supports only an Rserve instance running on a separate supported Linux host for integration with SAP HANA.

The Rserve integration allows users to submit R code in SAP HANA Studio, which is processed by the integrated R Linux host. All packages called in R code must be installed and active on the R host.

SAP Lumira and SAP Predictive Analysis

In 2012, SAP introduced a companion product called SAP Predictive Analysis that provides a frontend tool for visualization and calling both PAL and SAP HANA-R algorithms. SAP Predictive Analysis also includes all of the functionality of the SAP Lumira visualization tool. This tool provides a point-and-click interface to generate, save, and store various visualizations, including bar charts, line charts, pie charts, and even word clouds and geographic pie and choropleth charts. It allows users to interact with data stored in SAP HANA information views and create presentation-ready exhibits directly from data in SAP HANA. Figure 13.1 shows several different visualizations available in SAP Lumira.

SAP Predictive Analysis includes the same PREPARE and VISUALIZE panes from SAP Lumira shown in Figure 13.2 but also includes the addition of the PREDICT pane shown in Figure 13.3, which holds all of the predictive functionality. (Notice the toggle functionality at the top of both figures to move between panes.)

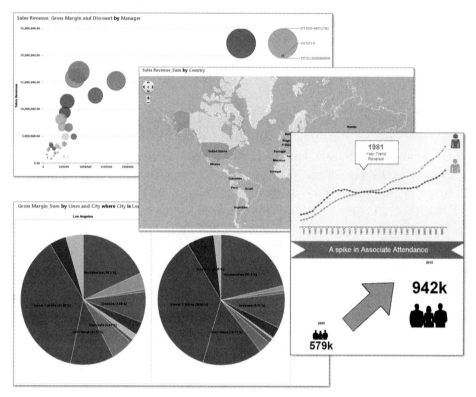

Figure 13.1 Sample Visualizations from SAP Lumira

On the PREDICT pane, you can build a predictive workflow by dragging and dropping predictive algorithm modules from the ALGORITHM tab on the top half of the screen into the predictive workflow designer on the bottom half of the screen. Each predictive module requires configurations specific to the algorithm prior to running, including selecting predictors and dependent variables. After configuration, you click the RUN ANALYSIS button, and you are notified after the analysis has been run. Upon completion, the RESULTS tab in the PREDICT pane is available and holds the result data and visualizations for all predictive modules that were run in the predictive workflow. In addition to predictive algorithms, there is also a module available to write the predictive result data set back to a table in SAP HANA.

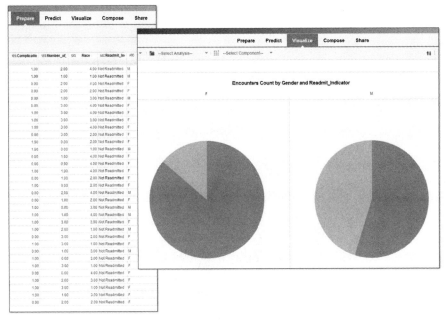

Figure 13.2 SAP Predictive Analysis: Prepare and Visualize Panes

Figure 13.3 SAP Predictive Analysis: Predict Pane

Now, we'll walk through an overview of the installation and configuration of each of these predictive tools that integrate with SAP HANA.

13.2   Integrating with SAP HANA

R integration and AFL are available for any SAP HANA implementation, but you'll need to install and configure these pieces before users can access the predictive content.

13.2.1   Installing the Application Function Libraries

After you've installed SAP HANA, install the AFL using the Unified Installer and start the scripting server so users can access PAL functions. In addition, if you'll be using SAP HANA Studio's Application Function Modeler, the SAP HANA client must also be installed to the local machine, and you must connect SAP HANA Studio to the *regi.exe* file in the SAP HANA client folder.

13.2.2   Deploying Rserve

To install the SAP HANA-R integration components, you must configure the R Linux. If the Linux host is running SUSE Linux with an active support agreement, you can download and install R and Rserve via the update repository. In this situation, there is no need to compile the R code. If the Linux host must be configured manually, the Java Developer Connection (JDC) (version 1.5.0_18 or higher) must be installed and configured. After Java is configured, R must be installed and compiled from its source code. SAP recommends R version 2.15 or higher.

Next, install Rserve on the R Linux host and all R packages for the algorithms that will be used for predictive analysis in SAP HANA. After the Linux host is configured, SAP HANA must be configured to interact with the R host. In SAP HANA Studio, the R server IP addresses and ports must be entered.

> **Additional Resources**
>
> Instructions for installing the AFL (which includes both the PAL and BFL functions) are included in the SAP HANA Installation Guide with SAP HANA Unified Installer, available at *http://help.sap.com/hana/SAP_HANA_Server_Installation_Guide_en.pdf*.

Installation and user instructions for HANA-R integration are found in the *SAP HANA R Integration* Guide, available at *http://help.sap.com/hana/SAP_HANA_R_Integration_Guide_en.pdf*.

User instructions for configuring and using the Application Function Modeler are found at the SAP HANA Academy site: *http://www.saphana.com/docs/DOC-3851*.

13.2.3 Leveraging R and PAL to Produce Predictive Results

You can run R code in SAP HANA Studio by creating a procedure with R code wrapped by `LANGUAGE RLANG AS BEGIN <R Code> END;`. In the R code, the return data must be a data frame object, so it's common for the output to be converted using `as.data.frame(<output data matrix>)` in the R code. An R procedure can also be called from another procedure—for example, one written in SQLScript.

To use PAL algorithms in SAP HANA Studio, the `afl_wrapper_generator` procedure must be created. This function is used each time a PAL procedure is built and takes in the procedure name, PAL function name specifying the algorithm and function to be used, and a table referencing the input and output table types. After the PAL procedure has been created, it can be called using a simple `CALL _SYS_AFL.<procedure name>(<procedure inputs and outputs>);` statement. In addition to the predictive functions, the PAL includes some scoring and diagnostic functions that may be called more regularly using the PAL procedures.

Using the SAP Predictive Analysis application with an SAP HANA online data source automatically generates the table types, formats, tables, and procedures required for either PAL or R algorithms. We've included examples of R and PAL algorithms using both SAP HANA Studio and SAP Predictive Analysis methods in the case studies in this chapter.

Additional Resources

For additional details on syntax, specific function availability, and usage, SAP has provided user guides with examples for calling R, PAL, and BFL functions:

- SAP HANA R guide:
  http://help.sap.com/hana/SAP_HANA_R_Integration_Guide_en.pdf
- SAP HANA PAL reference:
  http://help.sap.com/hana/SAP_HANA_Predictive_Analysis_Library_PAL_en.pdf
- SAP HANA BFL reference:
  http://help.sap.com/hana/SAP_HANA_Business_Function_Library_BFL_en.pdf

13.2.4 Installing SAP Predictive Analysis

Installation of the SAP Predictive Analysis client tool is straightforward and easy. After downloading the installation file from the SAP site, you simply click through the wizard, which has no configurations required except for entering the license key. There is no additional configuration required to run algorithms on data located on SAP HANA using either the PAL or SAP HANA-R; you must simply enter the database and connection information, as shown in Figure 13.4, to connect to the SAP HANA server and select analytic content.

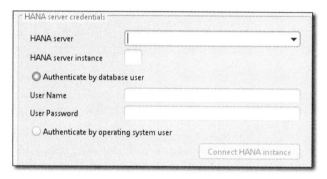

Figure 13.4 SAP HANA Server Credentials in SAP Predictive Analysis

In addition to running predictive algorithms on SAP HANA, SAP Predictive Analysis can operate on data stored locally on the user's workstation, using a local installation of R. To be used in this SAP HANA offline or local mode, a local installation of R must be on the same workstation, and SAP Predictive Analysis must be directed to look for it in the correct installation folder.

13.2.5 User Privileges and Security with SAP Predictive Analysis

In addition to having SELECT, EXECUTE, and WRITE permissions on any analytic content, tables, and schemas that will be used for predictive analyses, you'll need special privileges for both PAL and SAP HANA-R execution access. To manage this access with minimal manual configuration for new users, one best practice is to create a predictive user security role that is allocated to any users who need to access predictive content. Table 13.4 and Figure 13.5 show the security settings required to execute algorithms in each of the different predictive toolsets available in SAP HANA.

Predictive Functions	Permissions Required
BFL	▸ `AFL_SYS_AFL_AFLBFL_EXECUTE` system privilege must be granted.
PAL	▸ `AFL__SYS_AFL_AFLPAL_EXECUTE` system privilege must be granted. ▸ `AFL_WRAPPER_GENERATOR(SYSTEM)` stored procedure must be created. ▸ `AFL_WRAPPER_GENERATOR(SYSTEM)` SQL privilege execute must be granted. ▸ `_SYS_REPO` must have `SELECT` privileges with ability to grant to others on predictive users' schema.
SAP HANA-R Integration	▸ `CREATE R SCRIPT` system privilege must be granted.
Application Function Modeler	▸ `REPOSITORY_REST (SYS)` object privilege `EXECUTE` must be granted ▸ Root package (`REPO_PACKAGE_ROOT`) package privilege must be granted (`READ`, `EDIT`, and `MAINTAIN`).

Table 13.4 Security Provisioning for Predictive User Role

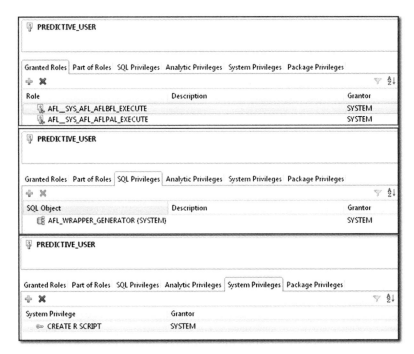

Figure 13.5 Predictive User Role Security Settings

In addition to creating the predictive role with all access required to run predictive algorithms, we recommend that a limited number of users run predictive algorithms, especially those run through SAP Predictive Analysis. Some of the access privileges granted to predictive users have far-reaching effects, so we recommend minimizing the use of these privileges outside of predictive functions.

In addition, supporting tables for many algorithms are created in the user schema that runs predictive algorithms. These tables can accumulate over time, and while their size isn't typically an issue, the presence of dozens or hundreds of tables, stored procedures, and views can make the predictive user's schema difficult to navigate. Therefore, we recommend that you store any data used for predictive algorithms in schemas separate from the predictive user's schema, which you should clean out on a regular basis to minimize the accumulation of these support tables.

We'll now move on to discuss several methods of implementing predictive models created using any of the SAP HANA predictive tools in an SAP HANA and SAP BusinessObjects BI environment.

13.3   Integrating with SAP BusinessObjects BI

Integrating predictive models back into the business process is often a stumbling block as organizations attempt to make predictive insights operationally actionable. This section discusses several ways to implement models in an existing BI environment.

13.3.1   Exporting Scored Data Back to Databases

The most straightforward method of implementing predictive models is to score the data in the predictive software and then write the scores back to a table in the database. For predictive models run in SAP HANA Studio using PAL or SAP HANA-R algorithms, this simply means taking the result set from the PAL or SAP

HANA-R algorithm and storing it in the BI environment. Using SAP Predictive Analysis, predictive model result data can be written back to the SAP HANA database using the SAP HANA `Writer` transform. This result table written back to SAP HANA can be used as a source for an analytic view or SAP BusinessObjects BI universe, which makes the predictive results available to users. SAP Predictive Analysis stores the predictive workflow, so each time new data must be scored, the SAP Predictive Analysis document can simply be reopened and rerun, replacing the original score table.

This method of writing predictive algorithm result scores back to the database has the advantage of being one of the fastest ways to implement predictive results and make predictive information available to everyone across the organization. Essentially, as soon as a model is approved by the executive team, scores can be written back to the database and integrated into BI environments. This also ensures that predictive results are relatively stable and all scores are refreshed at the same time.

However, the drawback of this method of implementation is that scores can't be calculated on demand in a business application; predictive results are essentially calculated and written on a batch basis (either automated or manually triggered). This means that scores aren't immediately available on new records added to the database and that scores can't be calculated in real time and used for immediate decision support.

This type of implementation is sufficient and effective for many applications. If new data can be scored regularly (e.g., weekly), the delay may be sufficiently small for many applications, such as batch marketing, for which marketing prospects for solicitations are selected based on model scores.

13.3.2 Exporting Algorithms

If simply exporting the scores for a predictive model is insufficient, the scoring algorithm, or method of assigning the predictive value, must be exported from the modeling tool and integrated into a business application or database. This is necessary in situations when real-time scoring is required—for example, insurance or financial risk models, where customers are applying for an insurance or financial product and expect immediate answers on whether they are accepted and what their rate will be. In these cases, batch processing won't suffice because customers expect results in a few seconds when contacting companies via web or phone. Similarly, customers expect that a change in their input data should result in an immediate impact on their return decision of acceptance or price level. To provide this type of response, the model scoring equation must be available either within an application or as a service that can be called by the application. This can be implemented as a web service, or the function can be made available in the database or application.

There are a few ways to program a predictive algorithm in a database or application on SAP HANA:

▸ **Code the algorithm logic**
The first option is to extract and understand the actual modeling equation or logic of the fitted predictive model and code it into a function available to the target application, such as a stored procedure in SAP HANA. The complexity of the final predictive model determines how complex the scoring algorithm is. For example, a simple decision tree can be coded in a few nested if-then statements, which is relatively easy to implement in almost any language. However, more complex algorithms, such as clustering and neural networks, may be very difficult to code. This method of implementation is one of the most labor-intensive because the algorithm must be fully coded and tested prior to implementation. Additionally, the SAP HANA scoring algorithm must also be updated any time the model is refitted or changed.

▸ **Predictive Model Markup Language export**
Predictive Model Markup Language (PMML) is an XML-based modeling format developed by data mining industry groups in an attempt to standardize predictive model representations. PMML defines both the predictive model and some limited preprocessing algorithms and supports the most common predictive models, including clustering, association, regression, time series, and decision trees.

While most predictive modeling tools (including R, PAL, and SAP Predictive Analysis) can export PMML models, very few databases or applications can accept and execute them. SAP HANA is slated with a future release to be able to accept PMML model formats. After this feature is available, the PMML method may be the best way to create a predictive algorithm in the SAP HANA database. The PMML file is exported directly from the modeling software to the database with no manual interventions, minimizing development and testing resource requirements.

► **Call the predictive scoring function**

In predictive software, there is typically stored model scoring functionality available for most algorithms. This allows a model to be fitted and saved in a proprietary format that can be scored only by the predictive software. Therefore, the model can effectively be scored by writing a stored procedure to call the predictive software from the target application or database.

For SAP HANA, this could mean creating a stored procedure that calls an R or PAL scoring process on a saved model object. While this doesn't require that the actual model function be coded in SAP HANA, it does require some effort to create the stored procedure; however, future updates would require minimal changes because no details of the actual model (such as coefficients or weights) are included in the stored procedure. As of version 1.0.11 of SAP Predictive Analysis, a stored procedure that calls a PAL model scoring function can be exported directly from the SAP Predictive Analysis predictive workflow for any saved models from PAL algorithms.

To illustrate some of these predictive concepts, we'll build and implement predictive models to assist with customer relationship management for the Adventure-Works Cycle Company. These models will use the data that was provisioned using SAP Data Services and modeled using SAP HANA Studio.

13.4 Case Study 1: Clustering Analysis

To increase Internet sales, the AdventureWorks marketing team has requested an in-depth analysis of its customers to understand common customer profiles and how to identify valuable customers early in their lifecycles. Based on this request from the marketing team, we'll first run a customer clustering analysis to better understand and segment customers.

Clustering is one of the most popular customer segmentation algorithms; it creates groups of similar customers based on numeric characteristics. While any numeric characteristic can be used to build the cluster, if you restrict the clustering algorithm to using only demographic (i.e., non-purchase-related characteristics), you may be able to evaluate a customer's potential lifetime value before the customer establishes a purchase history.

Therefore, for this initial analysis, we'll restrict the clustering algorithm to demographic characteristics, in an effort to allow the model to predict valuable customers without the benefit of transaction history. We'll use the R KMeans clustering algorithm to create our clusters in both SAP Predictive Analysis and through SAP HANA-R integration within SAP HANA Studio.

13.4.1 Preparing the Data

The first step to customer clustering is to ensure that the data is at the customer level prior to modeling. This means that there must be only one record per customer going into the modeling algorithm. In this case, we've created a calculation view on top of the Internet sales analytic view (ANLV_INTERNETSALES) created in Part III of the book. This calculation view simply aggregates order and sales metrics up to the customer level, creating customer-level aggregate data of the total number of orders per customer and total sales. While these sales aggregates aren't used in generating the cluster assignments, we'll evaluate the clusters based on these aggregated measures after they are created.

Create the First Customer Calculation View

First, create an initial calculation view with customer and order counters that are used in the clustering process by following these steps:

1. Launch the SAP HANA Studio application.

2. Right-click the `saphana.internetsales` package, and choose NEW • CALCULATION VIEW.

3. Enter the calculation view name "cv_internet_sales_order". You're creating a new calculation view using the graphical view type.

4. Add the analytic view ANLV_INTERNETSALES created in prior steps in the SELECT OBJECTS dialog shown in Figure 13.6.

5. Click FINISH, and define the rest of the calculation view manually.

6. In the TOOLS PALETTE dropdown box, select the `Aggregation` transform, as shown in Figure 13.7. This adds the `Aggregation` transform to the TOOLS PALETTE window. Connect the `Aggregation` transform from the ANLV_INTERNETSALES input element to the OUTPUT object.

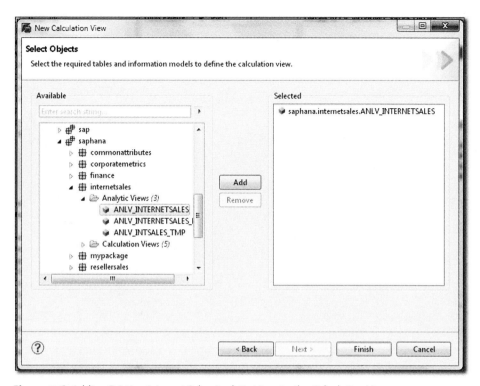

Figure 13.6 Adding Existing Internet Sales Analytic View to the Calculation View

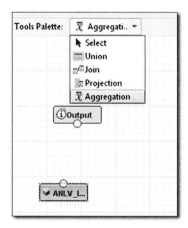

Figure 13.7 Selecting the Aggregation Transform

7. Click the `Aggregation` transform, right-click each element shown under COLUMNS in Figure 13.8, and click ADD TO OUTPUT to add the elements to the COLUMNS portion of OUTPUT OF AGGREGATION_1.

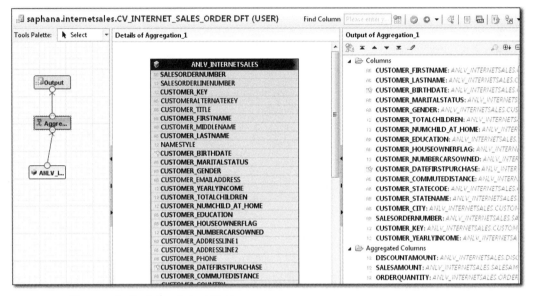

Figure 13.8 Configure Output Fields

8. Click the DISCOUNTAMOUNT and SALESAMOUNT columns, right-click, and select ADD AS AGGREGATED COLUMN.

9. Right-click CALCULATED COLUMNS and select NEW to create a calculated column for AGE, configured as shown in Figure 13.9.

10. Click the `Output` transform, right-click, and select ADD AS ATTRIBUTE for the list of variables shown under COLUMNS in Figure 13.9, as well as the new calculated AGE column. Right-click the SALESAMOUNT and DISCOUNTAMOUNT variables, and select ADD AS MEASURE.

11. Add counters for customers and orders by right-clicking COUNTERS and choosing NEW. Configure each counter as shown in Figure 13.10.

12. Click SAVE AND VALIDATE to save the view, and then click SAVE AND ACTIVATE to active it.

Figure 13.9 Creating a Calculated Age Column

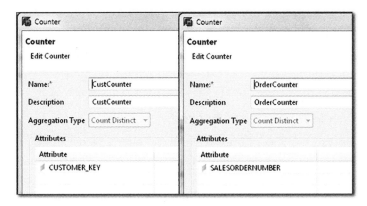

Figure 13.10 Creating Counters for Customers and Orders

Create the Second Customer Calculation View

Follow these steps to create a second calculation view with a single record per customer using the order-level calculation view created just before that will be used to fit the clustering model:

1. Right-click the `saphana.internetsales` package, and choose NEW • CALCULATION VIEW.

2. Enter the calculation view name "cv_internet_sales_customer". You're creating a new calculation view using the graphical view type.

3. Add the calculation view CV_INTERNET_SALES_ORDER created in prior steps in the SELECT OBJECTS dialog box shown previously in Figure 13.7.

4. Click FINISH, and define the rest of the calculation view manually.

5. Add and connect an `Aggregation` transform between the `Input` and `Output` transforms. In the `Aggregation` transform, add all customer fields, including `Age`, to the COLUMNS output by right-clicking and selecting ADD TO OUTPUT. SALESORDERNUMBER should not be in the output of the `Aggregation` transform. Add SALESAMOUNT, DISCOUNTAMOUNT, CUSTCOUNTER, and ORDERCOUNTER as aggregated column outputs.

6. Click the `Output` transform, select all customer fields, right-click, and select ADD AS ATTRIBUTES. Select the sales and discount amounts and counters. Right-click and select ADD AS MEASURE.

13.4.2 Performing Clustering Analysis

Now that the data has been prepared, you'll create the clustering model first in SAP Predictive Analysis and then later create the same model in SAP HANA Studio using SAP HANA-R integration.

Perform Cluster Analysis in SAP Predictive Analysis

The SAP Predictive Analysis tool has an intuitive user interface and visualizations where you'll create the predictive workflow and then visualize the cluster results. Although you're visualizing the data and creating the predictive workflow in the SAP Predictive Analysis tool on the user's local machine, the data is stored on SAP HANA, and the predictive algorithms are run on the configured `Rserve` instance. Follow these steps:

1. Open SAP Predictive Analysis, and click NEW DOCUMENT. Select a source type of HANA ONLINE. Enter the SAP HANA server address, instance name, and user name and password in the NEW DOCUMENT FROM HANA ONLINE dialog box, and click CONNECT HANA INSTANCE to open the content.

2. Navigate to the `saphana.internetsales` package, and select the customer-level calculation view CV_INTERNET_SALES_CUSTOMER. Click SELECT to open the data set in SAP Predictive Analysis.

3. The document opens to the PREPARE pane, with the attributes and measures from the calculation view visible on the left in the OBJECT PICKER. Click on the PREDICT button at the top of the application screen to move to the PREDICT pane. In the top half of the PREDICT pane, on the ALGORITHMS tab, locate the HANA R-KMEANS algorithm under the CLUSTERING category. Double-click the HANA R-KMEANS algorithm so that it's added to the predictive workflow, on the bottom half of the PREDICT pane, as shown in Figure 13.11.

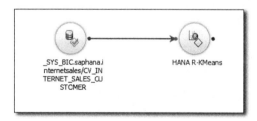

Figure 13.11 Predictive Workflow for Clustering

4. Right-click the HANA R-KMEANS module in the predictive workflow, and select CONFIGURE PROPERTIES. In the INDEPENDENT COLUMNS area, select the following fields: `CUSTOMER_TOTALCHILDREN`, `CUSTOMER_NUMCHILD_AT_HOME`, `CUSTOMER_NUM-BERCARSOWNED`, `AGE`, and `CUSTOMER_YEARLYINCOME`.

   Enter "3" for NUMBER OF CLUSTERS. The configurations should match Figure 13.12. Click SAVE AND CLOSE to return to the predictive workflow.

5. Right-click the HANA R-KMEANS module in the predictive workflow and select RUN ANALYSIS. Upon completion, a success message appears. Click YES to navigate to the predictive RESULTS pane.

6. On the RESULTS pane shown in Figure 13.13, review the result data, which should have the new `ClusterNumber` field included, and navigate to the RESULT CHARTS area to view the automated algorithm visualizations, shown in Figure 13.14.

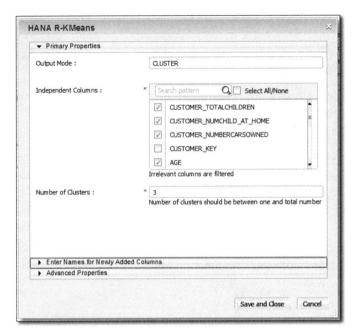

Figure 13.12 SAP HANA R-KMeans Configuration

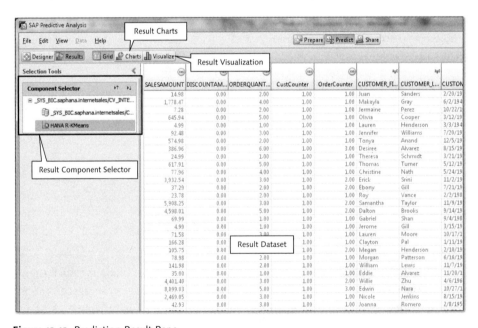

Figure 13.13 Prediction Result Pane

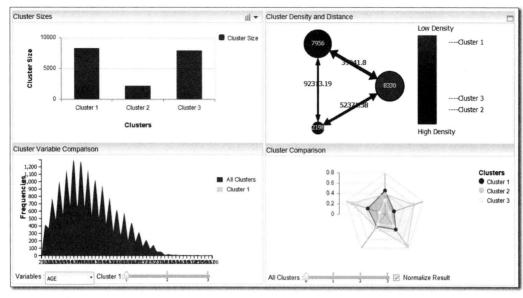

Figure 13.14 SAP Predictive Analysis Clustering Visualization

Cluster Model Evaluation

After you've fit clusters to the AdventureWorks customer data, you should evaluate them using both the automated output visualizations and by comparing key business metrics against the clustered customer groups. In Figure 13.14, the clusters are summarized, and you can see that there are two approximately equally sized larger clusters (1 and 3) and a single, much smaller cluster. However, on the radar chart in the bottom-right area of the cluster visualization, you can see that, while cluster 2 is the smallest in terms of customer volume, the cluster 2 customers are very different demographically from those of clusters 1 and 3. Cluster 2 customers have, on average, a higher income and almost twice as many cars, and are slightly older than customers in cluster 1 and 3.

The true test of the segmentation model is evaluating how well it segments customers' shopping habits. After reviewing the cluster segmentation compared to key metrics, including sales and orders, you can see that cluster 2 also spends significantly more than clusters 1 and 3. This higher spending is driven primarily by a higher average order amount, but cluster 2 also shops more frequently than clusters 1 and 3. Therefore, internal customer group names will be assigned according to the spending habits of each group—cluster 2 will be "Gold" level customers, cluster 3 is "Silver," and cluster 1 is "Bronze," as in Table 13.6.

7. After reviewing the cluster visualizations, note the R output shown in Figure 13.15 by clicking the center icon at the top of the predictive RESULTS CHARTS pane. While this text output may not look useful, it contains important information to re-create the cluster scoring algorithm in a database or other application. The data labeled CENTERS in the R output contains the center point for each cluster and is used in the scoring algorithm later.

Perform Cluster Analysis in SAP HANA Studio

In the absence of the SAP Predictive Analysis client, the same clustering analysis can be performed by running R code in SAP HANA Studio. This process effectively runs the same predictive process as SAP Predictive Analysis, with predictive algorithms run on the configured `Rserve` instance. Because this data is being transferred between servers, it's critical to transfer only the data that will be run through the algorithm to the R server, and not include any extraneous fields. Follow these steps:

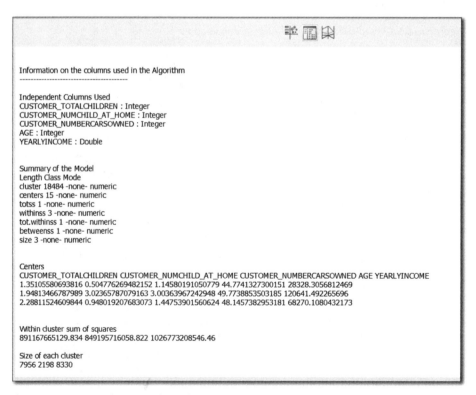

Figure 13.15 SAP Predictive Analysis Clustering R Output

1. Open SAP HANA Studio, and create three new tables to hold the modeling input data and output data with structures, as shown in Figure 13.16.

   Note that these tables need to be created in a separate schema called PA with the Predictive User role to isolate the predictive content generated by predictive algorithms. Table 13.5 offers a summary of these tables and the purpose for each.

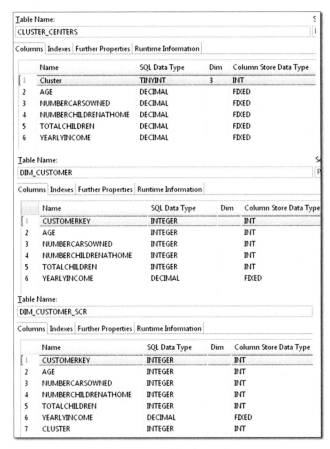

Figure 13.16 Input and Output Tables for R Clustering in SAP HANA Studio

Table	Purpose
CLUSTER_CENTERS	A model output table with the centers for each customer cluster. It's used in scoring new customers against the existing clustering model at a later time.

Table 13.5 Input and Output Tables for R Clustering in SAP HANA Studio

Table	Purpose
DIM_CUSTOMER	The model input table, which is a slimmed-down copy of the DIM_CUSTOMER table from the BOOK_USER schema with only the five clustering variables and the CUSTOMER_KEY field.
DIM_CUSTOMER_SCR	The model output table, which has the same fields as the model input table, with one additional column for the predicted cluster.

Table 13.5 Input and Output Tables for R Clustering in SAP HANA Studio (Cont.)

2. Populate the DIM_CUSTOMER modeling input table with the data required to build the clustering model in R, shown in Listing 13.1.

```
INSERT INTO "PA"."DIM_CUSTOMER"
select
    "CUSTOMERKEY",
    floor(days_between("BIRTHDATE", now())/365.25),
    "NUMBERCARSOWNED",
    "NUMBERCHILDRENATHOME",
    "TOTALCHILDREN",
    "YEARLYINCOME"
from "BOOK_USER"."DIM_CUSTOMER";
```

Listing 13.1 SQL to Populate the Modeling Input Table

3. As shown in Listing 13.2, create the R procedure ClustScr to cluster the input table customers and return the customer scores and cluster center information.

```
delete from "PA"."CLUSTER_CENTERS";
delete from "PA"."DIM_CUSTOMER_SCR";
DROP PROCEDURE ClustScr;
CREATE PROCEDURE
    ClustScr(
        IN train "PA"."DIM_CUSTOMER",
        OUT resulta "PA"."DIM_CUSTOMER_SCR",
        OUT resultb "PA"."RCLUSTER_CENTERS"
)
LANGUAGE RLANG AS
BEGIN
 custclust <- kmeans(train[,2:6], centers=3, nstart=1000);

 resultb <- as.data.frame(cbind(Cluster=1:dim(custclust$centers)[1],
custclust$centers));

 resulta <- as.data.frame(cbind(train, CLUSTER=custclust$cluster));
```

```
END;

CALL ClustScr(
      "PA"."DIM_CUSTOMER",
      "PA"."DIM_CUSTOMER_SCR",
      "PA"."RCLUSTER_CENTERS"
) WITH OVERVIEW;
```
Listing 13.2 R Code to Run Cluster Analysis

4. Review the cluster distributions by either running the SQL in Listing 13.3 or opening the data preview for the DIM_CUSTOMER_SCR table, which should return the results shown in Figure 13.17.

```
select
    CLUSTER, count(*)
from "PA"."DIM_CUSTOMER_SCR"
    group by CLUSTER;
```
Listing 13.3 SQL to View Distribution by Cluster

CLUSTER	CUSTOMERKEY_COUNT
1	2198
2	8330
3	7956

Figure 13.17 Cluster Data Preview Results

Cluster numbers generated by the clustering algorithm are randomly assigned, so although the clusters were named differently between the SAP Predictive Analysis run and the SAP HANA Studio run, the clusters are constructed identically. After the clustering algorithm is accepted in the organization, the cluster names 1, 2, and 3 should be altered to reflect organizationally accepted names.

To evaluate the value of the cluster algorithm you've created, let's review key metrics against the cluster breakdowns. Table 13.6 shows sales and orders per customer for each of the three clusters. While the clustering algorithm doesn't take into account any of these purchase-based metrics, it does effectively differentiate customers by purchase levels, with cluster 2 identifying a relatively small group of customers with a much higher than average order size and frequency. This analysis could be extended further to evaluate profitability per customer and then drive investment in acquiring and retaining these customers.

Cluster	Customers	Sales/Customer	Orders/Customer	Sales/Order
1—Bronze	7,956	1,327	1.42	$935
2—Gold	2,198	2,195	1.65	$1,330
3—Silver	8,330	1,678	1.53	$1,097
Overall	18,484	1,588	1.50	$1,061

Table 13.6 Key Metrics by Cluster

13.4.3 Implementing the Model

Because this model is built using only demographic characteristics, a customer's cluster can be assigned immediately when the customer is added to the customer database. Therefore, you can implement a scoring algorithm in the database that allows you to assign new records to the appropriate cluster. For some R algorithms, there are R functions that consume a saved R model object created during the fitting process, as well as new observations, and score them in R; for these algorithms, one implementation option is to call the R fitting algorithm to score new observations. However, the KMeans clustering algorithm doesn't have a scoring procedure, so you have to program your own scoring algorithm in SAP HANA.

To score a clustering model, you must calculate the Euclidian distance between a customer observation and the centers of each of the three clusters developed in the model. Euclidian distance is the straight-line distance between two points in n-space; in this case, there are five dimensional vectors for the customer and each of the cluster centers. An example calculation for the Euclidian distance between a customer observation o and cluster 1 center is shown in Figure 13.18.

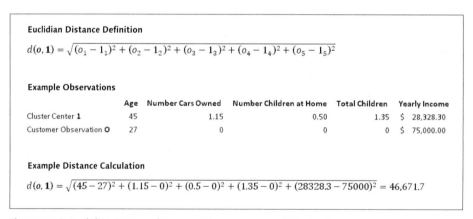

Figure 13.18 Euclidian Distance between Observation o and Cluster 1

The Euclidian distance calculation is repeated for each cluster, and the new observation is assigned to the cluster with the minimum Euclidian distance from the observation.

Now you can implement the process just described to assign new observations to clusters in the SAP HANA database using the following steps:

1. Create a score table to hold the cluster scores, which will be keyed on the CUSTOMERKEY field. An example creation statement for this table is given in Listing 13.4.

```
CREATE COLUMN TABLE "PA"."DIM_CUSTOMER_CLUSTER_SCORE"
("CUSTOMERKEY" INTEGER CS_INT NOT NULL ,
    "CLUSTER" INTEGER CS_INT,
    "SCORE_DATE" date CS_DATE,
    PRIMARY KEY ("CUSTOMERKEY")
    );
```

Listing 13.4 SQL to Create a Cluster Score Dimension Table

2. Create a table in SAP HANA with the cluster center information. This can either be the PA.RCLUSTER_CENTERS table that was created with the HANA-R KMeans clustering output generated previously or entered manually using the R output from SAP Predictive Analysis shown earlier in Figure 13.15.

3. Create a view to calculate the Euclidian distance between each observation in the customer table and each of the three clusters. An example of this calculation is included in Listing 13.5. Although there are several ways to perform this calculation, this solution attaches the cluster center information for each of the three customer clusters to each customer record, calculates the Euclidian distance for each cluster, and returns the cluster number for the cluster with the minimum distance.

```
create view "PA"."CLUSTER_SCORE" as
select
a.CUSTOMERKEY, a.AGE, a.NUMBERCARSOWNED, NUMBERCHILDRENATHOME,
TOTALCHILDREN, YEARLYINCOME,
SQRT(age1diffsq+cars1diffsq+cah1diffsq+totchild1diffsq+inc1diffsq)
clust1dist,
SQRT(age2diffsq+cars2diffsq+cah2diffsq+totchild2diffsq+inc2diffsq)
clust2dist,
SQRT(age3diffsq+cars3diffsq+cah3diffsq+totchild3diffsq+inc3diffsq)
clust3dist
```

```
 case when
SQRT(age1diffsq+cars1diffsq+cah1diffsq+totchild1diffsq+inc1diffsq)
<SQRT(age2diffsq+cars2diffsq+cah2diffsq+totchild2diffsq+inc2diffsq)
  and
SQRT(age1diffsq+cars1diffsq+cah1diffsq+totchild1diffsq+inc1diffsq)<SQRT
(age3diffsq+cars3diffsq+cah3diffsq+totchild3diffsq+inc3diffsq) then 1
  when

SQRT(age2diffsq+cars2diffsq+cah2diffsq+totchild2diffsq+inc2diffsq)<SQRT
(age1diffsq+cars1diffsq+cah1diffsq+totchild1diffsq+inc1diffsq)
  and
SQRT(age2diffsq+cars2diffsq+cah2diffsq+totchild2diffsq+inc2diffsq)<SQRT
(age3diffsq+cars3diffsq+cah3diffsq+totchild3diffsq+inc3diffsq) then 2
  else 3
   end Cluster
 from

 (
 select
cust.*,
c1."AGE" as AGE1,
c1."NUMBERCARSOWNED" as NUMBERCARSOWNED1,
c1."NUMBERCHILDRENATHOME" as NUMBERCHILDRENATHOME1,
c1."TOTALCHILDREN" as TOTALCHILDREN1,
c1."YEARLYINCOME" as YEARLYINCOME1,

c2."AGE" as AGE2,
c2."NUMBERCARSOWNED" as NUMBERCARSOWNED2,
c2."NUMBERCHILDRENATHOME" as NUMBERCHILDRENATHOME2,
c2."TOTALCHILDREN" as TOTALCHILDREN2,
c2."YEARLYINCOME" as YEARLYINCOME2,

c3."AGE" as AGE3,
c3."NUMBERCARSOWNED" as NUMBERCARSOWNED3,
c3."NUMBERCHILDRENATHOME" as NUMBERCHILDRENATHOME3,
c3."TOTALCHILDREN" as TOTALCHILDREN3,
c3."YEARLYINCOME" as YEARLYINCOME3,

POWER((cust.AGE-c1.AGE), 2) as age1diffsq,
POWER((cust.NUMBERCARSOWNED-c1.NUMBERCARSOWNED), 2) cars1diffsq,
POWER((cust.NUMBERCHILDRENATHOME-c1.NUMBERCHILDRENATHOME), 2)
cah1diffsq,
POWER((cust.TOTALCHILDREN-c1.TOTALCHILDREN), 2) totchild1diffsq,
POWER((cust.YEARLYINCOME-c1.YEARLYINCOME), 2) inc1diffsq,
```

```
POWER((cust.AGE-c2.AGE), 2) age2diffsq,
POWER((cust.NUMBERCARSOWNED-c2.NUMBERCARSOWNED), 2) cars2diffsq,
POWER((cust.NUMBERCHILDRENATHOME-c2.NUMBERCHILDRENATHOME), 2)
cah2diffsq,
POWER((cust.TOTALCHILDREN-c2.TOTALCHILDREN), 2) totchild2diffsq,
POWER((cust.YEARLYINCOME-c2.YEARLYINCOME), 2) inc2diffsq,

POWER((cust.AGE-c3.AGE), 2) age3diffsq,
POWER((cust.NUMBERCARSOWNED-c3.NUMBERCARSOWNED), 2) cars3diffsq,
POWER((cust.NUMBERCHILDRENATHOME-c3.NUMBERCHILDRENATHOME), 2)
cah3diffsq,
POWER((cust.TOTALCHILDREN-c3.TOTALCHILDREN), 2) totchild3diffsq,
POWER((cust.YEARLYINCOME-c3.YEARLYINCOME), 2) inc3diffsq

from
 (select
CUSTOMERKEY,
floor(days_between(BIRTHDATE, now())/365.25) AGE,
NUMBERCARSOWNED,
NUMBERCHILDRENATHOME,
TOTALCHILDREN,
YEARLYINCOME

  from "BOOK_USER"."DIM_CUSTOMER") cust cross join
  (select * from "PA"."RCLUSTER_CENTERS" where "Cluster"=1) c1 cross
join
  (select * from "PA"."RCLUSTER_CENTERS" where "Cluster"=2) c2 cross
join
  (select * from "PA"."RCLUSTER_CENTERS" where "Cluster"=3) c3
) a
```

Listing 13.5 SQL Query to Score DIM_CUSTOMER against the Clustering Model

4. Update or replace the score history table with the results of the view as appropriate for the implementation of the cluster score dimension. This view can be used in an SAP Data Services extract, transform, and load (ETL) job or SQLScript such as the one in Listing 13.6 to insert new values. In this case, truncate the DIM_CUSTOMER_CLUSTER_SCORE table and keep only the most recent score.

```
delete from "BOOK_USER"."DIM_CUSTOMER_CLUSTER_SCORE";
insert into
   "BOOK_USER"."DIM_CUSTOMER_CLUSTER_SCORE"
select
   CUSTOMERKEY,
```

```
CLUSTER,
now()
from "PA"."CLUSTER_SCORE";
```
Listing 13.6 SQL to Populate the Cluster Score Dimension Table

5. Repeat the previous step only when the organization has determined that clusters should be recalculated on each customer.

6. Include the new DIM_CUSTOMER_CLUSTER_SCORE table in the existing customer attribute view in SAP HANA Studio by navigating to the saphana.commonattributes content package and double-clicking ATVB_CUSTOMER. Drag and drop the new table DIM_CUSTOMER_CLUSTER_SCORE into the DATA FOUNDATION area, as shown in Figure 13.19.

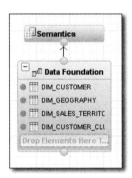

Figure 13.19 Customer Attribute View with Clustering Score Added

7. Drag a connection between DIM_CUSTOMER.CUSTOMERKEY and DIM_CUSTOMER_CLUSTER_SCORE.CUSTOMERKEY to connect the new table to the existing dimension tables. Click the CLUSTER field in the DIM_CUSTOMER_CLUSTER_SCORE table to add it to the attribute view.

8. Create a calculated column by right-clicking CALCULATED COLUMNS in the OUTPUT area of the Data_Foundation object, and click NEW. Use a case statement to translate the cluster numbers into organizationally accepted names for each customer group, as shown in Figure 13.20.

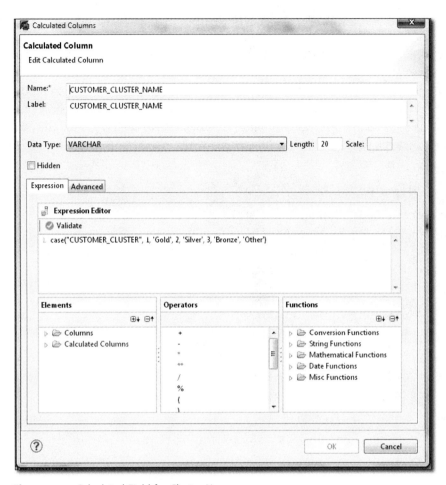

Figure 13.20 Calculated Field for Cluster Name

The clustering scores are now available in the common customer attribute view and can be added to dependent analytic views, SAP BusinessObjects BI universes, and end-user reports as necessary. The scoring algorithm you just developed can also be created as a stored procedure to score new records in the database.

13.5 Case Study 2: Product Recommendation Rules

AdventureWorks Cycle Company has also requested a method to identify likely companion purchases based on items already in a customer's online purchase basket. To determine which products to suggest, we'll develop an association model to suggest companion products to show on the website during the purchase process. These product suggestions should be prioritized to include items the customer is most likely to purchase, with a target of increasing average purchase size.

13.5.1 Preparing the Data

Unlike for the clustering model, the data from the existing Internet sales analytic view can be used for the Apriori algorithm that will suggest associations between items. Therefore, we'll access the ANLV_INTERNETSALES analytic view created in Part III of the book as the input for this algorithm.

13.5.2 Performing Apriori Analysis

The Apriori algorithm examines correlations and patterns within groups of items and is commonly used to develop item sets that are selected with high frequency; therefore, if a customer has already expressed interest in a portion of that item set, suggesting the remaining items may result in a high likelihood of acceptance.

In this case, we'll perform this Apriori analysis in both SAP Predictive Analysis and SAP HANA Studio, with both processes using the same Apriori algorithm from the PAL.

Perform Apriori Analysis Using SAP Predictive Analysis

Follow these steps to devise the Apriori suggestion rules by using SAP Predictive Analysis to run the PAL Apriori algorithm and review the visualization results:

1. Open SAP Predictive Analysis, and click NEW DOCUMENT. Select a source type of HANA ONLINE. Enter the SAP HANA server address, instance name, and user name and password in the NEW DOCUMENT FROM HANA ONLINE dialog box, and click CONNECT HANA INSTANCE to open content.

2. Navigate to the `saphana.internetsales` package, and select the analytic view ANLV_INTERNETSALES. Click the PREVIEW AND SELECT DATA checkbox, and

then click ACQUIRE to open the data set in SAP Predictive Analysis. In the field selection window, select only product-related fields (product_key and product_name, at a minimum) and the salesordernumber transaction key. Optionally, include a measure such as salesamount if you want to perform any visualizations in SAP Predictive Analysis. Click OK to create the new SAP Predictive Analysis document.

3. Proceed to the PREDICT pane, and add the SAP HANA Apriori transform in the ASSOCIATION category of the ALGORITHMS tab to the predictive workflow. Right-click on the SAP HANA Apriori transform in the workflow, and select CONFIGURE PROPERTIES. Adjust the configurations for the transform to match those shown in Figure 13.21.

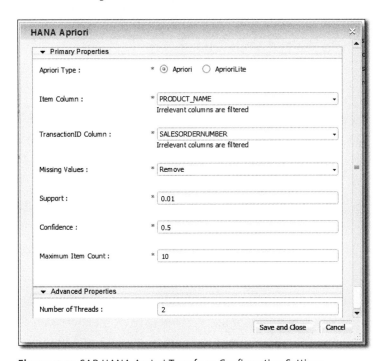

Figure 13.21 SAP HANA Apriori Transform Configuration Settings

4. Navigate to the DATA WRITERS tab, and double-click the SAP HANA Writer transform to add it to the predictive workflow. Right-click the new transform, and select CONFIGURE PROPERTIES. Enter the target table schema name (BOOK_USER) and table name (APRIORI_RESULT), and select the OVERWRITE checkbox.

5. Click on the RUN ANALYSIS button to run the predictive workflow. When you recieve the success message, click YES to proceed to the RESULTS pane, and then click CHARTS to view the automated visualization output, shown in Figure 13.22.

6. Reopen the configuration window for the SAP HANA `Apriori` transform, and enter "PRODUCT_KEY" in the ITEM COLUMN prompt. Rerun the analysis to generate the output table with keys rather than names for integration with the e-commerce application.

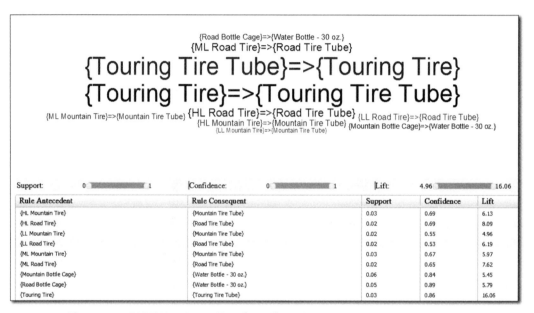

Figure 13.22 SAP HANA Apriori Transform Charts Output

In reviewing the results of this analysis, you'll see several pairings that make sense; for example, there are several tube and tire combinations, when customers purchasing a tire are also purchasing a corresponding type of tire tube with a confidence of 60% or higher. This may seem like common sense, but simply making this suggestion available prior to the completion of the Internet transaction to customers who purchase only a tube or only a tire could drive significant sales at little to no cost to AdventureWorks. You can also review the output table that was created as a part of this process in Figure 13.23.

AB Rules	12 Support	12 Confidence	12 Lift
{535} => {528}	0.01728189739325355	0.5545243619489559	4.955602367413949
{540} => {529}	0.02154813984598142	0.6946386946386947	8.086284366587396
{539} => {529}	0.0219096858165157	0.6544276457883369	7.618187817701856
{538} => {529}	0.02006580136664377	0.5316091954022989	6.18845906381826
{541} => {530}	0.02921291442206876	0.8641711229946524	16.06324535679374
{530} => {541}	0.02921291442206876	0.543010752688172	16.06324535679374
{536} => {528}	0.02805596731624426	0.6683893195521102	5.97317615169364
{537} => {528}	0.0345999493835641 2	0.6855300859598854	6.126357559794659
{479} => {477}	0.05499114212372103	0.8884345794392523	5.790106511006192
{478} => {477}	0.06117357822047073	0.8355555555555556	5.445483296680282
{478,485} => {477}	0.01182255323764417	0.8341836734693877	5.436542465713901
{477,485} => {478}	0.01182255323764417	1.0	13.65876543209876

Figure 13.23 BOOK_USER.APRIORI_OUT Table

Perform Apriori Analysis Using SAP HANA Studio

You can perform the same Apriori analysis from the SAP HANA Studio client by calling the PAL Apriori procedure via code using the following steps. These steps will create the Apriori function and then run it to retrieve the same Apriori rules output table generated by SAP Predictive Analysis.

1. Open SAP HANA Studio, and then open a new SQL window to run the table type creation and function generation scripts included in Listing 13.7.

```
SET SCHEMA PA;

DROP TYPE PAL_DATA_T;
CREATE TYPE PAL_DATA_T AS TABLE(
"CUSTOMER" VARCHAR(20),
"ITEM" INTEGER
);

DROP TYPE PAL_RESULT_T;
CREATE TYPE PAL_RESULT_T AS TABLE(
"PRERULE" VARCHAR(500),
"POSTRULE" VARCHAR(500),
"SUPPORT" DOUBLE,
"CONFIDENCE" DOUBLE,
"LIFT" DOUBLE
);

DROP TYPE PAL_PMMLMODEL_T;
CREATE TYPE PAL_PMMLMODEL_T AS TABLE(
"ID" INT,
"PMMLMODEL" VARCHAR(5000)
);
```

```
DROP TYPE PAL_CONTROL_T;
CREATE TYPE PAL_CONTROL_T AS TABLE(
"NAME" VARCHAR (50),
"INTARGS" INTEGER,
"DOUBLEARGS" DOUBLE,
"STRINGARGS" VARCHAR (100)
);

DROP TABLE PDATA;
CREATE COLUMN TABLE PDATA(
"ID" INT,
"TYPENAME" VARCHAR(100),
"DIRECTION" VARCHAR(100) );
INSERT INTO PDATA VALUES (1, 'PA_DEMO.PAL_DATA_T', 'in');
INSERT INTO PDATA VALUES (2, 'PA_DEMO.PAL_CONTROL_T', 'in');
INSERT INTO PDATA VALUES (3, 'PA_DEMO.PAL_RESULT_T', 'out');
INSERT INTO PDATA VALUES (4, 'PA_DEMO.PAL_PMMLMODEL_T', 'out');

GRANT SELECT ON PA_DEMO.PDATA to SYSTEM;

call SYSTEM.afl_wrapper_generator('PAL_APRIORI_RULE', 'AFLPAL',
'APRIORIRULE', PDATA);
```

Listing 13.7 PAL Apriori Function Creation

After the PAL_APRIORI_RULE function has been created, you must create a table with the transaction and product information, as well as shell tables for the function output results. Finally, call the PAL_APRIORI_RULE function to populate the PAL_RESULT_TAB with the result table. The table creation and function script is found in Listing 13.8.

```
DROP TABLE PAL_TRANS_TAB;
CREATE COLUMN TABLE PAL_TRANS_TAB(
"CUSTOMER" VARCHAR(20),
"ITEM" INTEGER );
insert into PAL_TRANS_TAB
   (select SALESORDERNUMBER, PRODUCT_KEY from "_SYS_BIC".
"saphana.internetsales/ANLV_INTERNETSALES");

DROP TABLE PAL_CONTROL_TAB;
CREATE COLUMN TABLE PAL_CONTROL_TAB(
"NAME" VARCHAR (50),
"INTARGS" INTEGER,
"DOUBLEARGS" DOUBLE,
"STRINGARGS" VARCHAR (100)
);
```

```
INSERT INTO PAL_CONTROL_TAB VALUES ('THREAD_NUMBER', 2, null, null);
INSERT INTO PAL_CONTROL_TAB VALUES ('MIN_SUPPORT', null, 0.01, null);
INSERT INTO PAL_CONTROL_TAB VALUES ('MIN_CONFIDENCE', null, 0.5,
null);
DROP TABLE PAL_RESULT_TAB;
CREATE COLUMN TABLE PAL_RESULT_TAB(
"PRERULE" VARCHAR(500),
"POSTRULE" VARCHAR(500),
"SUPPORT" Double,
"CONFIDENCE" Double,
"LIFT" DOUBLE
);

DROP TABLE PAL_PMMLMODEL_TAB;
CREATE COLUMN TABLE PAL_PMMLMODEL_TAB(
"ID" INT,
"PMMLMODEL" VARCHAR(5000)
);

CALL _SYS_AFL.PAL_APRIORI_RULE(PAL_TRANS_TAB, PAL_CONTROL_TAB,
PAL_RESULT_TAB, PAL_PMMLMODEL_TAB) WITH overview;
```

Listing 13.8 PAL Apriori Table Creation and Function Call

2. Review the results in PAL_RESULT_TAB, as shown in Figure 13.24.

SELECT * FROM PAL_RESULT_TAB

	PRERULE	POSTRULE	SUPPORT	CONFIDENCE	LIFT
1	478	477	0.06117357686161995	0.8355555534362793	5.445483684539795
2	479	477	0.054991140961647034	0.8884345293045044	5.790106296539307
3	535	528	0.017281897366046906	0.5545243620872498	4.955602645874023
4	536	528	0.028055967763066292	0.6683893203735352	5.9731764793396
5	537	528	0.034599948674440384	0.6855300664901733	6.126357555389404
6	538	529	0.020065801218152046	0.5316092371940613	6.188459396362305
7	539	529	0.02190968580543995	0.6544276475906372	7.61818790435791
8	540	529	0.021548138931393623	0.6946386694908142	8.086283683776855
9	530	541	0.029212914407253265	0.5430107116699219	16.063243865966...
10	541	530	0.029212914407253265	0.8641711473464966	16.06324577331543
11	478&485	477	0.011822553351521492	0.8341836333274841	5.436542510986328
12	477&485	478	0.011822553351521492	1.0	13.65876579284668

Figure 13.24 PAL Apriori Function Output

Alternatively, you can achieve the same output by opening a new Application
Function Modeler project, adding the Apriori algorithm, and connecting the same
PAL_TRANS_TAB created above as the source table, as shown in Figure 13.25.

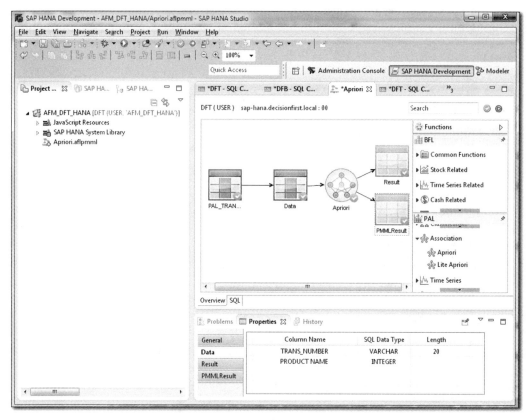

Figure 13.25 SAP Application Function Modeler

The user simply drags the source table to the DATA input, and then creates the RESULT and PMMLRESULT output structures graphically, matching the structure expected by the algorithm, as shown in Figure 13.26 and Figure 13.27.

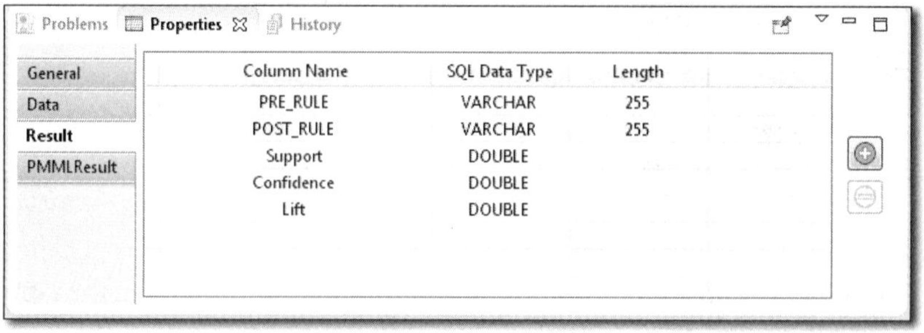

Figure 13.26 AFM Result Table Specification

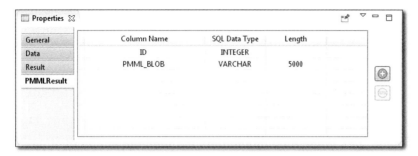

Figure 13.27 AFM PMML Result Table Specification

After validating, activating, and running the function, you can hover over the source or result tables and click OPEN DATA PREVIEW to view the results, which should be identical to those shown in Figure 13.24.

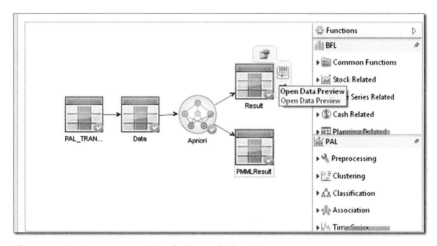

Figure 13.28 Viewing Apriori Results through the AFM

13.5.3 Implementing the Model

To make the suggested products available to the web application, the Internet team requested the ability to send one or more product keys and be returned with a list of items that should be displayed to the customer.

There are three possible ways to execute this using SAP HANA:

1. Employ the SAP HANA XS Engine to develop a web service that returns data from an SAP HANA table.

2. Connect from the e-commerce application directly to the SAP HANA database over a JDBC connection or other appropriate database connection configuration to access the table directly.

3. Create a Query as a Service (QaaS) web service through SAP BusinessObjects Web Intelligence using the product table created by the Apriori algorithm.

Because the SAP BusinessObjects Web Intelligence web service uses SAP BusinessObjects BI tools that already exist in the system, we'll employ this third method. This web service will be passed in one or more item keys that are currently in the customer's e-commerce basket and return the Apriori output table records for any suggested products for those input product keys. In this case, use the PAL_RESULT_TAB output table created previously, and execute the following steps:

1. Create an SAP BusinessObjects BI universe with only the Apriori result table PAL_RESULT_TAB and all fields from this table included as attributes, as shown in Figure 13.29.

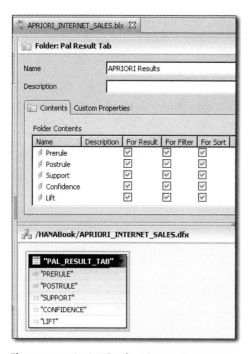

Figure 13.29 Apriori Product Suggestion Universe

2. After the universe has been created, create a new SAP BusinessObjects Web Intelligence report using this universe, which returns all of the fields in the universe and uses a prompt for the `Prerule` field, as shown in Figure 13.30.

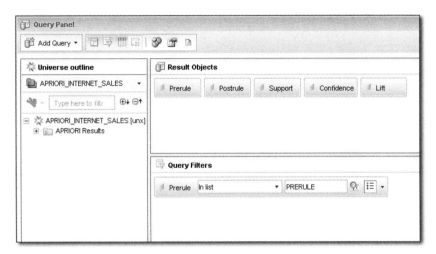

Figure 13.30 Apriori Product Suggestion Query

3. Click RUN, select any input from the list, and view the query results. After the report has generated, as shown in Figure 13.31, select the entire report table, right-click, and select PUBLISH AS WEB SERVICE.

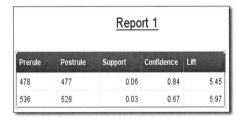

Figure 13.31 Product Suggestion Report

4. Click through the web service creation dialog, selecting the PRERULE prompt (see Figure 13.32), adding a name and description for the new web service (see Figure 13.33), and creating the service on the appropriate server. Finally, click PUBLISH.

747

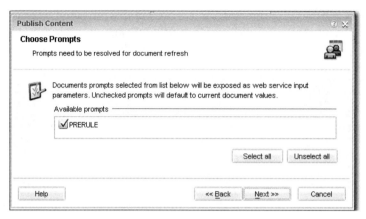

Figure 13.32 Apriori Product Suggestion Query

Figure 13.33 Web Service Name and Description

5. Test the web service by clicking the TEST button in the WEB SERVICE PUBLISHER pane, shown in Figure 13.34. In the APRIORI_RULE web service testing interface, enter in the values "539" and "540", as shown in Figure 13.35, and click SEND to review the web service functionality.

Figure 13.34 Web Service Publisher Pane

Figure 13.35 Web Service Testing Interface

This web service can then be exposed to the e-commerce application and return a list of potential products to display to customers. The web service can use the returned keys to link to existing product information, including images, descriptions, and names, and prioritize these suggestions by the confidence metric that is also returned to decide which items should be displayed first.

13.6 Summary

This chapter explored the tools available for performing predictive analysis in the SAP HANA database. By leveraging SAP HANA-R integration and PAL algorithms, you leverage the processing power of SAP HANA and existing BI infrastructure without the need to waste staff and system resources to transfer data among them or maintain a separate predictive tool.

While there are powerful tools that can be accessed directly in SAP HANA Studio, SAP has provided a powerful visualization tool with a user interface that allows easier access to the SAP HANA predictive tools, enabling business and statistical users access to tools typically reserved for highly specialized technical resources. Furthermore, these predictive tools allow unparalleled integration with the SAP BusinessObjects BI toolset, which allows business users and executives to act quickly on predictive model. Predictive models can often yield significant improvement on key business metrics, such as acquisition rates and marketing expenses, so implementing models in days or weeks rather than months can impact revenue by tens or hundreds of thousands of dollars.

Harnessing the transactional power of SAP HANA with the functionality of a well-designed dashboard can provide unique and attractive insight into key performance indicators as businesses have never before seen in tabular analytics.

14   Professionally Authored Dashboards with SAP HANA

The phrase *professionally authored dashboard* (PAD) is a relatively new term that describes an old concept. Historically, dashboards were developed by trained professionals with knowledge and experience in developing visualizations of this type. The original process was to gather specific requirements and develop a dashboard based on them. As requirements changed, these dashboards sometimes didn't reflect the most up-to-date requirements, and the dashboard projects usually failed as a result. A newer, more agile methodology called *Scrum* then became the popular design methodology. The major difference in Scrum methodology is that the requirements are gathered in a series of iterations (usually three) rather than one all-encompassing iteration. After the requirements are gathered, the dashboarding professionals then build a prototype to display to the end-user team. Any changes that are made to the dashboard would be made by the dashboarding professionals until a final design is achieved, agreed upon, and signed off.

These professional processes can take anywhere from weeks to months, depending on the complexity of the dashboard and the location within the project pipeline at which the dashboarding project falls. The amount of time that it typically takes for a PAD project lends a major disadvantage to these types of dashboards. This is because, at the end of the dashboard project, business processes may have changed, and the business questions answered by the dashboarding project may no longer be required.

So, if project duration is a major disadvantage of a PAD project, why should you undertake a PAD process to start with? One reason is aesthetics. Consider the use case in which an executive is a stickler for design and envisions the dashboard being released to the shareholders of the company to monitor the state of the business at a glance. It's apparent that the look of the dashboard is extraordinarily important, so the executive may need to request a PAD due to the tight design constraints.

Also consider the case in which the business has decided to implement increased transparency of the company to its employees. As part of this initiative, the company has installed multiple large screens around the office. These screens will rotate a series of dashboards containing metrics describing the performance of the company overall. In an effort to provide a polished look to the visualizations, the company requests a PAD. Figure 14.1 provides you with an idea of a PAD that, at a glance, gives information on the sales in a company while allowing for a drillable experience into sales rep performance. Meanwhile, Figure 14.2 gives information on the top ten customers and a focus on the key performance indicators (KPIs) of each one.

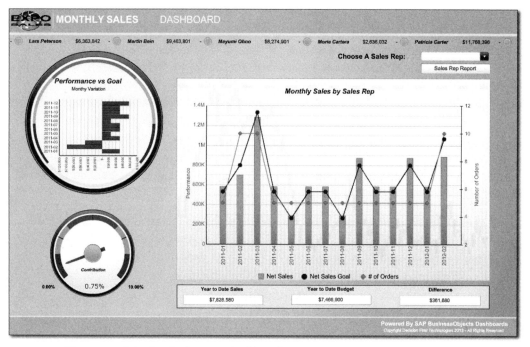

Figure 14.1 Sales Rep Performance Dashboard

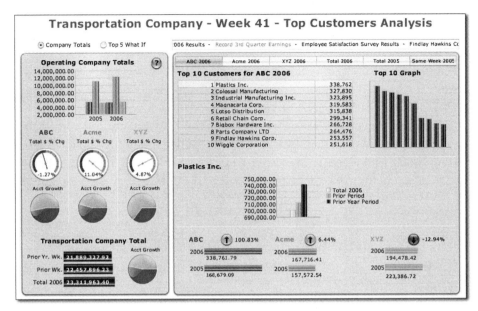

Figure 14.2 Top Customers and KPIs

SAP BusinessObjects BI provides two tools for designing PADs: SAP BusinessObjects Dashboards and SAP BusinessObjects Design Studio. Both tools are client-side installations that are separate from the core SAP BusinessObjects BI client/server installation. Each tool requires its own unique skill set in designing the dashboard; however, the overall graphical design of the dashboard requires a set of skills common to both tools.

In this chapter, our focus is on the methods by which you can connect SAP HANA to Dashboards and Design Studio data. For a full discussion of Dashboards, we recommend the SAP PRESS book *Creating Dashboards with SAP BusinessObjects: The Comprehensive Guide* (Li, DeLodder, 2012). For a full discussion of Design Studio, we recommend the SAP PRESS book *Getting Started with SAP BusinessObjects Design Studio* (Hacking, van der A, 2014).

> **Note**
>
> Distinguished from PADs are *self-service dashboards*, designed in SAP using tools like SAP BusinessObjects Explorer and SAP Lumira. We'll discuss SAP HANA and these types of dashboards in Chapter 15.

14.1 SAP HANA as a Data Source for SAP BusinessObjects Dashboards

Dashboards is a fully featured dashboarding tool that allows experienced designers to develop polished, professional-looking dashboards with little more than a drag-and-drop motion. Figure 14.3 is an example of what can be produced with SAP BusinessObjects Dashboards. Dashboards works in conjunction with Microsoft Excel to provide interactivity across multiple components that, together, form the dashboard and leverages Adobe Flash technology as the rendering engine to present the content to the users. It's the interactivity of these components and the data that they represent that changes available insight into data in ways that are immediately recognized and usable.

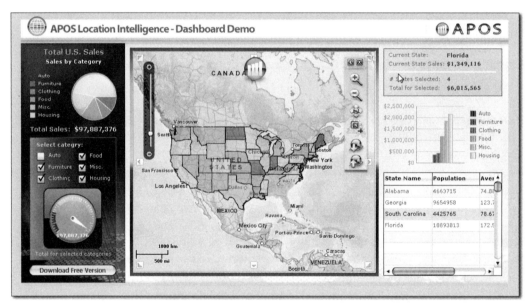

Figure 14.3 An Example Dashboard

When Dashboards was initially created, the only way to pull data into a dashboard was to hardcode the data directly within the embedded instance of Excel. The next generation of the tool offered options to dynamically update this data by binding *Query as a Web Service (QaaWS)* or *Business Intelligence Web Service (BIWS)* connections to the Excel document. There were also several other industry standard connection options supported that could also be bound to the Excel document. If you look at the Data Manager, shown in Figure 14.4, you can see a listing of the different ways that a dashboard designer could connect dynamically to data.

Figure 14.4 Connection Methods Currently Available from Dashboards

These connection options will allow you to access data within SAP HANA. You can, for example, build a universe on top of an SAP HANA instance, which can then take advantage of information views. The universe can also tap directly into the columnar tables that reside within the SAP HANA database. A QaaWS connection could then be developed on this universe to provide dynamic access to data within your dashboard. In fact, you can also build an SAP BusinessObjects Web Intelligence report on an SAP HANA–based universe and then expose the report data using BIWS, which can be consumed in Dashboards just like the QaaWS connections. In summary, the connection options listed in Figure 14.4 give developers a lot of flexibility when connecting to data that resides in SAP HANA.

With the release of SAP BusinessObjects Dashboards 4.x, SAP introduced a new connectivity option commonly referred to as *direct binding*. This connection option allows a developer to directly connect a Dashboards component to a universe and bypass the Excel layer. With this option, accessing data within SAP HANA is as simple as building a universe on SAP HANA and then adding a query in the Dashboard's QUERY panel.

Working with the new direct binding feature is quite simple. To bind data to a component, we first must select a universe. To select a universe we must enable the QUERY BROWSER panel. Once selected, the designer is presented with a dialog that asks the user to log on to an SAP BusinessObjects BI platform. After logging on, the designer is shown a listing of universes or BEx queries that have been published to the platform, as shown in Figure 14.5. Please note that SAP BusinessObjects Dashboards supports direct binding via the UNX– based universe or universes created within the Information Design Tool (IDT). With that in mind, it's important to note that the listing of universes presented doesn't include the legacy universe format (UNV).

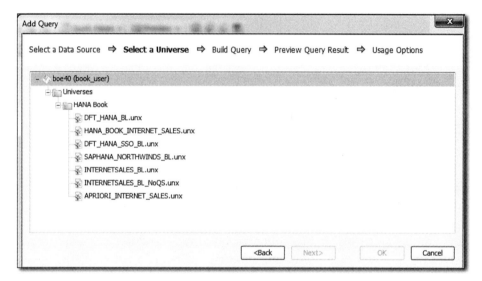

Figure 14.5 Listing of Universes on the SAP BusinessObjects BI Platform

After the designer selects the appropriate universe, a dialog is presented that allows the user to build a query like the one shown in Figure 14.6. The design of the dialog shows the objects from the business layer of the universe on the left side. The right side contains three panels: RESULTS OBJECTS, FILTERS, and RESULT SETS. The designer pulls objects from the business layer listing to the RESULTS SET panel. These objects will be available within the dashboard for projection into the dashboard components. To filter the data, the designer pulls the objects from the business layer listing to the FILTER panel. To perform a filter, the designer must select an operator and an operand (i.e., OBJECT: YEAR OPENED, OPERATOR: EQUAL TO, or OPERAND: 2001). The data is filtered out on the database level, and only the matching records are returned. Finally, the designer can click the PREVIEW window to pull back 200 records (default) to see how the data set will appear before committing to the creation of the query.

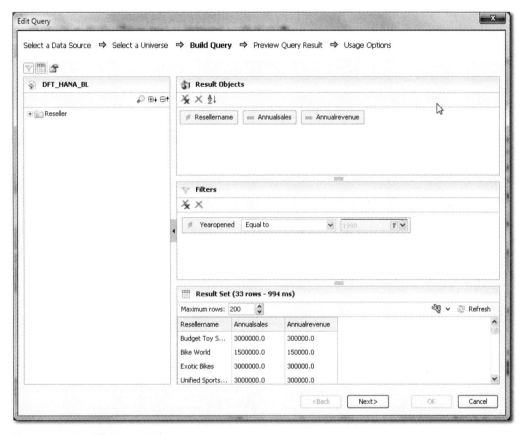

Figure 14.6 The Edit Query Dialog

When the designer completes the query and continues on, two other screens are presented: a full window preview and the query options.

Finishing up the QUERY BROWSER process, the designer is left with a query that can be used to bind directly to various components in the Dashboards application. As of SAP BusinessObjects 4.1, there is a dual mode button that allows a designer to bind data directly to a range of cells with Excel. Figure 14.7 gives an example of the dual mode binding button. This has been the traditional method of interacting with data within the dashboard. The other, newer method is binding directly to a query that is built in the QUERY BROWSER. When binding a component to a query in the QUERY BROWSER, the designer effectively removes the instance of Excel from the binding path in the dashboard. Data is executed directly against the data source through the objects referenced in the query. The data is returned and displayed in the appropriate areas in the bound component.

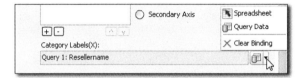

Figure 14.7 The Binding Menu: Spreadsheet or Query Data

Figure 14.8 shows an example of the dashboard at design time after the data is bound. Notice that the data associated with the direct bind is automatically displayed within the component. The result is an increase in performance and a decrease in the potential for error with binding to ranges of cells within Excel.

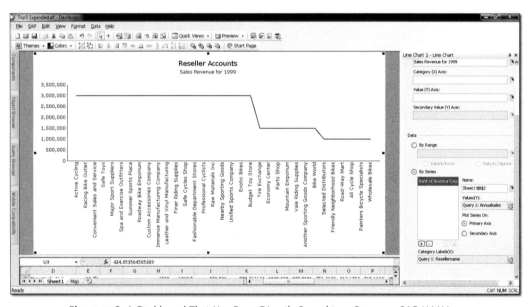

Figure 14.8 A Dashboard That Has Been Directly Bound to a Query on SAP HANA

While there are multiple ways to connect SAP BusinessObjects Dashboards to SAP HANA, technically SAP HANA is just another data source and requires no special consideration, apart from understanding how to properly query the SAP HANA source.

14.2 SAP HANA as a Data Source for SAP BusinessObjects Design Studio

Design Studio is a tool by which designers can develop dashboards with a polished, professional look. Design Studio was developed by SAP under the code name Zen. It was released in an initial version in 2012 and officially changed its name to Design Studio. The application is based on the open-source Eclipse integrated development environment (IDE).

Users familiar with the BEx Web Application Designer will notice a similarity between the familiar Web Application Designer and the new Design Studio. Design Studio is considered the next release of the application, and SAP will eventually encourage existing users to migrate to the new application. You can see how Design Studio currently looks in Figure 14.9.

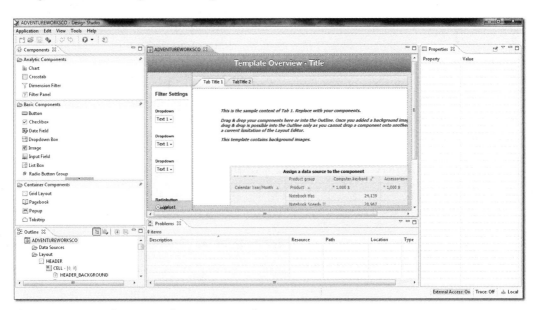

Figure 14.9 A Typical Design Studio Designer Interface

Design Studio allows you to connect to SAP HANA in three ways: to SAP BW on SAP HANA queries, to SAP HANA data sources, and to the SAP HANA XS Engine. Using these connectivity methods, you can achieve better performance over the traditional Excel/Flash-based Dashboards. We'll explain all three connection options to you and then explain how to consume the SAP HANA connections in Design Studio.

14.2.1 Connecting to SAP BW on SAP HANA

Upon launching Design Studio, go to the TOOLS • PREFERENCES menu item. In the PREFERENCES dialog, choose BACKEND CONNECTIONS. The BACKEND CONNECTIONS option lists the available SAP BW systems, as well as the existing SAP HANA sources.

To add a new SAP BW system, you must have the SAP GUI installed on your local machine. On entering the SAP logon interface, you add a new system. After the system is added, Design Studio picks up on the new addition and adds it to the listing of available systems. When a new Design Studio application is created, Design Studio uses one or more data sources that will be used within the application. Right-click DATA SOURCES in the OUTLINE area in the bottom-left part of the screen, and choose NEW. Enter the connection information by clicking BROWSE and selecting the appropriate SAP BW system. The interface asks for credentials to access the system, and then you can select a specific data source. Finally, after the data source is added to the application, you can apply the new data source to one or more existing components.

14.2.2 Connecting Directly to SAP HANA Data Sources

This process can also be applied to SAP HANA data sources. The first step is to install the SAP HANA middleware on the local machine. After the middleware is installed, an Open Database Connectivity (ODBC) source is created that connects the local machine to the SAP HANA instance. In Windows, go to the ODBC Data Source Administrator. See Figure 14.10 to see how the ODBC data source looks after the SAP HANA middleware has been added. (We discussed the SAP HANA middleware in Chapter 12.)

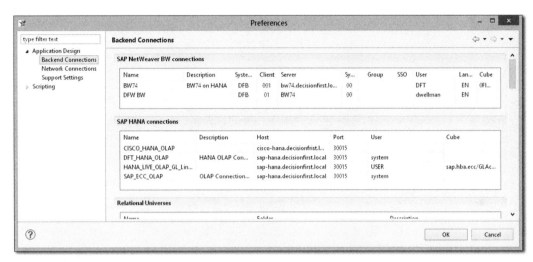

Figure 14.10 The Backend Connections Dialog Box after ODBC Is Added

14.2.3 Connecting to the SAP HANA XS Engine

A newer feature of the SAP HANA system is the XS Engine. The XS Engine is a web server that runs on the SAP HANA device that provides the ability to host applications without the need for a separate web server. Design Studio now has the ability to connect directly to the SAP HANA system through the XS Engine. This provides users the ability to connect to the same analytic and calculation views available through ODBC. The addition, however, is the ability to publish Design Studio applications to the XS Engine.

To connect directly to the SAP HANA system via the XS Engine, open Design Studio and select TOOLS • PREFERENCES, and then select APPLICATION DESIGN. In the GENERAL section on the right side, change the PREFERRED STARTUP MODE to SAP HANA. See Figure 14.11 for an example of the PREFERRED STARTUP MODE dialog. After clicking the OK button, you're prompted to restart Design Studio. You also have the option to save any changes that have been made to the active dashboard.

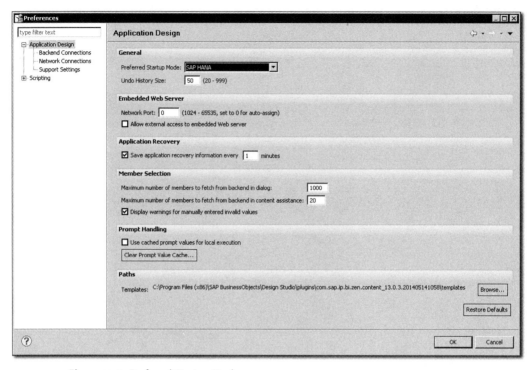

Figure 14.11 Preferred Startup Mode

When the application restarts, you are presented with a logon screen for SAP HANA, as shown in Figure 14.12. Enter a valid user ID and password for the SAP HANA system. The XS Engine URL is simply the name of the SAP HANA server where the XS Engine is installed and the port on which the XS Engine is listening for requests. In this example, the XS Engine URL is *http://sap-hana.decision-first.local:8000*.

Once the user logs on to the Design Studio application, the method of selecting an analytic or calculation view is the same as the selection from an ODBC data source. When the user creates a data source, a dialog is displayed requesting an analytic or calculation view, along with a data source name. The only difference between the selections of the data source with ODBC versus XS Engine is that the

ODBC method requires the user to select a valid ODBC connection before the selection of the view.

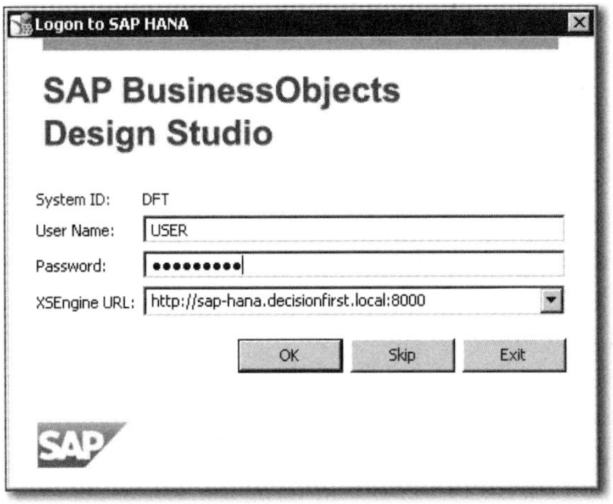

Figure 14.12 Logging On to the SAP HANA XS Engine

14.2.4 Consuming the SAP HANA Connections

After the ODBC data source has been created or the SAP BW on SAP HANA entry has been added in the SAP GUI, check the Preferences dialog in Design Studio to make sure that the data source is available. If Design Studio was open when the data source was created, simply click the Reload All Connections button on the Backend Connections dialog.

After the connection is created and visible in Design Studio, right-click Data Sources in the Outline panel, and then select New. Click Browse beside the Connection box, and select the proper SAP HANA connection. When the connection is selected, the application prompts you for credentials—user ID, password, and language—to log on to the system. Once validated, click the Browse button beside the Data Source box, and select the desired analytic view or calculation view. After the data source to SAP HANA has been added, the available connection appears as shown in Figure 14.13.

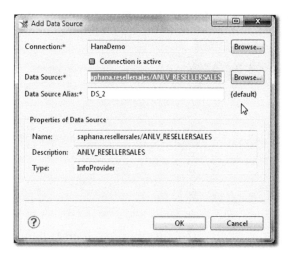

Figure 14.13 A Completed Add Data Source Dialog

14.3 Case Study: Exploring Data with SAP BusinessObjects Design Studio on Top of SAP HANA

In this case study, we'll give you a brief overview of dashboard design with SAP BusinessObjects Design Studio, including the process of connecting to SAP HANA. For more detailed information about Design Studio, we recommend the SAP PRESS book *Getting Started with SAP BusinessObjects Design Studio* (Hacking, van der A, 2014).

14.3.1 Gathering Requirements

AdventureWorks Cycle Company is in the business of building and distributing bicycles. The bicycles are created by the company and distributed via multiple regional distributorships, each managed by a regional manager. The company wants to monitor the system to determine overall sales figures and proactively respond to fluctuations in specific KPIs. The resulting dashboard will be made available to the regional managers and executives.

In our case study, a project manager, a dashboarding/visualization expert, two expert users/end users, and a database administrator are gathered in a conference room. The two experts state that the sales figures for the entire country have dipped over the past year. They want to use a dashboard to track sales revenues for the entire country, along with the regional breakdowns of the same data. They want to include month-over-month trending to determine whether there are any regions that are trending negatively (i.e., where sales are decreasing).

With a simple metric to be captured, they can then begin visualizing the data on a whiteboard, considering how the data will be used. The AdventureWorks team wants the initial view of the data to include a visual of a map of the continental United States, with a range of color codes (a choropleth map) showing the different sales figures for the various states. Regional icons can also be toggled to show the appropriate sales numbers.

14.3.2 Laying Out the Components

First, the designer must decide what tool to use to build the dashboard by considering the requirements (slicing data, graphical map, and color-coded icons) and the capabilities of the dashboarding tools available from SAP. Design Studio is an application that can project tables and a range of charts and that has the native capability of going mobile on non-Flash mobile devices. Due to the rich feature set available through Design Studio and the out of the box mobile capabilities, it is an ideal solution for this dashboard.

The designer opens the Design Studio application and begins laying out the components according to the sketches derived from the requirements phase. To begin laying out the components, follow the steps below:

1. Open Design Studio and go to TOOLS • PREFERENCES. Ensure that the preferred startup mode in the APPLICATION DESIGN tab is set to LOCAL MODE.

2. Go to APPLICATION • NEW and provide a name and an optional description. In the TARGET DEVICE field, select DESKTOP BROWSER.

3. According to the whiteboard drawing, lay out the components to provide a view of the dashboard. For this dashboard, we will add radio buttons (STATE and REGION), two crosstabs (one state and one region), a mapping component (custom built), and a pie chart.

4. Next, drag the component's borders to change the sizes according to the whiteboard.

5. Save the dashboard for presentation to the project team.

The result of this session is a dashboard that can be presented back to the original group for discussion and improvement (see Figure 14.14).

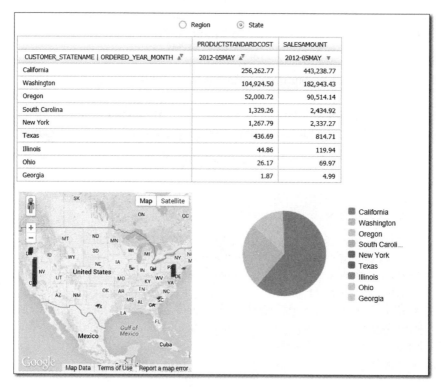

Figure 14.14 The Dashboard Result of the First Iteration

14.3.3 Connecting to SAP HANA

Now that the dashboard has been built, it's possible to add data to the components and further refine the dashboard. The SAP HANA team has made available an analytic view that contains all of the data necessary to drive the regional and state components: ANLV_INTERNETSALES in the `saphana.internetsales` package. To add data from SAP HANA to the dashboard, follow these steps:

1. Open the dashboard.

2. In the OUTLINE window, right click the DATA SOURCE folder and select ADD DATA SOURCE.

3. Click BROWSE beside CONNECTION and select the previously created ODBC data source.

4. Next, click the BROWSE button beside the DATA SOURCE text box and select the SAPHANA folder. Then select INTERNETSALES.

5. Pick the ANLV_INTERNETSALES analytic view and click OK.

6. Finally, click OK to add the data source to the listing of available data sources.

At this point, the data source has been added to the dashboard. For these requirements, we will add two data sources. Each data source will be derived from the same analytic view (ANLV_INTERNETSALES). However, one view will focus on data for states while the other will focus on data for regions. The data sources will be called ANSALESSTATE and AVSALESREGION. Since the two data sources are built on the same analytic view, the data that is available to each are identical. You need to set the INITIAL view in each data source so that you see state and region data in the appropriate data source. To set an INITIAL view, follow these steps:

1. Right click the AVSALESSTATE data source and select EDIT INITIAL VIEW.

2. In COLUMNS, ensure that PRODUCTSTANDARDCOST and SALESAMOUNT are added as measures.

3. In ROWS, ensure that CUSTOMER_STATENAME is added.

4. In BACKGROUND FILTER, add CUSTOMER_SALESTERRITORYCOUNTRY and a restriction for United States only (right click the filter name, select FILTER MEMBERS, and double click UNITED STATES).

5. Repeat these steps to set the INITIAL view for AVSALESREGION but use CUSTOMER_SALESTERRITYREGION for the rows (see step 3).

The data sources are now added and their INITIAL views set, which means they are currently available for use but are not wired to any components. (The term *wired* is a general dashboarding term; it means that a component is connected to a data source.) To wire a component to the recently added data source, follow these steps:

1. Left-click the first component on the canvas to wire up to display its properties. In this case, start with the first crosstab.

2. In the PROPERTIES window, pick the dropdown beside the DATA SOURCE property.

3. Select the AVSALESSTATE data source; the component immediately updates with the data from the INITIAL view.

4. Repeat these steps to assign the AVSALESREGION data source to the second cross tab.

5. Next, assign the AVSALESSTATE data source to the map and the pie chart. These will populate these components with state-related data. This can be

programmatically changed on the ONSELECT function of the radio button using JavaScript.

6. Finally, add three placeholders for an image and two bits of texts. The image for the top left corner is the AdventureWorks logo, the first bit of text is the title of the dashboard (top right of the dashboard), and the second bit of text contains the copyright text (bottom center of the dashboard).

The designer applies the branding and logos to the dashboard and binds all of the data to the components and spreadsheet. The final result can be seen in Figure 14.15.

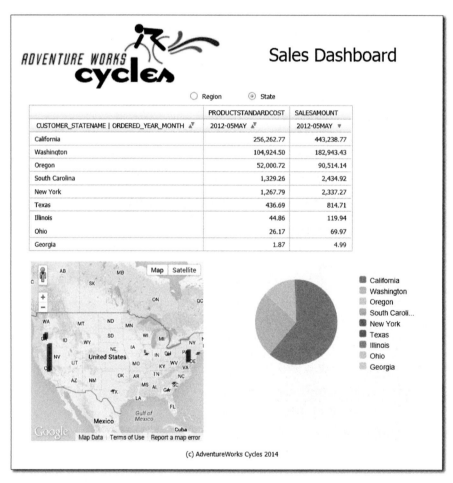

Figure 14.15 Final Dashboard

14.4   Summary

In this chapter, we introduced the concept of professionally authored dashboards (PADs) and explained how to connect the SAP BusinessObjects BI tools for PADs to SAP HANA.

In the next chapter, we turn our attention to using a self-service business intelligence solution powered by SAP HANA.

Unleash the power and flexibility of a self-service business intelligence solution powered by SAP HANA for easy access to massive data sets in real time.

15   Data Exploration and Self-Service Analytics with SAP HANA

Throughout most of the history of BI, end users and data analysts were beholden to IT or a dedicated data warehousing BI department to provide them with information. This usually resulted in users specifying report definitions to IT, followed by IT spending possibly weeks implementing these requests with a traditional reporting tool such as SAP Crystal Reports.

In later years, ad hoc query and analysis tools, such as SAP BusinessObjects Web Intelligence, came on the market. These tools allowed some sophisticated data analysts to do their own reporting and querying of the data warehouse environment. However, these tools still required a high level of end-user training to leverage them fully, and the time it took to answer relatively straightforward business questions was still too high.

Roughly parallel with the development of ad hoc query and analysis tools was the introduction of online analytical processing (OLAP) tools. These tools offered relatively good user experience for slicing and dicing data and performing analysis, but they required extensive pre-calculation of results and didn't allow for the easy addition of new data into the analysis. They, too, suffered from a fairly steep learning curve.

This situation left a hole in the BI toolbox—a hole that is filled today by a class of tools that provides users the ability to easily explore and filter data; perform analysis and visualization on that data; and rapidly expand and integrate additional data into the analysis when necessary, without the need to go back to IT for additional resources.

Within the SAP BusinessObjects BI portfolio, this need is satisfied by two tools: SAP BusinessObjects Explorer, a tool aimed at the general business consumer, and SAP Lumira, a tool that can be used by everyday business users as well as dedicated data analysts or power users. This chapter will discuss how to leverage these tools in conjunction with an SAP HANA appliance, including how this scenario provides significant benefits over the use of these tools in a standalone configuration. The chapter will conclude with a case study that shows a brief example of SAP Lumira in action. For a full discussion of what SAP Lumira is and what it can do, we recommend the SAP PRESS book *Getting Started with SAP Lumira* (Ah-Soon, Snowdon, 2015).

15.1 SAP HANA as a Data Source for SAP BusinessObjects Explorer

Explorer was first introduced to the Business Objects product suite near the end of the XI R2 product line. Business Objects acquired the tool before SAP, in turn, acquired Business Objects, and the tool was originally referred to as Polestar. You may still see some documentation and files reference the Polestar name. Initially, the tool was designed as its own standalone BI tool, but Business Objects later integrated it into the broader Business Objects platform and added support to the tool for accessing Business Objects universes. In the most recent editions of the tool, support has been added for direct access to SAP HANA and SAP BW Accelerator (BWA) systems. The addition of support for SAP HANA vastly increased the amount of data that the product can access and the speed with which that information can be delivered to end users.

Explorer uses a number of terms and concepts that aren't seen in other BI tools:

▸ **Information Space**
As one of the two main content types produced with Explorer, an Information Space represents a set of data consisting of measures and dimensions. End users "explore" an Information Space using Explorer. You can think of an Information Space as simply the results of a large query presented to the user in an accessible manner.

▸ **Exploration view set**
The second of the two main content types produced using Explorer consists of a set of visualizations that are based on one or more Information Spaces. The visualizations are organized into individual pages called *views*.

- **Facet**

  This is a synonym for a dimension in other BI tools. The reason for the unusual name is historical and comes from one of the underlying technologies that Explorer is based on: Apache Lucene.

- **Index**

  This refers to the collection of the index files generated by Explorer for each Information Space. The index stores metadata describing the structure and content of the Information Space, such as the list of facets and their values. For the non–SAP HANA scenario, the index also stores a cached version of the data set for the Information Space. Indexing is the process by which an index is generated, and it is performed by the index server.

With these basics out of the way, we'll discuss the indexing and user exploration processes in more detail and see how those processes differ between standalone Explorer and Explorer with SAP HANA. We'll also look at the necessary system configurations that must be made to establish a connection between Explorer and SAP HANA, the Information Space creation process when using SAP HANA, and finally, some of the benefits of the SAP HANA scenario for end-user experience.

15.1.1 Exploring and Indexing

Recall that, whenever users interact with the Explorer application, they are consuming data from an Information Space. The metadata describing that Information Space—and in the case of a non–SAP HANA scenario, the data itself—is stored in an Explorer index that was generated by the indexing server. Note that the distinction between metadata describing the Information Space and the data itself is important. It's what separates the Explorer on SAP HANA scenario from the standalone Explorer scenario.

When you consume an Information Space built on an SAP HANA data source, the Exploration Service prepares and executes calls to the SAP HANA appliance to provide all of the necessary data instead of consuming local data from the index. When you're exploring an Information Space created from a traditional database, the database can't typically respond fast enough to support the style of interaction necessary for the Explorer UI. Therefore, the index server must cache all of the data ahead of time and store it locally on the Explorer server. This is in contrast to the SAP HANA–supported scenario in which the index server merely stores the description of the Information Space (i.e., a list of facets and measures). Using SAP HANA as the live data source for the Exploration Service significantly reduces the load on the SAP BusinessObjects BI server hosting the Exploration Services and allows for the consumption of Information Spaces that are orders of magnitude larger than what is physically possible without SAP HANA. This method also supports near-instant feedback to the user, providing a superior user experience. Figure 15.1 walks you through the process of retrieving data from an Information Space backed by an SAP HANA data source.

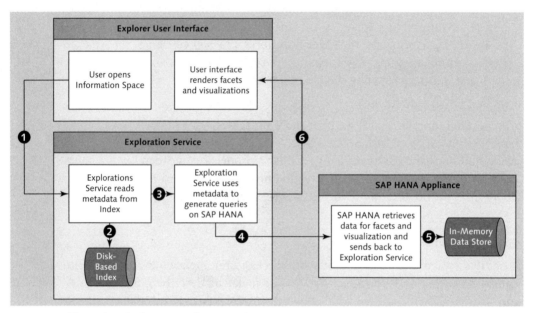

Figure 15.1 Exploring an Information Space on SAP HANA

Another significant benefit of the Explorer on SAP HANA scenario is that the data presented to the user is always as current as the data in the SAP HANA appliance. If you're using a real-time or near–real-time data load strategy, then users have access to the most current records. Because the non–SAP HANA scenario requires an extra indexing step and local storage of data in the index server, the user receives data that is only as fresh as the most recent indexing. Although this can be kept fresh with regular re-indexing, it adds an extra layer and complicates the data management process.

If you look at the server hosting the Index Service, you can actually locate the constituent files that make up an index. On a typical Windows installation of Explorer, the indexes are stored in the following path:

<SAP_BUSINESS_OBJECTS_ROOT>\SAP BusinessObjects Enterprise XI 4.0\Data\ Polestar\index\<SIANODE_NAME>.ExplorerIndexingServer\Published\Exploration Indexes

Inside this folder, you'll find one or more cryptically named folders. Each folder stores one index. The cryptic name is the internal ID of the index. At the next layer down, you'll find a date- and time-stamped folder representing a specific version of the index. Finally, inside that folder, you'll find the actual index files. Figure 15.2 shows an index based on a non–SAP HANA source.

Figure 15.2 Explorer Index on a Non-SAP HANA Data Source

Notice that this index contains folders to store values for the fact and facet values. As shown in Figure 15.3, these elements are missing from an SAP HANA–based index.

If you look at the space required to store an SAP HANA Explorer index, you'll see that it's a very small amount of data, no more than a few kilobytes. On the other hand, an index on a non–SAP HANA data source can easily run into the hundreds of megabytes. When you consider that the Exploration Service must load and process the index into memory, it's evident how much faster it is for the system to process the SAP HANA index.

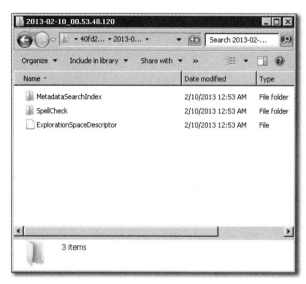

Figure 15.3 Explorer Index on an SAP HANA Data Source

This physical storage of the index on disk and the loading and unloading of the data from memory on the Exploration Service are two of the main limiting factors of the standalone Explorer solution. As a general rule of thumb, an Information Space of average complexity (10–20 facets) should have no more than one to two million rows of data. That may sound like a lot, but in the age of big data, when information accumulates by terabytes and petabytes, it's easy to devise scenarios that exceed this limit, even for medium-sized businesses.

Meanwhile, the SAP HANA Information Space can easily process a billion rows of data—and do it with better overall performance to the end user. It's important not to underestimate the value of end-user performance in scenarios like this. Even if the data presented to users is of high value, if they have to wait very long to access it or if they feel the UI is unresponsive, that data will likely go unused.

15.1.2 Connecting SAP BusinessObjects Explorer to SAP HANA

To take advantage of the Explorer on SAP HANA scenario, you must make some initial configurations to the SAP BusinessObjects BI platform to allow the Exploration Services to connect with the SAP HANA appliance. In the non–SAP HANA scenario, the Information Spaces are generated either from static Excel documents or against queries generated from an SAP BusinessObjects BI universe. In the SAP HANA scenario, the Information Spaces are designed based on either analytic views or calculation views in the SAP HANA appliance. To access these data elements, the Explorer system must know how to communicate with the SAP HANA appliance.

There are two methods for defining the connection information: one uses the advanced configuration properties for Explorer in the Central Management Console (CMC), and the other uses connection objects defined using the Information Design Tool (IDT). Of the two methods, the latter is preferred; the former is primarily a legacy option, so we'll detail only the solution using IDT.

To define the connection information, follow these steps:

1. Open IDT by choosing START • ALL PROGRAMS • SAP BUSINESSOBJECTS BI PLATFORM 4 • SAP BUSINESSOBJECTS BI PLATFORM CLIENT TOOLS • INFORMATION DESIGN TOOL.

2. Open the REPOSITORY RESOURCES window by choosing WINDOW • REPOSITORY RESOURCES.

3. Connect to the SAP BusinessObjects BI platform by opening a session. You'll need to authenticate to the platform as a user that has the rights to create connections.

4. Select and then right-click the folder you plan to store the SAP HANA connection in. Choose INSERT RELATIONAL CONNECTION.

5. At this point, the NEW RELATIONAL CONNECTION wizard appears. Walk through the wizard, giving your connection a name and description and providing the necessary connection values, as listed in Table 15.1. Figure 15.4 shows an example of the connection configuration process.

Field	Description
DATABASE MIDDLEWARE DRIVER SELECTION	Select either JDBC (choose SAP • SAP HANA DATABASE 1.0 • JDBC DRIVERS) or ODBC (SAP • SAP HANA DATABASE 1.0 • ODBC DRIVERS).
AUTHENTICATION MODE	▸ Use specified user name and password. ▸ Provide values for a hard-coded system account that will be used for all communication with the database. ▸ Use SAP BusinessObjects Credential Mapping. ▸ Use credentials mapped to individual SAP BusinessObjects BI user accounts to connect to the SAP HANA appliance. ▸ Use single sign-on (SSO) when refreshing reports at view time. ▸ Use SSO to the database to pass through credentials.

Table 15.1 New Relational Connection Values

Field	Description
USER NAME	The name of the database user account, if using a specified user name and password.
PASSWORD	The password of the database user account, if using a specified user name and password.
SERVER (HOST:PORT)	The server host name and port number that the SAP HANA appliance is listening on. The port number can be found using SAP HANA Studio.

Table 15.1 New Relational Connection Values (Cont.)

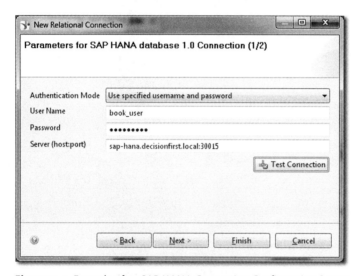

Figure 15.4 Example of an SAP HANA Connection Configuration Screen

15.1.3 Creating an Information Space on SAP HANA

After you've established a connection to SAP HANA, you can begin construction of your Information Spaces. As mentioned, the content types within SAP HANA that you can access using Explorer are analytic and calculation views. These appear in the Explorer interface inside their respective packages. This is the same structure in which you organize the content within SAP HANA Studio.

Information Spaces are created using the MANAGE SPACES view in the Explorer UI. In the SOURCES area, you'll find the SAP HANA appliance node, as shown in Figure 15.5. If this is expanded, you should see the connection name that you defined with the IDT. Finally, inside that node, you should find the list of views you can access. Unfortunately, all views are displayed at the same level in the tree, with their full paths, including package and view names, concatenated together. We can only hope that future versions of Explorer will improve on this small UI element to make navigation easier.

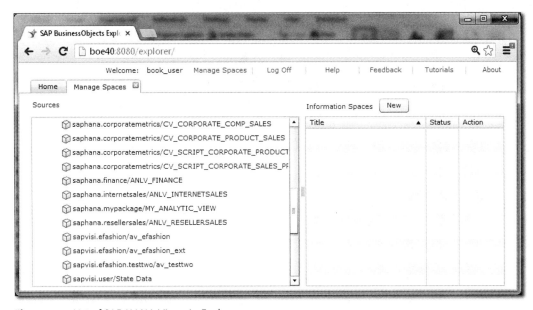

Figure 15.5 List of SAP HANA Views in Explorer

To create the new Information Space you need, select the appropriate source view, and then click the NEW button at the top of the screen. This takes you to the Information Space Creation Wizard. As you proceed through the wizard, you'll give your Information Space a name and description and select a location to store the Information Space in the SAP BusinessObjects BI repository. The location in which the space is stored affects which users have access to view the Information Space.

The majority of the work to create an Information Space is carried out on the OBJECTS tab. Here, you'll select which dimensions and measures from the SAP HANA view you want to make available to end users. Facets are organized on this screen by the attribute view or hierarchy they were created from, while measures are simply listed at the root of the object tree.

The last steps for creating your Information Space are to validate the definition on the OBJECT tab and click the OK button to save the Information Space, with the final step being to index the Information Space one time so that the metadata describing the Information Space can be stored. The other two tabs in the Information Space creation screen, Scheduling and Personalization, aren't really pertinent to an Information Space created on SAP HANA. Scheduling is unnecessary because the Information Space needs to be indexed only once, and Personalization is unnecessary because row-level security of data can be handled by the SAP HANA appliance using analytic privileges.

> **Additional Resources**
>
> We've definitely not covered every nuance and best practice in Information Space design, nor have we covered exploration views. Many of these elements are general to all Explorer scenarios, and not just Explorer on SAP HANA. For more information on designing content with Explorer, see the *SAP BusinessObjects Explorer User Guide* at *http://help.sap.com/businessobject/product_guides/boexir4/en/xi4_exp_user_en.pdf*.

15.2   SAP HANA as a Data Source for SAP Lumira

SAP Lumira is a desktop-based application that provides powerful analytic and predictive capabilities. SAP Lumira connects to a variety of data sources, including CSV files, Freehand SQL across different databases, Excel spreadsheets, both types of universes (UNV and UNX), and SAP HANA. Each of the connectivity methods has its own advantages and disadvantages. Although you can use any of the connectivity methods for analysis and visualization, our discussion is primarily concerned with connectivity to SAP HANA.

SAP Lumira provides capabilities that have, in the past, been associated with Explorer. Explorer is a web-based application that provides quick and easy access to data. SAP Lumira takes similar functionality in a familiar interface and provides a desktop application within which you perform analysis and visualizations. It represents the data that is stored in a data source. Like all of the other visualization and analysis tools, SAP Lumira doesn't require changes to the underlying data. The data stored in the data source is simply queried and represented within the interface. Manipulation tools are presented within SAP Lumira to provide for the modification of the data, but the changes live only within the SAP Lumira session and aren't written back to the data source.

SAP Lumira also provides a series of more advanced computational and visualization tools for use on the various data sources. When a new visualization is created on a data source, all of the fields within the system are linked into the visualization as measures, hierarchies, and attributes. The measures and hierarchies that are displayed are derived from the information views created in SAP HANA Studio (see Part III of the book). Creating the measures and hierarchies in SAP HANA Studio provides a unified view of the data with a single version of the truth, as opposed to providing a more loosely defined view that can be manipulated by the author of the visualization.

After the objects are imported from the data source, you have advanced tools available for use. First of all, the aggregation of measures can be modified. The default is SUM, but, you can select MIN, MAX, AVERAGE, COUNT, and COUNT DISTINCT. You can also create measure objects that take advantage of running SUM, running COUNT, and running AVERAGE. Dimensions that contain a geographical component such as county, state, and city can be mapped into a geographic hierarchy like the one shown in Figure 15.6. The creation of a geographic hierarchy enables you to analyze data in the form of a map that is either built in to SAP Lumira or hosted on the ESRI ArcGIS online web service (this applies only to SAP Lumira 1.18 and above). In addition, if you've created a measure based on a numeric field and also created a time-based hierarchy, a visualization showing the projected values for a time in the future can also be displayed, as shown in Figure 15.7. For instance, if you have five years' worth of sales revenue on a monthly basis, you can use forecast or linear regression to calculate the next six months' worth of sales revenues. These powerful tools provide a wide range of analytic, visualization, and predictive functions for you to take advantage of while working with the data directly within an application on your desktop.

Visualizations inside of SAP Lumira have received some massive upgrades since around versions 1.17 and 1.18. SAP completely reworked the COMPOSE room so that the visualizations that are created become more than just a series of charts and tables arranged in a grid. You are now able to create slide shows, immersive infographics, and reports inside of the COMPOSE room. Using these new visualization capabilities within an end user tool such as SAP Lumira puts a lot of power back in the hands of the business community.

In future releases, SAP has announced that visualizations created by end users in SAP Lumira will be able to form the foundation of a full SAP BusinessObjects Design Studio dashboard. This will potentially change the way that both ad hoc dashboards and professionally authored dashboards are designed and used within the context of a full business intelligence system.

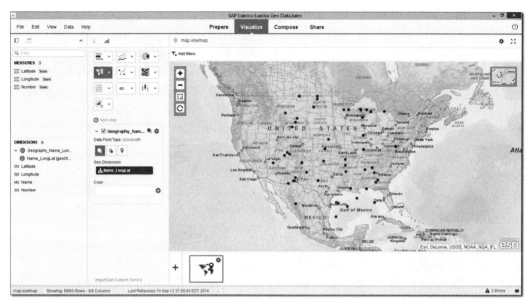

Figure 15.6 A Geographic Visualization of Tabular Data on an ESRI Base Map

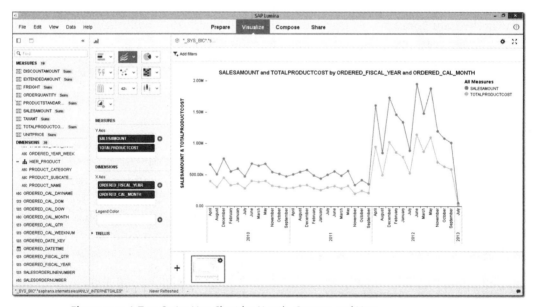

Figure 15.7 A Two-Series Line Chart by Month, Quarter, and Year

SAP Lumira provides the ability to connect to SAP HANA in two different ways: connecting to SAP HANA (online) and downloading from SAP HANA (offline). Let's take a look at each of the methods, as shown in Figure 15.8.

Figure 15.8 Options for Connecting to Various Data Sources

15.2.1 Online Connectivity

The most popular method of connectivity is connecting to data online. Connecting to online data sources enables you to take advantage of the speed and capacity of the SAP HANA system. You can connect to SAP HANA online to analyze thousands to millions of records of data in seconds.

The only disadvantage to the online connectivity method is that you must be online and have the ability to connect to the SAP HANA server. Connecting to SAP HANA online provides access to calculation views and analytic views that were created in SAP HANA Studio.

To connect to SAP HANA online, follow these steps:

1. Start by opening SAP Lumira.

2. Click NEW DOCUMENT, and then select SAP HANA ONLINE.

3. Enter the credentials that correspond to the SAP HANA installation to which you're connecting (See Figure 15.9).

4. Click CONNECT HANA INSTANCE. A listing of analytic and calculation views appears.

5. Select a desired view, and click CREATE.

Figure 15.9 Connecting to SAP HANA Online

The data is read into the SAP Lumira interface, and you're immediately forwarded to a visualization interface that allows for visualization of the data source.

15.2.2 Offline Connectivity

Alternatively, you can connect to SAP HANA data sources as an offline data source. At design time, you are connected to the SAP HANA system and can take advantage of the speed and resources of such a server. However, when the visualization is saved, the data is saved in a local instance of SAP (Sybase) IQ. The index of the data is stored along with the definition of the visualization.

On launching an instance of SAP Lumira, you are presented with eight options for connecting to data:

- Excel
- Text
- Copy from clipboard
- Connect to SAP HANA
- Download from SAP HANA
- Universe
- Query with SQL
- Connect to SAP BW

To connect to SAP HANA, follows these steps:

1. Select DOWNLOAD FROM SAP HANA from the list of available connections (see Figure 15.10).

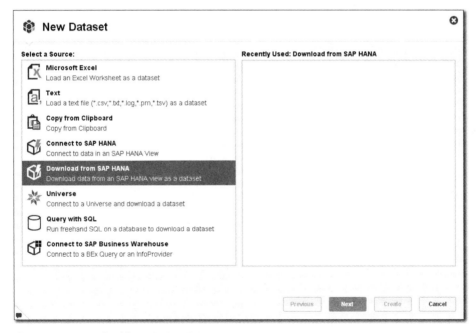

Figure 15.10 Download from SAP HANA

2. Provide the SAP HANA server name, instance number, user name, and password, and click CONNECT (see Figure 15.11).

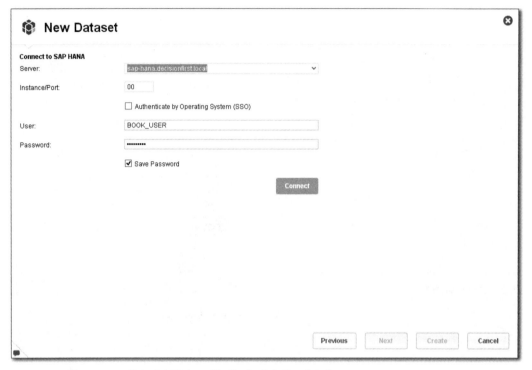

Figure 15.11 Data Set Dialog with Credentials Populated

3. Select the desired data source from SAP HANA from the left side of the dialog (see Figure 15.12).

4. Click the CREATE button. A dialog displays, showing the number of records downloading and the current download status and estimated wait time (see Figure 15.13).

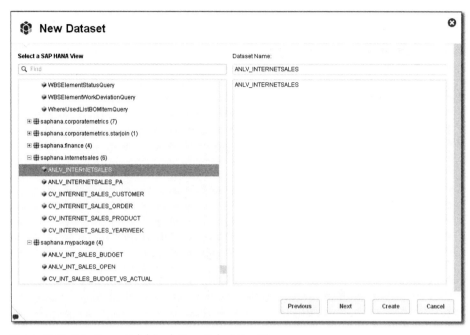

Figure 15.12 Selecting a Valid Analytic or Calculation View

Figure 15.13 The Data Download Status

5. Behind the scenes, an instance of the SAP (Sybase) IQ Network Server is launched on your machine. This service (*iqsrv15.exe*) is a local instance of the SAP (Sybase) IQ database server that will be used to store the offline data retrieved from SAP HANA.

6. After the *iqsrv15.exe* instance is launched, SAP Lumira scans the SAP HANA data source for the overall size of the data. If the cells in the SAP HANA source number more than 30 million, a warning is displayed with that information. You can then continue or cancel the request.

7. If you continue, the full record set is then downloaded from the SAP HANA data source into the local instance of SAP (Sybase) IQ, and the visualization in SAP Lumira can begin.

The SAP HANA offline connectivity method is typically used when the data sets are relatively small. The speed at which the data is downloaded can vary with the overall bandwidth between the SAP HANA system and the local machine that is downloading the data. In our benchmark tests, it took approximately 10 minutes to download 10 million rows of data from SAP HANA.

This results in a potentially huge LUMS file. This also eliminates the advantage that SAP HANA brings to big data analysis. When the visualization is saved locally, the resulting LUMS file is essentially a renamed ZIP file. If you rename this file as *.zip*, the file can be opened, and the data component can be extracted. If this extracted data file is given the *.csv* extension, it can be opened in any application that supports a CSV.

SAP HANA is synonymous with big data—a CSV file isn't. An SAP Lumira file that is stored using the SAP HANA offline connectivity method eliminates the speed, and the result is a visualization that performs poorly. The advantage to an offline dashboard is the ability to analyze the data while disconnected from the SAP HANA data server. If the visualization is filtered to the point that just a few hundred thousand records of data (or fewer) are imported, then an offline method is acceptable. If there are any more records than this, then the SAP HANA online method should be used, and the dashboard won't have the capability of being disconnected.

SAP (Sybase) IQ

Let's take moment to zoom in on SAP (Sybase) IQ. SAP (Sybase) IQ is a columnar data-store that has the capability to handle large amounts of data in a compact database management system. It is installed alongside SAP Lumira to facilitate SAP HANA's offline data visualization capabilities. The SAP (Sybase) IQ system uses a database called *Hilo.db*. Hilo is the developmental code name for the SAP Visualization Project. The databases are stored on the directory *C:\Users\<username>\AppData\Local\SAP\Lumira\ DataBase* and can be deleted at any time to free up drive space or clear out issues with any inconsistencies in the databases. The database will be reinitialized when the SAP Lumira application is loaded.

It's important to remember that the data sets aren't actually stored within the Hilo database. The data sets are persisted within the LUMS files and are loaded into the SAP (Sybase) IQ in-memory database on the fly when the LUMS file is loaded into SAP Lumira.

Keeping a visualization stored locally opens a wide range of offline capabilities to data visualization when connections back to the server aren't possible. You can open a new visualization disconnected from scratch. The data is streamed from the LUMS file and loaded into the SAP (Sybase) IQ in-memory database, and the visualization opens in SAP Lumira. If you then decide to open a new visualization, the data is retained in the in-memory SAP (Sybase) IQ database for faster retrieval, in case you decide to reopen the SAP HANA offline file.

15.3   Case Study: Exploring Sales Data with SAP Lumira on Top of SAP HANA

The sales management team at AdventureWorks Cycle Company has been tapped as the pilot business unit to leverage the new BI platform based on SAP HANA. As part of the pilot project, the BI team has modeled and loaded the company's sales data into the SAP HANA appliance and provided access to the SAP BusinessObjects BI platform tools. In previous chapters, we've covered the initial phases of the project where data was loaded and modeled in SAP HANA. Now, we'll examine the specific business analytic options using SAP Lumira.

As in the previous chapter, the focus of this case study is the business intelligence solution running on top of SAP HANA—in this case, SAP Lumira—as opposed to SAP HANA itself. We will therefore keep the discussion short; our goal is just to show you an example of what you can do if you do decide to implement SAP Lumira on top of SAP HANA.

15.3.1 Business Requirements

AdventureWorks Cycle Company operates two sales distribution channels: a direct-to-customer sales channel via the company's website, and a traditional retail reseller channel. Resellers are all independent retail operations spread throughout North America, Europe, and the Pacific. Resellers are organized into sales territories, with a reseller representative assigned to manage the relationship of each reseller with AdventureWorks. Most resellers have relationships with multiple brand manufacturers, so the reseller representative relationship is important to driving product sales.

As part of the pilot program, the North American reseller sales team wants to construct a better sales tracking and performance management solution. To date, the team gets only periodic updates on total sales metrics at the close of each month. Their ability to react to shifts in the market or downward trends is limited by the delay in data access. They want access to daily updates of sales trends and the ability to make comparisons to prior periods.

Finally, the sales team is sensitive to the sharing of data across different sales territories and reseller representatives. Therefore, they want to leverage the security features of the platform to ensure that each user sees only data appropriate to his role.

15.3.2 Planned Solution

To satisfy the pilot program's requirements, the BI team plans to leverage SAP Lumira to do the deeper analysis of data, look for trends and patterns, and help identify areas of interest for the end users to focus on. The BI team will work with a business analyst from the sales team to conduct a number of working sessions in which they will explore the data together. In these sessions, the business analyst will get an opportunity to become familiar with the SAP Lumira tool, hopefully leading to a point when the analyst can transition to a self-service model.

It's Monday afternoon, and AdventureWorks employee Bob is about to leave for the day. He knows that there is some analysis work that is required for tomorrow's 10 a.m. meeting, but he must leave for a dinner party with his friends this evening. (We all wish we were Bob, right?) He opens SAP Lumira and creates an offline connection to the SAP HANA system.

Bob enters credentials to connect to the SAP HANA system. After he connects, he selects the analytic view that the administrators have made available to him. By clicking the CREATE button, he sees that all of the latest data is included in the data set. Because the data is displayed in descending order, he can see from the highlighted record that the order data dates are loaded as of June 2012.

Now that Bob has been able to connect to the data and import it into SAP Lumira using an offline connection, he can save the visualization to a local file and disconnect to leave the office for the day. Because the data is saving to a local database in SAP (Sybase) IQ, the visualization takes a little time for the save to complete.

After the data loads within the application, Bob is able to start his analysis of the data from the train on his commute home. First, he begins by analyzing the total sales and order quantities by region for all years. It's very easy to see in Figure 15.14 that the Southwest region has had the highest sales of all regions. This could be attributed to multiple factors, such as a milder winter season, which allows people to engage in outside activities for more days out of the year.

Bob already knows that bikes constitute a large portion of corporate sales. However, comparing the total sales amount to the total number of orders reveals several interesting facts. First of all, when looking at the chart in Figure 15.14, Bob sees that the total sales amount per quantity ordered is actually higher for only one region: the Northwest. All other regions are showing nearly equivalent or lower sales per order. It appears that the Northwest region spends more per order than anywhere else in the country, which means that Bob can tell the regional sales manager about this fact to potentially run marketing ads to increase the total sales on bigger-ticket items. If he looks at the overall sales and order quantities, he can clearly see which items constitute a higher sales price per order. Bob stores both of the visualizations that he has generated for future use.

Figure 15.14 A View of All Sales and Orders by Region in the United States

Next, Bob throws in a time-related hierarchy so that he can analyze the data over a range of periods. Because he can see that the BIKES category is providing the bulk of the sales revenue, he'll focus on that category (see Figure 15.15).

By projecting the sales amount and order quantity on two different vertical axes and then changing the horizontal axis to the date hierarchy and selecting YEAR-QUARTER, Bob can see a trend in total sales amounts from one quarter to the next as he moves through the years (see Figure 15.16). He begins seeing trends in the data as the weather warms in the United States. Bob can also see that the sales and order quantities fluctuate depending on the time of year. However, he can't adequately see an overall trend, whether positive or negative. In this case, Bob can add a running average to show the quarter-to-quarter average that displays a more precise overall trend. The overall trend is shown to be moving slightly positive over the four-year study period, from $2.3 million in 2009 to $3.7 million in 2012.

Figure 15.15 Sales and Orders by Category

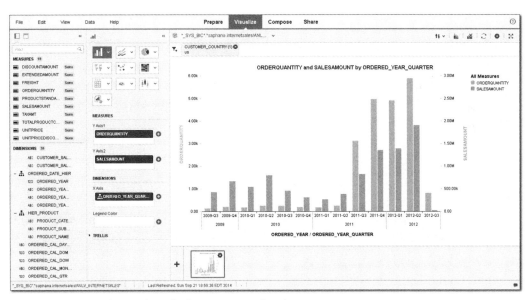

Figure 15.16 Quarterly Trending of Sales Amounts and Order Quantities

Bob returns to the office the next day a little groggy from the late-night dinner party but ready to share what he has found. He opens the saved visualization from the day before. While he does have the ability to refresh the data against the data source, he wants to share what he has found with this data intact. Inside SAP Lumira, he switches to the SHARE mode at the top of the application. Selecting the visualizations that we've seen in this case study, he can email them to his colleagues. Finally, he can take the data set as he worked with it and publish it back to SAP HANA for further analysis.

To publish a data set back to SAP HANA, Bob goes to the SHARE room and selects the downloaded data set from the DATASETS column. This activates a listing of options in the toolbar across the top (Figure 15.17). He selects PUBLISH TO SAP HANA and enters his credentials into the login window (Figure 15.18). Bob then selects the package where he would like to publish the data set, clicks the NEW VIEW button and enters a view name. He then clicks PUBLISH (Figure 15.19). SAP Lumira then takes the data set from the local SAP (Sybase) IQ instance, creates the table in SAP HANA, and publishes the data set. Anyone with the correct security can then access Bob's analyzed view and continue working with it.

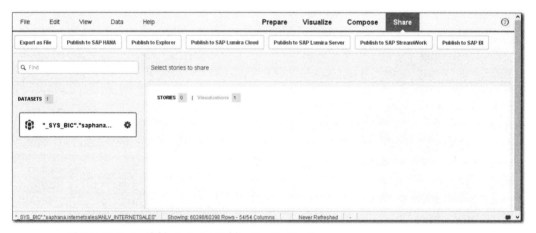

Figure 15.17 Available Data Set Publication Destinations

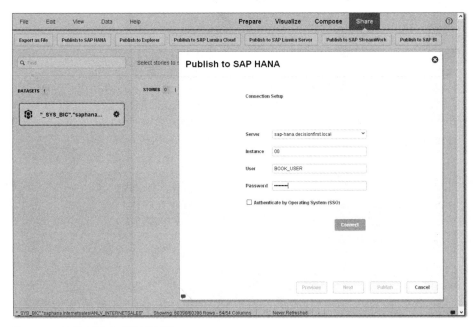

Figure 15.18 Publish to SAP HANA

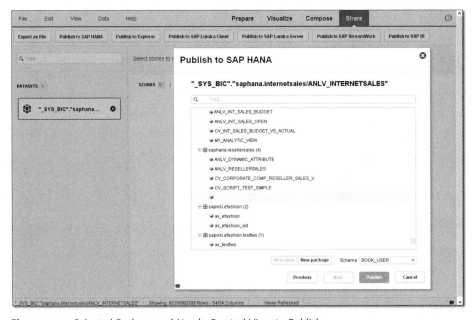

Figure 15.19 Selected Package and Newly Created View to Publish

15.4   Summary

As you've seen throughout this chapter, the combination of SAP BusinessObjects Explorer, SAP Lumira, and SAP HANA provides a powerful toolkit to deliver information to a variety of user populations. The speed and power of the SAP HANA device delivers one of the key features of the solution. In this mobile era, users expect a solution that provides responsiveness in seconds. Combined with the user-friendly interface of SAP BusinessObjects Explorer and SAP Lumira, you can deliver a compelling user experience.

In the next chapter, we'll introduce SAP BusinessObjects Web Intelligence. We'll discuss methods of connecting to SAP HANA and reveal several optimization methods that can be implemented on the report and universe to enhance the performance of reports.

Ad hoc reporting with SAP BusinessObjects Web Intelligence puts the power of SAP HANA into the hands of the users who need it most.

16 SAP BusinessObjects Web Intelligence with SAP HANA

The concept of reporting has inherent advantages and disadvantages. Reporting technologies provide access to data, allowing a wide range of viewers to make informed decisions from thoughtful and timely access to that data. Reporting allows users to build their own analytics and visualizations for quick access, in addition to the ability to request highly formatted reports that project a more professional image.

In this chapter, we'll explain how to connect SAP BusinessObjects Web Intelligence to SAP HANA (Section 16.1) and then focus on the features that can be applied on the universe level and within SAP HANA to optimize queries and performance in Web Intelligence on top of SAP HANA (Section 16.2). We'll conclude the chapter with a use case outlining each of the elements that were covered within the chapter (Section 16.3). For a full discussion of what Web Intelligence is and what it can do, we recommend the SAP PRESS book *SAP BusinessObjects Web Intelligence: The Comprehensive Guide* (Brogden et al., 2014).

16.1 Connecting SAP BusinessObjects Web Intelligence to SAP HANA

With the on-the-fly nature of data within Web Intelligence, you can see the obvious advantage of having real-time data available when and where you need it. But there are things to consider when you build reports in Web Intelligence against such large (and fast!) data sources.

First of all, you need to connect Web Intelligence to SAP HANA. In other chapters, we've discussed ways to connect to SAP HANA. In Web Intelligence, you connect to SAP HANA via a universe by installing the client middleware. Recall from Chapter 12 that, after the client middleware is installed, you can create either an Open Database Connectivity (ODBC) or Java Database Connectivity (JDBC) connection to the SAP HANA system. The administrator of the SAP HANA system should provide you with a server name, port number, user name, and password with which you can log on to the system, as shown in Figure 16.1.

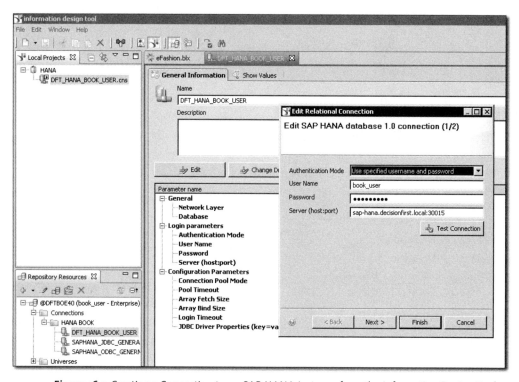

Figure 16.1 Creating a Connection to an SAP HANA Instance from the Information Design Tool

After the ODBC/JDBC source has been created, you create the connection to the SAP HANA system using the Information Design Tool (IDT). We discussed these steps in Chapter 12. Next, you determine whether you'll allow your users to connect to the raw tables in the user's schema or whether views will be implemented. The two types of views are analytic views and calculation views, which are available in the _SYS_BIC schema. After the raw tables and/or views are discovered, simply lay them out in a data foundation and create the associated objects in the business layer. Ensure that the objects from the SAP HANA system have appropriate names. For instance, we previously used the topic of sales revenue. If the sales revenue measure is kept in a raw data table called HANA_SALES_DATA in a field called SLS_REV, simply drag the SLS_REV field to the appropriate class in the business layer and provide a name that is descriptive of what is contained within the field (i.e., sales revenue). Finally, you systematically move from object to object and qualify each as a dimension, detail, or measure, as defined here (for more details, refer back to Section 12.2 in Chapter 12):

▶ **Dimensions**
Fields that contain data represented as text (e.g., street names, customer names, and product categories).

▶ **Details**
Fields that provide more information about a dimension. A detail is typically attached to a dimension (e.g., street number or telephone area code).

▶ **Measures**
Fields that can be aggregated (e.g., sales revenue, taxes paid, and quantity).

Now that you've created the connection to the SAP HANA system and have generated a universe in the IDT, the universe should be published to an SAP BusinessObjects BI repository. The act of publishing a universe makes the objects available to the various tools within the suite, of which Web Intelligence is one.

The Web Intelligence application, as mentioned earlier, has two forms: Rich Internet and Rich Client. To access the universe based on SAP HANA in Web Intelligence online, simply log on to the platform via a compatible browser, such as Internet Explorer 9. The standard URL follows this format: *http://<SAP BusinessObjects Host>:8080/BOE/BI*.

Note
Consult the Product Availability Matrix for further information on compatible browsers, operating systems, databases, etc.: *http://service.sap.com/pam*.

After opening the Web Intelligence application, click the NEW REPORT button. A listing of available data providers is presented. The web client can be built without a data source (that is, it can be used as a template) or connect to a universe. The Rich Internet Application can use no data source, universe, BEx queries, or analysis views. The desktop-based Rich Client can take advantage of the same data providers as the Rich Internet Application, plus personal data providers such as CSVs or Excel spreadsheets.

At this point, click UNIVERSE, and navigate through the listing of universes built in both the Universe Designer and the IDT. Web Intelligence reports can be built from this point against SAP HANA tables and views, as with any other data source available through a universe.

It may come as a surprise that, from a Web Intelligence perspective, there are no special skills needed to build reports against data loaded into SAP HANA. However, there are many known features of Web Intelligence that you can take advantage of to optimize the performance of Web Intelligence with larger data volumes. Let's turn our attention to these next.

16.2   Report Optimization Features with SAP HANA

In this section, we'll talk about several features of the universe and Web Intelligence on top of SAP HANA that can be used to optimize performance within Web Intelligence reports. Let's take a closer look at each of these features.

16.2.1   Usage of JOIN_BY_SQL

On the universe level, a feature is available that has existed since the very early versions of pre-SAP Business Objects. Recall that running multiple queries is expensive on the reporting engine side, so it's recommended that the designer move as much processing to the database server as possible. For this reason, we don't recommend using merged dimensions on an SAP HANA data source.

So when using two or more queries returning large sets of data, one feature to consider is the JOIN_BY_SQL parameter in the Universe Designer and IDT, which is shown in Figure 16.2.

The JOIN_BY_SQL function is a parameter that instructs the middleware to execute a report using multiple queries on the database level rather than in the report engine. By setting this parameter, the universe designer is making the decision that all queries generated by the reporting application are to be pushed down on the database level. This is advantageous in cases where you have large data volumes—such as when you use SAP HANA.

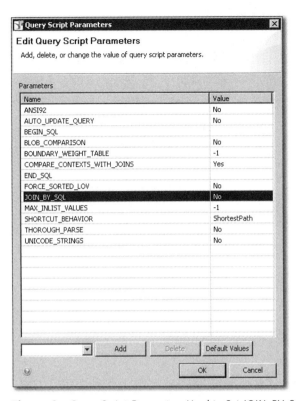

Figure 16.2 Query Script Parameters Used to Set JOIN_BY_SQL

For instance, look at the queries in Listing 16.1 and Listing 16.2.

```
SELECT
    Table__7."PRODUCT_NAME",
    sum(Table__7."SALESAMOUNT")
FROM
    "_SYS_BIC"."saphana.internetsales/ANLV_INTERNETSALES/olap"  Table__7
GROUP BY
    Table__7."PRODUCT_NAME"
```

Listing 16.1 SQL Statement Returning Sales Amounts for Internet Sales

```
SELECT
    Table__7."PRODUCT_NAME",
    sum(Table__8."SALESAMOUNT")
```

```
FROM
  "_SYS_BIC"."saphana.internetsales/ANLV_INTERNETSALES/olap"  Table__7,
  "FACT_RESELLER_SALES"  Table__8
GROUP BY
  Table__7."PRODUCT_NAME"
```

Listing 16.2 SQL Statement Returning Sales Amounts for Reseller Sales

Using merged dimensions, these two queries would be executed independently on the database server, and the results sent back to the reporting engine to be merged into a single result set. This approach introduces latency delays because of the slower speeds of the reporting engine. We do, however, take advantage of the speeds of in-memory database processing because of the speed at which the result sets of the two queries are returned. The bottleneck in this case is the merging step required on the reporting engine level.

Now let's have a look at the same query when using the JOIN_BY_SQL statement, as shown in Listing 16.3.

```
SELECT
    COALESCE(F__1.Axis__1,F__2.Axis_1),
    F__1.M__1,
    F__2.M__1
FROM
    (
SELECT
  Table__3."ENGLISHPRODUCTNAME" AS Axis__1,
  sum(Table__4."SALESAMOUNT") AS M__1
FROM
  "DIM_CUSTOMER"  Table__1 INNER JOIN "FACT_INTERNET_SALES"  Table__4 ON
(Table__1."CUSTOMERKEY"=Table__4."CUSTOMERKEY")
    INNER JOIN "DIM_PRODUCT"  Table__3 ON (Table__3."PRODUCTKEY"=Table__4.
"PRODUCTKEY")

GROUP BY
  Table__3."ENGLISHPRODUCTNAME",
  Table__1."CUSTOMERKEY",
  Table__1."SUFFIX",
  Table__1."TITLE"
)
F__1
FULL OUTER JOIN
(
SELECT
  Table__7."PRODUCT_NAME" AS Axis__1,
```

```
            sum(Table__8."SALESAMOUNT") AS M__1
      FROM
            "_SYS_BIC"."saphana.internetsales/ANLV_INTERNETSALES/olap"  Table__7,
            "FACT_RESELLER_SALES"  Table__8
      GROUP BY
            Table__7."PRODUCT_NAME"
      )
      F__2
      )
```

Listing 16.3 A Combined SQL Statement from JOIN_BY_SQL

You can see that the two SQL statements are still generated by creating the same two queries on the reporting level. However, when the SQL is created, it's immediately generated as a combined SQL statement, taking advantage of an outer join. The single SQL statement is then passed to the database for processing. The result set is then sent back to the report for display.

With this definition, we'll now show how to set the JOIN_BY_SQL parameter in the universe level. Begin by following the steps provided in Chapter 12 to generate a universe on an SAP HANA data source. These steps remain the same.

After the connection, connection shortcut, and data foundation layers are created, you select the data foundation in the PROJECT EXPLORER. Ensure that the properties for the data foundation can be viewed on the bottom-right corner of the screen. If not, click the DASH button underneath the layout of the data foundation. Click the PARAMETER button. You'll see a dialog with a listing of parameters available to your database. One of these parameters is JOIN_BY_SQL. Simply change the value from No to Yes by clicking the arrow beside the value. Save the data foundation and continue with the development of the universe.

> **Note**
>
> If you forget to set the JOIN_BY_SQL parameter before creating your business layer, just go back into the data foundation and set the parameter. It doesn't need to be set at any specific point in time during the development of the universe; just remember to publish or republish your universe after setting the parameter.

16.2.2 Merged Dimensions versus Analytic/Calculation Views

When you're building queries, data requirements sometimes dictate that you use multiple queries to pull data into the report. When multiple queries are required, you have two choices of location for the queries to be built and executed: on the report server or on the database server. Typically, when a query is created, you try to put as much processing on the database server as possible because database servers are usually resourced to have many more processors and more memory than a typical report server. The database handles the query and returns the data set.

When a report generates two or more queries based on the selection of objects, the reporting engine is responsible for stitching the results of the multiple queries together. This is usually the slowest route because one data set for each query is pulled. There is at least one common dimension that ties each of the queries together so that the report engine can match the resulting data sets. The data is then made available to be used in the report. The common dimension in Web Intelligence is called a *merged dimension*.

The concept of merged dimensions as they relate to every data source is the same as the relationship to SAP HANA. The queries built on the data sources on SAP HANA are built in the same manner as any other data sources. However, consider where the queries are being stitched together. When the multiple queries are executed, each query pulls back a data set and holds it in memory. Each data set has its own location in memory. Now, consider that SAP HANA systems are attributed to very large and very fast data sets. When you're working with an SAP HANA data source, it's typically a best practice to build views in SAP HANA, and then access those views in the universe as opposed to manipulating separate queries and merging the data together.

> **Note**
>
> Minimize or eliminate the usage of merged dimensions on SAP HANA data sources. Build views that serve the data through the universe to Web Intelligence to maximize performance.

16.2.3 Query Drill

Another feature of Web Intelligence that is discretely enhanced by using SAP HANA is *query drill*. Query drill is used when you're drilling into data that doesn't exist in memory in Web Intelligence. When you're creating a query in Web Intelligence, you specify a listing of dimensions and measures that are to be used in the report by adding them to the RESULT OBJECTS section of the QUERY panel. The inferred SQL is generated by Web Intelligence and passed to the database level when the query is executed. The data returned by the database server is held in memory and is available to the Web Intelligence report. (Remember that not all of the objects in the RESULTS OBJECTS section will necessarily be used in the report.)

To enable query drill for the current document, you access the properties of the document. Simply click the PROPERTIES tab on the top-left corner of the report designer, and then click DOCUMENT. You'll see a list of properties that are available for the current document, including QUERY STRIPPING, AUTO MERGE DIMENSIONS, and QUERY DRILL. Click the checkbox beside QUERY DRILL to enable the setting. Leaving this unchecked prevents a query drill from occurring in a report. This setting should be considered during the standard report design process due to the potential for increased traffic on the SAP HANA server. If drilling isn't required by the document, turn off query drilling so that unnecessary (and potentially incorrect) queries aren't required of the SAP HANA database.

When drilling is enabled in a report, you click on the underlined text to drill down into more detail. Hovering over the underlined text displays what happens when you click the text. However, if you click text that drills into an object that doesn't exist in the RESULTS OBJECTS area, you see (NEW QUERY) appended to the end of the tooltip. This means that Web Intelligence doesn't have enough data to provide the required level of drilling and must create a new query to pull the data into memory. Depending on the data source being used and the volume of data, this can run quickly, or it can take a long time.

Consider this same scenario when you're using SAP HANA as a data source. SAP HANA, with its in-memory capabilities, can be very quickly queried, and data can be returned much faster than with a conventional database. The idea here is that query drill is used without any scope of analysis (i.e., SCOPE OF ANALYSIS is NONE). When designing the query for the report, don't bring any unnecessary objects into the report. This reduces the amount of memory required by the report on the SAP BusinessObjects BI server. Because the data is available within a second or so on demand, take advantage of query drill for all drilling requirements.

Let's have a look at an example scenario of creating a report that uses a time hierarchy. You start on the year level and show the total sales by year. The requirements for this example dictate that you drill into quarter, month, and week. When you design the query, the only objects requested are YEAR and SALES AMOUNT. Leave the query filters blank because you don't want any data filtered out of the query. Click the SCOPE OF ANALYSIS button and ensure that SCOPE OF ANALYSIS is set to NONE. You'll see YEAR in the SCOPE OF ANALYSIS window, but you shouldn't see any of the other drillable dimensions. Click RUN QUERIES, and view the report.

Now, turn on drilling and hover over YEAR. A tooltip displays with the text DRILL TO MONTH (NEW QUERY). When you click YEAR, a new query is generated that pulls the sales amount aggregated by month. The report is then redrawn to replace the YEAR column with MONTH. Using a conventional data source such as SQL Server or Oracle could take seconds, minutes, or hours to return this data, depending on the amount of data being aggregated. This example isn't using summary tables or aggregate awareness that is generally attributed to drilling scenarios. However, with the optimizations of the SAP HANA data source, the transactional data is queried on demand. The transactional data is queried, and the appropriate result is returned to the report in real time.

The advantages here are twofold. First of all, the design of the report is simpler. Only the data required by the report is pulled into the reporting engine. The data volumes typically associated with an SAP HANA implementation are possible because data that isn't immediately required by the report isn't queried.

Second, the depth of drilling is dictated only by the requirements of the report, not by the resources available to the SAP BusinessObjects BI server. Because the data held in the SAP HANA data source is queried and returned almost immediately, the data held by the reporting server is reduced or made available to handle larger sets of data that are immediately required.

16.2.4 Query Stripping

The cardinal rule when designing a report in any tool is that if the data isn't required, don't pull it into the report. Pulling too much unnecessary data into a report not only increases the memory use on the report server responsible for generating the report, but also increases the load on the database server responsible for providing data to the report server. A feature of Web Intelligence that has, in the past, applied only to online analytic processing (OLAP) data sources is *query stripping*. This feature existed for OLAP data sources only. Starting with SAP BusinessObjects 4.1, query stripping was added for SAP HANA data sources to automatically reduce the number of data cells returned by all database queries. The concept of query stripping in a report means that you shouldn't request an object's data from the database if that object isn't used in the report. The SQL statement is rewritten so that the unused objects aren't included, and the data isn't retrieved.

Query stripping can be enabled in the DOCUMENT PROPERTIES section of a Web Intelligence report. Click the PROPERTIES tab on the top-left corner of the reporting interface, and click DOCUMENT. Select the QUERY STRIPPING checkbox to enable the functionality.

Let's look at an example of query stripping in a Web Intelligence document. Enabling the QUERY STRIPPING checkbox in a Web Intelligence document tells the report engine that if an object isn't used in the report, don't request it from the database server. For instance, consider the case in which you bring in full_name, Address_1, Address_2, Email_Address, and Sales Amount. In the report, you build a block that displays full_name, Email_Address, and Sales Amount. In a standard query without query stripping, all of the objects in the query results window are used to build the inferred SQL statement. That query is shown here:

```
SELECT full_name, Address_1, Address_2, Email_Address, Sales Amount
FROM INTERNET_SALES
```

The SQL statement is passed to the database server, and the full set of data is returned. The result is a block with 3,500 records and five columns resulting in approximately 17,500 cells of data.

But with query stripping enabled, the SQL statement is modified to pull only the objects that are referenced in the report. The resulting SQL statement with the unnecessary fields stripped away appears like this:

```
SELECT full_name, Email_Address, Sales Amount
FROM INTERNET_SALES
```

The result of this SQL statement is 3,500 records of data, but this time with only three columns of data. This SQL call results in 10,500 cells of data, which is just over half of the original request.

While these smaller results sets won't mean a lot of savings in total data consumed by enabling query stripping, consider cases when your queries return hundreds of thousands to millions of records of data. If you were to multiply the returned rows in the example that we just gave by 1,000, the benefit of query stripping becomes obvious. It's much better to return 10.5 million cells of data than 17.5 million cells. The memory savings on the reporting side is considerably less if the data isn't needed and isn't retrieved.

Let's modify the report once again. This time, add the `Address_1` field that you added in the query results pane of the QUERY panel. It doesn't matter where the `Address_1` field is added in the report; it can be a field in one or more tables, an axis in a chart, or even referenced in a report filter. Because the dimension is referenced in the report, the SQL is updated to include the `Address_1` field with query stripping enabled, as follows:

```
SELECT full_name, Address_1, Email_Address, Sales Amount
FROM INTERNET_SALES
```

This results in the number of cells returned increasing by the number of rows returned by the query. The benefit to query stripping is that it returns smaller result sets if they aren't used within the report. This is done automatically after query stripping is set in the DOCUMENT PROPERTIES. No other intervention is required by the user.

16.3 Case Study: Exploring Sales Data with SAP BusinessObjects Web Intelligence on Top of SAP HANA

The AdventureWorks Cycle Company global sales manager, Dave, is interested in learning more about the company's sales figures. Although Dave can request that the reporting team handle the creation of the report for him, he knows that that the reporting team is overtasked, and he might wind up waiting a long time before his report is created and returned to him.

Rather than waiting for the reporting team, Dave decides to take advantage of Web Intelligence to get quick answers to his questions. As a manager, he's savvy enough to know how to log on to the Web Intelligence application but has no knowledge of databases and doesn't want to learn. Although he doesn't know that the industrious BI team has invested in SAP HANA, he has heard that there have been phenomenal response times reported.

Dave wants to begin by building a report showing the various products that were sold via both the Internet and resellers. He doesn't know anything about the location or type of the database. All he knows is that a universe called INTERNETSALES has been created.

So he opens the SAP BusinessObjects BI portal and launches an instance of Web Intelligence. On creating a new report, he is presented with options of data source connections: No Data Source, Universe, BEx, and Analysis View. He selects Universe and receives the list of universes stored on the system, as shown in Figure 16.3.

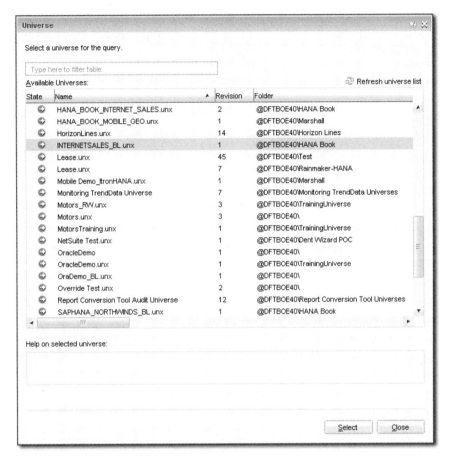

Figure 16.3 A Listing of Available Universes

Dave sees the *INTERNETSALES_BL.unx* and assumes that this is the correct Internetsales universe that the BI team told him about. When he picks the universe, he sees familiar objects organized into classes named in terms that he understands. Dave navigates through the classes and objects and pulls a few of the objects out into the Results Objects area, as shown in Figure 16.4.

Dave can now run this report. He starts by performing a query showing the different product names by sales amount and quantity for both the Internet sales and reseller channels. When he runs the report, the results of the query populate the body of the report as expected. He can then analyze and share the report as he sees fit.

Note that Dave simply selected a universe for INTERNETSALES—that is, he didn't need to know about the location, format, or structure of the underlying database. He simply ran the report and received the data.

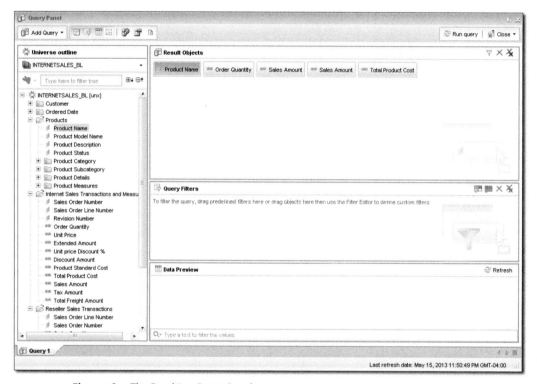

Figure 16.4 The Resulting Query Panel

With the query that Dave executed, the sales information for both the Internet sales and reseller channels consists of two different contexts in the universe. He could have viewed the SQL and seen that the result set is generated by the union of two different queries and different SQL statements, as shown in Figure 16.5. These two statements are executed independently, and the results are returned to the reporting engine. It's then the reporting engine's responsibility to bring the two queries together and deliver the results.

For smaller result sets from the two queries, this would be difficult because the resulting query would return data relatively quickly. The load on the report server is higher because the two SQL statements must be stitched together. On queries where the result set is much larger, there is a much larger load placed on the reporting engine as it attempts to union the queries together. It's better to push the processing down to the database server in cases like these.

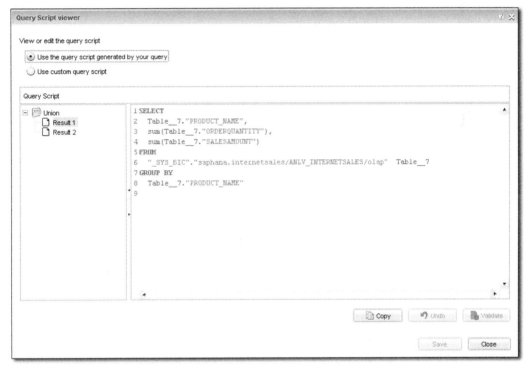

Figure 16.5 Two Separate Queries in the Query Script Viewer

Because the database being used is SAP HANA, the universe designer can take steps to ensure that the queries are processed on the database server as much as possible. These two queries are executed, then unioned together on the reporting engine level. In the universe, the universe developer understands that this sort of query can occur due to the sort of contexts that are available. The universe designer sets a parameter in the universe that unions the two queries together on the universe. The parameter is called JOIN_BY_SQL, and it's set on the data foundation in the universe. After the JOIN_BY_SQL parameter is set, the query is then reformulated, as shown in Figure 16.6.

Given this statement, the two individual queries are executed and then unioned together on the database server, as opposed to the two different queries being unioned on the report server. This results in much faster query times due to the extreme speeds possible from an SAP HANA data source.

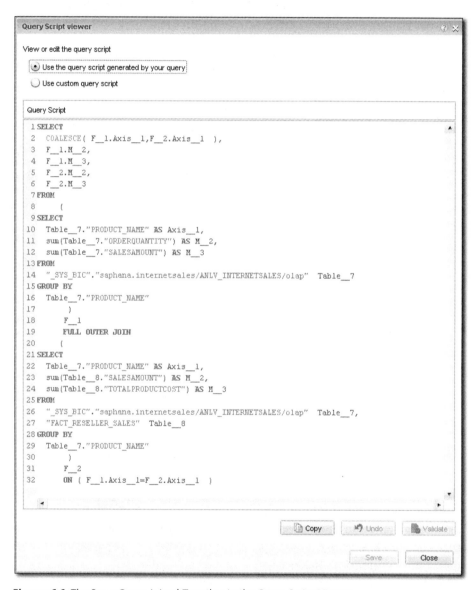

Figure 16.6 The Same Query Joined Together in the Query Script Viewer

Dave has been chatting with some Web Intelligence developers. He has heard of a Web Intelligence feature that can further enhance the query performance by removing objects from a query if they aren't used in the report. He's been told that the feature is called *query stripping*, which can be found in the DOCUMENT PROPERTIES of a document on which he is currently working. He opens the DOCU-MENT PROPERTIES and finds the QUERY STRIPPING checkbox. He ensures that the checkbox is enabled and runs his query again. There isn't a visual indicator that the setting is working other than query times being decreased even more.

Finally, Dave will be drilling into the report. In the existing product report that he has developed, he can currently drill down into the next level of detail, which is product model name. He can open the QUERY panel and set the scope of analysis as he typically would by opening the SCOPE OF ANALYSIS panel and selecting the levels. These will bring more data into the microcube in the server memory to make it available for the report to use as soon as he clicks on the next drill level.

Because he is using an SAP HANA data source, he can take advantage of query drilling to modify the underlying query to directly pull data from the SAP HANA database rather than the microcube in server memory. Query drilling is traditionally used when there are calculations on the report that can't be easily recalculated when the report is drilled into, such as database delegated averages, ranking, statistical functions, and the like. Query drilling passes the calculation of these measures back down to the database so that the correct context can be derived and the calculations can be accurately completed by the database server. You can take that one step further here by taking advantage of the increased speed of the SAP HANA data source to quickly request the next level of data that is required by the report. Coupled with query stripping, query drilling can provide your system with an SQL statement that is quick and concise and that returns the necessary data within a very short interval while minimizing the amount of memory used on the SAP BusinessObjects BI server.

The combination of the techniques given in this case study can provide the end user with a report that not only takes advantage of best reporting practices when using an SAP HANA database, but also minimizes the execution time and the amount of data required on the server. A Web Intelligence designer has no control over the JOIN_BY_SQL parameter, but a well-informed designer can have a look at the inferred SQL in the QUERY panel to determine whether multiple SQL statements are used. The designer can then question the universe designer to determine whether the JOIN_BY_SQL parameter should be used. The other two techniques—query drilling and query stripping—are controlled by the developer in the DOCUMENT PROPERTIES panel of the Web Intelligence report. The utilization of all of these items will push as much of the processing back to the database server as possible while ensuring that the reports run as quickly as possible for the end users.

16.4   Summary

SAP BusinessObjects Web Intelligence is an extraordinarily powerful tool that puts data into the hands of those who need to use it, when they need to have it, and how they need to see it. The tool provides enterprise-level reporting and analytics capabilities so that everyone from seasoned report writers to quickly trained executives are able to access the reports and manipulate the data. SAP HANA takes the power of Web Intelligence and shoves it into overdrive by allowing for superfast queries and quick and easy analysis of the resulting data.

Delivering operational and external reports in the age of big data can be a significant challenge. SAP Crystal Reports powered by SAP HANA can help bring things under control.

17   SAP Crystal Reports with SAP HANA

Throughout this book, we've examined the many advantages that SAP HANA's in-memory solutions bring to highly interactive visualizations and analytic BI content. As exciting as these new delivery mechanisms are, substantial portions of the world's BI content and usage scenarios still require traditional operational reporting content, as well as the external delivery of highly formatted reports. Although these use cases may not be as exciting and "sexy" as newer, interactive delivery mechanisms, they still form the backbone of many information delivery solutions.

So, with the advent of SAP HANA and highly interactive and visual information delivery tools, is there still a need for traditional reporting solutions? The answer is yes. It's true that some use cases that have been traditionally handled with reports may move entirely to newer, more visual and interactive interfaces; however, there are still many use cases that are best suited to a traditional report delivery mechanism. There are also cases wherein the newer interactive visualizations may serve simply to augment and enhance, but not replace, the traditional reports.

We find these use cases in almost every industry—in health care, in the delivery of lab results to patients, in manufacturing or wholesale, and in the performance reports sent to out to resellers. Cash flow is an excellent example of a scenario in which newer interactive visualizations can serve to augment but not replace a traditional report. Cash flow monitoring dashboards are a common use case for newer dashboard development tools, but traditional cash flow statement reports aren't going anywhere.

Because traditional reports aren't going to disappear, is there any value brought by the SAP HANA platform to this type of reporting, or is this a case in which SAP HANA is just another database? Here, too, the answer to the first part of this question is yes. SAP HANA brings a number of features that enable new innovations in the area of traditional report delivery.

The first of these is raw speed. Delivery of externally facing reports is often a very time-consuming process in the BI landscape; the generation of possibly thousands of documents for clients or partners can take hours in large, overnight batch jobs. A significant portion of the execution time for these jobs is often the backend query execution. This may be queries implemented in the reports themselves or large batch SQL procedures that prepare the data for the reports. Both of these can be greatly enhanced by a solution such as SAP HANA, whereby it may be possible to execute reports in real time as requested by end users without the need to manage a complex scheduling system, or at minimum, reduce the total execution time of scheduled jobs if reports must still be sent out ahead of time.

Second, and more specifically to operational reporting, is the direct implementation of application databases on SAP HANA. Operational reports typically need access to transactional details in real time. These reports therefore often run directly against application databases. In traditional systems, this can cause a number of problems — negative performance impacts to the application caused by reporting, the need to run reports against a replicated copy of the application database, and/or the requirement that the reports wait for the data to move into a warehouse solution via extract, transform, and load (ETL) — causing them to lag behind real time. With the move by SAP to implement its entire suite of business applications on the SAP HANA platform, as well as the option to load in real-time operation tables via tools such as SAP Landscape Transformation (SLT), operational report authors now have the ability to access application data directly without as many performance concerns. This brings us to SAP Crystal Reports.

SAP Crystal Reports 2013 vs. SAP Crystal Reports for Enterprise

If you're familiar with the SAP BusinessObjects BI platform, you probably know that there are two different versions of SAP Crystal Reports: the 2013 version and the version for Enterprise.

When SAP started work on the SAP BusinessObjects BI platform, one major goal was to harmonize the user interface (UI) and functionality across the various BI tools. However, because SAP didn't want to rush into rolling out a radically altered SAP Crystal Reports solution and risk alienating the substantial customer base that exists today — as well as cause complex migration paths from prior versions to SAP BusinessObjects BI — as a compromise, the decision was made to offer up two flavors of SAP Crystal Reports.

SAP Crystal Reports 2013 is the tool offered to the existing user community with essentially no UI changes in an attempt to make the migration path as smooth as possible. Although it doesn't offer much in the way of new or enhanced features, it does offer a stable and safe path forward for users with heavy existing investments. SAP Crystal Reports for Enterprise is the tool offered to new adopters of SAP Crystal Reports. It has a significantly reworked UI that was the product of usability studies attempting to make SAP Crystal Reports into a more user-friendly tool. SAP Crystal Reports for Enterprise also received the new platform enhancements that SAP Crystal Reports 2013 lacked, such as 64-bit support and tighter coupling to the SAP BusinessObjects BI platform universes, BEx queries, and SAP HANA information views. The development client has also been completely rewritten as a Java desktop application.

Given that you have two tools to choose from, which should you use to construct reports with when using SAP HANA data sources? The answer is generally going to be SAP Crystal Reports for Enterprise. It will receive the focus of new development and enhancements; its new UI, although possibly requiring a transition stage for older SAP Crystal Reports developers, is an overall improvement on usability, and it has the 64-bit architecture necessary to function in the modern era of big data.

SAP Crystal Reports for Enterprise is the focus of this chapter. We'll talk about connecting SAP Crystal Reports for SAP HANA and then walk you through a case study that shows SAP Crystal Reports in action.

17.1 SAP HANA as a Data Source for SAP Crystal Reports

In this section, we'll look at the options for connecting SAP Crystal Reports for Enterprise to SAP HANA data. The first UI element that sticks out is the ribbon interface that is common to many of the tools in SAP BusinessObjects BI. This interface, like the ribbon interface in current versions of Microsoft Office, categorizes the different application functions into groups. In theory, this makes elements easier to find for beginners because the ribbon headers use plain text labels instead of cryptic icons. Some long-time SAP Crystal Reports users may find that it takes a few more clicks to reach functions that were merely one click away in the old UI.

The second major interface convention of SAP Crystal Reports for Enterprise is the dock on the left side of the screen. If you're familiar with SAP Crystal Reports 2013, you'll notice that many of the wizards and so-called "experts" from SAP Crystal Reports 2013 have their counterparts located here. This interface is very similar to the dock of panels in SAP BusinessObjects Web Intelligence. The most significant of these panels for our purposes is the DATA EXPLORER panel, which is at the top of the list of items (see Figure 17.1). From here, you can establish connections and create queries, as well as add results from queries to the report layout. Once again, you may recognize the same grouping structure as SAP Crystal Reports 2013, and most of the report layout concepts are the same. The STRUCTURE and PAGE view modes are equivalent to the DESIGN and PREVIEW modes in SAP Crystal Reports 2013.

Figure 17.1 SAP Crystal Reports for Enterprise User Interface

SAP Crystal Reports for Enterprise has several methods for connecting to SAP HANA. The most recent type of connection allows for direct OLAP connectivity to analytic and calculation views created in SAP HANA. The addition of this OLAP connection method includes any hierarchies and variables that have been created in the view.

The complete list of connection options for SAP HANA is as follows:

▶ ODBC

▶ JDBC

▶ UNX universe (i.e., universes created with the new Information Design Tool)

▶ Relational connection from SAP BusinessObjects BI platform

▶ Direct OLAP connectivity to analytic and calculation views

Creating connections in a report is done using a wizard accessed via the DATA EXPLORER panel or initiated at report creation time. The wizard categorizes connections into three groups: PREVIOUS CONNECTIONS, SAP BUSINESSOBJECTS BUSINESS INTELLIGENCE PLATFORM, and CONNECTIONS BY VENDOR. The last of these is where you'll find direct connections to databases by vendor middleware.

The SAP BUSINESSOBJECTS BUSINESS INTELLIGENCE PLATFORM category is where you'll find the two additional connection choices available to SAP Crystal Reports for Enterprise. Selecting this option requires you to authenticate to the SAP BusinessObjects BI platform. From there, you have the option of selecting UNIVERSES, BEX QUERIES, or RELATIONAL CONNECTIONS. For connecting to SAP HANA, you can use the UNIVERSE or RELATIONAL CONNECTION option.

In this section, we'll walk you through the four main ways of connecting SAP Crystal Reports for Enterprise to SAP HANA.

17.1.1 Configuring ODBC and JDBC Connections

To leverage SAP Crystal Reports for Enterprise with SAP HANA data, you must create a connection to the database. From the perspective of SAP Crystal Reports, SAP HANA is just another database. That means the process you go through to connect is really no different from connecting to Oracle, SQL Server, or any other vendor's database product.

Like with all database connections, you need a set of database driver middleware to mediate the connection between the SAP Crystal Reports developer client and the database. For SAP HANA, there are two driver options to select from for use with SAP Crystal Reports: JDBC and ODBC.

At development time, it doesn't really matter whether you choose Open Database Connectivity (ODBC) or Java Database Connectivity (JDBC), but when it comes time to deploy your report to be processed on the server, this choice does matter. Windows server environments are typically best served by ODBC driver configurations, whereas UNIX server environments are best served by JDBC driver configurations. If you're unsure of the deployment architecture for your environment, check with your SAP BusinessObjects BI server administrators before committing to one driver or the other.

One advantage to ODBC configurations is that they externalize configuration details, such as server addresses, from the report definitions and BI applications. This generally makes dealing with migration of content among development, test, and production server regions easier. Something similar can be achieved with JDBC by using a host name alias in the JDBC URL and then using the operating system's HOST file to configure connections to an appropriate database server for the current region, but it requires more manual work on the server.

Setting Up ODBC Connections

To use an ODBC connection in SAP Crystal Reports, you first need to define the connection as an ODBC system connection in the 32-bit ODBC configuration panel. Only then can you create a connection in SAP Crystal Reports for Enterprise by following these steps:

1. Ensure that the 32-bit SAP HANA database client is installed, as done in Chapter 12.

2. Configure a 32-bit SAP HANA connection in the ODBC configuration panel accessed from either the CONTROL PANEL on 32-bit Windows or from the SYS-WOW64 directory on 64-bit Windows (*C:\Windows\SysWOW64\odbcad32.exe*) if on the SAP BusinessObjects BI server.

3. Provide the data source a NAME and DESCRIPTION, as shown in Figure 17.2. The SERVER:PORT field entry should be the same value that you used when configuring SAP HANA Studio. Remember that SAP HANA listening ports are configured as 3<*Installation Number*>15. So for a typical SAP HANA installation on instance 00, the port would be 30015.

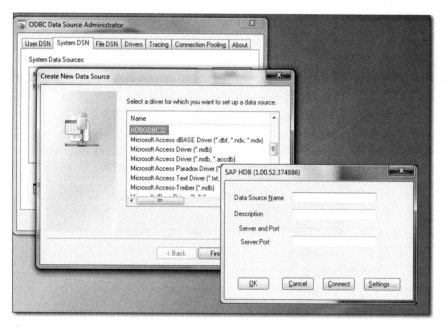

Figure 17.2 Creating ODBC Connections

Now, you have everything in place to configure a connection from SAP Crystal Reports for Enterprise to SAP HANA. To do that, you need to open SAP Crystal Reports for Enterprise, create a new blank report, and then use the Choose a Data Source Connection dialog to configure your connection by following these steps:

1. From the Choose a Data Source Connection dialog, select Connection by Vendor.

2. Navigate to SAP • SAP HANA Database 1.0 and choose ODBC.

3. Click Make New Connection, and select the connection name you created previously. Enter a user ID and password to connect to SAP HANA. Figure 17.3 shows an example of this process.

You can now start selecting objects based on the connection to construct your report.

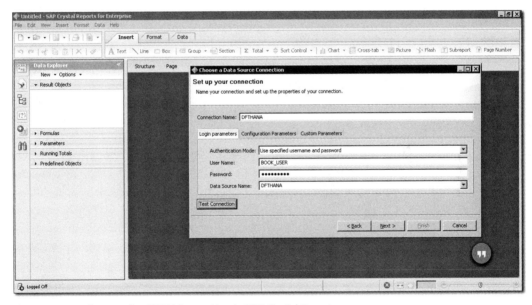

Figure 17.3 Configuring the ODBC Connection in SAP Crystal Reports

Setting Up JDBC Connections
Unlike ODBC connections, JDBC connections don't require any OS-level pre-configuration. Creating a JDBC connection in SAP Crystal Reports for Enterprise starts just like creating an ODBC connection, but this time, you choose JDBC instead of

ODBC. The configuration values for JDBC are also slightly different; instead of selecting an ODBC Data Source Name, you enter the values listed below:

▸ Host Name: your-hana-server-name

▸ Instance Number: <INSTALLATION NUMBER> (e.g., 00)

After you've entered these values and your user name and password, you'll be ready to retrieve data from the SAP HANA system. From this point forward, there is no distinction between JDBC and ODBC connections.

> **Note**
>
> If you're familiar with SAP Crystal Reports 2013, you may recall that the *CRConfig.xml* file needed to be updated to point to the installed SAP HANA JDBC drivers. SAP Crystal Reports for Enterprise has the necessary JDBC drivers included, so this file does not need to be updated for SAP Crystal Reports for Enterprise.

17.1.2 Using SAP BusinessObjects IDT Universes

In addition to using a platform-managed connection to SAP HANA directly, SAP Crystal Reports for Enterprise can leverage IDT-based universes constructed on top of SAP HANA. This approach is appropriate mostly when you're connecting to base column tables, as opposed to connecting to information models—that is, analytic and column views.

If you're leveraging base tables directly, then using a universe (as opposed to crafting SQL statements by hand) is generally considered the best practice. The universe layer offers the BI team the opportunity to construct reusable business definitions instead of recreating the wheel in each report. Because SAP Crystal Reports for Enterprise was designed from the start to work with universes, you don't have the drawbacks that older versions of SAP Crystal Reports had when working with universes, where the integration between the two tools was more of an afterthought.

The question of whether to use base tables or information models configured in SAP HANA is more ambiguous when you're considering SAP Crystal Reports for Enterprise. We addressed some of those questions in Chapter 12, where we compared the options of constructing models in SAP HANA versus universes.

The steps to establish a report connection to a universe in SAP Crystal Reports for Enterprise are nearly identical to the steps for connecting to a platform-managed relational connection, until you connect to the repository and choose the type of object to connect to. From that point forward, follow these steps:

1. Select DATA SOURCE TYPE • UNIVERSE, and then choose the universe from the repository.

2. You are presented with the EDIT QUERY panel, which is shown in Figure 17.4. This is the same panel you would be presented with for querying any type of universe, not just SAP HANA. Its UI is common across all SAP BusinessObjects BI products that support universe queries.

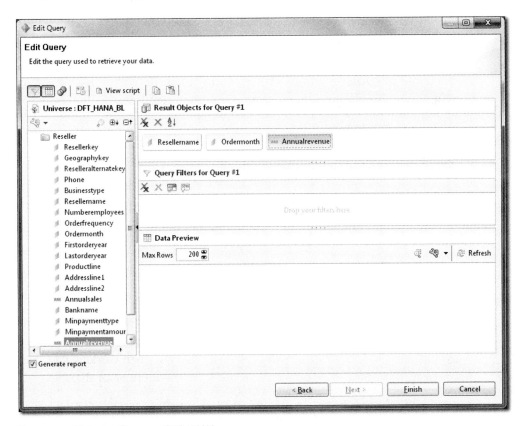

Figure 17.4 Universe Query on SAP HANA

3. Craft your query by dragging and dropping universe objects into the RESULT and FILTER areas.

4. At this point, you can construct your report just like any other data source.

17.1.3 Using SAP BusinessObjects BI Relational Connections

A major advantage that SAP Crystal Reports for Enterprise offers is the ability to let the SAP BusinessObjects BI platform manage connection metadata instead of configuring and storing this data in each and every report. This vastly improves the manageability of SAP Crystal Reports and facilitates migrations of content between environments. Therefore, instead of directly configuring a connection to SAP HANA using ODBC or JDBC in your report, you can instead configure the connection just once using the Information Design Tool (IDT) and storing the connection in the SAP BusinessObjects BI repository. Behind the scenes, this connection still uses either the ODBC or JDBC SAP HANA drivers, but the report authors can be abstracted from this detail.

To create a report using a platform-managed connection using SAP Crystal Reports for Enterprise, you must first create the connection object with IDT (covered in Chapter 9). After you have a connection object in place, follow these steps:

1. Either start a new report FROM DATA SOURCE or click CHOOSE DATA SOURCE from the DATA EXPLORER.

2. From the CHOOSE A DATA SOURCE CONNECTION wizard, select the SAP BUSINESS-OBJECTS BUSINESS INTELLIGENCE PLATFORM • BROWSE REPOSITORY link, as shown in Figure 17.5.

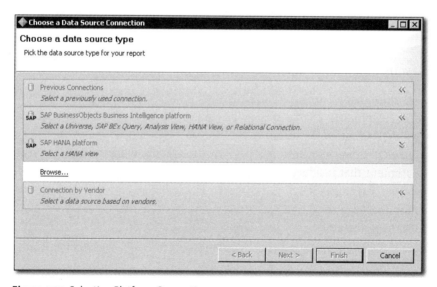

Figure 17.5 Selecting Platform Connections

3. Authenticate to the platform.

4. Select DATA SOURCE TYPE • RELATIONAL CONNECTION, as shown in Figure 17.6.

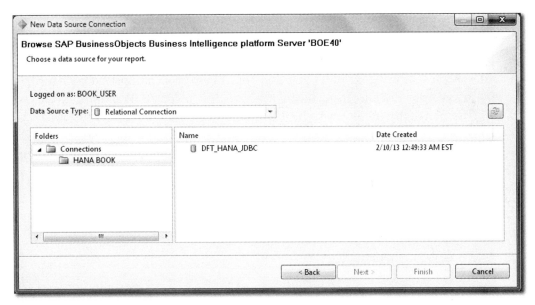

Figure 17.6 Selecting a Relational Connection

5. Navigate to the repository, and choose the connection you created with IDT.

6. The connection is opened, and you're presented with the same view of the SAP HANA catalog that you would see if you had created the connection directly against ODBC or JDBC (see Figure 17.7).

One new feature that emerged with SAP Crystal Reports for Enterprise is the ability to create custom SQL commands. After connecting to a relational connection, there is an SQL COMMAND button to the right of the ADD CONNECTION button. Clicking the SQL COMMAND button brings up a dialog allowing the user to create an SQL statement that results in a table that can be added to the data explorer in SAP Crystal Reports. The SQL COMMAND can also take advantage of PARAMETERS that prompt the user for data. This prompt filters data on the database level, thereby reducing the amount of data displayed in the report.

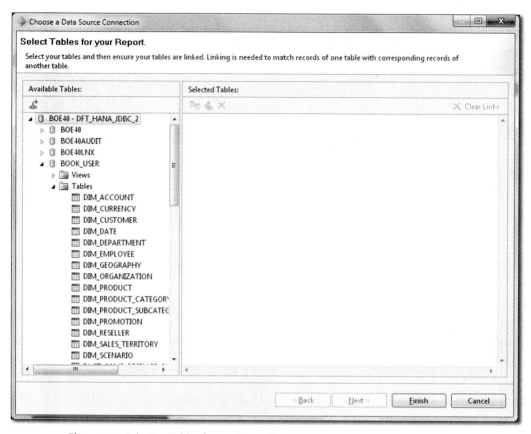

Figure 17.7 Selecting Tables from a Connection

17.1.4 Direct OLAP Connectivity to Analytic and Calculation Views

In August of 2013, SAP BusinessObjects BI 4.1 was released. With this release, SAP Crystal Reports for Enterprise gained the ability to connect to SAP HANA views through a published, or managed, OLAP connection in the SAP Business-Objects BI repository. Then, in June of 2014, the support pack 4 update to the SAP BusinessObjects BI 4.1 platform was released. With this release, SAP Crystal Reports for Enterprise gained the ability to natively connect to an SAP HANA server directly.

We'll discuss the steps for both of these processes next.

SAP HANA Views Connectivity via Managed OLAP Connection in the Repository

To connect to SAP HANA via a published OLAP connection, simply follow these steps:

1. In the CENTRAL MANAGEMENT CONSOLE, click the OLAP CONNECTIONS option in the ORGANIZE section. Alternatively, an OLAP connection can be created in the Information Design Tool and published to the repository. These connections can be used to directly connect to SAP HANA or build a universe on an OLAP data source.

2. In SAP Crystal Reports for Enterprise, create a new server connection to the SAP BusinessObjects BI platform server. Then, perform the following steps:

   ▶ In the EDIT menu, select SERVER CONNECTIONS.

   ▶ Select SAP BUSINESSOBJECTS BI PLATFORM on the left-side window.

   ▶ Click the ADD button and enter a display name, the web services server name, the server port, context (usually */dswsbobje/services*) and a valid user name and authentication type.

   ▶ Click TEST CONNECTION and enter the password for the provided user (see Figure 17.8).

   ▶ If the connection fails, ensure that the SAP BusinessObjects BI platform is correctly installed and configured, and try again.

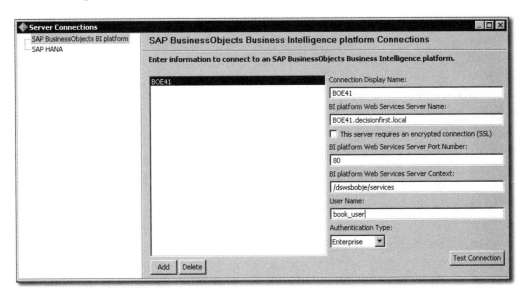

Figure 17.8 A Completed SAP BusinessObjects BI Platform Connection

3. In SAP Crystal Reports for Enterprise, create a new blank report.

4. Click Browse Repository under the SAP BusinessObjects BI Platform section of the Choose a Data Source Connection dialog box.

5. Select the newly created SAP BusinessObjects BI connection.

6. Enter the valid password for the provided user name.

7. Change the Data Source Type to HANA View (See Figure 17.9).

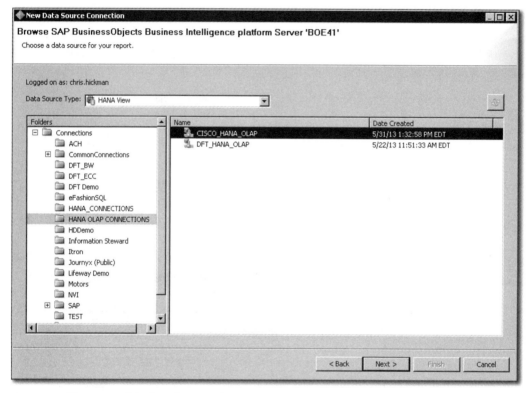

Figure 17.9 A Listing of Managed OLAP Data Sources

8. Navigate through the folders for a published OLAP connection based on an SAP HANA data source. Select a data source on which a report will be built.

9. You are presented with a listing of analytic and calculation views that your user ID has access to view. Select a view.

10. You can now pull out dimension and measures and select hierarchies as usual in an OLAP connection. Click Finish to run the query and build the report.

> **Note**
>
> You can check the web services URL by logging on to the CMC, going to APPLICATIONS, and viewing the PROPERTIES of the web services application. You may also paste this into a browser to validate the URL.

SAP HANA Views Connectivity Directly to the SAP HANA Platform

Direct connectivity means that users do not need to create or maintain links within an SAP BusinessObjects BI repository or have a repository at all. SAP Crystal Reports for Enterprise can connect directly to an SAP HANA server.

To connect directly to SAP HANA, simply follow these steps:

1. In the Central Management Console, click the OLAP CONNECTIONS option in the ORGANIZE section. Alternatively, an OLAP connection can be created in the Information Design Tool and published to the repository. These connections can be used to directly connect to SAP HANA or build a universe on an OLAP data source.

2. In SAP Crystal Reports for Enterprise, create a new server connection to the SAP BusinessObjects BI platform server. Then follow these steps:

   ▶ In the EDIT menu, select SERVER CONNECTIONS.

   ▶ Select SAP HANA on the left-side window.

   ▶ Click the ADD button, and enter a display name, the server name, the server port, and a valid user name.

   ▶ Click TEST CONNECTION, and enter the password for the provided user (see Figure 17.10).

   ▶ If the connection fails, ensure that the SAP HANA server is correctly installed and configured, and try again.

3. In SAP Crystal Reports for Enterprise, create a new blank report.

4. Click BROWSE under the SAP HANA PLATFORM section of the CHOOSE A DATA SOURCE CONNECTION dialog box.

5. Select the newly created SAP HANA data source.

6. Enter the valid password for the provided user name.

7. You are presented with a listing of analytic and calculation views that your user ID has access to view. Select a view. See Figure 17.11 for a sample listing of views.

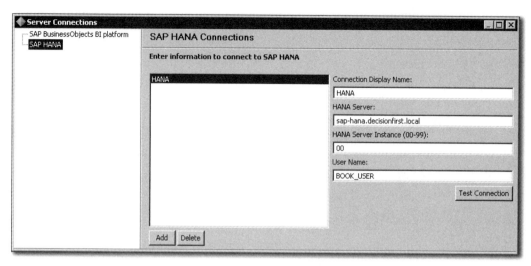

Figure 17.10 A Correctly Configured Connection to SAP HANA

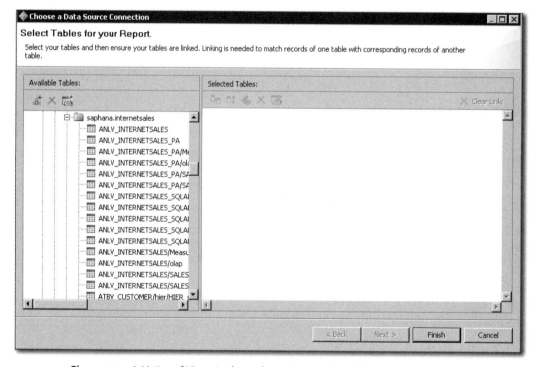

Figure 17.11 A Listing of Views in the saphana.internetsales Schema

8. You can now pull out dimension and measures and select hierarchies as usual in an OLAP connection. Click FINISH to run the query and build the report.

As you can see, these two connection methods are very similar to one another. The biggest difference is in the backend architecture. Connecting to an SAP HANA view from a managed OLAP connection in the SAP BusinessObjects BI repository requires an SAP BusinessObjects BI repository to be installed and configured in order to connect to an SAP HANA data source. Connecting to an SAP HANA view directly from SAP Crystal Reports for Enterprise requires only an SAP HANA server with no SAP BusinessObjects BI platform required.

Saving Reports to SAP HANA

Connecting to the SAP HANA repository allows the capability to save reports directly to the SAP HANA platform. Using the XS Engine running on the SAP HANA platform, SAP Crystal Reports for Enterprise can be saved to and opened from the SAP HANA repository without the need for an SAP BusinessObjects BI platform. In addition, users can now access reports created in SAP Crystal Reports for Enterprise within SAP Lumira Server.

17.2 Case Study: Exploring Data with SAP Crystal Reports on Top of SAP HANA

AdventureWorks Cycle Company offers its products through two primary channels: a self-hosted Internet sales channel that is direct to customers, and a reseller sales channel that works with independent sports retailers throughout the world. Competition for access to reseller floor space within the cycling sports industry is very high. Therefore, reseller relations are a key strategic initiative at Adventure-Works.

To help maintain positive relationships with its dealer network, AdventureWorks engages in multiple forms of outreach. One of these methods is providing marketing data and analysis to resellers based on AdventureWorks' own direct-to-customer sales. Currently, this data is delivered as a set of scheduled reports that are mailed out on a monthly basis.

The reseller relations team wants to achieve a higher level of engagement with resellers. To help achieve this goal, they have started an initiative to construct a reseller access portal that brings together all of the interactions that Adventure-Works has with its resellers into a single, one-stop shop. The hope is to provide live data content to resellers leveraging the enhanced performance that the newly implemented SAP HANA data warehouse provides. One of the first pieces of content to be delivered on the new platform will be a new version of the Reseller Marketing Report that is currently delivered as static content.

The new report will be implemented as an SAP Crystal Reports for Enterprise document. The marketing team doesn't want to expose the resellers to the complexity of the SAP BusinessObjects BI Launch Pad as a UI, so they run the report in the interface on a monthly basis to validate the data prior to the distribution of the final report.

The information delivered to the resellers will consist of product sales trends tailored to the geographic region that the reseller operates in. Product sales in the cycling industry are highly regional due to different materials and riding styles popular in more rugged areas versus flatter geographies.

The report header will consist of overview charts showing recent order volumes by product category/subcategory in the region. The rest of the report will focus in on the details of which products are sold in the region by month.

For this implementation, we opted to construct the report using the direct connection to the analytic and calculation views created on the SAP HANA platform. The connection to either the SAP BusinessObjects BI platform or SAP HANA is inconsequential for this case study because hosting the report is not a requirement.

17.2.1 Connecting to Data

The first stage of development is to connect to the data source. Because you're building the report off of a view in the SAP HANA system, select the Browse link beneath the SAP HANA source. After you authenticate to the SAP HANA system, select the SAP HANA package, and then navigate to the view that provides the necessary data. In this example, the universe is stored in the package `saphana.internetsales`, and the view is named ANLV_INTERNETSALES, as shown in Figure 17.12.

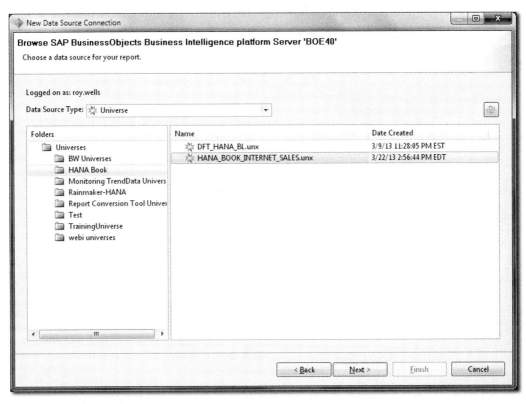

Figure 17.12 Selecting the Report Data Source

17.2.2 Designing the Query

After you've selected a source, you need to construct the query. You're presented with the EDIT QUERY panel, where you can select the characteristics and key figures for the result set and choose appropriate filters to limit the data. In this example report, make the selections listed in Table 17.1.

Hierarchy	Characteristics/Key Figures
ATBV_PRODUCT.HIER_PRODUCT	PRODUCT_CATEGORY, PRODUCT_SUBCATEGORY, PRODUCT_NAME
ATBV_ORDERED_DATE_ HIER.ORDERED_DATE_HIER	ORDERED_YEAR_MONTH

Table 17.1 Selected Values

Hierarchy	Characteristics/Key Figures
N/A	ORDERQUANTITY
N/A	SALESAMOUNT

Table 17.1 Selected Values (Cont.)

17.2.3 Limiting Query Results with Filter

The usage of filters can greatly improve the performance of a report by limiting the amount of data that is presented within the report. The general rule of thumb is that if the data is not needed, you should not pull it from the database. In this report, a single query filter has been defined on CUSTOMER_STATECODE within the ATVB_CUSTOMER.HIER_CUSTOMER_LOCATION hierarchy. This provides the runtime filtering necessary to connect the reseller portal to the report, allowing you to show just the data appropriate for the current reseller's region. Make the selections shown in Figure 17.13.

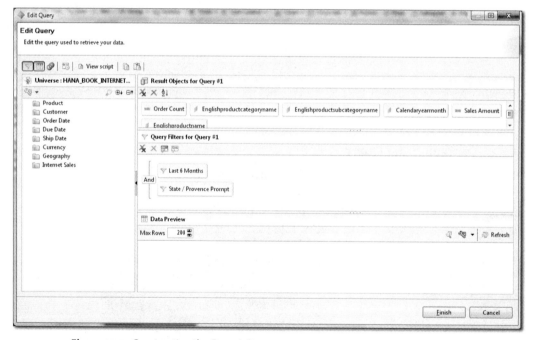

Figure 17.13 Constructing the Report Query

17.2.4   Formatting the Report Display

After the data is selected, you can lay out the report as described earlier. Place a report title in the REPORT HEADER section, and use some of the drawing tools to provide visual separation. You can then set up the report grouping structure to prepare for adding charts and data. To show an overview of data by product category on the first page, make that the first group. Inside that group, add a chart showing the top five products sold by order count. Use the SAP Crystal Reports TOP N sorting feature to limit the results in the charts. The final page layout is shown in Figure 17.14.

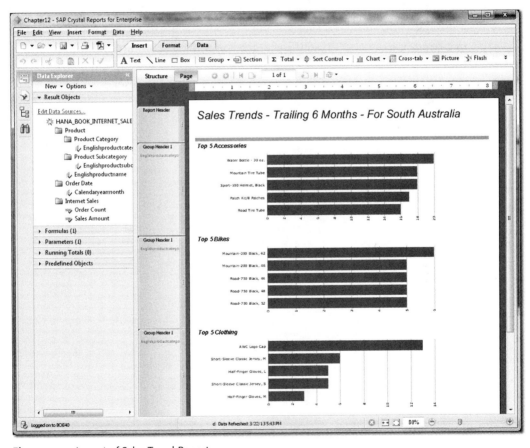

Figure 17.14 Layout of Sales Trend Report

From this point forward in the report design and development process, the same procedures that are used for SAP Crystal Reports development against any data source would also apply here. Keeping in mind the record and group layout of standard SAP Crystal Reports development, along with drilling and sorting, develop the report as you normally would.

17.3   Summary

You've seen in this chapter that there are still uses for traditional reporting tools despite the move to in-memory computing and interactive data visualization. SAP Crystal Reports has been near the top of the BI toolbox for a generation, and its latest rendition in SAP Crystal Reports for Enterprise still brings value to the table, especially when run on top of SAP HANA.

As an extension of Chapter 4, this appendix focuses on preprovisioning data with SAP Information Steward.

A   Source System Analysis with SAP Information Steward Data Insight

In Chapter 4, we discussed the steps to take before you provision data into SAP HANA, including why you should perform source system analysis (SSA), what you can achieve by analyzing a source, what the all-important principle of data quality is, and how to avoid fast trash in SAP HANA.

These topics were all discussed in the context of what SAP Data Services offers as a profiling tool. SAP Data Services has two primary profiling mechanisms: column and relationship. These are great because they are shipped with SAP Data Services—but they are not the primary focus of SAP Data Services. In fact, SAP has a separate solution that *is* designed around the concept of data quality monitoring: SAP Information Steward.

SAP Information Steward is a business user–targeted tool that is focused on being the central hub of the organization for data quality, metadata, and data cleansing activities. For example, you can create business rules to render scores on data quality dimensions, such as completeness or accuracy, as shown in Figure A.1.

However, you can also perform complex data profiles, collect metadata, organize a data dictionary, or create cleansing packages to fix data issues with SAP Data Services and SAP Data Quality Management. SAP Information Steward is a flexible application with many purposes and five distinct modules (shown as tabs in Figure A.1):

▶ **Data Insight**
This robust module offers complex data profiling and data scorecarding capabilities. You can also implement validation rules created by business users that can be shared in SAP Data Services as custom validation functions for ETL developers.

▶ **Metadata Management**

This is the metadata hub for the organization. You can capture metadata from most SAP tools, including SAP BusinessObjects BI and SAP Data Services. In addition, these capabilities can extend to practically any metadata-creating tool from other vendors if multisource integration licensing is procured.

▶ **Metapedia**

This is designed to house corporate data dictionaries by housing business terms and categories. A workflow process is enabled with user security so that proper approvals must be maintained before terms and categories are shared with the organization.

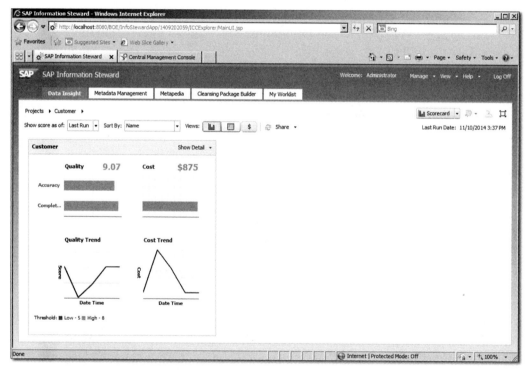

Figure A.1 SAP Information Steward's Data Quality Monitoring

▶ **Cleansing Package Builder (CPB)**

This is the only module specifically designed to work with SAP Data Services. CPB is used to create and maintain custom data cleansing package contents (both logic and dictionary values) to provide a true organization-specific data cleansing platform.

► **My Worklist**

This module is the central hub for the workflow approval process for all of the other modules containing workflow functionality. Business users may also use this module to review match results and fix errant matching data linkage results from SAP Data Services and SAP Data Quality Management data flows.

Because there are many different aspects to SAP Information Steward, in this appendix, we'll limit the scope of our exploration to only the Data Insight module of SAP Information Steward. Data Insight contains many powerful tools for the data steward, but our goal for this appendix is to focus on SAP Information Steward elements that support SSA for implementing SAP HANA, as well as the types of data profiling it offers.

SAP Information Steward's Data Insight module performs a variety of different tasks. Data quality scorecards are often the first capability of Data Insight highlighted and touted because they are so powerful. With the scorecard functionality of Data Insight, business users can create customized validation rules for a metadata-driven connection, much like a datastore in SAP Data Services. These rules are then scored against that connection to provide a baseline index of the score of the rules. Then, the rules may be gathered together on a scorecard as shown in Figure A.1, which is really just a composite score value of all of the scores assembled in Data Insight on three different data domains: customer, sales, and direct materials. These data domains are completely customizable and are used to measure almost any facet in the enterprise. Companies are using this functionality to actively monitor data quality in systems ranging from SAP Business Suite to data warehousing systems. The performance is quite good against SAP systems, and customers are exploiting this to give a dramatic view of what is going on in their operation systems to provide data-driven key performance indicators (KPIs) on the quality of their data.

This powerful functionality makes for many attention-grabbing demonstrations with the product, but the complex data profiling capabilities are often overlooked. SAP Information Steward also has several means of profiling your data, and it's this functionality that is important for supporting our quest of SSA for the organization. We'll explore these different types of profiling in detail in this appendix to see what unique insights they shed on our data to save valuable coding and development time for procurement into SAP HANA.

The six types of profiling in the Data Insight module are both unique to SAP Information Steward and very useful for SAP HANA data procurement. These profiling types go well beyond basic column and relationship profiling using SAP Data Services:

► **Column profiling**
Column profiling profiles numerous attributes of a column's data. This is much like SAP Data Services, but there are many more options available.

► **Address profiling**
Unique to SAP Information Steward, address profiling uses the SAP Data Quality Management engine to quickly tell a user if an address is valid, invalid, or correctable from a deliverability standpoint using certified postal service delivery supplementary data.

► **Dependency profiling**
Dependency profiling is much like SAP Data Services profiling, but multiple columns may be used to show the dependency of any of the columns contained within two tables.

► **Redundancy profiling**
Redundancy profiling can determine the degree of overlapping data values or duplication between two sets of columns.

► **Uniqueness profiling**
The uniqueness profiling task returns the count and percentage of rows that contain non-unique data for the selected set of column(s).

► **Content type profiling**
The content type profiling option returns only an assignment of a metadata type to the attribute column(s) selected and is used as a starting point for other types of SAP Information Steward profiling and Data Cleansing Advisor tasks. Because this type of profiling wouldn't be used for preprovisioning data for SAP HANA, we won't discuss it in this appendix.

As you can see, there are many data investigation tools that can be used to support and extend SSA activities for an SAP HANA data mart project, but there is also another feature of Data Insight that makes it uniquely suited to an SAP HANA project: Data Insight profiling can be scheduled over time. An SAP HANA project does not happen overnight, so multiple profile tasks must be manually run over time using SAP Data Services.

While this is not a difficult task, per se, it's another task that must be maintained and executed while in the midst of a complex project. SAP Information Steward takes care of that functionality for the developer because it is designed to be set and scheduled. Then, whenever the developer needs to investigate a column's contents and metadata, he or she always has an up-to-date view. This allows the SAP HANA development to capture more scenarios because more will be uncovered with constant and consistent data collection. This can be replicated with a regular push of a button in SAP Data Services profiling, but it's unrealistic to think that the manual run will be as consistent as a machine-scheduled task. This functionality, as well as the different types of data profiling, make SAP Information Steward a great choice for an SAP HANA development project. Let's explore these profile types in more detail.

A.1   Column Profiling

Column profiling, which is shown in Figure A.2, is the first of the profile task types and arguably the most useful profiling task to support SSA activities in an SAP HANA project.

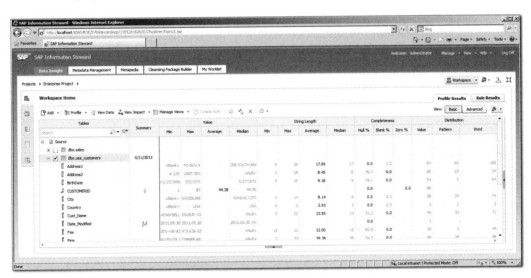

Figure A.2 Column Profiling Details in SAP Information Steward

You can use the column profiling task to examine the values and characteristics of columns in a table. The profile task returns many characteristics of the attributes of a table, ranging from simple (e.g., properties) to complex (e.g., distribution). These attributes are shown in Table A.1 in increasing levels of complexity.

Column Profile Element	Category	Description
Type	Properties	Data type of the column
Description	Properties	Text metadata business description of the column, if present in the source connection
Min	Value	Minimum value present in the column
Max	Value	Maximum value present in the column
Average	Value	Average value present in the column
Median	Value	Median value present in the column
Min	String Length	Minimum string length in the column
Max	String Length	Maximum string length in the column
Average	String Length	Average string length in the column
Median	String Length	Median string length in the column
Null %	Completeness	Percentage of NULL values in the column
Blank %	Completeness	Percentage of blank values in the column
Zero %	Completeness	Percentage of zero values in the column
Value	Distribution	Number of distinct values present in a column
Pattern	Distribution	Number of distinct patterns of data present in a column
Word	Distribution	Number of distinct words present in a column

Table A.1 Column Profile Elements Available in Data Insight

You can see the usefulness of the WORD data profiling element exemplified in Figure A.3. Not only are the words broken out in an easy-to-see distribution and pattern, but you can also click the word percentages link and see the data in the pane below, which makes up the word count and distribution.

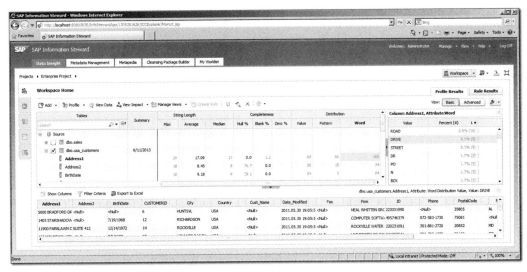

Figure A.3 Distinct Words Shown against a varchar() Column

This is powerful functionality, but it's actually even more powerful than it seems. This isn't simply a white space break to separate words. The software is actually using data quality functionality that breaks down the words to their individual components. This is much like how data cleansing works, but the complexity is performed at the click of a button. This is much more than can be accomplished by simply profiling using SAP Data Services alone for your SAP HANA project.

A.2 Address Profiling

Address profiling is a complex profiling task that quickly identifies whether address data within a record set is valid, invalid, or correctable for delivery, as described in the following list:

- Address data is *valid* if the address data in the record is a deliverable address.
- Address data is *invalid* if the address data in the record is a non-deliverable address.

▸ Address data is *correctible* when there are enough elements present in the
address data that the SAP Data Quality Management software in SAP Data Services can fashion the incorrect address into a correct deliverable address.

This is possible because the address profiling task uses the SAP Data Quality Management engine to process the data and return accurate results via supplementary
data from various postal services and agencies. After processing, the data is rendered into a graphical chart format with the details of all three results. As shown
in Figure A.4, you can select anywhere on the chart to see detailed data for any of
the three results.

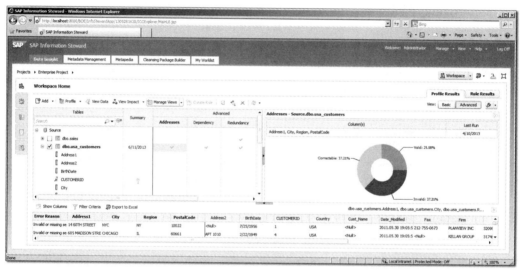

Figure A.4 Address Profiling Showing Invalid Addresses in SAP Information Steward

Because this is a quite complex profiling task result that is being performed, it's
sometimes assumed that the setup and running of the profiling task is difficult as
well. However, the opposite is true. SAP Information Steward offers just a *single*
input screen to map the address elements and a one-click execution, as shown in
Figure A.5.

All you need to do is open the screen shown in Figure A.5, give the profiling task
a name in the NAME field, and map all of the fields from the connection to the

address fields. Then, either save the task by clicking SAVE, or execute the task by clicking SAVE AND RUN NOW.

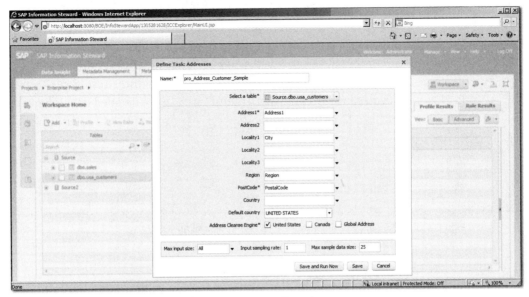

Figure A.5 Simplicity of the Input Screen for Address Profile Tasks

A.3 Dependency Profiling

The dependency profiling task is another powerful and complex profiling task for identifying attribute-level relationships in the data. The dependency profiling task shows true dependencies, not just the relationship of one table.

The dependency profiling task finds the values in one or more dependent columns that rely on values in a primary column in another table. For example, for each state (primary column), you can find the corresponding city name (dependent column) and report on the number of related cities to states, as well as the percentage of the relationship. Just as in SAP Data Services, these columns don't have to be related in the database or application. The tables and columns exist as metadata divorced from the source systems. You define the relationship, as well as the connection. Figure A.6 illustrates this process with an example of a postal code to region dependency profile.

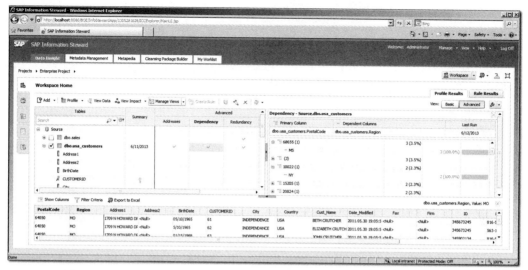

Figure A.6 Dependency Profile Results in SAP Information Steward

A.4 Redundancy Profiling

The redundancy profiling task is used to determine the degree of overlapping data values or duplication between two sets of columns in two different tables. The results will list all of the matching and non-matching values between the set of columns. Each set can contain one or more columns to use as comparison columns, and as with all of the other SAP Information Steward profiling tasks, there is no relationship at the database level required on any of the columns. The databases can be on different platforms and of differing connection types, as this is all metadata driven.

This type of profiling aligns most closely with relationship profiling in SAP Data Services, but it's more flexible because redundancy profiles show any types of related columns—not just one relationship per table noting orphan records, as in SAP Data Services. You have the concept of a main table and a comparison table, and you may select as many comparison columns as makes sense between the two tables.

Figure A.7 shows redundancy profiling between a customer table (usa_customers) and a table containing sales information (Sales), comparing the primary key of the customer table CUSTOMERID with the foreign key CUSTOMERID from the Sales table.

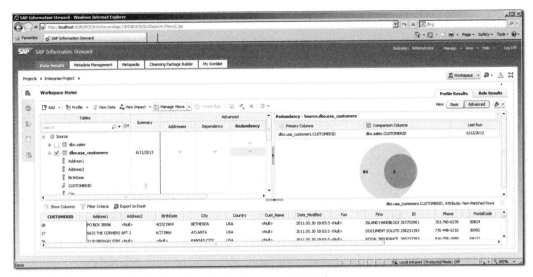

Figure A.7 Redundancy Profile Results in SAP Information Steward

A.5 Uniqueness Profiling

Uniqueness profiling is the final type of profiling task in SAP Information Steward; it returns the count and percentage of rows that contain non-unique data for the selected set of column(s). For example, you can run a uniqueness profiling task on an employee ID column to ensure that each employee has a unique ID. An example of uniqueness profiling is shown in Figure A.8. The title column in the figure is mostly duplicated or non-unique, with a representation of 89% of the column's row count. This tells you that the column doesn't have very many unique values.

Uniqueness profiling is particularly useful for determining the cardinality of columns (i.e., uniqueness of data) in a particular table. Because multiple columns may be run against the same table, it's easy to report on the relative cardinality of data in a number of columns. This is very useful to an SAP HANA initiative. Recall from Chapter 3 that cardinality is important for calculating join cost and determining the level of denormalization required when you design the data model for high performance in SAP HANA. This is just one example of another great SAP Information Steward profiling use case for SAP HANA.

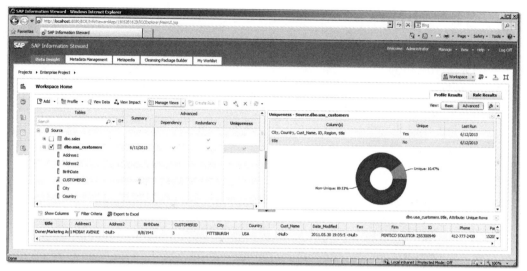

Figure A.8 Uniqueness Profile Results in SAP Information Steward

A.6 Summary

In this appendix, we discussed many options for profiling tasks in SAP Information Steward that are helpful to better understand your data before you provision that data into SAP HANA. SAP HANA is an immensely powerful platform, but it's only really useful with data that is of a high quality. Discovering the information quickly is only advantageous if the information is worth discovering and actionable.

Profiling your sources is important because it saves time and money. You can use SAP Data Services for your profiling tasks as you get a runtime license for an enterprise-class data integration tool, complete with enterprise-class profiling and SSA capabilities. However, many more types of profiling are available with SAP Information Steward, which, even though a separate license is needed, may be quite valuable to your pre-provisioning tasks.

Preprovisioning data is one step in the process that you don't want to skip. Not performing proper source system analysis up front in the process can lead to costly mistakes in your development cycle. Performing proper source system analysis shows you the real story behind your data and makes sure that you aren't just loading fast trash into SAP HANA. It's only after this step that you're ready to begin the process to provision your data into SAP HANA.

B   The Authors

Jonathan Haun currently serves as the lead SAP HANA consultant and consulting manager with Decision First Technologies. Over the past two years, he has had the opportunity to help a number of clients implement solutions using SAP HANA. In addition to being certified in multiple SAP BusinessObjects BI tools, he is also an SAP Certified Application Associate and SAP Certified Technology Associate for SAP HANA 1.0. Jonathan has worked in the field of business intelligence for more than 10 years. During this time, he has gained invaluable experience while helping customers implement solutions using the tools from the SAP BusinessObjects BI product line. Before working as a full-time business intelligence consultant, he worked in a variety of information technology management and administrative roles. His combination of experience and wealth of technical knowledge make him an ideal source of information pertaining to business intelligence solutions powered by SAP HANA. You can follow Jonathan on Twitter at *@jdh2n* or visit his blog at *http://bobj.sapbiblog.com*.

Chris Hickman is a certified SAP BusinessObjects BI consultant and consulting manager at Decision First Technologies. His specific areas of expertise include reporting, analysis, dashboard development, and visualization techniques. Chris' software development background has enabled him to achieve proven effectiveness in architecting, developing, testing, and supporting both desktop-based and web-based applications for many customer engagements representing various industries. Chris also speaks globally at SAP and ASUG events.

Don Loden is a principal consultant at Decision First Technologies with full lifecycle data warehouse and information governance experience in multiple verticals. He is an SAP Certified Application Associate on SAP BusinessObjects Data Integrator, and he is very active in the SAP community, speaking globally at numerous SAP and ASUG conferences and events. He has more than 14 years of information technology experience in the following areas: ETL architecture, development, and tuning; logical and physical data modeling; and mentoring on data warehouse, data quality, information governance, and ETL concepts. You can follow Don on Twitter at *@donloden*. You can contact Don by email at *don.loden@decisionfirst.com*.

Roy Wells is a consulting manager at Decision First Technologies, where he uses his 15 years of experience in system and application architecture to lead clients in the successful implementation of end to end BI solutions. He is particularly interested in delivering innovative visualization solutions and developing customized end user experiences that enable business transformation. He also enjoys mentoring and speaking publicly about BI, software development, and system integration solutions at conferences and venues worldwide. You can follow Roy on Twitter at *@rgwbobj* or contact him by email at *roy.wells@decisionfirst.com*.

Hillary Bliss contributed Chapter 13 of the book. She is the analytics practice lead at Decision First Technologies and specializes in data warehouse design, ETL development, statistical analysis, and predictive modeling. She works with clients and vendors to integrate business analysis and predictive modeling solutions into the organizational data warehouse and business intelligence environments based on their specific operational and strategic business needs. She has a master's degree in statistics and an MBA from Georgia Tech. You can follow Hillary on Twitter at *@HillaryBlissDFT* or reach her by email at *hillary.bliss@decisionfirst.com*.

Index

- ▶ Explore your SAP BW on SAP HANA implementation options
- ▶ Get step-by-step instructions for migration, including pre- and post-steps
- ▶ Learn how SAP HANA changes data modeling, reporting, and administration for an SAP BW system

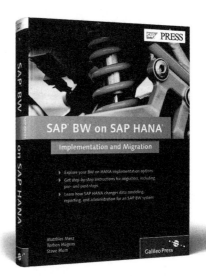

Merz, Hügens, Blum

SAP BW on SAP HANA

Implementation and Migration

If you're making the leap from SAP BW to SAP HANA, this book is your indispensable companion. Thanks to detailed pre-migration and post-migration steps, as well as a complete guide to the actual migration process, it's never been easier to HANA-ify your SAP BW system. Once your migration is complete, learn everything you need to know about data modeling, reporting, and administration. Are you ready for the next generation of SAP BW?

480 pages, 2015, $69.95/€69.95
ISBN 978-1-4932-1003-9
www.sap-press.com/3609

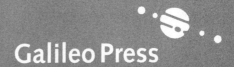

Galileo Press

Hanck, Chen, Hanck, Hertel, Lisarrague, Médaille

SAP Data Services

The Comprehensive Guide

It's time to extract, transform, and load your skills on managing enterprise data! With this book on SAP Data Services, you'll be an expert in no time. After learning about topics like planning, blueprinting, and integrating SAP Data Services, you'll get into the core of the book - detailed steps on how to perform Data Services tasks. Get the skills you need for your daily job, from basic tasks like designing objects, to advanced duties like analyzing unstructured text.

625 pages, 2015, $79.95/€79.95
ISBN 978-1-4932-1167-8
www.sap-press.com/3688

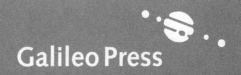

- ▶ Get up to speed on the next generation of SAP business intelligence
- ▶ Learn how to model and visualize data to tell a story
- ▶ Find out about options for desktop, mobile, and cloud deployment

Christian Ah-Soon, Peter Snowdon

Getting Started with SAP Lumira

The Comprehensive Guide

What story does your data tell? See what SAP Lumira can do and how to identify trends and find hidden insights in your business data. Get the details on progressing from data acquisitions to data manipulation to data visualization so you can add some color to your data. See how SAP Lumira fits into existing BI landscapes and which administration options are best for each setup. This introduction to SAP Lumira will help make each picture—or chart—worth a thousand words.

540 pages, 2nd edition, 2015, $69.95/€69.95
ISBN 978-1-4932-1033-6
www.sap-press.com/3645